Indochina

FROM INDOCHINA TO VIETNAM: REVOLUTION AND WAR
IN A GLOBAL PERSPECTIVE
Edited by Fredrik Logevall and Christopher E. Goscha

Indochina

An Ambiguous Colonization, 1858–1954

——

Pierre Brocheux and Daniel Hémery

Translated by Ly Lan Dill-Klein, with Eric Jennings,
Nora Taylor, and Noémi Tousignant

UNIVERSITY OF CALIFORNIA PRESS
Berkeley   Los Angeles   London

University of California Press, one of the most distinguished university presses in the United States, enriches lives around the world by advancing scholarship in the humanities, social sciences, and natural sciences. Its activities are supported by the UC Press Foundation and by philanthropic contributions from individuals and institutions. For more information, visit www.ucpress.edu.

University of California Press
Berkeley and Los Angeles, California

University of California Press, Ltd.
London, England

Library of Congress Cataloging-in-Publication Data

Brocheux, Pierre.
 [Indochine. English]

 Indochina : an ambiguous colonization, 1858–1954 / Pierre Brocheux and Daniel Hémery ; translated by Ly Lan Dill-Klein, with Eric Jennings, Nora Taylor, and Noémi Tousignant.
  p.   cm. — (From Indochina to Vietnam : revolution and war in a global perspective ; 2)
 Translated from the French.
 Includes bibliographical references and index.
 ISBN 978-0-520-24539-6 (cloth : alk. paper)
 1. Indochina—History—19th century.   2. Indochina—History—20th century.   I. Hémery, Daniel.   II. Title.
 DS548.B7613   2009
 959.7'03—dc22   2008047365

Originally published as *Indochine: La colonisation ambiguë, 1858–1954,*
© Éditions LA DÉCOUVERTE, Paris, France, 1995, 2001. This English-language translation includes additions and updates to the second French edition.

Manufactured in the United States of America

18   17   16   15   14   13   12   11   10
10   9   8   7   6   5   4   3   2

#265094867

The publisher gratefully acknowledges the generous support
of the Ahmanson Foundation Humanities Endowment Fund
of the University of California Press Foundation.

In memory of Jean Chesneaux and Georges Boudarel

CONTENTS

ILLUSTRATIONS

FIGURES

MAPS

TABLES

It gives us great pleasure to introduce Pierre Brocheux and Daniel Hémery's *Indochina: An Ambiguous Colonization, 1858–1954*. This work, by two world-renowned historians of French Indochina and Vietnamese nationalism, is the first full-length history of French colonialism and Vietnamese nationalism in the English language. Readers will find in the pages that follow an invaluable, engaging, and authoritative account of the history of French Indochina, viewed from the vantage points of both the colonized and the colonizers. Students of French colonial and Vietnamese history will find rich information on and analyses of the political, economic, social, cultural, and intellectual aspects of the making of the colonial experience in Indochina and its unraveling along national lines.

Indochina: An Ambiguous Colonization is much more than a simple *histoire événementielle* or a "textbook." At the heart of the work is an argument in favor of a more nuanced approach to the study of colonial Indochina than has been utilized in the past. Writing in the early 1990s,[1] as both the Cold War and the Third Indochinese conflict closed, Brocheux and Hémery distanced themselves from nationalist and anticolonialist approaches to history writing that had dominated in Vietnam and elsewhere during forty years of struggle for Indochina. They argued that the colonial period was more than just a fleeting moment or an artificial stage in the history of Vietnam, Laos, and Cambodia; it was also a crucial period of historical change and interaction and an integral component of French and post-colonial Indochinese pasts. Moreover, Brocheux and Hémery articulated this argument at a time when nostalgic and nationalist-minded French writers and associations were trying to recast colonial history as the record of a benevolent, civilizing project, and when French veterans' associations and nationalists forced the resignation of one of their colleagues at the Université de Paris VII, the late Georges Boudarel, a specialist on Vietnam.[2] Although they didn't deny the modernizing impact of colonial science and education, they rejected nationalist readings of the colonial past on both sides of the divide. Hémery and Brocheux emphasized instead the "ambiguous" nature of the colonial experience, the complexity of the colonial encounter, and the diverse nature of the interactions between colonized and colonizers. Daniel Hémery confided that the final choice of the title, using the term "ambiguous," was inspired by Georges Balandier's *Afrique ambiguë*.[3] "Ambiguity" marked an important shift in French colonial historiography on Indochina and set it on a track different from the more Saidian-inspired works of the time.[4]

Brocheux and Hémery's nuanced approach, rendered here in a translated and updated edition, responds nicely to the goals of the series we direct for the University of California Press, *From Indochina to Vietnam: Revolution and War in a Global Perspective*. Thematically, chronologically, and analytically, *Indochina: An Ambiguous Colonization* establishes a strong foundation for the series by providing a better understanding of the decolonization of French Indochina and the emergence of the modern nation-state of Vietnam. It examines the nature of the Vietnamese revolution and the war that accompanied it. Furthermore, Brocheux and Hémery situate the history of Indochina within its local, regional, and global dimensions between 1858 and 1954. This is a rare work of interpretative synthesis. Thanks to Brocheux and Hémery, readers will be better equipped to tackle in new and nuanced ways the complexities of the wars and revolutions in Vietnam, especially those less studied elements that this series seeks to bring to light.

Getting this volume ready for publication in English was not an easy task. We owe a great debt to Ly Lan Dill-Klein, who went far beyond the call of duty in performing the task of translation. She received invaluable assistance in this undertaking by Eric Jennings, Nora Taylor, and Noémi Tousignant. Special thanks goes to Cornell's Southeast Asia Program, the University of California Press, and the Groupe d'études sur le Vietnam contemporain for funding the translation. At the University of California Press, we would like to thank Niels Hooper, Rachel Lockman, and Monica McCormick. Peter Dreyer and Rose Vekony deserve special commendation for their meticulous and quite brilliant work as copy editor and project editor, respectively. The English-language version of this book would never have been possible without the myriad contributions of these individuals.

We have followed the original French book in omitting diacritics for Vietnamese words. However, interested readers will find a list of Vietnamese proper nouns used in the text with full Vietnamese diacritics at the back of the book.

Fredrik Logevall, Cornell University
Christopher E. Goscha, Université du Québec à Montréal

PREFACE

Until the 1950s, interest in French Indochina, though thriving, was confined to the discipline of colonial history, with its narrow Eurocentric and apologetic stance. During the decade of Dien Bien Phu and Bandoeng, however, curiosity about these peoples' past informed a new approach, one committed to the rediscovery of their cultures, social and anthropological structures, and movements and uprisings: to their rebirth, or birth, as nations. This anticolonial history brought a decisive shift in the historiography of the Indochinese peninsula, promoting the recognition, in these societies objectified by colonialism, of their own history at a time when they were asserting themselves as major actors in the future history of humanity. But for all its contributions, this approach also created a gap in our knowledge of the colonial events that make up their recent past, as well as the genealogy of our own past. This blind spot is intensified by the various nostalgias that have guided the construction of memory of Indochina—a false memory, of course. Ultimately, a history that relies on condemnation alone can never be adequate; historians must also strive to make sense of the past as a whole, to help us face the present and the future.

This constructed memory of Indochina is but one example of a more widespread phenomenon. Now more than ever, French society is struggling to come to grips with its colonial past, even as that past is a central historical pillar underlying the country's current mode of operation. In confused ways, this past is being brought back into fashion. Yet historians both in France and abroad still have trouble grasping the significance of colonization in terms of the historical development of these societies. They tend to minimize processes of expansion and external domination, relegating them to the rank of secondary or marginal explanatory factors. Many historians, French or otherwise, fail to include colonization as an integral facet of the history of France. Nor is the similarly biased and narrow approach of the "national histories" of former colonized societies well suited to an examination of the facts of colonization "from the inside." Implicitly based on a teleological view of the past, such history aims, more or less consciously, to celebrate and legitimate the nation-states that have been constituted since 1945.

Colonial Indochina has not been spared these distortions of the historian's lens. It has more often served as a prop to sustain various memories—generally selective, complacent ones—than as the object of comprehensive historical reflection based on a rigorous critical approach, devoid of self-indulgence. The highly scattered state of its academic historiography—now more fragmented than ever—eloquently illustrates this point. Despite their relative originality, neither anticolonial historiography nor its nationalist counterpart—and certainly not colonialist hagiography—is capable of going beyond this classic misunderstanding.

This book's ambition is to put forth the crucial project of transcending memory—a project that can only be undertaken through a history that is rigorous and critical, one that seeks to be as comprehensive as possible without eliminating narrative altogether. The time has come for a problem-based history. With this in mind, we have made several choices. First, we have chosen to approach Indochina as a historical construct, not only imposed and improvised from without, but also rooted—for the entire period under study—within the tensions and dynamics of the social and anthropological space of the peninsula. This was, of course, a colonial space, but that does not mean it lacked complexity. It was the site of an intermingling that brought colonizers and colonized into confrontation but also, inevitably, led to cohabitation; one where the relation of victors to vanquished was intersected by the equally significant relation of colonized to colonizer. We have also sought to approach Indochina through its multiple dimensions—political and military, economic, social, and cultural—and various temporalities, encompassing the long colonial period as well as the brief, violent ruptures of decolonization.

Beyond these choices, however, one must delve through the multiple historical layers of colonial Indochina. For what was colonial Indochina if not a meeting—characterized by violence and exploitation, as well as the day-to-day interactions of a self-confident European society—with the peoples, systems of power, and civilizations of Southeast Asia, in search of their own identities over the troubled course of the twentieth century? Perhaps even now we should not consider colonization to be completely over but instead recognize its obscure persistence in the collective unconscious.

This colonial contact has often been portrayed unilaterally: on the one hand, as fundamentally civilizing, even if faulty, by the older colonial historiography; on the other, as purely dominating, repressive, and exploitative, by the various anticolonial and nationalist historiographies of the more recent past and of today. Obviously, one must look beyond these black-and-white assessments to find the truth. For the colonial relationship was formed through more veiled modalities; it had unforeseen consequences and hidden resonances, as difficult to grasp as they are to measure. These are evident, for instance, in the appropriation by the colonized of the innovations imposed by colonization, in the reversibility of modes of domination as soon as circumstances permitted, and in the subtle investment in these modes on the part of subjugated societies who redirected and deflected them. Did this relationship not reach its limits—which, in any case, are harder to delineate than it seems—very early on, or else later than we think?

It is thus the ambiguity of the Indochinese colonial situation that we hope, on the basis of available sources, to shed light on. We present the current state of knowledge about Indochina's historical trajectory, from its construction by the French in the second half of the nineteenth century to its terminal crisis in 1945–1954. Given that our focus is on the colonial period itself, we limit discussion of the Indochina War of 1945–1954 to its overarching logic and essential points of reference. In any case, studies currently underway promise to bring new insights into the war. We have chosen instead to prioritize the internal assessment of the Indochinese colonial situation, the study of the dynamics of its power structure and economy and of its political and social movements. Needless to say, this assessment is nowhere near exhaustive; it remains provisional and subject to revision. Even now, we still know very little about many aspects of the colonial situation. Changes in ways of life and material civilization; transformations in attitudes and in the private and domestic spheres; everyday violence and great repressions; the history of both cities and rural areas, of coastal and mountain-dwelling societies; to say nothing of the vast realm of the economy—all remain largely unknown. May this book inspire further exploration of these areas and a lucid look at the tragedy of French Indochina.

A NOTE ON AUTHORSHIP

Pierre Brocheux and Daniel Hémery jointly conceived this book, its contents, and each chapter's approach. Together they wrote the preface, introduction, conclusion, appendixes, and bibliography. Chapters 1, 2, 3, 6, and 7 are by Daniel Hémery; chapters 4, 5, and 8 are by Pierre Brocheux.

Between India and China

At the Crossroads of Civilizations

It has become commonplace in the postcolonial historiography of the Indochinese states of Vietnam, Laos, and Cambodia to insist upon the ephemeral, artificial nature of French Indochina. Indeed, some have claimed that France had no coherent colonial project in Asia. The French colony of Cochinchina and the Indochinese Union created in 1887 are seen as a simple interlude in the long history of these profoundly dissimilar societies, which they brought together. Although this was an understandable reaction to the self-serving approach of the earlier colonial historiography,[1] the "colonial interlude" view seems highly reductive today, and the increasing availability of Indochinese colonial archives in the early twenty-first century, as well as the recent history of Vietnam, Cambodia, and Laos, have called it into question.

At the creation of the Indochinese Union, nothing was determinate, except perhaps the fact that the colonizers relied upon the prior historical expansion of the Vietnamese into Laos and Cambodia. However, to understand the context from which a French colonial state would emerge, it is important to take its historical and geographical aspects into account, especially the series of vast hydrographic basins formed by rivers flowing down from Tibet into the rich deltas to the southeast. Although geography does not create history, it does condition it. For several millennia, "Indochina" was sparsely populated and attracted migrant populations from beyond the region. It was one of the world's great historical frontiers, along which contacts and exchanges occurred among material cultures, myths and religions, various writing systems, and, of course, empires. It was within this complex region of intermingling civilizations that imperialist France constructed Indochina.

In light of a comprehensive recent "archaeological revolution," there is no longer any doubt that these Indochinese societies were part of a very ancient Southeast Asian civilization, which was marked by remarkable diversity. Their specificities, however, were for a long time ignored in the Western mapping out and categorizing of the geohistorical area that they constituted. Until the twentieth century, the Western representation of this area defined it above all in terms of the nature and the intensity of its cultural exchanges with the very different, larger Indian and Chinese worlds between which it existed, to the point where it was considered little more than a peripheral zone of contact between them. The first Western conceptualization of "Indochina" was elaborated from this distorted view in 1804 by one of the pioneers of geography in Europe in the romantic era, the Danish-born Conrad Malte-Brun (K. Malthe-Brüün, 1775–1826), who worked for the Napoleonic regime. In 1808, he was closely followed by the Scottish philologist and linguist John Leyden (1775–1811)—a pastor, surgeon, and professor of Hindustani employed by the English East India Company.[2] Leyden did not ignore the inherent "characteristics" of the "Indo-Chinese nations," but Malte-Brun carefully outlined their double and subordinate adherence to the Chinese and Indian domains in the context of his efforts in 1813 to define the geographical concept "Indochina" precisely. "This region," he wrote,

> does not have any generally recognized name. It is sometimes called a "peninsula beyond the Ganges," although it is not, strictly speaking, a peninsula. Several geographers have named it "exterior India"; this denomination is more characteristic than the first. But since these countries have periodically been subject to the Chinese empire and since most of the peoples who inhabit them resemble the Chinese—whether in physiognomy, height, and complexion or in their customs, religion, and language— we proposed, several years ago, that this region of the globe be given the new name— clear, expressive, and resonant—of "Indo-China." We were going to abandon this innovation when we learned that an English scholar, established in Calcutta, had had practically the same idea. This unforeseen concordance encouraged us to preserve this name until a better one is proposed.[3]

This first, purely geographic, linguistic, and anthropological—and by no means geopolitical—concept of "Indochina" quickly spread into the vocabulary of geographers and Orientalists. The term was then generally understood to refer to the continental region situated between the gulfs of Bengal, Siam, and Tonkin, the straits of Malacca and Singapore, British India, and the Chinese empire. John Leyden and others went further, attaching island Southeast Asia to this Indochinese realm. Moreover, this broad noncolonial definition of "Indochina" remained current until the middle of the twentieth century, although broadly superseded by the second, colonial sense assigned to the name toward the end of the nineteenth century.

Furthermore, if during the first third of the nineteenth century, the political future of the region became an international issue, several different formulas for grouping together its peoples have remained in circulation for a long time. One formula, for example, groups them in relation to the empire of Dai Nam or Annam—which during the period were the Vietnamese and Chinese names for what is today Vietnam[4]—or around Siam, which the Chakri dynasty tried to modernize around 1855, or even around the Burmese kingdom bordering British India. Moreover, starting in the sixteenth century, the English, Dutch, Portuguese from Macao, and especially Cantonese were infinitely more active than the French in the "voyage à la Cochinchine" and in the commercial opening of Vietnam: 168 ships from Macao entered its ports from 1773 to 1801, compared to only about 15 French ships.[5] Moreover, France repeatedly attempted to center its Asiatic expansion more to the west, in upper Burma and Siam.

However, if the future of "Indo-China" remained undecided for a long time, powerful historical forces strongly influenced the construction of colonial Indochina. Even today, these forces still make their effects felt, to the extent that Indochina, albeit neither a state nor a regional political grouping, is nonetheless much more than a simple geographical entity.

Far from being an artificial construct, French Indochina resulted from the global reorganization of the Far Eastern region as a whole following the decline of the "state-civilization" that was the Chinese empire—an empire that defined itself as the administration of *the* civilization—under the impact of the successive and concurrent advances of English and French imperialism, starting with the First Opium War of 1839–41. Indochina emerged from the ruins of this world system, whose southern periphery was formed by the Vietnamese and Khmer kingdoms and the Lao and Tai principalities, in addition to Siam and Burma, in the role of tributary states. The Chinese term *fan* (*phan* in Vietnamese) that was applied to them literally meant "hedge," as in "a dependency forming a hedge on the frontier."[6] One of the objectives of the French conquest in Indochina, as with the Opium Wars, was precisely to destroy this tributary relationship that had for centuries bound them to the imperial court in Beijing (twelve Vietnamese missions bearing tribute traveled to China in the period 1802–40 alone). It took half a century for this to take place—from 1858, the date of the first Franco-Vietnamese War, to 1897, the year when the pacification of central and northern Dai Nam was achieved. For roughly the next half century, until March 9, 1945, when the Japanese army overturned French colonial power, Indochina was in every sense both a colonial state structure and a regional economic entity.

Although the French colonial interregnum in eastern Southeast Asia lasted less than a century, it nevertheless had profound historical consequences for all those who lived within its colonial contours. There is, first, its impact on world history, inasmuch as the liquidation of colonial Indochina was a stake in a veritable "locally waged world war." Second, the stakes were high for France. If it is a bit exaggerated to say that the French Fourth Republic died at Dien Bien Phu in 1954, the French colonial empire certainly did. Finally, and most important, the colonial period influenced the historical development of the peoples of the peninsula who lived within this new colonial state. For them, French colonization meant forced entry into what is generally called "modernity"—the world of merchandise, wage labor, and the emergence of the modern state and its corresponding structures. It was often a brutal and radical rupture with their own past, with no conceivable going back, because of the coherence and strength of the power structures implanted by the colonizers, as well as their considerable intellectual and political advances over the organizational structures that local societies had hitherto produced.

INDOCHINESE SOCIETIES AND STATES
PRIOR TO COLONIZATION

The French who landed on the Indochinese peninsula in the second half of the nineteenth century, and who progressively annexed its territories in the east, found themselves in the midst of a mosaic of demographically unequal societies. In 1875, there were perhaps ten million Vietnamese and fewer than a million Cambodians. For thousands of years, these societies had emerged from and been shaped by the intersection of Austroasiatic (Viet and Khmer, both proto-Indochinese), Austronesian (Cham), Tai (Thai, Lao), and other, equally proto-Indochinese populations and cultures. It was upon this substratum of a supposedly aboriginal, or at least endogenous, civilization that the Chinese and Indian influences were grafted. Over time, this cultural complex gave rise to diverse collective entities—the peoples and states that we now call Vietnam, Cambodia, and Laos, among others.

These societies were different in their modes of organization (clans, autonomous tribes, and village communities federated in principalities of varying size, which were sometimes enduring states). Despite their differences, they had much in common. Their ecosystems, agricultural methods, and tools placed them in the category of "plant-based civilizations" *(civilisations du végétal)*. Rice was certainly the dominant crop, and it could be grown either on flooded or irrigated soils or on dry land using an itinerant slash-and-burn technique *(ray),* which burned the grass and fertilized the fields with the ash. This planting civilization was associated with gathering wild foods, hunting, and fishing. It also possessed craftsmen specialized according to their type of production and village of origin. Complementary exchanges connected the peoples of the plains with those of the forested highlands, as well as with places further afield, such as Singapore, Hong Kong, southern China, and Bangkok.

The religious and philosophical systems practiced by these societies shared many of the same origins, mainly Indian and Chinese, although different versions were adopted. In Cambodia and Laos, the prevalent religion was Theravada (or Hinayana) Buddhism, which stresses monastic service and assigns great importance to the use of canonical texts. In Vietnam, Mahayana Buddhism prevailed, which insisted upon the practice of charity in secular society. Unlike in the case of its neighbors to the west, Confucianism indelibly marked Vietnamese society, so much so that it became the official doctrine of the government. That said, neither Buddhism nor Confucianism ever completely did away with totemic and agrarian "animist cults." The "great" religions were juxtaposed to or superimposed on them, but never eradicated them entirely. The Vietnamese *than*, the Lao *phi*, and the Khmer *neak*—local genii and spirits—endured among the local peasantries, providing symbolic representations of the universe as well as instruments through which they could understand the world and tame it. Confucianism was similarly unable to eliminate the residual and altered Islam practiced by the Cham in today's central Vietnam. And in contrast to Buddhism, Confucianism failed to prevent Christianity from recruiting adherents among the majority Viet, or Kinh, population, and the need to protect these Christians became a latent pretext for foreign intervention. There were some four hundred thousand Vietnamese Christians on the eve of the French occupation of Cochinchina.

These peasant societies were essentially differentiated by the degree of their internal organization. Entrenched behind their "bamboo hedges," the eighteen thousand rural communities of Dai Nam, especially those in the northern and central regions, exploited the land under a system combining communal and private property, so that each family had at least a minimal holding, thanks to the periodic and equal (since an edict of Minh Mang's in 1840) redistribution of communal land. The village is generally designated by the term *xa*, which applies in fact to a number of villages in the anthropological sense of the term. The latter also have a variety of names, the most common being *lang*. A council of notables administers the village; it is generally composed of village scholars, former civil servants, and more or less affluent landowners. The social inequalities (between registered and unregistered residents, and between notables, the affluent, and the impoverished) were compensated for, at least partially, by communal and lineage solidarity, as well as by a sharp sense of belonging to the family and to the village. This was best seen in the cult of the local guardian spirit held in the *dinh* and by the fact that social relations were dictated by common law (*huong uoc*), generally written, which established the rules of the communities' social, cultural, and material life.

However, the image of a static, homogeneous, cooperative, inward-looking village is not to be trusted. This notion of a "built village," to employ John Kleinen's term,[7] is a legacy of the colonial ethnographic tradition. In reality, Vietnamese villages have long been influenced by large socioeconomic divides, and a floating population of wretched peasants exists in the countryside. The villages are divided into associations of mutual aid, *giap*, which organize feasts, ceremonies, and common labor, and often levy personal taxes. They are classified in a hierarchy according to criteria of seniority of residence, age, literary knowledge, land wealth, and ties to powerful lineages. This extremely strict hierarchy is symbolized by ritual and customary obligations.

Village autonomy in relation to the imperial state varied by region and according to the government's capacity to impose its authority. Thus, in the eighteenth century, the Trinh administration stopped nominating village chiefs. Lineages carried considerable weight in village communities, and the rural elite, who possessed not only an important share of the land but also another source of wealth in the shape of knowledge of the written word and texts, controlled the power. This elite had complex, changing ties with the mandarinal bureaucracy, which determined the extent of state levies on peasant production. By investing local spirits with official warrants, the Nguyen admittedly sought to tie their cults to imperial patronage. However, by honoring hidden divinities, the villagers maintained the tradition of autonomous management of village affairs.

The ties that bound the Khmer or Lao village families seem outwardly to have been looser and less collectivist than those among the Vietnamese. There, demography was less of a concern, and the gentleness of Buddhism was less likely to incite a productive passion and a coercive discipline. Nevertheless, social life was intense, thanks to the activities of the local *vat* (temple) and monastic festivities. In Cambodia, hierarchical networks, administered by officials *(okyas)* of the court and governors *(chaovay srok)* in the provinces, controlled nobles, their relatives, and their dependents, as well as those classified by the state as "slaves" (*kha* in Laos, *phnong* in Cambodia).

In all these societies, whatever the foundation of oligarchical authority, local power was in the hands of the elders. These village micro-oligarchies were also the conduits through which the central power shaped the identities of each of these societies—Vietnamese, Cambodian, and Laotian. The existence of this power allowed monarchs ("mandatories of heaven" in Vietnam) to play a role that was as much symbolic as real, since the ruler's virtues counted more than his actions. Through the ritual of the springtime's first plowing, for example, Khmer and Vietnamese kings summoned the blessings of heaven for the success of their harvests.

However, these states would never have existed or expanded had they not been able to levy and procure taxes from their peasantries. This taxation was most efficient in Vietnam, in whose thirty-one provinces a literate civil service bureaucracy instituted a cadastral (land registry) survey,[8] controlled taxes, wrote reports, and verified the population through censuses.[9] In Cambodia, the "mandarins" constituted a similar kind of bureaucracy, though their education and activities were subject to less formal rules and thus tended to be less efficient than in the Confucian world of Vietnam. Furthermore, the Khmer kingdom was less populous, and the proportion of slaves—whether by reason of debt or of heredity—was high: perhaps 150,000 out of a population estimated at 900,000 at the beginning of the 1880s.

The different nature of these societies allows one better to understand the reasons for the development of the dynamism that allowed the Vietnamese to assert themselves increasingly at the expense of the neighboring Cham and Khmer from the tenth century on. Cambodia began to lose its hold on the lower Mekong Delta to Dai Nam in the seventeenth century. Prei Nokor became Saigon in 1623. Vietnamese expansion was particularly strong in the nineteenth century under the Nguyen dynasty, in the framework of the Vietnamese "march south" *(nam tien),* deep into the rice fields of the Mekong Delta. This Vietnamese dynasty effectively severed Cambodia from its southeastern frontier, denied it access to the South China Sea, and consolidated its hold over what is southern Vietnam today. To the west and the north, Siam annexed the Cambodian territories of Tonle Repou, Saak, and Stung Treng. From the eighteenth century on, the territories annexed from Cambodia by the Vietnamese were divided into five administrative divisions *(tran)* and gradually colonized by ethnic Viet peasants coming from the poorer areas of the Nguyen kingdom. Meanwhile, the rice trade and its exportation, dominated by Chinese traders and immigration, contributed greatly to the development of the city of Gia Dinh (Saigon), a citadel and a merchant town. Its twin was the overwhelmingly Chinese city of Cholon, connected to the Mekong Delta thanks to the first canals constructed there. After 1750, Cambodia entered one of the darkest periods of its history. It became a kingdom "under the influence" of two foreign powers, constrained to balance Vietnamese pressure in the east with the influence of Siam to the west. The Vietnamese emperor Gia Long put it best at the time: it was "an independent country enslaved to the two other states." This dependence was at its apogee between 1835 and 1840, when Hue occupied the eastern and southern parts of Cambodia, renaming it Tran Tay (Commandership of the West), and attempted to "Vietnamize" its political structures, culture, and even its religion. A general revolt resulted in 1840, saving Cambodia from total annihilation. However, it did not prevent its transformation into a double tributary vassal to Siam and Dai Nam, sealed by the Vietnamese-Siamese treaty of 1846.[10] Similarly, the Nguyen sought to establish Vietnamese military and political control over the left bank of the Mekong: in 1830 they set up Vietnamese garrisons and stationed officers on the Tran Ninh plateau, and in 1831 the Luang Prabang principality was declared a dependency ("tributary state") of Hue.

Yet Vietnamese hegemony was not absolute. It manifested itself only in terms of the weakening of the Khmer kingdom, and in light of the extreme fragility, following the breakup of the former kingdom of Lan Xang, of the Lao principalities of Luang Prabang, Vieng Chang (Vientiane), and Champassak, whose populations were subjected to massive deportations to Siam, especially in 1827. Vietnamese society was also vulnerable to its own dysfunctions. For one thing, after winning the civil war against the Tay Son (1778–1802) and following the reunification of the country in 1802, the Nguyen maintained a strict state-controlled, formalistic, but rather corrupt monopoly on external trade (which flourished in Saigon). Rather than engaging the world outside via this trade (as the Siamese had long done), the Vietnamese court sought to limit the country's access to international trade (from the reign of Minh Mang on, Western ships only had the right to trade in Da Nang). Not only were the Nguyen fearful of Western schemes, but they also sought to prevent the emergence on the inside of an influential Vietnamese merchant class, of which a hybrid form (the "merchant-mandarins") had already appeared in the eighteenth century. The Nguyen dynasty thus had consolidated the supremacy of the Chinese merchant network under, it was hoped, state control. Second, population growth was a problem, despite the existence of a vast frontier open to settlers in the south. In 1836, for example, there were 1,737 rural townships in Cochinchina; in 1878, the French administration counted 2,387 villages and around 1,700,000 inhabitants, spread over 60,000 square kilometers, an average density of 28 per square kilometer. But the absence of improved technical innovations in agriculture made it increasingly harder to support the growing population, and the underdevelopment of transportation networks (especially when one considers the large distances separating northern and southern Vietnam) limited the rise of efficient productive forces and exchanges. Third, for a long time, the Nguyen monarchy had to confront the activities and pressures of foreigners throughout the Indochinese region, many of whom had been connected since the seventeenth century to the wider European trading sphere. This growing foreign intrusion coincided with the emergence within Vietnam of a more turbulent, numerous, and oppressed society. The state had particular trouble dealing with the independence and dynamism of the non-Vietnamese hunting and gathering cultures and itinerant farmers. These peoples, governed by their own authorities under the loose tutelage of Vietnamese mandarins, only offered an annual tribute to the Viet state, and they often rebelled. To give but one example, in 1802, Gia Long reconstituted, to the west of Binh Thuan, a Cham principality comprising Cham Muslims, Rhade, Kahauv, and Cru highlanders, named the Panduranga or Pradara. All of them were entrusted to a Cham prince named by Hue.[11] Things heated up, however, when a combination of increased Vietnamese immigration, Minh Mang's policy of Vietnamization, and the revolt of the southern Viet provinces in 1833 under Le Van Khoi triggered a local Islamic jihad in 1833–34—the famous "Po rasak" ("Wrath of God") movement led by a Cham hadji. The following year, the uprising of Ja Thak Va sought to restore an independent Panduranga outside of Vietnamese control.

Finally, social tensions became increasingly widespread. Banditry, vagrancy, intervillage violence, and peasant uprisings all weakened the Nguyen, who had, after all, only been in power for half a century and this in a country that had previously been divided for more than two hundred years (at least in the northern provinces, the preceding Le dynasty continued to be perceived as legitimate). Confronted with stagnant, irregular agricultural production, with the recurrent phenomenon of the appropriation of communal lands by rural "gentry" of powerful lineages, and with the growing numbers of landless peasants in the northern and central deltas, the Nguyen simply responded with an inefficient agrarian policy of land clearing to augment production. Not only did the Nguyen not look to directly prevent the appropriation of land for this purpose; in 1875, Tu Duc promulgated a fiscal reform favorable to it.[12] The peasantry, including Christian communities, fell increasingly victim to heavy fiscal and military requirements and religious prohibitions. The inequalities in the charges increased in tandem with the need to obtain more revenues for the state.

Many centrifugal forces were also at work, notably in the more heterogeneous southern society. From the reign of Gia Long (1802–19) to that of Tu Duc (1848–83), the Nguyen had to repress more than four hundred uprisings, such as those of Phan Ba Van and Nguyen Hanh (1826–27) in the region of Nam Dinh, that of Le Duy Luong, an authentic descendant of the Le lineage, in Ninh Binh (1833), and that of Ta Van Phung (1862–65). As Philippe Langlet has shown, notwithstanding its attempts to construct an official historiography and to legitimate itself through increasingly insistent references to Chinese culture and models, it was difficult for the Nguyen dynasty to situate itself in the national historical tradition and to have its legitimacy accepted by the literate elite.[13]

THE HISTORICAL INDOCHINESE TRIANGLE

Multiple conflicts thus arose in the peninsula, a state of affairs that favored a fall into dependency. This situation resulted from the discontinuous convergence of three factors that, after 1850, governed the development of the region for more than a century: the Chinese factor, the internal tensions of the region, and the entrance upon the scene of French imperialism in East Asia. These three factors were influenced by the wider world context of the long-standing competition between Great Britain and France.

The Chinese factor was determinant in two ways. Behind France's projects in Indochina during the nineteenth century was a larger design on China—above all, the desire to acquire privileged access to the immense market of the Chinese mainland. A latecomer to East Asia, France sought to catch up with its British rival by creating an outpost in the vast hinterland between British India and China. With the British dominating China's eastern coast, the French turned their attention to the great rivers flowing down from the highlands of western China into Southeast Asia. Opposed to the British "open door policy" in Canton and along the Yangtzi River, the French sought to develop a "river policy" based on exclusive, therefore colonial, control of the mouths of the Mekong and Red Rivers. They also aimed to control the Vietnamese shore of the South China Sea. China's influence thus played a decisive role—even though it was sometimes not directly present—in the making of French colonial Indochina. As noted above, the Indochinese states located on the Qing dynasty's southern periphery had long been part of China's economic, political, and cultural world. China had traditionally functioned as a protective power over regional tributary dynasties. Directly or indirectly, China had played a decisive military and diplomatic role in the outcome of conflicts throughout Southeast Asia. Before China's repeated military interventions of 1945–86, its last foray into the Indochinese peninsula was the war it waged against France in 1884–85 in a bid to prevent the French colonization of Nguyen Vietnam. Though weakened by European intrusions, the Qing dynasty had embarked on a process of modernization in the 1860s, and it had become a significant military and naval power in the region. In consequence, its failure in 1885 was the basis for a Franco-Chinese compromise, without which French control of Indochina would not have lasted. In other words, the eastern part of mainland Southeast Asia became French only because Chinese resignation finally allowed it.

A second cause of the discontinuities of French colonization of Indochina was the uneven resistance the French encountered. Almost everywhere, French colonial expansion ran up against armed opposition, much of it fierce. But nowhere did it face a state-controlled society capable of halting its expansion, much less rolling it back. That said, we must be careful not to accept at face value the traditional colonial representations of the future colonized societies as immobile, passive monarchies unable to modernize and cope with the stronger Western threat. In Cambodia, Kings Ang Duong and Norodom appeared anxious to modernize their country, and they looked for inspiration and a model to the example of Siam. This was also true of Minh Mang (1820–40) and Tu Duc (1848–83), the last two relatively strong-willed Vietnamese emperors of the nineteenth century. But in contrast to the situation after 1945, resistance to colonial conquest in the late nineteenth century was limited to the regional or local levels. Moreover, France succeeded in finding supporters or partners in the Khmer court and the Lao principalities. Though these were certainly wary and mistrusted the colonial power, they were also conscious of having no alternative. Facing the double threat of absorption by Siam and Dai Nam, they resigned themselves to a French protectorate, seeing in it a structure that would enable them to survive. A certain number of tribal authorities among the ethnic highlanders, such as the powerful Tai family of Deo Van Tri in northern Indochina, also adopted such a strategy.

The case of the Vietnamese state of Dai Nam was significantly different. Until the French expansion into Cochinchina in the late 1850s, the Nguyen state was one of the five main powers of Southeast Asia, along with Siam, Burma, Great Britain, and the Netherlands. Dai Nam, or Vietnam, as it would be better known in the twentieth century, resisted the French from the outset. It took a series of direct military clashes (1858–62, 1873, and 1882–85) before Hue finally yielded to the French. However, even in the case of Vietnam, the French obtained an alliance with the majority of the mandarin class and the court. This uneasy entente, stamped with bitterness and mistrust, began with the government of Jean-Marie de Lanessan (1891–94) and despite the fatal blows inflicted on the monarchy, lasted until 1945, if not 1954.

In fact, as in Qing China during the same period, the Vietnamese ruling class of literati, rural notables, and the court were faced with the difficult challenge of transforming an imperial Confucian state into a modern nation-state. They never clearly grasped the nature and importance of this challenge. Most of the important mandarins, undoubtedly in unison with the majority of the literati, opted first for uncompromising resistance to the French.[14] It was not that they were ignorant of the outside world. In Dai Nam, cultural borrowing from abroad had been a long tradition. The Hue court was probably just as aware of Western culture and techniques as the Qing, thanks to annual purchasing missions dispatched to Batavia, Manila, and Singapore, as well as to the Chinese merchants who dominated the foreign trade of Dai Nam. The Hue court also had access to the official newspaper of the Qing court, the *Jing Bao,* and to the English-Chinese press of Hong Kong. Since the First Opium War (1839–41), leaders in Hue had been well aware of the Western menace to the region. But like the Qingliu ("pure circle") in the Chinese bureaucracy, the Vietnamese mandarinate analyzed this threat through Indian and Chinese experiences and a Sino-Vietnamese looking glass, relying in particular upon the Confucian notion of the cyclic crisis of the celestial mandate and the intellectual categories traditionally applied to "barbarians." As a result, the Vietnamese mandarinate entirely misread the imperialist phenomenon and was unable to respond to it coherently. In marked contrast to the Siamese court in Bangkok, policymakers in Hue remained unaware of the opportunities created for them by the West and misjudged a succession of favorable conjunctures at the middle of the century, which eventually cost Dai Nam its independence.

However, the court and the bureaucracy did not remain passive in the face of the Western threat in general and its French variant in particular. Mandarins and scholars were well aware of the devastating potential that foreign activities, notably those of the missionaries, posed for the existing order, for the Confucian doctrine legitimizing it, and for their own social status. All of this weighed heavily on their decision-making. Throughout the nineteenth century, for example, the Nguyen undertook a continuous effort to reinforce and rationalize the state. In 1831–32, Minh Mang's large-scale administrative reforms generalized the system of provinces (*tinh*) throughout the entire country. Under Tu Duc (1848–83), Confucian reforms were undertaken: there were improvements in the selection of state officials; efforts were made to restore the balance between food production and consumption and the functioning of the irrigation system in Tonkin; and young scholars were dispatched to Saigon, Hong Kong, and France to study Western knowledge and ways.[15] In addition, during the nineteenth century, Vietnamese society slowly began to move down the path of modernization.

Again, it is important not to see the imperial government as a fundamentally reactionary entity, hostile to all innovation. There was, in fact, considerable debate within the bureaucracy on this question. The exchanges in 1840 between Emperor Minh Mang and the renowned scholar Vu Duc Khue, a conservative supporter of absolute isolationism, are a case in point. Tu Duc did not oppose borrowing Western methods, and certain mandarins recognized the necessity of adopting fundamental reforms, in particular, the Catholic scholar Nguyen Truong To (1828–71). Following the latter's journeys to France, Italy, Hong Kong, and Canton in 1858–61 and 1866, he addressed forty-three petitions to the court between 1863 and 1871 proposing a reform of the mandarinate, the encouragement of trade and industry, and cooperation with Western powers, in sum, the adoption of the limited modernization policy applied by Chinese officials.[16] Other mandarins, like Nguyen Hiep in 1879 and Le Dinh in 1881, returned from their missions to Siam and Hong Kong with similar reform-minded suggestions.

In the end, however, it was all in vain; these initiatives remained limited in scope. In the nineteenth century, the Vietnamese discoverers of the West were still rare. Any compromise with the outsiders, and with the sociocultural model they were pushing, seemed to be fundamentally impossible to most Vietnamese elites. In Vietnam, there was not even a limited technical and military modernization of a long-standing nature. This was in stark contrast to Japan's *Wakon yosai* (Japanese mind, Western technology) policy, or even China's *Yangwu yundong* (Western activities movement, 1861–75).

The Dai Nam social elite's persistent conservative attitude to fundamental changes—which the erudite and traditionalist emperor Tu Duc and many of his advisers (such as the great mandarin Trung Dang Que in the 1860s) embodied—is surprising, and it is still something of a historical puzzle. However, it is explained in part by the disastrous agricultural and demographic decline that occurred after 1870,[17] aggravated by the rise in prices caused by the increase, following the Opium Wars, of the value of silver in East Asia. To make matters worse, the constraints of dynastic legitimation led the Nguyen court to anchor its authority increasingly in the rituals and values of the past. This led the court to impose the Chinese model at the very time when it needed to be more flexible.[18] And in order to ensure the loyalty of the literati, notably in the north, the court defended Confucian ethics without concessions. On this note, the following passage from the 1877 doctoral dissertation of the future mandarin patriot Phan Dinh Phung is revealing of a widespread state of mind: "How can one give up, overnight, regulations that go back through the centuries, in order to throw oneself into the pursuit of the new? Acting precipitously in pursuit of an apparent advantage does not necessarily ensure that you will obtain it, and even if one does obtain it, how can one avoid being despised for having turned into a barbarian?"[19]

Finally, in addition to the risk of internal subversion—whose real threat should not be exaggerated—there was the short-term effectiveness of the court's isolationist policy. Significantly, Dai Nam, unlike Japan, China, or Siam, only faced one Western power, France, whose European setbacks were well known in Asia. Furthermore, in the absence of foreign commercial penetration and economic transformation, it might have seemed that Dai Nam's weakly differentiated society could unite effectively against external aggression. The refusal of all compromise with the foreigners therefore might have been seen as a reasonable strategy. In some ways, traditionalism seemed to provide the monarchy with strength, at least until the very end of Tu Duc's reign. However, it also condemned it to a perpetual oscillation between haughty intransigence and humiliating surrenders to the foreigners. Moreover, there was no serious internal social incentive to reach a cultural conciliation with the West, on the basis of which imperial Vietnam could have promoted needed internal reforms, which might have allowed it to preserve its independence. The court refused such reforms. In 1863, on his return from France, the ranking mandarin, Phan Thanh Gian, wrote: "Since the day when, sent as an ambassador to the capital of France, I saw Western civilization at work, I could not avoid a feeling of admiration coupled with fear. Upon returning to my country, I exhorted my compatriots to wake up, to emerge from the torpor in which they had been immersed for so long. Alas! In spite of my efforts to convince them, none of them believed the truth of my words."[20] Vietnam was one of the last Asian states to be conquered by the West. The tenacity of its resistance was equaled by the magnitude of its defeat. Conquered, Vietnam would be struck from the map of world nations for decades.

The last causal factor that influenced the development of the Indochinese peninsula in the nineteenth century was the discontinuity in the dynamism of French imperialism in East Asia after the First Opium War (1839–41). One fundamental fact explains this discontinuity: the primacy of Europe and the Mediterranean basin in the expansion of French capitalism in the nineteenth century, even after France's defeat in the Franco-Prussian War (1870–71) ended further annexations on the continent (like those of Savoy and Nice in 1860). After 1871, however, French territorial expansion in Europe was no longer possible, and France was in a defensive position in this respect. The financial and commercial interests that sustained France's Asian expansion remained limited for a long time. As a result, its ambitions in the Far East were tightly subordinated to its policies in Europe. Yet the factors inhibiting French imperialism in the Far East were offset by the need after 1850 for French capitalism to expand globally. French industrial growth ran up against a limited domestic market and the weak development of mass consumption. In fact, France's share of world exports declined seriously after 1860, falling from 12.8 percent in 1860 to 9.8 percent in 1890.[21] In the American market, which until then had been so important, French exports collapsed. Asia was henceforth increasingly viewed as a substitute with seemingly inexhaustible capacities for absorption. Such hopes were ultimately dashed, however. Asia would only absorb 3.5 percent of France's exports in 1910, as against 5.8 percent for Germany and 24.4 percent for Great Britain.[22] In other words, if there was no mechanical link between the short-term strategies of the business world and the French colonial enterprise in the Far East, Asia was nevertheless inseparable from the external economic expansion of French capitalism, in particular for the industries propelling its growth—textiles and metallurgy.

The preservation of French political power and prestige also counted. More than ever in the nineteenth century, maintaining great power status meant having global reach. An Asian acquisition was of central importance to France achieving this goal. "The political interest of this expedition," the Commission de la Cochinchine (Special Commission for Cochinchina) noted in 1857, "arises from the force of circumstances propelling the Western nations toward the Far East. Are we to be the only ones who possess nothing in this area, while the English, the Dutch, the Spanish, and even the Russians establish themselves there?"[23] The need to conquer areas that were still "free" in the Far East (and mainland Southeast Asia was one such) was considered in France to be indispensable. This was particularly the case between 1850 and 1880. The goal was "to make Saigon a French Singapore," as the Marseille Chamber of Commerce put it in 1865.[24] It was essential to competing with the British at the global level and allowed the Third Republic to compensate for France's decline as the greatest nation on the European continent after Germany asserted its hegemony.

Colonial Indochina therefore owed its emergence not to the hazards of the time but rather to the nineteenth-century conjunction of the forces that were destroying the old Asian order. Far from being an adventure, a historical aberration, or an epic, it was an enterprise governed not only by the strengths of a Western dream but also by the new rationality of the modern world, which was increasingly imperial and conquering. It was an enterprise deeply rooted in a history that was disintegrating: that of East Asia, and in a history that was taking shape: that of the global power relations of the contemporary world.

The Colonial Moment

The Making of French Indochina, 1858–1897

Yes, no matter what happens, a European nation will enter Annam in order
to take on a controlling influence there. . . . It will not last, I am sure of that,
but it is necessary to go through it: Annam cannot escape this fate.
—PAUL BERT, resident general of France in Annam and Tonkin, letter to the
Catholic scholar Truong Vinh Ky [Petrus Ky], June 29, 1886

Indochina, a marginal region that was nevertheless central to the French empire, emerged in the midst of war, following a series of military expeditions that did not fulfill their ultimate goals and whose outcome long remained undecided. There were two major periods of conflict, separated by fifteen years of peace. Between 1858 and 1867, the lower basin of the Mekong River, the southern provinces of Dai Nam—present-day Vietnam—and the kingdom of Cambodia came under the control of France. Between 1867 and 1882, the colonial undertakings in Indochina stagnated, with a failed attempt in 1873 to occupy the northern part of Vietnam. From 1882 to 1897, the expansion resumed with vigor: northern and central Dai Nam and the Lao states became protectorates of France (map 1.1), while a sphere of French influence was established in the southern Chinese provinces, Yunnan, Guangxi, and Guangdong. The unequal modern colonial relationship between the crises and the dynamism of a dominating industrialized society and subjected cultures and societies was thus regionally established. The same process led the latter to be forcibly inserted, as a dependent entity, into a world system whose construction at the hands of the great Western capitalisms was nearly complete.

But nothing was played out in advance. If the establishment of Western domination over the Indochinese geographic area was foreseeable from the middle of the nineteenth century, the colonial form this domination took was not inevitable, and the colonizers designed their projects very gradually. It took more than a third of a century of complex transformations for this colonial order to fully impose itself.

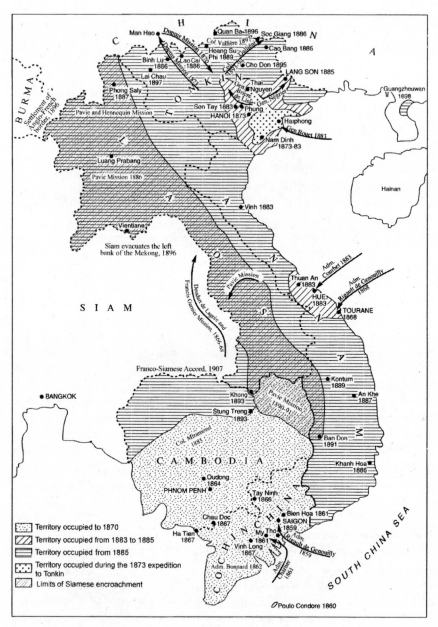

MAP 1.1. Stages in the making of French Indochina. (*Histoire militaire de l'Indochine*, vol. 3 [Hanoi, 1931].)

THE CONQUEST OF SOUTHERN INDOCHINA
(1858-1867)

The first advance of French Imperialism in Far East Asia was the annexation, in the context of the Second Opium War (1856–60), of the countries of the lower Mekong.[1] This advance is inseparable from the generalized civil war that, beginning with the revolt of the Taiping (1850–64), made it impossible for the Chinese empire to protect its southern tributaries. Furthermore, it was also determined by the nature of French and Southeast Asian societies. And, last, the competition between France and England was a permanent factor of French colonial expansion in the nineteenth century.

The Christian Question in Vietnam

Until the middle of the nineteenth century, there was no consensus in French society in support of new projects for Asian expansion. Heterogeneous, yet united, interest groups pressed for expansion into Indochina. The earliest urgings came from the missionary Church,[2] especially the influential Société des missions étrangères (Society of Foreign Missions), created by Monsignors Pallu and Delamotte-Lambert in 1658. Following their failures in China and in Siam, this society, along with the Franciscans of the Philippines, concentrated its efforts on Vietnam. The missionaries, the "teachers of religion" *(maîtres de religion),* created vigorous Christian communities in the six apostolic vicariates of Dai Nam and Cambodia, especially in the Spanish bishoprics of Bui Chu and of Western Tonkin (table 1.1). In Tonkin, their followers represented perhaps 3% to 5% of the population. These communities were strengthened by the support offered at the end of the eighteenth century by Bishop Pigneau de Béhaine and by a handful of French advisors to Prince Nguyen Anh, who became the emperor Gia Long, in the midst of the crisis that shook Vietnam following the great peasant revolt of the Tay Son (1771–79).

Their dynamism, however, was more the result of the clergy's vigorous action among the peasants, fishermen, boatmen, small merchants, and vagabonds, as well as among certain families of mandarins and semi-scholars who taught ideograms in the missionary schools, as has been shown by Alain Forest for the seventeenth and eighteenth centuries, and by Laurent Burel for the nineteenth century.[3] It was also attributable to the clergy's medical work; to the efficacity of the Association de la Sainte Enfance (Society of the Holy Childhood), which oversaw the care and baptism of sick or starving children and ran orphanages, a breeding ground for the Christian communities; to their agricultural colonies, founded on the French Catholic model of raising moral standards through work; and to the tenacious proselytizing of baptizing nuns.[4] Roman Catholicism—"a religion whose virtues are mightily prophylactic and protective," in Forest's words—both echoed local beliefs

TABLE 1.1   Members of Christian communities and French Catholic
missions in nineteenth-century Indochina

	1875	1886
Catholics	324,000	353,000
Baptisms	85,351	66,826
Missionaries	114⎤ 359	174⎤ 420
Native priests	245⎦	246⎦
Catechists	501	584
Churches and chapels	951	767
Schools	504	643

SOURCE: This assessment, taken from Vo Duc Hanh, *La place du catholicisme dans
les relations entre la France et le Viet-Nam de 1870 à 1886* (Bern: Peter Lang, 1993),
pp. 1405–10, is based on the archives of the seminary of the Missions étrangères de Paris,
of the *Annales de la Sainte Enfance*, and of the *Comptes rendus des travaux de la Société
des missions étrangères de Paris*.

and family rituals and simultaneously responded to a peasant society's desire not
only for salvation but for behavioral rectitude.

The Church's activities were tolerated under the reign of Gia Long (1802–20).
But afterwards, little by little, the missionaries lost ground in relation to the authorities. Indeed, the Confucian elite, for several valid reasons, considered Christianity a heterodox sect that could not be assimilated and that perturbed the global
system of cults and beliefs organized around the imperial figure. They equally
deemed it incompatible with other religious practices and with the official version
of Confucianism. Furthermore, certain missionaries sustained rebellions in the
hope of imposing a dynasty that would be favorable to them. Repression was instituted under the emperor Minh Mang in 1832. The first Catholic martyrs were a
Vietnamese priest and a French priest, Father Gagelin, both executed in October
1833. This was followed two years later by the torture and execution of Father Joseph
Marchand, who participated in the revolt of Le Van Khoi, adoptive son of the general governor of the south, in whom certain missionaries saw a new Nguyen Anh.
In 1836, an edict condemned European priests to death. Thousands of Christians,
including seven French and three Spanish priests, were martyred between 1833 and
1840. An inextinguishable conflict had opened up between the imperial power, the
dynasty, and the missions. This conflict occurred in the context of a genuine missionary offensive in Asia, supported by the financial power and energy of the
Œuvre de la Propagation de la Foi (Society for the Propagation of the Faith), created
in Lyon in 1822 by Pauline Jaricot. Fourteen new apostolic vicariates, of which seven
were assigned to the foreign missions, were created in China from 1844 to 1860.
From this arose an increase in tensions between the Roman Church and the Confucian states, which saw this barbarian religion as a cause of moral and social dis-

integration. The more Vietnam took refuge in a quasi-absolute isolationism, the more the ardor of the missionaries intensified.

The story of Monsignor Dominique Lefebvre is very representative of the Church's new Asian dynamism. Condemned to prison in 1845, then picked up by a French ship, he disembarked in Singapore and returned secretly to Vietnam the following year with Father Duclos. Both were captured. Duclos died in jail in June 1846; Lefebvre was condemned to death but not executed. In early 1847, he was back aboard a British ship, but he refused to be repatriated to Europe and disembarked in May 1847 in the Mekong Delta, where he evangelized clandestinely over the next several years. For the missionaries, Vietnam was a perfect mission country; besides the Philippines, it was the Church's only solid base in pagan Asia. They urged the government in Paris to impose religious freedom on the court in Hue, militarily, if necessary. The first serious incident took place in 1847 when, following an ultimatum demanding religious freedom, two French warships destroyed the coastal defenses and the Vietnamese fleet off Da Nang (Tourane). Emperor Thieu Tri put a price on the head of the missionaries and ordered the executions of Europeans, and his successor, Tu Duc, reiterated the edicts of persecution in 1848 and 1851. Even though these orders were not carried out, a threshold had been crossed. Henceforth, the missionary demand for a religious opening of the country was part of a new and irreversible historical logic, also clearly seen in China's difficult experiences during the same period. The establishment of diplomatic relations with outside powers on an equal legal footing resulted in the ruin of the tributary order of the Asian world; freedom of trade was instituted; and the Confucian literate class had to confront intolerable cultural competition, which was sustained in Vietnam by the widespread use of the transcription of the language into Roman characters (Quoc ngu), which the missionaries had invented in the seventeenth century. For Confucian Vietnam, the missionary challenge was of crucial importance.

At the beginning of the French Second Empire, the missionary campaign intensified. As early as 1852, eight bishops in the Far East sent a written demand to Prince-President Louis Napoleon Bonaparte for armed action against Hue. Charles de Montigny's diplomatic mission to Siam (Franco-Siamese treaty of August 15, 1856), Cambodia, and Vietnam in 1856–57 failed in the last two countries. The confusion of its goals and Montigny's tactlessness and arrogance came up against Siamese intrigues in Phnom Penh and a polite but nevertheless firm Vietnamese refusal in Da Nang. In spite of the naval bombardments of the forts of Da Nang, on September 26, 1856, and fifteen days of negotiations in January 1857, the French envoy obtained nothing. The mandarins exclaimed with joy: "The French bark like dogs but flee like goats." This failure implied that the future contained no other option than a military one. Some months later, on September 20, Tu Duc, emperor from 1848 to 1883, ordered the decapitation of Monsignor Díaz, a Spanish bishop in Tonkin; this was used to justify an expedition to Cochinchina. The tireless organizer of the missionary campaign was Monsignor Pellerin, an apostolic priest who had worked in northern Cochinchina and who, after his return to France in April 1857, with the help of Father Huc, intensified intervention with the Catholic hierarchy, Empress Eugénie, the Quai d'Orsay (the French Foreign Ministry), and the press. It was a note from Father Huc to the emperor that provoked the creation of the Commission spéciale pour la Cochinchine (Special Commission for Cochinchina, April 22–May 18, 1857) while the French-English expedition against China aimed at obtaining a revision of the unequal treaties of 1842–44 was being prepared.[5] The two priests were heard by the commission and received several times by Napoleon III.

Undoubtedly, it is necessary to avoid a mechanical identification of the Church with colonial imperialism. The missionaries working in Dai Nam were in fact more reserved than has generally been admitted regarding the French expansion after 1870. But earlier this was hardly the case. The missionaries legitimated the myth of a "Tonkinese" people ready to rise up against the Hue government, and of a sort of "liberating" conquest. They also played an irreplaceable role as informants and advisors. Thanks to their daily contact with the native populations, they were the only Europeans who could provide first-hand information about these societies. Familiar with indigenous social structures, and well aware of the decisive role played by the literati, the missions sought, at least until 1920, either to weaken those structures or to Christianize them, beginning with the imperial state.

The Church's actions were presented as part of a project that combined the propagation of faith, colonization, and an increase in France's national grandeur.[6] This convergence was the foundation for the progressive rallying of Catholic opinion to the colonial expansion project. For the Church, colonialism was vital, since it provided a response to the grave difficulties that accompanied its work in the societies of a newly industrialized Europe: the crisis of faith, threats against the papal state, the deterioration of the alliance with the French imperial regime after the war in Italy during 1859, and the rise of Republican anticlericalism. The development of ultramontanism dovetailed with the Church's increased overseas engagements, a path to a renewed universality, compensating for the slow decline of Christian culture in France that had been going on since before the French Revolution. "Precious Cross," Bishop Pigneau de Béhaine had said in 1799, "the French have knocked you down and removed you from their temples. Since they no longer respect you, come to Cochinchina."[7] Missionary action, the "colonization of souls," as a priest from Lyon would call it, also allowed the overseas coalition of the otherwise conflicting interests of the modern state and the Church, and was an effective restraint on their disputes back in France. It was henceforth one of the keys to the survival and the adaptation of a Catholicism that was on the defensive in France.

"Naval Imperialism"

The question of power was central for the big European states, and the role of the French military, especially of the Navy, which sought to grow along with the nation, was decisive in the first phase of French expansion in Indochina. The Navy was greatly inspired in this project by Justin Prosper Chasseloup-Laubat, who was minister of the Navy and the Colonies without interruption from 1860 to 1867, and who was succeeded as minister in 1867 by Admiral Charles Rigault de Genouilly, the conqueror of Saigon. It was Chasseloup-Laubat who persuaded Napoleon III to annex southern Dai Nam and who, in 1865, initiated the great mission to explore the Mekong led by Captain Ernest Doudart de Lagrée. Two of the five members of the Cochinchina commission of April–May 1857 were from the Navy: Admiral Léon Martin Fourichon and Captain Jaurès.[8] French Cochinchina was a product of "naval imperialism," and for twenty years, from 1859 to 1879, the Navy alone ran it; this was the so-called era of the admirals, of whom eight would eventually govern the colony after the treaty of 1862. As Prime Minister Jules Ferry put it in 1885: "It is also for our Navy that the colonies are created." Just as the Army had its officers in the *Bureaux arabes* (Arab offices) in Algeria, the Navy had its official administrators and indigenous affairs inspectors in Cochinchina after 1861, until the Gambettists put a civil government in place in May 1879. Even then, its first incumbent, Charles Le Myre de Vilers, was a former naval officer.

There was nothing fortuitous about the role of the Navy, which was more important in Indochina than in any other colony. This was confirmed at each decisive moment and proven by the centralization of power in the hands of Admiral Amédée Courbet in October 1883, and the appointment of admirals to the Haut Commissariat (High Commissioner's Office) of Indochina from 1940 to 1947. The Indochinese enterprise was, in fact, one of the important elements in creating a powerful fleet of warships with global range: the French Navy opted for steamships in the great naval building programs of 1846–51 and 1857, and by 1870, it possessed 339 warships, of which 45 were ironclads, as against 375, of which 42 were ironclads, for the British Royal Navy. It also greatly contributed to the development of the French Merchant Navy, whose rise was nevertheless slower.

In 1840, the Division navale des mers de Chine (Naval Division of the Chinese Seas) was created. This renewal of French maritime power necessitated the creation of a global network of bases able to provide coal, wood, and supplies. Without such a logistical infrastructure, it would be impossible for the French Navy to become independent of the omnipresent network of British bases. Fueling coal-fired ships' engines, in particular, was crucial. The acquisition of the mines of Hon Gai, already coveted in 1878 by the powerful China Merchants Navigation Co., was a driving motivation for the conquest of Tonkin. So, too, was the sensitive question of recruiting stokers and mechanics for the engine room. Only Asian, Chinese, Arab, and Indian sailors, it was thought, could stand the terrifying heat of the engine room in the tropics.

On September 20, 1880, the warship *Le Tonquin* embarked on the Saigon-Toulon crossing with the first crew of forty "Cochinchinese."[9] The occupation of the "Indochinese ports," remarkably well situated between the Indian Ocean and the Pacific, and the desire to create a French Hong Kong—many dreamed of Saigon, so close to the immense Mekong Delta, whose middle and upper portions were believed to be navigable—counted heavily in the French decision. At stake in the continuous pressure from the Navy was not simply the interest of a military lobby. There was also the possibility that French imperialism would gain importance in a global context. French colonization in the Far East was tied inevitably to the rise in the importance of the Navy, without which the global expansion of French commerce and the French state and the acquisition of the status of a worldwide, rather than just European, power would have been unthinkable. This was, in essence, the goal laid out by Foreign Minister François Guizot before the Chamber of Deputies on March 31, 1842: "To possess across the globe, at those points destined to become great centers of trade and navigation, strong, safe maritime stations that will serve as points of support for our trade. . . ."

The Pressure of Business Circles

The reservations of business circles about colonial action and the persistent misgivings throughout the century of liberal economists in line with Jean-Baptiste Say (1767–1832) have been emphasized for good reason. French historiography has often considered the search for new zones for the enhancement of capital and the role of economic factors to be negligible parts of France's Indochinese expansion. This is by no means certain. In fact, it might be argued that the combined pressures applied by the Navy and the Church in favor of colonial expansion, which had not been effective under the July Monarchy, succeeded under the Second Empire precisely because they then dovetailed with the expansionist dynamics of French capitalism, which after the economic crisis of 1847 entered an unprecedented phase of industrialization. Certainly, France had neither really invested in nor carried out commercial expansion in Asia prior to gaining complete control of the southern Indochinese peninsula: in 1840, only three French ships entered Chinese harbors, as opposed to thirty-four British and thirty-five American ships; the following year, French trade with the Far East was estimated at 40.5 million francs, whereas British exports raised some 310 million francs in China alone; in 1845, of the 108 Western trading firms installed in Chinese treaty ports, only one was French, against 68 British.[10]

In Indochina, however, as in the majority of France's colonial undertakings except Tunisia and Morocco, conquest was a necessary preliminary to investment.

After the initial fruitless attempts taken in relation to Dai Nam from 1816 to 1832, the interest of French business circles in Asia deepened as a result of the First Opium War (1839–41), the work of Consuls A. Barrot in Manila and Michel Chaigneau in Singapore, and, especially, the signature of the Franco-Chinese treaty of Whampoa in October 1844. Already in December 1843, an important mission from the chambers of commerce of manufacturing towns, composed of delegates representing Lyon silks and the wool and cotton industries, led by the diplomat Thomas de Lagrené, visited not only Canton and Shanghai but also Singapore, Batavia (Jakarta), Manila, and Tourane (Da Nang). The important survey it published on its return valued the trade of the "seas of Indochina" at a billion francs, half of which consisted of Chinese foreign trade.[11] From this arose the dream of a "French Hong Kong," for which the island of Basilan, in the archipelago of the Philippines, was considered in 1843. In addition, between 1840 and 1847, the Ministry of Agriculture and Trade dedicated some twelve issues of its *Documents sur le commerce extérieur* (Documents on Foreign Trade) to China and the Far East.

Though dominant historiography has downplayed these facts, this is an indication of the role of the economic forces at work and of the imagined economic stakes in France's first Indochinese expansion. Studies have shown that after 1840, cities with a stake in colonial trading—especially Bordeaux, which was deeply affected by the crisis of the Caribbean sugar economy—redirected their commercial and maritime endeavors toward the Maghreb, Africa, and Asia.[12] As early as 1858, the shipowners Eymond and Hewey opened a regular line from Saigon to Singapore, Hong Kong, Shanghai, and Manila. By November 1862, the company Denis Frères had settled in Saigon. Even Marseille capitalism, which, up until the middle of the nineteenth century, had done very little in the Far East,[13] started trying to expand its commercial horizons beyond the isthmus of Suez, especially after the opening of a branch of the powerful British Peninsular and Oriental Steam Navigation Company (or P&O) in Marseille in 1851.

However, there has been little systematic study of the colonial attitudes of the great industries of the time, metallurgy and textiles. Nevertheless, J.-F. Laffey, Pierre Cayez, and especially J.-F. Klein have revealed the tenacious efforts of the Lyon "Fabrique" (silk industry), which declined precipitously after 1852 because of the silkworm disease pebrine, to widen its sources of supplies in the Far East.[14] Lyon began to buy silk directly from China in 1851 and reached 2,000 tons in 1860, half of total French consumption. In the 1860s, half of Shanghai's raw silk exports and a third of Canton's were bought by the French, greatly profiting British shipowners, the masters of the Asian silk trade. As the case of Lyon shows, a true "municipal imperialism" with strong regional roots began to take shape. In 1854, the first Lyon silk merchant settled in Shanghai, joined in 1865 by Ulysse Pila from Avignon, who founded his own trading firm. At the end of 1874, out of sixty-three foreign trading houses in Shanghai, five were French. Between 1887 and 1892, Lyon on average imported from 6,000 to 7,000 tons of Asian raw silk annually. Though Lyon firms were limited by their dependence on the powerful British firm of Jardine and Matheson and the Hong Kong and Shanghai Banking Corporation, their Far East Asian activity was starting. From then on, Lyon capitalism would strive for the establishment of direct maritime links and French banks in the Far East.

The foundation of the Compagnie universelle du canal de Suez (Universal Suez Canal Company) and the beginning of the digging of the canal in 1859 strengthened the project of a new French expansion beyond India, structured around the Suez Canal. In 1860, a major bank, the Comptoir d'escompte, opened an agency in Shanghai, where a French concession was established between 1849 and 1856. The Messageries impériales, the future Messageries maritimes, the largest French shipping company and the primary transporter of Asian silk after 1870, inaugurated its Marseille-Saigon line in 1862. In its report of May 1857, the Cochinchinese Commission concluded that it was necessary to occupy the three principal Vietnamese ports in order to ensure the rapid development of French trade in China. To capture a part of the traffic from southern China and to reorient it toward a harbor under French control, preferably Saigon, which was already the center of rice exportation, was the underlying goal defined by the government of Napoleon III for the expedition to China prepared in accord with Britain the following year.

More generally, the new French expansion in Asia should be contextualized in the framework of the considerable development of European economic activities in the Far East from the middle of the nineteenth century on. Between 1800 and 1866, European exchanges with the Far East and India multiplied: in six years, from 1860 to 1866, they rose from 2,600 million francs to 4 billion (an increase of 45%), out of a world trade estimated at 52 billion francs in 1870; French trade with the region, in particular, rose from 285 million francs in 1866 to 638 million in 1888, representing a growth of 84.4% in two decades. In sum, if the real economic interest of French capitalism in the Far East was still fairly slight, a "demand for expansion" into Asia by a segment of business circles was, in fact, emerging. "We believe it is necessary to attract goods coming from the Far East to Marseille," the Marseille shipowner Rostand declared in the context of the great *Enquête de la marine marchande* (Report on the Merchant Navy) of 1863.[15] Chasseloup-Laubat echoed his words that same year, proclaiming: "It is a real empire that we need to create in the Far East."

The Fall of Saigon

In mid-July 1857, despite strong objections by his ministers, Napoleon III decided on a military intervention in Vietnam as a logical annex to the expedition to China. Spain joined the expedition in December with the dispatch of a corps of its Philippine army. Admiral Rigault de Genouilly's instructions were very "elastic."[16] He was to conquer a token territory, the port of Tourane (Da Nang), in order to negotiate a protectorate treaty or, by default, an "unequal" treaty similar to that which England had imposed on China on June 27, 1858 (and to the one it would impose on Japan on October 9, 1858). On August 31, 1858, a small expeditionary force, consisting of fourteen ships, two thousand French soldiers, and five hundred Spanish troops, backed by a few hundred Tagals, seized Tourane. They lacked the means to attack Hue, and the population did not rise up, as certain missionaries had predicted. Meanwhile, cholera decimated the units. The government of Hue refused to negotiate, and its troops resisted efficiently.

The French high command therefore decided to strike at Saigon, an essential supplier of rice for central Vietnam, located in the area that at the time was called "Basse-Cochinchine" (Lower Cochinchina), which unlike Hue was accessible from the sea. Simply put, the strategy was to blockade rice shipments to central Vietnam. Saigon was taken on February 17, 1859, but the ongoing war with China forced the evacuation of Tourane on March 30, 1860, and only allowed the maintenance in the south of a weak French-Spanish force of under a few thousand men. With difficulty they resisted the attacks of twelve thousand Vietnamese soldiers, reinforced by troops raised in the military colonies *(don dien)* of the delta. Saigon and its Chinese counterpart, Cholon, were defended throughout that year by the powerful fortified lines of Chi Hoa, supported by a defensive perimeter about twelve kilometers long blocking all the waterways, constructed under the orders of the skillful Vietnamese field marshal Nguyen Tri Phuong. Meanwhile, the persecution of Christians increased in the rest of the country.

It was the signature of peace with China (with the Beijing Treaty of October 29, 1860) and the end of the war in Italy that gave Admiral Léonard Charner the necessary means to take Saigon. The lines at Chi Hoa were taken on February 24–25, 1861; My Tho, a strategic key to the delta and to Cambodia, was taken on April 13; and French gunboats began penetrating the interior. In April, the provincial capitals of Ba Ria, Bien Hoa, and Vinh Long fell. The Hue court was split between realists—supporters of a "Siamese" strategy of negotiation that would allow more time and the modernization of the country—and diehards. Moreover, it was hampered by the interruption of the southern rice exports and by the serious revolt of the Catholic Ta Van Phung (Le Duy Phung) in the name of the Le, supported by the Spanish Dominicans, in the delta of the Red River. Obliged to choose between its enemies, the Hue court finally resigned itself to signing the treaty of June 5, 1862 (the Saigon Treaty), negotiated by Admiral Bonard, the first French governor of Cochinchina, and the representatives of the court, Phan Than Gian and Lam Huy Diep. Hue thereby ceded the three southeastern provinces of Dinh Tuong (or My Tho), Gia Dinh, and Bien Hoa, to France, along with the archipelago of Poulo Condore (Con Dao); granted freedom of navigation for French ships on all branches of the Mekong and opened Ba Cat, Quang Yen in Tonkin, and Tourane to trade; paid an onerous indemnity of four million dollars (piastres), or twenty million gold francs; and proclaimed religious freedom in the empire of Dai Nam, which also abandoned its suzerainty over Cambodia. Spain obtained only monetary compensation. The whole was a catastrophic treaty for Hue.

The annexation of the western provinces of Cochinchina, Vinh Long, An Giang (or Chau Doc), and Ha Tien was the logical continuation of this first stage of conquest. But in 1863, nothing was certain. As early as 1859, an active guerrilla war was already being organized among the peasants and the scholars in the occupied provinces, with the secret support of Hue. Go Cong was attacked on June 21–22, 1862. The insurgency, based in the swamps of the west, the coastal mangrove swamps, and along the border of the Plain of Reeds, and led by Truong Cong Dinh, a young *don dien* chief, was at its peak in 1862–63. However, although weakened by their leader's death in August 1864, the guerrillas resumed fighting at the start of 1866 in the western provinces and in the Plain of Reeds.[17] Moreover, Emperor Tu Duc considered the Treaty of Saigon no more than a tactical withdrawal.

In 1863, a Vietnamese diplomatic mission, directed by the remarkable mandarin Phan Thanh Gian, the chief proponent at court of a temporary compromise with France, attempted to negotiate the repurchase of the fallen provinces with Paris by exploiting the distrust of colonial wars of the French liberal middle class, who were dismayed at the cost of the conquest (140 million francs). The Vietnamese propositions—a fairly loose protectorate covering the entire south and the surrender of Saigon, My Tho, and Cap-Saint-Jacques, which amounted essentially to an Indochinese version of the granting of the treaty ports of Canton and Shanghai—seemed to a number of political figures to be more favorable to commercial penetration of Dai Nam than its annexation. Napoleon III, the *libre-échangistes* (partisans of free trade), and the Quai d'Orsay shared this point of view. The naval officer Gabriel Aubaret, an outstanding scholar and a great admirer of Chinese civilization, began negotiations in Hue and signed a treaty on July 15, 1864, that aimed at a restricted occupation. It was never, however, ratified because of the campaign unleashed in Paris by a coalescing colonial party backed by the Republican opposition, by Adolphe Thiers and Victor Duruy, and, in Saigon, by a Comité de développement industriel et agricole (Industrial and Agricultural Development Committee), jointly representing business interests and the Navy. For these, no longer just the commercial conquest of China but also control of a vast territory that was within cannon range—the paddy lands of the lower Mekong, an immense deltaic frontier, a "new Algeria" in the Far East—was at stake in the polemic.[18]

The decision reached in Paris to annex western Cochinchina had been anticipated a year before by the signature of a protectorate treaty with the Khmer king Norodom on August 11, 1863, at the initiative of Admiral Pierre de La Grandière, the French governor. Norodom, who was also challenged by the revolt of his stepbrother Si Votha in June 1861, hoped in this way to offset the reinforcement of the Thai threat following the lessening of the danger represented to his country by

Vietnam. Trapped in a situation in which it was threatened from the interior and exterior, the Khmer court had only one choice. The preceding sovereign, Ang Duong, had already sought French aid at the time of the Montigny mission to Kampot in 1856.[19] A "sanctuary" for the Vietnamese guerrillas of the south, and the key to the Mekong basin, Cambodia was crucial to control of the lower part of the river. Whoever intended to dominate southern Vietnam must also control Cambodia. This had been understood since the eighteenth century by the Vietnamese emperors, who had forced the weak Khmer state into a tributary dependence with the goal of consolidating their control of the delta. It was in essence this same "tributary" strategy that the French authorities took up. Through it, Cambodia was to become the base for an eventual expansion into Siam and toward the Mekong basin.

With the failure of Phan Thanh Gian's mission, the nonratification of the Aubaret treaty, and the advent of the protectorate over Cambodia, the fate of the last Vietnamese provinces in the south (Vinh Long, Chau Doc, and Ha Tien) was sealed. Between June 15 and 24, 1866, with the backing of Napoleon III, notwithstanding the hesitation of the Foreign Ministry, Admiral de La Grandière annexed the western provinces of the delta without warning. As Hue's imperial commissioner *(kinh luoc)* in the south, Phan Thanh Gian, who had sought a realistic temporary compromise in order to renegotiate the 1862 treaty and modernize the country, reluctantly gave in and then committed suicide. One year later, on July 15, 1867, a Franco-Siamese treaty confirmed the French protectorate over Cambodia in return for the transfer to the Bangkok government of the three Khmer provinces of Battambang, Sisophon, and Siem Reap.

Protests and awkward proposals for compensation by Hue were rebuffed by the French, who henceforth controlled southern Vietnam. Colonization had prevailed, in spite of the literati's refusal to collaborate, the administrative void created by the departure of the mandarins of western Cochinchina, and the resistance of peasant guerrillas—renewed in 1867 by the sons of Phanh Thanh Gian and continuing until December, through the uprisings of the Achar Sva (Sua) (1864–66) and the Buddhist thaumaturge Pou Kombo (June 1866–December 1867) at the frontier of Cochinchina and Cambodia—as well as the last serious revolt of 1872 in the region of Soc Trang, Tra Vinh, and Ben Tre.

INTERLUDE (1867–1878)

After 1867, French expansion in Indochina entered a period of remission, which persisted until the so-called Opportunist Republicans came to power in France in 1877. Napoleon III's disastrous Mexican adventure (1862–66); the Prussian defeat of the Austrian empire at Sadowa (1866); the battle of Sedan, when the French emperor and his army surrendered to the Prussians (1870); the Paris Commune (1871); and the sharp conflict between Republicans and monarchists in the years that followed all contributed to paralyzing the French colonial thrust. For France, European issues once again were the priority.

The Tonkin Crisis of 1873

This crisis exploded in the continuation of the great Mekong exploration that had begun in 1866–68. Led by two naval officers, Ernest Doudart de Lagrée and Francis Garnier, the expedition explored the course of the Mekong for 2,000 kilometers (as well as the course of the Yangtze River for 500 kilometers) and proved its impracticability as a navigable route into China. It discovered the existence of silk, tea, and textile exports from Yunnan via the Red River.[20] The commercial myth of Yunnan was thus born and would remain powerful until the end of the century, despite the fact that Consul Alexandre Kergaradec had proven the limits of the Red River's navigability after his two trips upriver in 1876 and 1877. From then on, acquiring privileged access to Tonkin became a necessity for French imperialism, particularly since Britain was exploring ground routes between Burma and Yunnan. It was the start of the race to Yunnan between the French and the British. An active lobby of French businessmen in China rallied to this project—notably, Jean Dupuis, who had been established in China since the Second Opium War (1858–60) and furnished arms to the Chinese imperial forces that put down the Yunnan Muslim uprising of 1855–73; and Ernest Millot, former president of the board of directors of the French Concession in Shanghai—as did the Catholic Missions, the Navy, and the colonial administration of Cochinchina.

In March 1873, Dupuis had successfully led an arms convoy to the Chinese Marshal Ma via the Red River into Kunming. A pretext for military intervention presented itself when Vietnamese mandarins detained Dupuis in Hanoi with his return shipment of salt from May to October. Dupuis's objective was to establish, with his Chinese partners, a two-way flow on the Red River of European products and minerals from Yunnan, in order to open the region to European trade under French control. Determined to intervene, Admiral Marie-Jules Dupré, the governor of Cochinchina, who had ordered the reconnaissance of the Red River in 1872, seized the opportunity. On October 11, he sent Francis Garnier to Hanoi with 222 men and four small ships to officially settle the Dupuis affair. Just then, a Hue delegation arrived in Saigon to obtain the restitution of the three Cochinchinese provinces annexed by France in 1867. In fact, Garnier's main mission was to obtain from Hue, by negotiations started in Saigon or by force, a new treaty that would grant the opening of the river to French trade, the annexation of western Cochinchina, and, possibly, a protectorate in Tonkin.[21] Dupré's strategy was aimed at finding an economical way to force Hue to capitulate, as had been done in 1858. In view of the Vietnamese refusal to negotiate anything other than the evacuation of Dupuis, Garnier, actively seconded by Monsignor Paul Puginier, the bishop of western Tonkin, decided to use force. He proclaimed freedom of navigation on the Red River under

French protection on November 17, 1873, and on November 20, he seized the citadel of Hanoi, followed by other strategic points in the delta. He also installed pro-French authorities in the provinces of Nam Dinh, Ninh Binh, Hai Duong, and Hung Yen.

It all failed, however. Garnier was killed on December 21 at the Paper Bridge by Black Flags, former Taiping insurgents who had taken refuge in North Vietnam and were hired by the Vietnamese administration to fight the French. In Tonkin, unrest was spreading throughout the country. The emergence, dating back to 1864, of a powerful anti-Christian movement among the literati (evidenced by demonstrations of candidates during examinations and calls for the massacre of Christians, "those French of the interior," and Prince Hong Tap's plot in 1864) culminated in 1874 with the Van Than movement.[22] Following the example of Monsignor Puginier, the Catholic communities had often helped Garnier. Hundreds of Christian villages were burned in Tonkin and in Nghe An. In Paris, reticence took hold: occupying Tonkin was out of the question. Instructions of January 8, 1874, enjoined Dupré to retreat.

Dispatched to Hanoi, Lieutenant Paul Philastre, who was very hostile to Garnier's initiative, signed a new, ambiguous treaty with the imperial government on March 15, 1874, under which France would evacuate Tonkin and promised military aid to Hue. In turn, the imperial city acknowledged the abandonment of the western provinces of Cochinchina, accepted the creation of joint customs houses and of concessions, temporarily entrusted the direction of its customs to the French, and legalized Christianity once more. It also agreed to the presence of a French resident in Hue and accepted French consulates, all protected by restricted garrisons, in Hanoi, in Ninh Hai, near the future Haiphong, and in Thi Nai (Binh Dinh). The commercial treaty of August 31, 1874, proclaimed free trade on and around the Red River. Through the treaty of March 15, Vietnam saw "its entire independence" from China recognized (art. 2) and was promised French military and naval assistance, in return for the acceptance of "French protection"—although the Vietnamese negotiators refused to allow the word *protectorat* to be used—and a vague agreement to conform its foreign policy to that of France.

In spite of the Hue concessions, the affair of 1873 was a serious setback for the defenders of the extension of colonization to all of Dai Nam. The monarchist government of the duc de Broglie had liquidated the Garnier expedition as cheaply as possible. The conservative majority in the National Assembly, which was committed to giving priority to "continental patriotism" and was strongly hostile to the politics of conquest, especially since it might lead to conflict with China, searched for a compromise in Asia. In 1877, reverting to Aubaret's approach, Minister of Foreign Affairs Louis Decazes declared that France had entirely renounced its protectorate over Annam. This final respite temporarily strengthened Dai Nam's Confucian monarchy. However, given the limitations of its own thinking, the Hue regime was only able to take advantage of this last chance in a traditionalist manner.[23]

The treaty of 1874, however, included several possibilities that never saw the light. The first of these was the establishment between France and Dai Nam of a relationship of noncolonial dependence, similar to the "unequal relationship of independence" that Britain was in the process of forming with Siam and China. The second was that of a final respite for the government in Hue, one that Tu Duc and his entourage, henceforth more open to reformist ideas, probably hoped to use in order to proceed, with French technical aid, toward a limited modernization of the empire along the lines of the Chinese *Yangwu yundong* (Western activities movement). They were undermined in this, however, by the echo among the literati of the anti-Christian subversion of the Van Than, and of their radical refusal of any reconciliation with the foreigners. Furthermore, the court never conceived of its relations with France as other than a vague tributary allegiance. The treaty of 1874 therefore inevitably led to a number of incidents. Hue, where the proponents of a traditionalist resistance quickly dominated once again, accumulated the barriers to the development of foreign trade in Haiphong and reinforced its tributary links with China. In 1876 and 1880, the court sent emissaries bearing tribute not to the border village of Nan Ning, as was customary, but directly to Beijing. In 1878, it solicited Chinese military aid against brigands and insurgents in Tonkin. The strength of the dominant political categories in Vietnamese society, the mobilization of Vietnamese literati against the treaty, as well as against Christians, pressure from the colonial lobby in Paris, and the chain of events probably at that point destroyed the possibility of imperial Dai Nam avoiding colonization. The brief encounter of the bureaucratic elite of Vietnam with European "modernity" came too late.

The Rise of the Colonial Idea

During the lull of the early 1870s, a decisive debate took place in France that led to the politics of colonial expansion abruptly accelerating after 1878. Without this, the annexation of the whole Indochinese peninsula would not have been conceivable. Nationalist ideology was reorganized around the colonial project, and the French imperialist doctrine took hold. Indeed, after 1871, colonization gradually became a central part of the collective vision of the national future. "Colonialism"—it would seem that the term was introduced into the French political vocabulary in 1895 by a fierce adversary of overseas expansion, the liberal economist Gustave de Molinari—made its appearance in the form of a vast movement of thought that saw the general functioning of French society, the future of the nation, and colonial development as intimately connected.

The essential texts were the economist Paul Leroy-Beaulieu's *De la colonisation chez les peuples modernes* (published in 1874 and reprinted five times by 1908) and Gabriel Charmes's *Politique extérieure et coloniale* (1885). Leroy-Beaulieu laid the theoretical foundation for the rallying of liberal economic thought, until then very reticent, to the colonial idea. During the 1880s, the majority of liberal economists, like Charles Gide, Frédéric Passy, and Léon Say, ultimately accepted colonization, all the while looking to promote free trade in the colonies instead of protectionism. For them, colonizing was no longer a marginal activity, but rather a response to the irreparable weakening of France in Europe, to the European crisis of French nationalism, and to the profound upset of the national consensus caused by the events of 1871. It was, furthermore, a legitimate response: Republican culture indeed took it upon itself, throughout the nineteenth century, to develop a messianic vision of liberating colonization that would propagate the Republic's founding trinity, science, progress, and democracy, to the ends of the earth. The "duty of civilization" to native peoples, Jules Ferry asserted in 1882, was "to proclaim the law of work everywhere, to teach purer morals, to spread and to transmit our civilization." It was "to deliver the blessing of the European civilization," as Admiral Charner had already put it in 1861.[24]

Between 1871 and 1880, the Republican idea, the ideal of the nation's self-representation, in the midst of reconstruction, was enduringly projected into colonization. Finally, the colonial dream corresponded, more prosaically, to the Republican preoccupation with the necessity of establishing a form of social regulation at the heart of industrial nations. For the "advanced" French Republicans, starting with Léon Gambetta (president of the Chamber of Deputies, 1879–81; prime minister, 1881–82), who truly inspired the resumption of overseas expansion, colonial imperialism would be the crutch of equality. It was the indispensable stabilizer of a nation torn apart by five revolutions in the short period from 1830 to 1870, the shock absorber of the fall in the fortunes of the traditional elite and the petite bourgeoisie, as well as the proletarianization of the peasantry. "A nation that does not colonize is bound irrevocably to socialism, to the war between rich and poor," Ernest Renan prophesized in 1871.[25] "Social peace, in the industrial age of humanity, is a question of outlets," Jules Ferry said.[26] Colonial administrators and theorists such as Paul Bert, J.-L. de Lanessan, Joseph-Simon Galliéni, Auguste Pavie, and Paul Doumer sprang not only from the new Republican bourgeoisie made up of the notables of commerce and industry, but also from the milieu of small manufacturing and small rural landowners, from the new social strata whose arrival Gambetta had predicted in a famous 1876 speech.

The colonial project, a historical new deal counterbalancing the disasters of recent French history, showed an unprecedented capacity to mobilize supporters, notwithstanding that it deeply divided opinion. It did so largely through the scientific movement: numerous scientific institutions, such as the Muséum d'histoire naturelle (Natural History Museum) and the influential Société nationale d'acclimatation (National Zoological Society), today's Société nationale de protection de la nature, founded in 1854 by Isidore Geoffroy Saint-Hilaire as the Société impériale zoologique d'acclimatation; learned societies dealing with political economy, such as that of Lyon; and most especially by the geographical movement. In the decade following 1871, ten geographical societies were created on the model of the Société de géographie de Paris, which rallied to the colonial expansion in the 1860s under the impulsion of its powerful general secretary, Charles Maunoir, and had 2,473 members in 1885. One of the most active was the Société géographique de Lyon, created in 1873. The representatives of the business milieu joined them, and their involvement created parallel societies devoted to commercial geography, which sought to stimulate prospecting for new outlets for French industry. A case in point is the Société de géographie commerciale de Paris (Paris Commercial Geography Society), which chose Dr. Jules Harmand, former companion of Francis Garnier in Tonkin, as its vice president in 1878. Already coming together before 1870, expansionist and intellectual lobbies and circles constituted themselves into an intricate network connected with the political and business milieus of France.

Indochina occupied a central position in the great colonial debates between 1873 and 1880.[27] More than virtually any other area of expansion, Indochina effectively condensed the entire colonial problematic, and one cannot overemphasize the decisive importance that it had for the future of French colonial imperialism in the 1880s, just as it did sixty-five years later, in the twilight of empire. Although rendering dependent what remained of Vietnam incited violent opposition in France, notably during the great Indochinese crisis of French politics in 1885, the defeat of this opposition, already foreshadowed in the previous decade, ultimately gave the French colonial project its true opportunity. Missionaries, officers, voyagers, and explorers, such as Jules Harmand during the course of his five journeys to the Mekong basin in 1875–77, preceded colonial possession with scientific possession, creating a new geopolitical imaginary. They "reinvented" Indochina, a new term whose former hyphen (Indo-China) was subsequently elided, the imagined territory where a colonial domain could be created out of a geographically unknown area.

Francis Garnier was especially active in this regard. In 1873, he published his *Voyage d'exploration en Indochine,* a remarkable account of his exploration of the Mekong from 1866 to 1868, which had a great deal of success. Between 1871 and 1874, he also published six articles and booklets on the necessity of commercial penetration of central China. The notes that he brought back at the beginning of 1873, detailing his journey to Sichuan were published in 1882 as *De Paris au Tibet.* Jean Dupuis's literary activity was also significant: he published fourteen articles and six books between 1874 and 1886; in 1877, in a speech to the Paris Geographical Society, he denounced the inertia of French politics in Annam. The Société académique indochinoise (Indochinese Academic Society) was established to promote the studies of "Trans-Gange India,"[28] and more or less romanticized narratives about the peninsula multiplied.

Not only did Indochina become part of the texture of the new national idea, it also became one of the priorities of the newborn Third Republic's foreign policy, as is shown by the imperialistic leanings of Gambetta's newspaper *La République française* at the time of the Garnier expedition. The campaign of the so-called Tonk-inois merged with what Raoul Girardet has called the *nationalisme d'expression mondiale* (global nationalism) of the Opportunist Republicans. This interest in In-dochinese affairs, as elaborated on in the writings of Jules Harmand, Paul Bert's son-in-law Joseph Chailley-Bert, Jules Ferry, J.-L. de Lanessan, Paul Doumer, and Albert Sarraut,[29] among others, would long remain central to the development of French colonial thought.

FRENCH CAPITALISM AND COLONIAL EXPANSION IN THE FAR EAST AFTER 1879

Certainly, the new colonial discourse was a vehicle for fantasies that intoxicated its authors as well as French opinion, myths that multiplied a hundredfold the promise of the fabulous Chinese market, or of a new Louisiana in Tonkin, which would be the source of many disappointments over the next twenty years. How-ever, the project of opening a commercial route to Yunnan and Sichuan via Tonkin strongly oriented the resumption of French expansion in the Far East.

Classic Colonial Interests

The resumption of colonial expansion in Indochina was part of a fundamental movement that one cannot simply limit, as the solidly installed cliché would have it, to the actions of a small lobby of opportunists and speculators aided by a hand-ful of officers and priests. It is not that their actions were negligible. The classic colonial interests were actually more active than ever. The new Gambettist ad-ministration; the merchants and the colonists of Cochinchina—a true *colonie colonisatrice* (colonizing colony); the colony's first civil governors, Charles Le Myre de Vilers (1879–83) and Charles Thomson (1883–85), Gambetta's former secre-tary; and the deputy Jules Blancsubé, republican mayor of Saigon and a friend of Gambetta's, all affirmed their position in favor of expansion into central and north-ern Indochina. Their dictum was, as the historian Alfred Rambaud, who was close to Jules Ferry, wrote: "Extending is the only means of preserving."[30]

The pressure from the business milieu and from the speculators should not be underestimated either, especially that of Dupuis and Millot, who were closely linked to the Gambettists and to Charles de Freycinet. In 1882, Dupuis founded the Société d'études et d'exploitation du Tonkin (Society for the Study and Ex-ploitation of Tonkin) with the view to investing, with the participation of Hong Kong capitalists, in the coalfields of northern Vietnam—plans also claimed by an-other group organized by a nephew of Ferry's, Bavier-Chauffour.[31] These milieus produced the myth of the "Tonkin mines," as well as several maps distributed dur-ing the parliamentary debates of May 1883, which bore fanciful captions such as

"Mung-tä-tchen-po: *grosses pépites d'or* [big gold nuggets]," "Muong-lou: *riches mines d'or* [rich gold mines]," and so on.

The interests of the French Army and Navy also should not be disregarded. Tonkin and Annam, in particular, offered points of logistical support, since they could supply the coal that would be required by a fleet with global range along the lines envisioned by the *Jeune école* (Young School) of Admiral Hyacinthe Aube and Commander François Fournier, which argued for a more mobile force based on cruisers, torpedo boats, and ships lightly armed with torpedoes.[32] The doctrine prevailed for a time with the nomination of a Republican naval officer, Admiral Jean Jauréguiberry, to the Ministry of the Navy and the Colonies in 1879–80, and again in 1882–83. In 1879, he proposed the first plan for occupying Tonkin, which called for a corps of 6,000 soldiers. More than ever, it seemed that possession of Indochina would determine the future of French naval power in the Indian Ocean and the Pacific.

Finally, after 1880, with the Church and the Republic increasingly at odds, territories that could be colonized also became indispensable grounds for compromise. Even though the Catholic missions were more reserved toward the conquest between 1870 and 1874, certain members of the hierarchy, notably Albert de Mun and Monsignor Charles Freppel, a monarchist deputy for Brest from 1880 to 1891, threw all their weight behind occupation of the whole of Indochina.

The New Economic Problematic

These influences, however, were only successful because they seemed to answer a more fundamental economic exigency. Certainly, the best historians often reject this type of explanation, with seemingly solid arguments to back up their point of view. We know, for instance, that Jules Ferry invoked the commercial imperative only after having taken the political decision to conquer Tonkin. It is also certain that we should not view the creation of the protectorate over Dai Nam and Laos as the work of financial capital (in the Hobsonian or Leninist sense of the term), born of the fusion between large industries and banks, and of large monopolist groups looking to divide the peninsula between themselves. These groups, which would be very active in Russia and in Turkey after 1900, hardly existed in France at the time, and they could in no way have been behind the Indochinese enterprise of the 1880s. There are however, two reservations to this evaluation. First, colonization of the peninsula was the springboard of the expansion into China for coalescing French financial capital. Second, Indochina was long the site of the accumulation and formation of important segments of this financial capital, in particular, of the powerful Banque de l'Indochine, today the Banque Indosuez. For these two reasons, the colonial Indochinese enterprise can in hindsight be said to have truly participated— by anticipation, if you will—in the imperialistic quest for new realms of profit.

Other data, in contrast, show the extent to which economic decisions were essential in the French colonial offensive in Indochina. French capitalism, along with all the industrialized economies, suffered a long depression in 1873–95, which reached its low point in 1884–85. The metropolitan economy faced both industrial stagnation—industrial growth rates were negative in 1873, 1877, 1879, and from 1883 to 1885—and a crisis in terms of profits and the exportation of merchandise. France had never known such a long period of economic uncertainty in the industrial era: between 1875 and 1905, its GNP at current prices augmented by only 10%, compared to 113% for Germany and 60% for the United Kingdom. All of the sector indicators confirm the depth and persistence of these difficulties. The mechanisms of profit accumulation and creation were undermined. The deterioration of profits followed the fall of returns on investments in the home market, which was itself caused, as Jean Bouvier has shown, by the hyperaccumulation of capital that had taken place around 1870. For example, the Crédit lyonnais, founded in 1863–64 with 10 million francs in deposits, had roughly 1,382 million in 1881. From then on, the export of capital became more critical than ever as a way of raising and regulating the rate of profit. Considerable before 1870 (700 million francs invested abroad on average each year) but hesitant from 1876 to 1885 (with a yearly average of 315 million), this export of capital underwent a recovery from 1885 to 1895 (with a yearly average of 469 million), before reaching a record level from 1896 to 1913 (with a yearly average of 1,200 to 1,300 million).[33] During the economic depression, colonies that could take their place among the principal outlets for these capital fluxes were viewed as solutions to the problem of finding sites for the profitable investment of excess capital. It was indeed precisely at the beginning of this cycle of recession, on January 21, 1875, through the initiative of the Comptoir d'escompte and the Société générale, that the Banque de l'Indochine—whose influence on France's Indochinese politics still needs to be elucidated—was founded.[34]

Compounding the crisis in profitability was the weakening of French foreign trade, whose key role in the sale of metropolitan products must be kept in mind. Over the nineteenth century, exports steadily increased as a proportion of France's physical product, but they slowed to around 4.25 billion francs a year between 1880 and 1904 (fig. 1.1). During the period from 1875 to 1914, French trade was at its lowest point in 1877, and in 1878, the commercial balance began to show a stubborn deficit (figs. 1.2 and 1.3).

French economic and political leaders thus saw the creation of captive consumer markets as an efficient riposte to a situation that was all the more serious because all of France's principal commercial partners, with the exception of England, adopted protectionist legislation in the 1880s. As J.-L. de Lanessan, the future governor-general of Indochina, noted in 1886:

Industry at first only worked for the home market, through exchanges between cities and the countryside; but soon this market became too narrow, and industry was compelled to manufacture for export, that is, for foreign nations. However, the

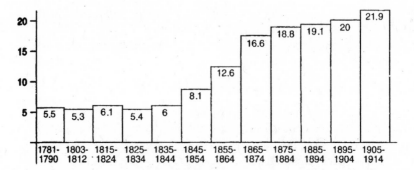

FIGURE 1.1. Relationship between French exports and production (percent), 1781–1914. (Based on data from J.-C. Toutain, "Les structures du commerce extérieur de la France, 1789–1970," in *La position internationale de la France: aspects économiques et financiers, XIXᵉ–XXᵉ siècles*, ed. M. Lévy-Leboyer [Paris: Editions de l'Ecole des hautes études en sciences sociales, 1977].)

same things have occurred in these nations, the same evolution has taken place in all civilized nations.... With the number of unindustrialized civilized countries decreasing every day, it is increasingly outside of them that manufacturers are obliged to search for consumers.[35]

Gambetta's decree of November 1881 transferring responsibility for the colonies from the Ministry of the Navy to the Ministry of Commerce, and his decision to place at the head of these two departments spokesmen for commerce from Marseille and Bordeaux, Maurice Rouvier and Félix Faure, were significant in this regard. No less revealing was the debate that ensued in the Chamber in 1883 under pressure from the textile industry of northern France, which wished to abolish the free trade that a Senate decree (*sénatus-consulte*) had established for the colonies in 1866. This debate led to a vote for the assimilation of the customs regulations of the colonies to those of the metropolitan France in November 1887, and then to the protectionist Méline customs tariff on January 11, 1892.

Jules Ferry would affirm forcefully that the most dependable "escape from the crisis," a necessary corollary to the resumption of growth, was through "colonial policy" that was "the daughter of industrial politics." This was not simply a commercial fantasy, as is frequently said today, even if the mirage of the markets of Tonkin and Yunnan had some misleading effects. In fact, the entire fabric of French industry and agriculture gradually formed strong ties with colonial markets, and many businessmen pushed for their conquest, or at least accepted it—which was already a great deal. Nevertheless, there was no automatic direct causal link between economic determination and the conquest of Indochina. It was this larger movement that gave unity to the conglomerate of businesses and the very heterogeneous

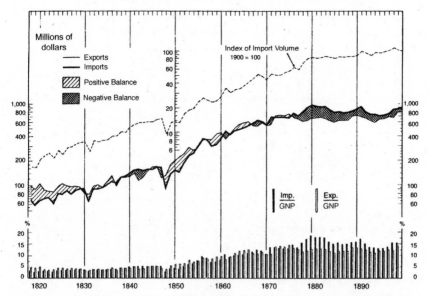

FIGURE 1.2. French foreign trade until 1900. (Based on J.-M. Jeanneney and E. Barbier-Jeanneney, *Les économies occidentales du XIXe siècle à nos jours*, vol. 1 [Paris: Presses de la Fondation nationale des sciences politiques, 1985], p. 240.)

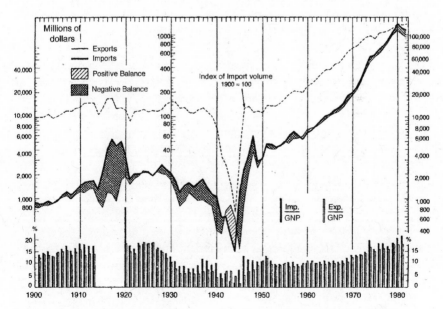

FIGURE 1.3. French foreign trade after 1900. (Based on Jeanneney and Barbier-Jeanneney, *Les économies occidentales*, 1:240.)

interests that would come together to form colonial capitalism. The main industries of the time pressured for Indochinese expansion. The cotton industry of the north, in Rouen and the Vosges, which in 1877 was still the third largest in the world; Le Creusot and Paris metallurgy; and the Lyon silk industry all demonstrated their interest in the endeavor.[36] Their goal remained China. It was a goal outlined by Francis Garnier, who wrote in an article posthumously published in 1882: "There is no possible future for our manufacturers if we do not claim our share of the Chinese market, or if we continue to pay British or American middlemen a high commission on Chinese raw materials."[37]

Thanks to Jean-François Klein's research, the Lyon case is now well known.[38] The Lyon silk industry was the only French industry whose production was dominant on the world market; it was endangered, however, by the rise of silk manufacturing in Milan and the Rhine port of Krefeld in Germany. Moreover, after the pebrine disaster, it became dependent on imports of Chinese raw silk. In 1877, 42% of the silk manufactured in Lyon was made with these imports; in 1900, 40.7%, and in 1910, 39.8%.[39] Inasmuch as Indochina was potentially a substitute source of raw silk, the Lyon trade was deeply concerned with its development. Its major firms invested in the activities of the Banque de l'Indochine and of the British Hong Kong and Shanghai Bank. In 1863, its silk merchants opened a silk-trading house in China directed by the young Ulysse Pila (1837–1909). In Lyon, the factory owners, the bankers, the silk merchants, and, with them, the ironmasters of the industrial basin of the Loire, their newspapers, the chamber of commerce, the Société géographique, and the Société d'économie politique constituted a powerful pressure group, directed by Pila and the banker E. Aynard, a liberal deputy of the Center-Left. Around 1883–84, this group, already in existence, converted to the Tonkin project of the Gambettists and Ferryists. At this point, they planned to penetrate and develop southern China commercially via Tonkin, which was strategically placed for the purpose and would only need to be equipped with economic infrastructure. Henceforth, they subscribed to the idea of a French protectorate at the southern frontier of the Qing empire, entailing colonization of Indochina based on free trade. To this end, the Lyon chamber of commerce and Société géographique, with the support of a dozen other chambers of commerce, organized Paul Brunat's mission for the commercial exploration of Tonkin in 1884–85. They leaned heavily toward military conquest. Allied to business circles in Marseille and Paris, and to the cotton industry of eastern France, they were jointly active in the Banque de l'Indochine, starting to invest before 1900 (perhaps around 15 million francs) in harbor and river infrastructure in Tonkin, as well as in the trading of Annam salt for Yunnan opium. Pila helped found some of the first businesses in the protectorate: Messageries annamites à vapeur in 1885; Docks et magasins généraux de Haiphong in 1886; and the Compagnie lyonnaise indochinoise in 1898. An active Republican, he became the counselor to his friend Paul Bert, with whom he maintained close ties after the latter became resident general in 1886. Pila also organized an important colonial exposition in Lyon in 1894. He was to be one of the true founders of French Indochina.

Ten years later, when the breakup of China was being planned, French business pressure for more aggressive economic penetration of southern China—"the greatest still unexplored market in the world," according to the British explorer Archibald Colquhoun[40]— intensified. The French focused on Yunnan, Sichuan, Guizhou, and Guangxi. As in the past, pressure was often applied by competitive business and the chambers of commerce that spoke for it. In 1894, at the initiative of the indefatigable Pila, those of Lyon, Marseille, Bordeaux, Lille, Roubaix, and Roanne established the Mission lyonnaise d'exploration commerciale en Chine, directed by Henri Brenier (1895-97). This time, however, powerful industrial and banking interests with links to the Quai d'Orsay and the Army also intervened. They took action not through the classic channels of the chambers of commerce but by going straight to the top of the government. Indochina was the base for their activity in China, where they, especially the Banque de l'Indochine, were readily tempted by the possibilities of cooperating with foreign capital in the creation of international consortiums—which were "ultra-imperialist," in a sense—aimed at equipping the country, notably with railroads.

In June 1896, the Compagnie de Fives-Lille obtained authorization from the Chinese to build a railroad from Longzhou to Dong Dang, extending the Hanoi–Lang Son line; but in the end, it was not built. The line from Yunnan (Haiphong-Kunming) was the object of a series of technical and economic missions to China. In 1895, the Comité des Forges (Ironworks Committee) created the Société d'études industrielles en Chine, which the following year sent out the engineer Dujardin-Beaumetz, an important member of the committee. This mission was completed by the Guillemoto and Belard missions in 1897-98, and those, much more prudent in their conclusions, of the consuls Auguste François (1899) and Haas (1900-1903) to the upper basin of the Yangtze. For its promoter Paul Doumer, who was closely tied to big business— particularly to the Union des industries métallurgiques et minières and the Compagnie générale d'électricité, over which he would preside in 1911—the construction of this railroad was a necessary prelude to the annexation of Yunnan. The decrease in orders for the construction of railroads in Europe helped to valorize the project for heavy industry and the large French banks. Because the Quai d'Orsay deeply disagreed with Doumer's methods, it was with difficulty that a consortium was created, in 1898, based on Guillemoto's hasty report, for the construction of the line, which gave birth to the Compagnie française des chemins de fer du Yunnan in June 1901. The consortium grouped together the main French banks (Comptoir national d'escompte, Société générale, Crédit industriel et commercial, Paribas, Banque de l'Indochine) and the major firms of the railway industry (Count Vitali's Régie générale des chemins de fer and the Société des Batignolles). A number of mining unions came into being in 1898-1900.

THE CRISIS OF TONKIN AND THE PROTECTORATE
OVER ANNAM-TONKIN (1880–1885)

The mechanisms to advance French colonization in Indochina were therefore established, particularly once the question of the political regime was settled in France after the crisis of May 16, 1877. Yet this advance would be singularly hesitant. Colonization was held up both by the complex decision-making process that accompanied it, composed of initiatives on the ground, as well as governmental decisions—the empire was being built both at its center and its periphery—and by the vigorous resistance it incited in France. Opponents included liberal economists like Gustave de Molinari; nationalists for whom the annexation of Tonkin signified the abandonment of Alsace-Lorraine; and monarchists, like the duc de Broglie, who disagreed that "colonial policies were in any way a compensation for the misfortunes experienced in Europe." De Broglie long remained attached to the idea of the primacy of continental issues, denouncing the entrapment of France in the "wasps' nest of Tonkin." Furthermore, the question of Indochina, the symbol of the colonial project, profoundly divided the Republicans. Like the Socialists, the Radicals, whose program of 1881 and electoral manifesto of July 1885 rejected all politics of conquest, denounced its risks and implications. They believed it was impossible to reconcile overseas expansion with the recovery of external dynamism within Europe, and, most important, that it signified the exclusion of all social reform policies and any hope of raising the standard of living of the popular classes of France. Colonialism was, in other words, the abandonment of radicalism's original great historical project in favor of external growth. "You want to found an empire in Indochina. We want to found the Republic," said Clemenceau, who lucidly celebrated "the best of the outlets, the interior outlet, much more powerful, much more desirable, more profitable in the true sense of the word, than the external outlets, so problematic and so costly."[41]

What ultimately came decisively into play in the dramatic engagement of the Republic in Indochina was French capitalism's commitment to growth. French opinion would never be unanimous on the subject of Indochina. More than any other colonial conquest, that of Indochina took place with very small parliamentary majorities: hardly four votes at the time of the great parliamentary debate on Tonkin on December 21–24, 1885. It unfolded against a backdrop of violent opposition, in particular, in 1885, after the fall of Prime Minister Jules Ferry's government on March 30, when it became the central theme of the October legislative elections.

With rare exceptions, however, such as Yves Guyot, a radical representative of the Seine and future minister of public works, this opposition was largely motivated more by power struggles, by what was at stake in metropolitan politics, than by any fundamental critique of colonialism, or even of the actual situation in Indochina. Only isolated individuals such as the Bonapartist Jules Delafosse, an elected representative from Calvados, carried out this kind of fundamental critique. As for the anti-colonialism of the Radicals, they did not challenge the principle of colonization, but rather its methods and the priority over social goals accorded to it by the Opportunist Republicans. Nor did they challenge the idea of a hierarchy of "races," the ideological pillar of colonization. In fact, denouncing the Indochinese policies of Ferry in their name, Camille Pelletan identified himself explicitly with this idea on December 29, 1885, when he asked: "Don't populations of the *inferior races* have as many rights as you? You abuse them, you do not civilize them!" It was a remarkable confusion: the opponents of colonization accepted its justification. Indeed, Clemenceau would write the preface for Auguste Pavie's book *À la conquête des cœurs*. Business opportunism, the abuses of colonial management, the collusion of France's policy of overseas expansion with the European strategy of Bismarck—all these were denounced. Indochina, however, was a luxury that would be accepted, if it were free of charge.

Much more important than this European-centered anti-colonialism was the conversion of the Opportunist Republicans, in power since 1877, to the Indochinese enterprise, and its insertion into the center of the dominant Republican project. Their conversion was above all the work of Gambetta and his political allies, Charles Freycinet, Jules Ferry, Maurice Rouvier, the young Théophile Deicassé, Jules Méline, Félix Faure, and Eugène Etienne. Between 1878 and 1880, Gambetta and Ferry seem to have rallied to the idea of a dynamic imperialism outside Europe. For them, it represented the only possible defense of France's status as a world power; as Ferry said, it "would not resign itself joyfully to playing the role of a big Belgium in the world." It was also the principal means of escape from the economic crisis, which worsened toward 1880, as well as the foundation for a consensus around the Republic. For them, Republican democracy, a return to prosperity, and the search for power and imperialism went together.

Henceforth, France could no longer abstain from taking part in the competition triggered in Southeast Asia with the thrust of the British from Burma toward the upper Mekong—in 1875, a British expedition to open a trade route between Bhamo in upper Burma and Shanghai, under Colonel Horace Browne, led to the murder of a British consular officer, R. A. Margary, evidently with the involvement of the Qing authorities—and from Singapore into the Malay Peninsula. "If, at any given moment, we do not snatch our portion of colonies, England and Germany will seize them," Gambetta declared in 1878. Numerous votes in the Chamber—notably on May 26, 1883, when the credits requested by Ferry for the expedition to Tonkin were approved unanimously by the 494 representatives present—showed that as long as the policies in Indochina did not have serious financial and military implications, they were largely approved. In any case, the tenacious resistance of Hue to the expansion of European trade in Tonkin hardly allowed Paris a choice other than the use of force.

At the Congrès international de géographie in 1878, the French delegation claimed Annam, Tonkin, and Siam for France. The following day, the campaign in favor of the revision of the Franco-Vietnamese treaty of 1874 became more pronounced. In the following years, national geographical conferences and the chambers of commerce of France's great industrial towns multiplied their resolutions in favor of annexation of Tonkin. "One must search there for new outlets to replace those that were lost through our disasters of 1870," the Douai Congrès national de géographie declared in 1882. Already in July 1881, during Ferry's first cabinet, the Chamber had managed to release an initial credit, but the Opportunist Republicans hesitated until the spring of 1883. The project for the complete occupation of Tonkin prepared by Gambetta's *grand ministère* in November 1881 was struck down in April 1882 in favor of a plan for more limited intervention in the delta, drawn up by Prime Minister Ferry and the governor of Cochinchina, Le Myre de Vilers, in September of the preceding year. Its prudent approach was in part the outcome of the crisis in Egypt and the resulting Anglo-French conflict. The plan aimed at deploying only limited forces to take control of the Red River in order to impose on Hue an interpretation of the 1874 treaty in favor of a *protectorat catégorique* (firm protectorate), in the words of Admiral Jauréguiberry.

Toward War

It was in this context that the Freycinet cabinet, formed in January 1882, sent Commandant Henri Rivière with three companies to Hanoi on March 26. Under pressure from French traders in Tonkin and Monsignor Puginier, Rivière attacked the citadel on April 25 on the pretext of neutralizing it. He handed back only a portion of the captured installations five days later. French policies, hesitant until early 1883, were clearly ready to exploit the general weakening of Dai Nam's empire. Paralysis was spreading throughout a power anchored in a conservatism divided between defenders of peace *(chu hoa)* and of war *(chu chien)*. A profound misunderstanding of the West equally blinded it: "His ignorance in all sciences is extreme," wrote Pierre Rheinart, the former French chargé d'affaires at Hue, of the influential minister of finance Nguyen Van Tuong in 1885. "His conversations with the French have taught him little, even about our country. He finds our institutions strange and does not even understand them. Industrial progress surprises him, but in and of itself, he finds little to envy."[42] Most important, however, Tonkin entered into a process of destabilization, linked to internal causes that are still poorly understood and to the indirect effects of the great revolts that had shaken southern China since 1850. This situation would allow interventionist lobbies to put an end to governmental hesitation.

The Chinese crisis, in effect, caused the migration of highland populations to the mountainous areas of Tonkin and Laos. Among them were Hmong groups who settled on the heights of Tran Ninh and Hua Phan toward 1845–50, as well

THE COLONIAL MOMENT 43

as masses of the poor fleeing misery and the civil war. Other groups followed after 1864: bands of Yunnan rebels, known under the generic name of Ho, and the remaining Taiping troops, who lived off the land, among whom were Liu Yong Fu's (Luu Vinh Phuc's) famous Black Flags.[43] They settled around Cao Bang and then Lao Cai on the upper Red River and were used by the Vietnamese authorities starting in 1872–73 against the rival Yellow (whose leader was Luong Tam Ky) and White Flags. Implicated in local conflicts between the Hmong and the Yao, they were joined in 1878 by around 10,000 supporters of a rebel military mandarin of Guangxi, Li Yang Kai (Ly Duong Tai). Northern Vietnam, ravaged by floods, famine, and bandits, was therefore on its way to being incorporated into the troubled space of southern China, and after April 1879, at the request of the Vietnamese, some regular Chinese troops arrived to fight the Chinese rebel forces, which were disbanded the following month.

On September 6, 1882, the Hue court decided to mount a military resistance to the French challenge. However, stuck between this challenge and the hostility of the literati, who blamed the court for the successive concessions to the foreigners, it was internally riven by grave dissensions regarding what attitude to take toward France. These disagreements heightened following the death of Emperor Tu Duc, who died childless on July 19, 1883. Ministers and regents disagreed about which policy should be followed: Nguyen Trong Hiep, the minister of foreign relations, favored a compromise and collaboration with France, while two regents, Minister of War Ton That Thuyet and Nguyen Van Tuong, were determined, as were the majority of the literati, to mount an uncompromising resistance. The two men were, however, enemies. Their division degenerated into pitiless struggles for influence that led to a serious dynastic crisis and a nearly total absence of imperial power. Four sovereigns succeeded one another over the course of two years. The first was the presumptive heir, Duc Duc (July 20–23, 1883), nephew and adoptive son of the defunct emperor; accused of incompetence and of involvement with the French, he was consigned by the regents to "close confinement" three days after his accession. The second was Hiep Hoa (July 30–November 30, 1883), his uncle, who was forced to poison himself for the second reason. Then came Kien Phuc (November 30, 1883–July 31, 1884), another nephew of Tu Duc's, enthroned by the resistance party that had been in power at Hue since July 1883, who died after a reign of eight months. Finally, Ham Nghi (August 2, 1884–July 5, 1885), Kien Phuc's thirteen-year-old younger brother, acceded to the throne.

The risk of an armed conflict with China, however, hampered French plans for exploiting the situation in Hue. On December 27, 1880, Beijing warned that occupation of Tonkin would entail war, and, in August 1881, the Chinese sent thirty thousand men there. For his part, on the eve of his death, in January 1883, Tu Duc appealed to China for help. The Qing regime was briefly tempted by the idea of a division of Tonkin as a way of assuring the survival of the tributary system that associated the Chinese empire with the peripheral states in a relation of superiority. When Rivière attempted, in March 1883, to occupy the principal towns of the delta, a threshold was crossed, and he came up against the Black Flags and the resistance of Vietnamese troops, which encouraged a Chinese military presence. It is clear that what was playing out in Vietnam, as would be the case half a century later, was a radical shift in the organization of the Far East: in this case, the establishment there of Western imperialist rule.

The Franco-Chinese confrontation thus had a determining influence on the outcome of the four successive phases of the crisis in Tonkin, whose Vietnamese, Chinese, French, and international dimensions were closely intertwined. After the negotiation in Beijing of a compromise based on the division of Tonkin into two zones of influence, Chinese to the north, French to the south (Bourée's convention proposal of December 1882), the second Ferry ministry, constituted on February 21, 1883, disavowed the Bourée convention on March 5 and opted, on March 16, for conquest. On March 12, Rivière occupied Hon Gai, where the engineer Fuchs had just discovered coal in 1880–82. Liu Yong Fu's Black Flags challenged, then killed Rivière on the Paper Bridge on May 19. His death dramatized the situation such that on May 26, the Ferry government obtained the necessary votes from the Chamber for the financing and consignment of an expedition "to organize the protectorate," commanded by General Alexandre Bouët and Admiral Amédée Courbet. On August 23, after the seizure of the forts of Thuan An, outside Hue, while Bouët overran the Red River Delta, Jules Harmand, named general civil commissioner on June 8, delivered an ultimatum to the Hue government. If it rejected his proposal: "The empire of Annam, its dynasty, its princes, and its court will have pronounced their own death sentence. The name Vietnam will no longer exist in history." On August 25, 1883, the regents were compelled to sign a drastic protectorate treaty with Harmand that was a prelude to pure and simple annexation. The Tonkin provinces, Thanh Hoa, Nghe An, and Ha Tinh, were to be placed under administration of French residents, along with the management of customs and external relations. Binh Thuan was conceded to Cochinchina, and a French resident was to be installed in Hue, with the right to audiences with the king.

The court, however, still considered all this merely a matter of gaining time. The war continued in the north, where the main Vietnamese fortress, Son Tay, fell on December 16. The regent Ton That Thuyet, the soul of the resistance, fortified Hue and secretly constructed a powerful camp entrenched in the mountains at Tan So, close to Cam Lo in Muong country, as well as building a mountain road toward upper Tonkin. Intending to revive the old strategy of national resistance to foreign invasion from highland bases, Thuyet had artillery, supplies, and a third of the imperial treasury transported to Tan So.

A second stage in the conflict, that of the semi-declared Franco-Chinese conflict, began after the summer of 1883. Convinced of the weakness of the Chinese army, Jules Ferry demanded on August 9 that it evacuate Tonkin. He was in fact seeking to confront both Beijing and the anti-colonial opposition in the French Chamber of Deputies with a fait accompli. This was why reinforcements, voted on December 15, were sent. These policies seemed to succeed: the fall of Son Tay and that of Bac Ninh, held by the Chinese, on March 12, 1884, led Li Hongzhang, the principal Chinese statesman, on May 11, 1884 (with the Fournier agreement), to accept the recognition of Franco-Vietnamese treaties, the opening of southern China to French trade, and the evacuation of Tonkin. Nevertheless, the conflict with China obliged Ferry's government to content itself with the formula of a protectorate over Vietnam and not to ratify the treaty negotiated by Harmand. Instead, a new protectorate treaty, the "Patenôtre treaty"—this one definitive—was signed in Hue on June 6, 1884. A fundamental charter for the protectorate until 1945, it too restored Binh Thuan and the administration of northern Annam to the imperial government, as well as confirming an administrative dissociation of Annam and Tonkin. In Tonkin, the treaty placed the provincial administrations under the control of French residents (through articles 6, 7, and 8). It envisioned France's direction of the foreign policy of Dai Nam and the installation of a French resident general in Hue, who was to have the right to personal audience with the emperor, a stipulation that represented a genuine profanation of the imperial function. For Vietnam, it was the end of the tributary relationship with Beijing. In Hue, the great seal of investiture granted to the Nguyen dynasty by the emperors of China was solemnly melted down on June 6 in the presence of the court assembly and replaced by a seal sent from France, carved from a meteorite. The protectorate of Annam-Tonkin had been established.

In parallel, following forceful action by the governor of the colony of Cochinchina, Charles Thomson, a much more coercive protectorate was imposed on King Norodom of Cambodia, with a view to the quasi-annexation of the country by the colony, under the treaty of June 17, 1884. The treaty envisaged the installation of French residents in the provinces, who were to control the Khmer governors, and, in contrast to the protectorate over Vietnam, it stipulated that the resident general would take charge of public order, economic services, and taxation, and proclaimed the institution of private property and an end to personal enslavement for debt. "Your protection is the cremation of the monarchy," Norodom apparently said.

In a third phase of conflict, the war with China revived, following an incident at Bac Le on June 22, 1884, when, in the absence of an order to withdraw, Chinese units resisted the advance of French troops. Beijing actually felt that a definitive retreat should only take place after a definitive resolution of the conflict. In Paris, intransigence prevailed in the euphoria born of the successes of the spring. The ultimatum of July 12 not only required the Chinese government to evacuate Tonkin immediately, but also demanded the payment of an indemnity of 250 million francs (making China finance the conquest of Tonkin). Since China refused to pay the indemnity, "There is nothing left to do but deliver a violent blow to that senile old lady, to take something as a forfeit, that is, to occupy Formosa [Taiwan] and then wait," Jules Ferry wrote on August 21.[44] Thirty-five ships of Courbet's squadron once again set up the strategy of territorial collateral. The bombardment of the great arsenal of Fuzhou took place on August 23–24, followed by the January 1885 occupation of Ke Long and Tam Sui, Formosa's two coal-mining harbors, which the Navy had long dreamed of acquiring. This was followed by a blockade of the island, then the February 1885 embargo on supply of rice to northern China, and finally a landing in the Pescadores in March.

Jules Ferry's maximalist strategy, however, failed because of a violent campaign of protest on the part of the Radicals and Conservatives, which reduced the government's ability to maneuver in the Chamber, and the discontent of the British, whose trade partially controlled the traffic in Chinese rice. Furthermore, Vietnamese and Chinese troops attempted a counteroffensive in the Tonkin Delta. Ferry initially had to come to some sort of compromise and accept unofficial British mediation and a plan for a peace resolution, secretly finalized by Duncan Campbell on March 15, 1885.

Then, suddenly, the unforeseen occurred in Lang Son. After having taken the city with a powerful column of eight thousand men and advanced beyond the border with the aim of neutralizing the Guangxi army, General François de Négrier, returning to Lang Son, was wounded on March 28 at the city walls. The Chinese were about to withdraw, but de Négrier's substitute, Lieutenant-Colonel Paul Herbinger, panicked and ordered an accelerated retreat, destroyed his baggage, and abandoned a battery. Militarily, this had no decisive importance, and diplomatically speaking the accord was almost signed in Beijing, but Jules Ferry, who had secretly asked Bismarck to intervene on his behalf with China, could not make public this fact. In Paris, on March 30, panic broke out following an anguished telegram from the new commander in chief, General Ernest Brière de l'Isle, who, fearing a Chinese offensive in the delta, asked for reinforcements. What weighed suddenly on Tonkin was the shadow of the events of Mexico during the Second Empire and the idea of a long war with China and of what Le Temps called a "colonial Sedan." In the Chamber, Georges Clemenceau and the Bonapartist Jules Delafosse led the assault against Jules Ferry, asking for his indictment before the High Court. Ferry was overthrown the same day, by 306 votes to 149, with 49 abstentions, "for a disaster that did not take place."[45]

The victory of the opponents of conquest was, however, short-lived, as is evidenced by the last phase of the Tonkin crisis, that of compromise. Charles Fourniau has demonstrated that it was not the colonization of Vietnam per se that was at stake during the crisis of Lang Son but rather three questions that greatly surpassed it: relations with China, the question of what limits to fix on the financial and military engagement of France in colonial expansion, and the future of the political project of the Opportunist Republicans, who aimed to provide a greater margin to the executive power in relation to the Parliament—Ferry's vision of a "strong government"—and whose failure was marked by the overthrow of Ferry in a climate of extraordinary violence.[46]

The Tonkin crisis squarely established parliamentary dominance—"The Tonkin question is only accessory: the true struggle is over France's domestic policy," wrote Le Télégraphe on December 25, 1885.[47] It ended with a compromise over Indochina. Many important chambers of commerce, town councils, and newspapers sought this solution. They had prematurely denounced a hypothetical evacuation that no one in the Chamber, not even Clemenceau, had called for. In contrast, 46 Radicals out of 143 voted for the 200 million francs and the dispatching of a reinforcement of 8,000 men requested by the new government headed by Prime Minister Henri Brisson and Minister of Foreign Affairs Charles de Freycinet, in so doing granting it the necessary majority. The Patenôtre protectorate treaty of June 6, 1884, was ratified on June 4, 1885, and ratification of the Franco-Chinese treaty followed on June 9, sealing the historic compromise between France and China on Indochina. France gave up all demands for an indemnity and its insular conquests, while China recognized the French protectorate over Annam-Tonkin, in effect abandoning its responsibilities as central power of the tributary system, and accepted the opening of Yunnan, Guangxi, and western Guangdong to commerce and the railroad. In August 1885, the Chinese troops, accompanied by Liu Yong Fu's Black Flags, evacuated Tonkin.

Certainly, anti-colonialist opposition remained powerful in France. The legislative elections of October 1885 were a defeat for the "Tonkinese." On December 18, the "commission des 33" ordered to examine the new request for credits for Tonkin by the Brisson government pronounced on the report of Camille Pelletan in favor of evacuation, and the credits were approved by a majority of only four during the difficult debate of December 21–24, 1885. However, the goal of this opposition stayed the same: to limit France's Indochinese action to Annam-Tonkin; to restrict the level of its military engagement, which the Freycinet government, constituted in January 1886, did; to establish limits on colonial policy; to assure direct management by the government of the initiatives on the ground; to establish parliamentary control of foreign policy and the colonial empire that was being formed. This was the thrust of Paul Bert's intervention in the debate. Colonization must be cheap and imply only a limited mobilization of France's military and financial means.

After the 1885 crisis, most political figures in the Third Republic, aside from the Socialists and a few Radicals like Pelletan and Clemenceau, rallied to what henceforth was the reality of Indochina, and more broadly, the reality of colonialism. In the legislative elections of 1893, only twenty-eight of those elected condemned colonial expansion in their policy statements. From then on, a consensus on the legitimacy of colonization was maintained through the formation of what would be called the "Colonial Party." This party was in fact an influential network of heterogeneous, often rival, colonial lobbies set up by Jules Ferry, Joseph Chailley-Bert, and Eugène Étienne. Its main organizations were the Comité de l'Afrique française, founded in October 1891, and the Union coloniale, founded in 1893; the latter's newspaper, *La Quinzaine coloniale,* and its Indochina section, the Comité de l'Indochine, were, together with the Comité de l'Asie française, founded in 1901, the essential elements. In 1900, two hundred deputies were members of the Chamber's colonial group, and in 1902, the Radicals held the Ministry of the Colonies for the first time in the person of Gaston Doumerge—a sign of their rallying to the colonial cause.

Henceforth deprived of any sympathetic response from metropolitan France, and cut off from China, imperial Vietnam's struggle against colonization was doomed. Nevertheless, it continued for another ten years, because in the field, the final and most difficult phase of conquest was just beginning.

RESISTANCE TO CONQUEST: THE CAN VUONG AND ITS DEFEAT (1885-1897)

Hue's Military Coup (July 5, 1885)

The long war of "pacification" in fact started following the arrival in Hue on July 2, 1885, of General Count Roussel de Courcy—"an idiot who can be a good warrior," according to Bernard Lavergne, the confidant of the Republic's president, Jules Grévy[48]—who had been appointed commander in chief and resident general in April. Brutal and ignorant of the real situation, and against the will of Freycinet's government and the Quai d'Orsay, which was in charge of the supervision of the protectorate, he was determined to forcibly annex Annam and Tonkin, as urged by the Ministry of Colonies, the Army, and Cochinchinese administration. The first step in this direction was clearly the elimination of the regents and the partisans of resistance within the court.

As early as November 1884, the strategy of a military coup against the Hue government had been prepared by Pierre Silvestre, the influential director of Affaires civiles (Civil Affairs) in Tonkin. He was well informed of the divisions within the court as well as of the regents Ton That Thuyet and Nguyen Van Tuong's secret plan to reach the fortified camp of Tan So, together with the young emperor, Ham Nghi, in order to call for a general uprising there against the French. General Brière de l'Isle, the commander in chief, had given his approval to the Silvestre plan, which prefigured the French strategy of December 1946 in Hanoi. It consisted of feigning ignorance of the Vietnamese preparations and taking advantage of the regents' and Ham Nghi's flight from the capital to proclaim the latter's deposition and replace him with a new emperor, one more docile and accommodating, selected from the imperial lineage.

In Hue, de Courcy made repeated provocations, forcing Thuyet into confrontation sooner than expected. On July 2 he ordered the regents to come to his own residence the following day, which Thuyet refused to do, and insisted he enter the palace for the imperial audience with his entire retinue through the "Middle Door," which was reserved for the sovereign. With no recourse, Thuyet took the initiative to start battle. On the night of July 4 to 5, 1885, imperial soldiers launched a preemptive attack on the French billets and the legation. By dawn, they had been defeated. The regents, with the fourteen-year-old Emperor Ham Nghi and the court, set out for the mountain bases of Tan So. Like Tran Hung Dao during the Mongol invasion in 1284, they sought to raise the nation against the invader, and on July 7 and July 13, they issued a call for general resistance—to help the king (chieu can Vuong), according to the title of the proclamation of July 13—as well as for the extermination of Christians.

The French victory in Hue, followed by the sacking of the Forbidden City and taking of the imperial treasure (perhaps 2.6 tons of gold and 30 tons of silver, a small part of which was subsequently restituted to the court), had resolved only the problem of the monarchy's submission—a matter that was finalized already on July 5, with the return to Hue of Regent Nguyen Van Tuong (who would be arrested on September 6 and deported), and then of the queen mother, Tu Du (Tu Duc's mother), and of the majority of the court. Certainly, the partisans of resistance quickly lost their supporters in the high mandarinate and in the royal family, who were determined to assure the continuity of the imperial regime and the social status of the ruling class at any cost, even dependence. With the help of some of the high mandarins, notably Nguyen Huu Do, the governor of Hanoi, who was promoted to grand chancellor and then to kinh luoc (imperial commissioner), de Courcy was able to impose the additional agreement of July 30, 1885, which extended the protectorate regime instituted in Tonkin to Annam and gave the resident general the right to preside over the Secret Council (Co Mat Vien). On September 14, he enthroned a new emperor, Dong Khanh (1885–89), a nephew of Tu Duc and future son-in-law of Nguyen Huu Do. This was a crushing humiliation for the dynasty, which was discredited in one blow.[49]

French control, however, was precarious. Outside Cochinchina, the expeditionary corps occupied only the principal towns of the Red River Delta, Lang Son, Hue, and three ports in Annam. Elsewhere, Thuyet and Ham Nghi's appeal, heard throughout the provinces, motivated a formidable resistance movement known as the Can Vuong (Help the King), which spread to Cochinchina, where several conspiracies would be discovered in 1885 in the region of Saigon. Thereafter, "Annam was put to fire and sword," as the new resident general, Paul Bert, telegraphed after his arrival in 1886.

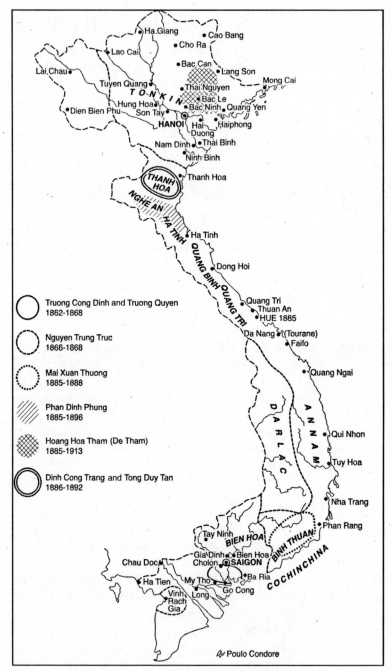

MAP 1.2. Vietnamese resistance to the French conquest, 1858–1897. (J. M. Pluvier, *Historical Atlas of South-East Asia* [Leiden, 1995], p. 45.)

Vietnamese resistance, moreover, developed simultaneously with major events in Cambodia, where a general insurrection broke out in January 1885 under the impetus of Norodom's longtime adversary, his stepbrother Si Votha.[50] Practically the whole of Khmer society entered into dissidence by protesting against the treaty of June 17, 1884, imposed on the king. The latter refused all cooperation with the French authorities, whose military helplessness was total, insofar as they could not fight on two fronts, Vietnam and Cambodia. The Can Vuong would force them to choose and to divide the military tasks. In August 1886, Saigon and Norodom signed a new agreement, the third, putting aside the treaty of 1884. After a series of tours through the provinces, the king obtained the submission of the insurgents. Cambodia had escaped annexation pure and simple.

National Resistance

The Can Vuong movement, remarkably analyzed by Charles Fourniau, was a genuine national insurrection. The French authorities denied its importance and applied to it, as they had to the Chinese rural banditry of the high region of Tonkin, the Vietnamese notion of "piracy" (*giac*), which in the mandarin tradition was a way of defaming any rebellion. This allowed for the double legitimization of repression, in terms both of the Confucian order and of the Republican vision of a pacifying and civilizing colonization. "What enables us to say," Jules Ferry would write, "that piracy is in a way only an accident, and that it will only have a relatively short duration, is that it is not inspired by a feeling of patriotism and independence. The Annamese has almost no national spirit."[51] Negating the existence of a Vietnamese nation was a way of justifying the colonial theories of an antagonism between the "Tonkinese" and the "Annamese" or between the peasantry and the mandarins, as well as projects to convert them from a protectorate to a regime of direct rule like that in existence in Cochinchina. Until 1887, in fact, Cochinchina, on which the protectorate of Cambodia already depended, tried to annex the two southern provinces of Annam, Binh Thuan and Khanh Hoa, and to constitute an Indochinese Union centered in Saigon.[52]

High commissioners and officers did not all agree, however, and some saw that it was refusal to recognize the national character of the Can Vuong movement that led the policies of pacification from one defeat to another until 1891 (see app. 1). Men like the former general commissioner of Tonkin Jules Harmand (see app. 2), Colonels Armand Servière and Théophile Pennequin, Captain Gosselin, and especially Governor-General J. L. de Lanessan had a clear-sighted view of the movement. The conclusions that de Lanessan, then a Radical deputy, came to in 1887 following his mission to Indochina were categorical: "It is in the name of patriotism that Annam rose up after July 15, in the same way that Tonkin had already revolted."[53] This was a lucid assessment of an uprising that was a response to the unprecedented national crisis that the installation of the protectorate and the partition of Tonkin had precipitated within Vietnamese society. The imperial court surrendered to a "barbarian invasion" that it did not have the conceptual means to effectively evaluate. With this capitulation, it was not only the dynasty's supposed celestial mandate that was shaken; the entire collective psychological fabric was ripped apart. The cosmic order suddenly began to unravel: "Now the sky is low, the earth is high,"[54] as a popular song proclaimed. In the midst of this terrible moral trauma, the only viable response was to follow the call of legitimate power. "In the eyes of the people, Emperor Ham Nghi, exiled in the provinces of Quang Binh, represented the homeland struggling against the foreigner," Colonel Fernand Bernard noted.[55]

The Can Vuong movement was widespread, but it remained fragmented in chronologically staggered and poorly coordinated regional uprisings (see map 1.2). Strictly speaking, "Can Vuong" designates only the uprising that took place in central Vietnam between 1885 and 1888 on the part of those loyal to the fugitive king. But it can be applied to the entire Vietnamese resistance in the sense that their leaders often referred to an ideal royalty as the incarnation of the country's independence. There were four main centers of insurrection. In Annam, where colonial activity was, in 1885, still unknown, the entire society rose under the direction of its intellectual elite, in a sense in complete legality, to defend the throne. This was notably the case in northern Annam, where supporters of Ham Nghi, organized from Ha Tinh and Quang Binh, and especially around the natural bastion of the high valley of Song Giang, from where it was relatively easy to reach Laos, had controlled the neighboring provinces of Nghe An and Thanh Hoa, where the dynasty originated, starting in February 1886. There, Christians, considered internal enemies, were massacred en masse, especially in Quang Tri in September 1885, following the cry of "Binh tay, sat ta!" (Hunt the Westerners, kill the Catholics!). These atrocious reprisals, which resulted in around 40,000 dead and the destruction of a large part of the Christian communities, left a long-lasting mark on the collective conscience. After the departure of Thuyet for China in early 1887, the insurgents of northern Annam were nevertheless defeated, and Muong warriors delivered Ham Nghi to the French on October 29, 1888. But one year later, in Thanh Hoa, the Hung Linh movement (1889–92) developed, under the direction of the prestigious Tong Duy Tan, while the great La Son uprising broke out in Ha Tinh and Nghe An in 1890, led by the former imperial censor Phan Dinh Phung until his death in December 1895.

In southern Annam, less than one hundred kilometers from Hue, where French presence was sporadic, the two provinces of Quang Nam and Quang Ngai rose up in a general revolt starting in July 1884. More than five thousand Christians were ferociously massacred in Quang Ngai in mid-July. In 1886, the resistance to the mandarin collaborators spread to Khanh Hoa and Binh Thuan. It collapsed the following year, however, under terrible blows from the mandarins rallied to Dong Khanh, Nguyen Thanh in Quang Ngai, and Tran Ba Loc and troops coming from farther south in Cochinchina.

In the provinces of the Tonkin Delta, on the other hand, the resistance was somewhat different. Ravaged for a quarter of a century by revolts, Chinese bands, then the war of 1884–85, the country was in fact under no one's control. The intolerable burden of provisioning the large colonial army, its violence, and the incessant recruitment of carriers—for instance, there were 1,200 coolies charged with carrying 20 to 27 kilograms each for 800 fighters when the Borgnis-Desbordes column fought near Cho Moi in February 1889—mobilized the peasantry as much as the royal summons. Still, the action of the energetic mandarins Tan Thuat, in the east, and Nguyen Quang Bich, in the west, was also essential. A situation of dual power was established very quickly in most of the delta, especially in the vast plain of Bai Say between Hanoi and Hung Yen: indigenous authorities won over to the colonizer were replaced at night by the clandestine power of patriotic leaders. The insurgents were organized in several scores of armed groups, rarely smaller than two hundred and fifty men, and supported by the walled villages, which, according to General Henri Frey, were "surrounded for the most part by a double or triple enclosure, made up of a strong bamboo hedge, reinforced on the inside with an earth wall, which creates a most serious hindrance; between these two successive enclosures lay deep ponds; narrow, twisting alleys, through which a buffalo can barely pass, divide the village into innumerable islands, which when necessary can become as many distinct little forts and centers of resistance."[56]

The mountain ranges that surrounded the delta, Dong Trieu, Bao Day, Tam Dao, Yen The, covered with dense forests, were the most lasting bastions of guerrilla warfare. "They have a permanent core, hardened, disciplined, maintained by unceasing incursions, and joined, at the leader's call, by contingents provided by villages of the region," Frey wrote. "They are consistently organized in Annamese style into sections, companies, battalions, and even armies, which they have pompously named: Army of the Vanguard, Army of the Rear Guard, Right Wing of the Faithful Army."[57] The guerrillas, clothed in uniforms consisting of blue shirts hanging to mid-thigh, short trousers, gaiters of strong canvas, espadrilles, and straw hats, were all equipped with modern rifles—quite often Winchester repeating rifles, whereas the French still had single-shot Gras rifles—machetes, and revolvers for the group leaders.[58] The chiefs were Vietnamese and given military mandarins' titles: *doc* (Chief) Tich (Nguyen Van Hien), a minor scholar from the province of Hai Duong, who would be exiled to Algeria; *doc* Ngu (Hoang Dinh Kinh, also called the *cai* Kinh), in the province of Lang Son; *doi* (Noncommissioned Officer) Van in the province of Bac Ninh, who would be executed in 1889; and *de* (Commanding Officer) Tham, the renowned Hoang Hoa Tham (who combined rural banditry with patriotic resistance), in Yen The. Some were Chinese, like Luong Tam Ky (the head of the Yellow Flags), son of a Taiping, who was installed in the region of Cho Moi, in the north of Thai Nguyen. In the heart of the jungle, these guerrilla troops constructed the powerful fortified systems described by Colonel Joseph-Simon Galliéni in his *Trois colonnes au Tonkin* (Three Columns in Tonkin).

Finally, the upper region, close to the border with China, was in the hands of Chinese bands that had hardly any relations with the Can Vuong. Certain bands, permanently installed, were made up of former Taiping or imperial soldiers. Others were itinerant and recruited from Hunanese and Hakka from Hainan who had settled in Guangxi and Guangdong. Among these was Luong Tam Ky's band, equipped with a thousand rapid-fire rifles, which operated in the Dong Trieu in 1892. These were professional bandits, small-scale local warlords who controlled the frontier traffic in opium, arms, and women and children sold in China as slaves.

With the exception of the Chinese bands, these movements had common characteristics. Their chiefs made open appeals through posters and placards to Emperor Ham Nghi, corresponded with his entourage, which had taken refuge in Muong country, and were certified mandarins. At Quang Nam, for instance, Nguyen Dung Hieu, one of the most important figures of the Can Vuong, was vice-minister of the war while acting as governor of Quang Nam and Quang Ngai.[59] It was, in fact, a segment of the imperial political system that resisted—more or less overtly depending on the region—in the name of the legitimate ruler. Chiefs of the resistance taxed villages, recruited men, and ordered work duties, organizing a truly parallel administration. When Nguyen Dung Hieu was captured in Quang Nam, five seals, two hundred and fifty blank official certificates for mandarinal nominations, and nine hundred tax registers were seized. Numerous mandarins, even in the court at Hue, secretly aided the uprising or at least offered some cautious support, while many others resigned, to the point of provoking an administrative void in Tonkin. This was only partially compensated for by the nomination of mediocre, venal civil servants, who, as Jean Dupuis noted, took refuge in duplicity:

> Alongside the official mandarins named by the French authority and therefore too embarrassed to overtly conspire against us, there were at this time in every province of Tonkin former mandarins who had been removed for having previously taken up against us and who, in the heart of villages where they were hidden among their parents and friends, were the real depositories of royal authority, governing as in the past, although in hiding, and organizing their rebellion as best they could. The official mandarins, who knew them well, naturally kept them informed of everything that pertained to the cause of the resistance and acted only in concert with them.[60]

The Guerrilla War

The resistance—its guerrilla warfare, its mobilization and dispersal of forces—was remarkably well carried out. Overall, confrontation remained limited to the level of local guerrilla warfare, but the leaders of the Can Vuong repeatedly attempted to move beyond this stage and rise above the provincial setting. This was the case at the end of 1886, when they organized a fortified base in the heart of Thanh Hoa, in Ba Dinh, threatening the French military apparatus at the strategic junction of its Tonkin sector and central Vietnam, located between the plains and the Muong country. At Ba Dinh, where the Can Vuong reached its peak, there was an unsuccessful attempt to "transition to a generalized and coordinated war."[61] The village fortress measured 1,200 by 400 meters and was constructed in the three villages of My Khe, Thuong Ta, and Mao Tinh (Ba Dinh: "the *dinh* of the three villages"), in the middle of rice fields that were inundated under several meters of water, connected to solid ground by four narrow dams. It was strongly protected by several buried enceintes topped with bamboo. Commanded by a remarkable military chief, Dinh Cong Trang, it was defended by about three thousand men. Three thousand five hundred soldiers—among them Captain Joseph Joffre, the future commander in chief of the French Army in 1914–16—were needed, as well as five thousand coolies, twenty artillery pieces, and a siege of two months, beginning in December 1886, to capture it, which the French did on January 21, 1887.[62]

Certain chiefs organized audacious raids. In July 1891, the *doc* Ngu (Nguyen Duc Ngu) installed himself in the villages on the left bank of the Red River, opposite Hanoi, and his men opened fire on the French concession, provoking panic among the Europeans. It took an hour to gather fifty colonial infantrymen to respond, and the incident cost Governor General Georges-Jules Piquet his job. Nevertheless, generally, the movements of armed groups did not extend beyond the theater of two or three provinces (there were twenty-three of them at the time in Tonkin), and their objectives remained limited. The resistance did not expand beyond a rural war fought by partisans.

The Can Vuong movement's troops were in fact mostly peasants. Several of its chiefs came from among the notables or the wealthy peasantry. Others came from marginal elements of rural society, like the chief Lo in the region of Son Tay, a young peasant who became a *tirailleur*, then a deserter, and was assassinated in 1889 at the instigation of the authorities. The same was true of the renowned De Tham (Hoang Hoa Tham), born around 1860; he was a buffalo herder until he was enlisted by the Black Flags in 1882. He resisted until 1896 in the heart of the impregnable forest of Yen The, with three hundred men armed with modern rifles, supported by the surrounding villagers. "A hero who merits our complete admiration, just as he has that of all the Annamese," General Pennequin said of him in 1911.[63] Galliéni captured his forts in November 1895, and De Tham became a *chef soumissionnaire* (under the authority of the French) in 1897. He resumed the struggle in 1913, until his assassination by Luong Tam Ky's men, who were allied to the French. It was indeed the peasantry that had to be fought, and it was to the *xa,* the Vietnamese village community, so solidly organized, which supplied the resistance with men and provisions, that the colonial army brought the war. The "forest war" was difficult in the mountains, and no less so in the rice fields, where attacks had to be made against large Vietnamese villages situated in the middle of the waters,

entrenched behind impenetrable bamboo hedges, so that they could only be reduced through artillery and fire. The central feature of the war of pacification was
undoubtedly the battle to secure the submission of the rural community.

But it was the literati, a "hostile class par excellence" according to Francis Garnier,[64] who furnished the royal insurrection with the majority of its greatest leaders: Mai Xuan Thuong in Binh Dinh; Nguyen Dung Hieu in Quang Nam; the great
mandarin Nguyen Quang Bich, one of the most famous scholars of his time, in
the region of Son Tay; Nguyen Thieu Thuat, former governor of the province of
Hai Duong, in the Bai Say; and the most remarkable of the chiefs of the resistance,
Phan Dinh Phung, in northern Annam. In 1895, he disposed of at least 1,200 to
1,300 rifles. In ancient Vietnam, the literati were the true managers of a still homogeneous rural society, the equivalent of a "lower clergy,"[65] whose social functions and influence were immense. Often of peasant ancestry, having competed
in literary examinations, they were numerous in villages, to which mandarins of
high rank customarily retired. Almost all of them dedicated themselves to the administration of schools, and they possessed great moral authority. They were, according to de Lanessan, "the most intelligent, active, and the only influential group
in the country, the ones blindly followed by the workers in cities and the farmers
in the rural areas, the ones who represented, and even the missionaries admit this,
the national party."[66] While the mandarinate, at least in its upper echelons, seems
mainly to have lent a strong hand to pacification, especially after 1891, a part of
the village elite directed the insurgency until the end and gave it its traditional and
patriotic character, as well as its strength, because it mobilized the village networks
of authority, especially the powerful and solidly organized lineages. Frédéric Baille,
the former resident of Hue, wrote in his memoirs of the actions of Nguyen Dung
Hieu in Quang Nam:

> This man, still young and of a rare energy, who gradually exhibited a renowned and
> near legendary heroism, ended up carving out a true royalty in this province. . . . He
> succeeded in giving to the insurrectionary movement of the Quang Nam the di-
> mension and prestige of a national movement. It seems that he aroused patriotic fire
> in minds that up until then were ill prepared for this idea. His influence in the province
> was extraordinary. On his orders, villages depopulated themselves, peasants set fire
> to their *cagnas* [Annamese peasant houses] to leave a void before our columns.[67]

Nguyen Dung Hieu was captured in September 1886 and beheaded.

The Colonial War

Until 1891, the protectorate army was held in check. The overly large expeditionary
corps—it consisted of 42,000 men at the end of 1885 and, with troop rotation, tied
up a total of 100,000,[68] whereas the British conquered upper Burma during the same

period with only 22,000—revealed itself to be poorly adapted to the political and strategic situation it was supposed to master. These mediocre troops, in part recruited from dubious units—the "zephyrs" of the disciplinary companies, the Foreign Legion, sometimes those convicted by military tribunals—were chronically ravaged by epidemics, such as cholera in August through September of 1885, which killed 4% of the corps.

The French commanders were long incapable of analyzing their adversaries, whom they indiscriminately called "pirates." "They only understand the cannon," Colonel Gustave Borgnis-Desbordes declared of his colleagues. They oscillated between a strategy of launching heavy columns in pursuit of the rebels—more than two hundred in Tonkin between 1885 and 1891—and creating a network of 259 dispersed military stations (postes) to police specific areas, which devoured reserve units.[69] They were also torn by rivalries between the Army and the Navy, between generals and high-level civil servants. Starting in 1885, these rivalries aggravated the permanent conflict between the Ministry of Foreign Affairs and the Ministry of the Navy and the Colonies; the residents general, under orders of the former, were determined to maintain the protectorate, whereas the latter favored creation of a direct administration.

In a report dated March 1888, General-Governor Jean Constans (1887–88), subsequently minister of the interior during the Boulangiste crisis, deplored the sterility "of this regime of small military stations that cover the territory and multiply indefinitely" and "the unceasing comings and goings of columns seeking adventure, the unannounced requisitioning of coolies, which removes able-bodied men from cultivation to make them beasts of burden who die in pain and leave the roads strewn with their corpses."[70] The Red River Delta in fact experienced all the horrors of colonial war: requisitions of coolies, of supplies, and of livestock, the sacking of the dinhs (common houses), the burning of villages, summary executions, baïonnettades (as de Lanessan called them) ordered by General de Négrier, not to mention the epidemics, the decrease in production, the flight of peasants. As the resistance grew, repressive violence became widespread, as is testified by innumerable narratives, such as this "ordinary" activity log of the Bay Say column during the dry season of 1885–86, which is eloquent in its terseness:

18/9: the manhunt did not find anything, but on its return it picked up two small groups of Annamese installed amid the rushes in shacks built on stilts—these stray people were executed.

19/9: a flying column of 70 legionnaires search a village: a large number of pirates leave at full speed and run away northward, led by two men on horseback. These groups fall under our fire. . . . A good number of them are left on the field. At 6:15, the village is invaded. . . . A group of 25 pirates escape. . . . Half of them are executed, shot from the exterior observation stations.[71]

From 1885 to 1888, the French Army and the Vietnamese militia it recruited succeeded only in preventing the concentration of guerrilla troops; in occupying certain points along the border, notably, the sectors of Cao Bang, Lang Son, and Mong Cai; and in capturing Ham Nghi on October 29, 1888, though this did not prevent the perseverance of the resistance carried out in his name. It was necessary to negotiate with several guerrilla chiefs. Through such negotiations, the Chinese Luong Tam Ky became *chef soumissionnaire* in the summer of 1890 and was granted the administration of the region of Cho Chu, the right to arm 500 *linh co* (soldiers), and an annual salary of 150,000 francs.[72]

There was no progress until 1890—in fact, quite the opposite. As Charles Fourniau has shown, during the dry season of 1890–91, the Can Vuong reached its highest point, a fact explained by the rejection of foreign domination by a peasantry that was deeply weakened by the burden of the colonial war. Colonization faced a situation of intense crisis, of extreme upheaval and misery, aggravated by the terrible floods of the Red River. Famine appeared. In the upper region, the French confronted close to ten thousand men armed with rifles, while in the delta more than two thousand five hundred were organized into thirty-seven guerrilla groups.[73] "Tonkin," Resident Louis Bonhoure wrote, "is an immense Vendée [alluding to the great peasant uprising in that region against the revolutionary National Convention in 1793] where the insurgent bands appear at night and disappear in the morning, dispersing and gathering in the blink of an eye."[74] For the resistance, after the failures of 1888, it was the beginning of a second wind, which was marked by the movement of Phan Dinh Phung in Nghe Tinh (1890–95).

Nevertheless, the resistance of the mandarins was defeated. The interpretations invoked a century later to account for this failure can never fully explain it. Who can provide an account of the rupture and unrest that explains how an uprising against foreign domination yielded to national lassitude and resignation? Undoubtedly, the major strategic weakness of the Can Vuong was its dispersal, the impossibility of a coordinated effort on the part of the forces of Tonkin and Annam. This was linked as much to France's military superiority in its conflict with a numerically limited adversary, which, deprived of Chinese help, often did not have firearms—the colonial war brought two "unequal" technologies into conflict— as to the exploitation by the French authorities of the horizontal divisions of Vietnamese society and the internal weakness of the Can Vuong. David Marr has well demonstrated that the Can Vuong movement was strongly influenced by regionalisms and remained dependent on existing structures of authority. The audiences of its leaders were often limited to lineages and villages where they were rooted.[75] The uprising was confronted with a wait-and-see policy on the part of the rural elite that is difficult to evaluate. It is plausible that in Tonkin, the members of this elite ultimately resigned themselves to accepting foreign domination in the hopes that it would put an end to the violence that was ravaging the rural areas.

Furthermore, extensive dissidence provided precious support to the colonial power. The Christian villages were a considerable help to the French troops that disembarked in 1883, and were especially efficient, since their clergy solidly organized them and their very existence was being threatened. Victims in Annam, but not in Tonkin, of the atrocious massacres of 1885—there were perhaps forty thousand victims, in the course of the summer, out of about a hundred and forty thousand Christians in the protectorate of Annam—the Christians participated in terrifying reprisals against the intellectual elite and rebel peasants and provided many coolies to the expeditionary corps (more than five thousand during the battle of Ba Dinh). In addition, the conflicting relationships between the montagnard minorities and the imperial administration weakened the resistance precisely in those regions where French troops would have had difficulty maneuvering, although the Tai of Lai Chau and the Muong showed evidence of a significant loyalty to Ham Nghi and Ton That Thuyet. Finally, the desire to defend the Nguyen was not unanimous, for example, among the patriots of the Binh Dinh, who seem to have preserved a vivid memory of the struggles of the Tay Son insurgents of the eighteenth century.

Above all, in spite of its popular following, the Can Vuong was not a modern national movement that included a project of social transformation and general modernization. It was therefore not capable of assuming the historical challenge of "progress" posed by French imperialism and colonization. In fact, this question was only asked by colonization. Even if some within the movement were sensitive to the problematic of modernization, the primary ideal of the resistant mandarins and their partisans was defense of the Confucian order and its guarantors, the imperial state and the village community, against the Western barbarians. They addressed themselves above all to the controlling class of literate civil servants, property owners, and rural notables. A proclamation found in a refuge of the Yen The in 1890 reads:

> The Western demons will not disturb the kingdom any longer. May all those who provide them with fish and meat come to our ranks, may students and the scholarly elite of the north and the south, the mandarins who have positions and those who are awaiting one, the children of the mandarin families, may those who are preparing for the undergraduate examinations and those who have passed them, may all the district chiefs and all the village chiefs gather in troops and pursue the pirates [the French].[76]

Patriotism, as vigorous as it was, defined itself in Confucian terms of the prince-subject relation as fidelity *(trung)* and loyalty *(nghia),* two virtues linked to that of filial piety *(hieu trung).* It was fundamentally attached to the past, conservative, and loyalist. Thus, when the literati seized the citadel of Quang Ngai in July 1885, they quickly sought to legitimize their action by naming as their leader Prince Tuy Ly, the uncle of Tu Duc, who had been exiled to the town by Regent Thuyet.[77] As Charles Fourniau has remarked, unlike the great Chinese popular revolts of the middle of the nineteenth century, the Can Vuong did not make even the smallest of social claims. Its only source of legitimacy was imperial power. The resistance of the intellectual elite and part of the peasant society was tied to the existence of a nation-state, certainly ancient, but also of a "royal nation," whose organizing reference point was a monarchical state, which had separated a millennium before from the empire-world of China. The nation identified with the dynastic state, but a modern national ideology did not exist. At the turn of the nineteenth century, it was still the case that the reigning conception of Vietnam implied an emperor, dynastic loyalty, and a Confucian vision of human relations, a double legitimacy that found itself hijacked, through the formula of the protectorate, in service of the foreigner. Suddenly, the political reference points of this national consciousness became confused.

Therein resides the fundamental contradiction of the Can Vuong, which was in a position to exploit colonization from the moment it sought and attained an alliance—an obviously conflicting one—with the dynasty and the majority of the mandarinate. In this regard, colonization in Vietnam was not simply a conquest by the outsider, but just as much an internal process in which a relatively large number of Vietnamese to some extent participated. It was therefore necessary for the colonizers to abandon their dream of a pure and simple annexation of the country.

A first step in this direction was sketched out empirically by the great physiologist Paul Bert, who was named resident general of Annam and Tonkin on January 31, 1886, by Freycinet, at the same time as the two residents superior of Annam and Tonkin, Charles Dillon and Paulin Vial, who were highly perceptive Catholic administrators. Bert was a Gambettist deputy from the Yonne, the inspirer of the educational laws of 1880–82 in France, ex-minister of public instruction in the "great ministry" of Gambetta in 1881–82. He was ambitious and imperious, and imbued with the Republican faith in the trinity of democracy, science, and progress, which according to nineteenth-century French Republican culture were to be universalized through colonization. He was also a brilliant scholar, who in 1869 had succeeded Claude Bernard as the chair of physiology at the Faculté des sciences de Paris and had discovered animal transplants. Once he entered into politics, he believed in the grafting of the Republican model onto the civilizations of the Far East: Indochina was founded as much by the Republic of scientists as by that of military officers and merchants. Along with his team (Antony Klobukowski, Dumoutier, Pène-Siefert, Joseph Chailley), he was favorable, especially when it came to Tonkin, to annexationist theories and was fundamentally hostile to the mandarinate. He installed the regime of the protectorate, laid out by the decree of January 27, 1886, which confided its control to the Ministry of Foreign Affairs and subordinated military power to civilian power. He also installed the apparatus of the provincial residents.

Above all, it was imperative, in Bert's mind, to develop political dialogue with a part of the Vietnamese society and its elites—"to make the Annamese nation our associate."[78] During his short Indochinese mandate—he died in Hanoi in November 1886—this policy was, however, undermined by the propagation of the simplistic idea of an opposition between the Tonkinese and the Annamese, set in motion by the establishment of the function of the *kinh luoc* (imperial commissioner invested with a delegation of imperial power), imposed on Hue on July 27, 1886, in Tonkin. This act removed the north of the country from the direct control of Hue and organized the partition of the country, a division that would be the foundation of French Indochina until its collapse in 1945. What did Paul Bert recommend? "In Tonkin, we must have a democratic policy, pacify through the peasant natives . . ."—hence the convocation of an ephemeral commission of elected notables—"in Annam, we must reassure the literati, rebuild the prestige of the king, pursue an aristocratic policy, pacify through the literate natives."[79]

Paul Bert's approach failed, but not completely. It pushed him to "Vietnamize" pacification, which he dared confide regionally to mandarins like Nguyen Than, whose ferocious campaign of 1887 put an end to the resistance in Quang Ngai and who in 1895 crushed the insurrection of Phan Dinh Phung. Influenced by the British model of the Indian Army—native units led by a European officer corps—the protectorate would increasingly call on local troops. Starting in the summer of 1888, the number of European troops fell to fourteen thousand men, supported by twenty-two thousand Vietnamese soldiers.[80] In Annam, there would never be more than 500 European troops in a territory that was a thousand kilometers long.[81] In Tonkin, in 1894, there were only 5,000 European soldiers and officers in comparison with 12,000 colonial infantrymen. Indochina was controlled and held by a military apparatus largely composed of the colonized. Bert laid the fiscal, budgetary, and structural basis for the protectorate, established the Garde indigène, inaugurated the facilities of the port of Haiphong, and sketched the first outlines of a railroad.

The failure of the annexationist and assimilationist theories to provide the foundation for the colonial regime led little by little to the idea that to counter national resistance, war must first and foremost be a political act. This idea appeared with Governor-General Richaud (1888–89), who, although he was won over to the strategy of heavy columns, discerned that the key to pacification was the village community, whose notables had to be won over one way or another. It triumphed with J.-L. de Lanessan, a deputy of the Republican Alliance, nominated governor-general on April 21, 1891, at a point when colonization was at a complete impasse. In that year, this former naval physician, an important botanist and zoologist, editor of the works of Buffon, professor at the Faculty of Medicine in Paris, and an atheist, materialist Republican who initially belonged to the radical extreme Left,[82] regained control of the situation. Through his action, a new intellectual configuration was brought to bear on colonial administration, based on a "scientific" reading of the relationships that had to be established with subject peoples, inspired by the two fundamental theses of "transformist" French anthropology of the end of the century: the hierarchical classification of societies on the ladder of progress, and the law of competition and solidarity that was believed to rule the living and govern the social.[83]

De Lanessan's project conceived of colonization as the "transforming agent" of backward countries. Revived by Durkheimian moralism, it led in 1905 to the affirmation of a new concept in Republican colonial policy: association. De Lanessan was one of the first to experiment with it, before formulating its theoretical content in 1897: colonization was a phenomenon that was natural and historic, composed simultaneously of competition and cooperation, and by the production of a "directed" complementarity between Europeans and "native" peoples in pursuit of the development of the world.[84] He founded his politics on the triple recognition of the unity of the Vietnamese people, the national character of the resistance, and the organic ties that united the Confucian mandarinate to the rural society and elite. What was his project? "To govern Annam and Tonkin by depending on all the active powers of the country: the king, the court and the Secret Council, mandarins, and the literati elite"[85]—in short to define the terms of a compromise with the political structures of Dai Nam and mobilize what it preserved of its social legitimacy, even if this meant reestablishing the unity of both the protectorates of Annam and Tonkin. He argued that the French should "govern with men from the national conservative party, with those who are considered representatives of the Annamese nationality and of the integrity of the empire," such as the regent Nguyen Trong Hiep, who had a great deal of influence. The protectorate had to make sense to the Vietnamese, and this political offer would be understood by their elites.

Through this project, villages benefited from a lightening of recruitment and requisitions, as well as from certain aspects of a developing program of public works, and taxes were standardized. Pacification operations were entrusted to the Garde indigène and to the *linh co* recruited in the villages, and as little as possible to the regular army. At the same time, adopting the strategy recommended by an exceptional officer, Colonel Théophile Pennequin, and continued by the next generation of officers—Armand Servière, Joseph Galliéni, Hubert Lyautey, Pierre Famin, and others—de Lanessan avoided the mistake of occupying only the lowlands, while superficially overseeing the highlands, which in fact strategically commanded the deltas. In August 1891, the mountainous periphery, populated by Tai, Tho, and Nung minorities, was divided into four military territories, entrusted to the administration of officers. The "policy of races," of which Galliéni made himself the theorist,[86] valorized the linguistic, social, and political ethnic minorities and acted to reinforce them through moderate taxes, the reduction of work to a minimum, the eviction of Vietnamese mandarins, and the restoration or consolidation of the power of customary chiefs *(quan lang)* and administrative tolerance of their control of contraband opium. This allowed for the creation of an efficient counter-guerrilla force through the distribution of ten thousand rifles, duly checked, to the Tai and Muong villages. The war in Indochina, then, was the beginning of a vast change in the thinking of the French military elite, which, following the Galliéni-Lyautey school of thought, ended up creating a theory of colonial war, conceived of as a war that was as much political as military. It was a theory presented by Lyautey in his famous article "Du rôle colonial de l'armée" (On the Colonial Role of the Army) in the *Revue des Deux Mondes* in February 1900.

Finally, the attitude of China was no less decisive. The retreat of the Chinese troops and the Black Flags in 1885 deprived the resistance of vital support. The support that China granted to the authorities of Tonkin following the Sino-Japanese war of 1894 and the 1894 Galliéni missions to Marshal Su, military commander of Guangxi, deprived the Chinese bands of a part of their supplies and the indispensable "sanctuaries" in Chinese territory. A line of bunkers was rapidly built to block the border, while a second line of militia stations encircled the Red River Delta. The Franco-Chinese convention of May 7, 1896, instituted an efficient mixed police system that would assure the control of the border until 1940. In Tonkin, the Chinese were photographed and forced to carry identification cards. Every military territory was methodically "cleansed" by the slow advance of a line of provisional posts—the tactics of the "oil stain" defined by Pennequin—and opened up by the construction of a network of roads and mule paths. The mountainous zone was thus pacified between 1892 and 1896.

In the meantime, the mandarinate, until then hesitant, seems to have responded, for complex reasons having to do with its culture of service to the state and management of society,[87] to de Lannessan's offer, as proven by the attitude of the influential regent Nguyen Trong Hiep (1834–1902). The mandarinate moved toward collaboration starting in 1891–92. Its role would be decisive. The brief participation of the respected personality Hoang Ke Vien in the pacification of Quang Binh in 1885 was one of the earliest signs of the potential rallying later incarnated in the figure of Hoang Cao Khai, the *kinh luoc* of Tonkin. De Lanessan sought to reinforce the authority of the court and reaffirmed its sovereignty over Tonkin. The Vietnamese civil servants, through the network of influences and domestic and personal relations that united them to the great lineages, local literate elites, and notables, were in a position to purge village communities. Thus, in 1892, the relationship of political forces was reversed. Leaderless, cut off from external aid, and hunted in the Tonkin Delta, the resistance was forced to withdraw into the middle region, where it became fragmented and separated from the villages. Its political and military horizon gradually narrowed to the mountaintops where it camped.

The defection of the court deprived the resistance of any credible political project. From that point on, it could no longer achieve victory solely by mobilizing an elementary patriotism, particularly since peasant support weakened as the peasants themselves became exhausted after such sufferings.

After 1891, struggle was hopeless. At the end of 1895, Phan Dinh Phung's guerrilla band was destroyed. In December, the great resister died in the forest of the high valley of Song Giang, in Quang Binh. After the defeat of the La Son movement, of which Phung was the leading light, the last of the major resistance forces, military initiative passed to the French, where it would remain for a long time. The government was able to pay for the submission not only of authentic bandits such as Luong Tam Ky but also of the last leaders of the anticolonial guerrilla war, like the De Tham in Yen The, first in April 1894 and then again in 1897. The final campaign against the last pockets of resistance in the highlands took place between 1895 and 1896. The following year, French forces controlled the entire country.

THE OCCUPATION OF LAOS AND THE FORMATION
OF A ZONE OF FRENCH INFLUENCE IN SOUTH CHINA

Once Vietnam was conquered, the problem of closing off the Indochinese frontiers to the west came to the fore. The tributary strategies of Hue and Bangkok had long been in confrontation in the vast Lao and Shan hinterland: in 1830, Siam had annexed the small state of Vientiane, deported a part of its population to the west of the Mekong, and then imposed a tribute on Luang Prabang; the principality of Xieng Khouang and northeastern Laos, however, became dependent on Vietnam in the middle of the century.[88] By the end of 1885, France's vague initiatives in Burma—the Franco-Burmese commercial treaty of January 15, 1885, the Deloncle mission to Mandalay in May, and the initiatives of Consul Haas—had failed. The British occupied the country in November, which displaced the Franco-British-Siamese confrontation more to the east, to the Mekong basin.[89]

At stake in the question of the Mekong from then on were three major issues. The first of these was the future of the Lao principalities, the deeply weakened descendants of the ancient kingdom of Lan Xang and the Tai domains *(seigneuries),* which fell under a system of "multiple tributes" that maintained their autonomous existence. The region was divided between the royal principality of Luang Prabang, a tributary of Siam, Vietnam, and more loosely of China; the surviving princely powers of the ancient states of Vientiane, Xieng Khouang, and Bassac; the principality of Chiang Khaeng, a tributary of Siam, whose capital was the small center of Muong Sing, which controlled the passage between Burma and Yunnan; the confederation of Sipsong Panna (the "twelve principalities") on the high banks of the river, a tributary of China and Burma; and the confederation of Sipsong Chau Tai, organized in domains *(muong)* in the hands of hereditary princes, the *chao fa,* who belonged to aristocratic lineages, located on Laotian-Vietnamese border near the Black River and controlled by the Tai aristocracy, especially by the powerful Deo Van Tri family in the region of Lai Chau. The second issue was the regional status of Siam, which was then on the path of modernization, and whose military posts had advanced after 1885, thanks to the weakening of Vietnam, onto the left bank of the Mekong toward the Annamese cordillera, to the plateau of Tran Ninh and the high banks of the Black River. The last issue raised by the Mekong conflict was the opposition between Paris and London. France claimed the "right" to the empire of Dai Nam, whereas the United Kingdom, whose commercial interests in Siam were considerable, hoped to connect the principalities of the upper Mekong to Burma or, at least, to make them into buffer states between British India and French Indochina.[90] The British also hoped to extend their trade to Yunnan, even though after 1885 London had abandoned the Colquhoun plan of building a railroad between Moulmein (Burma) and Simao (Yunnan), which was supported by the chambers of commerce of London and Manchester but ran into major topographical and climatic obstacles. Nonetheless, Tonkin was in danger of suddenly losing its geographical and economic importance.

After 1890, the Colonial Party of Eugène Étienne and Théophile Delcassé; a "Laotian" lobby (the Syndicat français du Haut-Laos) organized in 1888 by a future deputy of Cochinchina, François Deloncle; and also Gabriel Hanotaux, the influential minister of foreign affairs from 1894 to 1898, and his entourage of diplomats connected to imperialist politics, pressured France into abandoning its former plans to neutralize Siam by transforming it into a buffer state between the British and French colonial domains. In Paris, the Indochinese Union would be considered for a time as the initial base for a vast Southeast Asian empire, encompassing Siam and the Lao principalities. Auguste Pavie, vice-consul to Luang Prabang in 1886, then general commissioner to Laos, had explored the country. Pavie, a fascinating self-taught freethinker and nonconforming colonist, was in the midst of conducting the most systematic study of central Indochina up to that time, for which he traveled some 75,000 kilometers and explored 675,000 square kilometers during his two major scientific missions of 1890–91 and 1895.[91] He was named vice-consul of Luang Prabang in 1885—he arrived in February 1887—and disputed the claims of the Siamese over this land. During an attack by the Tai of Deo Van Tri against the principality in retaliation for Siamese raids against Lai Chau, as well as during forays of the Chinese bandits (the Ho) into the principality, he managed to persuade Oun Kham, the king of Luang Prabang, caught in the crossfire, to ask for France's protection. In the beginning of 1888, Son La, Lai Chau, and Dien Bien Phu in the Tai country were occupied by military columns and, thanks to the action of Pavie, the Tai aristocracy, in particular the powerful Deo Van Tri family, rallied to the French in April 1890. In February 1892, Delcassé announced, following a report from Deloncle and a petition signed by two hundred deputies, that France "was taking back" the left bank of the Mekong.

A Franco-Siamese crisis ensued in 1893–95. From April to May 1893, gunboats traveled up the middle region of the Mekong, while three military columns escorted the Siamese garrisons beyond the river. In spite of the dispatch of British ships to Bangkok, a French fleet occupied Chantaboun, in the Gulf of Siam, on July 13, 1893, and Pavie, sent as consul general to Bangkok the previous year, delivered an ultimatum to the Siamese government on July 20. Delcassé's objective was to impose a protectorate on Bangkok. This explains the French demands, the application of a naval blockade, and the threat of occupation of the provinces of Angkor and Battambang, which had been ceded in 1867. Tension was strong between the French and the British, and compromise was late in coming. Through the treaty of October 13, 1893, under pressure from London, Bangkok accepted the evacuation of the left bank of the Mekong and the demilitarization of a zone of 25 kilometers on the right bank. A combined Franco-British commission was elected to negotiate a settlement on the question of the upper Mekong. It was a difficult confrontation, since toward the end of 1894, pressure grew in Paris from the Colonial Party and the general government of Indochina; both were in favor of a protectorate in Siam, in view of the general dividing up of the Far East that the Sino-Japanese war of 1895 seemed to herald. "Bangkok could be part of the prize reserved for us," wrote Gabriel Hanotaux in June 1895.[92]

It was finally the risk of a military confrontation with Britain, the protector of Siam, at a time when tension was increasing regarding the upper Nile, the African counterpart of the Mekong question, that led France to accept the British proposition of October 1895 calling for a condominium over Siam. The French-British agreement of January 15, 1896, led to the resolution of the conflict to the advantage of Indochina; but France abandoned its project of a protectorate over Siam. The upper Mekong would form the border between Burma and Indochina. The principality of Chiang Khaeng was split in two along the river: the western half was included in British Burma and the eastern half in French Laos. The chao fa of Chiang Khaeng, Sali No, could do nothing but protest; his function would be done away with in 1916, during the plot of the last holder of the title. Siam was divided into three zones: a central buffer zone, the valley of Chaophraya, in which the two countries committed themselves not to send troops or acquire privileges, and two zones of influence on either side, British to the West and the South, French to the East. The advantages, granted by China to France and Britain concerning Sichuan and Yunnan, would be expanded to the nationals of both powers.

This was in effect a vast regional trade-off between the basin of the Mekong, henceforth French, and the west and south of the Malay Peninsula, henceforth under British influence. In 1895, after the departure of Pavie (nominated in 1893 commissaire général of Laos and president of the commission to delimit the upper Mekong frontier), the Lao principalities were regrouped into two territories and entrusted to two general commissioners: upper Laos, with Luang Prabang as its capital, and lower Laos, of which the chief town was Khong. On April 19, 1899, they would be merged into a single superior residency, installed in Vientiane. Subsequently, Siam would have to cede territory that had been recognized in 1893 on two occasions: the province of Champassak and the harbor of Krat in Laos in 1904; the two provinces of Battambang and Angkor in Cambodia and that of Sayaboury in Laos, in return for the restitution of Krat, through the treaty of March 23, 1907. The latter was confirmed by the 1926 agreement confirming the demilitarization of the Mekong frontier and specifying the borders along the river. The division of the Indochinese peninsula, then, was finally completed on this date.

Finally, during the same period, the initial goal of the conquest of Indochina, the penetration of the Chinese market, "the only reserve the future holds for us," according to Ulysse Pila, was achieved but revealed to be somewhat disappointing. The Beijing convention of 1887 opened three cities in southern China to French trade and granted the latter most favored nation status. In 1889, the consulate of Mongzi in Yunnan was created, of which the first two incumbents, Émile Rocher and Dejean de La Batie, were efficient promoters of French interests. When a group of Paris banks, with governmental guarantee, granted a loan of 400 million francs to Beijing to finance the war indemnity that China had to pay to Japan in 1895, this allowed France to gain recognition, through the agreement of June 20, 1895, of the transfer of Muong Sing on the upper Mekong, the priority for the mining concessions of Yunnan, Guangxi, and western Guangdong, along with the right to extend railroad lines from Tonkin into Chinese territory. As a result, stimulated by the Quai d'Orsay and by the Ministry of the Colonies, French capital became interested in equipping China. Vast projects of liaison between the Yunnan tin, copper, and iron mines and the Tonkin coal mines emerged following various exploratory missions in southern China, from 1895 to 1898, sponsored by the Comité des forges.[93]

The action of Paul Doumer, ex-minister of finances, who became governor-general of Indochina in May 1897, was decisive in this regard. Following his journey to France in the summer of 1898, he garnered support from politicians and businessmen for the railway and mining projects in South China and campaigned for the annexation of Yunnan. Some would go so far as to dream of a successful variant of the ongoing confrontation at Fashoda (on the banks of the White Nile in the Sudan, where the British and French were then politely deadlocked) on the upper Yangtze. With the accords of June 12, 1897, and April 10, 1898, Beijing ceded to the pressure, committing itself not to alienate any territory to a foreign power in the three provinces adjacent to Tonkin all the way to the mouth of the Xijiang, conceding to French interests the Lang Son–Nanning and Lao Cai–Kunming railway lines, and granting France a 99-year lease on the bay of Guangzhouwan, so that it could build a coaling station there. In several months, the bases of a vast zone of French influence were thus established in southern China.

. . .

At the end of this half century, thanks to the emergence of a new Asian order, France was assured of the control of an immense territory of 740,000 square kilometers, the most populated of its new colonial empire, and of a group of ancient civilizations and states. Through Indochina, as much as through its colonies in North Africa and sub-Saharan Africa, France, now republican, succeeded in converting itself into an "imperial society" *(société imperiale),* to use Christophe Charle's term.[94] On the Indochinese peninsula, the management of the relations between peoples had been profoundly changed. A mode of recognition between political entities and authorities based on symbolic relationships—like the rites of legitimization practiced by the first "masters of the earth," such as the Souei in Cambodia; the borrowing of royal titles from Indian traditions; the possession of talismanic protective images, or palladia; tributary allegiances to the Chinese empire (in the cases of Dai Nam and of the *muong* of Luang Prabang) or Siam (in the case of the Khmer monarchy)—was replaced by the modern delineation of borders, the signing of international treaties, and the imperialist organization of Indochinese space. French Indochina, far from being an artificial construct, was the result as much of the dynamic of events, of the shock of antagonistic initiatives, as of a program traced out in advance. In metropolitan France, the arrival of a certain cultural configuration, the new scientific, industrial, and Republican culture, made this "Indochinese moment" possible. This configuration, in turn, found itself consolidated by the creation of Indochina. Indeed, between 1867 and 1884, the "other" possible path— that of noncolonial imperialistic expansion in Asia, notably by French imperialism, carried out through the transformation of the native states into dependent partners of the West, all the while maintaining their political independence—was only progressively put aside in the Indochinese realm. France ignored this other path not only because of international constraints and the multiple demands of nineteenth-century French society but, just as much, owing to the inability of the Vietnamese elite to conceive of their future in this "other," noncolonial vision of Western expansion.

Reducing the Khmer kingdom to a dependency was certainly a difficult task. The uprising was so widespread in 1885–86 that the colonizers, in order to keep Vietnam—their principal objective—had to resort to royal mediation and abandon their project of a pure and simple annexation. As Alain Forest and Milton Osborne have shown, they were unable to capture the mechanisms of Khmer political power without reinforcing the king's symbolic power as the "master of existence."[95] In Cambodia, colonization had to be patient, and the identification of the nation with its royal rulers would continue to be reinforced.

It was different in Vietnam, where the French had to defeat a lengthy armed opposition and to break the monarchy morally, ideologically, and politically. The result of this difficult power struggle was largely determined by the attitude of the Chinese empire. Constrained to give up its tributary system in Southeast Asia by the war of 1884–85, Beijing outlined what would be China's Indochinese policy until 1950: while respecting the Franco-Chinese compromise as essential, it sought to control France's Vietnamese adversaries through calculated and limited aid, postponing long-term southbound expansion and the transformation of the peninsula's future modern nation-states into satellites.

The ambiguous and contradictory attitude adopted from 1884 to 1888 by the Vietnamese Confucian monarchy and bureaucracy, prisoners of their own ideological tradition, had dire consequences. The actions of Ton That Thuyet, Ham Nghi, and some mandarins and scholars certainly legitimized the resistance, which would evidently not have had the same impact without it. On the other hand, the final rallying of the court and the mandarinate to the protectorate with the aim of preserving the monarchy, the dynasty, and Vietnam's Confucian hierarchy, no matter at what cost—a logical corollary to the Franco-Chinese accord of June 6, 1885— weakened and probably shattered the nation's dynastic and royal affiliation. In the eyes of the literate elite, the Confucian monarchy was permanently discredited, and a breach opened between it and popular patriotism that would never close. The result was the opposite of what was established in Cambodia: the nation, the dynasty and, as a consequence, the monarchy were separated. Not only did the dynasty lose its "celestial mandate," but its maintenance on the throne by the foreigners made any continuation of this mandate impossible and potentially disqualified the royal function. Patriotism had to look for other paths.

Thus, from 1896 to 1897, the Vietnamese resistance found itself in an ideological void—a state of moral, political, and cultural searching. This was all the more serious for colonization, inasmuch as the Can Vuong had passed on a fierce spirit of denial to the defeated Vietnamese society. In 1900, a perceptive officer, Colonel Fernand Bernard, thinking of the long-term consequences of the defeat of the literati, underlined the emotional violence he saw appearing: "This whole period," he wrote, "has left a hatred that the years will not ease in the hearts of the Annamese and the Europeans."[96] Bernard saw in the defeat of the literati the origin of a political psychology common to most Europeans: "We can conclude that this finally subdued people will not recover the powerful instinct that, so often in its history, has raised it up against the invader. We believe that we possess the ultimate method for keeping it in submission." However, he added, "repressed feelings persist in the depths of souls. In the countryside of Annam, they are still thinking of the proscribed emperor, of Ham Nghi and his counselors, of Thuyet and Phan Dinh Phung. A naïve legend has already been created suggesting that they still live in the mountains, ready to emerge when the moment arrives."

The Structures of Domination

Regardless of what we do, the government we want to establish in lower Cochinchina will be based on racial superiority.

—CAPITAINE DE VAISSEAU JOSEPH D'ARIÈS,
  Senior French Commander in Cochinchina, 1861

According to the influential Radical party leader Albert Sarraut, a future governor of Indochina (1911–19) and later twice (1933, 1936) prime minister of France, "colonies are states in the making."[1] The period of French colonization therefore represented a fundamental break in the history of the political systems of Indochina: along with colonization, modern state structures were irreversibly implanted by foreign powers. Their grafting was improvised in the throes of conquest and in turn affected by the veiled yet long-lasting resistance of the colonized societies. At stake was nothing less than the definition of the mechanisms that were to be used to control these societies; but this construction also evolved amid contradictions. In Indochina as elsewhere, colonization was never an unchanging, homogeneous process, and the major decisions were made reluctantly, indecisively and apparently contradictorily, one after the other. The whole combined the specific historical investments and the aims of a part of the sociopolitical forces of metropolitan France that were more or less linked to the "Republican compromise." Colonization was ambiguous, not at all monolithic, split by innumerable conflicts of interest and orientation, the first of these being the near permanent opposition between the French colonizers of Indochina and the Indochinese administration, whose arbitration by colonial authority was especially difficult.

Moreover, colonial power was subject to a major political constraint, which was the result of the profound indifference that ordinarily separated French politics from the Indochinese undertaking. This constraint involved two long-standing requirements. On the one hand, colonization in Indochina must never cause any political waves in metropolitan France: in other words, colonization must not cost France a thing, which implied resorting largely to an "inexpensive" mode of domination—the protectorate. This was the meaning of the contentious vote in the Chamber of Deputies in December 1885. On the other hand, setting in motion and creating colonial profit and investment, simply put, the "development" of the colony, depended on it becoming rapidly profitable and capable of creating budgetary surpluses. This in turn presupposed a vigorous intervention of the colonial state apparatus in the internal workings of the subjugated societies. As a result, the state in Indochina long vacillated between two tendencies: the extension of structures of direct administration, following the African model, versus the maintenance of a protectorate based on the British model of "indirect rule."

THE LONG-LASTING UNCERTAINTY OF THE POLITICAL AND ADMINISTRATIVE MODEL, 1858–1897

From its earliest stages, colonization encountered a nearly irresolvable dilemma. Until after 1884, the Vietnamese imperial state, the Khmer royal power, and the Laotian political systems, not to mention the customary powers of the ethnic minorities, all remained intact and irreplaceable. Yet leaving them in place presented two risks: harming the dual imperative of pacification and profitability, and exposing French sovereignty to dangerous competition. These risks revived the old debate—started during the Second Empire concerning the status of Algeria—between the supporters of direct rule, theorized by Arthur Girault in his *Principes de colonisation et de législation coloniale* (1895), and those who endorsed "association," an actual protectorate supported by the Quai d'Orsay. The latter group included men such as Jules Harmand and the influential Joseph Chailley-Bert, who served as a deputy from 1906 to 1914 and was a leader of the Colonial Union and the designated spokesman for the colonial budget in the Chamber of Deputies. Jean-Louis de Lanessan, Albert de Pouvourville, General Théophile Pennequin, Louis Vignon, Albert Sarraut and many others would all contribute original ideas to this ongoing debate. These issues were nothing but the refractions within Republican colonial circles of the very real challenge facing the colonial administration: the necessary distortion of the doctrinal conceptions of the administration by the responses of the conquered societies, continually slipping away from colonial rule, which controlled them with difficulty.

Direct Rule or Protectorate?

At the outset, direct administration was the stronger of these two tendencies due to the resistance stemming from the Vietnamese monarchy and scholars. In this regard, the experience gained in Cochinchina under the nine consecutive admirals who ruled from 1861 to 1879, and then under a civilian government, was crucial in defining the political form of the colonial regime.[2] The widespread withdrawal

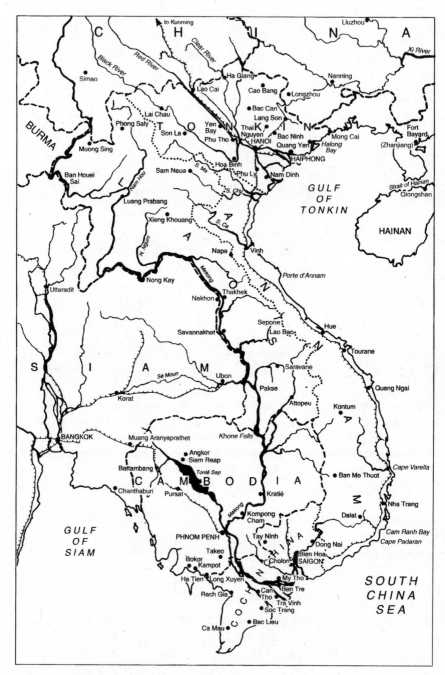

MAP 2.1. Administrative map of French Indochina.

of the mandarins from provinces conquered between 1858 and 1867 created a political and cultural void that thwarted any attempt at indirect rule, such as that which Admiral Bonard instituted on a trial basis in Bien Hoa province, inspired by the Dutch example in Java and by Napoleon III's ideas about an "Arab kingdom" in Algeria aimed at preserving indigenous administration below the provincial level. It was therefore necessary to create a substitute provincial administrative system managed by the inspectors of the Indigenous Affairs Department. Organized by Admiral Pierre de La Grandière (1863–68), these inspectors were selected from among Navy officers up until 1873; Émile Luro, Gabriel Aubaret, Paul Philastre, Francis Garnier, Paulin Vial, and Antony Landes were some of the most brilliant. Supported by the Catholic missions, this corps coordinated a dual political structure, which was, however, authoritarian and centralized in the hands of the admiral-governors, superimposing a small number of French provincial and district administrators onto the village institutions of the twenty provinces. These administrators were first trained at the Collège des stagiaires (1874–76), created by Luro. The great Cochinchinese scholar Petrus Ky—a southerner who had studied as a seminarian at the Collège des missions étrangères in Penang—taught there, assisted by a staff of Vietnamese secretaries and interpreters.

The direct control of the colonized society was certainly facilitated by southern Vietnam's cultural profile. This area was less impregnated by Confucian culture than the northern and central regions, and a Southeast Asian tradition—both mystical and Buddhist, eclectic and hybrid—was well established. These historical conditions permitted a stronger penetration of the colonizer's culture, values, and political and legal practices into the society of the south, whose ties with Vietnamese tradition would slacken from then on. These conditions facilitated the expansion of French law—despite the efforts of Paul Philastre, the French penal code replaced the Gia Long code in March 1880, and the French civil code was promulgated in part in October 1883—the French language, and especially Quoc ngu, the romanized transcription of Vietnamese, which as early as 1882 replaced ideograms as its official written form. The advent of a new Republican colonial staff around 1880 reinforced the policy of direct rule. The military regime disappeared in Cochinchina with the nomination of a civil governor and the creation of the Colonial Council of Cochinchina on February 8, 1880, and of a deputy's seat in July of the following year.

As early as 1885, the military regime also gave way in Annam, sanctioning the creation of the position of resident general of Annam-Tonkin on January 27, 1886. The residents superior of Hue and Hanoi were accountable to this office. Its first incumbent, Paul Bert (April–November 1886), convinced of the opposition between the "Tonkinese people" and the "Annamese mandarins" was resolved to detach Tonkin from the control of the imperial court. He hoped to pacify it by using the "indigenous peasantry," that is, by attaching the village councils to the colonial government, while also really applying the protectorate in Annam with the help of the "indigenous scholars." Fundamentally, the project was a way of transferring the colonial structures of Cochinchina to northern Vietnam, as well as to Cambodia. From this perspective, the question of how to deal with the mandarins—there were around fifteen hundred in the protectorate as a whole in 1896—was of central importance, since they made up the backbone of the Confucian society that had to be neutralized.[3] After a project to annex Tonkin in exchange for maintaining the independence of Annam was forsaken, the key measure in this regard was the royal edict of June 3, 1886, through which Emperor Dong Khanh delegated the totality of his powers in Tonkin to an imperial commissioner *(kinh luoc su)*— Nguyen Trong Hiep was chosen—to whom the northern mandarins were henceforth to be held accountable. "A prodigious change," Joseph Chailley-Bert commented, "which, under the appearance of a simple convenience, prepared the actual separation of the two countries."[4] The administration of Tonkin was thus removed from the Hue court and subjected to the strict control of four residents and eleven French deputy residents, who kept "a file on every influential mandarin, scholar or influential individual."[5]

In May 1886, the Garde indigène was created and placed under the supervision of the residents; it was an effective tool of repression. In Tonkin, Paul Bert endeavored to establish direct ties between the residents and the village communities by instituting, on April 30, 1886, a council of Tonkinese notables, who were elected by the canton and deputy chiefs, as well as provincial consulting commissions—bodies destined to rival the mandarin hierarchy, which still needed to be maintained for a time. The discredited imperial dynasty and the court were placed under financial tutelage. The imperial treasury, which had been confiscated by General de Courcy, was returned to Dong Khanh in 1886, but Paul Bert withheld half of it as security, invoking the cost of the pacification process in Annam. In 1889, the protectorate, which already administered the customs in Annam, acquired the additional duties of overseeing the Chinese poll tax and the opium monopoly, as well as other rights, including, in 1892, the collection of new direct taxes that de Lanessan had obtained the right to enforce. Finally, starting in June 1887, the French representative in Hue began to attend the meetings of the Regency Council, and especially those of the Secret Council (Co Mat Vien), then became its president in June 1895. He countersigned all the rulings of the Hue government, a practice ratified by the convention of February 28, 1889, and the royal ordinance of June 13, 1895. As noted earlier, the Cambodian convention of 1884 was, in fact, a measure intended to lead to annexation pure and simple.

Although direct rule was the predominant tendency until 1889, it also encountered insurmountable difficulties. "This experiment almost cost us dearly," wrote Captain Louis Rouyer.[6] In Cambodia, direct rule provoked a general uprising; in Annam, it incited the obstinate resistance of people trained by the educated class; in Tonkin, it encouraged the noncooperation or dissidence of the educated class. Even though vanquished, the Can Vuong prevented an annexation. Moreover, the abolition of the precolonial states resulted in unanimous indignation because, as de Lanessan noted about Vietnam: "the emperor is the ritual (in Europe, one would say constitutional) personification of the Annamese people."[7] This experiment also ended up being too costly. In 1885, in Cochinchina, Le Myre de Vilers estimated that the presence of 100,000 men was necessary; but the cost of creating 900 military posts and of maintaining 50,000 men amounted to at least 100 million francs. Finally, the linguistic barrier and widespread ignorance about the functioning of the colonized societies made the mediation and collaboration of indigenous authorities indispensable, because the idea of recruiting new employees from among interpreters, officers of the Annamese troops, and even among house boys, was quickly abandoned. The protectorate policy was a prolonged, durable compromise with national realities. It sought to maintain the dynasties and the indigenous state structures and was advocated by the Quai d'Orsay, whose authority Annam and Tonkin came under from January 1886 to October 1887. In the end, it temporarily prevailed around 1891, though it meant running the significant risk of seeing a monarch stage an uprising, as Ham Nghi had done in Vietnam in 1885 and as Duy Tan would do in 1916.

Governors-General Georges-Jules Piquet (1889–91) and especially J.-L. de Lanessan (1891–94) gave this policy a deeper meaning: the establishment of a strong alliance with the court and the Vietnamese mandarinate; the same would hold true in Cambodia and Laos. The alliance was actively sought after with the faction of mandarins de Lanessan named "the national Annamese party,"[8] which in 1885 had not entirely chosen between Dong Khanh and Ham Nghi. This group included men such as Hoang Ke Vien and Nguyen Trong Hiep (who were elected to the Secret Council in 1887); even though involved with the foreign power, these mandarins defended the imperial regime "as the sole protector of the Vietnamese nation."[9] The ideas expounded by de Lanessan, and also by higher officials such as Residents Superior Rheinhart and Baille in the 1890s, as well as those of officers such as Pennequin, were relatively audacious. They constituted, without a doubt, the inception of the most advanced policy that France had ever practiced in Indochina, tolerated as long as it concerned only the pacification of the Can Vuong, then quickly denounced and aborted with de Lanessan's dismissal in December 1894. These ideas inaugurated a tradition, which would remain in the minority, of "liberal" colonization founded more or less confusedly on the long-term acceptance of a possible shift in the colonial relationship toward a gradual decolonization and on the will to modernize indigenous societies. Built on recognition of the existence of the Vietnamese nation, de Lanessan's policy saw the protectorate as the creation of a genuine and lasting historical compromise between French imperialism, the conservative national elite, and the monarchy.

De Lanessan restored a large part of the mandarins' prerogatives, entrusted them with the command of militia units, and endeavored to instill into French personnel a respect for the cultural values of Vietnamese society. Above all, he was determined to reverse the separation of Tonkin and Annam. This farsighted policy led to the restoration of more satisfactory relations with the mandarinate, as well as enabling the mobilization of strong Confucian values, such as the loyalty of civil servants to the king, to aid in pacifying society and overcoming armed resistance. It did not, however, resolve the problem of colonial development and economic exploitation. Furthermore, it faced strong opposition from metropolitan politicians, the military, the Church, and the colonizers. The logic behind de Lanessan's policies lay in the idea of partnership with the ruling class and the Vietnamese bureaucracy, as well as their Khmer homologues, along the model of British India. In fact, this sort of evolution had already been rendered impossible not only by the need to balance the budget of the Indochinese Union but certainly also by the growing influence on French policy in the Far East wielded by significant financial and industrial interests whose chief concern was guaranteed profit. In any case, the dynasty had not really regained its authority, and the monarchy had already become a mere shadow of its former self. Beginning in 1885–86, the emperor was generally perceived as France's pet. "In fact, national monarchy was dead," Charles Fourniau writes.[10] De Lanessan should "stop in his tracks and recognize, pragmatically, the need to rule the provinces more directly and extensively, allowing French governmental action to reach beyond the boundaries of our protectorate treaty," Lieutenant Colonel Louis de Grandmaison suggested.[11]

Around 1894, it became clear that none of these opposing approaches were entirely effective. The protectorate regime in Annam, Tonkin, and Cambodia remained poorly defined and had achieved only an unstable and unequal compromise between the authoritarian policy of direct rule and recurrent attempts to renew the power of the indigenous rulers.

The Indochinese Union

The major preoccupation of the French authorities, maintaining their tenuous control of Vietnamese society, also exacerbated the conflicts of interests that divided colonization. These were all the more acute in that, until 1887, there were two separate French rulers of the peninsula: the governor of Cochinchina, who fell under the Ministry of the Colonies and had authority over the resident general in Cambodia, and the resident general in Annam-Tonkin, who fell under the Ministry of Foreign Affairs and, as of January 1, 1887, was given his own budget. The clash between civil and military authorities, the rivalries between ministries in Paris, the dispute between the undersecretary of state for the colonies and the Foreign Ministry over the administration of the Annam-Tonkin protectorate, the conflict between Indochinese merchants and French industrialists over customs tariffs, and the missions' desire for preferential treatment—all of these conflicts remained unresolved for ten years.

Above all, following the institution of a civil administration in Cochinchina, the local colonists—around 2,000 French settlers in 1880, and 4,852 in 1901, of whom 400 were Indians from Pondicherry, speculators and merchants, minor public officials, and various clergy—were gaining considerable power and autonomy. The keystone of their new situation was the Colonial Council, created on February 8, 1880, and elected by the community of colonists and by a limited number of indigenous voters, which was largely in control of determining the budget, most expenditures, the assignment of concessions of land and procurement contracts, subsidies, and clerical stipends. The colonists were organized into a powerful political clique, which was sharply in favor of annexation, although divided into rival factions. The spokesmen of this group—notably Deputy Jules Blancsubé and the planter Paul Blanchy, who owned a near-monopoly of pepper plantations and served a seemingly unending term as president of the Colonial Council from 1882 until his death in 1901, as well as being mayor of Saigon in 1895—defended the colony's autonomy with regard to customs and budgets in the name of democracy. This group long succeeded in obstructing the political centralization of Indochina under the direct authority of the government.

The decrees of October 17 and 20, 1887, that created the Indochinese Union were an attempt to produce this political centralization, which had become indispensable to ensuring the arbitration between divergent conceptions and interests.[12] This Union became completely connected to the administration of the Ministry of the Colonies, the stronghold of Opportunist Republicans, by a later decree of April 21, 1891. The Indochinese Union brought together, under the authority of a governor-general who was vested with political and administrative power and was also the administrator of its common budget, the lieutenant governor of Cochinchina and the residents superior of the protectorates of Cambodia, Annam, and Tonkin (the protectorate of Annam-Tonkin was effectively divided on May 9, 1889, into two distinct superior residencies). Later on, the superior residency of Laos, created on April 19, 1899, became part of the Indochinese Union, as did the territory of Guangzhouwan in January 1900.

As Paul Isoart has shown, in 1887 Indochina was still merely a hybrid compromise, which succeeded in establishing only a relative financial solidarity among the different territories of the Union, each with its own "local" budget, with Cochinchina making generous contributions to the military spending of Annam and Tonkin.[13] The Colonial Council of the southern colony retained control of its budget, the largest in the Union, for obvious reasons. This council, elected by officials, merchants, and colonists, had a clear agenda: to grant contracts to entrepreneurs and land to settlers, and to manage payment of the civil servants. As de Lanessan wrote, "it is an elected assembly that pays its electorate with the money of those who are unable to elect it."[14] The governor-general—whose budget was created in October 1887 and eliminated as early as May 1888, under pressure from Cochinchina—was,

TABLE 2.1 Costs of the French settlement in Indochina, 1859–1895

	Francs (1914 rate)
Cochinchina, 1859–1895	155,748,000[a]
Tonkin and Annam, 1874–1895	594,239,000
TOTAL	749,987,000[b]

SOURCE: Budget commission report on draft legislation for the provisional regulation of finances for the Annam-Tonkin protectorate in 1895 (Krantz Report), quoted by L. Salaun, *L'Indochine* (Paris, 1903). In his *Histoire des finances coloniales de la France* (Paris, 1938), p. 210, Albert Duchêne, the former director of political affairs for the Ministry of the Colonies, estimates the amount at 3 to 3.5 billion francs (1938 rate; about 468–546 million 1914 francs).

[a] Does not include the amount spent by the colony on the other Indochinese budgets (i.e., 117,155,000 F).

[b] Roughly 8.9 billion francs at the 1984 rate.

in fact, the administrator of only Annam and Tonkin (whose superior residency was even done away with from 1895 to 1897). In fact, around 1897, the political structure of Indochina did not yet exist.

A "Financial Lang Son"

Finally, and above all, the pacification of Annam and Tonkin cost much more than the initial conquest of the territory. Taking possession of Cochinchina cost 80 million francs in all from 1862 to 1867.[15] From 1859 to 1895, France spent a total of roughly 750 million (1913) francs in Indochina (table 2.1).

The prevalent illusions in 1885 about the financial potential of Annam-Tonkin were quickly abandoned. In 1887, Ernest Millot, an associate of Jean Dupuis, estimated the possible revenues of Tonkin at 150 million francs, of which 40 million could be "easily" obtained after three years.[16] In fact, by 1887, Tonkin yielded only 15 million francs.

Requesting French subsidies proved to be an increasingly difficult endeavor, since the Protectorate was strongly contested in the metropole until the early 1890s. Every budgetary debate gave rise to the anticipated opposition from monarchists, radicals, and socialists. The Opportunist Republican government could only keep its Asian acquisition by reducing its drain on the metropolitan budget. From 1887 to 1891, 87 million francs were set aside for it from this budget, and during the same period, military spending exceeded 242 million; all of this for a negligible 2 million a year gained from the export of French goods.[17]

Indochina therefore needed to finance its own pacification, insofar as possible. The formula Camille Pelletan hurled at the Chamber of Deputies in December 1885 summed up the problem well: "You want a protectorate when cost is concerned but an annexation when it comes to profit!"[18] Cochinchina was called on to contribute:

its tax revenues increased from 6.9 million francs in 1868 to 18.8 million in 1879; land tax, paid in Annamese currency in 1864, was paid in silver piastres starting from 1868; and corvée labor was partially converted into silver. The Cochinchinese colony provided the equivalent of 41 million piastres to the protectorate of Annam-Tonkin from 1887 to 1891. Paul Bert attempted to reduce military spending in the Protectorate by reducing the number of European troops and, most important, sought to increase the returns of the imperial tax system. In this he came up against the problem of the poor returns of precolonial tax structures. This problem was aggravated by agricultural uncertainties and fluctuations in the price of paddy, which led to an erratic fiscal income.

In Vietnam, the tax system was based on the lists of registered individuals (*dinh bo*), which determined personal taxes, the payment of taxes through labor, and the levying of soldiers. The only individuals subject to taxation were the male members of the village population between the ages of eighteen and sixty who owned property and were listed on the registers kept by the village authorities. As for land taxation, it was based upon the *dia ba,* the cadastral register collected under Gia Long, which had not been updated since the great reappraisal undertaken by Minh Mang. The registers were only used to determine the total amount to be paid by the community, which was then divided among the inhabitants by the notables. It was, then, the village community that paid the tax. The imperial state did not recognize the individual. Furthermore, there were numerous exemptions offered to the mandarins and their relatives, the graduates of the triennial examinations, subordinate agents of the central and local governments, and so on. Toward 1884, according to the French authorities, the number of individuals registered in Annam and Tonkin represented only one-third of the able-bodied, taxable population. The conquest therefore led to the reappraisal of the old fiscal compromise between the imperial power and the village authorities. In order to augment the budgetary revenues in Tonkin, the circulars of 1888, 1890, and 1894 required villages to increase the number of those registered by 10 to 20 percent.[19]

They had little success. This is why the Cochinchinese tax system, founded on the supremacy of indirect taxation and on monopolies, was progressively extended throughout Indochina through the creation of concessions of the state monopoly on gambling in Tonkin, starting in 1886, and the extension of metropolitan customs tariffs throughout Indochina in 1887, of the farming of opium in Cambodia in 1884, in Tonkin in 1888, and in Annam in 1889, and of the salt tax in Tonkin in 1886. The fiscal returns of Annam-Tonkin increased, albeit slowly, from 2,608,000 piastres in 1886 to 6,700,000 in 1894.

Indochina's deficit was no less catastrophic: 20 million francs for the five fiscal years from 1887 to 1891. "It is a financial Lang Son!" interim Governor-General Bideau remarked in April 1891 (referring to General François de Négrier's brush with disaster in 1885—see chapter 1 above).[20] In the end, Tonkin cost the metropolitan budget nearly half a billion gold francs from 1882 to 1891.[21] In 1896, the colony's liability reached 43 million. On February 10, 1896, Parliament, which had advanced 30 million francs to the Indochinese budget the previous year, was obliged to authorize a state-guaranteed loan of 80 million francs to absorb the Indochinese debt and finance a series of public works. Still, the liabilities of Annam and Tonkin continued in 1896. Even Cochinchinese finances were unbalanced by more than half a million piastres in 1896, and by close to a million in 1897. These accumulated deficits postponed the development of the entire colonial economy.

THE COMPLETION OF THE INDOCHINESE STATE, 1897–1911

A new phase in Indochinese history began with the arrival of Paul Doumer to head the Gouvernement général in 1897. Doumer, an important figure on the Left, as well as in the Radical Party, which played a decisive role in the administration of Indochina, had been minister of finance in the cabinet of Léon Bourgeois (1895–96). This self-made man, a manual laborer turned professor and treasurer of the Grand Orient de France, one of the main branches of French Freemasonry, was a vigorous and authoritative personality, linked to the Comité des forges. Colonization gained momentum with the recovery of the world economy, and the end of armed resistance allowed Doumer to straighten out the administrative apparatus, establish a productive fiscal system, and make investments. Without a doubt, Doumer was chosen for his financial capacities and his strong will by Prime Minister Jules Méline (1896–98), a right-wing Republican against whom Doumer had fought, with the result that Méline preferred to distance him. Governors-General Paul Beau (1902–8), Antony Klobukowski (1908–11), and especially Albert Sarraut (1911–14) would fine-tune or add to the colonial regime Doumer had put in place, without ever modifying its essential features.

The Reorganization of the Indochinese Union

The colonial state organized by Paul Doumer and his counselors had as its "central core" a powerful political-administrative structure with a double function: to integrate all the Indochinese political structures into the French state-controlled system and to neutralize the former Vietnamese, Khmer, and Lao states, as well as the political structures of the montagnards, and convert them into subordinate apparatuses that could be used to control the colonized populations.

Workaholic, ambitious, energetic, and highly competent, Doumer would be the true creator of the Gouvernement général and the state structure of Indochina.[22] On the eve of his departure in 1891, de Lanessan had succeeded in obtaining from the government the April 21 decree making the governor-general the "trustee of the Republic's powers in French Indochina," with the right to order the enactment of laws and metropolitan decrees, subject to governmental sanction. He was also given military authority, the right to correspond with all French diplomatic agents in the Far East, to organize the civil service, to designate a portion of civil servants, and to draw up the Union's budget and get it approved by the metropolitan authorities. Unity of command was thus established. The decree was inspired by approaches borrowed by Jules Harmand, the first civil commissioner in Annam in 1883, from Dutch practices and, especially, from the British model of domination in India, which was founded on the autonomy of the administrative and financial management of the Indian empire from the metropole and aimed at creating what he called a "vice-state." "The great possessions," Harmand wrote in 1891, "should be organized as true states, provided with all the structures necessary for the survival and the functioning of states, and made to possess all the characteristics that define states, except one: political independence."[23]

In reality, however, the decree of 1891 was applied only in Annam and Tonkin. The administrative and budgetary fragmentation resulting from the process of gradual conquest was preserved in its entirety. Cochinchina still fell outside the authority of the governor-general. It had been necessary to dismember Vietnam to subdue it, but this resulted in the fragmentation of colonial power. Indochina was a juxtaposition of territories foreign to one another, connected by a somewhat vague "personal union," in which protected states preserved their own financial autonomy. In the absence of a common budget, any rather large expenditure was impossible. Although a governor-general existed, a general government did not.

Between 1897 and 1902, the latter took shape with the institution of departments of Finance, Customs and Rules (1897), Public Works (1898), Agriculture and Trade (1899), Posts and Telegraphs (1901), and the General Secretariat (1902), which split responsibilities with the department of Political Affairs and General Security in 1922. With the governor-general, a staff of high commissioners, representatives of major interests, and a pair of Vietnamese notables formed the Superior Council of Indochina. This was the decision-making structure, replicated throughout the five territories of the Indochinese Union, of a powerful central apparatus, which would remain stable until after 1945, even though its various components experienced numerous overhauls.[24] It was at this level that residents superior in the four protectorates and the lieutenant governor of Cochinchina conducted the business of day-to-day government.

The French Indochinese Civil Service, created in 1899 on the model of the British Indian Civil Service, successfully recruited personnel by offering high salaries. On July 31, 1898, the general budget was created, subsidized by indirect taxes collected in the Indochinese Union, largely (95 percent in 1913) from state monopolies (opium, salt, alcohol) and customs duties, and intended to finance the shared expenses of development and the improvement of the colony's infrastructure. The direct taxes, meanwhile, remained at the disposal of the "local budgets," which were used to cover the expenses of the daily functioning and of the development of each of the five parts of the Union. Since the indirect fiscal system was largely dominant, the Gouvernement général had at its disposal the majority of the Indochinese finances. The institution of the Gouvernement général and the general budget, which the southern settlers had relentlessly resisted, delivered a decisive blow to Cochinchinese autonomy. Indeed, it reduced by more than two-thirds (67.3% in 1899) the revenue of the local budget, managed by the Colonial Council of Cochinchina. Nevertheless, Cochinchinese colonization preserved its particular features and remained relatively important politically. It elected a deputy, and Saigon was the only city in Indochina to possess a municipal council elected by universal suffrage. This made it necessary to compromise with the French settlers of the south; the Colonial Council succeeded in preserving almost complete management of direct contributions and allotment of land concessions of less than five hundred hectares.

In this way, a coherent state-controlled apparatus was created. From the outset, however, it was weighed down by its own inertia. Doumer's reforms succeeded in creating a rigid centralization, which Sarraut sought to attenuate in 1911–12 by decreasing the number of civil servants and decentralizing general services. The reforms also reinforced the tendency to *fonctionnarisme*—the constitution of a large civil service bureaucracy—the critique of which was the leitmotif of proceedings devoted by Parliament to the colony. Certainly, the European staff was relatively small in Annam and Tonkin: seven hundred European civil servants for more than ten million inhabitants around 1895, to whom must be added several thousand Vietnamese subordinate civil servants. Jules Harmand believed that Indochina, like India, could not avoid the development of a bureaucracy. "India" he wrote, "is no more than a vast bureaucracy."[25]

But the cost of the colonial state and the French colonial Civil Service represented a considerable weight for the colony (table 2.2), certainly greater than for its British or Dutch counterparts. By 1900, Cochinchina—which before the conquest had been run by fifty mandarins of all ranks, assisted by a smaller staff—had 290 European civil servants and more than 1,000 other French officials, or 1 for every 7,900 inhabitants, as compared to 1 for 76,000 in Java.[26] Adolphe Messimy, who reported the budget of the Colonies in the French Chamber, noted that in Phnom Penh in 1910–11, there were "fourteen French civil servants currently employed in post offices that were not at all busy." He continued: "In Singapore, where the volume of work was perhaps ten thousand times greater, since this city is a center of intense circulation and the point of arrival for eight large telegraph cables, there are only eight English civil servants in all."[27] The number of European civil servants continued to grow. There were 2,860 in 1897, and 5,683 in 1911, as compared to the 12,200 "indigenous" civil servants in 1914. "We can affirm," Messimy's successor, Deputy Albert Métin, wrote in 1911, "that the European staff in Indochina costs more than 35 million every year, which is 25% of its budget's revenue."[28]

TABLE 2.2 Cost of Indochinese administrative management, 1913–1938
(percent of administrative expenditures in the local budgets
of Indochina; personnel expenses are in parentheses)[a]

Region	1913	1920	1930	1931	1938
Cochinchina	55.9	49.6	45.7	46.1	38.3
	(35.8)	(30.4)	(27.5)	(29.6)	(24.5)
Annam	66.7	56.5	53.3	68.4	68.1
	(51)	(41.6)	(32.6)	(42.5)	(57)
Tonkin	60	59.4	55.2	61.9	66.4
	(42.8)	(39.9)	(38.4)	(41.4)	(32.9)
Cambodia	56.8	58.2	50.7	58.8	66.6
	(44.2)	(40.5)	(37.5)	(40.2)	(43.5)

SOURCE: CAOM, Aix-en-Provence, Fonds des Affaires économiques du ministère de la France d'outre-mer, 58.

[a] Figures for Laos and for the general government of Indochina are missing.

Converting the Protectorates into Cogs
in the Colonial Machine

Today, it is difficult to grasp the power system of the protectorates, its architecture, its degree of efficiency, and its internal workings. De Lanessan had attempted to create a "genuine" protectorate, which left open the possibility of Vietnam and Cambodia remaining subject to international law. After his dismissal in December 1894, however, this policy became obsolete. This change was marked by the increasing preeminence within the government in Hue of Nguyen Thanh, the brutal conqueror of Phan Dinh Phung and a key supporter of unconditional collaboration, who was elected regent in 1897. Three years later, Paul Doumer managed to strip the Nguyen monarchy and Khmer royalty of their remaining political autonomy, turning their territories into protectorates that were simply extensions of the colonial structures of the French state.[29] The protectorates, deprived of individual status in the eyes of international law, were under the sole control of French constitutional law.

The public and private law they continued to create was subordinated to the authority of the French Parliament and the regulatory power of the governor-general and of the president of the Republic. However, although the colonial regime was repeatedly tempted to suppress the empire of Annam—for example, when it deposed Thanh Thai on September 3, 1907, and then his son, the young emperor Duy Tan, on May 3, 1916, during the latter's attempted uprising, linked to a plot by Phan Boi Chau's Viet Nam Quang Phuc Hoi (see chapter 7)—it could never resolve to do so. The protectorate was the most economic mode of control, and it was impossible to replace the administrative apparatus of the mandarins and the monarchy.

At first, Tonkin was entirely detached from Hue. The office of the imperial commissioner *(kinh luoc su)* maintained the fiction of an official liaison between the northern provinces of Vietnam and the court. Clearly, this relationship had hardly any practical incidence—"the function had been created by us and the incumbent was our pet," wrote Doumer[30]—but the choice of the mandarins depended on the imperial commissioner and was therefore subject to his "secret and generally bad influence."[31] On July 26, 1897, the young emperor Thanh Thai (1889–1907) granted Doumer the suppression of the functions of the imperial commissioner and their transfer, notably with regards to the choice and the promotion of the mandarins, to the Tonkin resident superior's office, which thus came to possess the imperial power in northern Vietnam. In this way, the approaches that Jules Harmand had infused into the aborted treaty of 1883 found their practical application. In Tonkin, the mandarin administration became directly bound to the resident superior, the head of the French administration.

In Hue, political power passed into the hands of the resident superior of Annam. The imperial order of September 27, 1897, reformed the central Annamese government. The Council of Regency was abolished, and the two regents, Nguyen Thanh and Hoang Cao Khai, became ministers. The former Secret Council (Co Mat Vien), created by Minh Mang in 1834, was transformed into a Council of Ministers, whose presidency, like that of the Council of the Royal Family, belonged by law to the resident superior. All autonomous deliberation disappeared. French civil servants were delegated to each of the seven ministries, and the resident superior retained the right to veto imperial decisions, and, obviously, laws he proposed could scarcely be ignored. The administration of justice and, especially, of finances and the Treasury was controlled by the French residence. On January 1, 1899, the imperial budget was integrated into the budget of the Annam Protectorate created the previous year, although in principle it remained autonomous, and the levying of taxes that de Lanessan had passed on to the French provincial residents was definitively entrusted to them.

A similar organization was established in Cambodia. The turning point was the 1891 fusion of the royal treasury with the protectorate budget. A royal ordinance of July 11, 1897, established a Council of Ministers presided over by the resident superior, who had to countersign all royal documents and "in law as in reality . . . was in fact the head of the Cambodian government."[32] The protests of King Norodom's son Prince Yukanthor during a visit to Paris in 1900 were unavailing.[33] After King Norodom's death, in April 1904, the French even imposed their own candidate, Sisowath, as his successor. Other measures followed, in particular the suppression of the system of provinces *apanagées* exclusively assigned to the queen mother, to the heir-designate to the throne *(obbareach),* and to ministers. Destroying powers that rivaled those of the monarchy—dominated by Minister Thiounn, a man who was loyal to the French—indirectly reinforced the king's prestige over time, but it had the immediate effect of transferring the political management of the provinces to the French residents. Finally, the Laotian *muong* (domains) were unified in 1899 under a new superior residency based on the Annam-Tonkin model, since it comprised nine provinces where the Lao administration (that of the *chao muong*) answered to the French residents, while the kingdom of Luang Prabang was placed under a protectorate regime similar to that of Annam.

With this final seizure of power in 1897, the last vestiges of the former states' independence faded away. In Vietnam, the function of the empire, along with the former national structure organized around imperial ideology, the dynasty, and the mandarinate were doubly impacted by Doumer's initiatives. The ties between the southern population and Hue and its bureaucracy had been severed since the mid-nineteenth century. The social space of Vietnam, already culturally heterogeneous during that century, was dismantled and broken into three zones of different political status, integrated into a powerful political structure that overshadowed them: Indochina. Henceforth this space functioned only in a fragmented manner, with no connections between the three regions except those mediated by the foreign administration. Furthermore, the territories of the three main cities, Hanoi, Haiphong, and Tourane (Da Nang), were set up as concessions and entirely ceded as property to France by the royal ordinance of October 3, 1888. The judiciary organization and legislation in effect in Cochinchina were applied there. Vietnamese administration was done away with in areas populated by montagnards—the minority groups of the highlands—in the Military Territories created in the north, as well as in the "Moï" (i.e., peopled by "savage" montagnards) country in central Vietnam, which henceforth became the new provinces of Kontum (1913), Upper Donnai and Lang Bian (1920), Plei Ku (1932), and Darlac (detached from Laos in 1904).

The imperial government was the victim of a veritable political "phagocytosis." It was exploited and dispossessed of the power of initiative and decision, which was transferred to a parallel decision-making center, the superior residency. The head of the residency directed the deliberations of the new Co Mat and approved all of the imperial government's decisions, rendering them enforceable. Colonization had captured the dynamism of the central Vietnamese state. From the end of the nineteenth century on, the emperor became nothing more than a "sacred idol."[34] Not for long, however; the former cosmological conception of a celestial mandate imported from China, associated with the notion of ancestral rules, was distorted and devitalized by the Protectorate. This traditional conception portrayed the emperor as the "Son of Heaven" *(thien tu)*—the mediator between the universe and the society of men, the "mother and the father of the people"—and, through the delegation of executive powers, also transformed the administrators into "mother-father civil servants." The Protectorate maintained the image of the celestial mandate; however, it was virtually divested of meaning. The Protectorate also weakened the other royal Vietnamese tradition, best expressed through the term *vua* (king or genius): a monarchy that was not only the vector of a Chinese state-controlled model but also the summit of a bureaucracy that was much closer to the rural population than in China and was the guarantor of national existence. "The transformation of dangerous functions into honorary functions" that Jules Harmand had recommended in 1887[35] had been realized. The monarchy was hardly more than the instrument of the occupier, even if the handling of the emperors, Thanh Thai and Duy Tan, in particular, would sometimes prove difficult. The national contract that had tacitly united the monarchy to the society was thus broken. The forms through which the nation was to be represented had to be redefined; a crisis of legitimacy was triggered. "The king is still there, but the homeland is no longer. Without a homeland, what good is a king?" the modernist scholar Ngo Duc Ke asked in 1924.[36]

In the Mekong basin, by contrast, colonization confronted societies in which the state was slowly disintegrating, as in the case of Cambodia, or was very weak, as was the case in Laos. In these areas, there was no dismemberment of the previous political space. In Cambodia, the royal institution, with its symbolic function of "controlling the existences," remained at the center of the collective identity, while the dominant elite of princes and officials saw their powers reinforced.[37] However, Khmer royalty ostentatiously retired from political decision-making and focalized on its ritual and symbolic functions. Therefore, it became de facto hardly implicated in the Protectorate's choices—especially since, from very early on, the proportion of Vietnamese subordinate office workers in the bureaucracy of the French superior residence was extremely high: in 1937, they numbered 4,600.

In Laos, the main challenge was taking charge of an immense area that was three-quarters forested, whose population was oriented toward Bangkok, and whose principal historical center, Luang Prabang, was a journey of thirty days from Saigon and forty-five days from Hanoi.[38] Here, colonization was bound by heavy constraints. First among these was the lack of human settlers—at the time when Pavie traveled through the country, there were fewer than two inhabitants per square kilometer. Then there were the effects of extreme ethnic heterogeneity—in 1931, there were 485,000 Lao and, at least officially, 459,000 non-Lao. Finally, there was the imperative of setting up a system of management with minimal costs—in 1914, upper Laos was administered by two hundred and twenty-four officials, of whom only twenty-four were French.[39] This necessitated preserving and coming to terms with units of local and regional power, in particular, Thai political structures. The latter were concentrically organized into a "nesting system"[40] in which several villages *(ban)* maintained exchanges founded on reciprocity and competition in the horizontal setting of intervillage networks (*tasseng*: canton). These then nested together into greater units, the *muong* (lordships), which were in the hands of hereditary aristocratic lineages who benefited from taxes paid by free men and the work of servile groups and dispensed protection. The *muong* were in turn grouped into the three Lao "kingdoms."

Under these conditions, the only possible colonial strategy was to patiently construct a minimal, central, state-controlled structure, while transforming the *muong* authorities into civil servants and trying to incorporate the courts of the Lao princes into a modern system. Among the montagnards (proto-Indochinese in central and southern Laos: Sedang, Bahnar, Jorai, Edde, Rhade, Mnong, Phnong, Stieng, Maa, etc.; Tai from the mountainous regions of northern Vietnam; Hmong, Khamou, and Lu of the upper Mekong), the colonial authorities found no other solution than to manipulate the tribal and aristocratic hierarchies and to play on ethnic antagonisms, relying on the most numerous minorities of the region: the Lao, and the Khmers in the south. So, for instance, the village chiefs who managed the Lamet tribe were submitted to the Lu authorities of a Lamet *muong* created especially for this purpose, which in turn answered to a Lao district chief.[41] Tai and Lao officials and tax collectors controlled the Hmong, who received a quasi-monopoly on poppy growing in the Union. The system remained efficient for a long time: in 1938, three French civil servants, two civilians, and one military official were all it took to manage the 596 villages of the province of Saravane.

However, at the same time, the colonial administration strongly favored safeguarding the autonomy of the mountain populations within the framework of their own administrative structures—the "Moï delegations" in southern Annam—and preserving their distinctive cultures. Léopold Sabatier (1877–1936), a strong-minded individual who was named *délégué administratif* (administrative representative) of the Rhade of the Darlac (Dak Lak) plateau in 1914, theorized this approach in terms of political ethnography.[42] In 1923, Sabatier managed to persuade the resident superior in Annam, Pierre Pasquier, to transform Darlac into a sort of "Moï reservation," where Vietnamese immigration was prohibited. He resigned soon afterward, however, victim of a violent, slanderous campaign of defamation led by the planters and European speculators.

Finally, the middle and lower echelons of the previous administrative systems were incorporated into the colonial state as subordinate structures assuring the direct control of the population. In Vietnam, the mandarins, who played so prestigious a role in the old Confucian universe, were submitted in the long run to a humiliating tutelage, reduced to the rank of mere civil servants executing the decisions of a foreign power. Their role was little by little debased by the distribution of honorific mandarin titles to zealous servants of the new regime—low-level secretaries, yard supervisors, retired *tirailleurs,* sometimes even domestic servants of high-level French civil servants.

At the same time an inverse process took place, through which the progressive "destruction" of the imperial function had the effect, as Phan Chu Trinh would point out, of giving the local mandarins a discretionary power over the people. In this way a "neo-mandarinate" was born progressively, reorganized on the model of the European civil service. In 1897, the Hau Bo School, devoted to training the new mandarins of the protectorate, opened in Tonkin; it became the School of Mandarins in 1898, then the School of Law and Administration. The triennial examination of Nam Dinh included tests in both French and Quoc ngu. The granting of ranks was submitted to new regulations, and a board tracking promotions was established in 1904. The residential administration of Tonkin judged the appeals of the mandarin courts' verdicts. In 1909, the mandarinate was divided into two bodies, the first judiciary, the second administrative. In 1912, the mandarins of the schools formed a specialized corps. In Cambodia, starting in 1902, a body of Cambodian civil servants was organized, trained in the Kromokar [Civil Servants] School, which opened in 1914 and became the School of Cambodian Administration in 1917. It was split up into two sections, one for administrative staff and the other for judicial staff, by the ordinances of 1917 and 1922, and received a statute in 1933. A similar separation of the civil servants of the Protectorate into two distinct bodies started in Laos in 1927.

This should not, however, mislead us. In Vietnam, the apparatus of the mandarinate, the offices of the *tong doc* and *tuan phu* (governors of the provinces), and those of inferior circumscription, *phu* and *huyen* (districts), continued to operate—with their subordinate employees, their stamps and their seals, their ceremonies and messengers—with relative, though perhaps declining, efficiency at least until the 1930s, and probably beyond in the sixteen provinces of Annam and the twenty-one of Tonkin. They continued to be governed by the old Chinese principle of unified authority and the nonspecialization of officials.

Emmanuel Poisson's recent account of the Tonkin Protectorate's mandarin administration between 1884 and 1920 challenges the image, so solidly established by anticolonialist historiography, of a bureaucracy that was servile, distant from society, corrupt, inefficient, and under the sway of the colonial state.[43] In fact, the mandarins were still very much physically present in society, even if their numbers remained limited. In 1896, there were 418 mandarins and 858 subordinate employees administering the 148 prefectures of the first and second categories in Tonkin, along with the twenty-one *chau* (mountain districts populated by non-Viet minorities) of the Protectorate. This meant that, on average, there was one for every 4,000 to 5,000 inhabitants. This was certainly not a large staff, especially since the employees of the provincial offices always made up 60% of the personnel, and 90% of them were recruited in the north, primarily in a small number of *huyen* (prefectures of the second category) and source villages. More than half the provincial mandarins had started their careers before 1885 and had passed the traditional literary examinations, and they continued to associate bureaucratic rules and principles with ethical ones at least until the 1920s, even though their duty of loyalty to the emperor was interrupted during the war years. The possession of a diploma in the traditional Confucian examination system continued to be required for all recruits (there were still 13,000 candidates for the examinations in 1900). Traditional careers, although often accelerated by collaboration with French repressive operations, were much more common than the simple promotion of creatures of the colonial power. Selection by the "forging ground of talents" (the prestigious schools of Hanoi or Nam Dinh), the play of lineage patronage, recommendation, and unofficial solidarities still regulated the process of recruitment, selection, and promotion. The intellectual production of the mandarins certainly did not disappear, and this was equally true of their administrative activities, their *évergetique* (a sort of patronage) function, and their conception of "harmonious" management of social affairs.

The investment of communities (villages, families, lineages) in the mandarinate remained nearly intact for a while longer, just as during Dai Nam's independence. In a way, the establishment of the Protectorate made possible a kind of historic revenge for the literate elite of the north, who seem to have lost a lot of ground at the highest levels of the state under Minh Mang and Thieu Tri and later found themselves in the position of unavoidable partnership with the Protectorate authorities. Given the mandarins' knowledge of the country and the need for the French to go through them to modernize and reform Vietnamese society, a large part of the Tonkinese mandarinate, like the regent Nguyen Trong Hiep considered itself a feasible "third party."

The mandarinate's relationship to the French was therefore complex. It was one of collaboration, certainly, and also of corruption, but not of servility. There was a capacity for autonomous decisions, for making propositions, which the French residents had to adapt to in formulating their projects and carrying out their actions. Poisson notes the persistence within the mandarinate of a solid culture of administrative reform that went back to the nineteenth century and included a struggle against the corruption of the lower levels of the bureaucracy, the weakening of networks of clients, and improvements in the training of administrators in both intellectual and practical terms. It was a tradition the Protectorate took up in seeking to modernize the mandarin culture. Starting with the promulgation of the mandarin status in 1912, an individual's position, rather than rank, determined his salary. The bureaucracy was not passive in this reform effort and was able to take initiatives and make itself heard. Most important, a number of mandarins participated actively in modernization, notably at the Dong King Nghia Thuc school in Hanoi in 1907. There was therefore a convergence, at least for a time, from 1900 to 1920, between the reformist tradition of the imperial state, the modernizing colonial project, and the reformism of the Vietnamese social elites. The ideals of service to the state and of responsibility were still strong within the mandarinate, and there was a recurring temptation to take on the role of a sort of "third party" that would bear the destiny of the nation and would be an autonomous partner of colonization.

In sum, during the first thirty years of the Protectorate, the continuities probably outweighed the ruptures in the management of the administration. In confronting the difficult problem of the "governance" of the colonized society, the colonial power was prisoner to local inertia and resistance. In order to ensure its domination, it had to work through the bureaucracy and, just as important, the infra-bureaucracy of the offices that had long administered the connections between the state and the village. Undoubtedly, it had to establish (and respect) a complex and evolving historical compromise with a Vietnamese mandarinate that was far from on its last legs in the first decades of the twentieth century and relatively open to administrative and social innovation. Farsighted colonial administrators understood that "you don't govern against the elites." The colonial regime maintained itself only by proceeding with a minimum of reforms. That was its contradiction: modernizing too fast meant the risk of undermining the social legitimacy of the mandarinate, while modernizing too slowly meant fossilizing oneself in inefficiency. It was a difficult dilemma and perhaps an ultimately unsolvable one.

Still, the political-administrative impulse, and the flow of authority, originated in the residencies. It was a strange model for the colonial state, one that, at least in the protectorates, was essentially dualistic. At its points of convergence, it seized the existing network of internal powers and governed by exploiting and manipulating the precolonial state-controlled systems. It also preserved, and truly "protected," what Governor-General Pierre Pasquier shrewdly called "this admirable provincial administration that makes a marvelous instrument for the government."[44] In Indochina, this provincial administration was the mechanism through which the colonial regime kept its hold on the colonized. This is why, after 1900, the French authorities pursued a consistent policy of defending it, despite strong opposition.

In two decades, from 1897 to 1918, the entire distribution of power was overturned and entirely reorganized in the peninsula. Neither the court nor the mandarins tried genuinely to resist this hurricane that swept through Vietnam during the dark days of the end of the century. "It is they who were the first to be morally conquered," Doumer wrote. "With a few exceptions, they completely accepted the sovereignty of France and are serving her with devotion."[45] In the absence of any alternative perspective, it seemed to them that colonization was the only appropriate historical path. They formed a privileged, honored oligarchy, exempted from taxes and living off the country—Hoang Cao Khai, the former imperial commissioner of Tonkin was rewarded for his cooperation with the title of regent of Annam. Mandarin salaries were increased twice (in 1900 and 1906) in Tonkin and once in Annam and Cochinchina. In Annam, the pay of a first-class *tong doc* (governor of a province), which had increased before the political reform of 1897 to 870 francs and 300 measures of rice per year, reached 1,500 piastres in 1900 and 4,000 in 1906 (a piastre was then worth around two francs). This was the equivalent of the salary of a civil service administrator in France.[46] Notables in the townships maintained their control over communal life and the levy of direct taxes, which they collected from peasants according to the quota of registered persons allocated to each village by the administration. The prime minister of Annam summed up the political philosophy of the highest sectors of the mandarins when he declared to a journalist from *Le Temps:* "Since the pacification, everyone has understood that resistance is vain and the best thing is to make do with the new state of affairs."[47]

The Profitability of Colonial Finances

As early as the spring of 1897, Paul Doumer completely reorganized the finances of Indochina. Optimizing the taxation of peasant production was an immense challenge, because the mode of taxation affected all of Vietnam's sociopolitical structures, notably that of the village. Tax policy was thus the principal lever of in-depth transformation, the success of which—that is to say, of colonial capitalism in Indochina—depended on the capacity to invest and to borrow.

The principal thrust of Doumer's strategy was to rationalize and increase indirect taxation and individualize the direct taxes inherited from the precolonial era (personal and land taxes, corvée) in order to raise their output. The individual, in the modern sense of the term, appeared in Indochina in the form of a taxpayer. Previously, in Cochinchina, the decree of November 15, 1880, which fixed personal tax at three francs "per able-bodied man," had implicitly repudiated the impersonal notion of the enrollee, but in November 1882, Le Myre de Vilers had instituted the registration of all male residents between eighteen and sixty years of age, who were henceforth compelled to pay the personal tax, though its amount was reduced.

The essential elements of Doumer's reorganization were the decrees of June 1 and 2, 1897, which established the new direct tax regime in Tonkin, which was in turn taken up in Annam by the royal order of August 15, 1898. Those hitherto unregistered were subjected to a personal tax of 0.40 piastres (2.50 piastres for registered persons). In the protectorates, two-thirds of the corvée (already transformed in Cochinchina since 1881 into a redeemable service that could be incorporated into the personal tax), fixed at thirty days per year and per registered person since 1899, could be redeemed at the rate of 0.10 piastres per day of labor and merged with personal tax (in 1918 for Annam and in 1920 for Tonkin). However, as Deputy Adolphe Messimy would note in 1910, "the fact that a native has avoided his corvée through payment does not shelter him from requisitions. This form of payment is too often an expedient invented to fill the treasury of the provincial budget, which it largely nourishes."[48] The basis of the land tax was reorganized through the formation of four classes of rice fields and six taxable land classes. All the taxes in Annam were collected by the protectorate, which then paid a subsidy to the royal government (925,000 piastres in 1899). In Cambodia, corvée continued at least until the great peasant uprising of 1916. Payment of taxes in currency became the rule in 1897–98.

The repression of tax fraud, a new step toward individualization of taxes was facilitated by the extension in Tonkin in 1897 and Annam in 1913 of the tax card, or "acquittance card," already instituted in Cochinchina in 1884. Issued by village chiefs *(ly truong)*, who were paid 0.02 piastres per card and were thus encouraged "to manage their tax cards with the zeal of lady patrons selling lottery tickets for their charity work,"[49] it served as proof of identity, and all men were required to carry it at all times, under penalty of a fine. However, in the absence of a rural civil state and a modern cadastral register (in November 1911, only 725 out of the 2,011 Cochinchinese villages were registered; in Tonkin, the levied area did not exceed 207,000 hectares in 1912), the collection of personal and land taxes remained entrusted to the village commune in Vietnam and the canton *(khum)* in Cambodia. Their amount was still determined, as previously under the former monarchies, on the basis of the count of registered individuals and of the land registers of each village.

On the other hand, the amount fixed for direct taxes was continually on the rise and often criticized in France. The basis of the land tax was overestimated due to concerns about the tax yield. Population figures, the basis for the calculation of personal taxes, were also exaggerated. Estimated in 1902 at 20 million by the Direction générale des douanes et régies (Customs and Excise), then at 16 million (the figure reported by Henri Brenier in his 1914 *Essai d'atlas statistique de l'Indochine française*),[50] the population was in fact smaller—19 million according to the first census, conducted in 1921. Given the impossibility of precise knowledge of "indigenous" production and trade, Doumer's administration focused mainly on the indirect taxation that fed the general budget.

Indeed, the principal income of the Gouvernement général came from customs returns, as well as state-controlled companies: the salt *régie* (1897), based on the existing monopolies of imperial Vietnam; the alcohol *régie* (1897), which controlled small-scale indigenous production, using sticky rice *(nep)* in Vietnam and palm sugar in Cambodia, and traditional techniques to make an alcohol used in offerings and in ritual celebration everywhere; and lastly, the opium trade (1899). In combination with official licenses and large-scale state alcohol wholesalers, these *régies* constituted a global mechanism for extracting money from the peasant economy—the salt monopoly taxed the consumption of fish and brine; the alcohol monopoly taxed village sociability; and the opium monopoly taxed rural trade and usury, inasmuch as it chiefly affected the Chinese community, which controlled them; the 20,000 Chinese opium smokers—out of a total of 90,000 Chinese in Cochinchina in 1907—consumed five times more than the Vietnamese.[51]

Here again, as Chantal Descours-Gatin and Philippe Le Failler have shown, the Cochinchinese experience served as a testing ground. Drawing on the model of Singapore, the triple monopoly—namely, on the purchase, manufacture, and sale of opium—was seen, together with the creation of the alcohol monopoly, as the only

STRUCTURES OF DOMINATION   93

practicable means of building up the budget for the economic development of the south. The monopoly was first established in Cochinchina in January 1862 in the transient form of rights licensed to the powerful Chinese secret societies *(bang)*— in 1864, to the Cantonese Wang Tai, and the following year, to the Fujianese Bang Hap—before taking final form as a direct *régie* (1881).[52] Although Francis Garnier regarded all these as "artificial and paltry" sources of income, from 1864 to 1881, the opium monopoly provided 18%–23% of Cochinchina's revenue; after 1881, opium and alcohol provided 20%–25%.[53]

In Cambodia, Norodom created the licensing system in 1863. In Annam and Tonkin, the contract established in thirteen provinces by Tu Duc at a late date (in 1862) was taken over by the protectorate, in Tonkin in 1888, and in Annam in 1892 in favor of the racketeer Saint-Mathurin, and then transformed into a *régie* in Tonkin and Cambodia in July 1893. Opium provided about 15 percent of the protectorate's income from 1887 to 1897. The opium *fumeries* (1,513 official smoking houses in 1918), the alcohol shops, and the salt storehouses were in fact all institutions that served to collect taxes. Some years later, loans motivated the expansion of the *régies* by Doumer: "Indochina has just contracted a loan of 200 million. . . . It has been necessary to include a global credit for 41,676,000 francs in the general budget in order to ensure its service. The governor-general thought he would be able to find [this money] in the establishment of a monopoly on alcohol."[54]

The system of *régies* was a form of taxation at several levels. Production (except in the case of opium, which was purchased in India and Yunnan, but nevertheless conditioned in the "boilers" of Saigon) and acquisition and sale to consumers were state monopolies, farmed out—since the government did not have the capacity to manage all the functions of the monopolies itself—to entities like the powerful salt syndicate of Bac Lieu and large companies like the salt works of Cana in Annam, whose profits hinged on the fiscal exploitation of the village. The monopolies were essential. From 1899 to 1922, opium, the most important of the state-controlled products, represented on average 20% of the general budget's revenue. The net returns of the *régies* in the direct resources of the general budget was consistently high, but after having leveled out between 1913 (36.5%) and 1920 (44%), with a peak in 1916 (48%), it stabilized at around 17%–20% until 1930 (18%). The figures then decreased steadily in the interwar years (9% in 1933) and rose again during World War II (14% in 1942).

This *régie* system has often been denounced for its immorality, for price increases and the violence caused by the *régie*'s management, notably from 1900 to 1913. Taxes on salt increased from 0.08 piastres in 1897 to 1.00 in 1899, 2.00 in 1904, and 2.25 in 1906, an increase of 2,712%. The process of establishing an alcohol *régie* in Tonkin resulted in the destruction of the ancient craft of rural distillation (four hundred distillers paid license fees around 1880), which was associated with raising pigs and produced alcohol at very low prices (0.04 to 0.05 piastres for a liter of plain alcohol around 1895), exporting its surpluses to China.

The administration chose to concentrate the production and sale of alcohol in order to tax consumption. First, in July 1897, a monopoly of sales was established, at first contracted out to a few wholesalers *(débitants)*; overnight, retail sale prices jumped to 0.18–0.22 piastres per liter. Village distillers were subjected to harassment and persecution. Alcohol revenue shot up from 126,000 piastres in 1893 to over a million in 1901.[55] The struggle against village distillation by the administration was facilitated by Dr. Albert Calmette's process—the patent for which was acquired by the Auguste Fontaine Distilleries in 1898—which doubled output, increased alcohol content, and permitted the use of ordinary rice. This led, in December 1901, to the granting of a ten-year monopoly of sale in the two Vietnamese protectorates to the Compagnie générale du Tonkin et du Nord-Annam, which already held the monopoly on salt and opium. Then, in March 1903, a ten-year monopoly on manufacturing was granted in the same region to the Société des Distilleries du Tonkin (of the Fisher group) and to the Société des Distilleries de l'Indochine (of the Fontaine, Calmette, Debeaux group). The contract granted to the latter, renewed in 1913 and 1923 and maintained until the abolition of the monopoly in July 1933, created one of the most powerful Indochinese business groups. In central and southern Annam, as well as in Cochinchina, the monopoly was divided between diverse Chinese and European producers and distillers. The concessionaries' profits were astonishing: in 1909, the socialist deputy Francis de Pressensé told the Chamber of Deputies that the Fontaine group expected a provisional net profit of 2.3 million francs for a capital investment of 3.5 million.

A complete repressive system was put in place in 1897 to increase the output of the monopoly and to combat the illegal village distillation that was the peasant society's response to "Debeaux's bottles." Mobile squads carried out searches in villages, denunciations were encouraged, and village notables were given the collective responsibility of paying fines inflicted on clandestine distillers or collectively on villages. There was widespread brutality. "In many villages, contraband was a communal enterprise. The alcohol needed for the celebration of the local feast was made on behalf of the village by a hired distiller, almost always a poor wretch, sometimes an unfortunate leper, a sham smuggler, whose main role was to serve time in jail instead of or in place of his principals, who remained in the background."[56]

At the beginning of the twentieth century, the opium monopoly was shaken by a series of new factors: prohibition campaigns and international conferences, opium smuggled from China, repeated attempts by the Chinese authorities to fight against the drug, and frequent ruptures in supply. The number of opium houses fell to 1,224 in 1929. However, the *régie* revenues remained stable, originally, thanks to existing stocks, and later, during World War II, when production in Tonkin and Laos was encouraged, especially among the Hmong. The monopoly was maintained until 1950 and only disappeared with France's ratification of the Drug Convention of the United Nations.

This general reorganization of taxes, founded on the multiple taxation of peasant consumption (matches, boats, wood, tobacco, betel nuts, etc.), had the effect of considerably raising the yield and increasing the tax burden, less perhaps because of the rise of tariffs than because of the streamlining of the entire fiscal system. In Tonkin, direct taxation produced 30% more in 1902 than in 1897. Taxes were henceforth regularly collected, clearly defined, and entirely monetarized, becoming less random but more of a burden. For the peasantry, they were the principal form of daily oppression, the hardest of the new disciplines imposed on its daily life.

The number of activities and the size of the population that was taxed—perhaps 17% of Cambodians were actually taxed in 1921—continued to increase.[57] In Vietnam, before 1885, the imperial Treasury's returns were modest: estimates of the 1878 returns vary from 12.6 million francs, according to the French consul at Hue, Louis de Champeaux, to 40 million according to Émile Luro. A half century later, in 1912, the Indochinese population—"the indigenous multitude that is silent and that pays"[58]—contributed more than 150 million francs to the budget of the Gouvernement général. The former Dai Nam contributed close to 135 million to this sum. Toward 1911, the average tax was officially estimated at 8.96 francs per inhabitant,[59] but it is in fact difficult to determine its real economic weight. In 1931, the total of the general budget and the local and provincial budgets rose to 130.9 million piastres, which comes to 17.5% of the total value of Indochinese production, using the figure for the latter of 750 million piastres suggested by Paul Bernard for that year.[60]

Bernard estimates the tax burden at 35% of income per person in Cochinchina, 18% in Cambodia, 17% in Tonkin, and 16% in Annam.[61] These are very high figures, but they suggest the need for further in-depth research, as do the estimates of the contributions per family proposed in table 2.3, whereby the total amount of taxes in 1929 would equal 33% of that year's paddy production.[62] This total seems very high if one compares it to the official estimates of average annual production of paddy per person (two hundred kilos in Tonkin around 1932, or roughly a ton per family; and six hundred kilos in Cochinchina, or three tons per family) or with the estimate that Bernard provides for the production in 1931 of a farming family of five people in western Cochinchina (four tons of paddy per year). Based on the figures in table 2.3, 15–16%, on average, of this income would have been paid to various Indochinese budgets during the period 1926–30. Above all, the collection of these taxes would have been very dependent on economic risks, especially since it reached its maximum during the worst years of the Great Depression. While these calculations may have the merit of outlining a set of questions for research, they are too rough to be convincing. One thing, however, is clear: the tax burden was very unequally distributed between the countries, to the detriment of Cambodia, according to Alain Forest's calculations (see also table 2.4).[63]

TABLE 2.3 Tax burden in Indochina, 1913–1943: a provisional estimate

Year	Direct revenue[a] (in millions of piastres)	Official population estimates[b]	Taxes per inhabitant (in piastres)	Taxes per family of five	
				In piastres	Equivalent in kilos of paddy[c]
1913	63.7	16,395,000	3.88	17.25	452
1920	78.8	18,806,000[d]	4.19	20.95	323
1925	103.7	—	5	25	423
1926	113.2	20,491,000	5.52	27.6	421
1927	131.7	—	6.42	32.1	521
1928	134.7	—	6.57	32.85	592
1929	142.8	—	6.65	33.25	467
1930	144.1	—	6.71	33.55	515
1931	130.9	21,452,000	6.1	30.5	790
1932	113	—	5.26	26.3	848
1933	102.6	—	4.78	23.9	1,043
1934	100.6	—	4.36	21.8	1,159
1935	103.2	—	4.48	22.4	903
1936	110.4	23,030,000	4.79	23.95	801
1937	127.2	—	5.52	27.6	582
1938	149	—	6.46	32.3	488
1939	179.2	—	7.78	38.91	556
1940	189.3	—	6.82	34.1	451
1941	232.9	—	8.39	41.95	640
1942	272.8	—	9.83	49.15	713
1943	—	27,728,000[e]	6.11	30.58	—
AVERAGE, 1925–1942					663

SOURCE: *Annuaire statistique de l'Indochine, 1913–1942.* The figures obtained provide only an extremely simplified view of the actual tax burden. They do not take into account the payments into communal budgets or the taxes paid by the Europeans and the Chinese, which should be deducted from the total taxation.

[a]Combined revenues from the general budget, local budgets, and (beginning in 1931) provincial budgets.

[b]The figures are from the official censuses, known to have a very wide margin of error. Their results have been spread over four periods: 1925–1928 (1926 census), 1929–1933 (1931 census), 1934–1938 (1936 census), and 1939–1942 (1943 census).

[c]The preceding column multiplied by the annual average wholesale price of paddy in Saigon.

[d]1921 estimate.

[e]1943–1948 estimate.

There were even more evident fiscal inequalities between social groups. The European settlers paid very little. Before the creation of European personal tax in 1920, there was no provision for progressive taxes according to income, except in the case of land taxes. In the absence of rural *état civil* registers, the tax remained an apportionment tax distributed among villages, with its levying entrusted to rural notables or the customary authorities, and this aggravated various problems. Income taxes would not be instituted in Indochina until 1937. This basis for taxation

TABLE 2.4 Direct taxes per inhabitant, 1897–1930 (in piastres)

	1897	1902	1904	1921	1925	1930
Annam	.25	.55	.77	.78	.93	1.16
Cochinchina	—	—	1.76	2.25	2.11	2.34
Tonkin	—	—	.81	1.36	1.43	1.51
Cambodia	—	—	—	1.71	2.83	3.23
Laos	—	—	—	1.27	1.39	1.60

SOURCE: Exposition coloniale internationale, 1931, Gouvernement général de l'Indochine, direction des Finances, *Les impôts directs en Indochine* (Hanoi, 1930).

created clear injustices and was one of the key factors behind the constraints on the monetarization of village economies and the increase in usury and of social differentiation among the colonized peasantry. It was the latter, certainly, who financed the development of the colonial economy. Anti-tax agitation would become a permanent factor in peasant movements.

Indochina no longer drew anything from the French budget, except in the general budgets for 1905 and 1906. Starting in 1897, the budgets of Annam and Tonkin operated with a surplus and, that year, Treasury reserves, crucial for the financing of loans, were created in the two protectorates. In 1900, the surpluses of the local budgets and the general budget exceeded 4 million piastres, and in 1913, the amount in the reserve fund of the general budget rose to 14.5 million piastres. All budgets continued to operate with a surplus until 1922. Later, from 1922 to 1927, withdrawals from the Treasury reserves covered the deficits in the general budget generated by the dramatic increase in public spending. In 1938, Indochina was second only to Algeria among the French colonies in its financial importance. Its general budget (930 million current francs) was three times that of the AOF (Afrique occidentale française) or Madagascar. It was the only colony to contribute a significant share of France's military budget (181 million gold francs from 1899 to 1913) and to metropolitan expenses (supplying 12.3 million piastres in 1929, 13% of the colony's general budget, which was nearly the cost of the new public works there). It contributed to the additional pay for military men serving in the colony and to military pensions, financed French activities in the Far East, and contributed innumerable subsidies to bodies and institutions in France.

In 1887, Jules Harmand designated the objective of the colonization of Indochina as the "constitution of a new state, with large budgets."[64] The financial law of April 13, 1900, decreed the budgetary autonomy of the colonies and required them to make annual contributions to France's budget. By then, Harmand's goal had been reached: not only had Indochina's credit been established, but loans and economic investment had become possible.

1911-1930: AN IMMOBILE STATE?

Until their destruction by the Japanese in March 1945, the great political and administrative structures remained essentially intact, exempt from any substantial modification. For a century, the high Indochinese administration and the Colonial Ministry had as a tacit rule, if not an ideal, an extreme distrust of political reforms, and they sought to promote only those changes that followed initial colonial logic, despite the fact that many favored the policy of association outlined by de Lanessan. A galaxy of high civil servants, often erudite and lucid and always conservative, incarnated this ideal: Jules Bosc, Pierre Pasquier, René Robin, Louis Marty, Jean Przyluski, Paul Blanchard de la Brosse, and many others. Between 1909 and 1928, it certainly seemed that the political status of Indochina was apt to evolve, especially because of the political innovations of Albert Sarraut (see chapter 7). This strategy, one that created a slight opening for the modernist and conservative trends of nationalism, nevertheless led to political immobility at the end of the 1920s. There were at least two causes for this. First, after 1918, French imperialism reached its zenith, and it had no reason to substantially change the status of its colonies. Second, after 1930: the colonies became vital for France's survival, and the question of their political status became taboo. The concept of the Indochinese Federation did not emerge until the end of World War II; between 1944 and 1947, there was an attempt to establish such a federation. Starting in the 1920s, French colonization was clearly politically far behind the general rise of Asian nationalism.

Personal and Property Law

This is not to say that there were no changes in Indochina. Those changes that did occur however, obeyed the general logic of the colonial enterprise. Until 1930, the Indochinese authorities effectuated changes that centered foremost on the status of the person and on the social relations at the heart of the colonized societies. What we know today is incomplete and sketchy. It is undeniable that colonial action, amid its confusing array of objectives, tried to transform the "communal man" of Indochinese societies into an individual subject. It did so by inculcating a new moral economy, new lifestyles and social relationships, all of which produced a modern subjectivity, adaptable not only to a market economy but also to the constraints of the colonial capacity to govern. This is true of the transformation of customary or legal norms of social life through the creation of new laws: the partial enactment of a civil code in Cochinchina (1883); the codification of Lao customs (1908); the establishment of a civil and a penal code in Cambodia, inspired by French law (1920 and 1924); the creation of a civil code in Tonkin (1931); the new Laotian codes (1927); and the penal (1933) and civil (1936) codes in Annam, which revised the code of Gia Long (1812).

We also know very little about the procedures of "individuation," such as the institution, at least in theory, of *état civil* registers (in Cochinchina in 1883, in Tonkin in 1923, and in Cambodia in 1925), or about the tenacious colonial policies of substituting private property for the traditional notions of property. The latter were governed by conceptions of state property and precarious familial possession based on the cultivation of the land and the payment of taxes. These concepts made ancestral land a place of solidarity between generations and anything but an alienable commodity. These notions were still very prevalent outside the Vietnamese regions. In Vietnam itself, with the exception of Cochinchina, communal land, periodically redistributed between registered families *(inscrits)*, preserved a considerable importance.

How could laws based on the occupation of land be transformed into a European law of property? How could apparently "vacant" land be seized? The registration of landownership—without which European-style private appropriation of land could not triumph—was most difficult in Cambodia, as suggested by the successive failed attempts made in 1884, 1908, and 1911 to institute it. However, the decree of May 8, 1931, on the mandatory establishment of cadastral matrixes seems to have been implemented. In Cochinchina, from 1862, unoccupied lands became state property, and their sale started in 1865. The concession regime was organized there in 1882, throughout Tonkin in 1888, and in Annam in 1899, following the loss of the emperor's demesne property rights to the protectorates in 1897. From 1902 to 1928, numerous texts authorized the alienation of communal lands under certain conditions. In Tonkin, land registration was generalized in January 1924 (at least in principle, since the enforcement of the law ran up against the absence of cadastral surveys), as it was in Cochinchina in 1925. The decrees of July 21, 1925, were meant to promulgate a true property code for all of Indochina. They instituted the "Land Book" in Cochinchina and in the French towns of the protectorates, and therefore the registration of the entire area. In the four protectorates, however, it seems to have been possible only to apply a transient regime destined to lead to a general cadastral system.

The cadastral system was, along with direct control of village management and the rural *état civil,* a key element for the growth of tax revenues. This remained, after Doumer, the essential goal of the colonial administration's innovations, particularly in response to the enormous financial needs of the colonial economy's large-scale expansion from 1920 to 1930. The administration persistently tried to identify the colonized populations individually; to promote the social status of the modern individual, largely ignored in these societies; and to individualize the direct fiscal system in order to widen the tax base. As part of this project, identity papers were made obligatory on November 9, 1918. However, until 1945, the personal tax card with photo and fingerprints was a legal alternative for the majority of the population. The former registration system underwent new and serious attacks in 1920 in Tonkin (with the ordinance of August 26) and in Annam (with that of October 30): all able-bodied men between eighteen and sixty years were henceforth required to pay a personal tax of 2.50 piastres. Other policies shared these objectives. There was a massive reduction of exemptions from personal taxes and *corvée* labor—social privileges that were deeply appreciated in rural society—and the 1920 measures in the two protectorates, along with a 1937 law in Cambodia, fused payments in labor with capitation, creating a "simple and productive tax" (Vu Van Hien). In 1920, Tonkin was equally obliged to register the unregistered, which suddenly increased the personal tax revenue by 150%, from 2,544,000 piastres in 1920 to 4,100,000 piastres in 1921.

Always with the goal of increasing fiscal productivity, the colonial authorities also had a policy of generalizing the European ownership regime—systematized by the decree of July 21, 1925. This policy rendered the soil alienable and established a land market. It did away with the sacred aura surrounding the ties between the people and the land by transforming the old Vietnamese *dia ba* (register of rice fields and cultivated land), levied under Gia Long, into a modern register of landownership. However, these policies were actually only taken up in Cochinchina (a territory under French law); the Cadastral Office was created there in 1869, but the cadastral system was only officially generalized in 1894. It was fully implemented in April 1938 in two towns and ten provinces (Saigon and Cholon, and the provinces of Gia Dinh, Tan An, Cholon, Go Cong, My Tho, Ben Tre, Can Tho, Rach Gia, Chau Doc, and Bac Lieu), and its establishment was very advanced in the provinces of Long Xuyen, Sa Dec, and Soc Trang; there were a total of 3,167,000 hectares registered on the cadasters, as against 1,321,000 that were not. But in the rest of Indochina, in 1940, only embryonic cadastral drawings existed, mainly in plantation zones or in regions close to towns.

Colonization and the Villages

It was from the same perspective, primarily fiscal, but also to attend to a crisis of the structures of the peasant framework, that colonization tried to use these structures. This was the case with the robust but opaque Vietnamese village community, actually a conglomerate of two to five "hamlets" *(thon)*, administered by a council of notables and called the *xa*, or *commune*, the somewhat misleading term used by the French.[65] The goal of the colonial administration was to put an end to village administrative autonomy, whose power was summed up in a famous adage: "The king's law cedes to village customs." It did this by transforming the councils of notables into an administrative substructure. The authorities believed that in so doing, they had the means to obtain precise knowledge concerning the demography and the village system of landownership; they could also thus influence the village hierarchies and divisions in the hopes of encouraging the emergence of a new peasant elite. They seem to have succeeded in Cochinchina, where the destruction of village autonomy was extremely precocious, though not complete. A point of no return had perhaps been crossed there with the work of the 1903 commission and the ordinance of August 27, 1904. The latter defined the status of the councils of communal notables; organized their composition into a strict hierarchy of twelve executive high notables and nine minor notables, establishing their co-optation and in consequence their clientalization by the new class of large landowners who were rising socially; and submitted the communal administration (budgets, law and order, collective works) to the administration's strict control.

It was probably in 1905 that the district chiefs and subchiefs, previously simple elected notables, became low-ranking civil servants,[66] and in 1909 that the communal budgets were instituted. "In Cochinchina," the lawyer Nguyen Huu Khang wrote in 1946, "the *commune* is no longer anything but an administrative district, the smallest of all, almost without its own life, administrated by 'half-civil servants' chosen from the landed rural class."[67] In fact, the crisis of the village community in the south seemed to go back at least to the 1880s, when the registration system was changed, and administrative tutelage weighed increasingly heavily on the villages. From 1900 on, official reports expressed alarm at the discrediting of notables and the difficulties in recruiting them, noting that affluent and influential families were increasingly avoiding their functions. These families, who had previously provided the majority of notables, preferred to delegate their clients to serve on the village councils and to devote themselves to the management of their property. A dangerous political and institutional void slowly opened up in the south, into which, in the twentieth century, the leaders of the illegal rural movements would forcefully enter.

On the other hand, in Tonkin, the members of the village community *(xa)* were able to stall the efforts made by the colonial administration to penetrate their structures of governance, albeit in a limited fashion. It is likely that after the conquest, extortion by notables increased considerably, if for no other reason than because of the deterioration of mandarin authority and of the penetration of mercantile logic in the countryside. The village community therefore entered into a slow, and poorly understood, process of destabilization. Generally speaking, the village authorities became direct agents of colonial tax levying. However, French efforts to take over villages were less successful. Starting in 1909, the administration tried to promote the codification and writing of customary laws *(huong uoc)* and the establishment of communal budgets. The ordinance of August 12, 1921, sought to displace the existing systems of village power, abolishing the former council of notables, which had been co-opted by the traditional, rural elite,[68] as well as the distinction between those who were registered and those who were not. It also instituted a communal administrative council, the council of the *toc bieu* or council of lineages *(hoi dong toc bieu)*, elected by the chiefs of the *ho* (patrilineal lines) or by the *giap* (generational associations). This council chose the *ly truong*, the communal agent who dealt with the administration, as well as the others responsible for village power. The same reform required that communal budgets be controlled by the administration, and in 1923, the revision of the customary laws in accordance with official models was decreed.

The reform nevertheless failed to achieve its aim. While, at least officially, 1,188 villages (out of more than 6,000 recorded) had budgets in 1923, and 4,053 had a council of *toc bieu*, the former notables quickly refused to participate in the new councils, while their secret influence was sufficient to neutralize them. Peopled with members of influential families, the councils were simply façades behind which social solidarity and traditional power were still exerted, albeit now clandestinely. The customary laws drafted according to the administrative models—which existed in only half of the villages in Tonkin in 1937—went unheeded. The bamboo hedge remained largely intact. Local reform, moreover, had the unexpected effect of creating disorder in the village administrations, sometimes incurring serious division while unleashing electoral contention and corruption, and shaking the authority of the class of notables and landowners and bringing them into a silent opposition.

By 1927, it was necessary to change direction and return to the former system of the *ly truong*. The ordinance of February 25 abrogated those of 1921–22, and reconstituted, alongside the council of the *toc bieu*, the former co-opted council notables *(ban ky muc)*, who were to approve the decisions of the *toc bieu* and the communal administration. As a result, this second council manipulated the legal managers of the village at will, and all the more freely because of the fact that it no longer had an official role. The perverse effects of the reform of 1921 would continue to worsen. Finally, on May 23, 1941, the most traditionalist of solutions was chosen: suppression of the administrative councils of 1921, abolition of rural elections, and restoration of total power over the village to the council of notables. After two decades of struggling, the process had returned to its starting point.

In Annam, there were the same initial aims, the same struggles, and the same results. The royal edict of 1924, which reinforced the scope of the small executive notables, displeased the major notables and compelled them to weak collaboration with the provincial mandarins, as became clear during the troubles from 1930–31 on. "Elements of disorder," one high-level civil servant wrote, "were implanted especially easily in the villages of northern Annam, since the individuals whose influence could have efficiently fought their activity remained hesitant or neutral, or even secretly favorable to it."[69] The circulars of the Co Mat in September 1930 and March 1931 aimed to restore the authority of the council of the grand notables by simply adding the representatives of the *ho* to it. Once more, the goal was to use the village community as a means of transmission for the colonial administration and to reconstruct its internal structures. In spite of the establishment of an obligatory *état civil* registry in Annam through the civil code of 1936, the Protectorate had to put up with

STRUCTURES OF DOMINATION   103

the continuation of the system of registered individuals for the periodic distribution of local land, of which they were the sole recipients, as well as for the determination of the basis for direct taxes and for the recruitment of notables.

During this interval, there was a radical change in the meaning and the practice of village power in Annam and Tonkin, as analyzed by Philippe Papin.[70] The function of the *ly truong* (head of the *xa*), elected by the registered inhabitants and those who were exempted from taxes, hardly conferred any prestige at the beginning of the twentieth century. This function led, at the best, to a possible election to a subordinate position of canton head, and it entailed many risks. It was strongly valorized by colonial reforms, and around 1940, it became a true career, a very profitable post, and a source of social authority. The *ly truong* freed itself from the control of the council of notables. It was henceforth bitterly fought over by the important lineages because the *ly truong* exerted a growing part of village power and demanded payment for administrative acts, which were ever-increasing. This function was more and more reserved for major lineages, and social access to village power tended to be reduced. In fact, colonization was for a long time the captive of the very thing that was the basis of its functioning—the "traditional" village. Within this rural space, it amplified the mutations of the rural elite into an exploiting social stratum.

In Cambodia, where the village, very dispersed, was actually organized around the Buddhist monastery *(vat),* and where the former customary organization of patronage seemed to become blurred between 1890 and 1905, the colonial regime attempted to create a territorial village community on the Vietnamese model, which they believed less difficult to control. A royal ordinance of August 21, 1901, instituted a council in each *srok* (canton), directed by a *mesrok* chosen by the inhabitants, who was in charge of tax collection; another, of June 5, 1908, abolished the *srok* and created the *commune (khum),* administered by a council elected every four years by the "registered" and overseen by an elected *mekhum* endowed with a budget. Elections took place in 1909, and the *état civil* was declared mandatory in November 1911. However, the failure of the project of the Cambodian *commune* was quickly apparent.

It became evident that the *khum* were incapable of establishing communal budgets or of organizing rural police, and were in fact artificial structures. The 1919, 1925, and 1929 ordinances tried again to do so, but without much more success. At the same time, the protectorate endeavored to fix the territorial limits of villages and to regroup hamlets along major roads.

The Cambodian *commune* lacked a life of its own, however. The functional structures of the peasant social space remained the *phum* (the inhabited space, generally a hamlet), organized in a sacred order by the allegiance of its inhabitants to the tutelary genius of the space *(neak ta)* and the local networks constituted around a *vat.*[71] The *mekhum* took up the administrative tasks of increasing importance that were imposed on them, and from which they profited, but the hidden power of the powerful families was barely reduced. In this way, a gap opened between the Franco-Khmer administration and the peasantry, which henceforth had no recourse to real power other than the force of its inertia. The peasantry's protests could not find any lasting means of expression. It was an evolution that benefited the colonial administration, but one that was in the long term fraught with terrible tragedies.

In the same perspective, the colonial regime superimposed itself on the hereditary chiefs of the montagnards, allowing them—exactly as Hue had done in the past—to maintain their customary powers, for instance, that of the *tao,* the seigniorial class, in Tai-dominated regions. The regime attempted, without much success, to "tribalize" the Proto-Indochinese forest peoples by installing chieftainships in villages that had never known them, such as those of the Mnong Gar studied by Georges Condominas.[72] The colonial authorities also attempted to mold the social spaces of the highlands into a network of cantons and districts. From the beginning of the 1920s, the French tried to create among the highland minorities an elite educated in the schools of Ban Me Thuot, Pleiku, Dalat, and Kontum in Annam and at Veun Sai and Camp Le Rolland in Cambodia. A handful of students had access to secondary schools or the *primaire supérieur* educational system. Moreover, sections of highland *tirailleurs* were created in the 1930s. This effort fell in line with Léopold Sabatier's policy, which consisted of two aspects: an administration based on tribal customs and the establishment of an administrative autonomy. This was translated by the writing down of these customs, by the creation of medical centers, and in 1939, by a General Inspectorate of the Moï country, which supervised the administration of the highlands. Starting in 1926, after Sabatier was called back to France, the Darlac (Dak Lak) was, however, opened to Vietnamese migrants, who created villages and small urban markets there. Around 1940, the provinces of Pleiku, Kontum, Darlac, and the High Donnai comprised an unstabilized population of plantation workers and shopkeepers, many of whom were contract workers.[73]

The control of rural Indochinese societies by the colonial regime therefore never went beyond a certain level, although it is difficult to pinpoint with certainty, given the lack of solid studies, especially concerning the little-known elites. The material civilization and the peasant culture remained almost intact until the 1930s. In this regard, the fiscal history of the 1920s and 1930s is significant: it reveals to what extent Indochina's fiscal structures were fragile when the economic situation became difficult. In 1928, on the eve of the Great Depression, the financial crisis of the colonial regime began when the reserve fund *(Caisse de réserve)* of the general budget ended up nearly empty because of the withdrawals that had been necessary since 1922 to cover the rising deficits of the Indochinese budgets. Given the impossibility of raising customs taxes on imports due to opposition from France's industries, it became necessary in 1927 to increase taxes on alcohol and shipping and to create a domestic tax of 2% on all merchandise, other than rice, produced in or brought into the colony. This was the price of temporarily restoring the balance of the general budget and rendering Indochina capable of participating in the great intercolonial loan of 1930, but it gave only a brief respite. The system of traditional taxes and the three *régies* no longer had any flexibility.

With the economic crisis of the 1930s, this system rapidly fell into disarray. This evolution was, in the end, the result of the impossibility of the colonial state moving beyond its dependence on the mediation of the various dominant groups in the countryside: the dominant classes of the rural areas who controlled the base of the fiscal system, especially in Vietnam, the class of landowners and of rural notables in the north and the center, and the large landowners in the south. Colonization was only able to clientalize them and give them an interest in its own operations. But the burden of its taxation of the peasant economy, however, probably affected village solidarities. Even in Tonkin and Annam, the relative cohesion of the former *communes* was shaken—but according to what regional rhythm? On a national level, colonization destroyed the political influence of the class of notables and petty landowners. As a sort of compensation, it may have precipitated that class's transformation into a sort of rural gentry of the Chinese type, exploitative and on the road to increasing discredit. Such was, it seems, the basis of a distrustful alliance, more or less conflictual according to the varying circumstances, that associated the rural elite with the colonial regime in an unequal exercise of authority over the peasant world, and that constituted, beyond the European society and the Chinese community, the true social foundation of the colonial state in Indochina.

The Protected Monarchies

It was therefore structurally impossible for the colonial regime to transcend its historical logic. In fact, despite a certain number of "liberal" periods in its history, this logic was maintained until the final hour in 1945. It led the colonial authorities to carry out the complete political disempowerment of the indigenous monarchies. The agreement of November 6, 1925, imposed on the Co Mat by Resident Superior Pasquier following the death of Emperor Khai Dinh, presented not as a treaty but as a simple decree of the governor-general, transferred the entire political and administrative power in Annam, along with the nomination of the mandarins, to the resident superior. The Co Mat kept only the right to be consulted with regard to residential ordinances. The emperor lost the little appearance of the exercise of power he still had, keeping only the right to appoint ministers, and the power to regulate rituals, grant pardons, and deliver honorary distinctions and royal patents *(sac phong)* to guardian spirits honored in village temples *(dinh)*. This was how his political dispossession, to say the very least, was consummated. The ritual and symbolic weight that the imperial function preserved in appearance, its sacred dimension, was deprived of its social value by the very fact that colonization separated the accomplishment of rituals and the exercise of real power, without which the former has no meaning.

The void left at the summit of the Confucian state thus signified a rupture of the historical contract that bound the people to their elite, not only with the Nguyen dynasty but also, and even more so, with the monarchy per se. "Because of its abdication, the royal figure ceased to be perceived as a referential axis around which society organized itself," Nguyen The Anh writes.[74] The dynasty persisted in responding to this void with the same vain solutions it had adopted as the protectorate established itself: coupling its successive capitulations with an attitude of historical awaiting composed of veiled reticence and murmured criticisms concerning the colonizers' decisions, grounded in royal decrees. The dying emperor Khai Dinh and his heir, the young Bao Dai, who succeeded him in 1925, considered this dual attitude capable of ensuring the survival of the monarchy and of the dynasty during a phase unfavorable to the dynastic cycle, all the while preserving over the long term their function as the nation's final recourse until a conjuncture propitious to the full and utter restoration of the imperial mandate.

In the same year, in Luang Prabang, the Laotian Royal Council was transformed into the Council of Ministers, presided over by the resident superior. The Protectorate administration confirmed the legitimacy of the Luang Prabang dynasty, whose sovereign, King Sisavang (r. 1904–59), had studied at the École coloniale in Paris. What became of the former elites—Vietnamese mandarins, provincial governors (chauvay khet), provincial civil servants (kromokar), Khmer balat and mekhum, Muong chao and Lao civil servants, chiefs of lam (montagnard fiefs within the military territories), village notables, and subordinate Indochinese civil servants of the French administration? By 1930, the "indigenous" state apparatuses, the intermediaries through which the colonial regime implemented its decisions in the colonized society, were in the hands of a "hybrid bureaucracy."[75] It was modern in appearance; its typical representatives were, in Cambodia, the former interpreter Thiounn, who in 1902 was minister of the palace and always loyal to the French in his work in the royal government, which he dominated for twenty years;[76] and the brilliant minister Pham Quynh at the court in Hue after 1930. In fact, power was concentrated in the foreign political machine. French colonization led to a profound crisis of the former ruling classes, to which it was in the end scarcely in a position to come up with anything but a highly conservative response.

Political Innovation and Its Limits

The dispossession of these groups was not compensated for by an in-depth political modernization of the dominated societies. Certainly, it is crucial here to avoid oversimplification. In Indochina, the colonial power was not unaware of the national and democratic aspirations of its subjects: the enormous political documentation that it left behind is sufficiently convincing in this regard. Colonial power had searched, from the outset, to gain legitimacy in their eyes, to place itself in the context of the long history of the Indochinese peoples, for example, by highlight-

ing the historical relations between the emperor Gia Long and the French in Dai
Nam in the early nineteenth century, and by presenting itself as the renovator of
Khmer identity through the restoration work of its archaeologists at Angkor in
Cambodia, as Agathe Larcher-Goscha has shown.[77] Many of the figures responsible for colonization were conscious of the need for the evolution of the political
status of Indochina. Why, then, was there so little opening of the colonial power
in Indochina to the logic of political reform, and to compromise with its adversaries, at least until the advent of the Vietnamese nationalist movement in the 1930s?

We can perhaps answer this question by identifying several of the constraints
of the approach Jules Harmand outlined in 1892:

> The government and administration of this possession cannot be constituted the same
> way as in Europe, and must take on a paternal form, in the political sense of this
> word. . . . We must never allow anyone to question our right and our firm intention
> not to share any of the roles of leadership and action that are necessarily the privi-
> leges of the conqueror, and which he cannot abandon without compromising his dom-
> ination. The English . . . have already appreciably gone beyond this limit. It is already
> difficult for them to go back, and perhaps they will never be able to regain the lost
> ground. Let us make sure we know how to take advantage of these warnings in order
> that we may define, from now on, the limits we should never exceed.[78]

It was not the rejection of change per se but the will to retain absolute control
over it that was the limit of colonial reformism. Furthermore, events and conjunctures became openly unfavorable to it after 1929. Throughout the colonial
period, immobility was strongly favored by the centralization of the Indochinese
regime: the concentration of power in the Gouvernement général, a substructure
of France's global empire, whose only limit, Harmand asserted, was "le contrôle de
la métropole"—the Chambers, ministers, and press of Paris.[79]

Pushing in the same direction was the extreme fragmentation of colonial interests in France, which were far from having a unified voice. What most today call the
"Colonial party" was, in fact, a mere conglomeration of lobbies, institutions, and associations. Within this amorphous congeries, various French and Indochinese business interests—themselves profoundly divided into unstable networks and coalitions
by the vagaries of monetary, trading, or commercial conjunctures—opposed one another, often ferociously. Pressure by the Indochinese colonists was to some extent
ineffective, as Gilles de Gantès has shown for the Belle Époque.[80] In spite of the intensity of the public debate on Indochina, basic decisions were always difficult, and
involved, at the highest levels, the laborious arbitration of conflicts that opposed diverse components of a sort of decision-making pentagon: the high colonial administration; the great French economic lobbies (banks, cotton, metallurgy, wheat, etc.);
the great financial and industrial groups active in Indochina, in part but not always
represented in the Colonial Union; local enterprises and colonists gathered together

in chambers of commerce and agriculture, in unions representing the planters, and others represented by the Committee of Commerce and Industry of Indochina (the Indochinese section of the Colonial Union); and finally the influential colonial politicians, who all took turns writing their views in the Indochinese and metropolitan press. Indochinese colonists, civil servants, and local businessmen could only exert strong pressure when they joined their demands to the views of major figures in the colonial decision-making structure. The campaign of denunciation of the management of Governor-General Antony Klobukowski (1909–11) and the remarkable report of the socialist deputy Maurice Viollette in 1911, followed by his interventions in the Chamber of Deputies, demonstrate this. The long absence of the forms of modern civil society among the colonized and the prolonged weakness of what slowly constituted the Vietnamese elite after 1900 completed this picture.

Finally, among these factors contributing to inertia, we must take into account the vision of auto-legitimation on which officials expounded without respite to the colonized, whose influence has been overly ignored. This was two-pronged, combining the contradictory discourses of progress and tradition. The first was arranged around the theme of the unavoidable long phase of tutelage the Indochinese peoples had to go through in order to attain progress, which for some—for example, for several of France's proconsuls between 1880 and 1920 (who were often Freemasons), such as Bert, de Lanessan, and Sarraut—included the eventual adoption of elements of Western democracy. In March–April 1887, a miniature model of Bartholdi's Statue of Liberty was exhibited at the Hanoi Exposition before being erected, as the culmination of an initiative on the part of individuals of the township of Hanoi and of La Fraternité tonkinoise, the Masonic lodge in the city, in a pagoda at the Petit Lac.[81] But Liberty never actually came down from her pedestal. The myth of progress, in its colonial version, was very quickly shrunk down to its technical, cultural, sanitary, and economic dimensions. This reduction was nourished by the discourse of tradition rooted in the counterrevolutionary thinking that had flourished in France since the beginning of the nineteenth century, an ideological tradition that was highly influential in the culture and bureaucracy of the colony. Many French officials in Indochina identified the colonized as "natural" communities of the type dear to counterrevolutionary thinkers like Joseph de Maistre (1753–1821) and Louis de Bonald (1754–1840), and they aspired to protect these "organic societies" from the degradation they were believed to have suffered in Europe.

Early ethnographic, geographic, and Orientalist works gave many of these officials an idealized, ahistorical view of the extended family and the Vietnamese village, which they saw as harmonious, closed, immobile micro-societies: "organic cells of society," in the words of the resident superior of Tonkin in 1941. Moreover, in a sense, colonization contributed greatly to the "invention" of the national tradition and furnished several major themes central to the modern national ideologies then gestating among the colonized elites. This political philosophy was essentially shared by all the officials in Indochina in the 1930s: whether they were Radicals believing in solidarity; Conservatives influenced by the thought of Jacques Maritain, like the influential director of political affairs, Georges Grandjean; or even those—was Pierre Pasquier among them?—who did not situate themselves far from the counterrevolutionary monarchist postulates of Charles Maurras, the leader of the neoroyalist Action française in the metropole. The colonized elites could only rediscover themselves, it was believed, through this vision of a present, which must be governed by the past. It was a vision that inspired this definition of the "fundamental Annamese institutions" by Pham Quynh in 1941, for example: "You know them: it is the patriarchal family, it is the oligarchic township, it is the monarchic state; they rest upon the traditions of order, discipline, hierarchy, and authority that are the foundations of the Annamese society. They make up what is referred to as the social order of the land of Annam. This social order has as its tutelary guarantor of political order the French Protectorate."[82]

From top to bottom of the colonial apparatus, the dominant sentiment, at least after 1929–30—for the three previous decades, the question needs to be reconsidered— was that colonization had to take into account the broader movement of the time, which would not end for quite a while, and that a total rupture with the past would be dangerous. "In a country as traditional as Annam," an anonymous administrator wrote in 1937, "nothing of lasting value will be accomplished by breaking with the past."[83] This traditionalist vision of history, highly influential in the upper levels of the Indochinese administration, was legitimized by the sincere idealization by officials of the Indochinese civilizations, by a sort of conservative romanticism, paternalistic and attached to the past, elaborated by thinkers, writers, and French Orientalists who were fascinated by the history of these civilizations. The latter thus served, in the colonial discourse, to "archaeologize" the present. Pierre Pasquier, a remarkably cultivated high-ranking civil servant who was conscious of the need to open up a historical perspective for conservative Vietnamese nationalism, formulated the central theme of this colonial romanticism: the defense of the "Annamese identity" and the vision of a "traditionalist future."

> Allow a friend of these people, of their ancient customs, their respectable traditions, to believe that in studying the past one can learn how to lead a race that the chances of evolution has placed under our control into the future. Learning to know one another will be the best way to like one another. Let us not destroy anything of the ancient Asian edifice. Let us respect the "character" in which a system of thought quivers. Let us work as adapters and not destroyers! So that, in a century, France does not have to face reproach for having destroyed, under a pitiless centralization, the originalities of this faraway country. . . . Let us leave this garden as we found it. . . . Let us preserve the gentle poetry of Annam, the ponds where lotuses die, the subtle images, the songs between girls and boys on summer evenings, the scholars with long beards, and the mandarins in their ancient and colorful costumes.[84]

In this vision, modernization was made up only of calculated and limited modifications; progress was only tradition in motion. "To support and ... to restore everything that remains compatible with progress in the customary constitution of the village," was what was needed, a high civil servant wrote in 1937, echoing Pasquier. "It is only after having finished this preliminary work that it will be possible to build further, on solid foundations, and to proceed with the necessary reappraisals."[85]

From this arose the hypertrophy of the coercive practices and devices of the colonial state, a necessary compensation for its lack of legitimacy. The regimes of the *indigénat* and the collective responsibility for villages were instituted in Cochinchina from 1881 to 1903, in Annam and Tonkin in 1897, and in Cambodia in 1898, although it was progressively limited or even abandoned there, it is true, after 1903. The law of 1900 officially created colonial army units. The Garde indigène (Garde civile in Cochinchina) was also created in 1900 and given the responsibility of the surveillance of the peasantry. On June 28, 1917, Albert Sarraut created the Sûreté générale indochinoise, a fearsome police force, which was, among other tasks, deployed against the nationalist movement, and from it a true political police force, the Police spéciale de sûreté, emerged after 1920. There were also indigenous courthouses that replicated the French courthouses; special jurisdictions, with Criminal Commissions that, from 1896 on, punished attacks on the security of the protectorates; and, finally, the prison system.

In consequence of colonial racism and the indigenous prison tradition, the modern type of prison based on disciplining and rehabilitating the condemned was not created in Indochina by the French, as Peter Zinoman has shown.[86] In 1933, there were eighty-nine provincial prisons, five central penitentiaries in the major cities, and around ten penal colonies *(bagnes)*: Lai Chau, Lao Bao (1896), Cao Bang (1905), Ha Giang, Thai Nguyen, Ban Me Thuot (1932), Kon Tum (1931), Son La, and, especially, Poulo Condore (1862), as well as deportation to the Inini penal colony in Guyana (where 523 political deportees arrived on June 3, 1931). All of these institutions were key building blocks of social control. At the beginning of 1933, the Indochinese prison system contained 4,895 prisoners in its penal colonies, 3,440 in the central prisons and 19,416 in the provincial prisons, for a total of 27,751 prisoners in all. This meant that 160 people were incarcerated for every 100,000 inhabitants, a ratio that was two to three times higher than in the Dutch Indies, in Japan, or in France. The prisons, ravaged by epidemics, were sordid, dilapidated, chaotic, and anarchic. Between 1930 and 1940, an average of 4% of prisoners died each year. Penal labor, often contrary to the legal regulations, was the rule: the beach resort of Cap St-Jacques (Vung Tau) and a number of public buildings were built by the prisoners of Poulo Condore and other prisons in Cochinchina. The same was true elsewhere. The prisoners' resistance strategies were facilitated by the disorderly management of the prisons and also by the mix of "political" and "common law" prisoners. The history of the penal colonies, as with the ordinary prisons, was punctuated by bloody revolts—Poulo Condore in 1890 and 1918, Lao Bao in 1915, Lai Chau in 1927, and, especially, Thai Nguyen in 1917—and by raids perpetrated by criminals or sects in order to free prisoners.

This hypertrophy of the means of coercion was not really numerical, even though expenditures on the Garde indigène, the police, and prisons amounted to 19 percent of the budget in Tonkin (as against 14 percent for education) and 16 percent of the budget in Cochinchina (against 11 percent). A case in point is the Sûreté, which had a very limited personnel. In 1934, there were only 68 French policemen and 242 Vietnamese in its political branch, the Police spéciale, whose remarkable Service central de renseignements et de sûreté générale (Central Service of Information and General Security; SCRSG), mobile brigades, and external branches in China, Thailand, and France, combined with an efficient network of secret informants and modern techniques, gave it a lasting historic advantage over its adversaries, as Patrice Morlat has shown.[87] The Sûreté's *services d'identité* (identification services), for example, were organized as early as 1897 in Cochinchina, 1908 in Tonkin, 1913 in Cambodia, 1922 in Annam, and 1930 in Laos, and listed all those accused, convicted, or suspected of crimes, as well as foreigners, seamen, and "boys," using the Bertillon method, creating 52,000 files in 1927–28 and 237,000 in 1940–41.[88] "Indochina," the *chef du service* in Tonkin would write in 1942, "can boast that it is ahead not only of France but of most countries in Europe as well."[89]

The political influence of the security services preponderated, notably that of the Sûreté générale, which was connected to the colony's principal information and policy assessment agency, the Direction des affaires politiques (Political Affairs Directorate), established on February 10, 1922. Since it could hardly muster much support from the colonized, the scope of the colonial state's ideological apparatus and activities was limited. As in other colonies, however, state violence was hard to regulate, and it was invariably above the law. Hence the numerous "excesses" and, above all, the overwhelming fact that the colonial state functioned primarily through coercion and violence. Brutality and torture were common practices for the Sûreté—as early as the 1930s, the *gégène* (electrical torture), the *retournement du gésier* ("turning the gizzard inside out"), and other forms of "questioning" were used in its "slammers." These practices were reported by many of the accused during their trials, and confidential reports acknowledged the same. Repressive columns launched during conflicts combed the countryside, their passage all too often punctuated by summary executions. "Ordinary violence"—striking and beating—and assaults were part of daily life in the prisons and the camps. The protests and efforts of a certain number of civil servants and officers, of certain Christian circles, of the League of Human Rights, and of the French Left had only a limited effect and did not modify the profound nature of the colonial state: it was first and foremost a "police state."

This helps explain the timidity and the indecisive prudence of political reforms. These reforms cannot be ignored, however, for a series of Western political institutions had been introduced. Indochina was the only French colony where, as in British India, there was genuine representation of the colonized elite, established between 1900 and 1930. But it was only a pale imitation of the metropolitan model and functioned very differently from the way it did in France. The colonial assemblies (see app. 3) were all elected with a restricted suffrage, and the mixed assemblies were chosen by a system of two electoral colleges of unequal importance and confined to a merely consultative role. The only exception was the Conseil colonial (Colonial Council) of Cochinchina, which granted all concessions of more than twenty hectares and voted on the local budget. The Cochinchinese provincial councils, established by Le Myre de Vilers in 1882, elected by notables, and presided over by administrators of provinces, were effectively nothing more than instruments for the semi-bureaucratization of the village authorities. The indigenous Consultative Chambers of the protectorates, the first of which was created by Paul Bert in Tonkin on May 4, 1907, only expressed their wishes on strictly limited questions. Urban democracy was atrophied. The three mixed town councils of Saigon, Hanoi, and Haiphong had a narrow margin of decision and initiative. The mayors of Hanoi and Haiphong were designated by the administration, and their range of action was very limited; Saigon at first had a real power, but it was dismantled by the creation, in April 1931, of a regional *préfecture* for Saigon-Cholon, which was endowed with all the essential powers on the Paris model. Their management, furthermore, was chaotic and interrupted by a number of dissolutions: there were five different mayors of Hanoi from 1901 to 1907, eleven town councils and three municipal commissions in Haiphong from 1898 to 1908, and four municipal temporary administrative commissions in Saigon (1914, 1922, 1929, 1931), instead of the municipalities.

All of these elected institutions were consistently paralyzed by the tutelage of the Gouvernement général. Restricted to French colonists, the former dominant classes (notables, principal landowners, mandarins, and civil servants), the modern intellectual elites, and the new Vietnamese middle class, the colonial assemblies were places where the compromise between the dominant minorities of the colonized societies and French imperialism—the historical pact on which French Indochina was founded—was reproduced throughout the sessions and debates, which nonetheless remain of great interest. The colonial order found legitimacy in these assemblies, at which it viewed itself in the exotic mirror of its local clientele. They were chiefly devoted to the difficult task of managing conflict between the different colonial interests and social partners present. Things were, of course, not predetermined; the reform of Indochina's management was an almost constant preoccupation, but it proved to be "feasible" only within very limited constraints. Between 1905 and 1930, as J.-D. Giacometti has shown,[90] the Indochinese debate established itself around four intertwined concerns, namely: the definition of "indigenous" policy; the definition of the customs, monetary, and financial relations to be established between Indochina and the metropole; the choice of a form of development; and the issue of Indochinese ties with the Pacific basin. Schematically, this debate highlights two opposing orientations. The first advocated autarchy and was tied to the main French industries exporting to Indochina (the Vosgian and Alsatian cotton industries, for example), sometimes joined by Indochinese companies looking for markets in France and the rest of the empire. They supported an "imperial bloc," as well as the tightly knit integration of Indochina into the metropole's economic and political sphere. The second group defended autonomy, notably concerning customs and monetary issues, which they deemed necessary to consolidate Indochina's entry into the economy of the Far East. They were also often open to the perspective of an evolving political compromise with the modern Indochinese elites. Paul Claudel, France's ambassador in Tokyo from 1923 to 1925, summed up this second group in the formula: "Indochina, second metropole." "Indochinese dominion" was another expression summarizing this perspective that was influential in business circles, as well as at the higher levels of the Indochinese administration in the 1920s. Presented skillfully by Albert Sarraut in 1921 in his famous Plan for the Development of the Colonies,[91] this program was better and better defined up until 1930, at the cost, however, of numerous battles behind the scenes and of ongoing indecision concerning the conflict between these opposing views, without a global option ever fully coalescing.

Changes in the political status of Indochina were therefore minimal in spite of the periodic affirmation of the multiple intentions of an effective yet divided colonial reformism. Between 1911 and 1927, this reformism attained its maximum vigor, under the governments of Sarraut (1911–13; 1916–19), Maurice Long (1919–20), and Alexandre Varenne (1925–27). It did not, however, manage to shift political power to the colonized elites in any significant way. The projects for the creation of a representative assembly for the Indochinese Union, inspired by the Volksraad of the Dutch Indies (presented through the Long project for an upper chamber in 1920, the Merlin project for an Indochinese congress in 1924, the Varenne project for a popular assembly, and the Pasquier project of 1928 for the creation of *délégations financières* [financial organizations]), only led to the creation, on November 4, 1928, of the Grand Conseil des intérêts économiques et financiers (Grand Council of Economic and Financial Interests), a purely consultative and restrained creation on the part of business. As for the admission of the colonized to Indochinese public office, it was made official in February 1921 with the creation by Maurice Long of the so-called *cadre latéral* (lateral framework) for public services other than Justice and the Civil Service, but only a handful were truly admitted.

The state of the press is a good indication of colonial political immobility. Undoubtedly, colonization had introduced the press in societies where it did not exist, and there were hundreds of journals published in Indochina, at first through administrative initiative, by the settlers and the missions, then, increasingly, starting in the 1920s, by the new Vietnamese intelligentsia, to the point where the latter possessed a veritable hegemony over the system of Indochinese newspapers around 1936–39.[92] But fiercely repressive legislation that was transferred to Indochina hobbled and paralyzed freedom of speech. The French law of 1881 governing the press applied only to Cochinchina and only to French-language newspapers. Vietnamese- and Chinese-language papers fell under the decree of December 30, 1898, which subordinated their publication to prior authorization by the Gouvernement général and established censorship. In the protectorates, the press was restricted by the need for prior authorization, a required deposit, and censorship according to the decree of October 4, 1927: any newspaper could be forbidden by administrative decree, and only French-language newspapers published by Frenchmen benefited in 1935 (through decree of June 30) from the law of 1881. It was only in 1938 (by decree of August 30), that the Vietnamese- and Chinese-language press was no longer obliged to obtain prior authorization to publish. It was a regime worthy of the Second Empire. Rudyard Kipling declared that the Ten Commandments did not apply east of Suez. Nearly all of the Indochinese subjects of colonial France remained unaware of the rights of citizenship.

Small islands of limited democracy existed in the Indochinese political system, however, essentially in Cochinchina and in the large towns. The French Left was periodically active there, in particular, the Masonic lodges—the Grand Orient de France had founded seven lodges in Indochina, of which the oldest, the Réveil de l'Orient (Awakening of the Orient), was organized in Saigon in 1868, and the most active was the Fraternité tonkinoise (Tonkin Fraternity), created in 1887;[93] the Ligue des droits de l'homme (League of the Rights of Man), constituted in Hanoi and in Saigon in the decade 1900–1910;[94] sections of the Radical party; and especially the SFIO (Section française de l'Internationale ouvrière, the French Section of the Workers' International, which later became the Socialist party). The first socialist group was organized in Saigon in 1905. It had 123 members and presented a candidate at the legislative elections in the same year.[95] Socialism, influential among the civil servants around 1927–30, after a short eclipse, regained a genuine dynamism between 1936 and 1940, through two federations close to the Pivertiste left wing of the SFIO Socialist party, in the Indochinese north and south.[96] We should not underestimate the importance of this "colonial democracy," since it introduced another political model in cultures until then closed off to the modern notion of politics. But the years 1925–32 constituted a threshold that was not crossed. After 1930, democratic space did not really expand, as is shown by the timeline of the creation of Indochinese assemblies. Except during the otherwise ambiguous experience of the Popular Front, the colonial regime locked itself into a fundamentally defensive attitude, focused on the renovation of monarchic structures and the pure and simple repression of new political forces that contested its authority. This is made clear by the fact that, in the period between the two world wars, the essential center of political decision-making was the leadership of the powerful Sûreté générale, whose head was director of the Affaires politiques (Political Affairs) department, the key figure in the colonial government, author of political reports to Paris every month or every three months. It was a fusion of politics and policing that underlined the repressive orientation that colonial politics had definitively taken.

French colonial rule long prevented the maturation of a modern political society in Indochina outside of the cities, omnipotently dominating the indigenous societies on which it was built, to the point where it was able to survive without political reform. But as a result, the colonial state possessed only fragile legitimacy at best and had an extremely small social foundation, so that by 1930, at a time when hope of political reform was fading throughout East Asia, it had all but lost the consent of those it ruled. It was a state without a future.

3

Colonial Capitalism and Development, 1858–1940

With colonization, Indochina inserted itself into the world economy, to a greater extent than any other part of the French empire aside from Algeria and Morocco. The history of this entry can be summed up in one phrase, replete with meaning: the term *mise en valeur*—"development" or "exploitation"—was central to everything from speeches to confrontations. The idea that colonization meant bringing "progress" to the colonized was certainly a major trope of imperial self-legitimizing discourse. For their part, the adversaries of the colonial regime disputed the validity of this trope by arguing that while Japan was industrializing and Siam had begun to modernize, the colonial regime in Indochina was actually a hindrance to "development." This interpretation ended up prevailing.

A provisional assessment shows that Indochinese colonization in fact involved three dimensions of "development."[1] The first was a quantitative growth in production; in 1925, Fernand Leurence, the first director of the General Statistical Service, estimated this growth at 50% between 1899 and 1923,[2] an annual increase of 2%. The second dimension consisted of the modernization of economic practices, modes of thought, and social relations, and the disciplining of minds and bodies according to the norms and the requirements of industrial work. The third entailed the setting in motion of multiple local processes that destroyed the existing socioeconomic structures and the progressive industrialization of a part of production in correlation with the increase in exchanges for money and the penetration of science and productivist values into modes of production. Moreover, there was a constant, effectively implemented will to "develop." For Indochinese peoples, subjugation certainly constituted a real and painful economic revolution.

This process, however, involved the forced intrusion of an exogenous capitalism into a historically hostile environment: that of agrarian societies still poorly integrated into the Asian market space whose developmental logic did not lead in the direction of industrialization. Furthermore, it involved a colonial mode of commercial development whose driving force was necessarily the search for high profits by focusing on developing sectors that produced goods for foreign markets. The new Indochinese economy would therefore function as one element in the colonial regulation of metropolitan capitalism up until 1930. Subsequently, the combination of this developmental dynamic and that of Indochina's peasant societies led not only to the economic crisis of Indochinese capitalism but also to a grave situation of underdevelopment.

COLONIAL DEVELOPMENT

Colonial development took place essentially in four domains that were, until the end of World War II, the leading branches of the new Indochinese economy: rice and indigenous crops grown for food or other uses and destined for exportation; basic facilities and infrastructure; industries and agro-industries; and foreign trade. These four areas developed in complex interaction with one another, with the growth of the infrastructure and of foreign exchange preceding or following, depending on the circumstances, that of production. It is, however, possible to distinguish three interconnected main economic cycles, which crudely coincide with the three long-term movements in world economy: 1873 to 1895 (phase B, or recession), 1895 to 1929 (phase A, or expansion), and 1930 to 1950 (phase B). "The *mise en valeur* of the colony is achieved gradually through successive steps, with different domains introduced at each new stage," Charles Robequain observed in 1939.[3] These stages began with a period of rice exports that started in the 1860s. Then, following the application of Paul Doumer's economic strategy in 1897, there was a period of industrial, mining, and plantation development. This was followed in turn by a lengthy depression of the colonial economy, which affected its various branches unequally after 1930.

But the economic history of Indochina remains to be written, and a complete study should look at the history of firms, better distinguish the various contexts, expose the networks through which innovation took place, identify the driving sectors, and explore the relations between manufacturing and the peasant economy. It would also be necessary to determine the innumerable unsuccessful economic starting points and short-lived enterprises. This was notably the case in the Cochinchina of the admirals, where, up to the beginning of the twentieth century, attempts to create industrial establishments or plantations, such as French rice mills between 1862 and 1900 or sawmills between 1870 and 1885, nearly all failed, because they were competing with vigorous small-scale Vietnamese production and

Chinese capitalism. Capital, a spirit of enterprise, and settlers were long absent in Cochinchina, where in 1906, there were no more than thirty-six European industrial enterprises.[4] In 1901, the electoral list of the Chamber of Agriculture of the colony included only sixty-eight holders of land concessions and four settlers subsisting entirely off their land.

Agricultural colonization developed in an anarchical manner, at least until the decade between 1928 and 1939. It grew sporadically and aimlessly. "There isn't any planning; there never was any!" Agricultural Inspector Yves Henry wrote in 1924. Among the many failures were those of Cochinchinese coffee and indigo, Cochinchinese sugar manufacturers (such as the Indochina Sugar Company, created in 1870), and the Société d'études pour la culture du coton en Indochine (Company for the Study of Cotton Crops in Indochina) (1923–27), launched by the untiring Colonel Fernand Bernard with the backing of French spinning mills and large banks, despite whose efforts Indochinese exports barely reached 900 tons in 1937.

One of most bitter setbacks was that of silk spooling and spinning fabrics (the factories of the Société franco-annamite de textile in Nam Dinh and the Delignon establishments at Phu Phuong). These were founded after 1910 with Lyonnais capital and financial help from the administration with the aim of decreasing the costly importation of Chinese and Japanese raw silk to France (which rose to almost 3 billion francs in 1928). In Lyon, in February 1921, the Compagnie générale des soies (General Silk Company) was created with the support of political figures such as Édouard Herriot, Adolphe Messimy, and Louis Pradel. It built a spooling and spinning factory in Phnom Penh, with subsidies and technical support from the Protectorate, in the hopes of using superior Cambodian silk. But because of the incompetence of both the company and the administration, the plantations of mulberry trees they created were derisory, and by 1927, the Phnom Penh factory had to import a significant number of its cocoons. In spite of the export subsidies instituted in 1902 in Tonkin, and then made general throughout Indochina in 1909, Tonkin silk was 20% more expensive than silk from Canton in 1922. Sericulture in colonial Indochina had proven a fiasco.

The two protectorates of Cambodia and Laos were regions of disappointment par excellence for colonial enterprise. Only a few French settlers established themselves in Cambodia (twenty-three between 1897 to 1920) before the appearance around 1920 of the big rubber tree plantations in the red-soil zone.[5] By 1920, the entire modern industry of the protectorate, which represented only around a million francs of investment, consisted of a silk-spinning mill (founded in 1917), a cotton-ginning factory, a rice mill (founded in 1919), and a distillery (founded in 1914).[6] In Cambodia, colonial development was strictly commercial, focused on the shipment to Saigon of corn, rice (some 150,000 tons in 1910–20), salted fish, pepper, livestock, cotton, and latex. Cambodian imports added up to only 25,400 tons in 1920.[7] "Almost nothing has been done to develop this beautiful and fertile region," Doumer noted in 1897.[8]

As Alain Forest has shown, this assessment remained accurate during the entire colonial era. Between the two world wars, there was only embryonic industrial development. Aside from electric plants in the major cities, cigarette manufacturers, distilleries, breweries, the two silk-weaving mills of Phnom Penh, and the Ksach Kandal cotton-ginning mill (1892), development was of a rather "proto-industrialization" sort, with rural micro-industries dispersed in the small provincial centers (Siem Reap, Battambang, Kompong Cham, etc.). These micro-industries, rarely mechanized, were managed by small companies, often Chinese: rice-processing factories, brine and *prahok* plants, lime kilns, brickyards and tile works, manual sawmills, small boatyards, and mechanical sawmills (four in all, the main one being the large mill of the Compagnie forestière du Mékong at Chhup). They kept a principally Vietnamese and Chinese working population busy.

In 1908, an estimated 5.5 million francs were invested in the Protectorate's industries. The Comptoir de l'industrie cotonnière, which operated a cotton-ginning mill in Chhup in 1919, and the Compagnie des grands lacs de l'Indochine, which tried to introduce industrial fishing on Cambodia's Great Lake, the Tonlé Sap, in 1925, were two short-lived attempts to graft large enterprises onto this economic fabric. The only successful attempts were the five large rubber plantations set up on the red basalt lands of the provinces of Kompong Cham and of Kratié: Chhup, established in 1925 by the Compagnie du Cambodge (1921); Mimot, in Stieng country (Société des plantations réunies de Mimot, 1927); Prekkak (Compagnie des caoutchoucs du Mékong, 1927); Chamcar Andong (SCKT); and Snuol (Société des plantations de Kratié, 1927). In 1945, there were 22,179 hectares of tapped trees, out of 30,157 planted hectares. The 800,000 to 900,000 hectares of Battambang's plains are naturally fertile, because they are flooded during long periods when the Mekong is high; which is why they were chosen as the site of a "New Egypt," to use Resident Superior Ernest Outrey's 1912 expression to describe a project that started during the great rice-planting boom of the 1920s, yet never extended past Battambang. There was also the project to turn Phnom Penh into Saigon's hinterland twin in the context of a vast dual port system. It was to be an important emporium, aimed at the southern Chinese market; however, this never saw the day, despite the construction of a river port there. Around 1930, the use of coal was limited to Phnom Penh; Mekong launches, locomotives, distilleries, and even electrical plants were all fueled by wood.

What is striking in Cambodia, however, is the vitality of the peasant economy, with its premodern technical basis and high demands for human labor in its two oldest forms: rice planting on the flooded banks and rear banks, both dependent on the Mekong's water levels, and the multiple cultures of the *chamcars*. Small-scale domestic handiwork production, seasonal fishing on the Tonlé Sap, and temporary wage labor all complemented these agricultural activities. This material civilization ensured the slow "peasant recovery" of the river plains of the Tonlé Sap and of the

"Mesopotamia" of the southeast by clearing as well as by digging *prek* (irrigation channels) between the mounded banks of the Mekong and *beng* (small permanent ponds fed by the river via the *prek*) in the rear. The *prek* technique spread during the Protectorate period. Peasant society entered the economic logic of a primary rural capitalism. Several fundamental changes attest to this, including the expansion of speculative corn farming on the ridges of the Mekong, aimed exclusively at export, and the generalization of Chinese networks for collecting agricultural production, rice, corn, dried fish, and forest products (Chams and Malays controlled the cattle trade). This collection was associated with usury and massive debt on the part of peasant families; more generally, it was linked to the establishment of a Chinese commercial monopoly throughout the country.

The formula could have applied to Laos as well, this "barren hinterland of a stupendously prosperous shore,"[9] where, until World War II, a rudimentary barter economy *(économie de traite)* was dominant. It was based on the exchange of livestock and products from hunting and gathering (rubber, gum benzoin, cardamom, lac resin) for manufactured goods, and carried out by Chinese, Tai, and Lao tradesmen established in the Muong capitals, who generally represented large establishments in Kunming, Bangkok, and Hanoi. The sizeable tin mines of Nam Patene (1923) and the plantations of the Boloven plateau were the only industrial enclaves entirely embedded in the Laotian socioeconomic fabric. In 1935, foreign trade was minuscule (12.6 million francs' worth of imports, 1.4 of million in exports). For colonial capitalism, the "profitable" Indochina centered on the Vietnamese highlands and deltas.

THE CYCLES OF ECONOMIC DEVELOPMENT

The Rice-Growing Cycle

Between the beginning of the 1860s and the first years of the twentieth century, colonial development was founded on Cochinchinese rice.[10] This occurred in the context of the emergence, as of the 1790s, of a world rice trade based in Bengal, Java, and lower Burma, and it depended on the exploitation of the comparative advantages of the Cochinchinese economy: a relatively small population and a vast reserve of land suitable for rice cultivation. It did not involve the establishment of rice growing on the modern Japanese or Italian models. Rather, it was based on the turning outward of peasant production and on a partial capitalistic transformation of native systems of agricultural exchange. This transpired in the wake of the rapid expansion—which had in fact started at the beginning of the nineteenth century—of rice growing out from the central provinces of Cochinchina and toward the virgin territories of the Mekong Delta, essentially those to the west of the colony (Transbassac). It also depended on the insertion of this rice production into the vast Far Eastern rice market that was formed after 1850 around five poles: Hong

Kong and southern China, Japan, Singapore and Malaysia, the Dutch East Indies, and British India and Ceylon. Despite efforts at modernization undertaken by the authorities and by certain French and Vietnamese property owners, there were no modifications in cultivation methods. Outputs were the lowest in Asia. Chemical fertilizer was practically unknown. Cultivated varieties were very numerous (more than 240 in 1910), and the composition of exported rice was thus very heterogeneous; the ratings for the "Saigon no. 1" variety were generally 15% to 30% lower than those for the "Burma 2 star" and "Garden Siam" varieties. Hulling methods remained archaic, but five steam-powered rice-processing factories were constructed between 1869 and 1883; the first Chinese factory was established in Cholon in 1877.

On the other hand, there was a change in the modes of exploitation. This involved the growth of a form of tenancy based on small plots that associated the indebtedness of the *ta dien* or farmer (due to a system of advances granted at usurious rates for the means of subsistence and cultivation) to a system of protection/patronage relations exercised by the big landowners *(dien chu)* and legitimized in Confucian terms. Labor relations functioned along the lines of traditional domination, but land appropriation was capitalistic. In central Cochinchina, the larger landholdings, exploited either directly or through tenancy, remained relatively modest. In the West, meanwhile, the large latifundia (worked by tenant farmers, *ta dien*), which had been evolving since before the French conquest, quickly expanded through the auctioning of newly cultivated lands. But there were few owner-operated farms and few genuine French colonists, aside from some remarkable individuals: the consolidation of rice fields and revenues took place through a form of "latifundia capitalism" that only began to modernize itself after the 1930s. The Chinese businessmen of Cholon and the French capital had absolute control over equally capitalist structures, such as the collection and processing of paddy (387 rice mills and mechanical huskers in 1939) and rice export.

This hybrid capitalistic development had as its condition, besides the equipping of the colony's harbors, the digging of drainage, irrigation, and transport canal networks in the delta, which continued work undertaken by Vietnamese emperors at the beginning of the nineteenth century (the canal from Long Xuyen to Rach Gia in 1817, and the Vinh Te canal in 1820). This permitted the control of a delta that, unlike that of the Red River, which had been shaped for centuries by an old peasant civilization, was still a "new land,"[11] a true frontier, in 1860.

The construction of canals began in 1866 with the use of corvée (forced labor). In 1879, three engineers—Renaud, Combier, and Thevenet—began studying the delta and establishing a plan for its development. In the following years, the engineers invented the "basin flushing" *(bassin de chasse)* technique. The successful bidders for dredging contracts, companies like the Société française industrielle d'Extrême-Orient (1900) and Société française d'entreprises de dragages et de travaux publics (1912), made steam-powered dredges standard. After 1893, vast five-year programs of public works were launched. Aided by mechanization, they accelerated construction and created 600 kilometers of canals (at least 2.5 meters deep at low tide) and 2,000 kilometers of secondary canals, which were intended to drain flooded areas and permit the transportation of harvests to Cholon, the center for husking mills, and Saigon, one of the world's biggest harbors for rice exportation. Around 1930, separate canals were built for drainage, transportation, and irrigation. However, as elsewhere at the time, the ecological effects of the digging of these canals and of rice monoculture were seriously neglected. The dredging of rivers and the construction of canals, financed by the colonial budget, were the decisive factors in the rise of rice growing in southern Cochinchina, because they permitted cultivation in its western provinces, where the acreage of rice fields increased by a factor of 21 between 1869 and 1946. These quickly became large export provinces (with roughly one ton per hectare around 1930). In total, the cultivated acreage in Cochinchina increased from perhaps 315,000 hectares in 1836[12] to 2,303,000 in 1943. Production weighed in at 3,100,000 tons in 1940 (out of 6 to 7 million tons for all of Indochina), of which an average of 1,740,000 tons (say 1,250,000 tons of rice, plus by-products) were available for export. Indochinese rice exports (Cambodia was able to supply 60,000 to 200,000 tons toward 1940, and Tonkin 50,000) increased thirtyfold between 1860 (when perhaps 58,000 tons were exported) and the record year of 1928 (1,797,000 tons).

In this way, a significant, ethnically diverse, large-scale capitalism of landlords, merchants, and manufacturers was established in southern Vietnam. Ownership of latifundia was primarily Vietnamese and secondarily French (in 1931, 253,000 hectares belonged to companies or to owners with French status, of which around 100,000 belonged to 120 French-born colonists). In contrast, it was Cholon's powerful Chinese middle class that controlled the complex system of paddy collection and storage, the small river craft for transportation, Cholon's factories (seventy-two in 1939, of which fifty-five had large capacities), and pricing and sales. They also controlled the four official *Congrégations* and scores of more or less secret business syndicates, in particular, the powerful syndicate of paddy merchants (with eighty members in 1930) who financed and concentrated on the collection of paddy from inland. In 1930, some forty Chinese trading houses and, especially, eleven French concerns controlled more than 80% of exports. Finally, the overall financing of production—loans, investments in property, and usury—was the province of the French banks. It was said in Cochinchina that "Cholon belongs to the Banque de l'Indochine through the intermediary of the Chinese." All of these structures participated in a barter economy based on the exchange of agricultural products furnished by an impoverished peasant society in return for basic products (lamp fuel, European cotton fabric, items of everyday consumption purchased in China) imported or produced there by a local capitalist industry. This exchange was organized in the context of the commercial monopoly held by the French and Chinese colonial import-export houses and through a vast network of Chinese intermediaries who purchased agricultural products and distributed basic consumer goods. Agricultural income was unequally distributed among rice exporters, absentee landowners, and the majority of the *ta dien*.

In Tonkin, as Ta Thi Thuy has shown, a similar development of rice growing was attempted between 1890 and 1900 on the northern fringes of the delta, which had been depopulated during "pacification."[13] Abandoned land there was assigned to French settlers and then brought back into cultivation by Vietnamese sharecroppers, who were sometimes its former owners, established in villages in the concessions; 198,000 hectares were conceded in this way to Europeans. However, by 1898, the attempt had failed, and there were no more than 30,000 hectares of European-owned rice fields in Tonkin in 1937. Only the coffee plantations were well maintained. On the other hand, in southern Indochina, many other activities stemmed from the barter economy: trading in Cambodian cattle, which were exported live to the Philippines, Singapore, and Siam; production of salted or dried fish from the Tonlé Sap and the Mekong Delta; traffic in cinnamon from the "Moï" plateaus of Quang Nam; that in forest products from the peripheral provinces of Cambodia; and especially the export of Cambodian corn, which was developed from 1903 with the help of the taxation policy on foreign grain entering France.

Paddy trade underwent an impressive development in Cochinchina, in contrast to Cambodia and Tonkin, which furnished at best around 300,000 to 400,000 tons out of an average Indochinese annual exportation of 1,331,000 tons between 1919 and 1923. This trade reached its zenith in 1922–30, when on average 46,000 hectares were brought into cultivation annually in the Mekong Delta. The elevated price of paddy considerably increased the revenues of landowners. As long as it was above 2.37 piastres per picul (60 to 65 kg), the landowners of Transbassac and the *ta dien* recovered their outlays without having to resort to modern inputs. From this resulted an enormous increase in the amount of credit invested in rice growing: the debt of Cochinchinese rice growers was estimated at 600 million francs in 1930 and it was especially heavy in Transbassac (340 francs on average per hectare in the province of Bac Lieu, and 540 francs in Go Cong).[14] The entire system of rural mutual credit served to finance the expansion of extensive rice growing. Around 1930, Indochina was the source of roughly a quarter of rice exports worldwide, second only to Burma; up until that year, rice almost always contributed more than 60% of its export earnings (61.7% in 1913, 74.5% in 1921, and 69% in 1929), and it supplied China with 30% to 40% of its imported rice.

The Cycle of Mines, Plantations, and Manufacturing Industries

In the meantime, starting with J.-L. de Lanessan's pro-consulate (1891–94), new channels of development were added to rice exports, opening a new cycle of colonial capitalist expansion, this time in all of Indochina. The 1890s represent an important turning point: colonization settled into a rational exploitation of tropical natural resources. Furthermore, starting at the beginning of the twentieth century, Western speculation on Chinese economic development reverted to more realistic views. This likewise occurred in French business circles as they focused their investments and their global strategy on Indochina, without, however, abandoning their Chinese ventures.

Essentially industrial, the cycle was oriented around the trinity of collieries, plantations, and industries that did not compete with those of the metropole. At the end of the nineteenth century, the first Asian industrialization and development of coal imports in Japan and coastal China lent value to the Quang Yen basin of coal fields in Tonkin, which contained anthracite deposits of exceptional quality, exploited through strip mines (at Hatou, Campha) on the coast. To these would be added the two small basins of Phan Me to the north of Thai Nguyen (1910) and Nong Son to the south of Tourane (1900–1920). Quang Yen was operated by two powerful companies: the Société française des charbonnages de Tonkin (French Tonkin Coal-Mining Company), or SFCT, founded in 1888 and controlled by the Crédit industriel et commercial (Industrial and Commercial Credit Corporation), which had the concession of the deposits of Hon Gai, and the Charbonnages de Dong Trieu (Dong Trieu Coal-Mining Company), or SCDT, founded in 1916 and controlled by the de Redon family and the Banque nationale de crédit (National Credit Bank).

Starting at the beginning of the century, Indochina exported 200,000 tons of coal. By 1939, it exported 1.8 million tons and was the principal exporter after Manchuria in the Far East. Around 1905, the exploitation of nonferrous minerals in the upper region of Tonkin also commenced, leading to a veritable fever of prospecting between 1926 and 1930. Out of this developed a zinc industry, based in the mines of Cho Dien acquired in 1920–21 by the Compagnie minière et métallurgique d'Indochine (Mining and Metals Company of Indochina). In addition, there was the extraction of tin from the deposits in Tinh Tuc, close to Cao Bang, and those at Nam Patene (in Phon Tiou) in central Laos, prospected by the Société d'études et d'exploitation minières de l'Indochine (Indochinese Mining Studies and Exploitation Company) and mined by the Compagnie fermière des étains d'Extrême-Orient (Tin-Mining Company of the Far East). Following the mining rush of 1925–29, minerals and metals became an important Indochinese export sector.

Processing industries were the second sector that developed during this period of growth from 1895 to 1930. In 1907, they included some eighty-five enterprises in Tonkin, representing an investment of 41.7 million francs.[15] Their development, however, had been severely limited by pressure from metropolitan industries with which they competed. "No colony has been given the possibility of freely developing its industries," the geographer Charles Robequain wrote in 1939. "The very possibility of this kind of development has long appeared paradoxical and inconceivable. Indochina has not escaped this rule."[16] These industries, therefore, turned to exporting to Asian markets or to those domestic markets that metropolitan French industry could not supply. A first group of enterprises, located immediately downstream from the mines, included primary users of mining products, such as the factories producing *agglomérés* (briquettes) in Hon Gai; the Hon Gai and Uong Bi power stations; and factories that consumed a great deal of coal and had assured outlets in the colony or in East Asia. In the latter category was the powerful Haiphong cement factory of the Société des ciments Portland artificiels de l'Indochine (Portland Cement Company of Indochina), founded in 1899, which exported between 20 and 80% of what it produced.

A second set of companies comprised industries born of urbanization and the policy of infrastructure development. In this category, one finds the forty-two power stations (1935), which were all low-power but supplied a rudimentary electrical network, the railroad assembly and repair workshops, the naval arsenal in Saigon, the small naval yards of Haiphong, glassworks, and manufacturers of porcelain. A third set consisted of industries of consumption, tied to the activities of the *régies* (state monopolies), such as—during the 1930s—the five alcohol distilleries of the Société des distilleries de l'Indochine (Indochina Distilleries Company), or linked to the rise of colonial agriculture, like the oil refineries, soap factories, breweries, the three large sugar refineries of the Sucreries et raffineries de l'Indochine (Sugar Factories and Refineries of Indochina), the four manufacturers of tobacco, and, especially, the cotton industry.

This process of limited industrialization resulted from the insufficiencies in French industry, which created a space for local development. The cotton sector, studied by Irene Nørlund, illustrates this well.[17] It was able to develop as an industry of substitution, selling its cotton thread to an active class of Vietnamese craftsmen and benefiting from the customs duties imposed on imported Indian fabrics. A transposition of the old model of the French textile *fabrique*, it combined the use of the large mechanized cotton mill with widespread weaving done in homes or workshops embedded in the heart of the peasant economy. In 1940, the four modern cotton mills of the Société cotonnière du Tonkin (Tonkin Cotton Company) (14,000 workers) supplied the 50,000 weavers of the delta, but the latter group gradually developed their own complete cotton complex by building three weaving plants in Nam Dinh. In Tonkin, factories and workshops employed at least 120,000 cotton workers. In Saigon, the factory of the Société cotonnière du Saigon (Cotton Company of Saigon), opened in 1924, had 10,000 spindles and 400 looms.

The agro-industrial plantation sector came into existence under de Lanessan, with the adoption of a policy of agricultural concessions in Tonkin and Annam, and the perfection of the concession regime through ordinances of 1913, 1928, and

1929. These limited the size of free concessions to 300 hectares, beyond which concessions were only granted after the adjudication of the Gouvernement général, and foreign and Chinese planters were excluded. In 1926, a colonization program was put in place. The total acreage exploited by European colonists and planters increased from 11,390 hectares in 1890, distributed among 116 mainly Cochinchinese farms, to 322,000 hectares, of which 198,000 were in Tonkin, in 1900. It reached 1 million hectares in 1937, 110,000 in Tonkin and 610,000 in Cochinchina, of which 400,000 hectares were effectively exploited. The future of the plantation economy remained uncertain for a long time. It was vigorously initiated during the conquest of Tonkin with the cultivation of the *Arabica* coffee plants (the first plantation was created in 1888 close to Ke So), cultivated in connection with the raising of cattle for manure on the banks of the delta, west of Hanoi and Son Tay, as well as closer to the coast toward Phu Ly and Ninh Binh, in Annam in the red soil zones of Thanh Hoa and Nghe An, and in the high plateaus of the south between Kontum and Djiring. In 1937–38, 13,000 hectares yielded around 1,500 tons of coffee. Tea plantations were developed in the red soils of southern Annam (in Kontum, Plei Ku, Darlac, and upper Donnai) starting in 1924, with limited results: in 1938, 3,000 hectares yielded 812 tons of black tea, which was exported to France and North Africa.

Rubber trees played the biggest role in the expansion of the Indochinese plantation economy and stood out as its greatest success.[18] The period of latex harvesting in the forest lasted until around 1915. But the era of the rubber plantation had already begun in Cochinchina, as in the rest of Southeast Asia, in 1897–98. It was there that the first attempts to acclimatize *Hevea brasiliensis* were undertaken, along with the creation of experimental plantations. These were tied to the initiatives of the administration in the trial gardens of Ong Yen, and in particular to the work of Dr. Alexandre Yersin and the agronomist Vernet at the plantation they created in Suoi Giao in 1897. The first generation of plantations, typically less than one hundred hectares in size, were developed starting in 1909 on the gray soils (composed of alluvium on top of laterite) close to Saigon. In spite of the elevated rubber price (its historic record was attained in 1910), the planted acreage did not exceed 15,850 hectares in 1919, and production barely amounted to 3,500 tons; scientific and technical investment was almost nonexistent, and productivity was low.

Yet, around 1907, some big commercial plantations were already engaged in large-scale cultivation on the red basaltic soils that extended over an area of about three hundred kilometers by forty kilometers between Kratié and east of Saigon, between the sandstone plateaus of Cambodia and those of southern Annam. Some of these were the Société agricole of Suzannah (1907), the Société des plantations of An Loc near Bien Hoa (1909), Quan Loi, Xa Trach (1907), the Société des plantations of Phu Quoc (1908), and the Société des caoutchoucs (Rubber Company) of Indochina (1910) near Thu Dau Mot. In 1913, fifty-one plantations covered 70,000 hectares, with a total of 2 million trees, but the majority of these were not yet producing. In spite of a slide in global consumption after 1919 (although France's doubled in four years, from 35,700 tons in 1926 to 71,400 in 1929), the organization of world production into cartels within the framework of the Stevenson Plan (of November 1, 1922) provoked a new rise in the rubber market in 1924–25 and stemmed the decline of prices until 1928. In Indochina, a veritable boom in rubber began in 1926 and continued until 1930: between 1925 and 1929, the cultivated acreage jumped from 18,000 hectares to 78,620. The industry employed a total of 70,000 "coolies," contractual workers from Tonkin and Annam and free workers recruited on-site. By 1942, 133,000 hectares were cultivated, of which 103,000 hectares were in Cochinchina and 28,600 in Cambodia.

In contrast to the situation in Malaysia and the Dutch East Indies, large commercial plantations dominated in Indochina. Vietnamese plantations, all under fifty hectares, occupied less than 7% of the acreage in 1943, and the sixty-three small European plantations (generally between thirty and fifty hectares in size), overseen by a Vietnamese *caporal,* were no more significant. In 1937, 68% of the cultivated land belonged to twenty-seven companies controlled by French holdings. Three large financial and industrial groups controlled close to two-thirds of production in 1944: the Rivaud-Hallet group (31%), also strongly established in Malaysia and Sumatra; the Michelin group (11%); and the group of the Banque de l'Indochine (Société indochinoise des plantations d'hévéas, et al., 29.6%).

Plantations were set up much to the detriment of two groups. The first were the peoples of the forest highlands, who were deprived of a part of their territory and saw the destabilization of their economy, based on hunting, gathering, and slash-and-burn agriculture *(ray).* The second was a poor proletariat whose members, recruited under contract in Tonkin and northern Annam, were for all intents and purposes prisoners on the plantations. They were forced to endure the brutal and ferocious exploitation of the companies for 0.30 to 0.40 piastres per adult per day until the adoption of a first "contractual labor" regulation in 1927 and the organization of the first workers' resistance movements by clandestine communist unions. Mimot in Cambodia figured at the top of the list of the worst plantations. Workers of "red rubber" endured an uncommon martyrdom there. The resident, E. De-senlis, noted in 1927 that its workers were "treated like human cattle, terrorized by the overseers."[19]

Because they appeared rather late, the Indochinese plantations benefited from technical advances achieved elsewhere. After 1929, they systematically grafted their own trees from the best specimens, and in 1942, they had the highest proportion of grafted acreage in the world (42%). They followed the model of scientific and industrial plantation outlined by Vernet before 1914, and perfected in Sumatra and Malaysia, and drew moreover on the expertise of the agronomists who had contributed to the elaboration of this model, such as the Dutch scientists van Pelt and P. J. S. Cramer. The plantation of the 1930s became a genuine agro-industrial factory due to many factors. There were the agricultural aspects such as the homogeneity of trees and seasonally alternated tapping. Other, more technical aspects included the use of increasingly advanced technology by planters, the systematic employment of engineers and agronomists, truck fleets, electrified factories for the manufacture of the rubber "partitions," the support of laboratories and continuing research, and the Taylorization of labor. Finally, other factors contributed to this search for maximum productivity: rigorous management of accounts, the geometric planning of space, and a methodical antimalaria campaign started in 1927. After the crisis of the 1930s, the Indochinese plantation was the most modern in Asia and the most competitive in the world. Since there is an average six-year delay between the planting of the tree and the first latex harvest, and eleven years for maximal production, it follows that the growth of exports occurred only after 1930. In 1929, 10,000 tons were exported; in 1938, 60,000; and in 1942, 75,200. Two-thirds of this came from a group of nineteen companies. Indochina was then the third-largest exporter in the world, but far behind Malaysia and the Dutch East Indies, with 6.5% of the sales. Up until 1940, more than 1 billion current francs were invested in the cultivation of rubber, whose future total revenue was then estimated at more than 2 billion.[20]

Colonial Public Works

This second period of colonial development was preceded and accompanied, through the 1930s, by the construction of a modern transportation infrastructure. "Indochina . . . was built by steel and by money: with the steel of rail and the money of the general budget," *La Quinzaine coloniale* asserted on May 25, 1902. Equally, though, it was developed by road and on water. Small steam-powered craft made their appearance, particularly in Cochinchina, where towing considerably increased the numbers of trips that could be taken by the junks. Neither the traditional small craft nor the "indigenous" coastal trade was, however, fully eliminated: the latter represented a third of the tonnage of maritime traffic of Indochina in 1936–37. The Messageries fluviales de Cochinchine (Cochinchinese River Transportation Company) opened its river lines of motor-driven boats very early. They went as far as Khone in 1890 and thereafter were expanded to the navigable reaches of the Mekong from Savannakhet to Vientiane. In 1930, about two hundred motor launches and more than a hundred thousand other boats circulated on the channels of the lower Mekong. Boats traveled up the Red River to Lao Cai, eight hundred kilometers in the interior.

The period of railroad construction began with the so-called Doumer program, a vast plan for 1,700 kilometers of railroad, progressively elaborated between 1891 and 1898 on the model of the Freycinet plan (1878–86) in France. Doumer conceived of the railroad primarily as an instrument of imperialistic penetration into China, but also as a means of connecting the multiple sites of the peasant economy with the new industrial poles and regional and foreign markets. In 1942, 2,767 kilometers of one-meter rail lines were in use, to which was added the 464 kilometers of the Yunnan line (from Lao Cai to Kunming), which compensated for the difficulties of navigating the upper Red River.

Most railroad lines were constructed at exorbitant cost, with considerable budget overruns: the 384 kilometers of the Haiphong–Lao Cai line required nearly 200,000 francs per kilometer instead of the planned 130,000, for a total of 78 million francs instead of the budgeted 50 million. They were financed and managed by a public enterprise, the Compagnie des chemins de fer de l'Indochine (Indochinese Railroad Company). The only exception involved the Chinese segment of the Yunnan line, constructed between 1901 and 1911 by the private Compagnie des chemins de fer du Yunnan (Yunnan Railroad Company), which had been granted the franchise of the line and itself received enormous subsidies from the general budget. Until 1914, the construction sites mobilized approximately a hundred thousand workers, toiling under frightful conditions. The largest construction was the Transindochinois railroad (1,860 kilometers), opened in successive stretches: Lang Son–Vinh (1905), Tourane–Hue (1906), Hue–Quang Tri (1908), Saigon–Nha Trang (1913), Vinh–Dong Ha (1927), and Tourane–Nha Trang (1936). On the other hand, the projected construction of a rail junction between the Transindochinois and the Mekong, and another between Saigon and Phnom Penh, was not accomplished. Only lines that penetrated in a limited way into the interior—Saigon–My Tho (1885), Phnom Penh–Battambang–Mongkolborey (1932)–Poipet (1940), Saigon–Loc Ninh (1933), the line from Nha Trang to Da Lat, and the Tan Ap–Xom Cuc line, which was extended toward Laos by a cable car to the mountain pass of Mu Gia—were constructed.

Investments in railroads, which were very high (in 1908, the initial estimate for the construction of the Yunnan line exceeded its budget by 72% during construction), ultimately yielded disappointing results. Unlike in the case of European networks, profits garnered from passenger traffic were for a long time greater than those from freight, which had to compete with the waterways. In 1937, only 1,171,000 tons of merchandise was transported, and the railroads barely broke even. From 1903 to 1935, they operated with a deficit. But, whatever the critics of the Transindochinois may have said, what D. W. Del Testa has aptly called this "Imperial Corridor" in fact contributed to the generation of a new geography of production and exchange, to a new collective vision of the world, and, in the Vietnamese case, to the unification of the national space.[21] With the completion of the Hanoi–Vinh section (321 kilometers) in March 1905, traveling from one city to the other took less than 24 hours, as opposed to five days. As early as 1920, the fourth class reserved for "natives" made up 93.5% of the passengers.

In 1911, a coherent road construction program was launched. It was believed that roads were better fitted to accelerate exploitation and to bring Laos and the high Vietnamese plateaus out of isolation. As of 1918, the program was premised on the distinction between local roads, under the jurisdiction of the different territories of the Indochinese Union, and colonial roads to be financed by the general budget. Its essential elements included the Route coloniale 1 from Hanoi to the border of Siam (a distance of 1,285 kilometers), which roughly followed the ancient "Mandarin road," the dense networks of the dam roads in the Red River and Mekong deltas, the four great axes of penetration toward Mong Cai, Lang Son, Cao Bang, and Ha Giang in the north, the three Savannakhet–Quang Tri, Vinh–Thakhek, and Vinh–Luang Prabang axes that headed toward Laos, and the roads of the high plateaus of southern Annam (Kontum–Plei Ku–Qui Nhon, Ban Me Thuot–Nha Trang, Saigon–Da Lat). In 1943, with 32,000 kilometers of roads paved with stone and 5,700 paved with asphalt, an automobile traffic of 18,000 vehicles, and a traffic of 40–50 million travelers, Indochina boasted one of the finest road networks in East Asia.

The takeoff of the colonial economy was tied to the rise of the two great delta ports. Haiphong, located on the Cua Cam, one of the mouths of the Thai Binh, began as a modest depot of the China Merchants Navigation Company in 1874.[22] The landing point of the expeditionary corps, the port was built up through the construction of the first docks in 1886 and an arsenal in 1888. In spite of the site's disadvantages (notably silting and the existence of a double bar at the entrance to the Cua Cam), which required costly dredging and forced boats to discharge at Ha Long Bay, the port, complemented by its coal annexes at Port-Redon, Hon Gai, and Campha, functioned as point of junction between maritime navigation and the French lines of the Far East and the active fleet of small craft in the delta, and constituted the largest outlet for Yunnan and Tonkin, with a traffic of 1.2 million tons in 1937.

The growth of Saigon, located on the right side of the river of the same name and eighty kilometers from the sea, was considerably greater. It was taking place at least as early as the beginning of the nineteenth century, with the development of the Chinese merchant town of Cholon, whose port Saigon was. Admiral Page's decision to declare Saigon a free port on February 2, 1860 (a status that should have been suppressed in 1887 by the application of customs tariffs), accelerated the expansion of the port. French conquest and the opening of commercial lines from Europe to China—as early as 1858, the Eymond and Henry shipping company of Bordeaux created a regular line traveling to Singapore, Manila, Hong Kong, and Shanghai—established it as a port in the European and Chinese traffic in the Far East. This is particularly true with regard to its trade with Hong Kong in rice (which was booming by 1860), pepper, and European products. In 1867, close to five thousand Chinese and Vietnamese junks, of all tonnages, frequented Saigon's harbor, along with approximately a thousand oceangoing ships.[23]

Large-scale trade propelled the growth of French trading houses, notably those of Bordeaux, such as the powerful house of the Denis Brothers, created in Saigon in November 1862, and those of Roque, Sensine and Chalès, and Renard, as well as those of British and German companies. Colonization created an urban area (with 450,000 habitants in 1941) and a modern harbor about six kilometers downstream from the city. There the intense river traffic—converging on Cholon from Cambodia and the provinces of Cochinchina along a nearly twenty-five-kilometer span of the Arroyo Chinois (and the canals that flanked it after 1906)—met with ocean-going ships.

Saigon was the most active port on the northwestern shore of this "Asian Mediterranean," the South China Sea. Its high level of activity was the result of the linking together of the flow of merchandise, of capital and currency, and of men coming from or going to the four interconnected economic spaces—a study of their linked dynamics would be of great interest: Marseille and Europe, Hong Kong and China, Singapore and the Malaysian world, and finally southern and central Indochina up to southern Laos. The port of Saigon's traffic (2,140,000 tons in 1937) made it the sixth-largest French port. Between Haiphong and Saigon, no other important harbor centers developed, because of the lack of a sufficiently active hinterland: Nha Trang, Qui Nhon, Tourane, and Ben Thuy were only stops or outlets for the small coastal deltas of Annam. The same was true of the small river ports of the Mekong, from Vientiane to Phnom Penh, which were simple wharves animated by the traffic going to or coming from Bangkok.

Through these great cycles of the colonial economy, an irreversible upheaval of the Indochinese space occurred. The relative uniformity of the precolonial systems of production and exchange had been replaced by a strong differentiation into unequal domains of economic and social development. Once structured in this way, Indochina was henceforth a multiple and an indelible historical reality. The most visible change was the vast displacement in the geography of exchange. Previously, this had taken place along north-south routes, by coastal traffic or via the succession of navigable lagoons of northern Annam—a kind of reduced replica of the Chinese imperial Grand Canal—which connected the delta of the Red River to Hue. Upon this general design, which privileged regional and interregional trade, was superimposed a new network of exchange that took place along west-east axes and converged on the two principal colonial ports. Secondly, the exchange between Siam and the Mekong countries was weakened, and Cambodia was economically welded to Cochinchina. Moreover, the developmental gap between the regions of the Mekong and those of Vietnam was abruptly intensified in the course of a few decades. Until 1954, the Mekong areas, with the immense mountainous ridge of the north and center of the peninsula, comprised a vast reserve of land, used for foresting and mining, and submitted to the more or less effectual management of the colony's great technical administrations, notably the Service forestier (Forest Service), and, to a relatively large degree, to military administration. To this Indochina of "reserves" was opposed that of the Vietnamese deltas, where externally focused economic structures were implanted: the rice "trade economy" *(économie de traite)* on the Mekong Delta, the mining industry in the north, the agro-industries of the plantations in the highlands of the peripheries of the deltas. But, here again, the gap deepened between the Cochinchinese deltas, where production was mostly intended for the Asian market, and the deltas of the center and especially the north, which remained dominated by intensive, inwardly focused, small-scale rice growing.

Technical and Scientific Modernization

For indigenous societies, colonization certainly represented an irreversible entrance into the modern capitalist era. This shift was accompanied by a transfer, limited though significant, of the technical and scientific knowledge of industrialized societies, which proved indispensable to the management of the colonial economy. Within a few decades, the historic horizon of the Indochinese societies was altered, and they passed without transition from the *civilisation du végétal* (plant-based societies) into the era of the submission of nature, the railroad, the car, the airplane. The vast majority of the colonized hardly benefited and were only distant spectators to this shift, basically a shift in the relationship between mankind and nature.

As in the Dutch East Indies, science and colonial scientists—who were closely linked to the Muséum d'histoire naturelle (Museum of Natural History), the Jardin colonial (Colonial Garden), and the École d'agriculture coloniale (School of Colonial Agriculture) in Nogent, on the outskirts of Paris, as well as to the upper reaches of the administration and the men of the "Colonial party" (notably Joseph Chailley-Bert)—were of crucial importance in the definition and application of development projects and promoted a technical and rational form of colonial exploitation of nature. Colonization was a "scientific" enterprise, focused on the acquisition of knowledge, the beginning of the scientific possession of the Indochinese biosphere, while dominating and exploiting its populations. Essential in this regard was the activity of botanists—such as Guillaume Capus, who was appointed by Doumer to the position of the director of the Department of Agriculture and Commerce in 1897, and, especially, Auguste Chevalier, a brilliant scholar from the Muséum, appointed by Sarraut to head the Inspection des services agricoles (Agricultural Services Inspectorate) in 1914—as well as of agronomists such as Yves Henry (who headed the Inspectorate after 1923), of engineers of the Corps des Ponts et Chaussées and of the Inspection des travaux publics, and of scientists from the Institut Pasteur, such as Albert Calmette and Alexandre Yersin.

The rise of numerous scientific institutions and projects was no less important: the Botanical Gardens of Saigon (1863) and Hanoi (1886), which started out as experimental gardens; the Mission scientifique de l'Indochine (Indochina Scientific Mission), created by Doumer in 1902; a number of exploratory missions such as those of Pavie and his collaborators throughout Laos (1879–94); the Service géologique (Geological Service, 1898), the Service forestier (Forestry Service, 1901), the Institut océanographique (Oceanographic Institute, 1922); the organization of agricultural competitions, which took place starting in 1894 in Tonkin; expositions and museums; agricultural and industrial fairs in Saigon (1880), Hanoi (1902), and Hue (1915); and the Conseil des recherches scientifiques (Scientific Research Council).[24] Indochina would become one of the important centers for the creation and application of colonial science.

Following the broad outlines of Doumer's project, science and the sectors of colonial production were brought together, while an influential ensemble of economic institutions was put in place: chambers of agriculture, the Direction de l'agriculture et du commerce (Directorate of Agriculture and Commerce), reorganized in 1925 into the powerful Inspection de l'agriculture et des forêts, and the Services de l'agriculture (Agricultural Services) of Tonkin (1897), of Annam and Cambodia (1898), and of Cochinchina (1899). This apparatus was enlarged through the creation of planters' and rice-growers' unions, and by a significant scientific network, all agronomic in nature: laboratories for agricultural and technical chemical analysis in Saigon (1898) and Hanoi (1899), experimental gardens and fields, agricultural stations, the École vétérinaire de Hanoi (Hanoi Veterinary School, 1917), the École supérieure d'agriculture et de sylviculture (College of Agriculture and Forestry) in Hanoi (1918), which trained native technicians, the Centre agricole de Bokor (1918), and the Institut d'agronomie coloniale (Institute of Colonial Agronomy, 1918), which became the Institut des recherches agronomiques et forestières de l'Indochine (IRAFI; Indochinese Institute of Agronomic and Forestry Research) in 1925 and was composed of specialized stations (Can Tho and Battambang for rice; Ong Yen, Gia Rai, and the Boloven for rubber plants; Plei Ku for tea and coffee). The Gouvernement général organized a corps of agronomic engineers (10 in 1900, 55 in 1929) and created the Service statistique générale de l'Indochine (General Statistical Service, 1922), which published the Bulletin économique de l'Indochine and the ten Annuaires statistiques de l'Indochine (1913–42), as well as the Bureau de climatologie et de météorologie agricole (Agricultural Climate and Meteorology Bureau, 1927), which in 1934 assembled observations from 490 stations. The government also created the Laboratoire d'hydraulique et d'étude des sols (Laboratory of Water and Soil Studies) at Phu An, the Office indochinois du riz (Indochinese Rice Office, 1930), which was in charge of improving cultivation methods and factory techniques, seed stations, and model silk farms in the silk-producing provinces (six in Annam), and the Institut du caoutchouc en Indochine (IRCI; Institute of Rubber Research in Indochina, 1940). From 1920 to 1930, the practice of scientific agronomy was imposed on the plantations and the colonial agricultural enterprises, and there were numerous attempts here and there to gradually introduce it into the realm of peasant agriculture.

As tools of colonization, these institutions were far from perfect. Many were ephemeral, like the Institut scientifique de Saigon (Saigon Scientific Institute, 1919), conceived by Auguste Chevalier on the model of the Paris Muséum as a site for basic research, then incorporated by Yves Henry in 1923 into the IRAFI and reoriented toward applied research. Others, like the University of Hanoi, never got beyond the infrascientific stage before the 1940s. The colonial state was not a bloc; it was formed amid debates and conflicts that ultimately focused on the choice of development strategies and the assessment of their social and political costs. In fact, applied research carried the day between the two world wars. In 1924, the agronomist Yves Henry denounced the serious deficiencies of the agricultural services: the ignorance of hygrometric requirements for crops, of the biochemistry of flooded soils, and the evolution of agricultural productivity, along with a total detachment from peasant practices of cultivation, the absence of programs for the selection and standardization of paddy, the rivalries between scientific groups, the inertia and the weight of the services, and the minor effect their actions had.[25] Nevertheless, these efforts were not entirely in vain, at least in some areas, such as the struggle against the great livestock epidemics from 1929–30 on. At the same time, a vast project aimed at transferring and acclimatizing plants (gutta-percha, rubber trees, coffee, forest species) and understanding and transforming the productive systems was carried out, along with the collection of specimens; a scientific inventory of Indochinese ecosystems had been put together by the 1860s. As in the West, nature was henceforth the object of classification and insatiable intellectual appropriation.

In many of the areas of the peninsula (deltas, mid-altitude zones, urban zones), colonization simultaneously imported species and extended fragile, specialized ecosystems, introducing both its ideas of nature conservation and predatory land reclamation. The Indochinese forests, one of the great wooded massifs of the intertropical zone (in 1922, they comprised 31 million hectares, out of a total surface in Indochina of 75 million), were placed under minimal state-controlled management directly inspired by the ideas of the French forestry school. The scientific inventory of the forests began with the publication between 1876 and 1906 of the monumental *Flore forestière de la Cochinchine* by Louis Pierre (J. B. Louis), who had explored the lower basin of the Mekong and the peninsula of Malacca for thirteen years. A seven-volume *Flore générale de l'Indochine* was published by Henri Lecomte between 1907 and 1943.

The industrial exploitation of the forests was under way. While colonization seems to have upset or destabilized the situation of relative forest homeostasis, adding its effects to those of the peasant clearings, it also brought with it, very early, the introduction of conservation projects, motivated by the need to preserve forest ecosystems associated with commercial forestry. As early as the end of the nineteenth century, colonial conservationists denounced the slash-and-burn agriculture *(ray)* of the upper region of Tonkin. At the same time, the confinement of highland minorities took place and the first forest reserves were constituted: 444 existed in 1930, totaling 2,250,000 hectares. In Tonkin, in 1921, the forester Jean Prades estimated that the forest had shrunk from six million hectares in 1900 to five million in 1909. At this early date, he had already evaluated at 1,200,000 hectares the deficit of forested land necessary to ensure an average supply of two cubic meters of wood per inhabitant per year, while maintaining the minimum of forest-land desirable in the tropics: 40% of the total area of the protectorate. The general tendency was to "tropicalize" European forestry, overriding the knowledge and customary practices of local forest populations, to whom part of the forested area— seldom much more than one-tenth of the total—was assigned as a reserve. For colonial engineers, these were necessary corollaries to the "durability" or "sustainability" of the forest's exploitation.[26]

French colonial development was, however, unable to exceed stubborn historic limits: obsolete economics and colonial capitalism's crushing and lasting emphasis on the export of raw materials led to a growth rate inferior to that in the British and Dutch colonies in Southeast Asia, with numerous shortfalls in comparison to the latter—there was no fertilizer industry, no metallurgy, no hydroelectric power, no jute industry, mechanization was restricted to certain sectors as a result of the very low level of wages, and modern inputs were lacking in the peasant economy. Most important was the total inability to move on toward diversified industrialization. In 1939, only 63,480 people used electric power.[27] The consumption of electricity per inhabitant was estimated at 2 kW/h in 1935 (as compared to 39 in France), and it was only in 1933 that a high-power electricity supply from Hanoi's power plant started to become available in the Red River Delta. Modern processing industries employed 150,000 workers at most in 1939.[28] According to a 1937 study, the production of these industries, combined with that of the mines, comprised only 19.6% of Indochina's national revenue.[29]

Relatively speaking, Indochina was the least "underindustrialized" of the French colonies: its portion of the empire's private industrial investments, excluding the Maghreb, increased from 19.2% in 1916 to 32.5% in 1940.[30] Starting in the 1920s, there was already theoretical consensus in colonial circles on the principle of the colony's industrialization. "Our Indochina will soon be the first among the industrial countries of Asia," Governor-General Maurice Long declared in 1921.[31] But the numerous development projects of this relatively industrialized colonial capitalism did not have an outcome that was fundamentally different from those of the other colonies. This is true, for instance, of the Sarraut plan of 1921, the Maginot program of 1929, the plan to equip the colonies elaborated by the Imperial Conference of 1934–35, the Programme quinquennal de travaux publics (Five-year Public Works Program) of 1939, the Vichy government's ten-year development plan of 1942, and lesser-known projects such as the vast program of investment defined by the Jeancard mission in 1918 in Tonkin, which projected the construction of a port in the bay of Ha Long and a powerful five-hundred-hectare industrial complex in Quang Yen. Major accomplishments took place mostly in the realm of infrastructure expansion and transportation, designed both to combine the three Vietnamese *ky* into a single, strategically and geopolitically integrated market and to emphasize exports.[32]

The economic model that those responsible for Indochinese colonization attempted to replicate was that of Java—a modern colonial capitalism, focused on the export of raw and semi-processed products, with high technical productivity and an elevated financial output; they never attempted to follow a model of general industrialization and development closer to the example of colonial India, the China of the lower Yangtze, or Japanese Manchuria until after 1945–46, and by then it was too late. These strong tendencies of colonial development persisted well beyond World War II. This historical inertia can be explained by the massive obstacles that industrialization encountered not only in the existence of very active peasant civilizations but, just as much, in the form of constraints and blockages specific to the foundational structures of the colonial capitalism established at the end of the nineteenth century.

THE STRUCTURES OF INDOCHINESE CAPITALISM

The first constraint on Indochinese capitalism was that it used a currency other than the French franc and interlocked with Asian financial structures. Indochina was the only large French colony where it was necessary to exchange money in transactions both with foreign countries and with France. This was true even for the administration, whose expenses were partly paid in francs.

The Unpredictable Piastre

Imposed by the necessities of colonial development in the Far Eastern context, this system was put in place, starting in 1858, by the transformation of the dual monetary systems—still very poorly understood—that had governed exchange in the Indochinese area since the beginning of the eighteenth century. These structures included, on the one hand, innumerable local currencies: the copper *latt* and iron ingots in Laos, the Siamese *tical,* the Cambodian *fuang* and *att,* and especially the ancient Vietnamese currency, *sapèques (dong)* made partly from copper but principally of zinc, whose individual units were worth very little, and which circulated in abundance in Vietnam and, in combination with bar silver *(nen),* were used in the majority of domestic transactions.

At Dai Nam, following Minh Mang's reforms, the striking and issuance of copper and zinc coins, of bars, ingots, and, since 1832, silver and gold coins had become a strict state monopoly, carried out in the monetary workshops of Bac Thanh, in Hanoi, and of Hue. But there was not enough money issued to meet the needs of the regional markets, and a sizeable counterfeit production subsisted. As a result, foreign silver coins also circulated in the Indochinese peninsula since the seventeenth century. Called dollars or piastres, these coins had a value of 5.30 to 5.50 francs: the Spanish piastre (also known as the *carolus* dollar), the Indian rupee, the British trade dollar, minted in Hong Kong, the American trade dollar, and especially the Mexican dollar or piastre. These were of similar weight and quality (ranging from 24.26 grams of refined silver for the British trade dollar to 24.43 grams for the Mexican piastre) and were used both for important domestic exchanges and in transactions with the exterior. At the end of the nineteenth century, the Mexican dollar was probably the most widespread coinage in the world and was hegemonic in all of East Asia.

The colonial reorganization of this monetary complex was slow and chaotic due to the impossibility of generalizing the use of the franc in a colony that was economically connected to the Asian area and dominated by silver money and the parallel circulation of the *sapèque* and the piastre. The use of the latter would increase rapidly with colonial conquest (an April 10, 1862, proclamation made its use compulsory; the principle of paying taxes in piastres was adopted on May 15, 1874; the first bills of 5, 20 and 100 piastres issued by the Banque de l'Indochine went into circulation on January 8, 1876; and the budget of Cochinchina was established in piastres in 1882), but would coexist for a long term with the *sapèque*. This coexistence became troubled following the end of regular *sapèque* minting in copper (1894) and in zinc (1903),[33] and the depreciation of silver after 1873, which had unleashed considerable speculation within the internal exchange market and caused the revaluation of the *sapèque*, a rise in domestic prices, and the impoverishment of peasants whose salaries were paid in *sapèques*. Meanwhile, the price of rice was fixed in piastres (1 piastre was worth 4,800 zinc *sapèques* in 1896, and between 2,100 and 2,400 in 1913).

Following an attempt to tie the *sapèque* to the piastre in 1902, and after the demonetarization of the former in 1914, monetary substitution was achieved, although not entirely, since brass *sapèques* were issued under Khai Dinh (1916–26) and once again in 1933; they were still used in rural Annam and Tonkin after 1939. The substitution was accomplished to the advantage of the piastre and its lower multiple, the cent. In effect, the efforts to impose the franc (in 1864 and 1878, and through Doumer's project of September 1897) by fixing a single legal exchange rate in francs for the different coins in circulation failed because of speculation. This consisted of the foreign purchase of low-value Mexican piastres and their exchange in Indochina for five-franc coins whose legal value was, in Cochinchina, lower than their intrinsic value. In September 1886, the Banque de l'Indochine was authorized to issue a French piastre, the so-called trade piastre, in the form of coins containing 24.3 grams of refined silver and notes that could be converted into metal. Once the Mexican piastre was demonetized (through the decrees of 1903 and 1906), this became the Indochinese monetary unit until the end the colonial period. After the decree of January 3, 1905, the import of foreign piastres was prohibited, as was the export of Indochinese piastres.

From then on, Indochina was integrated for a long time into the East Asian system of the silver standard, centered on the Chinese market. But, given that a number of countries in the region slowly abandoned the silver standard when the value of silver fell—either in favor of the creation of national currencies tied to the Gold Exchange Standard (India in 1893, Japan in 1897, the Philippines in 1903) or, more frequently, in favor of the Sterling Exchange Standard (the Straits in 1906, Siam in 1908)—Indochina actually found itself in a mixed monetary space organized around silver currencies, at least for as long as China and Hong Kong continued to use the silver standard, and around the pound sterling.[34]

The rate of the piastre was henceforth defined by three parameters: the relation of silver to gold, that of the franc to gold, and the evolution of the balance of payments in Indochina. Colonial currency would experience fluctuations inherent in the silver standard (fig. 3.1). All the monetary effects of silver fluctuations would accumulate in Indochina. They started with the catastrophic collapse that occurred between 1873 and 1914 and the resulting depreciation of the piastre in relation to the gold franc: from 6.25 francs in April 1864, it fell to 5 francs in 1876, 4.20 francs in January 1886, and 1.92 francs in November 1902. This in turn caused the inflation of domestic prices and enormous losses in exchanges with countries using the gold currency, though these were tempered by the countermeasures taken by the Gouvernement général from 1903 to 1905 (prohibition of exporting piastres, etc.). There was also the revaluation, from 1915 through the end of 1921, of silver and therefore of the piastre (between July 1915 and February 1920, its exchange rate with the franc increased by around 633%) amplified by inflation in France. This inflation caused difficulties in exportation to countries that used gold currency, so that it was necessary to establish the obligatory use of banknotes as legal tender in 1920–21. And, finally, there were the new decreases from February 1920 to the end of 1921, and stabilization until 1925. But after 1919, the repercussions of silver's volatility were compounded by the franc's depreciation, which provoked a fantastic increase in the piastre-franc exchange rate until July 1926 (27.50 francs to 1 piastre), which was ended by the stabilization of the franc in December 1926.

What we can see from this set of data is the increase in the risk of exchange, which translated into the extraordinary instability of the piastre's commercial rates on the currency market. This risk had three principal effects. First, scarcities of currency, repeated at the peak moments in monetary demands in the Far East and for foreign exchange, were often extremely brutal, as was the case in 1905, 1906, 1907, 1908, and 1919–21, for example. Second, there was permanent speculation that sought to draw profit from exchange, which was "detrimental to trade, with the exception of that of the banks,"[35] notably at the time of the devaluation of the franc.

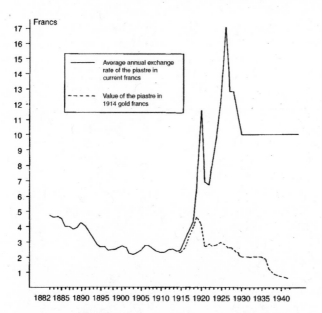

FIGURE 3.1. Fluctuations in the exchange rate of the piastre, 1882–1942. (Based on *Annuaires statistiques de l'Indochine, 1941–1942*; A. Touzet, *Le régime monétaire de l'Indochine* [Paris: Sirey, 1939], pp. 216–17.)

The piastre then acted as a currency of refuge. Thus, the devaluation of the franc in May 1938 was accompanied by massive purchases of piastres, practically equal in the course of the one month of May to those of the entire year of 1937. "Indochina," the governor-general marveled, "thus finds itself, accidentally and strangely, taking its place among the stopping places of errant capital."[36]

A final constraint occurred as a result of the risk of exchange: the necessity for all capital investments and all commercial operations to constitute an exchange reserve, often drawn from the financial reserves of companies and corporations, in order to absorb the possible losses at the time of the transfer of funds to the markets of western Europe. This exchange reserve could transform itself, in the context of certain situations or favorable exchange rates, into a fruitful basis for monetary profits. Monetary and commercial profit was thus overvalued, to the detriment of productive investment. Every decrease in the value of the piastre—the dominant tendency except during the interlude of 1915–26—favored the export sectors and hurt the expenditures of the administration, as well as the incomes of civil servants, whose salaries were fixed in francs but paid in piastres. It also incited the repatriation of revenue and capital to France in order to escape the consequences of the continuous fall of the exchange rate, weighed on Indochina's capacity for loans, imports, and consumption and burdened the movement of French investment in the colony with the threat of its eventual devaluation. In contrast, the rise of the piastre—for instance, during the good period from 1921 to 1926—made it an investment shelter for speculative metropolitan capital and increased the profits of exporters, and of rice growers in particular (because of the stable rates for rice), with an exchange bonus. In France, under the leftist majorities, the *mur d'argent* ("wall of money") gladly played Indochina off against the franc. In sum, risks and monetary profits weighed heavily on productive investment.

Until 1929, all the attempts at monetary reform favoring French investment through the adoption of the gold standard and a strong currency connected to the franc came up against the coalition of colonial interests. Reform was backed by supporters of an economically integrated colonial empire, as well as occasionally by the Indochinese Chambers of Commerce and the Commission monétaire (Monetary Commission) of 1920. Colonial interests in opposition were bound to the maintenance of the silver standard and of an autonomous currency for Indochina. It would also seem that the Banque de l'Indochine was opposed to the gold standard, inasmuch as premiums and profits from exchange constituted one of its main sources of income. "The leaders of the bank," one high-level civil servant wrote, "were well-placed to speculate either on the rise or the decrease of the piastre, with the certainty of success; they could, so to speak, never make a mistake, and as a result, every time that there was a change in rate, up or down, the bank always made a profit."[37] The crisis of the franc that opened up with the war of 1914 long deferred the pegging of the piastre to the gold standard or to the franc.

The conjunction of the stabilization of the franc in 1926 and its devaluation in June 1928, the fall of silver rates and of the piastre-franc exchange rate (17 francs in 1926, 11.46 francs in 1929), five years of massive investment of French capital in the colony, and China's preparation to abandon the silver standard, however, made the reform of Indochinese currency an unavoidable issue. Invested capital, after all, melted away at the same time as the exchange rate, and colonial loans in preparation could only be compromised by the weakening of the currency that the budget used to gage them. In 1928, in concert with the Gouvernement général, the Banque de l'Indochine converted to the gold standard, "a monetary system both flexible and powerful enough to be advantageously substituted for the present system, which has served us well, but whose time appears to have come and gone," as the bank's director, René Thion de la Chaume, wrote.[38] On May 31, 1930, the piastre was pegged to the franc at the rate of 10 francs, and therefore to the gold standard, which had the effect of maintaining the exchange rate of the franc to the piastre at an elevated level for several years. "The gold standard has restored security to external capital whose eventual use in Indochina is envisaged," the *Dépêche coloniale* declared.[39]

The Empire of the Bank

A second constraint weighed just as heavily on the development of the colonial economy: the credit structures implemented during the last quarter of the nineteenth century. If the modern bank appeared precociously—in 1863, with a Saigon branch of the Comptoir national d'escompte de Paris—the network of modern banks remained limited. In 1940, besides the Banque de l'Indochine (with eleven branches in Indochina), which functioned as a currency-issuing institution, there were seven other banks in operation in the colony: two British banks (the Hong Kong and Shanghai Banking Corporation and the Chartered Bank of India); the Banque franco-chinoise (BFC), created by Paribas with the support of Chinese capital, as well as a prudent and modest participation of the Banque de l'Indochine, to take over the business of the Banque industrielle de Chine, which went bankrupt in 1922; a small Vietnamese bank (the Société annamite de crédit, created in 1927); and three Chinese banks. But in 1940, the Banque de l'Indochine oversaw 50% of exchange operations, the two British banks 40%, and the Chinese banks 8%.[40] One feature that characterized these banks is that they only gave loans to the large French or Asian trading houses: in 1938, the BFC only had 108 current account debtors, while those of the Banque de l'Indochine's three branches in Saigon, Can Tho, and Phnom Penh numbered 433.

Discount credit was weakly developed, and average-term credit even less so; letters of exchange were rarely used, and the price of borrowing was elevated. The image of French banks common in the Chinese business milieu was "that they offer an umbrella when the weather is good and withdraw it as soon as it rains." On the other hand, there was a bubble in loans on jewelry and on gold, though essentially only in Cochinchina, notably on the part of the pawnshops formed by two powerful companies—Ogliastro, Huibonhoa, et Compagnie (1885) and Crédit mobilier indochinois (1930)—whose thirty-four branches made 704,000 loans of an average of 30 piastres (300 francs) in 1938.[41] Indochina did not possess a single investment bank per se, but there were speculative investments, rather considerable ones, in fact, by metropolitan French financial groups. Until 1945, all projects to create an investment bank, which would have fitted well into the direction of Sarraut's policy to "develop the colonies," remained in limbo: the Indochinese activities of the Crédit colonial (Colonial Credit) established by Paul Reynaud in August 1935 were minute, and the 1936 Moutet project to create a Fonds colonial (Colonial Fund) never left the files of the Ministry of the Colonies.

At the origin of this situation was the quasi-monopoly held by large-scale French banking capitalism united within the powerful Banque de l'Indochine, one of the two historic foundations of the present-day Crédit agricole Indosuez group. Remarkable studies by Marc Meuleau and Yasuo Gonjo provide rich analyses of its history.[42] Its power was rooted in its singular status: a private establishment, it was at once a currency-issuing institution, a commercial bank, a financial company, and a business bank. Its creation resulted from the initiative not only of the state, but of two large private banks: the Crédit industriel et commercial (CIC, 1859) and the Comptoir d'escompte de Paris (1848),[43] later transformed into the Comptoir national d'escompte de Paris. In the wake of the conquest, and in the context of its "merchant strategy" to develop a network of agencies along the main intercontinental commercial paths between 1860 and 1869,[44] the Comptoir opened nine agencies in the Far East along the French Marseille-Shanghai maritime route, including one in Saigon. This provides added proof that the most modern French business milieus were precociously involved in colonization.

Because the particular status of both of these institutions limited their banking operations, in 1873, they elaborated—in concert with the state but independently of each other—two projects for the development of a great Asian financial establishment with multiple functions, capable of financing the colonial economy that had to be created. In November 1874, they merged these projects, and with their respective allies (including Paribas, the important Paris bank, and funds from Lyon, Marseille, Strasbourg, and Belgium) invested 8 million francs in initial capital. The Banque de l'Indochine was created on January 21, 1875. Supplementary capital was contributed by Paribas in 1881; by the Société générale, which had been tempted for a time by the privilege of issuing money in Tonkin, in 1888; and by the Crédit lyonnais in 1896; all three obtained seats on the Banque de l'Indochine's board of directors. At this point, the bank acquired its definitive structure: that of a private bank playing the dual roles of issuing money and of acting as a central bank. It succeeded in uniting the large French banks in Asia against the British banks, and this unity translated into a system of co-management by five banks, instituted between 1888 and 1896.

Endowed at its creation with the renewable privilege of issuing currency for twenty years, the Banque de l'Indochine exercised unusually broad functions— discounting promissory notes (escompte), credit, advances, exchange, deposits— and had the right to found branches not only in all French possessions in the Far East but throughout Asia. Though often conflict-ridden, the marriage of convenience between the bank and the French state quickly assured it of remarkable prosperity. Starting in 1879, gross profits and dividends took off, though between 1885 and 1898, the earnings of Asian branches weakened under the effect of the depression of the Far Eastern economy, of the ultraprotectionist tariff of 1887, and of the crisis of the piastre. Over the long haul, turnover increased sevenfold in gold francs between 1898 and 1924, and the statements of accounts increased eightfold between 1898 and 1929. A colonial bank like any other from the outset, the Banque de l'Indochine was unusual in having branches in many places. This enabled it to become one of the first French banking networks overseas. Indeed, it covered an immense area: the bank of Cochinchina and India until 1887, it spread its activities to New Caledonia in 1888, then to the remainder of Indochina (Hanoi in 1887, Phnom Penh and Tourane in 1891), to Hong Kong (1894), to China, to Siam (1896), to Singapore (1905), and to Djibouti, issuing five different currencies.

In its management, the power of the founding banks—whose points of views often diverged—remained essentially intact until the Vichy law on banks (December 1940), which is why, unlike other colonial banks, its seat was located in Paris. In 1917, two hundred to two hundred and fifty shareholders owned 51% of the capital, among whom the top hundred made up the general assembly. Until 1931, the French government had no representative on the bank's board of directors (table 3.1), only a government commissioner with observer status, lacking any right of veto. The bank's managing director only exercised authority in the name of the board, and the arrival of six directors nominated by the state in 1931 hardly modified power relations in the establishment's upper echelons. After 1918 and especially during the 1930s, these echelons attained increased autonomy through staff that rose through the ranks in its central administration, dominated by several personalities: Stanislas Simon, director since 1888 and president of the bank in 1927; Octave Homberg, a surprising financier, the son of a regent of the Banque de France and former collaborator of Théophile Delcassé's at the Foreign Ministry, who was the secretary-general of the bank in 1907; and René Thion de la Chaume, who came from the Inspection des finances (Financial Inspectorate) and the cabinet of Joseph Caillaux, who was secretary-general in 1909, then director in 1920.

A power that dealt with the government of Indochina as an equal, the Banque de l'Indochine preferred increasing its capital (as it did five times between 1875 and 1919) by selling new shares at a premium and granting the privilege of preferential subscription to the first shareholders, rather than by issuing bonds or appealing to the fraction of non-liberated capital (the invested capital was only equal to a quarter of the nominal capital until 1919, a date when the latter was 95% liberated, but through an allocation from the reserves), in order to increase its securities in the stock market (a share worth 500 francs reached 12,000 francs in 1931, or 2,400 gold francs) and especially to preserve the control of large Paris banks in defining its orientations. Until 1931, it did not have to pay any fees to the state. Owing to its political clout, reinforced by its director's role; its relations with politicians like Raymond Poincaré and Albert Sarraut; and the presence in its headquarters of numerous *inspecteurs des Finances* (inspectors of finances), who during the 1930s included Paul Baudoin, Jean Laurent (a former member of Poincaré's staff and future director general of the bank from 1945 to 1952), and François de Flers, the Banque de l'Indochine's privileges were extended without great difficulty until 1920.

But at that point, its relations with the state became strained. The bank was opposed to all attempts at reform: the project of December 1917, the Sarraut plan of

TABLE 3.1 Board of directors of the Banque de l'Indochine, 1927

Composition of the board[a]

President	Stanislas Simon, former managing director of the Banque de l'Indochine, president of the Compagnie des chemins de fer de l'Indochine et du Yunnan
Vice president	Paul Boyer, president of the Comptoir national d'escompte de Paris
Members	Émile Bethenod, honorary president of the Crédit lyonnais;
	Alphonse Denis, president of the Denis Frères companies of Indochina and Bordeaux;
	Charles Georges-Picot, vice president of the Société générale;
	Henri Guernaut, honorary assistant governor of the Banque de France, honorary president of the Société générale;
	André Homberg, president of the Société générale;
	Octave Homberg, president of the Société financière française et coloniale;
	Jules Rostand, vice president of the Comptoir national d'escompte de Paris;
	Ernest Roume, former governor general of Indochina;
	Edgar Stern, director of the Banque de Paris et des Pays Bas;
	De Trégomain, former director of the Mouvement général des fonds at the Ministry of Finances, honorary governor and administrator of the Crédit foncier de France
Director	René Thion de la Chaume, former inspector of finances
Assistant directors	Maurice Lacaze, Gaston Mayer, Jules Perreau
Government commissioner	André You, honorary director in the Ministry of the Colonies, former state adviser

Distribution of the board's 16 seats

Société générale	4
Comptoir national d'escompte	2
Crédit lyonnais	1
Banque de Paris et des Pays Bas	1
Crédit foncier	1
Colonial big business	1
Staff of the Banque de l'Indochine	5
Senior colonial officials	1

[a] Note the weak representation of industrialists and the general absence of investors (with the exception of Octave Homberg) within the board of directors.

June 1922, and especially the Daladier project of 1924–25 aimed at creating a new currency-issuing institution that would establish control over discount rates, institute the remittance to the state of a part of its profits, with the goal of financing colonial development, and allow for the choice of its leaders by the government.[45] These interventionist projects, in particular that of a new currency-issuing bank, although supported by Paribas, the Banque de l'Union parisienne, and the Homberg group, only slowly and partially become a reality through the convention of

November 16, 1929, confirmed by the law of March 31, 1931. These projects gave the state definitive control over 20% of the Banque de l'Indochine's capital, the right to nominate 30% of its administrators and its president, and the right to a royalty and treasury advances granted to those colonies in which the bank exerted the right of issuance. But in actuality, this was only a rearrangement of the relations between the bank and the state. The director was still nominated by the board and the power of the small leading group of the establishment was hardly undermined: Stanislas Simon remained president, and his friend Thion de la Chaume retained his position as director. The latter became president in 1932, after the death of Simon, and was not relieved of that function until November 1936—the only success of the reformist intentions of Marius Moutet and his director of economic affairs, Louis Mérat, whose project to create a public currency-issuing institution didn't even reach Parliament.[46] The bank preserved control of its short-term credit rates and the amount of its advances, that is, of its essential functions.[47]

The judgment of the economist William Oualid in 1923 remained entirely valid ten years later: "The Banque de l'Indochine is an oligarchic organization, in which the appearance of nominal sovereignty of a shareholders' meeting . . . actually masks the omnipotence of the group of the large banks that created it, whose unity is only sometimes broken by rivalry and difference of interests in other domains, and where the omnipotence of private interests, however highly respectable, is not counterbalanced as in all another establishments of issuance by a constant intervention on the part of the state."[48] Until the convention of July 1947, which withdrew the privilege of issuance from the bank (though it was not applied until January 1, 1952), and in spite of the marked hostility of a certain number of large Parisian business banks (Paribas, Union parisienne), the issuance of Indochinese currency was the work of a powerful subsidiary of a syndicate of large French banks based in the metropole and created under the Second Empire (see table 3.1). "In sum," Oualid concluded, "financial interests prevail over colonial interests."[49]

This image is certainly confirmed by a brief examination of the bank's Indochinese activities, which put into place, rather than a dynamic investment policy, a "financial strategy" focused on research and on the security of banking profits in the strictest sense. Certainly, this verdict could be somewhat mitigated. The Banque de l'Indochine directly supported the financing of Doumer's infrastructure development program by successfully placing Indochinese loans on the French market. It provided credit to large Indochinese enterprises placing their securities. But it invested little. Prior to 1930, it only very cautiously used its right to involve itself in the creation of companies, granted by the reform of its statutes of May 16, 1900. These statutes made it a universal bank, but its Indochinese investments were limited to secure businesses. In 1928, it was only involved in eighteen of the Indochinese firms quoted on the Paris stock exchange (mines, distilleries, electric companies, credit companies). But it remains true that it was allied to the powerful Société financière française et coloniale (French and Colonial Financial Company, a holding company, founded by Octave Homberg, that had interests in twenty-three companies in Indochina in 1929), which it bailed out in the years from 1930 to 1935. It is also true that it played an advisory role with new companies and that it assured them of the indispensable banking services necessary for their growth. But it was only after the crisis of 1929 that the Indochinese investments of the bank became more systematic.

The Banque de l'Indochine's essential activities were twofold. First, it focused on exchange operations: the buying and selling of commercial drafts on bills for goods, in order to pay for the transactions, both in France, where it had at its disposition its central office and the network of CNEP branches, and in foreign countries. Second, it also handled operations with exchange premiums nourished by the fluctuations of exchange rates between Far Eastern currencies (table 3.2). Exchange alone, notably with China, represented two-thirds of the bank's operations in 1914, nearly three-quarters in 1922, and 70% in 1923.[50] In Saigon, at the end of the 1920s, it carried out more than half of all exchange operations.[51] Situated at the heart of an immense international network at the hinge between the gold and silver monetary systems, the "French Bank" was a true generator of currencies that maintained control of the means of payment from the colony to foreign countries, fixing their price and premium. To obtain exchange outside of Indochina, one had to go through the bank, which profited considerably from exchange operations such as the ability to buy remittances (remises) when rates were low and sell the drawings (tirages) when the rates were high. From 1875 to 1914, the premium for the exchange of the piastre for the Hong Kong dollar was on average 2.50%, with variations of around 14%. Both types of operations procured, without great risk, substantial banking charges (agios) and exchange profits (arbitrages). These amounts are difficult to isolate in the establishment's accounts; however, according to Oualid—an author highly critical of the institution, it is true—they constituted 80% of profits in 1920. According to the Lasserre report of 1937 "[they] assured enormous benefits due to the very elevated margins of banking charges and exchange premiums in the Far East."[52] Certainly, this was one of the Banque de l'Indochine's main sources of profit.

The Banque de l'Indochine's actual credit operations essentially took the form of discounted credit advances for periods of up to six months on real securities (merchandise, warrants, pledges, etc.). Discount credit was relatively restricted: it comprised around a third of its total operations in 1919, against two-thirds in the other French colonial banks, and in 1921, it only amounted to half of its advances.[53] As for average and long-term credit, it was insignificant, hindered through the bank's legal obligations, which resulted from its twofold function as an institution of monetary issuance and credit. The central mode of financing in the Indochinese economy was that of six-month renewable credit. Interest rates, especially on short-term

TABLE 3.2 Operations of Indochinese branches of
the Banque de l'Indochine, 1919 fiscal year

Operation	Amount (in current francs)	Percent
Loans, discounts, advances	1,492,521,842	19.3
advances = 1,016,713,190		
Deposits to checking accounts	2,952,013,923	38.2
Exchange	3,273,879,993	42.4
issuances = 1,578,416,211		
remittances = 1,695,473,781		
TOTAL	7,718,415,758	

SOURCE: W. Oualid, *Le privilège de la Banque de l'Indo-Chine et la question des banques coloniales* (Paris, 1923), p. 99.

loans, were higher than those in France (the average interest rate of the Banque de France did not surpass 4% from 1875 to 1913), higher than in the other colonies, and higher than those in other places of the Far East:[54] 6% to 12%, for example, in 1919, as against 8% in West Africa. More moderate during the Great Depression, the interest rate on short-term loans was nevertheless maintained at between 5% and 7% from September 1933 to August 1937.

These high rates, along with the lack of cash, became grievances that settlers directed at the bank, often supported by the administration. Certainly, one should examine these complaints carefully, since the risks incurred were high. But there is no doubt that short-term loans and advances were granted unequally to different sectors of the colonial economy. Moreover, no more than fifteen towns in all of Indochina had banking facilities. In 1921, 47.1% of banking operations concerned trade, 30% industry, 12.5% mines, and only 10.3% agriculture.[55] The great majority went to European enterprises (84% of the total of 1921 versus 14% to Asians). It was therefore the export of products to the world market that profited most from these operations—domestic trade received very little credit from the bank, receiving 4% of the total discount rate in 1938[56]—leaving large profits from the commissions paid and allowing profitable speculation on exchange rates and on prices of raw materials.

The Banque de l'Indochine essentially financed the colony's foreign trade—more than half of rice exports from the port of Saigon—and very little agriculture. This constituted the second major grievance directed at the bank's directors by settlers and by the Vietnamese bourgeoisie. Agricultural credit represented only 10.7% of the bank's Indochinese operations at the end of 1927, and 18.9% in 1929,[57] and this was mostly in the form of rediscounted loans to the Cochinchinese SICAM, whose principal beneficiaries were the large Vietnamese rice growers. The amount of the loans guaranteed by harvests—in principle, one of the primary reasons for its existence—was minuscule: from 447,000 francs in 1890, it fell to 15,000 francs in 1899, and reached 255,000 francs in 1919 (while during the period, the same loans rose to 2 million in Martinique) and 580,000 francs in 1938.[58] The bank only participated in the agricultural economy of Indochina on a small scale, and it survived the crises of that economy, notably those from 1920 to 1921 and 1929 to 1935, without many problems. "The bank has not been of any use to agriculture."[59]

Furthermore, the size of the Banque de l'Indochine's Chinese activities indirectly weighed on the growth of credit supply in Indochina. Initially, these did not arise from a strategic engagement on the part of the bank, but from a choice of the political power structure, specifically, Gabriel Hanotaux, then minister of foreign affairs, who imposed them against the will of the bank's leaders in November 1897.[60] Following an agreement to partition the Chinese financial market between the Quai d'Orsay and the Banque russo-chinoise (Russian-Chinese Bank), the bank was pressed by the government to take responsibility, after July 1898, for the penetration of French banks into China south of the Yangtze; with Belgian support, the Banque russo-chinoise was granted access to the northern half of China. Since its foundation in 1894, the Banque de l'Indochine's Hong Kong branch had been highly autonomous on the financial level, and it was soon directly linked to the bank's Paris office. A Shanghai branch was opened in July 1898, soon followed by those of Canton (1902), Hankow (1902), Tianjin, and Beijing (1907). As "the financial arm of French imperialism in Asia" (Meuleau), it was no longer only a colonial bank but one of the most active commercial and business banks in China, deeply involved in railroad projects and in the investing of the Chinese state. This created a breach in British banking hegemony in Asia. As early as 1900, the Banque de l'Indochine played an important role in the creation of highly profitable businesses like the Yunnan railroad.

The Banque de l'Indochine very rapidly became autonomous in relation to French politics, merging diplomacy and business. In 1908, it allied itself to the Hong Kong and Shanghai Banking Corporation and to the Deutsche Asiatische Bank, and in 1909–13, it became the French leader of the famous Consortium international des affaires chinoises (International Consortium of Chinese Affairs), which attempted to put the Chinese Republican Government under financial tutelage. It also participated in the second Consortium launched by Washington in October 1920 to counterbalance Japanese expansion. An adversary of the Banque industrielle de Chine (Industrial Bank of China)—established by Paribas with the support of Philippe Berthelot, the Quai d'Orsay, and Beijing, among other reasons, to combat the Banque de l'Indochine's influence—it drove its rival to bankruptcy in 1922,[61] and it was able to preserve its positions in China until 1948. As is shown in table 3.3, its nine Chinese branches constituted a privileged domain for the bank, which even temporarily opened a branch in Vladivostok in 1918. In 1913, 32.6%

TABLE 3.3 Percentage of the Banque de l'Indochine's operations
conducted by Chinese and Indochinese branches, 1920

Operation	Chinese branches	Saigon branch and Indochinese agencies
Discounts and receipts paid	37	43.7
Advances	30.6	43.5
Exchange operations	53	22.4
Deposits	45.2	27.9
Cash flow transactions, including notes/bills	57.1	16.6

SOURCE: Oualid, *Privilège de la Banque de l'Indo-Chine*, p. 103.

of the Banque de l'Indochine's regular operations were in Indochina, but 46.3% took place in China,[62] and the banking activities of branches in China, Bangkok, and Singapore represented 70% of its total activity in 1920.[63] Between 1904 and 1913, Indochinese profits represented 55% of the total, whereas Chinese profits represented 31.6%.[64]

It was Indochina—along with other colonies where the bank operated—that long provided the resources the bank drew on: 621 million piastres in 1920, of which 76% were banknotes, 8.8% deposits in Indochina and in the colonies, and 14.6% foreign deposits, to which should be added the investment in China of the account opened up for the Indochinese Treasury in August 1900, which almost always had a credit, containing 10 to 20 million piastres in normal periods. The profitability of the Can Tho branch (founded in 1926) exceeded, after 1928, that of the Chinese branches. "The bank, which gets more than five-sixths of its resources from the inhabitants of our colonies, carries out half of its credit operations outside of them," Oualid wrote in 1923,[65] a conclusion today shared by the Japanese historian Yasuo Gonjo: "In exporting the funds of the colonial Treasury, the bank essentially aimed to reduce the capital surplus of the Saigon branch . . . and to maintain a certain elasticity of banking profits in Indochina. These capital exports permitted the bank's total profits to be carried to their maximum, but also represented a reduction of capital destined for the colony's development."[66]

The desire to assure the stability of dividends and investments in China helps to explain the systematic policy of increasing its own funds by redeeming loans and creating large reserves, which was pursued very early on by the Banque de l'Indochine's staff (table 3.4). The amount of just those reserves in current francs increased from 0.7 million in 1884 (with a capital of 2 million actually deposited) to 48.6 million in 1914 (with 12 million in deposited capital), to 18.8 million in 1919 (with 45.6 million in deposited capital), and to 146.8 million in 1939 (with 120 million of deposited capital).[67]

TABLE 3.4 Transactions in amortization and currency reserves
of the Banque de l'Indochine, 1919 and 1921 (in current francs)

	1919	1921
Capital paid	45,600,000	68,400,000
Total reserves	23,307,000	75,052,000
Reserves toward endowment	4,400,000	50,000,000
fund for the agencies of China,	(18.8% of	(68.4% of
Siam, and Singapore	total reserves)	total reserves)

SOURCE: Oualid, *Privilège de la Banque de l'Indo-Chine*, p. 104.

The Banque de l'Indochine was a unique case, at once the issuing bank of the French empire, east of Suez (with the exception of Madagascar), the bank of the Indochinese state, for whose Treasury it acted, and a bank of business and commerce not only in these colonies but also in Hong Kong (the most important branch outside Indochina), in China, and in the rest of Southeast Asia. It was in fact a universal bank established at the key links in the vast financial circuit that united Europe and the Far East. Its strategy was multinational, based on arbitrations between locales, transfer and recycling of funds, notably in China and, after 1930, especially in France, then in Africa, of the profits accrued in Indochina. "It is an invincible temptation," wrote Oualid, "for it to use the resources of its privilege in such a way as to give it an advantage in its operations abroad. . . . As an issuing bank, it uses [its resources] in order to participate in colonial or foreign affairs it is interested in . . . without concerning itself with the specific interests of the colony insofar as they don't coincide with its own."[68] The Banque de l'Indochine weighed heavily on French colonial development. In fine banking logic, it was the central operator in the growth of a capitalism that exported products that were barely processed. In short, until the mid 1950s, the Banque de l'Indochine perpetuated a colonial economy that still marks the Indochinese region.

The Deficiencies of Agricultural Credit

Indochina's unusual credit structure—at once highly monopolized and extremely globalized—constituted a formidable obstacle to Indochinese economic development. The Banque de l'Indochine built an insurmountable dam that prevented the appearance of a modern national capitalism as in India, as is shown by the experience of the Société annamite de Crédit, the brainchild of Cochinchinese constitutionalist leaders. Created in February 1927, with a great deal of help from patriotic appeals, it languished, and was soon reduced to one branch, a mere Cochinchinese micro-bank. Moreover, the lack of participation of the Banque de l'Indochine in agricultural credit forced the majority of peasants to turn to usury, which swelled to unprecedented proportions with colonization.[69]

In Cochinchina, an entire network of lenders offering loans against the collateral of the harvest, at a minimum of 2% per month, was established by Chinese traders linked to the manufacturers and merchants of Saigon-Cholon. Large landowners, and the rural notables, as important in this domain as the Chinese lenders, were equally active in the three Vietnamese countries (Cochinchina, Annam, Tonkin). This network financed the harvests and subjugated the peasantry. Occasional loans were offered by professional Indian bankers, the *chettys* (of whom there were more than three hundred in Cochinchina in 1931), who invested in usurious loans, especially to rice growers, with capital coming from India or accumulated in Indochina. In 1932, the Service des prêts fonciers (Land Loan Service) estimated that debts to *chettys* and to Vietnamese and Chinese moneylenders totaled around 250 million piastres, half of all agrarian debt, or 13% of the amount of advances, discount loans, and other loans by the Banque de l'Indochine. Until 1945, Chinese and Indian moneylenders dominated the rural loan market in spite of the administration's efforts to organize inexpensive agricultural credit. Indochinese peasants were thus excluded from all access to modern credit, without which they were unable to modernize their production or stall their descent into underdevelopment.

In Cochinchina, the twenty Sociétés indigènes de crédit agricole mutuel (Indigenous Mutual Agricultural Credit Companies, SICAM; with 14,000 members in 1930), created by Albert Sarraut in 1912, only loaned small sums at 10% to 12%. The Crédit foncier (Land Credit), created in February 1923 by the great Indochinese companies and by the Banque de l'Indochine, only participated in urban investment. Its subsidiary bank, the Crédit foncier agricole (Agricultural Land Credit), created in 1928 (it became the Crédit hypothécaire de l'Indochine— Mortgage Credit of Indochina—in 1933), was more involved in agriculture, though rather late. But it only granted loans to large rice growers (a total of 90 million francs in 1931), and it primarily assumed the role of managing the exceptional loans granted during the Great Depression. In the protectorates, where the delay in drawing up cadastral surveys prevented the generalization of mortgages, the Crédit populaire agricole (Popular Agricultural Credit) (founded in July 1927), inspired by the Dutch example in Java, consented to small loans at 15%, but its impact was limited. In 1933, it had 90,000 members and loans totaling 375,000 piastres; in 1941, the totals were 184,000 members and 3.7 million piastres loaned, essentially in Annam and Tonkin.[70] As was shown by the government's survey in 1930, these initiatives only really benefited big landowners, landlords, and often also traditional bankers, who borrowed money from government agencies and reinvested it in the form of interest-paying loans.

Investments and Investors

In the absence of a true investment bank, the circulation of capital was therefore either the work of the colonial state or the result of speculative medium-term investments, which in combination were decisive in the historical development of Indochinese capitalism. The two principal features of investment in Indochina were its rigidity and the external focus of its effects: it engendered the emergence of economic sectors entirely oriented toward the global market and, furthermore, tended to dearticulate the various economic structures of the peninsula; its flows changed little in the long run. Still, many data remain to be collected by historians: we do not yet have satisfactory evaluations of the tides of capital that irrigated the Indochinese economy up until 1945, and we know even less of the period thereafter. Today, it remains difficult to assess with certitude the quantities of capital exported from France and the investments effectively realized with it—the amount in shares and bonds issued was far from being synonymous with invested capital, and like other faraway places, Indochina had its phantom companies, bluffing French investors. It is difficult to evaluate with any precision public investment, tax uses, the annual self-financing of enterprises, the gross structure of fixed capital, or profits, and to separate the latter into those transferred outside Indochina and those reinvested there. What are presented here are therefore only provisional evaluations, necessarily subject to revision.

Of all French colonies, Indochina was, after Algeria, the one that received the. most investment. Between 1896 and 1940, at least 52 billion 1940 francs of public and private funds were invested, roughly 6.2 billion 1914 francs,[71] according to the figures of the September 1943 investigation of the Secrétariat d'État aux Colonies (Office of the Undersecretary of State for the Colonies),[72] which were taken up again in 1947 by the Indochina Subcommittee of the Commissariat général au Plan.[73] According to the data available today, investments totaled between 2.9 and 6.7 billion francs (table 3.5). Like all the statistics given below, these figures are only provisional. Two facts can be determined from them. First, from 1914 to 1940, Indochina's share of France's total colonial investment—which ended up representing close to half of the French foreign investments in 1939—increased from one-sixth to close to one-fifth (table 3.6). Second, investment in Indochina presented trends analogous to those illuminated by Jacques Marseille for colonial investment in general,[74] notably the alternation of public and private investment according to the successive conjunctures in the development of the colonial economy (table 3.7).

The role of public capital (direct budgetary investments and the product of the seven Indochinese loans granted from 1896 to 1940), financed by the different budgets of Indochina, that is, by the taxation of the social product of the peasantry, was very influential from the beginning. For the period from 1890 to 1914, Marseille—who does not always specify his calculation methods—has estimated it at 300 million gold francs,[75] to which can be added the 425.9 million francs in loans granted by France to the Gouvernement général and guaranteed by Indochina's tax revenue, that is to say, a total of 726 million gold francs, or 77.3% of the total known investments from before 1914. The total amount of loans granted from 1896

TABLE 3.5 Investment in Indochina, 1880–1940: estimates compared

Investments	In 1939/1940 francs, current rate	In 1914 francs, adjusted for inflation
A. Public loans[a]	14,162,277,000 (1940 rate)	1,699,440,000
B. Private investments by companies		
1. Estimate of the 1943 public survey[b]	38,458,602,000 (1940 rate)	3,567,312,000
2. "Broad" estimate of Paul Bernard and Jean Bourgoin (1947)	33,400,000,000 (1939 rate)	5,010,000,000
3. Partial estimate of Henri Lanoue (1954):		
a. Direct investments (issuance of stocks and bonds), per *Annuaires statistiques de l'Indochine*	11,644,000,000 (1940 rate)	1,397,280,000
b. Issuance of stocks and self-financing since 1924, per *Répertoire des sociétés anonymes indochinoises* of 1944	10,074,000,000 (1940 rate)	1,208,880,000
TOTAL (A and B)		2.9–6.7 billion gold francs

SOURCE: Data for public loans are derived from table 3.7; for private investments, from table 3.9.

[a]The direct budgetary investment has never been the subject of comprehensive study.

[b]Issuance of company stocks and bonds, self-financing of companies, investments of unincorporated businesses.

TABLE 3.6 Indochina's place in France's colonial investment: a partial assessment

	Colonial investments in 1914 (in millions of francs)			Colonial investments in 1940 (in billions of 1940 francs)		
	Public	*Private*	*Total*	*Public*	*Private*	*Total*
Investments in the Empire, including North Africa	2,884.2	1,276.3	4,160.5	69.8	223.7	293.5
Investments in Indochina	425.9	230.6	656.5	14.1	39.1	53.2
	(14.7%)	(18%)	(15.7%)	(20.2%)	(17.4%)	(18.1%)

SOURCE: Statistics compiled by J. Marseille, with particular reference to the 1943 public survey by the State Secretariat to the Colonies on investments in the colonies ("La politique métropolitaine d'investissements coloniaux dans l'entre-deux-guerres," in *La Position internationale de la France: Aspects économiques et financiers, XIXe–XXe siècles,* ed. M. Lévy-Leboyer [Paris: Éditions de l'École des hautes études en sciences sociales, 1977]).

to 1940 would increase to 14,160 million 1939 francs, the equivalent of a little bit more than a billion of 1914 francs (see table 3.7).[76] Until 1914, the role of loans in public investments was considerable; the three great loans of 1896, 1898 (the large loan of 200 million francs destined for Doumer's rail program), and 1909 (409 million francs over thirteen years) financed more than 60% of infrastructure expenses. However, the part of these loans within public investments diminished rapidly

TABLE 3.7 Public loans and issuance of stocks in Indochinese companies, 1880–1940

Period	Public loans In 1914 francs adjusted for inflation[a]	Percent	Issuance of company stocks In 1914 francs adjusted for inflation[a]	Percent
1880–1914	425,969,000 (12,529,000)	39.9	211,894,000 (6,232,000)	19.1 }77
1915–1929	159,437,000 (11,388,000)	14.9	640,545,000 (45,753,000)	57.9
1930–1935	393,367,000 (78,673,000)	36.8	150,552,000 (30,110,000)	13.6 }22.8
1936–1940	88,469,000 (22,117,000)	8.2	102,731,000 (25,683,000)	9.2
TOTAL	1,067,242,000		1,105,722,000	

SOURCE: 1943 public survey on investments in the colonies, CAOM, Affaires économiques, 52. The survey, which uses a purely monetary deflator (the relationship between the successive gold values of the franc), gives the figures, in 1940 francs, of 14,162,277,000 for public loans and 17,837,602,000 for issuance of company stocks. The raw data of the present table have been deflated year by year following the method indicated in note 71 of the present chapter. We thank Mme O. Hardy-Hémery, professor at Université de Lille-III, for her advice in choosing a coefficient for the conversion of current francs to inflation-adjusted francs.

[a]Annual averages are given in parentheses.

after 1905 (fig. 3.2), even though Sarraut had obtained the vote for a fourth loan of 90 million francs on December 26, 1912. Meanwhile, direct budgetary investment little by little took over, furnishing 83.3% of the public funds mobilized between 1914 and 1923.[77] As for private investment, it featured an energy undoubtedly superior to that of public investment from 1915 to 1929 (see table 3.7), the latter guaranteeing the profitability of the former. It was well and truly the Indochinese peasantry, mostly Vietnamese and Khmer, who by their poverty and labor, financed the public investment through their taxes.

From 1920 to 1938, investment of public funds in Indochina (app. 4) probably reached 529,129,000 piastres (of which 165 million went to military expenditures), or about 1.2 billion 1914 francs.[78] It increased dramatically—in current piastres as in francs—between 1927 and 1934, and then fell back to its previous level (see fig. 3.3 below), but after 1930, particularly from 1931 to 1934, it was increasingly financed by loans. Between 1931 and 1934, such loans financed 81% of the expenditure on new public works.[79] With the collapse of the Indochinese budgets—in 1932 and 1934, it was necessary to take out two treasury loans, as had been the case in 1896—state-controlled investments were sustained during the Great Depression only with recourse to the French financial market. This was only possible after the vote in favor of the great Maginot program of colonial public works signed into law on February 22, 1931 (out of 3,600 million francs borrowed by six separate sec-

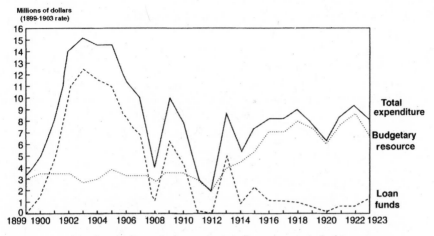

FIGURE 3.2. Actual expenditure on the economic infrastructure in Indochina, 1899–1923.

tions between 1931 and 1937, 1,372 million were allocated to Indochina, of which 705 had been raised by May 1935). Of this loan, 1,516 million francs were actually invested in 1940. The payment of the debt, until then slight, henceforth represented roughly 10% of the general budget.

The Economic Functions of the Colonial State

The orientation of this state "developmentalism" largely explains the paths followed by colonial economic growth. The economic initiative of colonial power was concentrated on the construction of railroads, roads, and ports, and on the valorization of sectors that were most profitable for private capital, that is, the export sectors. But the economic function of the colonial state cannot be considered purely instrumental. In fact, it became the site of confrontation between numerous contradictory requirements, none of which it could ignore: the interests of the French export industries, struggles for influence among the various investing sectors of French financial capitalism, the particular demands of the European landowning settlers and traders, the Chinese trading houses, the Vietnamese rural and commercial middle class, and the peasant societies' imperatives of social reproduction. From these arose innumerable contradictory pressures and, in times of crisis, particularly difficult arbitrations. Without doubt, beyond the often acute distrust and conflict among the different groups of colonial capitalism and the Gouvernement général, there was, in the long run, a complementarity to their initiatives and a profound compatibility between them. This is evidenced by the inverse synchronicity between the issuance of shares by companies and of public loans (see table 3.7). The latter prepared for and preceded the fresh supply of money from companies during the initial phase of equipping the colony from 1880 to 1914, and substituted for private investment between 1930 and 1935, when the latter was sagging. But the multiplicity of interests and the colonial situation gave the Indochinese state a unique capacity for initiative. In Indochina, as in other colonies, the state exercised much more than a simple function of support and compensation for private investments.

The state was in fact the permanent organizing structure for the accumulation of capital. The Gouvernement général had its own economic conceptions and especially its own development strategy, which often diverged from the practices of the principal Indochinese companies, as is evidenced by the numerous conflicts that opposed it to the Banque de l'Indochine. If there was a general understanding between them on essential issues, as is attested by the relentless policy of contracting credit and issuing currency, of "purifying" the fabric of colonial enterprises, that the government carried out during the crisis of 1929–34, today we are beginning to see that the colonial empire, far from being the site of economic intervention on the part of an archaic bureaucracy, constituted on the contrary a testing ground for modern forms of state economic action.

In this regard, Indochina was only a particular case of a universal trend. Thus, the appropriation of an immense territorial domain by the colonial state, this "colonial nationalization" of space, was the first stage in land concessions to an emergent landowning capitalism. It was a formidable expropriation for the land's real users, such as, for example, many peasant communities in the Middle Region of Tonkin between 1885 and 1897, following its military conquest. In Cochinchina, the administration's confiscation of lands considered abandoned, communal, or "vacant"—notably the forests where populations of hunter-gatherers and itinerant farmers lived—was undertaken starting in 1863, and in January 1902, state property already totaled 3.7 million hectares.[80] The policy of auctioning land (starting in 1865) was long tempered by another policy of free concessions granted on the condition that the land was cultivated (starting in 1889), favorable to small and medium-scale colonization, usually exploited through farming, by individuals. Some 400,000 hectares were given as free concessions as of 1911 to 254 Frenchmen, of whom 110 were civil servants, 42 colonists and planters, and 36 Catholic missionaries. But in December 1913, a new regulation, applicable to the whole of Indochina, generalized auction sales that favored large-scale capitalist exploitation; it was further reinforced by the measures of October 1924 and November 1928, completed by a lightened fiscal system (deferred taxes for seven years for rubber tree growers, etc.). Henceforth, free concessions limited to less than ten hectares were granted with more restraint. This basic policy achieved its broadest implementation between 1920 and 1930, a period during which 634,350 hectares were conceded in the three Vietnamese ky to European colonists (421,000 hectares

TABLE 3.8 Infrastructure expenditures, 1899–1923 (percent)

Agricultural hydraulics and inland navigation	15.3
Dredging	5.2
Railroads	36.3 ⎫
Roads	25 ⎬ 68.1
Ports	6.8 ⎭
Personnel and miscellaneous expenses	11.4

SOURCE: *Bulletin économique de l'Indochine*, no. 171 (1925): 138.

in Cochinchina, 149,200 in Annam, 63,350 in Tonkin), who possessed 1,025,600 hectares by 1931. Much of this land lay in the southern and central regions, famed for their rich red soils.

In 1942, 2,307,000 hectares were granted throughout Indochina: 905,500 to Europeans, companies or individuals, of which 566,800 were indeed developed; 1,397,500 to "native" concessionaries—essentially Vietnamese—of which 1,163,000 were developed. Three-fourths of the surface granted and 89.6% of the actually developed lands were in Cochinchina.

In another domain, the operations of the state, and particularly its fiscal policies, destabilized long-standing social relations and forced the poorest peasants into the proletariat, inducing the formation, at the heart of the Vietnamese peasantry, of a manpower reserve. Through labor legislation (the creation of a workers' handbook, the 1927 legislation on contract work, etc.) and the organization of recruitment campaigns in Tonkin and Annam, the state ensured the shift of this reserve to low-cost wage-earning work. The reputed "crutch of private investment,"[81] it also provided its guarantee and its subsidies to a number of large enterprises. A first example is that of the Yunnan Railroad Company, which received 64 million francs from 1900 to 1909—more than five times the amount of its original capital—in addition to a guaranteed annual interest of three million francs for seventy-five years. Another example is the Messageries fluviales de Cochinchine (Cochinchina River Transportation Company), which received 18 million piastres from 1900 to 1937.[82]

Finally, and most important, public investment served principally to finance the construction of infrastructure and the tools necessary for an export economy (cf. table 3.8, app. 4, and fig. 3.3). Public works represented the essential arena of this investment and absorbed 18% to 20% of the entire budget from 1900 to 1939, more than 6 billion 1937 francs (around 1 billion gold francs).[83] During this period, priority was given to roads, ports, and railroads, which—especially the railroads—generated only mediocre revenue. Railroads accounted for half of the loans contracted prior to 1914 and another 66% of the 1,752 million francs allotted through

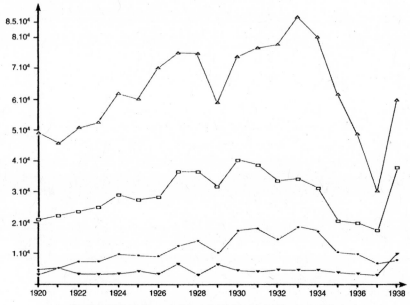

- ▼ -   Investment in hydraulics, agriculture, and animal husbandry (thousands of piastres)
- • -   Investment in public works (roads, railroads, ports, inland navigation) (thousands of piastres)

- □ -   Total investments (thousands of piastres)
- ▲ -   Total investments (thousands of 1914 francs)

FIGURE 3.3. Public investments in Indochina, 1920–1938.

the great program of public investment adopted in 1931. Starting in 1909, railroad debt rose to 250 million francs, the equivalent of 3.5 times the total general budget of Indochina. From 1914 to 1924, roads, ports, and railroads received 73.3% of investment resources,[84] to the detriment of hydraulic works, which received less than 15% of expenditure from 1899 to 1923. On the other hand, expenditure on sanitary and medical projects was comparatively very small: between 1920 and 1929, it oscillated between 1.65% to 3.78% of all the combined budgets.[85] It was only after 1931 that investment in water (27.5% of the program of 1931) and public health (6.4%) became truly consequential, prodded by increasing underdevelopment in the Vietnamese deltas.

Private Investment

This strategy of public investment explains why private investment was vigorous. But the strategy favored the concentration of this investment in the production of raw or semi-processed materials that were easily saleable on the foreign market, as well as in the financial sector. In the absence of systematic studies of the subject, the evaluation of private investment in Indochina during the period from 1880 to 1940 remains uncertain. Available estimates suggest private investment between a minimum of 1.4 billion 1914 francs, undoubtedly too low, and a maximum of 5 billion (with enterprises supplying their own capital by issuing stocks and bonds), adopted by the experts of the Commissariat général au Plan in 1947; the more reasonable average figure of 3.5 billion was suggested by the 1943 survey (table 3.9).

Whatever the exact numbers, Indochina (essentially Cochinchina and Tonkin, because Cambodia, Laos, and Annam only received fairly large investments in the years 1924–30) was clearly one of the major sites of export for French capital. This only became the case, however, starting in the 1880s. Until then, in the Cochinchina of the admirals, private investment stemmed from only three sources. The first of these was the investment of capital from the great French and European colonial ports and industrial centers, but also from Hong Kong, in the hulling, industrial processing, and trade in paddy and rice, which was booming in the Far East; in the importation of European products; and in traffic in Indian opium. This included Bordeaux shipowners (Roque, Denis, etc.) who organized maritime and river connections in Cochinchina.[86] In 1874, eleven large commercial houses—notably, De Clerville, of Nantes; Denis Frères, Roque, Renard, and Spooner, all four of Bordeaux; Speidel and Engler of Hamburg; Diethelm of Zurich; and Hale of London—were active in imports and exports, in rice, and in wholesale trade. In 1898, Descours et Cabaud, a big Lyon metals trading firm, established itself in Haiphong. It was to become the biggest Indochinese commercial group, with ten branches in Indochina, two in Yunnan, and one in Bangkok. Other major firms that set up shop in Indochina included Poinsard et Veyret (Comptoirs d'Extrême-Orient, 1920), Ogliastro, Optorg (1919), and the Union commerciale indochinoise et africaine (1904). In all, there were over forty large trading houses in Indochina.

In addition to their investments, there was some local accumulation from Chinese commercial networks, as well as from public works firms and from budgetary transfers executed for the profit of the members of the colonial civil service.[87] This was reinvested locally, notably through the mechanism of the Caisse de prévoyance de Cochinchine (Contingency Fund of Cochinchina), which operated from 1873 to 1887. This triple accumulation was undoubtedly important, but it was small in comparison to the flow of capital that occurred after 1890–1900 (fig. 3.4 and app. 5) and would be maintained past 1930. According to the investigation conducted by the Secrétariat d'État aux Colonies in 1943 for the period 1880–1930, the value of capital shares issued for Indochina alone reached 3 billion current francs (around 1 billion gold francs), and this figure is clearly too low, since it does not take into account the investments of unincorporated businesses, self-financing, or the elusive Chinese, Indian, and Vietnamese capital (app. 5).

TABLE 3.9 Private investment in Indochina, 1880–1940

A. Estimate of the 1943 public survey

Investment categories	In 1940 francs	In inflation-adjusted 1914 francs
Issuance of company stocks	17,837,602,000	1,105,722,000[a]
Issuance of company bonds	918,340,000	110,200,800
Self-financing of companies	15,516,660,000	1,848,000,000[b]
TOTAL	34,272,602,000	3,063,922,800
Investments of unincorporated businesses	4,186,000,000	503,320,000[b]
GRAND TOTAL	38,458,602,000[c]	3,567,242,800

B. "Broad" estimate of Paul Bernard and Jean Bourgoin (1947)

Investment categories	In 1939 piastres	In 1939 francs	In inflation-adjusted 1914 francs
French private capital invested in 1939	1,800,000,000	18,000,000,000	2,700,000,000
Self-financing of French businesses in 1939	1,540,000,000	15,400,000,000	2,310,000,000
TOTAL	3,340,000,000	33,400,000,000	5,010,000,000

C. Partial estimate of Henri Lanoue (1954)

Direct investments[d] from 1880 to 1940, per *Annuaires statistiques de l'Indochine*		Direct investments[e] from 1924 to 1940, per *Répertoire des sociétés anonymes indochinoises*	
In 1940 francs	In inflation-adjusted 1914 francs	In 1940 francs	In inflation-adjusted 1914 francs
11,644,000,000	1,397,280,000	10,074,000,000 (8,030,000,000 stock, 2,044,000,000 self-financing)	1,208,880,000

SOURCES: Part A: 1943 survey on investments in the colonies (CAOM, Affaires économiques, 52), conducted by the Banque de l'Indochine. The flaws of this survey, in particular the choice of a method that clearly exaggerates the volume of investments and of a deflator that is strictly monetary (the relationship between the successive gold values of the franc), have been aptly criticized by Henri Lanoue (see his article cited for part C, below) and by J. Marseille ("L'investissement français dans l'Empire colonial: l'enquête du gouvernement de Vichy [1943]," *Revue historique*, no. 512 [Oct.–Dec. 1974]: 409–32). We have corrected its results by deflating them following the method described in our note 71 to this chapter.

Part B: Commissariat général au Plan, commission de modernisation et d'équipement des Territoires d'outre-mer, sous-commission de l'Indochine, *Notes sur les données économiques et financières d'un plan d'équipement de l'Indochine*, by Paul Bernard and Jean Bourgoin, April 25, 1947, CAOM, Affaires économiques, 578.

Part C: H. Lanoue, "La vérité sur les investissements français en Indochine," *Cahiers internationaux*, Dec. 1954. We have converted the author's figures, in 1940 francs, to 1914 francs on the basis of the coefficients described in our note 71.

[a] Figure taken from table 3.7.

[b] The figures for self-financing of companies and investments of unincorporated businesses could not be deflated year by year, because the 1943 public survey gives only a general assessment for the whole period, which we have converted to 1914 francs using the average of the deflation coefficients cited in note 71.

[c] J. Marseille gives the figure of 39,198,000,000 in *Revue historique* (see source note above).

[d] Issuance of stocks and bonds; self-financing is not assessed.

[e] Issuance of stocks and self-financing.

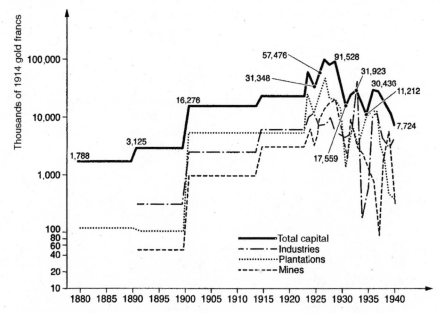

FIGURE 3.4. Mobilization of capital stocks by Indochinese companies in various economic sectors, 1880–1940 (in thousands of 1914 gold francs). (Based on data in appendix 5; the breakdown for transport, commerce, property and real estate, and banks could not be included here.)

This flow of capital reached its first plateau between 1890 and 1914. An official study valued private investments in 1903–5 at 126.8 million gold francs: 57% in industry, 10% in agriculture, and 33% in commerce,[88] more than 75% of which was confined to Cochinchina and Tonkin. It is noteworthy that, from the beginning, this flow included appreciable industrial and commercial investments, essentially from the great economic centers of France, especially Marseille, Lyon, and Bordeaux. The colonial development of Indochina, particularly in Annam and Tonkin, was thus pioneered by traders, bankers, and some Lyon manufacturers, boosted by Ulysse Pila.[89] With the support of Paul Bert, J. L. de Lanessan, and Armand Rousseau, the powerful Lyon Chamber of Commerce was converted to the colonial idea by two men: Pila and the banker Édouard Aynard, deputy of the Rhône department and president of the Chamber. They were both looking to build an integrated economic system in Tonkin directed at southern China that would combine railroads, banks, the opium trade, steamer navigation routes, insurance companies, and various other commercial and industrial enterprises.

In sum, the aim was to "Asianize" the entrepreneurial model of the great French industrialists Paulin Talabot and François Arlès-Dufour on the scale of the South

China Sea. That model encompassed the P.L.M. (Paris–Lyon–à la Méditerranée rail company), the Crédit lyonnais, a bank with its roots in the silk industry, the Marseille docks, the Suez Canal, the Indochinese route of the Messageries maritimes, the Compagnie lyonnaise d'assurances maritimes (Lyon Maritime Insurance Company), and the Comptoir d'escompte de Paris's first branches in India and China. This system was designed to connect Lyon directly to Chinese silk sources (1843–73), and it made Lyon Europe's most important market for Asian raw silks. Between 1884 and 1900, its businessmen created the Syndicat lyonnais d'études pour L'Indochine, the first factories, notably, the Bourgoin-Meiffre silk mill, and the Compagnie lyonnaise indochinoise (which was to become the Union commerciale indochinoise in 1904),[90] as well as a series of other enterprises, all with the same shareholders. Among the latter were the Société des ciments Portland artificiels de l'Indochine, which opened its main factory in Haiphong in 1899; the mills of the Société cotonnière de l'Indo-Chine of Haiphong (1898) founded by Mulhouse industrialists (Koechlin, Dolfus-Mieg), by the big Bremen shipowner, A. Rickmers, and by the Scottish rubber tire manufacturer Best-Dunlop;[91] the Docks et houillères de Tourane in Qang Nam (1899); and the Société lyonnaise de colonisation en Indo-Chine, which managed several agricultural concessions in Tonkin.

After having organized the Mission lyonnaise d'exploration commerciale in China (1895–97) with the goal of linking Tonkin and Yunnan together commercially, the Lyon capitalists, along with British interests, founded a consortium, the Anglo-French Yunnan Syndicate, to develop mines in Yunnan. They then invested part of their capital in the Yunnan Railroad Company (Compagnie de chemin de fer de Yunnan). After 1910, despite the partial failure of the vast Yunnan project, which was in part responsible for the disappearance of the Lyon colonial lobby, a small group of these companies and important investments continued functioning.

In 1912, the directory of colonial enterprises of the Colonial Union listed 138 commercial houses, 81 industrial enterprises, and 47 rubber-growing businesses. Among the large, durable investments were the cotton mills of Bourgoin-Meiffre et Compagnie in Hanoi founded in 1890; the Société cotonnière de l'Indochine (Cotton Company of Indochina) in Haiphong, founded in 1898, which were absorbed by the Société cotonnière du Tonkin (Cotton Company of Tonkin) in 1913, whose factory in Nam Dinh (1900) was founded by the industrialist A. Dupré with capital from Mulhouse and Lyon; the Compagnie lyonnaise indochinoise (Indochinese Lyon Company) of Ulysse Pila (1898); the Société des ciments Portland artificiels de l'Indochine (1899); the Est asiatique français (French East Asian Company, 1905), directed by Hely d'Oissel; the first two electric companies (1900 and 1902); public works companies like the Française d'entreprises de dragages et de travaux publics (French Commercial Dredging and Public Works Company, 1902); the Compagnie française des tramways (French Tramways Company, 1890) and the Compagnie des tramways de l'Indochine (Tramways Company of Indochina, 1911); and sawmills and match

TABLE 3.10 The creation of Indochinese companies by period
(based on a sample of 269 companies)

Before 1888	1888–1902	1903–1918	1919–1930	1931–1939
2	15	43	135	74
(0.7%)	(5.5%)	(15.9%)	(50.1%)	(27.5%)

SOURCE: J.-P. Aumiphin, *La présence financière et économique française en Indochine, 1859–1939* (Hanoi: Éditions des statistiques du Vietnam, 1997). Aumiphin classified by period the companies recorded in *Répertoire des sociétés anonymes indochinoises*, published by the general government of Indochina in 1944. This index lists only 295 companies, whereas the 1943 public survey on investments in the colonies lists 461 companies operating in Indochina: 118 industrial firms, 112 plantation companies, 112 commercial firms, 57 mining companies, 30 property and real estate companies, 23 transportation companies, and 9 others.

TABLE 3.11 Private investments by type of activity,
1914 and 1940 (percent)

Type	1914		1940	
Industries	13.8		20	
Mines	5.4	46.6	12.5	59.9
Plantations	27.4		27.4	
Transportation	15.2	24.5	12.9	25.1
Commerce	9.3		12.2	
Real estate	1	28.9	6.2	15
Banks	27.9		8.8	

SOURCE: Developed by J. Marseille on the basis of the 1943 public survey. See his "L'investissement français dans l'Empire colonial: l'enquête du gouvernement de Vichy (1943)," *Revue historique*, no. 512 (Oct.-Dec. 1974): 409–32.

manufacturers, such as the Société indochinoise forestière et des allumettes (Indochinese Forest and Matchstick Company, 1904). Colonization and limited but discernable industrialization went hand in hand. Toward 1908, according to Charles Robequain, close to 40 million gold francs were invested in Tonkin industries alone.[92] In total, in 1914, private investments amounted to at least between 212 and 357.7 million gold francs,[93] which approached the total of French investments in the Ottoman empire before 1914 (509 million gold francs). Indochina probably received over 20% of the private investment in the French colonial empire.

From 1911, the rhythm of this wave of private investments changed with the arrival of large French financial groups and the proliferation of companies (table 3.10), and was diversified through the development of plantations and the mining sector. Along with the industries, these two branches henceforth received the majority of invested capital. This phenomenon culminated between 1924 and 1930 (table 3.11): no fewer than 366 companies were created.[94] In five years, from 1924 to 1928, investment rose to more than 2.5 billion current francs—around 415 million 1914 francs—according to the statistician T. Smolski,[95] or more than 3.8 billion current francs according to the high estimate of Charles Robequain.[96] In total, during the decade 1920–30, Indochinese investment had reached at least 2.8 billion current francs (around 560 million 1914 francs), 41.8% of that of all of France's colonial companies, evaluated at 6.7 billion francs.[97] The peaks were attained in 1927, 1928, and 1929, with more than 90 million 1914 francs invested each year. This fabulous speculation can be explained by a series of contexts: the resonance of the Sarraut campaign for the development of the colonies and the propaganda activity of the Gouvernement général in France (for which the Agence économique de l'Indochine [Economic Agency of Indochina] was created in Paris in 1918), the exceptional prosperity, after the war, of the Indochinese budgets, whose reserve treasuries "overflowed with capital"[98]—their accumulated amount was six times more than that of the treasuries of the AOF (Afrique occidentale française) in 1922—the success of mining prospects, in Tonkin and especially in Laos, offers of metropolitan capital, and so on.

There were two especially powerful determining factors. First, the crisis of the franc from 1920 to 1928, along with the rise of the piastre, made the latter a currency of refuge and pushed speculative capital toward Indochina in search of secure investments: investing in the colony was a way of gaining value simply through the continuous rise of the piastre-franc exchange rate. Second, the rise in the price of raw tropical commodities such as tea, coffee, and sugar, and particularly the recovery of the rates of rubber (which increased from 16.3 cents a pound in 1921 to 72.4 in 1925), and therefore the rate of profit of plantation enterprises following the application of the Stevenson plan calling for production quotas (November 1922), drove the prodigious expansion of the mining industry and the plantations. In four years (1925–29), 700 million current francs were invested in the rubber plantations of the red soils of Cochinchina, Cambodia, and southern Annam, where the required investment, per planted hectare, was the lowest in Southeast Asia. This explains the concentration of investments in Cochinchina, which received 54% of this amount between 1924 and 1928.

The crisis of the 1930s broke the pace of private investment but did not eliminate it completely. Damaging though it was, the Depression did not cause French capitalists to lose interest in Indochina (see table 3.7 and fig. 3.4). Indochinese companies continued to issue shares at an appreciable rate between 1930 and 1935, and even as late as 1940. From 1931 to 1940, Indochinese companies issued shares valued at a billion current francs (around 205 million 1914 francs), equivalent to the twenty-five years from 1890 to 1915, probably a quarter of the total French colonial share issue during the decade of the crisis. Indochina did not experience a true withdrawal of investments until before the end of World War II. The thirteen companies included in fig. 3.6 (p. 173 below) raised additional capital on fourteen occasions, excluding the distribution of free shares, between 1930 and 1941. But the capital advanced was not necessarily invested. To come to a reliable conclusion on this matter, it would be necessary to survey the balances and accounts of firms and to understand the evolution of self-financing.

The Components of Capital

Until 1940, the initial tendencies of private investments were confirmed. Mines, industries exporting products with little added value (cement, hulled rice, rubber), or those connected with the development of the infrastructure of transport and towns (electricity, etc.) represented an increasingly intensive drain on private capital (see table 3.11). Through them emerged an Indochinese capitalism with genuine historic importance. To see this we need only look at the colonial roots of the contemporary Indosuez group, or the political-financial relations of men like Paul Doumer, Albert Sarraut, and Édouard Herriot—tied in the 1920s to the Compagnie générale des soies (General Silk Company)—and of Paul Reynaud and many families of the great French bourgeoisie, like those of Homberg, Bardoux, or Giscard d'Estaing, to this colonial capitalism.

The heterogeneity of the private capitalism that constituted, along with the great economic apparatus of the colonial state, one of the two elements of Indochinese capitalism should be emphasized. We can effectively distinguish at least three components that corresponded to the different generations of colonial enterprises. Industry, trade, the fitting out of the great ports of France, the French commercial and rural settlers, Chinese capitalism, and the Vietnamese system of latifundia were the oldest of these. The land owned by the Vietnamese upper middle class gave it a powerful foundation: the income generated by extensive Cochinchinese rice growing was considerable until 1930. The accounts of Transbassac rice-growing concerns published at the time reveal that as long as the average rate of a *gia* (20.4 kilos) of paddy was kept between 1.20 to 1.40 piastres, as was the case in the years 1928–30, when the production cost of paddy was stable at around 0.53 piastres per *gia*, landowners made enormous profits—on the order of 120% to 165% of their investments.[99]

The agricultural firms of lower- and middle-class colonists, often misunderstood,[100] played an equally pioneering role in Cochinchinese rice growing and in the plantation economy: for example, in the cultivation of coffee trees in Annam, generally practiced on plantations of less than one hundred hectares, and even in the cultivation of rubber. It was the plantation created by Commissaire de la Sûreté de Saigon (Saigon Security Police Commissioner) Belland in 1898 that first demonstrated the scope for rubber growing in Indochina. Until 1925, the majority of the rubber companies—such as the Société agricole de Suzannah (Suzannah Agricultural Company, founded in February 1907)—had been established with the aid of local capital, generally belonging to casual planters (civil servants, doctors, pharmacists, military men, etc.), who were not necessarily ineffective.

The major companies that managed different production monopolies and the sale of alcohol, salt, and opium were also funded by this type of capital. The chief of these was the powerful Société française des distilleries de l'Indochine (French Indochina Distilleries Company), founded in May 1901 by Auguste Fontaine, a former Douanes et Régies (Customs and Excise) official who was an especially influential figure in the colony, along with the Calmette brothers and Raoul Debeaux, owner of the Compagnie générale de Tonkin et du Nord-Annam. Other outlets were French participation in fifty small rice distilleries funded by mixed capital—French, Chinese, and Vietnamese—which still coexisted with the Distilleries de l'Indochine in 1937, the French rice mills owned by Gressier, the Rizeries indochinoises (Indochinese Rice Mills, 1910), and the Rizeries d'Extrême-Orient (Rice Mills of the Far East, 1910) of the Marseille traders Rauzy and Ville.

Even though the concentration of capital had taken place before 1914, as shown by the formation of the Fontaine group (involved in alcohol, tobacco, commerce), many businesses, though lucrative, remained of limited size, such as the Haiphong shipyards of Marty and Abbadie, the Raoul Debeaux Company, the Tonkin Distilleries, the Bien Hoa Industrial and Forestry Company, and the Indochina Tobacco Manufacturers. In 1912, there were still only twenty-six large enterprises. Starting with Doumer's government, many traders became involved in imports and exports, wholesale trade, and administrative markets by becoming associated with metropolitan firms. A little earlier, between 1890 and 1900, the steady rise of European rice growing started, generally cultivated, like the great Vietnamese rice fields, on lots of a few hectares rented to poor farmers *(ta dien)*, with usurious advances granted to the peasants. In 1931, Europeans owned 300,000 hectares of rice fields in the whole of Indochina, if one includes the reclaimed villages of the Catholic missions. How much colonists' internal savings and their reinvestment amounted to is unknown, but the figure cannot be taken as negligible, and the process never ceased. In 1929, Smolski evaluated its part in privately invested capital at 12% in 1924, 65% in 1927, and 54% in 1928.[101]

In this growth of Indochinese capitalism, the place of Indian and especially Chinese capital, which escapes all quantification, was no less considerable, since it dominated land loans and the trade and processing of corn, silk, numerous hand-picked products, and especially rice. According to Paul Bernard, the Indian *chettys*, traditional bankers who practiced usury, invested around 50 million piastres (around 500 million current francs) around 1930. As for Chinese activities, considerable before the conquest, they continued to spread after colonization. In Cochinchina, the annual number of Chinese immigrants increased from 44,000 in 1879 to 92,000 in 1902 and 156,000 in 1921.[102] Starting in 1885, the Chinese founded solid communities in Haiphong, the new town constructed by the French in Tonkin, and Chinese trade soon dominated the entire protectorate. But the big bourgeoisie of Cholon was the core of Chinese capitalism in Indochina.

In Cochinchina and in Cambodia, Chinese traders and their agents together exercised, starting in 1860, the five economic functions of the *compradore* system, in addition to participating in the farming of Cochinchinese opium, from which they profited until 1897. These functions were those of the intermediaries between Vietnamese producers of paddy and European exporters of rice; purchasers and processors of paddy, and exporters of rice produced in their own businesses, essentially destined for Hong Kong, as well as of corn, jute, fish, cinnamon, cardamom, *stick-lac* (tree resin), and so on; importers of and dealers in goods from China; intermediaries between French exporters, Indochinese industrialists, and the mass of native consumers; and, finally, financial backers and distributors—paired with the Indian and Vietnamese moneylenders—of credit. In 1874, forty powerful Chinese houses were already established in Cholon, with Cantonese capital from Hong Kong or Hokkien from Singapore, notably in the rice trade (Tan Keng Sing, Ban Joo, Ann, etc.). In 1938, the Chinese employers possessed twenty-five of the twenty-seven steam-powered rice mills of more than 100 horsepower and virtually all the junks that transported paddy on Cochinchina's canals. They controlled an immense, opaque commercial banking and moneylending network, which was widespread throughout Cochinchina, Cambodia, and Laos. Its power and the overlapping of its interests with French trading houses and banks were such that one can speak of a true symbiotic Franco-Chinese capitalism. As for strictly native investment and accumulation, their extent remains unknown, although their importance has been incorrectly overlooked. In 1947, Paul Bernard estimated that on the eve of World War II, Vietnamese investments alone, primarily in land, were worth 12 million piastres, 18% to 20% of the annual flow of French capital.[103]

The final component of Indochinese colonial capitalism, in every respect the most important, consisted of the industrial, agro-industrial, and metropolitan financial sectors, run by influential bankers, leading company directors, and other members of France's *patronat* (business establishment). There existed also a powerful Indochinese colonial *patronat,* with strong-headed individuals such as René Thion de la Chaume, president of the Banque de l'Indochine between the two World Wars; its general secretary Édouard de Laboulaye; Étienne Denis, the head of several groups, among which were Denis Frères of Bordeaux, the Brasseries et glacières de l'Indochine, the Société industrielle des eaux et d'électricité en Asie, and the Compagnie Indochinoise d'équipement industriel, which he founded in 1926; and the *polytechnicien* Jean Rigal, a remarkable general manager (since 1931) of the Société française de dragages et de travaux publiques, founded in 1902 by the engineer L. F. Dussoliers and the Société anonyme franco-belge. Originally the flagship of the Société financière française et coloniale group, the Société française de dragages et de travaux publiques was transferred to the control of the Banque de l'Indochine in 1931. Its fields of operation were the deltas of the Mekong and the Red River; equipping cities, irrigation centers, and the canals in Tonkin; and the construction of roads and railroads (for example, the Tourane–Nha Trang line). After the 1930s, the Société française de dragages et de travaux publiques became one of the largest European public works operations in China and Africa, as well as in France and elsewhere in Europe.[104]

These groups have been very little studied, except partially for the most important of them, the Banque de l'Indochine group. In the thirties and forties, the bank was directed, in Paris, by Thion de la Chaume, E. De Laboulaye, and its deputy general manager, Paul Baudoin—future minister under Vichy—and in Indochina by Jean Laurent and F. De Flers. The constitution of the Banque de l'Indochine group was rather belated because, until the 1920s, it only exercised direct control over a small number of big businesses, whose prototype was the Compagnie de chemin de fer du Yunnan (Yunnan Railroad Company), which it founded in 1901 with the Société générale and the Comptoir national d'escompte de Paris (CNEP). Its portfolio of securities totaled only 18.5 million current francs in 1923. But it grew larger during the 1920s, making twelve purchases in 1924, ten in 1925, and forty-six in 1928,[105] and especially during the crisis of 1929, which proved favorable to the restructuring of Indochinese enterprises. During this period, the Banque de l'Indochine's function as a business bank saw a rapid development (cf. app. 6).

Besides the Banque de l'Indochine, one should not neglect the mining consortia, more or less linked to metropolitan French metallurgic groups. These included the Société des charbonnages du Tonkin (Tonkin Coal Mining Company) and the Charbonnages de Dong Trieu (Dong Trieu Coal-Mining Company), which were among the best businesses in the Far East. There was also the Compagnie minière et métallurgique de l'Indochine (Mining and Metallurgic Company of Indochina), which had mined the zinc of Cho Dien since 1919 and profited from the rarity of this metal in the Far East. And, not least, there were the Société d'études et d'exploitation minières de l'Indochine (Indochinese Society of Mining Studies and Exploitation), which had mined tin at Nam Paten in Laos since 1920 and the Étains et wolframs du Tonkin (Tonkin Tin and Tungsten Mines) (1911), tied to de Wendel, who held the concession of the basin of Tinh Tuc.

A number of French industrial groups possessed subsidiary companies in Indochina. This was the case with Air liquide, whose subsidiary the Société d'oxygène et d'acétylène d'Extrême-Orient (1909) owned factories in a dozen cities in the Far East. Likewise, Michelin had since 1928 owned a concession comprising the three rubber plantations at Phu Rieng (5,500 hectares), Dau Tieng (8,700 hectares), and Ben Co (150 hectares), which allowed it to progressively liberate itself from having to purchase gum in pounds and dollars.

Finally, there were four holdings that were firmly implanted in the colony: the SICAF (Société indochinoise de commerce, d'agriculture, et de finances, or Indochinese Commerce, Agriculture, and Financing Company, 1919), which was involved in the plantations, and was controlled by the Banque de l'Indochine; the smaller Union financière d'Extrême-Orient (Financial Union of the Far East,

1929); the Société française financière et coloniale (French Colonial and Finan-cial Company) (SFFC); and the Société financière des caoutchoucs (SFC). The SFFC was created, with the support of the Lazard Bank and the Belgian house of Hallet, on November 12, 1920, by Octave Homberg (1876–1941), R. Thion de la Chaume's brother-in-law, acting secretary-general of the Banque de l'Indochine, and a "financial romantic."[106] He left this last institution to become the vice pres-ident of the Banque de l'Union parisienne, simultaneously serving in 1914 as Alexandre Ribot's principal collaborator in the Ministry of Finances. After a brush with bankruptcy in December 1930, the SFFC lost its autonomy; the Banque de l'Indochine, supported by a group of Paris establishments, bailed it out and then acquired control of 35% of its capital in 1932. In 1933, after the elimination of Homberg, the former inspector of finances Edmond Giscard d'Estaing (the fa-ther of the future President Valéry Giscard d'Estaing), who joined the holding company in 1926, took over its reins. By 1937, the SFFC was a powerful group of thirty-six colonial companies, primarily Indochinese and secondarily Madagas-can (see app. 7).

The last of these four holdings, the SFC, created in 1909, was an integrated part of a veritable international conglomerate of Franco-Belgian capital, the Rivaud-Hallet group, and was particularly active in the plantations of Malaya and Angola and the mines of South Africa. It was controlled by the Rivaud-Lebel bank, an important Paris banking establishment that specialized at the beginning of the century in the colonial and rubber industries in alliance with Belgian capital, no-tably the Financière des caoutchoucs, controlled by a Belgian family, the Fabri. At the death of Oliver de Rivaud, its founder, his son-in-law, Jean de Beaumont, became head of the group. The latter was a descendant of Colbert and the own-er of the Saigon *Journal d'Extrême-Orient;* he was elected deputy of Cochinchina in 1935, over Albert Sarraut's son Omer. In 1941, Rivaud-Hallet could boast of being one of the main plantation groups in the world, controlling through the SFC and its direct affiliates (Caoutchoucs de Padang, Compagnie du Cambodge, Plantations des Terres-Rouges, etc.) more than 56,000 hectares, of which 32,000 were planted with rubber trees, in Malaya, Java, and Sumatra, and more than 30,000 hectares of rubber trees in Indochina.[107] In 1937, the SFC controlled five plantation companies in Indochina, eleven in Malaya and the Dutch East Indies, eight in Central and East Africa, and eight mining companies in South Africa (app. 8). Indochinese rubber cultivation thus seems not only to have been par-ticularly concentrated—in 1938, twenty-seven companies of more than 1,000 hectares each possessed 68% of the 127,000 hectares planted, and five financial groups controlled 70% of the planted acreage (table 3.12)—but also integrated on an international scale into a vast system of technical and financial transfers, balancing risks and profits.

TABLE 3.12 Indochinese rubber company groups, 1944

Groups[a]	Hectares planted	Annual production potential (tons)
Rivaud-Hallet group (Société financière des caoutchoucs)		
Plantations des Terres-Rouges	17,587	16,350
Compagnie du Cambodge	15,613	12,000
Compagnie des caoutchoucs de Padang	1,553	970
TOTAL	34,753	29,320
	(37.25%)	(31%)
Banque de l'Indochine group		
Société indochinoise des plantations d'hévéas	11,877	14,200
Société indochinoise des plantations réunies de Mimot	5,538	6,900
Société des caoutchoucs de Kompong Thom	1,333	1,660
Compagnie des Hauts Plateaux indochinois	957	900
Caoutchoucs du Donai	2,466	2,850
Caoutchoucs de Phuoc Hoa	1,251	1,560
TOTAL	23,422	28,070
	(25.10%)	(29.68%)
Société française financière et coloniale		
Société des caoutchoucs de l'Indochine	7,567	7,240
Société indochinoise des cultures tropicales	4,063	3,280
TOTAL	11,630	10,520
	(12.46%)	(11.12%)
Union financière d'Extrême-Orient		
Société des plantations de Kratié	2,995	3,750
	(3.21%)	(3.96%)
Paribas (Compagnie générale des colonies)	2,411	3,015
Caoutchouc du Mékong	(2.58%)	(3.18%)

[a] Not listed are the plantations (Dau Tieng and Thuan Loi), belonging to the Michelin company, which accounted for 11% of the land under cultivation.

A Profitable Country

Under colonial domination, this external commercial development generated a considerable, if not exceptionally high, accumulation of capital. Of all the French colonies, Indochina was without a doubt the most profitable. This fact is often denied or seen as unimportant. The economist Jean Bourgoin estimated in 1947 that private investments in Indochina never yielded more than 1.52%: "That which it was agreed to call colonialism," he declared, "was above all a poorly financed and cheap colonialism."[108] Until now, no survey has seriously tried to evaluate the profits of Indochinese corporations, or the size of the failures—probably very numerous—and the investments lost through unsuccessful prospecting or during economic crises. Still, indications certainly suggest that capital remained exceptionally profitable for a long time in Indochina, which confirms what had already been suggested by authors writing between the two wars. In 1929, Henri Simoni estimated the profits of private capital invested in the colony at a staggering 400–500%.[109] For example, between 1900 and 1914, the profits of the Fontaine group were fantastic: 10–12 piastres for each of the 120,000 hectoliters sold per year, in other words 3 million francs in 1910 for a capital of 3.5 million.[110] Jacques Marseille has estimated that, in 1929, five Indochinese companies (Banque de l'Indochine, Distilleries de l'Indochine, Charbonnages du Tonkin, Financière française et coloniale, Eaux et électricité d'Indochine) alone earned 31.8% of the net profits of the twenty largest colonial companies.[111] Another indication: in 1947, the Commissariat général au Plan calculated, based on figures provided by the Banque de l'Indochine, that the profits, interest, and profit-based management bonuses from Indochinese companies distributed in 1938 (and largely transferred to the metropole) came to 780 million current francs. On a total investment estimated at 18 billion current francs, this corresponds to a very reasonable profit rate of 4.33%, or more than 7.8% if one compares it to Indochinese production overall, valued at 10 billion current francs.[112]

Figures 3.5 and 3.6 and appendix 9 reveal, although only for a sample of fourteen large companies, the size of the profit made, as well as its duration over time, which is also confirmed by the sums these joint-stock companies put in reserve annually. The rates of Indochinese profits were higher than the profit of corporations in France. The case of the Banque de l'Indochine is clearly extraordinary, to the point where it cannot be seen as representative. From 1876 to 1914, its cumulative (declared) net profits reached 107,311,000 gold francs for an invested capital of 12 million: in thirty-eight years, the latter had been reimbursed nine times. From 1876 to 1944, the activities of the bank officially cleared a cumulative profit of more than 393 million 1914 francs, 1,637% of expended capital (24 million 1914 francs), or approximately 4.75 billion 1990 francs. Its own funds (invested capital and the reserves included in the balances) increased from 15.9 million 1914 francs in 1905 to 55 million in 1910; they fell to 16.8 million (84 million current francs) in 1920, then rose to 44.2 million (242 million current francs) in 1930. "But," Marc Meuleau notes, "the Bank had at its disposal . . . substantial hidden reserves."[113] Its profit ratio reached 67.2% of capital in 1909 and 56.5% in 1914. For the bank, the two most prosperous periods had been 1898–1914 and especially 1921–31, during which the rate of profit remained higher than 50% of the effectively expended capital (fig. 3.5). Even in the heart of the Great Depression, from 1931 to 1935, its dividends remained higher than those of the prosperous years from 1923 to 1926 and, after 1937, its balance was close to the best of the earlier figures. "At the end of the decade," Meuleau observes, "the crisis was revealed to have been good business for the Banque de l'Indochine."[114] It is true that an important part of its profits came from branches and agencies in China and in French colonies in the Indian and Pacific Oceans, but their major source was still Indochina.

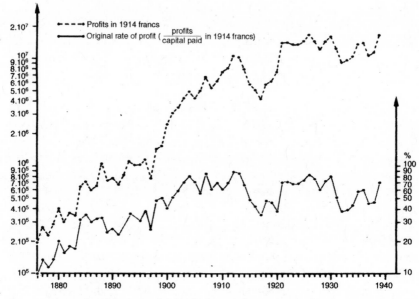

FIGURE 3.5. Profits of the Banque de l'Indochine, 1875–1939. (Based on data in appendix 9.)

Another important characteristic of Indochinese profit was that stock market capitalization of the Indochinese companies was extremely high, and stock exchange gains were therefore enormous. The Société des charbonnages du Tonkin, main developer of the Hon Gai coal mines, achieved a profit ratio of 62.8% of expended capital and 84.6% in 1913. In 1928, it had a stock market value of 2.8 billion current francs (448 million 1914 francs), fourteen times the capital invested (around 200 million current francs, or 32 million 1914 francs), and considerably higher than the best coal-mining values in France. This is explained by the volume of distributed profits (dividends, percentages, free shares): Indochinese corporations exported their profits on a large scale. In sixty-eight years (1876–1944), the Banque de l'Indochine distributed around 208.5 million gold francs, 868.75% of actual invested capital. Colonial salaries help account for this situation; they were derisory compared to metropolitan ones. In 1939, the nineteen companies responsible for two-thirds of rubber production declared a profit of 309 million current francs, more than seven times the total annual wages of the 40,000 workers on the plantations.[115] Table 3.13 shows that this was not an exceptional case. In 1947, the experts of the Commissariat général au Plan estimated that the average daily salary of 1939 stood at a paltry 0.22 piastres.[116] The capital gains *(plus-value)* in colonial Indochina bear no comparison to the results that metropolitan companies achieved during the same period. Undeniably, Indochina constituted one of the important zones for the accumulation of French capital.

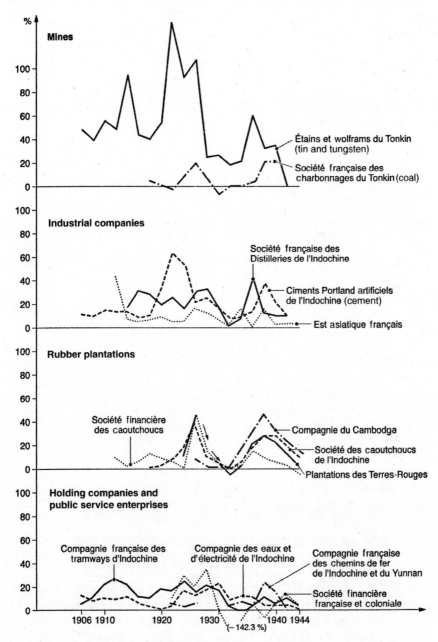

FIGURE 3.6. Rate of net profit for thirteen Indochinese companies, 1906–1914. (Based on data from *Annuaires de la Cote Defossés, Annuaires financiers France-Extrême-Orient*, 1922–1923, 1924–1925, and 1928. To determine the rate of profit, the sum of the net profits and of the capital raised was converted into 1914 gold francs, using the method indicated in note 71. The declared net profit was then divided by the capital issued at each period.)

TABLE 3.13 Profits and salaries for five companies, 1939

Companies	Declared net profits	Estimated annual salary expense	Relation of profits to salaries
Société indochinoise forestière et des allumettes (Vinh-Ben Thuy and Hanoi; 2,000 workers paid 3.50 F per day)	1,020,000 F	2,100,000 F	48.57%
Société des papeteries de l'Indochine (Viet Tri and Dap Chau; 3,000 workers paid 3.50 F per day)	1,915,000 F	3,150,000 F	60%
Société des ciments Portland artificiels de l'Indochine (Haiphong; 4,000 workers paid 3.50 F per day)	13,965,000 F	4,400,000 F	3.6 times
Société des distilleries de l'Indochine (3 factories in Tonkin, 1 in Cholon, 1 in Phnom Penh; 2,500 workers paid 5 F per day on average)	18,606,000 F	3,825,000 F	almost 5 times
Société cotonnière du Tonkin (mills in Haiphong and Nam Dinh; 10,000 workers paid 3.50 F per day)	52,414,000 F	10,500,000 F	5 times

SOURCE: The salaries are based on the average salaries of unskilled workers in *Annuaire statistique de l'Indochine, 1941–1942*, p. 209; the profits are the figures given in *Répertoire des sociétés anonymes indochinoises* (Hanoi, 1944).

Foreign Trade

In the final analysis, foreign rather than domestic trade was undoubtedly the principal source of colonial development. Domestic trade was, nonetheless, substantial. In 1909, the value of goods transported along the Cambodian and Vietnamese coasts—179.4 million francs—represented 34% of the total value of foreign trade.[117] Yet the tonnage transported by coastal traffic and the railroads remained lower than the amount exported (2.5 million tons as opposed to 4 million in 1935, for example). Foreign trade was the great "transformer" of the wealth produced in the peninsula into commodities that could be inserted into a global circulation of currency, products, and capital. In 1910, it had already reached the considerable sum of 519 million francs, a quarter of the total commerce of the French colonial sphere, which amounted to 2 billion francs. Certainly, the amount per capita (around 180 francs per inhabitant in 1937) was low compared to France (1,570 francs), the Dutch East Indies (310 francs), the Philippines (470 francs), and espe-

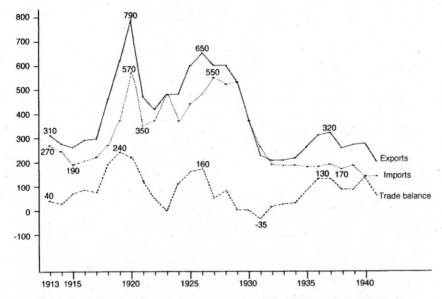

FIGURE 3.7. Indochina's foreign trade, 1913–1941 (in millions of 1913 francs). (Based on *Annuaires statistiques de l'Indochine 1941–1942*, p. 296. Beginning in 1933, these figures incorporate the value of merchandise declared for temporary admissions or reexported, but this value is always less than 6% of the total foreign trade value.)

cially British Malaya, including Singapore (5,100 francs), but it was equivalent to Siam's and surpassed China's and India's. In fact, the regional intensity of foreign trade was very unequal, since it was in the rice trade and plantations of Cochinchina and in the mining and industrial zones of Tonkin, for the most part, that the Indochinese economy's internationalization took place. In 1928, foreign trade represented around 600 francs per inhabitant in Cochinchina, as opposed to 125 in Tonkin and northern Annam.[118]

At least in Cochinchina, this commercial development dates back to the last two decades of the nineteenth century; it reached its historic peak during the 1915–29 period, apart from a brief crisis in 1921–23. The recovery of 1935–37 took place at a level much lower than that of 1929 (see fig. 3.7). What characterized this commercial development was the size of its surpluses. Indochina's trade balance was always favorable from 1891 to 1945, except from 1900 to 1906, during the infrastructure construction phase, and in 1922, 1930, and 1931. Exports pulled colonial economic growth as a whole forward, in particular during World War I: in four years, the trade balance reached a surplus of 442 million gold francs, with a peak of 240 million in 1919.

This situation was exceptional for a long time in the French colonial empire, with the exception of the Maghreb. Indeed, between 1913 and the start of the 1940s, the foreign trade of most French colonies was mired in deficits. Their cumulative trade balance became positive only from 1934,[119] and even then it was not positive with respect to foreign countries. In 1938, the value of Indochinese exports stood at 51% of Algerian exports and 9.48% of those of metropolitan France.[120] In 1932, they were equivalent to 42% of Ceylon's, 18.5% of the Dutch East Indies', and 33% of rich British Malaya's.[121] Thus, from 1928 to 1938, the balance of Indochinese foreign trade generated a positive cumulative balance of 3.8 billion current francs, as opposed to only 791 million for the rest of the colonies, except the Maghreb.[122] According to official Gouvernement général statistics, from 1913 to 1941, Indochina's foreign trade produced a total profitable balance of 2,325 million gold francs,[123] which was admittedly far from compensating for the deficit in France's trade balance. However, this cannot be regarded as negligible if one considers that the Indochinese commercial surplus represented around 23.2% of the French commercial deficit in 1928 and was still 7.30% in 1935 and 5.5% in 1937.

The result was that, placed in the larger framework of France's economic relations with the rest of the world, the surplus of Indochinese trade contributed to the balancing of France's foreign accounts. This is borne out by an examination of the geography of the foreign exchange and account balance. First, contrary to what a number of authors have written, these exchanges were characterized, early on, by their incomplete integration into the French system of protectionism, which was established starting in the 1880s. After 1887, Indochina was placed under the Méline law of 1892, which defined the regime of customs assimilation (a reciprocal customs franchise between the metropole and the colony and a common tariff, at least in principle); the sales of French industries in the colonies were strongly protected. But in practice, starting in 1921, and then with the derogation to the customs law instituted on April 13, 1928 (the "Kircher tariff," which reinforced customs assimilation between France and its colonies), and the special tariff adopted for Indochina by the texts of December 1928 and July 1929, completed by the Franco-Chinese trade treaty of May 1930, Indochina enjoyed a certain customs autonomy.[124]

Second, a distinct imbalance existed in the flow of commodities between the colony and its different commercial partners. Until 1930, Indochinese commerce with the Far East was greater than that with the metropole: exports to Hong Kong, China, Singapore, Japan, and the Dutch East Indies represented 58% of the total in 1913, 66% in 1929, and the purchases of East Asia from the colony greatly surpassed its sales (by 46% between 1908 and 1912 and 134% between 1924 and 1929). In fact, Indochina's principal markets were southern China (including imports to Hong Kong), which was the first outlet for Cochinchinese rice; the Dutch East Indies, which imported rice and exported gasoline to Indochina; Singapore, a market for fish, tin, and Indochinese rubber, which from there was sent on to the United States, Japan, and France; the Philippines, a market for Cambodian livestock and

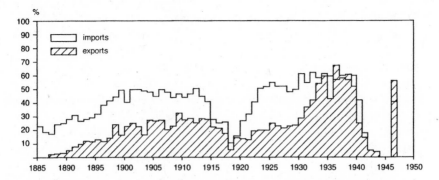

FIGURE 3.8. Trade between Indochina and France, 1885–1950 (percent of Indochinese exports and imports shipped to or from France and its colonies). (From I. Nørdlund, "The French Empire, the Colonial State in Vietnam, and Economic Policy: 1885–1940," *Australian Economic History Review*, no. 1 [March 1991], special issue, "Exploring Southeast Asia's Economic Past.")

Cochinchinese rice; and Japan, which purchased rice and especially coal and rubber. Indochina's sales to Japan were close to five times higher than its purchases between 1913 and 1932.[125] But China's role was essential. It was by far the primary market for Indochina, which was its most important supplier of rice. It also provided Indochina with traditional articles (umbrellas, earthenware, silk cloths, vermicelli, objects for religion and celebrations, tea, medicines). On the eve of the crisis of the 1930s, Indochinese sales represented 4% to 6% of total Chinese imports. Through Indochina, the French share in the Chinese import market was at least doubled.[126]

Finally, the United States absorbed an increasing amount of the rubber output after 1930: 34,000 tons out of 72,000 produced in 1940. In fact, in the long term, one effect of colonization was to integrate the Indochinese economy into the Far Eastern market and, more generally, to integrate Indochina, more so than any other French colony, into the global economy.

The Great Depression and the implementation of the idea of "imperial autarchy" through the close integration of the colonial empire into a French economic space, in the wake of the economic Conférence économique de la France d'Outre-mer (Economic Conference of Overseas France) of 1934,[127] certainly disrupted the geography of Indochinese foreign trade for some time. In parallel with the rise of the colonial market to the rank of France's primary commercial partner starting in 1928, Indochinese exports to France (57% of the total value of its exports between 1934 and 1938, as shown in fig. 3.8) surpassed those to the Far East (34%). A real, though temporary, disconnection between Indochina and East Asian economic space took place, which resulted in the preservation of profits of both Indochinese exporters and the Banque de l'Indochine during a phase of the global market's contraction. This also resulted in the maintenance of Indochina's capacity to absorb French industrial products. It was, however, a precarious situation, which was ended by the war: the law of October 15, 1940, granted customs autonomy to Indochina.

The essential factor was the asymmetry between the Indochinese–East Asian and Indochinese-French trade balances. The former was very favorable to Indochina until World War II. In contrast, as many works, notably those of Irene Nørlund, have shown, the customs assimilation instituted starting in 1887, reinforced by the Méline tariff of 1892 and further deepened by the Kircher tariff of 1928, which started a customs war with China from 1929 to 1935, enabled France to export much more to Indochina than it bought from it—over 60% more on average, for example, from 1908 to 1912. These were essentially manufactured products with a large added value, sold at prices generally much higher than those of identical foreign products. In 1934, Paul Bernard estimated that the prices of French imported merchandise surpassed those of equivalent foreign products by an average of 15%, and that the "Indochinese taxpayer paid an annual tithe of around 12 million piastres [30 million 1914 francs] to the exporters of France, with the sole purpose of offering them a privileged place in its market."[128]

So, throughout the period, Indochina played a role as a regulator of France's trade. The terms of exchange were largely unfavorable to Indochina, though this was probably less true during the crisis of 1930, because of the decrease in the price of imported consumer goods; the metropole's percentage of the value of imports into the colony continually increased until 1940. Imports from the metropole and those, less important, from the other French colonies, represented 29.6% on average of the total value of Indochinese imports from 1911 to 1920, and 43.2% from 1921 to 1930, whereas Indochinese exports to the metropole—rice, corn intended for consumption by livestock (whose rates were tied to those of oats), rubber, tea, a little coffee, pepper—leveled out at 19.6% of the total amount of Indochinese exports from 1911 to 1920, and 20.9% from 1921 to 1930.

Except during the Great Depression, profits from Indochina's balance of foreign trade rose steadily, far outstripping its equally growing deficits with the metropole and generating a considerable transfer of value to France, at the price of maintaining a very low standard of living among the colonized. Assimilation "obliged the indigenous peoples, who could have inexpensively acquired what they needed among their neighbors, to pay high customs and to have their imports sent from France burdened with transportation expenses on 15,000 kilometers."[129]

Indochina thus became, from the years 1908–12 on, one of the important foreign markets of French products—cotton fabric and, to a lesser extent, cotton threads of Rouen and the Vosges, rayon fabrics of Lyon, light and heavy metals, and automobiles. In 1938, fabrics (cotton and rayon), which were 90% French except from 1915 to 1922, represented 22.5% of Indochinese imports, and infrastructure goods, 21.3%. Indochina was, after Algeria, the principal colonial outlet of the French economy, notably for industries with lessening momentum like textiles; it accounted for 3.1% of the total exports of France and 4.1% of its imports. The case of cotton is especially revealing. As early as 1885, French threads and fabrics led Indochinese imports: 33% in 1911, 39% in 1913, 27% in 1922, and around a quarter from then on.[130] Indochinese imports of cotton fabrics absorbed 6% of France's production in 1913,[131] and up to 22% of French cotton fabric exports in 1938.[132] When the total of all products is considered, French sales to Indochina, around 500 million current francs in the low year of 1933, came just after sales to the United States (868 million), and before sales to Italy (492 million). They were equivalent in 1938 to 22.8% of the French sales to the Belgian-Luxembourg Union, France's largest client, 27% of sales to England, and 44% of those to Germany. The following year, Indochina was eighth among France's clients.[133]

Placed in a highly unequal relationship of exchange with France due to colonial domination, Indochina was definitely one of the important pieces of the complex system of external regulations that French capitalism constructed for itself during the nineteenth century, a system of "colonial regulation" that was so influential and yet has been so misunderstood in the writing of its history. The price of this situation for Indochina was its underindustrialization. Indochina constituted the eastern section of this global system that functioned through the compensation of regional balances (of products, currencies, capital). Its pole was Saigon, which was the center of a vast network of exchange whose other axes were the three emporiums of Hong Kong, Singapore, and Marseille. The scheme of this compensation was simple but effective: Indochina could buy from France more than it sold to it because it sold to Asia more than it bought from it. Thus, in 1930, the profit margin of its trade balance with Hong Kong, China, Singapore, Siam, the Dutch East Indies, and Britain's Asian colonies was 780.7 million francs, which more than compensated for the deficit of its balance with France and the other French colonies (592.8 million). Furthermore, the surplus in the Indochinese trade balance with countries of the Far East allowed the colony to buy in francs and, additionally, appreciably to attenuate the deficit in France's general trade balance. These surpluses, achieved in strong currencies (dollars, sterling, florins), also contributed somewhat to the balancing of French accounts.

Through Indochina, French capitalism appropriated a part of the profits produced by the Far Eastern market that Britain had organized since the nineteenth century. It was a phenomenon that we cannot fully measure, in the absence of any reliable reconstruction of Indochinese balances of accounts and payments.[134] We know that the Indochinese balances of accounts and payments in the years 1934–39 were negative,[135] because of the multiple and often elusive transfers of profits to France, but we can glean little more. These transfers included civil servants' salaries, the savings of the French in Indochina, profits of companies, annuities for

TABLE 3.14 Funds from Indochina brought back to France,
1928–1931 (in millions of current francs)

	1928	1929	1930	First half of 1931
Dividends; taxes, business overhead	200	150	100	50
Personal savings	400	350	300	150
TOTAL	600	500	400	200

SOURCE: *Note sur la situation monétaire de l'Indochine, 1930–1931*, CAOM, Affaires politiques, 2645 (5).

loans, the profits from speculation on the difference between the official rate and the commercial rate of the piastre, and on the fluctuations of monetary exchange, movements of funds executed by Asians to China and Southeast Asia. We possess only very partial assessments of all of these transfers in the 1930s (table 3.14), which doubtless were substantial. The profits derived from global investment in Indochina were largely sent back to France. The repatriated capital was valued at 600 million current francs in 1928, 500 million in 1929, and 400 million in 1930.[136] In 1939, Smolski estimated its total at 314 million in 1935, 241 million in 1936, and 764 million in 1937:[137] the drain therefore perhaps rose to more than 520 million 1914 francs for these six years.

These considerable figures give us only a partial indication of the value of the net transfers of capital from Indochina to France, but they demonstrate the truth of the following judgment on the part of the *Dépêche coloniale* in 1934: "Indochina is an essential part of France's equilibrium."[138]

4

Colonial Society

The Colonizers and the Colonized

French Indochina was a multi-ethnic society in the sense that the French conquered, annexed territories, and organized peoples whose cultures were different, some marked with the imprint of Chinese or Indian civilization, and others by the perpetuation of a proto-Indochinese foundation.

The reassembling of these ethnic groups under French tutelage was at first an administrative and political enterprise. Through transformations in economic and social structures, which associated the new with what persisted from the past, domination by a foreign, European nation imprinted a certain unity on, or at least gave a consistency to, the social and cultural heterogeneity of the peninsula. This is why we can consider that one society in fact existed in Indochina, whose essential characteristic was its organization through a hierarchy based on racial identification. The French occupied the top of the social ladder because they were the conquerors and the colonizers; the Indochinese were below them because they were the conquered and the colonized. There were, however, preexisting social and ethnic hierarchies, dividing the princely aristocracy, scholars and monks, peasants, artisans, and merchants. There were also the Cham and Khmer groups, subjugated by the Vietnamese, and the Lao and montagnards, who were under the protection, even if distantly, of the Vietnamese. The Chinese also had an economic power that was not negligible.

French domination did not erase these hierarchies, but rather integrated them into a new system. Over time, the result was the increasing complexity of the stratification and functioning of Indochinese societies. The pluralism of these societies must be taken into consideration, because Vietnam (more precisely, each of

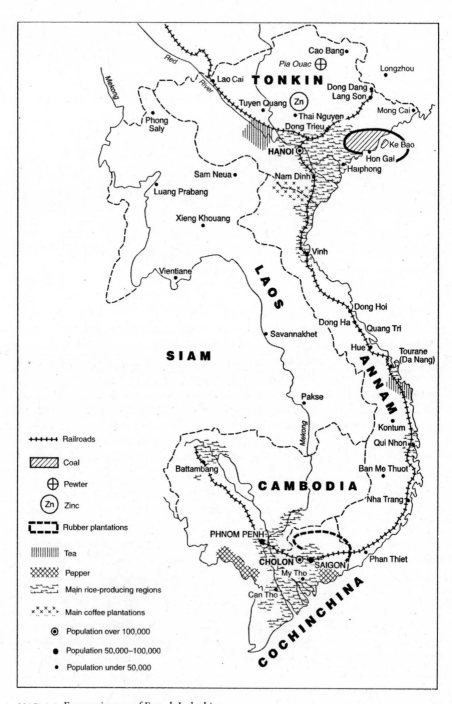

MAP 4.1. Economic map of French Indochina.

TABLE 4.1   French and total population of Indochina, 1913–1940

	1913 estimates	1921 census	1940 census
French population	23,700	24,482	34,000
Total population	16,000,000	20,000,000	22,655,000

TABLE 4.2   Geographic distribution of the French in Indochina, 1913–1940

	1913	1921	1940
Regions			
Cochinchina	7,357	11,429	16,550
Tonkin	5,338	9,643	12,589
Annam	1,676	2,125	2,211
Cambodia	1,068	1,515	2,023[a]
Laos	241	360	—
Urban centers			
Hanoi	4,488	6,121	5,856
Haiphong	2,000	2,096	2,350
Saigon-Cholon	7,580	9,278	17,364

SOURCE: Brenier, *Essai d'atlas statistique de l'Indochine française*; L. Cros, *L'Indochine française pour tous* (Paris, 1931). For 1940, see Centre des archives d'outre-mer, Aix-en-Provence, NF Indochine 1567.

[a] Figure for 1936.

the three *ky,* or countries: Cochinchina, Annam, Tonkin), Cambodia, and Laos all evolved at differing rhythms, thus acquiring specific features that nuanced, or even contrasted, different sectors that appeared seemingly unified under the name "Indochinese."

THE COLONIZERS

French demography evolved progressively in proportion to the expansion of its colonial possessions, the consolidation of political control, and the opening of new sectors of economic or extra-economic activity (table 4.1).

A Population of Managers and Bureaucrats

The French population had three permanent characteristics: it was concentrated at the two extremities of the peninsula; restricted to small, principally urban settlements in other areas; and resided mainly in large urban centers (table 4.2). Furthermore, half of the French population in these urban areas was comprised of civil servants (six thousand in 1929).[1]

As soon as the conquest was consolidated and the first occupiers had set up urban areas—central and mediating zones of colonial power, centers of expansion of French civilization—these towns became the main arenas of colonial settlement. The European population developed steadily; however, never to the point of fulfilling the following wish: "I have just indicated that it is desirable for the number of Europeans in the colonial countries to continually increase . . . this growth . . . alone can ensure a control of the nationalistic tendencies of the indigenous populations."[2] Parallel to the development of welcoming structures now able to receive more than just a male population, accustomed to the discomforts of military campaigns, and the temporary stays of traders or Christian missionaries, communication with France became easier. The regular steamship lines between Marseille and Saigon took thirty-six days in 1900 and thirty days in 1930. With the arrival of telegraph in 1921, and of airplanes that made the trip in ten days in 1931, and in five and a half in 1938, Indochina was no longer in an inaccessible location.

At the beginning of the century, Louis Imbert wrote that it was desirable for emigrants bound for Cochinchina to be married men and to bring their wives with them. "It is necessary for the French wife to go to the colonies to help, to console, and to support her husband, to watch over his well-being and his health," he explained.[3] By the 1930s, leaving France to be with one's husband and raise children in the colony, where conditions were close to those in France, did not require unusual daring. In fact, life in the colonies possessed certain attractions, namely, material advantages: "In any case, it remains certain: in an equivalent financial situation, in this colony, you can enjoy a way of life that is much more luxurious than that to which you could aspire in the metropole," Pierre Billotey observed.[4] There was also a heightening of social status, as Raoul Serène noted:

In Indochina, all French are somebody, all French have the right to consideration, to respect, to a rank . . . to servants, because all French are on a mission. At a family-run restaurant in a small village in the south of France, a professor who had been assigned to Indochina voiced his concern about knowing nothing of the life that one could lead there, while his wife was especially worried about what would be necessary for the house; one of his neighbors immediately replied that, having just spent twenty years in Saigon, he could inform them precisely: "For your house, Madame, you will have three servants: a bep for the kitchen, a boy for the service of the house, a coolie for the garden." The coffee had long been drunk by the time he finished speaking of grand dinners, soirees, and receptions.

"But what was your occupation?" wondered the professor.

"I was a barber."

Even if the barber was boasting, the story shows that if there was a shift in class in Indochina, it was upward.[5]

Urban Expansion

The urban nuclei created by the French reminded them of the towns that they had left behind. Already, in 1883, the view of Saigon "from afar" resembled Rochefort for Pierre Loti, who felt "an unexpected sensation, that of coming home. . . . I was on the shore, at nightfall, astonished after the exile of Tourane, to suddenly redis-cover the sound and the movement of a city, the open cafes, the women dressed in French style, the hum of cars."[6] A few years later, Henri d'Orléans wrote of "beau-tiful Hanoi,"[7] and *médecin-major* Charles-Édouard Hocquard waxed ecstatic about it: "I barely recognized this town; in place of a large dirty village surrounded by marshes that I described when I began the account of my journey, I find a neat city, well taken care of, complete with European-run hotels, which are relatively com-fortable. On all sides rise up villas and large trading houses."[8]

Forty-five years later, Hanoi was perceived as "certainly very French, owing to its new quarters, whose aspect is frankly Western; there are few or none of the ar-caded streets one finds in Phnom Penh or Hong Kong, nor verandas as in Saigon. The yellow-washed buildings bring to mind the old Spanish adobe style, and the roof terraces make one think of the Mediterranean, aside from their green-tiled balustrades. . . . It is only the Annamese houses, solidly built of bricks and white-washed under their brown tile roofs, that seem at all familiar to me."[9]

The Indochinese towns expanded rapidly in the decade that followed World War I. Governors-general conceived of ambitious urban projects. Just as Marshal Hubert Lyautey called on the architect Henri Prost, a first-place winner of the Prix de Rome, for such projects in Morocco, Maurice Long invited another laureate, Ernest Hebrard, to come to Indochina in 1921. The latter longed to give more co-herence to the colonial city with zoning that corresponded to urban functions—administration, business, residence—and at the same time for a style inspired by indigenous architecture that would be better adapted to the environment. What was needed was to preserve the old cities but install electricity and running water, Hebrard thought.[10]

The planning of Hanoi, which became the administrative, political, and cultural capital of the Indochinese Union, was the subject of a confrontation between two currents of thought. Some supported the conservation of the traditionally orga-nized urban space in which craft and agricultural villages, and the merchant city, were regrouped around a citadel; others wanted to start from scratch and build a single modern Western city.

The town of Hanoi grew by juxtaposing a European town to the Vietnamese one. The first privileged a neoclassical architectural style for its public buildings and a regional French style for its houses. The second preserved the old merchant town, but in altered form, introducing a mixed mode of construction, in which the *compartiment* (a low building that extended backward, with alternating open courts and enclosed rooms) was now built of stone and boasted two or three floors. Nevertheless, after the visit of Hebrard and his search for an "Indochinese style," the Vietnamese architects of the 1930s built villas in a modern Asian style in the districts where the Vietnamese middle class resided. Meanwhile, the growth of the population of Hanoi led to the formation, around this modernized urban area, of poorly organized conglomerations of precarious, unsanitary straw huts.[11]

In actuality, the functional distribution of districts in the cities of Indochina had occurred independently before the arrival of Hebrard, and not in obedience to governmental decree. The theory that the city should be built, first and foremost, for Europeans, certainly without excluding natives, but also without allowing them to mingle in the residential districts with Europeans, only ratified what was already the situation in practice.

With the exception of the city of Cholon, whose predominantly Chinese population ensured it a homogeneous and consistent character, in all the Indochinese towns, the location of residential and work areas depended on the place their inhabitants occupied in the colonial hierarchy, and therefore on ethnic criteria. Whether in Hanoi, Saigon, or Phnom Penh, there were precincts of villas surrounded with flower gardens for the European administrative and business officers and members of the liberal professions; the modest, intermediate villa districts were for the subordinate officers. Areas of mixed inhabitants were transitional between these and the purely Asian districts of the outskirts or the old towns (such as craft districts in Hanoi). Europeans of modest condition, "French from India," Eurasians, and Indochinese were intermixed there in rows of *compartiments* and dilapidated enclosed villas.[12] The Cité Heyraud on the outskirts of Saigon, the site of a terrible massacre of French in September 1945, was a typical example of such a transitional mixed district. Houses in these districts were constructed in stone and had running water, electricity, and sewage systems. Alongside, the poor districts extended, built on stilts, close to bodies of water or in conglomerations of straw huts, and in the absence of hygiene were victims of frequent epidemics (cholera, plague), fires during the dry season, and floods from the rising rivers. In 1937, 70% of the indigenous population of the Saigon-Cholon region (115,354 people) lived in straw huts.[13]

The same hierarchy was present in the little administrative agglomerations of the provinces or on the plantations. The most popular residential building was the bungalow, placed in an elevated or airy place, whose architecture, open veranda, and good ventilation were well adapted to the tropical climate. The gradual introduction, between 1920 and 1940, of kerosene and then electric lighting and refrigeration, the increase in the use of automobiles, the efficiency and the ease of acquiring quinine, then nivaquine against malaria, pushed back the limits of discomfort in the "bush." In 1925, Roland Dorgelès noted: "We shall no longer see the colonists and civil servants of the *Cercle vicieux* [vicious circle] on the terrace of the hotel in Cantho watching the river to see if they can make out a friend's boat—an event in their life as exiles. Now they all have their own cars and can cross the Bassac on a ferry powered by an engine; you can get to Saigon in one morning, when once it took days."[14]

The Colonial Lifestyle

There were compensations for the severity of the hot, humid climate, the risk of anemia, and the accelerated degradation of the human organism; those who had the right by contract or had the financial means took periodic holidays (every three or five years) in the metropole. Later, it was possible to find a substitute for the coolness of France and the curative spa waters of Vichy, which were believed to be good for the "colonial liver," in hill stations like Da Lat, where the Grand Hôtel was finished in 1922, Bana in Annam, Tam Dao in Tonkin, and Bokor in Cambodia. Da Lat, with its villas and hotels amid the pines and the magnificent *lycée* Yersin (a high school named for the Pasteur Institute doctor who had discovered the site in 1896), attracted not only French vacationers but also Chinese tradesmen, French plantation owners and livestock breeders, and Vietnamese commercial gardeners, who raised temperate-zone fruits and vegetables like carrots and strawberries there. Cap Saint-Jacques (close to Saigon), Nha Trang (in Annam), Do Son (in Tonkin), and Kep (in Cambodia) became popular as seaside resorts. A worldly social life also appeared very early in the big cities: "Having barely set foot upon the red soil, under the crimson poincianas [called "flames of the forest" in Malaya] of the Indochinese capital, new arrivals cannot restrain their joy when, after three or four weeks' liberty, they discover in the capital a village where they find themselves once again, an administrative capital where everything is in the style of a French city. . . . Finally, and especially, O French delight—the cafe! There are many lively cafes, overflowing under glass marquees and tents that stretch out to the pavement."[15]

Opinions, however, were divided. In a letter to his sister in 1894, Lyautey opined that Saigon looked like "cardboard decoration." The municipal theaters of Saigon and of Hanoi (whose central location and architecture copied the Opéra de Paris's Palais Garnier) inspired pride in the Europeans of those cities, but in 1910, the dramatist and academician Eugène Brieux dismissed the latter building as a "pretentious caricature of the Paris Opera House."

Corporate or regional associations appeared early, among them the Association des démobilisés de la marine et de l'armée de terre (Association of Veterans of the Navy and Army), that of the veterans of World War I, those of the former pupils of the Chasseloup-Laubat, Albert-Sarraut, and Sisowath High Schools, the Taberd School, and so on. L'Amicale des Corses was probably most active, Corsicans being numerous in Indochina and the French group that displayed the most solidarity. The horse races at the hippodrome in Saigon, football or rugby matches, cycling races, and wild game hunts all provided an extended range of entertainment without which the colonial tour of duty, with its disorientation, monotony, and idleness, ran the risk of ending in depression, alcoholism, opium addiction, or adultery. The Cercle sportif saigonnais (Saigon Sporting Circle) and its Hanoi equivalent catered to local high society—candidates for membership had to be sponsored—and offered a wide range of recreational activities, including bridge, swimming pools, tennis courts, gymnasiums, fencing, and dancing. In Saigon, at the "Boule Gauloise," games of *pétanque* and *belote* reigned. The Army and Navy clubs of the same town constituted another social center. All these groups were organized according to the internal hierarchical divisions of the European community.

Indochina was not an El Dorado, or a vocational haven, for everyone. Many who went there to find fortune, make a career, pursue a religious or secular mission, give free rein to a taste for adventure, or simply escape from an unhappy life at home were destined to be disappointed. The colony had its parasites and failures who lived quietly on the fringes of its conventional majority. At the other extreme were unique, eccentric personalities who acquired fame, sometimes fleeting, as in the case of Marie-Charles David de Mayréna, who established himself as "King Marie I of Sedang," or sometimes the beginning of lasting renown, as in the case of André Malraux. Others have been forgotten because of their modesty: for each Dr. Yersin, how many other physicians or hospitable nuns, devoted to their patients, have yet to see their names recorded by history? How many teachers were there who left an indelible mark on young Indochinese minds?

Social Cleavages

If, as a whole, European society was at the summit of the colony's social pyramid, it was nevertheless divided into socio-professional groups of unequal status. The community of the colonizers was also divided, according to the vocabulary of the time, by cleavages along "racial" lines (although the quality of being French was more a legal than an ethnic notion) and political differences.

Within the broader typology of the colonies, Indochina was not a colony of settlement but one of managers and supervisors. Certainly, the mythology of the colonial settler had its adepts and advocates; the colonizer was described, in terms more emphatic than lyrical, as a "superior being": "The colonial settler has a more developed brain than his counterpart in Europe. He is better armed for life's struggles. He is distinct, a legitimate son of nature. He is man in his greatest capacity."[16]

But with its tropical climate, and with rice growing dominant in the densely populated deltas, Indochina offered nothing that compared to the Mediterranean environment, even that of Algeria's Mitidja. In addition, the ideal of the soldier-laborer, exalted by Algeria's Governor-General Thomas-Robert Bugeaud, confronted an entirely different ecological and cultural setting in Indochina. Colonist farmers and plantation owners certainly existed, but they adapted themselves to Indochina and became, with a few exceptions, agricultural entrepreneurs who did not reside on their concessions. The immigrant French—the expatriates—were principally civil servants (both civil and military) or traders, or their employees. When soldiers and sailors got demobilized there, it was just a change of function (to the police or customs) for many of them, or they found work as business employees, plantation supervisors, or factory foremen.

Colonists against the Administration

The *colons* generally regarded the administration and its civil servants as a burden. They criticized the latter for being too numerous and for swallowing up sums of money that could have been used for the colony's economic development. What happened in Indochina simply reproduced the contradictions between the individual and the state, the administration and the individual. At the start of the establishment of the French in Cochinchina, Governor-General Admiral Pierre de la Grandière expressed his disdain in this way: "It is necessary to be here, and to hear them in all their pretentiousness and arrogance, to be in a position to judge them. Their insolence and clumsiness, their presumptuousness and bad faith would make God lose patience. There is not one good, honorable man among all the traders of Cochinchina. It is sad to say, but it is true."[17]

From then on, the conflict was unceasing. Echoes of it can be found in the records of the sessions of the Colonial Council of Cochinchina, a consultative body and a kind of "colonial" parliament that was chiefly a forum for expression that many governors sought to contain. The existence of this site in which governmental decisions were contested, and where governors and administrators were even sometimes attacked, without a doubt encouraged native Cochinchinese to question colonial authority. Colonists also possessed a press that did not treat civil servants with much tact. The marquis de Montpezat's *La volonté indochinoise,* Tirard's *Le colon tonkinois,* and P. Chêne's *Le paysan de Cochinchine* were frequently involved in polemics and sometimes attacked governors-general, especially when their political allegiances, as in the case of the socialist Alexander Varenne, displeased them. At the root of these confrontations was the fact that the administration regulated the relations between the *colons* and the natives and often opposed the abuses of the former (although the *colons,* likewise, opposed the administration's abuses).

The colonists were also opposed to the financial powers, more precisely to the privileged banking institution, the Banque de l'Indochine. The rise and prosperity of the monoculture of rice in the west of Cochinchina and the cultivated plantations (rubber, coffee, etc.) during the 1920s were based on massive indebtedness. The economic crisis revealed to public opinion that the most important creditor of the rice growers and planters was the Banque de l'Indochine, either directly or indirectly through its affiliate the Crédit foncier de l'Indochine (Land Credit of Indochina). The seizure of Mme de la Souchère's rubber plantations in 1932 triggered the indignation of the small and medium planters against the power of the banks. The stabilization of the Indochinese piastre in 1931, through the pegging of Indochinese currency to the gold standard, along with fixing the exchange rate at 10 francs to 1 piastre, crystallized an underlying conflict between the colonists and the Banque de l'Indochine. The rice growers, who had difficulty selling their rice because of the rate decrease, considered that this measure would aggravate their difficulties and hasten their demise. They blamed both the Banque de l'Indochine and the Gouvernement général. The attacks of the press and street demonstrations transformed the discontent of the major French and Vietnamese rice growers, now unified, into a class struggle. Certain pamphleteers even went as far as to brandish the threat of secession and the autonomy of Cochinchina.

But, despite these conflicts, the civil service also had a "positive" impact for some. Working in the administration was the goal of some young educated Indochinese. For the Europeans, there were advantages linked to income: the famous "colonial supplement" (seven-tenths of gross pay), which doubled the metropolitan salary, was the main privilege, but not the only one. Until 1926, a money-changing indemnity compensated for fluctuations in the piastre's exchange rate. Periodic vacations in France, accommodation, and social status were all elements that accentuated the disparities in status, salary, and standard of living between European and indigenous civil servants, including those who served colonial bureaucracy; those employed in public works, for example, collected salaries fixed at ten-seventeenths of those of Europeans.[18] With the progressive emergence of an Indochinese middle class, a demand originated from this for the equal treatment of those with degrees and those without degrees who occupied identical positions.

Differentiation between French social classes was based not only on the position one occupied in a profession or an institution, and on salary and wealth, but also on ethnic origins. From this point of view, French-Indochinese Eurasians and natives of the French territories in India (e.g., Pondicherry) and of the islands (Reunion and the Antilles) constituted a separate group among French citizens.

French Indians, to whom the generic name *Pondychériens* was applied, arrived early in Indochina. With regard to their French citizenship, they had an antecedence that was invoked by one of them in a reply to a magistrate at the Saigon courthouse who was of Corsican origin: "Sir, we were French one hundred years before you!" Their familiarity with French techniques and procedures qualified them to fill certain occupations, notably in the administration. There was a *Pondychérien* contingent in the police, customs, the *régies* (state-controlled companies), courthouses (among court clerks, lawyers, and even magistrates), the Treasury, and the accounting services of the administration and businesses. They should in no way be confused with Indian subjects of the British crown engaged in the textile business and financial trades, such as the caste of *chettys*, or *chettiars*, generically called "Malabars."

The concentration of French citizens from India in Cochinchina gave them considerable weight in the territory's diverse electoral councils (municipal, Colonial Council, legislative). The Cochinchina deputy Ernest Outrey was even accused by his adversaries of owing his mandate to the votes of Indians whom, his accusers claimed, he had rewarded with many favors. Whether this was simply slander on the part of the defeated candidates (also ready to benefit from the same votes) or the truth is not of particular importance. More significant is the way the Vietnamese perceived the disparity of status and rights that existed between them and those they judged as colonized, and to whom they denied a superiority that they were reluctantly willing to grant to the Europeans. The attitude of many, notably the Vietnamese, toward blacks, is clearly expressed in a letter written to the minister of the colonies on May 31, 1931, by M. Do Huu Thinh: "We have just learned with surprise that an Indochinese administrator of the black race is going to be appointed as our governor. . . . It would be impolitic to impose this on the Annamese population, who only barely yield to the superiority of the white race, but will never do the same to *hommes de couleur* [men of color] of the other colonies, . . . negro or mulatto civil servants will always be badly received in Indochina."[19]

French-Indochinese Eurasians were not a foreign component of the French population. Legitimate marriages accounted for only a minority; the majority were illegitimate children abandoned by their French fathers, unknown or known, who had returned to their homeland unconcerned with the fate of their offspring. In these cases, the children grew up in the indigenous environment of the maternal family, when there was one, and essentially became Vietnamese, Cambodian, or Lao, without ever completely losing the stigma of their double origin. Uprooted or caught between two cultures, those without family sank into delinquency: theft, prostitution, vagrancy. After 1907, orphans identified as Eurasian were taken in by private secular or religious associations, which ensured them a decent upbringing and a minimal European-style education. The goal of these charitable institutions was their integration into colonial society. With the exception of some cases in the administration and the liberal professions, they were placed in subordinate management positions: in the Army and the Navy, as plantation supervisors, public works foremen, police, and prison guards, and also in other tertiary occupations opened up to Eurasians. The École des mécaniciens de la Marine (School of Navy Mechanics) in Saigon and then the École des enfants de troupe de Dalat (Dalat Army Children's School) were specially created to accommodate them.

Eurasians were conscious of the ambiguity implicit in their double origin and conscious of not being full-fledged French citizens. Their determination to be integrated into the dominant group only accentuated the distance that separated them from the dominated and aggravated their rejection by the latter. Victims of a double-sided racism, they were often racist themselves. Without doubt, they were perceived differently according to the Indochinese society in which they lived: prejudices against them were more vigorous among the Vietnamese than among the Lao or the Khmer. The historic evolution of the French possession of Indochina, and the limited extent of the European population, did not permit Eurasians to become a permanent and lasting component of the population of Indochina, unlike in the case of the islands of the Indian Ocean, the Caribbean, and Latin America. They were destined to melt either into the Indochinese population or into that of the metropole.[20]

Humiliation

The relationships and internal contradictions of the French collectivity developed before the eyes of the indigenes. Very early on, the Vietnamese, Cambodians, and Lao realized that they were not facing a monolithic block: masters did not only have weaknesses, they were also opposed to one another on economic, political, religious, and personal grounds, all of which represented opportunities that could be seized by the colonized to contest their power and resist their domination.

The larger society in French Indochina functioned essentially around the relational axis of colonizer-colonized, but in the diversified space of the Indochinese Union, relations between groups and between individuals were neither identical nor unchangeable. The foundations of Franco-Indochinese relations were the historical conceptions, the mental images, and therefore the stereotypes of the colonizers. Certainly, these did not fully determine all collective and individual behavior, but they imbued it to various extents, when they did not dictate it. The French were in Indochina, they believed, in order to bring modern civilization to backward peoples. This credo, explained by Jules Ferry's famous July 28, 1885, speech on the *mandat civilisateur* (civilizing mandate), was the code of colonial conduct.

This article of faith, however, was interpreted and presented in different ways, depending on those who professed it and those to whom it was directed. So the Lao was represented as heedless and sensual, the Cambodian as passive and not particularly sharp, the Annamese as intelligent, proud, and secretive, the Chinese as active and shifty, and the Malabar as deceitful. Whatever the variants within this typology, they all tended to place Asians in a lower position that justified French tutelage. Bazin, a recruiter of labor for the southern plantations, described the coolies as credulous, improvident children. And didn't the French residents superior in Annam and Cambodia treat those countries' "protected" sovereigns and their entourages like mischievous or faceless children? The French resident superior referred to the emperor Duy Tan as "this little *con* [idiot]." A quarter of a century later, Admiral Jean Decoux announced with contempt: "All Annamese princes are made from the same tobacco [i.e., of the same stuff]." Governor-General Pierre Pasquier was one of the few to admire the character of the high mandarins of Hue, whereas the other French representatives saw the customs of the royal courts as a mass of imagined fantasies or a tangle of contemptible schemes. The journalist Andrée Viollis, who accompanied Minister of the Colonies Paul Reynaud in 1931, reported that the prime minister of the court of Hue, His Eminence Nguyen Huu Bai, was refused access to the official car and made to travel with the journalists.[21]

Even Raoul Serène, a Christian who pleaded for reconciliation and friendship between individuals, underlined the fact that by nature, the colonizer-colonized relation was one of master and servant:

> The French usually disembarked in Indochina determined to be on the best possible terms with the Annamese. It was only gradually, moving from one small misunderstanding to another, that they arrived at isolation, and a separation from the Annamese world; but while everything seemed to lead toward this separation, everything also led away from it. At worst, if they hardly knew Annamese people other than the *nhaques, beps,* boys, coolies, secretaries, and tradesmen, no one except the servants of whom they were the masters, they perceived quickly that this was a whole world with which it was easy to come to an arrangement. French and Annamese constituted two worlds in which each group got by; two worlds separated by a gap that one did not mind, as long as one got along well enough. The problem of connecting did not present itself.[22]

The young Vietnamese who studied in France noticed the progressive change in tone and attitude of the French with whom they traveled on their return: after the Red Sea was passed, the French were increasingly distant toward the Indochinese and *tutoiement* (use of the familiar/disrespectful second person address *tu*) progressively replaced *vouvoiement* (the formal/respectful *vous*). This *tutoiement* could be employed daily in regard to any indigenous person, whether he was a rifleman or a physician. It was only in 1941 that Governor-General Decoux officially prohibited its use in speaking to Indochinese.

The logic of colonial relations favored arbitrary and brutal conduct toward the natives, whether they were coolies, peasants, laborers, or white-collar workers. A European might believe he had the right to beat, sometimes fatally, a worker whom he perceived to be lazy or rebellious, or a random person who had not made way for him quickly enough or who had refused him his seat closer to the screen at the movies. The records are rich with incidents and even crimes that illustrate in a tragic and revolting manner the nature of relations between the French and the Indochinese, despite the advice given to those considering emigrating to become colonists in Tonkin, to whom it was recommended to treat the "docile and hardworking" laborers well and to "pay them regularly."[23] The lawyer Georges Garros, father of the famous aviator, gave in illustration a case in which a colonist's farmers ran away: "The European will, with legitimate spite, declare war on his indigenous neighbors. Sometimes even—this has been seen—his Chassepot rifle goes off 'by itself,' killing a peaceful *ta dien* [farmer] skirting his property who had committed no other wrong than to look like a marauder to the lord of the place. A human life sacrificed? Legal intervention, involuntary homicide, eight days in jail, suspended sentence: the European reappears the following day and goes back to his occupations and his rifle. The Annamese does not understand this solution."[24]

Twenty or twenty-five years later, the legal annals related similar incidents on rubber plantations, such as those that in November 1936 led *Procureur général* Dupré to instruct the *juge de paix* of Bien Hoa province: "It is imperative to repress without exception the acts of brutality inflicted on the coolies by European plantation assistants. These acts are too frequent. . . . To be viable and fertile, the act of colonizing must be accomplished in the spirit of human dignity."[25] In 1926, Governor-General Alexandre Varenne recommended "treating the Annamese with respect."[26] In 1930, Minister of the Colonies Albert Sarraut insisted on the application of equal punishments to the colonized and the colonizers, exhorting: "Watch out for racial verdicts!"[27]

Fortunately, the French did not permanently exercise an abusive or oppressive power over the natives. Neither their mentality nor their circumstances lent themselves to the generalization of violence and despotism. It is necessary to contextualize the polemical anticolonialist literature, though it founded its denunciations on real facts. Within layers of the population of equivalent status (large landowners, members of the liberal professions), there could be meetings between French and Indochinese for professional motives, convergence of interests, or simply because of social obligations. But there, as well, often enough, the "current did not flow" and the encounters were limited to an exchange of politeness and banalities. A young Vietnamese schoolboy observed that his French and Vietnamese teachers said "hello and goodbye" to one another and did not associate any further.[28] A Catholic Vietnamese lawyer, who himself had good relations with the French, depicted the situation in the Cercle franco-annamite de Longxuyen (Cochinchina), which was frequented by the provincial elite, thus: "Annamese and French mingle with one another there. But if there are outsiders, groups form. In those cases, it is preferable for the French not to be reserved and to take the lead in approaching the Annamese, whose shyness and relatively lower status keep them a bit on the defensive."

In the same town, however, Dr. Duong Van An, who also maintained good relations with the "advanced" French, nonetheless came into conflict with Europeans of lower positions. The former *conseiller colonial* Dang Van Dan, the largest landowner of the province (with eight thousand hectares of rice fields) expressed his grievances against the conduct of French subordinate civil servants toward the Annamese population. This was in 1943.[29]

The French novelist Marguerite Duras accurately captured the position of the Europeans in colonial society and the nature of the relations between the dominant minority and the dominated majority. Her novel *L'amant,* notably, depicts a love affair between a European woman and an Asian man, something that was a transgression of the colonial code of conduct. In another mode, Régis Warnier's 1992 film *Indochine* presents a fairly accurate picture of colonial Indochina, although it does this through a melodramatic plot that is not lacking in exaggeration or misnomers.

Individually, the French did not observe the tacit rule of separation from the Indochinese. There were, for instance, men who took native women as mistresses, and who were thus able to enter into the Indochinese milieu, although this was not the case with all those who took a wife or a local concubine. The idea was rampant in Indochina that the arrival of Frenchwomen in the colony was an obstacle to communication and a factor of separation between the Europeans and the Indochinese. It was common to imagine that the Indochinese woman, whether a legitimate wife or concubine, acted as an intermediary between communities. (These concubines were identified in Vietnamese as *con gai,* a notable example of the pejorative connotation that can be attached to a neutral word, which originally simply designated a person of the feminine sex or a little girl; the same is true of the neutral term *nha que,* meaning peasant.) The propagation of the European family was only a secondary and supplemental reason for colonial segregation. Mixed unions, however, did not necessarily imply closeness between communities, since they also obeyed the general logic of colonial relations.

In Tonkin during the 1920s, with his Tonkinese wife and collaborator, Amédée Clementi founded the magazine *L'Argus indochinois,* which attacked colonialism and openly advocated the independence of the "Annamese." After publishing around two hundred issues, he closed down the magazine and retired to Thai Binh, where the couple was murdered in 1945.[30] In Cochinchina, a Breton colonist named Le Nestour, who retired to his island of Tortue, kept the documents relating to a village spirit, which the French authorities wanted to seize because the village had chosen as its guardian spirit that of an individual who had resisted French conquest. Le Nestour spent his life fighting against the administration and defending the peasants who were his neighbors.

It was often ideology or politics that provided the grounds for understanding and cooperation between colonizer and colonized. A young Vietnamese man who completed his secondary education in the *collège* of Quy Nhon (in central Annam) at the end of the 1920s, despised M. Gabriel, his math professor, who had called the Annamese the "dirty race." But, along with all his friends, he liked M. Mariani, who taught history, and who, as a member of the Ligue des droits de l'homme et du citoyen (League of Rights of Man and Citizen), exalted the Revolution of 1789, the overthrow of monarchical despotism, and popular sovereignty. They waited for his class impatiently and "listened to him passionately."[31]

Freemasonry was also a locus for encounters and cultural interaction between French people and middle-class Vietnamese. Among the participants were Nguyen

Phan Long (leader of the Constitutionalist Party and director of the newspaper *Le flambeau d'Annam*) and Tran Trong Kim (inspector of Vietnamese primary schools, historian, and head of the independent government after March 9, 1945). In 1927, the Ruche d'Orient lodge in Saigon believed that it was necessary to establish equal rights between Vietnamese and French. This lodge deemed that the Vietnamese should participate in the administration of their country, since Freemasons had the duty to facilitate political evolution, and "to guide it so that it does not overtake us, and crush us while overtaking us."[32] Georges Coulet, historian of the secret Annamese societies, envisioned a fruitful cooperation between Freemasonry and these societies, once they had abandoned their conspiratorial goals.[33] Between 1925 and 1940, Vietnamese began being admitted into Masonic lodges. Two lodges, Confucius and Kong phu tseu, were even made up entirely of Vietnamese, and had to confront the hostility of the administration and the French lodges, who feared they would become centers of opposition to French domination. Many Freemasons would indeed join the revolution of 1945, the best known of these being the lawyer Trinh Dinh Thao and the doctor Pham Ngoc Thach.[34] During the same period, Paul Monin, a Saigon-based lawyer, co-published a magazine supportive of Annamese nationalists, with André Malraux as his partner.[35]

The Popular Front era gave French leftists opportunities to cooperate with Vietnamese revolutionaries. The journalist Ernest Babut, a member of the Section française de l'Internationale ouvrière (SFIO), the French branch of the Workers' International, and of the Ligue des Droits de l'homme, who had met Ho Chi Minh in Paris during the 1920s, waged a campaign against the excesses of the colonial regime alongside Phan Chu Trinh and other nationalists. Babut was imprisoned during Decoux's governorship (1941–45) and subsequently remained a target of anger and harassment by Hanoi colonists. As early as 1945, Babut supported the Democratic Republic of Vietnam. When he had a run-in with the Sûreté and a magistrate, the Vietnamese writer Nguyen Cong Hoan was able to look for help to R. Bréant, director of the French school of Nam Dinh and a "comrade" in the SFIO of Tonkin. Edgar Ganofsky, manager of the journal *La lutte* (1933) and then of *Tia Sang* (1939) in Saigon, was fired from his teaching post and finished his days utterly destitute, living in a straw hut with the family of a rickshaw driver. There were only four French people in the funeral cortege that accompanied his body to the cemetery in 1943. Clearly, the French who chose to transgress the invisible barriers that separated the colonizers from the colonized were no more than a fringe, outcasts regarded as traitors to the community of interests and the moral cohesion of the colonizers.[36]

THE COLONIZED

Within its political and administrative borders, the Indochinese Union assembled a multi-ethnic, multicultural population. The history and social organization of these various peoples rendered them more or less receptive to the contributions of the dominating nation. In consequence, the Vietnamese, Cambodian, and Lao societies, along with ethnic minorities, evolved at an uneven pace during the colonial period.

An Ethnic Mosaic

The Vietnamese, in spite of the division of their geopolitical space into three *ky* (Cochinchina, Annam, Tonkin), showed evidence of a demographic dynamism that was already one of their characteristics, and that propelled a tendency to geographical expansion. This tendency, stimulated and even organized by the French, enabled the Vietnamese to settle by the thousands in Laos and in Cambodia (193,926 out of 3,049,524 inhabitants in 1939),[37] where they were regrouped in cities and worked in the mining and forest industries. Thousands also relocated from Tonkin and northern Annam, not only to Cochinchina but also to New Caledonia and the New Hebrides.

These migrations were certainly part of the division of labor introduced by the colonial economy, but they were also the continuation of an earlier process that existed throughout the peninsula, as is illustrated by the presence of numerous Chinese communities there. It was also during colonization that the Vietnamese initiated or intensified their permanent settlement in the highlands of Tonkin (middle regions) and in central Annam (in the high plateaus) and completed their colonization of Transbassac (in the Mekong Delta).

The migration of peasants, fishermen, or the coolies who worked on plantations was certainly indicative of overpopulation, but also of an aptitude to adapt quickly to the new disciplines and work techniques of the rubber industry or tin mining. The Vietnamese also supplied white-collar workers for the bureaucracy and commerce, however, which suggests that they were faster than the Khmer or the Lao (or at least started earlier) in learning shorthand typing, modern accounting, the use of the wireless telegraph, and driving automobiles. They were the equivalent of the *Pondychériens* in relation to the other Indochinese.

Confronted with the industrious nature of the Vietnamese, which allowed them (since it was no longer a situation of military conquest) to impose themselves as indispensable guests for the orderly functioning of the economy and institutions, the Lao displayed a tolerant or insouciant hospitality. The Khmer, however, adopted the defensive withdrawal of a people who had witnessed the weakening of their material and political power since the fifteenth century. They showed a sensitivity and even hostility, capable of degenerating into murderous aggressiveness. In Cochinchina, which had once been Khmer territory, the Cambodians retreated in the face of Vietnamese colonization: they were only 330,106 in 1940. Still strongly regrouped in some provinces (Tra Vinh, Chau Doc, and Rach Gia), they had been unable to prevent the massive erosion of their positions elsewhere. Their land had been taken away, they were reduced to farming at the service of Vietnamese landowners, or forced to wander homeless. A revolt of the Cambodians of the village of Ninh Thanh Loi (Rach Gia) in 1928 testified to their grievances against the Vietnamese, while other incidents and conflicts punctuated interethnic relations in Cochinchina. All that was lacking was the existence of national states and nationalistic ideologies to confer a weight and gravity to the hitherto localized and episodic conflicts of the colonial period.

The French benefited from these more or less conflicting cohabitations: the 80,000 Cambodians in the Tra Vinh province constituted an "element of stability and peace," Administrative Inspector Renou wrote in 1943, adding: "There is no communist trouble." Elsewhere, that is, in the high plateaus of Annam and in the highlands of Tonkin, individuals of the Rhade, Hmong, Tai, and Nung communities were appointed by the colonial administration as guardians of stability and order. The center of the peninsula was an almost virgin domain; the last cartographic survey of the colonial period still showed white sections of uncharted and intractable territory. In 1934, the Moï, as they were known pejoratively, attacked the Le Rolland camp, an advanced post of French penetration. In 1937, other Moï, under the direction of Sam Bram, rebelled; a mobile column traveled through the region of Pleiku to repress them. Once intractable, then pacified and Christianized, these regions were a land of adventure for Marie-Charles David de Mayréna, who, on June 3, 1888, proclaimed himself King Marie I of Sedang (an evanescent statelet he founded among the tribes of the interior). The center was the domain of evangelizing Christians who were in constant conflict with the administrator Leopold Sabatier, who was anxious to preserve the territorial and cultural integrity of the Moï against the desires of colonists and Catholic missionaries.[38]

The bare-breasted women, totems, and sorcerers of the interior evoked strange, nostalgic imaginings from the Europeans, who contrasted their wild, ingenuous liberty with the refined culture of the people of the plains. Like their counterparts in the Sahara desert, young officers stationed in upper Tonkin experienced a feeling of freedom, of no longer being subjected to the prohibitions of their society, of being regarded as lords.[39] In 1911, Jean Ajalbert summed up what a European might feel "amid Indochinese nature": "I imagine that it is, especially, a feeling of being released from the complicated burdens of European life, of escaping from social constraints, of being self-possessed, of knowing an unsuspected independence, as well as the pride of danger, the discovery of oneself through the necessity of personal initiative, the pride of locating oneself apart, outside time."[40] Though the ethnic divisions favored them, the French were divided on how to treat the various groups. Some French preferred the temperament of the Lao and Khmer, whom they judged to be less "stubborn" than their neighbors; others could not conceal their preference for the Vietnamese, whom they considered more intelligent, more rational, and more industrious than the other Indochinese. Jean Marquet expressed this opinion powerfully in his book *Les cinq fleurs: L'Indochine expliquée.* Inspired by G. Bruno's (i.e., Augustine Fouillée's) famous patriotic textbook *Le tour de la France par deux enfants,* and published by the Direction de l'instruction publique en Indo-Chine (Office of Public Instruction in Indochina) in Hanoi in 1928, it depicted only Vietnamese characters and exalted their dynamism. Though Marquet celebrated the tutelary power of France and the Pax Gallica, he also recalled the existence of Vietnamese national heroes: the Trung sisters, Tran Quoc Tuan, Le Loi, and Dinh Bo Linh.

The Chinese were the sixth component of the peninsula's multi-ethnic population. Long established in the peninsula, and numbering 326,000 in 1940,[41] they occupied the professional "niches" left open by the natives: domestic and foreign trade, pepper growing, produce farming, mining zinc, tin, and coal, some sectors of the craft industry, and urban services (rice-field workers in Cholon, dockers in Haiphong). This caused Georges Groslier, who was responsible for the rebirth of traditional Cambodian arts, some concern: "Since ancient times, all of Cambodia's trade has remained in Chinese hands and today [in 1925] a Khmer store, even in Phnom Penh, is pretty much impossible to find."[42]

Omnipresent in Tonkin, Cambodia, and Laos, the Chinese participated in the colonization of Cochinchina in the seventeenth century: Cholon (Kwoo Loon, "the Great Market") and the port of Ha Tien (on the Gulf of Siam) were their creations. They preserved their ethnicity through endogamy, but they also mingled, through mixed unions, with the local populations.[43] The positions they acquired were essentially the result of deficiencies in certain sectors of activity. The European traders of Cochinchina finally resigned themselves to working with them, calling them "our indispensable enemies." All European commercial or industrial companies used some Chinese compradors, who were obligatory intermediaries for dealings with the network of their indigenous clientele. In Saigon, the comprador of the Banque de l'Indochine, Yip Pak Hung, had "ten women and three Citroëns."

Chinese population in French Indochina has been evaluated at 293,000 inhabitants in 1921 and rose to 418,000 in 1940. Migratory flows sporadically slowed down or even regressed due to the economic situation and regional politics, but the general trend was up. These givens, which should be used cautiously, represent a relatively small percentage of the total population, but the importance of the Chinese communities in Indochina should be evaluated in terms of the economic roles they played.

Work division according to ethnic identities facilitated daily cohabitation; the Vietnamese had irreverently changed the term *khach tru* (immigrant guest)—a term to designate the Chinese—into *khach chu* (guest uncle). The overall peaceful relations were shaken up every now and again by scuffles, without any extreme consequences. The newspapers and official chronicles mention only one violent conflict between the Vietnamese and the Chinese in a neighborhood of Haiphong in

1927. The majority of disputes were between employers and employees or active and silent partners, just as with those between Chinese and Chinese, Vietnamese and French, or Vietnamese and Vietnamese.

The Chinese entrepreneurial spirit stimulated that of the most active and ambitious Indochinese, that is, the Vietnamese. In the 1920s, an economic nationalism against the Chinese began to appear among the Vietnamese. It was only in 1976, however, that the movement to withdraw the Vietnamese economy from Chinese control would take a radical turn; this was something even Ngo Dinh Diem had failed to accomplish in 1956.

The French therefore conquered an Indochina where peoples different in their numbers, their dynamism, and their ambitions cohabited separately or interlinked. Their numbers were less important than the strategic positions they occupied in the territory (for instance, border or pioneer zones), in the economy, or in the bureaucracy. The system of interethnic relations, linked to power relations, was one of the factors that influenced the fate of Indochinese peoples. The colonizers, who had involved themselves in a game that was already under way, did not fundamentally modify the ethnic chessboard, but they made sure to retain control of its pieces. The Pax Gallica both nourished Indochinese conflicts and postponed their settlement.

The Peasants

An essential instrument of production and the main source of wealth, the land was the primary criterion of social status. It was the site of the implantation of the primordial and dominant element of social organization: the village. The Vietnamese village had a strongly integrated political organization and a distinctly defined territory. The Cambodian or Lao village was more loosely organized. But all were inevitably the nodal points for the impact of colonial policies, and subject to transformations that, although gradual, were profound.

Contrary to what some nationalistic authors imagined and some French believed, the Vietnamese village (xa) was not a village democracy. Oligarchies and gerontocracies retained the power at the heart of the villages in order to regulate—to their advantage—social relations between registered and unregistered persons and to negotiate relations with the imperial government. In any case, the inequality of internal relations was only important to those French who were imbued with democratic ideals. If the village functioned in such a way as to place some in power over others, through its privileges and its abuses, it also implied duties: for better or worse, the weak and dependent were not abandoned. The Cambodian system of patronage, where villagers were under the protection of a prince, comprised an analogous mechanism. A subordinate mandarin (tri huyen) explained the unequal effects of the great economic crisis by recalling: "What attenuates misery is that the good Annamese peasant does not refuse a bowl of rice to his poorest relative."[44]

During the same period of crisis, urban house renters in Saigon demanded a moratorium on rent and their arrears from their landlords by invoking a solidarity (or more appropriately an indulgence) due to the fellow citizens of a given community.[45]

At the time, some French officers, educated in the classical humanities, were seduced by the historical analogy with *La Cité antique* (the ancient city) that the French historian Fustel de Coulanges had analyzed so impressively. Most of all, however, the village offered an ideal instrument for the application of administrative decisions. Before Émile Luro had theorized this idea in the courses he gave to administrative trainees, Commandant d'Ariès had written, in December 1861: "It [the village] absorbs the individual into itself to allow only the collective being to subsist and it is this very remarkable and very important fact, in my opinion, that explains the role that the village plays in the Annamese administration."[46]

In each village, the French appointed a minor notable to be responsible for and an instrument of their administration, and who had an essentially executive role: the *ly truong*. The *grand notables,* holders of the moral authority and/or the real social power, hid themselves behind him. In Cambodia, the traditional *mesrok* (village head) became the *mekhum*.[47] The latter, like the Vietnamese *ly truong,* was viewed as similar to the mayor of a French *commune.* When there was no village council, as was the case in Cambodia, the French created one. It was essential for the colonial authorities to appoint individuals to carry out their instructions, and who could be charged with the responsibility for the tax levy, the performance of corvée, the military draft, and the maintenance of order.

Behind this organization, the villages continued to support relations of coexistence, solidarity, and antagonism. The grievances of the Vietnamese peasants about the discriminatory distribution of the local rice fields highlight family networks, with their debtors, and sometimes even their thugs, all participating in the disputes, rivalries, and sometimes vendettas. Yet the anonymous denunciations, the complaints and the signed petitions constitute proof that behavior was not completely homogeneous, and that the law of silence was sometimes broken.[48] As a general rule, however, the village united behind its notables to oppose the French colonists who came to settle in close proximity to them, or to obstruct the searches of customs officers.

Village cohesion could also be reasserted against a neighboring village during disputes over the sharing of water for irrigation or the occupation of alluvial ground that had emerged from the river, or under the pretext of the theft of livestock. Certain internal stakes crucially determined social relations. Among them, the redistribution of communal land was a source of grievances that troubled the harmony of the village or else highlighted its exceptional character. The rice fields or other communal lands created a counterbalance to private property, allowing the village to function as a community either in a social or a religious mode. Portions of the communal land were allocated every three years to soldiers, to widows and orphans, and to those who did not own a piece of land, or else as religious donations or for ritual purposes.

This institution, which maintained social equilibrium, was certainly challenged before colonization, an example being the assignment of the best land to the clients of the oligarchy of notables or the sale of rice fields to procure resources for the village. Nevertheless, its decline was particularly evident during the colonial period as a result of the combination of several factors. Not only in Cochinchina, a peculiar case, but also in Annam and Tonkin, where traditions were supposedly better maintained, a sharp reduction in communal property occurred. The introduction of a varied and more constraining fiscal system, connected with the extension of the monetary economy, stimulated the desire for wealth and a general mentality of private ownership. Simultaneously, material, and especially financial, enrichment allowed new fields of activity to be introduced that generated their own wealth. This enrichment was also a way of enhancing social status that had otherwise been devalued by colonial subjection.

The slow regression of a form of collective ownership clearly illustrated the conflict between individual aspirations and the dominant collective spirit that determined the codes of conduct. This conflict had existed for a long time in Vietnamese society. As soon as circumstances allowed, personal interests affirmed themselves. In 1882, the administrator of the district of Cholon brought the following incident to the attention of the *procureur général* of Saigon: a man asked a village to give back three parcels of rice fields (46 hectares) to him that his ancestor had given to the village "as a bonus for imperial soldiers." The claimant considered the donation as out of date, since the "benevolent French administration pays its riflemen and militiamen." It is important to note that the French administration was by then receiving a tax from the village equivalent to the one it had paid before colonization. The administrator warned the *procureur:* "Once again, I call your attention to the exceptional seriousness of this affair. It seems that an assault against the *cong dien* [communal rice fields] has begun in a number of judicial districts; if this evil is not energetically stamped out, we should expect a trail of lawsuits that will enrich the bar [i.e., the lawyers] but will annihilate the last source of support that remains for us in this country. The suppression of the *cong dien* represents the destruction of the Annamese village; three years will be enough for this to occur."[49]

This affair is exemplary, because it exposes one of the mechanisms that led to the alienation of property that was reputed inalienable, but also because it illustrates the economic rationality of a nineteenth-century Vietnamese individual. The courts of Cochinchina had to decide on many cases involving the sale of *cong dien* (rice fields) or *cong tho* (village commons) either to Indochinese or French individuals, or to legal entities (until the 1920s), often with new goals, such as the construction of a garage or a set of lodgings or the expansion of a plantation.[50] Rather than selling their communal lands, the villages of Cochinchina auctioned them off every three years. The social purpose of the communal lands was so undermined that in 1937, facing peasant demands, administrators had to offer them up for auction at low prices, giving priority to those peasants without land. The evolution, however, was irreversible, as it had been in Annam and Tonkin. Probably because of a runaway demography and the maintenance of tradition, at least formally, the erosion of the local land regime was slower there, but nevertheless inexorable, as is evidenced by the demands of the peasant movements of 1930–31. In 1937, the Radical Socialist secretary of state Justin Godart described how, during an unplanned stop in a village in the Tonkin Delta, the peasants told him that the distribution of communal lands had not taken place for twenty years.[51] In Tonkin, overpopulation and the diminution of communal land resulted in bitter procedural quarrels during the distribution of the *cong dien*.[52]

The tax system and the allocation of benefits were not controlled by the village notables, of course, but they could adjust the forms through which they were collected and could choose the contributors and those recruited for emigration according to sympathies and dislikes. The tax levies, the distribution of tax quotas, notably in relation to the classification of the rice fields, the establishment of the calendar, the distribution of duties such as watches and corvée (for the maintenance of levies and the construction of roads), and the recruitment of soldiers were all opportunities for the notables to make their power felt, express their preferences, and satisfy their rancor.[53]

Fissures appeared in the village consensus, more evident in Vietnam than elsewhere, particularly in the symbolic realms of village life such as the rituals that traditionally reunited the inhabitants. During the festivities honoring the tutelary spirit of the village, certain rituals of derision or sexual confusion acted as safety valves by provoking the temporary effacement of the hierarchy and social prohibitions. A feast (the *xoi thit*) followed. This demonstration of conviviality concretized the privileges of the mandarins and the notables and emphasized their social preeminence. The euphoria that flowed from the drinking of alcohol certainly helped the guests lose their psychological inhibitions, and even if they were of an inferior rank, they allowed themselves to question or insult others without taking into consideration the social rank of their target. Starting in the 1930s, however, the *xoi thit* were sometimes the occasion for egalitarian demands by the peasants, or they were subverted and the notables excluded by a few daring individuals. Certainly, such acts were still rare, but the authorities, when informed of such incidents, became alarmed, because they grasped the meaning and potential scope of the phenomenon.

It was in Cochinchina, with absentee owners of large expanses of land who were less inclined to submit to the practices of the village, that individuals affirmed themselves most in relation to the community. The majority of owners, however, understanding what was in their best interest, adopted a form of paternalism. Sometimes, they dragged their farmers along in their conversions to new forms of religiosity such as Caodaism and the Hoa Hao religion. They thus earned a sense of being part of a community of feeling.[54] The new religions not only revitalized traditional religions and practices (Buddhism, Spiritism), but also tried to renew the social contract, creating new networks of solidarity and interdependence.

Otherwise, the rituals and superstitions of yesteryear were still very deeply rooted. In Cambodia and the Lao territories, the leading form of religion was Theravada Buddhism; it had an official status and a popular presence that permitted it to maintain an enduring consensus and to effectively inform social and cultural life. Yet it didn't exclude the cults of the pre-Buddhist native local spirits (*phi* and *neak ta*); instead, it tolerated and accepted the popular religions and integrated them into its practice.

Rural Vietnamese society was on the path of increasingly deep social differentiation. We can even ask whether by the end of the colonial period, the Vietnamese village had become simply a setting of administration and worship, like the Russian *mir*, or village commune, after the reforms of Prime Minister Pyotr Stolypin (1906–11). It was an entity that became divested of its communal substance, but that nevertheless preserved its vitality through its confrontation with foreign domination. Its internal contradictions mutated, gradually, into causes of dislocation. When Secretary of State Justin Godart was sent on an inspection mission to Indochina by Léon Blum's Socialist government in 1937, he became convinced that it was urgent to create a peasantry of small landowners in order to ensure social and political stability in the country.[55] His recommendation was founded on the observation that small-scale farms were losing ground in relation to large properties, which were hidden in Tonkin and in Annam but quite overt and resembled latifundia in Cochinchina.

While the gap widened between the two extremes of the rural society, the poor became poorer. This can be seen from an examination of the available statistical data, although they are primarily from Tonkin or specific localities. We shall return to the great famine of 1945 in Tonkin, which is too particular to illustrate the typical characteristic of the fate of the Indochinese masses. Catastrophic climatic events (floods, typhoons, and droughts), linked to the division of land into small parcels and the chronic indebtedness of the landowning peasants and farmers, made them almost permanently vulnerable. Exterior risks and intrinsic weaknesses merged to keep peasants in a situation in which the line between poverty and misery quickly blurred, and where frugality and famine were near neighbors.

Destitution and backwardness were most apparent in the area of public health. Toward 1915, the director of the Service de l'hygiène et de la santé publique (Hygiene and Public Health Service) called for a greater financial effort on the part of the administration:

With regard to hygiene in the countryside, we can say that it is a completely unknown thing in most rural areas, even those that are comfortable or rich, not to mention among the thousands of poor in Tonkin and northern Annam. Above all, it is necessary to prevent these men from dying from hunger or from the cold. Even if the idea occurred to them, they would never have the means to buy the soap necessary to wash themselves. What is there that can be done in the domain of hygiene for these thousands of men of the northern provinces, where the population density reaches . . . 600 per km^2? For the time being, little or nothing.[56]

Twenty years later, *Médecin-colonel* Peltier reported that "infant mortality is always very high in Annam." It was the same in Tonkin, where Dr. Le Roy des Barres estimated that, out of every hundred infant deaths, fifty were due to destitution, thirty to abuse, and twenty to other causes.[57] In 1939, the Gouvernement général decided to create a body of hygienists oriented toward epidemiology and social hygiene, who were supposed to go to work in the countryside in 1940. Village midwives who had received minimal training were supposed to be paid through local budgets, but the latter were so modest that this decision was not applied. General and maternity hospitals existed only in the urban centers, and the poverty of most people in the rural areas prevented those who lived there from having access to them. When they were not completely helpless in the face of illness and death, they depended on untrained midwives and quacks.

There remained spontaneous emigration to the mines of Laos and to urban factories, as well as organized emigration to the plantations of southern Annam, Cochinchina, Cambodia, and New Caledonia. There were even some official, quite ill-fated, attempts to create settlements in Cochinchina and in the upper Tonkin region; in Thai Nguyen province, from 1923 to 1935, the result was derisory: there were nine settlement villages, with a registered population totaling 385 individuals.

Nevertheless, in the southern territories that did not have the same population overload, and whose soils and climates were more varied and more fertile, the peasantry was in a more enviable condition, sufficient in any case to retain many migrants from the north, who in principle had only come for the duration of a specific work contract. The middle-class peasants, represented in Vietnam by the image of "a tile roof and a jackfruit tree" *(nha ngoi, cay mit),* probably benefited from the colonial economy, because they took advantage of the boom in rice farming during the 1920s. But their insertion into the market economy exposed them to the risky fluctuations in prices and export levels. Those left behind by Cochinchinese prosperity were especially the Khmer Krom, Vietnamese settlers fleeing the control of the plantation owners, and the more unstable elements on the frontier. The impact of the economic depression of 1931 was weak on those groups, however, as it was among the poor of Tonkin, because, even if the price of rice fell, their condition had not created new needs (clothing, oil lights, recourse to Western pharmaceuticals). They continued as before to light their dwellings with bad oil, to eat field rats or snakes, to fish in the muddy waters of pools or of rivers for "small shrimp, frogs, crabs, snails, in short, whatever was enough for one or several meals."[58]

The peasants most active in the social movements were neither the poor of Tonkin and northern Annam nor the population of the extreme west of Cochinchina—those who had nothing to lose. The most rebellious peasants came rather from the sectors most deeply rooted in the countryside, even if they were poor. Apart from patriotic motives, which were often determinant, the peasants who resisted colonization did so because they did not want to lose the land they possessed, or to which they had the legal right, because of high rents or overly elevated taxes; they wanted to regain what they had been forced to leave in the hands of creditors, and they dreamed of affluence.

The generalization within the Vietnamese countryside of family networks based on male and patriarchal dominance helped both those who resisted colonization and the colonial administration itself, for instance, when the French established councils of lineage chiefs to serve as their intermediaries in Tonkin in 1921. The social gulfs based on real estate or investment fortunes, or on the status gained from being a member of the literati or holding honorific degrees, supplanted or obliterated the division between property owners and landless farmers or day laborers. Still, the system of relationships was partially structured by class adherence, through matrimonial alliances between powerful families of different villages. Patriarchal dominance often disappeared in the lowest stratum of the peasantry, replaced by a certain equality between the sexes. The networks of families and clients in turn provided revolutionaries with channels through which to spread their propaganda.[59]

This outline describes northern Vietnam. Was it applicable for the remainder of the country? The ambivalence and contradictions of the social organization are perceptible in the *hoi ky* (compilations of memories) written by the militant communists of the center and the south. On the one hand, their forms of recruitment, complicity, and connection were largely copied from the model of the family encompassing three or four generations (*tam dai dong duong* and *tu dai don duong*), used the practice of adoption, and were reinforced by the village associations such as the *giap,* which were under patriarchal control. On the other hand, the communists were fixated on the goal of making class contradictions evident and stirring up class antagonisms. This complex configuration explains why in the north and elsewhere, overlapping adherences to lineage and class, and to national liberation and class struggle, generated tensions and violent ruptures within families and lineages.

Urban Workers and New Economic Sectors

The mines, the plantations, and logging that the French developed required a large labor force. The population explosion in the Tonkin Delta and parts of northern

Annam—without a concomitant increase in resources—created a magnificent pool from which to recruit.

The Vietnamese were spontaneously drawn to work in the mines in northeastern Tonkin and the factories of Nam Dinh, Haiphong, and Vinh, or to cross the Annam cordillera in order to be hired in mines and lumber mills in Laos, because these regions were relatively nearby. In contrast, it was necessary to organize the migratory trends toward the plantations of southern Annam, Cochinchina, and then Cambodia. The Transindochinois railway was only finished in 1937, so it was necessary to ferry workers by water. Coolies recruited by specialized agencies on three-year contracts formed a category of indentured laborers that was different from that of the so-called free workers. Because it involved the same tasks that had traditionally been accomplished by Chinese manpower, this dissemination of Vietnamese manpower throughout the peninsula began to undermine the monopoly the Chinese had held until World War I. In this way, between 1915 and 1930, an Indochinese working class, which was in fact primarily Vietnamese, was created by the extractive, agrarian, and manufacturing industries. Service workers working in transport and the urban professions, as well as artisans, also were part of this group.

In 1929, among French enterprises, there were 53,240 workers in the mines, 81,188 on the plantations, and 86,624 in manufacturing and commercial enterprises, for a total of 221,052.[60] In 1940–41, this rose to around 88,724 in the mines and various industries (excepting the rubber and chemical industries), 219,234 in craft work (not including those on plantations or involved in trade), for a total of 307,958.[61]

Except in the large towns, these workers remained attached to the rural world, dividing their time between the rice fields and the factory or the mine: "Around May 15, a third of our personnel generally leave us for the harvest of the fifth month."[62] The same phenomenon was noted on the plantations that employed free labor from neighboring villages, in contrast to the indentured workers who devoted all their strength to plantation labor and who, anyway, were especially far from their villages. The latter sometimes attained their hope of returning home. Some left at the end of three years in order not to lose their part of the communal rice fields back home. Since most of these migrant workers remained where they had come to work, however, one can reasonably suppose that having broken their ties with their local communities, they were able to develop the sense of being part of a national community.

Similarly, the tens of thousands of Indochinese *ouvriers non-spécialisés* (ONS, or unspecialized workers) who served in France during World War I undoubtedly acquired a broader vision of the world when they discovered other ideas and other surroundings, and the same was true of Indochinese sailors—cabin boys, scullions, stokers—who were to play an important role in creating the international connections of the Indochinese Communist Party. The diminished importance of specialization, and thus, even more, of qualification, was an important character-istic of the world of modern work. The label ONS applied to workers recruited for France was meaningful in this regard. In mines and factories in Tonkin and north-ern Annam, there were two categories of workers, distinguished by the color of their garments: *cu nau* (brown-colored clothing) designated unskilled workers, and *ao xanh* (blue-colored clothing) designated specialized workers, or at least those with professional training. In certain companies, these categories were superimposed on the division between Vietnamese workers *(cu nau)* and Chinese workers *(ao xanh)*. Membership in the *ao xanh* labor aristocracy was sought after; it was, for example, necessary to pay a sum of money to certain foremen *(cai)* in the work-shop of the Truong Thi railroad (northern Annam) to be hired as an apprentice and to have the right to wear the much-coveted "blue."[63] The difference in salary, status, and ethnic origin between the two categories created a difference in behav-iors in regards to union organizing and politics. The Communist Party called on its militants to erase this distinction, which was contrary to class interests and pro-letarian solidarity.[64] The fact that the communists themselves recognized the *cu nau / ao xanh* distinction puts us on notice, however, that the Indochinese prole-tariat of that era was neither homogeneous nor uniformly miserable.

There were also differences in time and space. The workers on the rubber plan-tations provide us with a good example of this. The free workers, if they also cul-tivated a patch of ground in their village, had a more enviable situation than their indentured comrades, who, in principle, benefited from a monetary advance from the start, lodging, a mosquito net, food rations, and bonuses at the end of their terms. And though the indentured workers were protected against layoffs or wage de-creases during the great economic crisis, it is also apparent that they were prison-ers on the plantation, that any attempt at flight was punished severely under the laws on breach of contract. They did not have the possibility of changing their em-ployer themselves, even if they were victims of supervisors or a brutal *cai*.

The period of the reclamation and creation of plantations (1925–29) was diffi-cult for the workforce. The human cost was elevated because of malaria, workdays that were too long, poor treatment, insufficient food, suicide, or the fatal outcomes of escapes into the forest. Material conditions (lodging, food, medical care, the length of workdays) undeniably improved around 1930. The strikes and the protests of 1937, which expressed a refusal of wage decreases and an attack on the inhumane behavior of overseers, were the index of an overall improvement in working con-ditions and the existence of the possibility of being heard by the administrative authorities and the Inspection du travail (Labor Inspectorate).

In the absence of a systematic study of salaries and prices in Indochina, we must content ourselves with a few points of reference. The "survey of the working pop-ulation and salaries" conducted in Nam Dinh in 1928 reveals a variety of situations and categories, depending on the company and the kind of work (table 4.3).[65]

TABLE 4.3 Workforce and salaries in several Indochinese companies, 1928

Company[a]	No. of workers	Salaries[b] Men	Women	Hours per day	Daily wage or piece rate[b]
Société franco-annamite pour l'industrie de la soie	835	42 office staff • 15 accounting secretaries: 80–12 $/mo • 16 supervisors: 80–10 $/mo. • 2 electricians: 40–15 $/mo. • 9 mechanics: 80–15 $/mo.	622 workers: 0.35–0.12 $/day	12	Per day • 78 unskilled workers and others: 0.30–0.40 $/day Per piece • 93 weavers: 0.50 $/day
Société indo-chinoise d'électricité	78	35–12 $/day	—	8	Per day
Factory of the Société française des distilleries de l'Indochine	271	256 workers • specialized: 1.10–0.60 $/day • unskilled: 0.40–0.28 $/day	15 workers: 0.17–0.19 $/day	10	Per day
Société anonyme des transports maritimes et fluviaux de l'Indochine's company for bottling and shipping of native alcohol	227	155 workers • cai and guards: 18–15 $/mo. • specialized: 15–7 $/mo. • unskilled: 4–7.50 $/mo. • shallop owner, skipper, and sailors: 30–9 $/mo.	72 workers: 0.18–0.20 $/day	10	Per day • packers, washers, carpenters Per piece • crate manu-facturers and transporters

[a]Franco-Annamese Silk Industry Company; Indochinese Electrical Company; Indochina Distilleries Company; Sea and River Transport Company of Indochina.
[b]$ = Indochinese piastre.

The modesty of urban workers' salaries left them no option but to live in shantytowns made up of rudimentary straw huts, inhabited by "the poorest class, which provides the manpower indispensable for the economic development of the region, and in this capacity it is useful that it be granted the right to establish itself close to industries and trades that use it. This is why it is necessary to maintain and tolerate special zones for this kind of habitation, which the normal process of the extension of cities would progressively drive back toward the periphery of the urban region."[66] At least a straw hut provided a roof, as their sampans did for the *sampaniers*. Many rickshaw drivers, on the other hand, had no homes other than their vehicles, and many others slept on sidewalks, along the banks of rivers, or in the shade of a tree, such as a banyan or a poinciana.

When two or three families shared the same dwelling, it led to structural overload and promiscuity. The proletarian districts were breeding grounds for cholera, plague, tuberculosis, malaria, and venereal disease. Anti-social activities, from banditry to uncontrolled prostitution, were prevalent. A 1930 Indochinese Communist Party document describes the demoralization that reigned in the proletarian milieu of Hanoi, where the sentiment of despair was widespread and engendered alcoholism and opium and gambling addictions.[67]

Starting in 1937, groups of permanent, low-rent apartment buildings were put up in Hanoi (Brévié City) and Saigon (Aristide-Briand City), along the lines of similar cheap housing in France. A total of twenty or thirty families, drawn from the upper echelon of manual workers or minor civil servants, lived in each of them. Craftsmen (tailors, woodworkers, locksmiths, etc.) lived and worked in sections, often grouped by profession along certain roads or in certain housing blocks or yards. Whether they were bosses, employees, or apprentices, they worked and lived together. This kind of organization, which amalgamated familial and professional relations, assuaged tensions without necessarily overcoming them.

Conflicts erupted on the subject of salaries, general work conditions, and the behavior of managers and bosses. One such incident happened at the end of 1911, after the Compagnie des charbonnages of Trang Bach (Trang Bach Coal-Mining Company) in Tonkin failed to pay its six hundred workers for three months. The miners, who could not buy on credit at the Chinese grocer like the seven Europeans of the staff, plundered a field of potatoes, and a hundred and fifty of them went as a delegation to protest to the Haiphong *procureur de la République* (district attorney). The others returned to their villages, a natural fallback position.[68] In 1937, the French administration blasted metropolitan employers whose decisions were dictated by "cold economic considerations based on overhead costs," reproaching them for brutally firing workers who had requested that they be paid two days in advance, as had happened in Nam Dinh and Saigon.[69]

Strikes were spontaneously used against Asian as well as French employers. Unions were forbidden by French legislation, and were therefore underground and only founded at the end of the 1920s, most often inspired by communist militants. As the governor of Cochinchina saw it, "The social education here is too insufficient to allow workers—recent strikes have proved it—to clearly distinguish between professional demands and political questions."[70] The workers got around official interdictions by creating associations that were almost always legal fronts for clandestine unions. In this way, the first Amicale des ouvriers de l'Arsenal de Saigon (Association of the Workers of the Arsenal of Saigon) was founded in 1920 by Ton Duc Thang (1888–1980), a worker who had returned from France, where, according to his official biography, he had worked in Toulon.

Mandarins, Landowners, and the Urban Middle Class

The period of French domination noticeably modified the social landscape, both at the top and the bottom of the social pyramid. In 1915, when the French government suppressed the traditional examinations (written in Chinese characters and based on the study of Confucian classics), it confirmed its intention to change the education of those who it had selected to lead the people and make them follow the will of the colonizers. The School of Law and the Institute of Indochinese Studies in Hanoi trained classes of men who were more and more adapted to the spirit of French law and capable of understanding and applying the administration's instructions. Nevertheless, Annam, Tonkin, Cambodia, and Laos were administered throughout almost the entire colonial period by civil servants who were still imbued with ancient ideas, familiar with traditional mores, and inspired in their administrative relations by Confucian ethics and customs. Even so, charges of misappropriation, nepotism, and the abuse of power were well founded.

In 1934, in Annam, out of 899 mandarins in the civil service, 267 had received diplomas from traditional schools, 218 were literati without titles selected during the triennial contests, and 193 were graduates of training that was half traditional and half modern. Only 28 were graduates of metropolitan French or Indochinese colonial training.[71] Following the routine was the predominant approach of these individuals; it was a safeguard for some and a form of passive resistance for others. After the uprising of Nghe Tinh in 1930–31, the French administrators tried to place the responsibility for it on certain mandarins, whose passivity was equivalent, in their eyes, to actual complicity with the rebels. Analyzing the same events, the high mandarin of the Hue court blamed a protectorate regime that had crushed the will of its administrators and discouraged their initiative.

At the beginning of the century, the scholar Phan Chu Trinh denounced this fossilized mandarinate and called for its suppression, or at least its purging. After 1930, all the while deploring its minimal efficiency and integrity, the French accommodated themselves to it, because the mandarinate had become necessary in order to keep the revolutionaries at bay. A strong-willed mandarin always ended up coming into conflict with the tutelary power. This was the case with the young Catholic mandarin Ngo Dinh Diem. In 1931, the French resident superior in Annam praised the energy and intelligence with which Diem shielded his province of Binh Thuan (southern Annam) from communist maneuvers. Two years later, after having been called on to participate in the Hue government, Diem encountered resistance when attempting reforms and was forced to resign. The French much preferred Prime Minister Pham Quynh to Ngo Dinh Diem; the former was more moderate and more docile, although unappreciated by the mandarin aristocracy because of his plebeian origins.

Aside, perhaps, from the tone of regret, there is therefore nothing surprising about Admiral Decoux's 1941 report evaluating the Hue government during a ministerial overhaul: "The Annamese government will remain quite dull in the absence of true organizers, who are impossible to find among people currently likely to enter the Council."[72] Could it be any different with a government that functioned under the presidency of the French resident superior, and in a capital of which the journalist Andrée Viollis wrote: "Peace, mellowness, melancholy especially. . . . Hue is famous for its tombs that look like palaces, for its palace that looks like a tomb"?[73]

In the opinion of the French administration, it would be better for Diem to confine himself, like the governor *(tong doc)* of the province of Ha Dong, Hoang Trong Phu, to the promotion of industrial arts and crafts and to running the Société agricole de l'Indochine (Agricultural Society of Indochina). Ngo Dinh Diem belonged to a mandarin dynasty, and though his father had collaborated with the French right after the conquest, his national pride had not been suppressed. Other mandarins like Bui Bang Doan and Phan Ke Toai behaved likewise.

One could become a mandarin from father to son, but it was difficult to penetrate this class from the outside. French domination, however, opened up new possibilities for children of property owners and other social groups. The French presence incited the development of a middle class that oriented itself toward public functions, trade, industry, and liberal professions. The medium and large landowners were the source of this middle class. Certain among them remained tied to the land, while others became businessmen. Southern Vietnam attracted the majority of landowners; but there were also some in Tonkin, like Bach Thai Buoi. The possession of a considerable rice surplus that they could export led these landowners to become interested in related activities: transportation, manufacturing, and hydraulic pumping stations. Gradually, they financed consumer industries such as brickworks and then took the risk of putting money into banking: in 1927, a few of them created the Société annamite de crédit (Annamese Credit Company).[74] They quickly acquired a class consciousness[75] and even developed a genuine economic nationalism,[76] which was formed and strengthened in opposition to the hegemony of the Chinese middle class in the economic sphere.[77]

It was indeed impossible to launch a frontal attack on French economic supremacy, because it was based on political domination. However, there were also other reasons, which were clearly expressed by one member of the Vietnamese upper middle class: "The national middle class is thankful to the protectorate for having pulled it out of the feudal quagmire. It is not unaware that it is a vassal to the French upper middle class because of the lack of industrialization and the preeminence of agriculture in Indochina. But as it is more than thirteen thousand kilometers from France, and given that it dominates a large part of the national market, it benefits from an autonomy whose value it fully appreciates. It knows what it would come up against if it were to enter a competition to the death with a nearby imperialism that would flood the national market with all kinds of merchandise at 'dumping' prices."[78]

This declaration was a realistic account as well as a rational acceptance of dependence. Since the time of Gilbert Chieu, at the beginning of the century, the southern agrarian middle class and the business class had become wiser. Chieu was a prototypical member of the budding Vietnamese middle class. A civil servant, he acquired French citizenship, became a property owner in the west of Cochinchina, and become involved in the hotel industry, in commerce, and in journalism. After having denounced the economic power of the Chinese, he defended Prince Cuong De, who was in exile in Japan, against the French. In 1908, he was arrested and imprisoned for plotting against France.[79]

A decade later, the Vietnamese of the south made new attempts at economic development by manufacturing rice and silk, producing *nuoc mam* (fish sauce), and trading in commodities. These initiatives are linked to the names of Le Phat Vinh, Le Phat An, and Bui Quang Chieu, who took advantage of the favorable conjuncture created by World War I in Europe. After having completed his studies in France, Nguyen Phu Khai returned to Vietnam and was instrumental in the revival of economic activity. Khai founded a rice plantation in Cantho in 1915, an Annamese commercial society, and an Annamese bank, and he called on his compatriots to boycott Chinese trade. Simultaneously, and like Gilbert Chieu, Khai founded a newspaper, *La Tribune indigène,* to accompany the economic action and present the demands of this emerging middle class. The obstacles the latter encountered in finding "a place in the sun" drove it progressively to the brink of political action in the form of constitutionalism, although this was essentially a Cochinchinese phenomenon.[80]

It is true that the index of Indochinese corporations in 1944 included sixty-five Vietnamese administrators out of ninety-two, but another source on corporations from 1943 emphasizes that there were only nine fully Vietnamese corporations, in comparison to fourteen Franco-Vietnamese and four Sino-Vietnamese ones.[81] Progress was, then, rather slow. The French controlled 86% and the Chinese 14% of rice exports, a basic area.[82] In 1945, the Vietnamese economic and financial middle class was still in limbo.

The Vietnamese business class has been disparagingly characterized as a "rickety middle class." It is important to note that, in addition to its situation of dependency, which earned it the epithet of "comprador," the world crisis of the 1930s nipped its ascension in the bud. It was kept in an embryonic state by World War II, and then by the revolution of August 1945. Yet the rural middle class, at least that of Cochinchina, had opted for a modernization of customs that created new needs (e.g., in clothing, housing, and cars) and called for the sending of their children to establishments of secondary and higher education, including in France. The mandarin Pham Quynh took offense at this lifestyle and its materialistic mentality, oriented toward the acquisition of possessions, including superfluous ones.[83] The economic depression had serious consequences for several of these big property owners, who had gone into debt in order to modernize and hold onto their rank.[84] "In order to avoid losing respect in the eyes of their fellow citizens, the big property owners were obliged to maintain the lifestyle they had led. They could only minimally limit their expenses."[85] Despite all their attempts, they were forced to further restrict their expenses and resign themselves to seizures of their property. Some were even driven to suicide.

The two other elements of the middle class—the liberal professions and civil servants and other employees—came from the agrarian and merchant classes. Frequently, these middle-class individuals were also property owners, as can be seen in thirteen applications to the Chasseloup-Laubat High School in Saigon in 1931, which give the professional occupation, salaries, and other income of the parents (table 4.4).[86] The sampling presented here precisely situates the material situation of these middle-ranking civil servants and testifies to their strong desire to ensure that their children acquired French intellectual culture, since the Chasseloup-Laubat High School was, in principle, reserved for the French.

This desire was generalized throughout the upper levels of the Vietnamese middle class. In Cochinchina in the same year, 548 property owners and notables of Vinh Long province presented a list of wishes to the minister of colonies in which they requested the transformation of indigenous primary teaching into French primary teaching, with French as the main language of instruction and Quoc ngu as only one subject among others in the curriculum.[87] The ten civil servants on this list belonged to the upper category, however, and were therefore not representative of all civil servants (of whom there were about 500,000 in 1945). The difference in salaries between various ranks and levels was blatant. The Vietnamese adage "The civil servant gives orders; in the evening, he drinks champagne, and in the morning, cow's milk" (Quan phan, toi ruoi sam banh, sang sua bo) certainly did not apply to the majority, but it allowed them to fantasize.

In the milieu of the civil servants and subordinate employees, women worked on the side, such as in retail sales and sewing, to help provide for the needs of their families. The conditions of one Cambodian minor civil servant in Phnom Penh were as wretched as those of his counterparts in Hanoi or Saigon; his wife manufactured small cakes and sold them at the market three times a week.[88] Almost all such people were in debt.

The search for social promotion through education was, however, widespread in all social categories. This is illustrated by a document on the readmission of student-teachers of the École normale de Saigon, who had gone on strike on May 17, 1929. It provides a list of those who had signed the ten-year commitment of *normalien*

TABLE 4.4 Salaries and property of several civil servants, 1931

Name	Profession	Salary[a]	Property[a]
Pham Thai Hoa	Principal secretary-interpreter, Judicial Department of Indochina	1,428 $/year	250 ha of rice fields, 14 rental units, and his own residence. Property valued at 60,000 $.
Dang Nhu Nhon	Principal secretary (first level), Financial Office of Cochinchina	1,920 $/year	Renter, 55 $/mo.
Le Van Thanh	Clerk for lawyer Couget	120 $/mo.	One parcel of land and of a rice husking plant. Property valued at 4,500 $.
Do Huu Khai	Interpreter, Judicial Department	—	Buildings valued at 15,000 $ with an annual revenue of 2,800 $. His wife owns buildings valued at 30,000 $.
Ta Quang Huy	Principal secretary (fourth level), Postal Service	1,248 $/year	6 ha of rice fields valued at 9,000 $. Renter, 24 $/mo.
Huynh Van-Chan	Primary school teacher (second level)	1,248 $/year	0.25 ha of land and 4 rental units valued at 2,600 $.
Nguyen Dinh Tri	Former assistant-prefect, former municipal adviser of Saigon, first notary clerk	—	Renter, 40 $/mo.
Nguyen Van Dai	Secretary (third level), Saigon City Hall	87 $/mo.	—
Nguyen Van Duong	Owner of a shallop and two junks valued at 20,000 $	—	120 ha of rice fields valued at 40,000 $
Trang Quang Ba	Land registry and topography technician	207 $/mo.	6 ha of rice fields valued at 2,000 $
Tran Van Phu	Principal secretary-interpreter (third level)	1,344 $/year	One parcel of land, 800 m²
Le Van Phi	Secretary (first level), Customs and Monopolies	154 $/mo.	10 rental units valued at 12,000 $; other property

[a] $ = Indochinese piastre

students. Their professions were very diverse: the majority were certainly "farmers" (although the term *lam ruông* is generic and included very different categories), but there were also numerous other professions, including the most modest ones.[89]

The acquisition of French nationality was also much sought after, but the French government granted "naturalization" parsimoniously: in 1925, there were only thirty-one people naturalized, and in 1939, there were only three hundred.

A natural penchant for education, combined with a strong will, is what compelled certain young Vietnamese to apply for admission to the University of Hanoi or to embark for France. A middle class of liberal professionals thus slowly emerged. In 1937, there were 227 Indochinese physicians (who had obtained a diploma after four years of study in Hanoi and did not have the title of "doctor") and pharmacists. In addition, there were some who had returned from France with the title of "doctor." Combined with engineers, architects, and graduates of schools of humanities and law, this group probably exceeded five thousand people in 1940.

These graduates did not immediately acquire recognition of their social dignity and professional competence. It was said that a Corsican janitor of the University of Hanoi was better paid than a Vietnamese *agrégé*. Whether it is true or false, this story is interesting in that it illustrates the disparity of treatment between colonizers and colonized. These differences, rightly seen as flagrant injustices, were taken up in the 1920s. They were even discussed officially by the emperor of Annam, Khai Dinh. In 1923, he wrote to Governor-General Pierre Merlin stating that it was necessary to give young Annamese who had obtained degrees in France positions identical to those given to French who held the same degrees.[90] After 1938, those with law degrees could join the Indochinese Bar, and the French authorities planned to welcome as many Indochinese doctors as possible into the Assistance publique (Public Health Service).[91]

In addition to claiming their right to a social status equal to their French counterparts with the same expertise or the same position, the middle class had also to impose the respect of their status on French of lower rank. Many incidents were born of vexations or humiliations inflicted on the Vietnamese middle class, whom the French only wished to see as natives and inferior beings.[92] "The modern elite longs for social equality," Resident Superior Pierre Pasquier warned Governor-General Alexandre Varenne in 1926.[93] This opinion was shared by Varenne, who saw in this elite "an Indochinese *tiers état* [Third Estate, as opposed under the Ancien régime in France to the privileged estates of the aristocracy and the Church] to which we must grant a place if we want to avoid it demanding one."[94]

5

Cultural Transformations

Economic development, the formation of new social classes with diverse lifestyles and philosophies, and foreign influences all combined to produce new cultures and mentalities in Indochina. The experiences, ideas, and moral and religious values introduced by colonization found expression in literature, music, and the fine arts. They informed certain new behaviors, though never fully eliminating the preexisting ways of thinking or living, if only because they had an unequal effect on different peoples and social classes, and in different ways in the cities than in the countryside.

The Vietnamese, the Cambodians, the Lao, and the ethnic groups of the highlands all reacted to the new situation at different rates and to different degrees. Some reacted to modernization with stubborn resistance and rejection. At other times, however, they adopted it unknowingly, through ephemeral infatuations. The search for multiple syntheses between past and present, native and outsider, East and the West, was probably never successful. The form of interaction that took shape was, inevitably, syncretic. Full cultural comprehension and assimilation would take much longer to achieve than the eighty years of French colonization.

FRENCH CULTURAL INITIATIVES

Economic, social, and technical changes are agents of cultural evolution, but in a colonial regime in particular, the policies of the imperialist state are likewise influential. The state defined the direction of education policy, publishing, even the orientations of the press and cinema. Through subsidization or outright censorship, the state facilitated or hindered the circulation of people and ideas. The state also policed local customs and thus could accelerate or hinder changes in mentalities.

From Assimilation to Relativism

Did the colonial state in Indochina have a clearly defined cultural project that it carried out in concrete ways? Or was the state content simply to identify the direction that should be followed, one that could be inflected and even changed? Certainly, the spread of French civilization was the acknowledged goal. But did that really mean that French civilization would replace existing cultures? Even today, we ridicule the phrase "Nos ancêtres, les Gaulois" (Our forefathers, the Gauls), which Indochinese and African children were obliged to recite. However, in practice, teachers were not gullible enough to believe that they could inculcate into their students the belief that they were descendents of the Celts. The very traditions and the daily lives of the pupils themselves served to belie the recitation. Over the years, the phrase became more a symbol of educational routine than the accurate reflection of a political goal. What was scandalous was less the recitation of this phrase than the application of a teaching curriculum identical to the one being used in the metropole and the use of textbooks that were poorly adapted to the colonized milieu. Untangling these three interlinked elements of colonial cultural policy—the cultural assimilation of the colonized, the colonial desire to realize some sort of social genesis, and the political centralism of the Third Republic—would never be easy.

Over time, a better knowledge of Far Eastern civilizations forced the French rulers to change their cultural and educational approaches as they realized the absurdity of trying to turn the Indochinese into Frenchmen. Many French policymakers long established in the colony understood the irreducible originality of local civilizations. They conceded that there would be persistent resistance to the imposition of new psychologies and attitudes. And they worried that the spread of humanist, republican, liberal, and democratic components of French culture could have unforeseen repercussions on the colonized societies. In 1930, Governor-General Pierre Pasquier expressed his doubts to the journalist René Vanlande:

> For thousands of years, Asia has possessed its personal ethics, its art, its metaphysics, its dreams. Will it ever assimilate our Greco-Roman thought? Is this possible? Is it desirable? Until today, to our knowledge, it [Asia] has only proceeded by imitation. It has endeavored to take a path parallel to ours. There is juxtaposition. Can it be an intimate penetration? Where can one find the cement and the ties between Asia and ourselves? We, the Gauls, we were the Barbarians. And, in the absence of our own light, we illuminated ourselves, after some resistance, with the light that came from Rome. The glue of Christianity completed this fusion. But in Asia, without speaking of the distance between races, we find souls and minds molded by the oldest civilization of the globe.[1]

These remarks testify to a change within the French attitudes towards foreign cultures. Gwendolyn Wright has correctly pointed out that the cultural innovations that had appeared in France since the beginning of the twentieth century (the rebirth of French regionalism, the artistic movements of fauvism, cubism, etc.), had some influence on the governing powers in Indochina. For example, the famous Governor-General Albert Sarraut was an art critic and connoisseur. The new relativistic approach and questioning of the ideal of universal beauty—of which Europe was supposedly the depository—weakened French pretensions to cultural hegemony.[2] Pasquier's reflections on education were more concrete: "It must be admitted: we turn out batches of teachers and professors based on the educational philosophy that gave the Third Republic such an admirable pedagogical nursery. . . . But is this really what the old, conservative people of Annam want?"[3]

That said, it is important not to rely solely on the intentions proclaimed in official speeches. An examination of the cultural evolution of the Indochinese peoples under French rule—the initiatives of the colonizers and the responses from the colonized—is indispensable.

Colonizing Education

According to an anticolonialist slogan, France built more prisons than schools in Indochina. In reality, the French government made significant, sustained efforts to further education there. The statistics testify to a marked growth in the number of public schools, an increase in the size of the teaching corps, and a substantial rise in the number of students. To this, one can add the large number of private educational establishments in urban areas (see app. 10).

We can distinguish three major periods in the creation of the Indochinese educational system: 1860–1917, 1917–1930, and 1930–1945. The first phase was marked by the quest for an appropriate system. Between 1860 and 1917, the French were chiefly concerned with conquering the eastern part of the Indochinese peninsula and establishing their rule there. They were still too imbued with a sense of the superiority of their own culture to esteem the cultures—themselves different from one another—of those they were colonizing. At the same time, Republican France itself saw profound changes in the definition of both the means and ends of education.

The reforms of Jules Ferry not only changed France; as we shall see, they also had an impact on the colonies. Around 1890, when the question "What education for our colonies?" was being debated in the metropole, French colonial administrators on the spot simultaneously began to take into account Indochina's idiosyncrasies. The Public Instruction Code promulgated by Governor-General Albert Sarraut (1917–19) established "higher education and defined the programs and teaching cycles for each level" of the Indochinese schooling system, although it in fact did no more than create the legal context for it. The educational system that came into being under Governor-General Martial Merlin (1922–25), however, experimented with the single-school *(école unique)* approach before its metropolitan counterpart. "Pedagogical innovations had just started: the creation of a communal educational system in Annam, the renovation of the pagoda schools in Cambodia, then in Cochinchina, and finally in Laos, and education for the ethnic minorities. . . . Classes were no longer to be taught in French, but in the local languages. . . . Textbooks were written expressly for them. All aspects of primary education were experimented with to allow a widespread development of mass schooling."

The crisis of the 1930s, which assumed not only an economic dimension, but also a political one, was the start of a period of budgetary restrictions that slowed creativity and innovation. Only the educational sector dubbed "penetration" continued to develop, because the populations themselves took charge. Several upper schools were restructured, and the equivalency of French and Indochinese diplomas was established.[4]

For this, Cochinchina served as an educational laboratory, marked by the implementation in 1879 of Franco-indigenous education based on the French public school model.[5] The first modern schools spread from the south into the northern protectorates of Vietnam, such as the College of Interpreters in Hanoi (1886). These schools produced the first generation of intellectual cultural intermediaries, such as Truong Vinh Ky and Paulus Cua in Cochinchina, Nguyen Van Vinh (who founded the influential publication *Dong Duong Tap Chi* [The Indochinese Review] in May 1913), Pham Huy Ton, Pham Quynh, and Tran Trong Kim, among others. In the quest for a coherent educational policy, the colonial regime seems to have long tried to restructure the traditional education that had remained intact in Annam and Tonkin. In 1908, there were more than 15,000 schools in these two protectorates where Chinese characters were taught, with perhaps 200,000 pupils,[6] not counting the official schools in district and provincial seats. The French hoped to transform the traditional schools "into an immediate means of instruction and intellectual penetration."[7] This was certainly the aim of the May 31, 1906, reform elaborated by Governor-General Paul Beau and his director of education, Henri Gourdon. It opened the way for the creation of the first Conseil de perfectionnement de l'enseignement indigène (Council for the Improvement of Indigenous Education), created on November 14, 1905, under the direction of metropolitan and local Masonic lodges. The reform reorganized Franco-indigenous education—officially created in Tonkin in 1904, in Cambodia in 1905, and in Annam and Laos in 1906. It established the principle of one school for every village, and made Quoc ngu the mandatory written language of instruction in the ethnically Viet regions of Tonkin, Annam, and Cochinchina. Chinese ideograms became from that point no more than an object of study. To a larger extent, elementary aspects of French were introduced in upper-level primary schools *(primaires supérieures)* and teacher training colleges *(écoles normales),* and language skills were tested through a variety of literary contests.

TABLE 5.1 Number of public school students in Vietnam and
Cambodia, 1920–1945

Vietnam			
Years	Primary cycle	Primaire supérieur	Secondary
1920	1,126,000	2,430	—
1923	—	—	83
1929	—	—	121
1938–1939	287,500	4,552	465
1940–1941	518,737	—	5,637
1943–1944	707,285	—	6,550

Cambodia		
Years	Public primary	Renovated "pagoda schools"
1930	15,700	—
1939	—	38,000
1945	32,000	53,000

SOURCES: For Vietnam through 1939: G. P. Kelly, *Franco-Vietnamese Schools 1918–1938* (Madison, Wis.: Southeast Asia Publications, 1982); for Vietnam, 1940–1941: J. Gauthier, *L'Indochine au travail dans la paix française* (Paris: Eyrolles, 1949), p. 35; for Vietnam, 1943–1944: *Annuaire statistique de l'Indochine, 1939–1946*. For Cambodia: J. Delvert, "L'oeuvre française d'enseignement au Cambodge," *France-Asie* 125-126-127 (October–November 1956).

In 1907, in an attempt to combat nationalism, Paul Beau created the Indochinese University in Hanoi with three divisions for instruction in literature, law, and science. In its first year, however, the university counted only ninety-four students and seventy-four auditors. In January 1908, colonial circles, concerned by events in Annam (the anti-tax revolts in Quang Nam), closed the university, which was not reopened until 1917, when departments of Medicine and Pharmacy, Veterinary Science, Education, Watercourses and Forestry, Commerce, Finance, Law and Administration, and Fine Arts were added. In 1928, the School of Medicine became a fully operational faculty. The Indochinese University had as one of its distinctly affirmed goals the training of administrators. During World War II, when communications with France were interrupted, the university expanded and diversified its teaching, as well as its recruitment. In 1941, for example, it had a Science Department and also a Department of Architecture. In 1943–44, its final year (the university was closed when the Japanese ended French rule in 1945), the Departments of Law, Science, Medicine, and Pharmacy registered a total of 1,222 students: 837 Vietnamese, 346 French, 18 Cambodian, 12 Lao, 8 Chinese, and 1 unspecified. There were also 353 registered in other disciplines, for example, 130 in the Department of Fine Arts, 99 in Watercourses and Forestry, 46 in Veterinary Science, and 78 in other fields (Public Works, Architecture, etc.).[8]

TABLE 5.2 Students at the University of Hanoi, 1922–1944

Years	1922	1929	1938–1939	1941–1942	1942–1943	1943–1944
No. of Students	500	511	457	834	1,050	1,575

In the capitals and the towns, modern education was not without its successes. The Quoc Hoc College in Hue, founded in 1896 and reformed in 1905, is a case in point. It welcomed 787 students between 1899 and 1905. However, in the rural areas, modern education often failed: "In the course of my tours," Ha Dong's resident wrote in 1909, "I realized that the local schools for the most part existed only on paper."[9] Nevertheless, these modern schools, in tandem with the penetration of Western culture, led to the rapid retreat in the use of Chinese-based ideograms, as noted above. The traditional literary contests suffered from the competition represented by the new educational methods. Little by little, traditional exams lost their value, since, in the new context, they could no longer open the way to social promotion and professional advancement. In 1912, there were only 1,330 candidates taking part in the triennial contest in Nam Dinh, in Tonkin, as opposed to over 6,000 in 1906. The form of the examinations was modified in 1913, and the last triennial competitions occurred in Nam Dinh in 1915 and in Hue in 1919. The adoption of Quoc ngu and French as languages of instruction, combined with the demise of traditional examinations in the schools, shattered the essential mechanisms by which the ruling elite had been affiliated to the Confucian Sino-Vietnamese universe. It also dealt a blow to schools for the study of Chinese characters and the official government schools in Hue, which were in any case dismantled in 1919 and replaced by Franco-indigenous schools under the control of the Protectorate.

The Goals and Results of Colonial Education

The Règlement général de l'instruction publique of December 21, 1917, envisaged as the true "charter for Indochinese education," rationalized the entire educational apparatus. This set of regulations did not seek to exclude the colonized from modern knowledge and education, since these were among the colonial system's most powerful weapons. Rather, it aimed to channel the use of education into the service of three clearly conceived goals—to inspire and control the content and the transmission of written knowledge within the villages; to transmit to some extent a minimal modern mass education, on which the colonial system depended for its basic functioning; and, at the same time, to adapt the colonized elite to the functions assigned to them by the colonial system. Thus, while attempting to economize as much as possible (education represented 6% of the local and general budget expenses in 1930, and 7.8% in 1942), the regime adopted a strategy fairly close in its fundamental logic to that underwriting a similar school system in the metropole, one that excluded the masses from intellectual professions. In Indochina, the central concern was not the French school, which was only very marginally accessible to colonized youth, but a parallel network of Franco-indigenous schools (see table 5.1). This system prioritized primary teaching. In 1924, it was divided into an Elementary Primary Cycle (of three years) and a Primary Cycle (of two years, then three in 1927), extended by two highly selective examinations into upper primary and secondary "local" education. At the end of this, the latter provided a "local" *baccalauréat* (the French equivalent of the high school diploma), and, for a very small minority, admission to the Indochinese University. The system certainly produced a modern elite, but it was numerically a very restricted one, and most of its members had only a primary education. In 1930, 34,371 candidates earned an Indigenous Elementary Primary Studies certificate (as compared to 47,214 in 1942). Of this number, 16,933 received certificates indicating that they had learned French, and 4,379 received Franco-indigenous Primary Studies certificates (12,696 in 1942). However, of this total, only 648 received Franco-indigenous diplomas (1,124 in 1942), and only 75 earned the "local" *baccalauréat.*

From a social and political point of view, upper primary education was very significant. In the 1930s, it was the part of the educational system that generated the lower middle class of civil servants, employees, and professional revolutionaries. Secondary teaching played an analogous role, but tended to produce writers, journalists, or civil servants of a middle or superior rank. The high-school level was a seedbed for the Indochinese University in Hanoi and French universities and hence the antechamber through which those who entered into the liberal professions passed.

In 1932, there were 541 students, of whom 20 were French or foreigners, at the Indochinese University. In 1942, three law degrees and nine doctorates in medicine, pharmacy, and dentistry were conferred; there were 69 admissions to the first year of medical studies; and 42 certificates for advanced studies in the sciences were awarded. This was, however, a culturally truncated elite. Its largest groups, mainly Vietnamese, were civil servants (26,941 in 1941–42). Nearly all of them served as lower-level clerks and teachers (16,000 in 1941–42). Of the teachers, the overwhelming majority taught at the primary school level, and most of them were mere auxiliaries. This elite was long excluded not only from positions of command and organization, but also, in spite of the belated creation of the Hanoi School of Sciences, from theoretical work, especially scientific theory, which could only be studied in metropolitan France and was therefore only marginally accessible to the colonized. It was not until 1930 that the first scientific doctorate (in physics) was granted in Paris to one of the colonized, the Vietnamese Hoang Thi Nga, whereas Cambridge admitted its first Indian student as early as 1865. The Tata family had created the Indian Institute of Sciences in Bangalore in 1911—though in a country, it is true, that had been conquered since the eighteenth century. This elite was

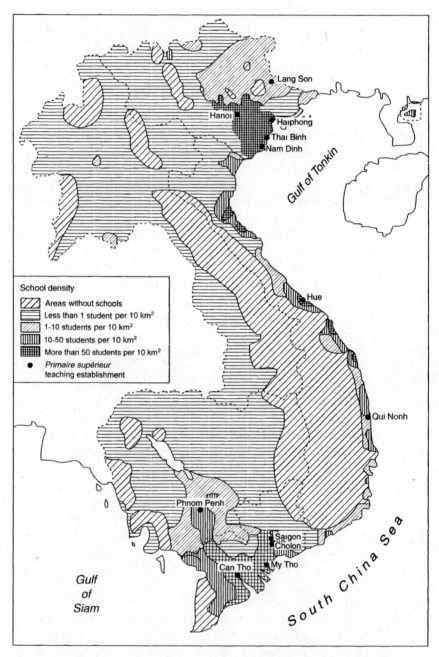

MAP 5.1. Distribution of public schools. (Exposition coloniale de 1931, Gouvernement général, *Le service de l'instruction publique en Indochine en 1930* [Hanoi, 1930].)

also under ideological surveillance, and indeed, viewed with suspicion by the colonial state. The minister for the colonies cautioned in 1919:

> It is advisable that we only go down the reformist road with extreme prudence. . . . It is precisely the natives educated in our methods and in our ideas who are the most dangerous enemies of our authority and the most resolute partisans of a *home rule* [said in English] in which we would have no place. There is no doubt, in fact, that the education provided in France does not correspond to any real need of the indigenous populations, or to their mentality. There, more than anywhere else, it is advisable not to open up the speculative domain of ideas too extensively, but, on the contrary, to encourage the acquisition of only the most essential knowledge.[10]

Although the number of Vietnamese children without schooling for lack of means (poverty, but also lack of schools and of teachers) can be estimated at around 100,000 in 1944, the schooling of youngsters increased constantly after 1930. Moreover, the important deficiencies that affected rural areas and the lower social categories in the cities cannot be attributed entirely to a deliberate Malthusian logic on the part of the French. In 1944, a critical assessment of the Association for the Diffusion of Quoc ngu (Hoi truyen ba quoc ngu)—a private Vietnamese and even crypto-communist initiative—underlined the geographical limitation of the group's actions to villages in the Hanoi vicinity, and blamed its failures on the psychological obstacles thrown up by the rural people themselves.

The Question of Language

A major educational problem was the selection of the language of instruction. While French would, of course, be preeminent, it was inconceivable that all Indochinese could be schooled in that language. It was thus necessary to maintain the vernacular languages as instruments of communication among the indigenous peoples. The organization of two categories of teaching, one reserved for French and the other called "Franco-indigenous," respected the linguistic duality of every territory of the Indochinese Union (Cochinchina, Annam, Tonkin, Laos, and Cambodia).

An example of this is the diffusion of Quoc ngu, the transcription of Vietnamese into Latin characters, which under the French became the national writing system of the Vietnamese. However, the ultimate success of this writing system was neither desired nor foreseen by either the colonizers or the colonized. Established in the seventeenth century by European Catholic missionaries, Quoc ngu was originally a means of transcription designed to facilitate evangelization. Although Alexandre de Rhodes undoubtedly played an active role in the perfection of Quoc ngu, Portuguese Jesuits played a central role in this endeavor by forging the new transcription on the basis of Portuguese.[11] During the colonial period, the French believed that the Chinese characters and the *nom* system (the demotic Vietnamese script based on Chinese characters) could not be instruments of modernization.

Besides, a rejection of the Chinese or *nom* characters allowed the French to end the cultural monopoly of the existing literate elites who used Chinese characters, thereby undermining their prestige and their authority. By replacing Chinese with French, the colonizers thus counted on creating a new cultural playing field tilted to their own advantage. This project was clearly stated at the time: "The Annamese within our Protectorate and under our direction are in fact influenced by China. More than ever, the literate class is intellectually under its dependence; it knows and thinks only through China, according to her and far behind her . . . its characters being the only vehicle of instruction for this class. This will be the case as long as the present situation endures, as long as it is not replaced by the national language in everyday usage and by French as the vehicle of higher education."[12]

In the 1880s, the French were still not conscious of the inherent difficulties of generalizing the use of French, although they quickly realized the importance of Quoc ngu as an intermediary language that would allow the Vietnamese to familiarize themselves with French. What was lost sight of was the vision of Gabriel Aubaret, a French Navy officer fluent in Chinese and Vietnamese, who negotiated the 1864 treaty ceding the three provinces of Cochinchina to France. Aubaret assigned a revolutionary role to the new roman transcription system: "This common language, solidified through our use of Latin characters, opens a clear path for our civilizing ideas to penetrate; and who knows whether it will be in this way that European science, so absolutely unknown in the Far East because of the insurmountable difficulty of terms, will be understood one day? We can hope that some of the Annamese people, whose future is in our hands, will acquire an incontestable moral superiority over the remainder of Cochinchina; to solidify a language through writing is, after all, a revolution almost comparable to the discovery of printing."[13]

Meanwhile, French was taught in all Indochinese schools. The certificate of Franco-indigenous primary studies (CEPFI), the end of the first level of colonial education in Vietnamese countries, included a dictation in French (five spelling mistakes resulted in elimination). As a result, until the 1930s, the failure rate sometimes reached as high as 70%. But opinions and practical arrangements surrounding this francophone principle varied. Gustave Dumoutier (1850–1904), who directed education in Annam-Tonkin at the turn of the century, reestablished the teaching of Chinese characters and introduced Quoc ngu in the schools of Annam and Tonkin. In 1930, an essay in Quoc ngu appeared in tests for the CEPFI, as well as an optional examination in Chinese calligraphy. Starting in 1930, it was decided that ethics, history, and geography did not have to be taught in French. Echoing Governor-General Pierre Pasquier, Alexandre Varennes, himself a former governor (1925–27), warned against teaching the natives that France "is their homeland," and cautioned: "Make sure they have an Asian education that is useful to them in their country."[14] In the same vein, a teacher named Émile Tavernier published a booklet in Saigon in 1933 entitled *De la nécessité d'écrire l'histoire de l'ancien empire d'Annam* (On the Necessity of Writing the History of the Ancient Empire of Annam). Reverence for Vietnamese culture was accentuated during World War II, so that the radical Vietnamization of teaching in 1945—which was clearly a voluntary break with the colonial past—can be considered as a logical, inevitable outcome of this earlier process, something which the most farsighted French had already conceded.

It was only in the aftermath of World War I that the Vietnamese, seeing that French domination was well established, decided they had to deal with the linguistic question. Several figures defended the idea of making Quoc ngu the national form of writing. This was notably the opinion upheld by the nationalist Phan Van Truong in 1912, when he created a Hoi than ai dong bao (Countrymen's Club) in Paris. It was at this time that he wrote a pamphlet that was a true "defense and illustration of Quoc ngu." According to him, this new form of writing was a tool for literary creation and scientific teaching, not just a simple means of communication between the French and the native population. Later, when he returned to his homeland, Truong continued to promote the diffusion and teaching of Quoc ngu, for example, to the Société cochinchinoise pour la promotion des études (Cochinchinese Society for the Promotion of Education) in 1925. The importance of the role that Truong played in the intellectual, and therefore political, history of his nation can hardly be overemphasized.[15]

Then, in the 1930s, Quoc ngu became a tool of political proceedings and modern Vietnamese literature. The initiatives of the colonizers also affirmed the rise of Quoc ngu. There was no precise cultural program in this domain, but Indochina's Gouvernement général did take note of two or three facts that incited it to take an interest in cultural questions. For one thing, the 1907 Dong Kinh Nghia Thuc (Dong Kinh [Hanoi] School of the Just Cause) had demonstrated that in the absence of governmental measures, the Vietnamese had the will and the capacity to establish a politically uncontrolled organization of modern popular education (see below). Second, Chinese reformist literature (Kang You-wei and especially Liang Qichao) had penetrated Vietnam and introduced the Vietnamese to the ideas of Montesquieu, J.-J. Rousseau, Darwin, Spencer, and so on. The Chinese Republican movement and the revolution of 1911 worried colonial authorities. And, lastly, German activity in the Far East in the early twentieth century alarmed the French.[16]

To take on these threats, the Gouvernement général relied on literary modernists and the supporters of a Franco-Vietnamese colonial contract, as embodied in the official policy of "collaboration and Franco-Vietnamese harmony." The first initiative was the creation of the magazine *Dong Duong Tap Chi,* which appeared between 1913 and 1920. Its moving spirit was Nguyen Van Vinh (1882–1926), an enthusiastic partisan of French culture, who was joined by Phan Ke Binh, Tran Trong Kim, Nguyen Van To, Pham Duy Ton, and the poet Tan Da. The magazine violently attacked the traditionalist literati, and the French therefore came up with a new magazine, *Nam Phong Tap Chi* (Wind of the South), which was officially launched on July 1, 1917. This was followed, two years later, by the creation of the Association pour la formation intellectuelle et morale des Annamites (Association for the Moral and Intellectual Education of the Annamese). The idea originated with Louis Marty, who was the interim director of the Indochinese Sûreté and a man with remarkable political skills. He became the mentor of numerous young Vietnamese radical intellectuals. Marty laid out the objectives of *Nam Phong Tap Chi* as follows:

> The subjects to be treated will be very freely chosen, so as to preserve sufficient independence and impartiality in this collection, without which this work of propaganda will suffer the fate of earlier similar attempts, which failed because of the naïve and clumsy administrative bias that inspired them. . . . The head of the Political Office of the Gouvernement général is its unofficial promoter. . . . The two main editors, Pham Quynh and Nguyen Ba Trac, took this magazine under their wing, so that it would preserve an exclusively indigenous character in the eyes of the public.[17]

Nam Phong received a monthly subsidy of four hundred piastres from the Gouvernement général, which decided to entrust the direction of the new enterprise to a remarkable man who, like Nguyen Van Vinh, had been trained at the School of Interpreters. Writer, translator, and essayist, versed in Chinese, Quoc ngu, and French, Pham Quynh and his mentor, Marty, touched a sensitive chord in linguistic nationalism. The magazine also played a fundamental role in the intellectual life of Tonkin and Annam until around 1924. It was an invaluable tool in the diffusion of Quoc ngu and cleared the way for the take-off of Vietnamese literature and language. As Pham Quynh wrote at the time: "To be Vietnamese, we must respect and cherish the language of our country. We must place Vietnamese above French and Chinese. I am someone who, because I truly love Vietnamese, has voluntarily dedicated his whole life to giving this language an independent literature, so that my people do not have to endure the eternal fate of studying and writing in a language borrowed from a foreigner."[18]

The initiators of *Nam Phong* wanted to channel the intellectual aspirations of the Vietnamese middle class their way and screen foreign intellectual contributions themselves. In this sense, Pham Quynh played the role of a Confucian scholar, monarchist, and elitist. His linguistic purism only allowed for borrowings from Chinese in the building of a Quoc ngu vocabulary. His monopolistic control over the selection of French authors published (though he excluded contemporary writers) greatly limited the influence of *Nam Phong* to the advantage of the radical publications that appeared after 1923, notably, *La cloche fêlée* (The Cracked Bell), edited by Nguyen An Ninh. These, paradoxically, were published in French.

With the same cultural preoccupations in mind, Pierre Pasquier founded the Buddhist Institute of Phnom Penh, destined to receive three thousand monks and to divert the Buddhist clergy from going to Siam. The Buddhist Institute, associated with the Orientalist Suzanne Karpelès, was not only destined to shield the Khmer monks from the influence of the Thai monasteries, it was also the crowning achievement of a cultural project that solidified a renaissance movement within Khmer culture. This began in 1914 with the creation of the School of Pali (the religious writing of southern India in which the Buddhist canonical texts had been written) in Cambodia, located in Phnom Penh. This was reorganized in 1922 and renamed the Pali School of Higher Learning. In 1924, these French initiatives were followed by the founding of the Royal National Library of Cambodia, whose director was Karpelès. The Buddhist Institute was opened shortly thereafter. These creations in the capital depended on a network of pagoda schools, some of which were progressively brought up to date. This was the case in the provinces, as well as in areas in Cochinchina inhabited by the Khmer Krom, the Cambodian inhabitants of the Mekong Delta, conquered by the Vietnamese in the nineteenth century. The first pagoda schools to be reformed dated from 1908–11, but they really took off only in 1930. The introduction of new subjects (arithmetic and geography, for example) into the curriculum pointed up the modernization of the traditional Cambodian education system. According to Pascale Bezançon, Louis Manipoud was the driving force behind this educational policy. He devoted himself to this reform with particular conviction and tenacity in the province of Kampot, where he was inspector of primary schools between 1924 and 1936.[19]

These educational institutions doubled the size of the network of schools without undermining it. Pupils sat for the Certificate of Elementary Indigenous Studies with a 48% success rate in 1935. In 1930, 3,332 students were enrolled in 101 renovated schools. In 1939, 908 reformed schools counted 38,834 students; and finally, in 1944, 47,555 students studied in 992 reformed schools. In Cochinchina, in 1941, 5,837 Khmer children attended this type of school. Such schools demonstrate the flexibility and adaptability of a French policy usually considered to have been assimilationist and unpragmatic.

The Revival of Arts and Crafts

Colonial authorities and individuals attempted to rebuild or to renovate other cultural domains in Indochina. These initiatives principally concerned traditional arts and monuments. In Cambodia, Annam, and Tonkin, the French tried to halt the decline of the arts and to stimulate their development. The situation had become particularly alarming in Cambodia. The artisan of the Cambodian arts renaissance, Georges Groslier, explained the reasons for this deterioration in a long report:

> For about the past sixty years, Khmer traditions have been subjected to the direct influence of the West. . . . By comparison to the European arriver, the highest mandarin

is no longer a great character in the eyes of the masses. He tries to acquire our superiority, which he only understands in its vain and superficial aspects, in order to reestablish his lost prestige in new garb. The Khmer aristocracy (and I mean by this term the entire ruling class), the only one that associates with the Europeans, quickly moved ahead of the people: it abandoned them . . . out of one and a half million inhabitants, ten thousand, if you will, have come over to our side. Therefore, on one side, there is an invariable popular mass, on the other, the rich, directing element, the motor, in the midst of a full Europeanization. . . . All these purchasers of puerile imported consumer goods—notables, well-to-do farmers, princes of all kinds of blood—stopped looking to the local craftsmen. Previously . . . all mandarin Khmer of some quality had their share of cabinetmakers and goldsmiths, troupes of musicians and dancers, sculptors and artists. . . . In 1909, I met . . . the last high mandarin who still had some actresses. And in 1917, only the king maintained workshops, which were in a distressing state of anarchy and disintegration. . . . The misfortune spread among the pagodas, for every monastery also had its artists. But monasteries started building with reinforced concrete, which only Chinese workers know how to do, buying paper flowers from the glass showcases of Western shopkeepers, importing glass chandeliers from the Bazar of the Hôtel de Ville in Paris in honor of the statue of the Buddha, and the popular artists, without any work, became rarer, receded into the background, and practiced their crafts less and less.[20]

Here, Groslier was alluding to a census of craftsmen. In 1917, there were a hundred and thirty of them located throughout the country. The majority, to subsist, had to rely on farming. In Phnom Penh, a town of thirty-five thousand Cambodians in 1925, there were only thirty-two artisans, of whom twenty were attached to the court.[21]

Although they did not decline so dramatically, Vietnamese arts and handicrafts showed similar signs of decline. The causes were comparable, the weakening of imperial patronage being one of the most important. In 1897, according to an anonymous colonial official, in Vietnam, "Working in jade and ivory was almost completely abandoned. As for the enamel work once practiced in palace workshops . . . its technique is lost, and there are no longer any enamel workers in Hue."[22] This decline, he added, was "especially caused by European influences of dubious taste," which had "brought about an incontestable degeneration of styles," leading to an "extreme scarcity of clientele." In 1937, the official French milieu finally agreed on the need to revitalize the Indochinese arts. This shift was founded on the recognition of their aesthetic value, but it can also be explained by the realization that they were expressions of cultural identity: "It seems that we must assume the role of conserving the artistic domain of the people whose education we have undertaken, the unique character and originality of their national art, to help them rediscover elements that they have misjudged or forgotten, and to emphasize their identity rather than impose our own. This is especially true with regards to the Far Easterners who have created unparalleled works of art and who have achieved very admirable results in all branches of art."[23]

Finally, in 1924, the Gouvernement général founded the École des beaux-arts de l'Indochine (School of Fine Arts of Indochina) under the direction of Victor Tardieu. Renamed the Higher School of Fine Arts of the Indochinese University in 1937, the establishment recruited new masters capable of training handicraft artists. It also taught Western techniques of sculpture and oil painting to student artists and included a Department of Applied Arts. There was a debate about the mission of the School of Fine Arts, which pitted those who wanted to train only craftsmen against those who strove, in line with the demands of a part of Vietnamese opinion, to make the school a training ground for artists devoted to what were known as the major arts.[24] From 1937, the choice leaned toward the second orientation, in the same way that "Indochinese Physicians" became "Indochinese Doctors." It can therefore not be said that colonial education was just an institution destined to shape performers and underlings, a kind of "discount education."

The colonial administration and the promoters of the renaissance and development of indigenous arts took care to associate the schools with museums, which brought together many ancient artifacts from French Indochina and elsewhere in the area. This provided sources of inspiration for artisans and artists and played a role in shaping public tastes. The Albert Sarraut Museum formally opened in Phnom Penh on April 13, 1920, and by 1924, it was already exhibiting 2,202 original objects, some dating to the classical period. In 1923, the Khai Dinh museum opened in Hue, whereas Hanoi was home to the Louis Finot Museum and Saigon boasted the Blanchard de la Brosse Museum.

The organizers of the art schools did their best to support the students they had trained and ensure them outlets for the sale of their artistic work. For example, the Office des corporations cambodgiennes (Office of Cambodian Corporations), founded in 1920, was an outlet for Khmer artisans. The corporate associations of Gia Dinh and Thu Dau Mot, founded in 1933, and the Société annamite d'encouragement à l'art et à l'industrie (Annamese Society for the Support of Art and Industry), created in 1934, did the same in eastern Indochina. These associations encouraged local artists to participate in exhibitions in Indochina, as well as internationally, in France (in Paris in 1925, 1931, and 1937) and in San Francisco (1939). They also organized contests offering prizes or diplomas.

The Modernization of Artistic Education

Restoration work had started earlier through the implementation of artistic education throughout the colony. The first school in Indochina was founded in 1917, in Phnom Penh. Its mission was to restore an original Cambodian artistic patrimony that was in danger of disappearing completely. The teachers were all Cambodian artists and were entirely free of French tutelage. A rigorous selection process admitted seventy students in 1937. Cochinchina possessed three provincial schools where so-called minor arts were taught. A school was founded in Bien Hoa in 1903 for artisans working in bronze and ceramics, which had fifty students in 1937. A school was founded in Gia Dinh in 1913 for the teaching of the decorative arts, design, engraving, and lithography, which had from seventy to ninety students in 1937. In Thu Dau Mot, a school was founded in 1901 for woodworking, cabinetwork, sculpture, and inlays of mother of pearl and wood.

The efforts accomplished in favor of artistic instruction and the promotion of the fine arts bore fruit. Traditional techniques such as lacquering and silk painting in the classic style were vigorously maintained. The principal innovations were oil painting and the introduction of European perspective in the composition of paintings. Although the realism of the traditional arts remained predominant, romanticism and even Western realism made themselves felt. One of the realist painters most appreciated by the Vietnamese and European public was Nguyen Phan Chanh. He received honors from *L'Illustration,* which reproduced several of his works in its special 1932 Christmas edition. Among the more eccentric artists was Ta Ty, the first Vietnamese cubist painter. Lastly, owing to French influence, caricature and humorous drawing found support from an expanding Vietnamese press. In the pages of the magazine *Phong Hoa,* the genre immortalized Ly Toet and Xa Xe, two fictional Vietnamese rustics invented by the poet Tu Mo, who are victims of their own naïveté.

The Introduction of Broadcasting and Cinema

Other forms and tools of modern cultural expression appeared relatively early in Indochina. Broadcasting was introduced at the end of the 1920s. In 1938, in Cochinchina, Vietnamese owned 59% of all radios, while the Chinese accounted for 17%. Two private radio stations in Saigon were particularly successful: Radio Boy Landry and Radio Michel Robert. They broadcast music programs and Asian theater, which took up more airtime than their French programs. As for cinema, there were, from 1932, twenty-seven public cinemas in Tonkin. The two French companies that owned twenty-two of these theaters projected 80 to 100 talking films and 150 silent films per year. In Annam, eleven cinemas showed films regularly; however, it was in Cochinchina that the cinema truly thrived and was most diverse, not only in the origins and genres of the films it showed but also in the audiences they attracted. Cochinchina had thirteen movie theaters, in addition to traveling entrepreneurs who showed films in the provinces. In all, Cochinchina ran a total of 100 talking films in 1932. As for Cambodia, it had seven cinemas, where 324 silent films were shown. Laos had only three. The clientele of the grand cinemas of Hanoi and Saigon was primarily French; elsewhere, however, it was mostly Indochinese or Chinese.[25]

Lenin was not the first to understand the ideological and political role that cinema could play. The French authorities were also concerned about the impact of the "Seventh Art" on the populations of the colonies. They paid attention to the content of each film, whether French or foreign. In 1932, the huge success of the American director Lewis Milestone's *All Quiet on the Western Front* (1930) in Hue worried the authorities, who considered the film to be dangerously pacifist. Although the Soviet filmmaker Vsevolod Pudovkin's *Storm over Asia* (1928) presented "French characters in a favorable light," a ban was recommended in 1938 because its subject matter dealt with violent revolt.[26] Chinese films that had the capacity to provoke anti-Japanese demonstrations were equally censored. Except in particular cases, a fairly liberal policy governed the importation of films on social topics, even if they were "bitter," as long as they were "not subversive." However, the authorities paid more attention to the effects produced by movies displaying naked women and prolonged kissing. One French official observed at the time: "The indigenous audience members react to certain somewhat daring scenes with loud hilarity that embarrasses the European viewers."[27]

Governor-General Pasquier was supportive of using movies in schools, and the local chief of education in Annam reported that, from 1926, films were used as teaching tools in the major educational establishments of Hue, Vinh, and Qui Nhon.[28]

THE INITIATIVES OF THE COLONIZED

In developing education, in restoring the monumental and artistic past with a success attested by the magnificent work accomplished at Angkor by the École française d'Extrême-Orient (French School of the Far East), and in encouraging intellectual publications, the French made it clear that they intended to influence the cultural evolution of the Indochinese. But France was but one side of the coin. The Indochinese were able to draw on different or contrary references within this same French culture and opposed countervailing values to those the colonizers officially attempted to instill into them.

Education, the Press, and Publishing

The Vietnamese attempted to attain the sources of modernity by themselves, while refusing or evading those that the colonizers filtered and then offered them. The first step toward seizing the opponent's secrets was the Dong Du (Voyage East) movement. From the outset, it combined a political project with a cultural program. Through the work of Phan Boi Chau, and inspired by the Japanese model (which was reinforced by the Japanese defeat of the Russians in 1905), this movement sought to maintain traditional moral values and politics. Chinese characters remained its language of expression. The principal effect of the Dong Du's cultural program was its contribution to the intellectual and political evolution of involved individuals rather than the elaboration of a new culture. By rubbing shoulders with Japanese and then Chinese reformers, the Dong Du confirmed to the Vietnamese that they were right to search for inspiration and suggestions from the West. This experience paralleled the rallying of intellectuals to Quoc ngu.

The earliest attempt at real, autonomous cultural development was the Dong Kinh Nghia Thuc (DKNT) movement mentioned above, which coincided not only with the French crackdown on the Dong Du and the expulsion of Vietnamese by the Japanese government but with numerous initiatives by Hanoi in support of popular education and periods of study in France, such as those by the Association d'aide aux Annamites pour des études supérieures et techniques en France (Association of Aid to Annamese for Advanced and Technical Studies in France) and the Association de soutien aux étudiants en France (Association of Support for Students in France). Thus began the phase that followed the Dong Du: that of the Tay Du (Voyage West).

On March 3, 1907, a group of "patriotic and progressive" literati founded the Dong Kinh Nghia Thuc in a room on Silk Street (Hang Dao) in Hanoi. Members paid a monthly contribution of five piastres. The school provided the paper, pens, and ink. Every evening, four to five hundred listeners hurried to conferences where one could learn characters, Quoc ngu, and French, as well as the main disciplines of the French educational curriculum. The latter request represented a Vietnamese desire to attain educational parity with the colonizer. Traditional customs were debated, as well as more purely intellectual questions. The Vietnamese thus familiarized themselves with Montesquieu's *L'esprit des lois,* Rousseau's *Le contrat social,* and the evolutionist writings of Darwin via Chinese and Japanese translations and commentaries. Numerous translations in Quoc ngu were completed, and the romanized language even served as the main vehicle of instruction. Women were admitted to DKNT classrooms both as students and as teachers. Several works published by the DKNT have recently been discovered, notably, the *Tan dinh luan ly giao khoa* (New Manual of Morals), *Quoc dan doc bao* (Reading Book for the People), and *Quoc van tap doc* (Book of Readings and National Literature). These books, which extol moral and civic virtues, patriotism, and national solidarity, reveal the extent to which ethics was at the heart of the DKNT educational program. Its leaders believed that morality was "the quintessence of national honor and the origin of education."

The DKNT thus assigned an important place to modern knowledge. However, this school associated it with the culture of so-called ancestral values and virtues in order to affirm the originality and cohesion of a Vietnamese nation linked by blood ties and consecrated through its 4,000 years of existence. This implied a cardinal and imperative duty: piety and loyalty to the sovereign and the homeland.[29] Unsurprisingly, in December 1907, the colonial authorities closed the school.[30]

The Dong Kinh Nghia Thuc nonetheless marked a cultural turning point in two ways. First, the classically trained literati (Luong Van Can, Tang Bat Ho, and Nguyen Quyen, for example) gave their stamp of approval to the use of the romanized Quoc ngu writing system, transforming an instrument of foreign penetration into a tool of internal communication and national cultural unification. Moreover, Quoc ngu was much more effective for facilitating mass education than Chinese-based characters had ever been. By teaching a syllabus very close to the one being proposed by the French and by studying Western philosophers, the organizers and their pupils broke away from cultural xenophobia. They distinctly separated Western culture from the enterprise of colonial conquest, thus abolishing traditional reticence about participating in Western or Western-derived schools.

The French government understood that it had an interest in not suppressing, and even in exploiting this local desire for modern knowledge. In 1909, the colonial state created the School of the Protectorate, a secondary establishment reserved for young Vietnamese. In 1913, it encouraged the launching of *Dong Duong Tap Chi* by Nguyen Van Vinh, who had likewise participated in the Dong Kinh Nghia Thuc. And ten years after it had closed, the government reopened the Indochinese University in Hanoi. Moreover, the Dong Kinh Nghia Thuc cleared the way for an intellectual collaboration that supplemented political or "supporting" collaboration with the colonizer. Later on, some of the translators for the magazine *Nam Phong* were men who had been active in the Dong Kinh Nghia Thuc, such as Nguyen Huu Tien, Nguyen Don Phuc, and Nguyen Van To, among others.

Thanks to the rise of Quoc ngu in particular and the spread of education in general, the publication of periodicals and books became a notable part of Indochinese intellectual life, above all in Vietnam. From 1924 on, despite obstacles stemming from government censorship, financial constraints, and lack of professional experience, the press witnessed a remarkable boom. Many modern writers started their careers in journalism before becoming well enough known to make their livings as novelists, poets, or essayists. The first newspapers were official organs, mainly destined to broadcast the colonial administration's decisions and authorized texts. The official and private media, even those printed in Quoc ngu, were originally French-owned. One of the most famous French newspaper owners and editors was François-Henri Schneider. Paradoxically, it was in this kind of publication that the first Vietnamese challenges to colonial domination appeared. For example, the famous patriot Gilbert Chieu wrote his major political harangues against colonial domination in the pages of the informational paper *Luc Tinh Tan Van* (The New Gazette of Six Provinces [i.e., Cochinchina]), which belonged to Schneider.

The most remarkable periodicals in terms of the talent of their authors and the ideas and debates they presented were, in Saigon, *La cloche fêlée,* edited by Nguyen An Ninh and Phan Van Truong (1923–28), *Dong Phap Thoi Bao* (1923–27), *Trung Lap Bao* (1924–33), *Duoc Nha Nam* (1928–37), and *Phu Nu Tan Van* (1929–34). In Hanoi, one could read *Trung Bac Tan Van* (1919–45), also owned by Schneider, *Thuc Nghiep Dan Bao* (1920–33), and *Khai Hoa Nhat Bao* (1921–27), among other periodicals. Huynh Thuc Khang succeeded in publishing *Tieng Dan* in Hue from 1927 to 1943 by himself, with scant resources.

During a short period of time corresponding largely to the duration of the Popular Front government in France, the legal communist and left-wing press experienced a brief but intensive expansion, which is addressed elsewhere in this work. In 1937, the Gouvernement général tallied a total of 110 dailies and 159 magazines and bulletins. In 1938, there were 128 daily publications and 160 magazines and bulletins. In 1939, 128 dailies and 176 magazines and bulletins were in operation.

The activity of the Indochinese publishers was, without doubt, the most sustained of all those in the French colonial empire. Thanks to laws requiring copies of all books to be sent to the Bibliothèque nationale in Paris, that library now holds a collection of some sixteen thousand works in Quoc ngu, mostly relating to religious matters. Vietnamese authors and editors, however, wrote on a great range of topics. Among these editors, Dao Duy Anh, a lexicographer whose French-Vietnamese dictionary is still a classic, had an extremely important role in popularizing philosophical ideas, notably Marxism. He edited a series of brochures to introduce the ideas of Jean-Baptiste Lamarck, Charles Darwin, Auguste Comte, Karl Marx, and H. G. Wells to Vietnamese readers. He also provided clarifying introductions with titles like "What Is Religion?" or "What Is Society?" or "What Is the Nation?" In addition, Dao Duy Anh attempted to collect documents relating to ancient Vietnamese history and to analyze these texts following the methods of the French historian Charles Seignobos.[31]

Many of these works contained a glossary of new words in Quoc ngu. In other areas, there was a medical encyclopedia published in Haiphong in 1930, followed fourteen years later by two medical dictionaries. Several books on applied sciences—electricity, physics, chemistry, agronomy—appeared between 1929 and 1934. Booksellers also offered practical guides on car mechanics, accounting, shorthand and typing, photography, and so on.[32]

The popularization of science is also evident in periodicals such as Nam Phong (1917–21) and Phu Nu Tan Van, to name only two major titles. After 1921, however, two magazines were published that were specifically devoted to the popular dissemination of scientific and technical knowledge. In Saigon, Khoa Hoc Pho Thong (Science) appeared from 1934 to 1942. In Hanoi, Khoa Hoc Tap Chi (Scientific Journal), edited by the agronomist and engineer Nguyen Cong Tieu, sold an average of two thousand copies between 1931 and 1940. Tieu was especially well known for his research on azolla, or duckweed fern, used as a green agricultural fertilizer. He was admitted to the Scientific Council of Indochina, which depended on the governor-general. There, he sought to reconcile the scientific spirit (i.e., rationalism) with Confucianism.[33] The success of the popularization of sciences, notably applied sciences, testified to the open mind of the urban Vietnamese and perhaps pointed up a certain scientific naïveté.

Meanwhile, the illiteracy rate remained very high. The rise in the number of publications in Quoc ngu should not prevent us from seeing that they were essentially destined for the urban middle class. Nevertheless, lectures, public commentaries, and oral transmission of information and opinions should be taken into account when trying to gauge the actual spread of new intellectual knowledge during the colonial period.

Changes in Customs and Ideas

An anecdote related by the French journalist Andrée Viollis illustrates the gap between two Vietnamese generations:

> In one of those towns I found out that an Annamese dignitary wanted to make my acquaintance. His son, a fellow student of my daughters' at the Sorbonne, had visited me in Paris. He is a tall, handsome boy, of studied elegance, with slicked-back hair, who seemed to attend dances no less assiduously than he did classes. Then there is the father, a classic mandarin, dressed in his refined robes, his hands in his sleeves, bowing with dignity; he does not even know French and his customary compliments are translated by an interpreter, as he repeatedly bows. It is impossible to associate this character straight out of a Chinese screen with the very Parisian image of the young regular of the Boul' Mich' [Boulevard Saint-Michel, in the heart of the student quarter in Paris]. Separated by years, but also by the insurmountable barrier of ideas, customs, and habits, how will this father and son be able to understand and listen to each other? I am told that this excellent civil servant, who has made significant sacrifices for the education of the young man, patiently awaits his return. Is the young man also eager to return to his country? Will he rebel against the tyranny of his indigenous environment or against the French yoke and its constraints? It is a moving problem that evokes serious reflection.[34]

This narration ends with a question. But Governor-General Pasquier recounted to the journalist René Vanlande how the son of a mandarin had ridiculed his father by accusing him of having conceived him in a moment of drunkenness. One can imagine how monstrous such a statement must have seemed in a society where filial piety was a capital virtue. Without a doubt, the reported case is extreme. Nevertheless, a cultural malaise existed, and not only among those "returning from France." At one point, it even became fashionable to speak only in French. The writer Nam Xuong wrote a satirical piece that was an adaptation of Molière's Le bourgeois gentilhomme. The principal character, a "French Annamese" rejects his parents because they have an "indigenous odor" and resorts to an interpreter because he is ashamed to speak in his native tongue. There were also some ephemeral infatuations like the creation of a Tino Rossi club in Hanoi by about twenty young Vietnamese "fans." Beyond this, and more profoundly, a new way of living was emerging, one that increasingly collided with the values that had been cultivated for centuries in Vietnam.

The French conquest first of all disrupted the notion of political duty by raising the important question of to whom obedience and loyalty should be directed— to the sovereign who had surrendered to the invader, to the monarchy, independent of the sovereign, or to moral beliefs in themselves? One either had to accept the new rulers or fight them to the end. This predicament eventually forced the Vietnamese to begin to separate politics from ethics. This was new.

Parallel to the political questions created by the colonial process were cultural issues that threatened the very soul of the nation *(quoc hon)* and its national essence *(quoc tuy)*. Confronted by superior foreign power, traditional ideology could be perceived as the cause of weakness and, consequently, of defeat and servitude. It could also be held responsible for delaying modernization, since Confucianism was sometimes seen as impermeable or even hostile to the scientific and technical spirit. It could even be written off as "feudal," a hindrance to the renaissance of the nation. But did this mean it was necessary to accept the values that the colonizers sought to impose on the colonized, or accept those unleashed by the colonizers' very presence? Whatever the topic of a debate—linguistics, philosophy, literature, history, education, or ethics—and whatever the theme of a literary work, one always encountered the question of the nation's destiny, whether it be decadence, disappearance, or rebirth. All movements, all organizations, all intellectual schools or currents inevitably had to deal with this matter.

During the 1920s and 1930s, as seen by the malaise among the youth and the debates on the status of women, Vietnamese society was shaken in its key institution— the family. What seemed most menacing to the cohesion of the familial and national collectivities—which were inseparable in the Vietnamese context—was the emancipation of the individual. This constant conflict imposed limits on all movements whose objective was the transformations of relations between the generations and the sexes.

The main Vietnamese women's organization was created in 1926 in Hue. Placed under the patronage of a man, Phan Boi Chau, and directed by Mme Dam Phuong, the Association des femmes pour l'étude et le travail (Association of Women for Work and Study) adopted as its primary goal equal rights in education and preeminence in familial responsibilities. The latter point was portrayed as the foundation of patriotic sentiment. The ideal of the liberated woman was best symbolized by the Trung sisters, heroines who had taken part in a tenth-century insurrection against the invading Chinese armies.

Other militants went farther by pronouncing their rejection of "feudal customs," meaning arranged marriages, one-sided chastity, and especially the "Three Submissions" and the "Five Virtues." These questions were debated within the narrow circles of the urban middle class. Furthermore, it was in Hue, the imperial city and capital of conservatism, that women were the most active. The weekly *Phu Nu Tan Van* (Feminine Gazette, or Modern Women's News) reached a peak circulation of 8,500 copies, progressively expanding the themes it treated in its pages. The importance of these themes was reflected in the fact that the paper's audience consisted of as many men as it did women. The control of the magazine by the Marxist Phan

Van Hum, starting in 1933, put an end to its eclecticism. From that point on, it emphasized less the obligations owed to the national community than the social duties owed to hard-working, underprivileged women. In this sense, the liberation of women was only conceived of to the degree that it was in line with collective obligations. The point of view expressed by the Indochinese Communist Party situated itself within an analogous perspective. The emancipation of women was inseparable from the liberation of the proletariat. This was an important departure from conservative positions and official wishes as they were expressed by the author of a work on *La femme dans la société annamite* (Woman in Annamese Society): "The Annamese woman has in all times been a model of great purity. She is the guardian of a high moral culture; in the setting of the family, she has fulfilled herself for millennia, independent of our social and national adventures."[35]

At the end of 1930, the colonial administration reduced the Association of Women for Work and Study to a simple patronage association, and *Phu Nu Tan Van* ceased to appear in 1934. In the meantime, other groups of women from Cochinchina and Annam were forbidden to meet or had their associations dispersed.

If the ideological battles revealed what moved hearts and minds, we know very little about what actually happened in the families themselves. It is reasonable to imagine that few radical changes occurred, since even "French naturalized" families continued to observe local customs in the family domain and in the relations it generated. Through the legal and economic changes, and even under the appearance of French manners, cultural identity persisted.

Nevertheless, the young men and women of the urban middle class began to move down the path of physical and intellectual transformation. Physical education, sports (and notably European football), swimming, tennis, and traditional martial arts, but also English boxing, progressively developed. This occurred first in scholarly establishments, then spread with the expansion of sporting associations. In 1937, the first summer camps allowed a still modest number of schoolchildren (four to five hundred in each *ky*) to go to the beach or the mountains.[36] The first municipal swimming pool reserved for Indochinese opened in Saigon in 1937.[37] The first Boy Scout groups were started in 1930, and the first Girl Scouts emerged in 1936. Beginning in 1935, the Scouting movement, which numbered eight thousand members, as opposed to only a hundred in 1930, possessed its own magazine. La Fédération des scouts d'Indochine (The Federation of Scouts of Indochina) was formed in 1937 and opened a school for leaders in Bach Ma (close to Hue). The Scouts provide us with an interesting case: conceived as an organization fit to instill discipline, fidelity, and respect for hierarchy, it simultaneously gave young Indochinese an opportunity to acquaint themselves with modern techniques of organization and action. It taught them to take the initiative and to help others. It allowed them to become familiar with the rural population when they came to the aid of the poor or victims of disasters.

In 1932, a group of young girls from Hanoi organized a march to Haiphong. While few reached their destination and many were the objects of ridicule, the event garnered a great deal of attention, because it was understood that girls from good families did not travel by foot. In 1936, some girls from Saigon decided to start cycling, and one of them attempted to ride the 1,800 kilometers from Saigon to Hanoi.

Indeed, in traditional society, physical exercise was considered scandalous, let alone exposing parts of the body to the sun and to the eyes of others. This cultural reticence was only overcome very slowly and with great difficulty. In 1936, Mme Françoise Brachet, principal of the Hanoi Teacher's Training School for young girls, recounted that

> in fifteen years, ideas have changed. When I arrived to Hanoi in 1921, all of my students wore a black *cai ao*. It was so sad that I tried to allow them, at least, to wear a violet *cai ao*. The families there were violently opposed to this. However, today violet is the color of the uniform of the Annamese women. Today, my students wear colored dresses. Another thing: in attempting to give them gymnastics lessons and let them sing to the harmonium, I almost unleashed a revolution. In this office, I saw mothers kneeling . . . in protest. Only the *Kham Tien,* prostitutes, sing and make gestures with their arms. Now, all my pupils sing. Every morning, they have half an hour of physical education. Their professor is a young French noncommissioned officer and the families approve.
>
> But there is something more important. Shaped by our ideas, the young Annamese no longer accept what was the rule for their mothers. No one is willing to become a "second-rank spouse." On this point, they do not give in, whatever the insistence or the threats of their parents.
>
> They have acquired a sense of their personal dignity. They require an independent budget, and one now sees an astounding thing, in Annam: young couples get settled in their own houses, and the young woman frees herself from the authority of her mother-in-law.[38]

Although her remarks are limited to the modest proportions of a particular social stratum (teachers), the observations of Mme Brachet provide us with a window into social changes in colonial Vietnam. Incontestably, some transformations had occurred within the span of a decade. To Tam, the heroine of a melodramatic novel by Hoang Ngoc Phach published in 1925 (said to have been inspired by the 1848 novel *La Dame aux camélias* by Alexandre Dumas *fils*), who is forced by her parents to marry a man she does not love, and who dies as a result, was perhaps not quite representative of that generation. To Tam chooses submission; other young people chose suicide, whether because of love or because they could no longer tolerate domestic discipline. The son of a provincial judge explained his suicide in a letter published in *Phu Nu Tan Van* of May 25, 1931, as follows: "Can one imagine that a man of twenty-four years, married and the father of a family, still living at the expense of his parents, would be obliged to ask for their permission every time he wanted to spend a coin or take a step out of the house, never daring to do anything according to his own will? Such a life is not worth living."

The essayist Truong Tuu (born Nguyen Bach Khoa) provided his own insightful commentary on the evolution of the young: "Individualism and Western romantic literature surge into our country like a hurricane carrying away all the souls. In the long-cleared soil of Vietnamese sensitivity, these two spiritual factors have found sufficient conditions to take root and develop themselves. Waves of youngsters who grew up amid the collapse of Confucianism move away from the rationalistic spirit to go straight to art and love. They forget reason. They know only nature and the heart."[39]

After a period of withdrawal from traditional values, the philosophical and religious men and doctrines redeployed and redefined themselves around the challenges caused by the intrusion of French culture, as well as by social and political tensions.

The "Return" to Traditional Values

Working in the neotraditionalist Chinese style of the 1920s and 1930s, Tran Trong Kim, Freemason, scholar, and primary school inspector, attempted to adapt Confucianism to the modern world by associating intuition with reason, while allowing them their respective and separate domains. But the metamorphosis of Confucianism into metaphysics considerably weakened its impact on social reality. Pham Quynh, on the other hand, cultivated a Confucianism of an "ethical order," using Charles Maurras to counter the critical approach of Jean-Jacques Rousseau and the ideas of French liberal thought in general. A deep connivance developed between this conservative current and the colonial authorities as they faced the intellectual and political evolution of the youth and the social and political movements of the peasantry and the workers in the early 1930s in particular. Using a lexical approach to the elementary school textbooks published by the chancellor's office of the Hanoi Education Department between 1925 and 1930, the sociologist Trinh Van Thao has arrived at the following conclusion:

> The crushing hegemony of the cultural and moral values derived from the conservative milieu and the Confucian ideology (focused on the master-king and the father), the ramifications of a familial and patriarchal system, which insisted heavily upon the omnipresence of paternal authority (notably through the three feminine submissions), underscored by an essentially agricultural economy and a rural and communal civilization, leaves no doubt as to the cultural impregnation exercised by the *Nam Phong* group on our authors, with whom they maintained privileged relations (creating a literary and philosophical, if not political, community). . . . [T]he undeniable success of the manuals (*Quoc van giao tu*), and their resonance in the collective Vietnamese memory during the years of humiliation and contrition (1925–45), suggest a people nostalgic for the traditional values of conservative Confucianism, which were taken, rightly or wrongly, to be the authentically national values.[40]

The stakes were equally high for Vietnamese Buddhism, which found itself confronted with similar challenges. Given the historical role that Buddhism had played in the history of the Vietnamese state, it could not remain indifferent to the cultural and societal transformations taking place during the colonial period. The rapid rise of the Cao Daist religion in the mid 1920s, for example, coincided with the uproar caused by the trial of Phan Boi Chau and the death of Phan Chu Trinh, the economic crisis of 1929, and the loss or muddling of moral landmarks. Similar factors gave rise to the revival of Buddhism in Asian countries such as Burma and Siam, where religion was associated with national movements or the monarchy. A spiritual reform movement developed in Vietnam in response to modernity, material progress, and advances in science and technology. Quoc ngu literacy and publication took on new importance as means of spreading religious doctrine and training a clergy capable of assuming these new tasks. Above all, religion became integral to philosophical-political debates, such as Nguyen An Ninh's 1937 *Critique du bouddhisme* (Critique of Buddhism), which posed the question "God or the poor?" (underlining the permanent tension in Buddhism between the quest for enlightenment, or personal salvation, and collective salvation). In the 1930s, Cochinchina, Annam, and Tonkin all had Buddhist associations, and sometimes even provincial sections. In 1937, the Association bouddhiste du Tonkin (Buddhist Association of Tonkin) announced that it had two thousand monks and nuns and ten thousand adherents. Annam was said to have three thousand monks and nuns. Attempts to federate the associations into a national body did not, however, succeed. The Buddhists had varying attitudes to French domination. They were mostly apolitical, but certain provincial associations in Cochinchina sheltered young patriotic monks, such as those of the Phat giao tan thanh nien (New Buddhist Youth) association of Saigon. In contrast, the Société des études bouddhistes de Cochinchine (Society of Buddhist Studies of Cochinchina) was regarded as pro-government, according to the historian Tran Van Giau.[41]

The Vietnamese Catholic community comprised 1,300,000 adherents (not including 74,000 in Cambodia) out of a total Vietnamese population of 15 million in 1931. Evangelization rarely reached into Laos. Of its 1,500,000 inhabitants only 18,964 were Catholic (and the overwhelming majority of these were ethnic Vietnamese). In Vietnam, the Catholic community stood out not only for its large number of believers but also for the growing importance of the indigenous clergy, who, with 1,062 priests and 3,129 nuns in 1931, outnumbered their European counterparts. From 1933 to 1938, three Vietnamese acceded to the rank of bishop: Monsignors Nguyen Ba Tong, Ho Ngoc Can, and Ngo Dinh Thuc.[42] Catholic educational works saw a particular expansion after 1934, along with the Jeunesse étudiante chrétienne (Christian Student Youth) and the Jeunesse ouvrière chrétienne (Christian Youth Workers), not to mention the Scouts. And Vietnamese national literature proudly includes the Catholic Han Mac Tu (1912–40) among its greatest romantic poets.

The Vietnamese were drawn to religious novelty. This was especially the case in Cochinchina, a "frontier" region and fertile ground for acculturation, where the Cao Dai and Hoa Hao religions developed quickly.

Millenarianism and Messianic Movements

Cao Dai, the Great Religion of the Third Period of Salvation, was born in 1926 within a narrow circle of spiritualists founded by the prefect Ngo Van Chieu. When Le Van Trung, a French-naturalized civil servant, former member of the Cochinchina Conseil de gouvernement, and colonial counselor, and the "pope" *(pape)* Pham Cong Tac took over the leadership, Cao Dai changed. From an esoteric circle, it was transformed into a religion, attracting thousands of members. Its structure was comprised of a clerical hierarchy, which built its Holy See *(Toa thanh)* near the town of Tay Ninh. Caodaism incorporated Buddhist, Confucian, and Taoist elements, unified by the catalyst of prophetic spiritualism. This, more than syncretism and the invocations of the exotic spirits of Victor Hugo, Joan of Arc, and Jesus Christ, was undoubtedly the reason for its popular success. One could interpret this doctrine as a means for the new Vietnamese upper class to affirm their equality with the French. Spiritualism was a transcultural common denominator, symbolically represented in the narthex of the Holy See in Tay Ninh by a fresco of three historic figures: the Tang-era Chinese poet Li Tai Po, the sixteenth-century Vietnamese scholar Nguyen Binh Khiem, and the nineteenth-century French poet and novelist Victor Hugo.

But although it was a religion of landowners and middle-class civil servants, Caodaism penetrated the peasant world, where it presented itself as the bearer of new social relations founded on mutual trust, notably between landowners and farmers. Cao Trieu Phat, on his return from France, where he was a sergeant-interpreter from 1914 to 1918, founded an ephemeral labor party, followed by the Caodaist sect of Bac Lieu in 1926. Phat asked his farmers to address him as "Brother," rather than "Sir." When the nationalist revolution of 1945 came, he joined the Viet Minh.

French incomprehension and suspicion of this new outpouring of local elite aspirations put the two on a collision course. In the 1930s, the Tay Ninh Cao Dai sect established relations with Prince Cuong De through the intermediary of the Japanese businessman cum spy Mituhiro Matushita. Police repression, the closing and the occupation of the Holy See in 1940, and the exile of Pham Cong Tac to the island of Nosy Lava (near Madagascar), conferred great prestige on Caodaism, as well as political power under favorable circumstances.[43]

The historical conjuncture was equally important in the growth of the Buddhist religious sect called Hoa Hao, named after the birthplace of its prophet, Huynh Phu So. Historians identify it, like Caodaism, as a political-religious sect, due to the role it played in the first Indochinese war. In fact, its political-military apparatus was only a superstructure, which did not survive historic vicissitudes. If the religious current of Hoa Hao was momentarily orientated toward temporal objectives, it did not exist any less as a cluster of beliefs and rituals destined, like all religions, to put people in harmony with nature and one another, and to organize these relationships.

Huynh Phu So was the guide of what might have remained a local sect, like so many others that emerged in Cochinchina. However, his charisma, his alleged healing powers, and his gift of prophecy attracted scores of peasants to his movement, and not just the poor. Moreover, his murder by the Viet Minh in April 1947 conferred on him that all-important martyr's halo. During his lifetime, he presented himself as the reincarnation of the Master Buddha of Peace in the West (Phat Thay Tay An). Doan Minh Huyen, the first known incarnation, appeared in 1849 in the hills around Chau Doc, located along the frontier between present day Cambodia and Vietnam. Distributing amulets bearing the four ideograms *buu son ky huong* (mysterious fragrance from the precious mountain), he preached the religion of Dao Lanh (The Good). At once a mystical current and a communal organization that devoted itself to the clearing of virgin land, Dao Lanh was inevitably drawn into the resistance to the return of the French to the Mekong Delta. The millenarianism and the messianism of this religion also found an additional objective in a war against the French. It allowed the Hoa Hao prophets to identify the apocalypse and the advent of the "Era of Justice and Light" with Vietnam's national liberation. What was exhibited was therefore a form of the dominant Buddhism purified of cultural pomp and without a clergy. The Hoa Hao religion became implanted in a very specific terrain located at the confluence of Khmer, Viet, and Chinese pioneer zones, where the "orthodox" framework of the Confucian literati was weakest, if not nonexistent. The local population expected a great deal from the Hoa Hao's claim to be "those who take care of people" *(cuu dan do the)*. Every reincarnated Buddha was both a minister to the soul and a healer of the body. Indeed, both the vigor and the weakness of this religion resulted from the charisma of one figure. This explains its ups and downs, and also the fact that it remained circumscribed within narrow geographical boundaries.[44]

Cambodia and Laos probably offered a deceiving appearance of tranquility because of the absence of dramatic events and an apparent continuity in social and mental structures. Popular Buddhism, inseparable from the local setting, assured religious homogeneity. The Buddhist monarchies in western Indochina, even though dependent, had not, as in Vietnam, undergone the double dissociation of the institution from the ruler, on the one hand, and the monarchy from the nation, on the other. Lao and Khmer monarchs do not seem to have suffered a similar erosion of their prestige in the eyes of the people. Modern education was neither the locus nor the instrument of upheaval, since it only touched a handful of the aristocracy's sons and daughters. Was it not symptomatic that, until World War II, the sons of Khmer or Lao nobility prepared for the *baccalauréat* by attending high schools in eastern Indochina—Albert-Sarraut (in Hanoi), Chasseloup-Laubat (in Saigon), or Yersin (in Dalat)?

The Rise of Modern Literature in Vietnam

The advent of modern literature in Vietnam was preceded by a long tradition of writing by the literati that was strongly influenced by the Chinese model and written in Chinese characters.[45] The Vietnamese masterpiece *Kim Van Kieu* written in the first years of the nineteenth century, affirmed the existence of original Vietnamese literature through its verse and its title. This literature was always lively in the nineteenth century, producing the notable works of Nguyen Dinh Chieu and the nonconformist poet Ho Xuan Huong.

In the period 1913–30, the flourishing of journalism established Quoc ngu in print, and in so doing forged and sharpened the instrument necessary for the creation of modern literature. Newspapers and magazines were the original vectors of this blossoming literature, thanks to their publication of poems, novellas, and serial novels. The magazine *Dong Duong Tap Chi* published the works of Tan Da (alias Nguyen Khac Hieu, 1889–1939), considered a pivotal writer, who ensured the transition from classical poetry to what was called "new poetry" *(tho moi).* In 1939, the writer Phan Khoi recalled:

> I have known M. Nguyen Khac Hieu (Tan Da) since 1918, when I came to live in Hanoi and wrote for the *Nam Phong* magazine. On a cold spring evening, I was lying down, reading, upstairs from the office of the magazine, on Cotton Street—the floor reserved, at the time, as lodging for Nguyen Ba Trac. A visitor arrived. M. Trac made the introduction: "This is M. Nguyen Khac Hieu." At that moment, it was as if an electric current passed through me. I felt dread and fright. I got up quickly! This is true. The name of Nguyen Khac Hieu, at that time, was no small thing, and this name had even more solemnity for me than for others. When I heard it, I shivered. This is true. Consider that literary writings in Quoc ngu in this period were still very rare, and literary creation was even rarer. Yet I had already read texts in the *Dong duong tap chi* such as "The Internal Content of Every Being." I had just arrived in Hanoi when "The Small Dream" *[Giac mong con]* was published, and I could not have had a greater admiration for the author, who was truly talented. I said to myself of him: "Pham Quynh and Nguyen Van Vinh only write following the books and thoughts of the French; as for this guy, he writes his own thoughts; it is he who is truly a creator."[46]

It is generally agreed that Tan Da was the greatest Vietnamese poet of the first half of the twentieth century. French literature influenced Vietnamese writers through translations or the reading of texts in French. The choice of French authors was varied, ranging from Abbé Prévost to Victor Hugo. But the poetry Tan Da wrote was primarily romantic. It portrayed the self and its passions as a source of scandal, and therefore something that created a rupture with the conformist heritage and environment. The southern writer Ho Bieu Chanh used the novel to moralize about social reality. Playwrights were familiar with Corneille's *Le Cid* and *Horace,* and with the plays of Molière, translated and published in *Nam Phong.* The success of the performance of Molière's *Le Malade imaginaire* in Vietnamese on April 25, 1920, was an important event.

After 1930, literature became both a mirror of and a catalyst for social change. That year saw the start of a second period in the development of Vietnamese literature. Its rise was marked by the supremacy of the "Autonomous Literary Group" (Tu Luc Van Doan; TLVD) and the "New Poetry" movement. Described as romantic, the two literary trends affirmed themselves through breaks with the past and its literary traditions. The starting point of New Poetry was the publication of the poem "The Old Lovers" by the reformist scholar Phan Khoi in March 1932: "We are not spouses but lovers. Why therefore speak of fidelity and eternity!"

Taking up the perspective of the "returnee from France," Hoang Tich Chu extolled the adoption of French syntax in the writing of Quoc ngu. TLVD writers used a concise, clear style, taken from classic French literature. They tried as far as possible to avoid Chinese terms, turns of phrase, and literary allusions, such as the unchanging images of wind, snow, flowers, and the moon.

Gathering together the novelists Khai Hung, Nhat Linh, Hoang Dao, and the poet Tu Mo around the publishing house Doi Nay (Our Times) and the magazine *Phong Hoa* (Mores and Customs),[47] the TLVD was a powerful agent of cultural renewal. *Phong Hoa* not only published literary works but also took the initiative in publicizing ideological debates, such as the polemics on the emancipation of women, the implications of Confucian ethics, and controversies (during 1935–39) between advocates of "art for art's sake" (such as the romantics Luu Trong Luu, Thieu Son, and Hoai Thanh) and those of "art for life" (the Marxist critic Hai Trieu is a good example). The artist-designer of the group, Nguyen Cat Tuong, reformed the traditional costume of Vietnamese women, making it essentially what it is today.

Not only did the TLVD poets—The Lu, Xuan Dieu, Luu Trong Luu, Che Lan Vien, and Huy Can—adopt a French style of verse that was freer than that of Chinese, but their poetry was also lyrical. They sang of love and nature and exalted the role of the poet. "We, the poets of today, we do not want to, indeed we cannot, feel and be moved in his way [that of Tan Da]. Our deep feelings are much more complex, we suffer, we feel much more, and when we burst with joy, the joy also takes on strange colors and nuances."

Already in 1930, a clear and vigorous realist trend had begun. During the period marked by the economic crisis of 1929 and the social and political uprisings rocking Indochina in 1930, the writers Vu Bang, Vu Dinh Chi, and Vu Trong Phung published numerous suspenseful novels about the urban proletariat, prostitution, and usury, among other things. Meanwhile, Vietnamese readers increasingly gained access to the works of Balzac, Flaubert, Tolstoy, Dickens, Barbusse, Gide,

Dostoevski, and Goethe. Between 1936 and 1939, the prestige of the TLVD declined, because it not only had to compete with social realist writers who benefited from greater press and publishing liberty, but also to take into account the social and political questions that were now on the agenda. The novelists Ngo Tat To, Nguyen Cong Hoan, Nguyen Hong, and Nam Cao chose to write about the people, notably those in rural areas, and the class oppression that was overwhelming them. They expressed a social critique, like novelists of the TLVD, but in a populist and Marxist vein.

Nhat Linh and his friends also attacked the "feudal," mandarin, and bourgeois society, which oppressed the individual. The literature of the TLVD was an affirmation of the "I" in the face of the collective. The literary controversies, like the one around *Kim Van Kieu*, were underpinned by different beliefs about the nature of Vietnamese society and the role of intellectuals in society. The cultural debate was deepened by political rifts. In 1939, *Ngay Nay* (Today), the other magazine of the TLVD, reproduced the French press's approval of André Gide's *Retour de l'URSS (Return from the U.S.S.R.)*. It was not only a confrontation between literary movements, but also an ideological war between communists and their sympathizers, on the one hand, and intellectual "bourgeois individualists," on the other. Not all the novels, poems, or essays, however, fell into the previously cited movements. There were original and unclassifiable writers such as Nguyen Tuan (born in 1913), who excelled at nostalgic chronicles of an introspective and intimate character. And there was also a militant literature that flourished in prisons. In the late 1930s, the young poet To Huu became famous for his revolutionary lyricism. Popular literature also thrived in the shape of *ca dao* (anonymous couplets) and *cheo* theater, in its renovated urban forms. The classical theater of the *tuong* and the modern *cai luong* (reformed theater) always drew large audiences.

In contrast, modern literary creations were largely absent in Cambodia. One can only cite one modern novel. In 1938, Rim Kin (1911–59) published *Suphat*. The reasons the author provided to explain his decision to write shed light on why Khmer literature developed slowly. Rim Kin was a student at the Sisowath High School, where Vietnamese were as numerous as Cambodians, if not more so. The markets in Phnom Penh teemed with Vietnamese books, and Rim Kin decided to take up his pen in order not to be "disgraced before foreigners."[48]

An Unfinished or Impossible Fusion?

An overview of Vietnamese intellectual and artistic creation during the "eighty years of French colonization" would be incomplete if nothing were said of the existence of works written in French by Indochinese, as well as those written by French authors in, or about, Indochina.

Among the first group, the names of three men stand out, to whom modern Vietnamese culture is indebted even if, until 1933, nationalist opinion viewed them unfavorably and minimized their role. Two Catholics, Truong Vinh Ky, better known by the name of Petrus Ky (1837–1898), and Huynh Tinh Cua, also known as Paulus Cua (1834–1907), were intermediary figures between traditional culture and that imposed from the outside. As scholars trained in Sino-Vietnamese studies and interpreters for the French government, they made scholarly contributions in the domains of philology and lexicography. Paulus Cua produced an important dictionary, *Dai Nam Quoc am tu vi* (1895). They did not, however, confine themselves to this area. Both transcribed and translated Chinese and Vietnamese works into Quoc ngu. Furthermore, Paulus Cua founded the first newspaper printed in Quoc ngu, *Gia Dinh Bao* (1865). What the third man, Pham Quynh, did to assure the vitality of national writing has been described earlier in this chapter.

These three figures, along with others, laid the foundation of modern Vietnamese culture. Other writers, however, wrote their works in French rather than their mother tongue. Given this, should we count them as Vietnamese (or Cambodian, in the case of the poet Princess Yukhanthor) creators, or should they be included under the heading of francophone literature? The novels and poetry of Nguyen Tien Lang and Pham Van Ky are part of a context of cultural mingling that some have claimed they desired themselves.[49] In contrast to what happened to those who adopted European techniques in the plastic arts,[50] in literature, the tool of expression they used propelled them to the margins of their national culture. Consequently, with the exception of militant nationalists who wrote polemics in French (Nguyen Ai Quoc, alias Ho Chi Minh, and Nguyen An Ninh), Indochinese writers of the French language have been placed with the cohort of French writers of colonial literature.

The domain of Indochinese French literature is extremely rich. As early as 1930, René Crayssac inventoried the archival and fictional production. The authors "are legion," he wrote, and the list of works that he presents is indeed impressive—and will certainly grow longer in the future.[51] Through a great quantity and variety of genres, and a range of quality and talent, these works include examples of descriptive and often superficial travel literature; of exotic literature, at its best, a quest for initiation into the world of the Other; as well as colonial literature, which was predominant. The latter was the mirror of the colony, as well as the bearer of the colonial ideology that saw the Indochinese as the "property" of the colonizers. Certain authors, however, tried to penetrate the indigenous world and explored the problems posed by European intrusion. Sympathy and even empathy were not absent. Some authors were highly perceptive, among them Albert de Pouvourville and especially Jean Marquet, Herbert Wild, and Mme Chivas-Baron. All demonstrated a true consciousness of the colonial situation, of its contradictions and injustices.

In the end, literature and the fine arts found literary themes and sources of inspiration in Indochina: the exotic scenery, certainly, but also an affirmation of universal ethical values. However, this colonial literature created by French writers was tied up with the destiny of the empire. "It is remarkable, for example," one author has noted, "that the literature of the quests and protests of the 1930s for the first time took into account misery, injustice, repression, protests, and revolts, without ever arriving at an acknowledgment of the contradictions of a colonial system, whose legitimacy was never questioned. . . . From this point of view, [Louis] Malleret's dream of a fusion of the East and West, manifested in art and literature, remained an illusion."[52] The same author, with good reason, identifies the novelist Jean Hougron (1923–), who was writing during France's final war in Indochina, as a privileged witness of the fall of "white power." Was their audience mainly French or Indochinese? Did they influence the Indochinese, in particular, the artists? In terms of artistic influence, Victor Hugo, Molière, André Gide, and suspense novels had the greatest impact on Indochinese and especially on Vietnamese readers.

The questions raised about the French writers of Indochina resurface with regard to those working in the plastic arts. Were they only colonial artists, for whom Indochina was nothing more than an inspiration? Did they, at best, simply popularize European art (methods and aesthetic), or at worst, merely propagate the politics of foreign domination? Or were they influenced to the point where their stay did not leave them untouched and they became "orientalized"? One analysis of their work concludes:

> One does not find in their paintings any strained sentiment: there is only harmony. The effects of sickness, death, and old age are absent. The paintings also leave aside the tensions born of colonization. André Maire, for example, overlooks the war, although he remained in Vietnam until 1958; his paintings represent Indochina in such a way as to invoke the image of a country imprinted with the serenity of the "Asian philosophies." Seduced by Indochina, these artists wished to provide an enticing image of it. Their role was not to attain objectivity but rather to paint with all their sensibility. . . . They were fascinated by Indochina, and their paintings translate what they felt naturally, without the pressures of propaganda, which, in official commissions, demanded of painters that they idealize the image of Indochina.[53]

On the other hand, Indochina did not bring France a renewal of plastic arts comparable to that which Japanese and African art inspired among European impressionist and cubist painters. The meeting and blending of two cultures, their interactions, have yet to studied; it is a wide-open field for historians.

6

The Impasses of
Colonial Development

In the 1930s, at the close of a phase of vibrant growth, the new Indochinese economy—an especially advantageous and profitable component of French capitalism's colonial regulation—faced a critical historic situation. Colonial development was itself a key factor (though not the only one) in the underdevelopment of the peninsula's peasant societies, and ultimately it provided no alternative to the serious destabilization it had caused. When it was undermined by the crisis of the world economy, its inner logic prevented all responses other than that of a basic modernization of its structures, impeding any transition to a different mode of capital accumulation.

THE COLONIZED SOCIETIES: DEMOGRAPHY, PRODUCTION, EXCHANGE

It is still difficult to provide a reliable assessment of the economic and demographic evolution of the colonized societies of Indochina. Numerous authors have characterized this evolution using the concept of a dual economy and have sought to outline the opposition between two economic sectors.[1] On the one hand, they suggest, there was the "modern sector"—the dynamic capitalist exporting sector of the industrial zones, mining, harbors, and plantations. On the other, there was the "traditional" economic sector, which consisted of small-scale family rice-growing based on subsistence production. This agriculture, with artificial irrigation systems, was dominant in the Vietnamese deltas. While it was equally predominant in the Laotian and Cambodian plains, they were irrigated only by the flooding of the rivers. Along the Mekong, this second sector was coupled with farming of the river's banks and fisheries, and everywhere with small-scale trade. In the highlands, itinerant slash-and-burn agriculture dominated, combined with the ethnic minorities' hunting and gathering. Others have sought to discover the inner dynamics of Vietnamese peasant society. For J. C. Scott, the "moral economy" of the Vietnamese village was resistant to the logic and the dynamic of the market developed by colonial capitalism. S. L. Popkin, in contrast, insists that the village economy adapted to this dynamic.[2] All these analyses, however, underline the astonishing continuity of the peasant economies of the peninsula, which is very clear in the Vietnamese states, where the economic units represented by families and village communities preserved their dynamism until the end of the twentieth century.[3]

This research and these debates have the advantage of outlining the unequal integration of the different material cultures of the dominated societies into the channels of colonial capitalism, and of examining the interconnections between them. In fact, entire sectors of peasant production—Cochinchinese and Khmer rice growing, Khmer and Vietnamese cultivation of corn, pepper growing on the Cambodian coastline, livestock breeding in Cambodia, the fisheries of Cambodia's Great Lake, the Tonlé Sap, and the lower Mekong, and so on—overlapped in the sphere of exports. This type of overlap typified the *économie de traite* (barter economy) found throughout Europe's tropical colonies in this era, based on exporting the surplus products of a barely modernized peasantry, whether agricultural or crafts, over more or less long distances.

Peasant production also constituted the essential source of Indochinese capital accumulation, notably because it financed public investment through the taxation of the village's surplus production. The peasantry, especially in the deltas of northern Annam and Tonkin, also served as a source of cheap manpower for factories and plantations. Beyond the obvious dualism of the economy, the determining consideration was the subordination of peasant modes of production and consumption to the capitalist mode of production in its colonial form. This provoked a lasting situation in which villages were socially abandoned in favor of modern colonial cities leading to impoverished peasantries. The "traditional" economy, it seems, received no more than 20% of total investment in the course of the colonial period. In 1937, for instance, Governor-General Jules Brevié assessed the accumulated amount invested in hydraulic works and river transportation between 1920 and 1936 as equivalent to only 55% of the contribution paid by Indochina to France's metropolitan budget during the same period.[4]

Demographic Change

Colonial development necessarily left a profound mark on the material civilization and the anthropological structures of the Indochinese peasantry, and, most important, on the complex but fundamental relationship between population movement, the availability of arable land, and the production of grain. The management of this relationship, an essential function of the precolonial states, was one of permanent challenges that the colonial regime had to assume after the conquest. In this respect, the demographic growth generated by colonization was an important feature of this period. This process must be placed in the context of the remarkable demographic explosion in Southeast Asia during the nineteenth and twentieth centuries: the entire region counted some 80 million inhabitants in 1900, versus 530 million in 2000—that is, an annual average growth of 6.6%, compared to 0.6% in Europe (excluding Russia).

Although it is difficult to know precisely, it is plausible that colonization caused the Indochinese societies to enter this broader process of demographic transition. From before 1921, there are only general population assessments, with the exception of the Cochinchinese census of 1901. Registration under the *état civil* system was compulsory in Cochinchina starting in 1883, and in Tonkin starting in 1924, but it is not a reliable source of data, outside of the cities and of Cochinchina. Because of the methods of assessment used, the data provided by the four general colonial-era censuses (1921, 1926, 1931, and 1936) have also proven extremely unreliable, even those provided by the two relatively conscientious surveys done in 1921 and 1936. The colonial administration, though aware of the deficiencies of the census methods, did not really improve them. In 1921, in Cochinchina, Cambodia, and the big cities, a card was supposed to be filled out for each house or boat. Everywhere else, however, the most common method utilized until 1926 consisted of multiplying the number of registered persons on each village's personal tax roll (which in the Vietnamese states included all able-bodied men between 18 and 60) by an arbitrary coefficient, generally 6 to 8, which was often too small. Throughout the colonial period, censuses depended solely on the declarations of village authorities, who "feared in every manifestation of this order an increase of charges concerning taxes or recruiting." Consequently, they probably deliberately underestimated the actual population, perhaps by as much as 10 to 15% according to some authors.[5]

The geographer Pierre Gourou wrote of the Red River Delta in 1936, "The [estimated] birthrate would be 34‰ and the death rate 14‰; the annual population excess would be thus 20‰. Obviously, none of these numbers, and none of the resulting reports, are exact. We may be sure that the actual birthrates are much higher than 34‰ and reach the highest maxima observed in the world. It is also evident that mortality is much higher, perhaps double the percentage that we have obtained. The annual surplus is not 20‰, which would ensure the doubling of the population in thirty-five years, but is rather between 10 and 15‰."[6] In 1939, land surveys conducted by the medical services of Annam showed that the official figures had to be increased by 27%, while the health services assessed the population of Indochina at 25,086,850.[7] There are, then, innumerable contradictions between various series of statistics. In Tonkin, the censuses of 1926, 1931, and 1936 were certainly an improvement, since villages were required to fill out domestic forms.[8] According to T. Smolski, head of the Statistique générale de l'Indochine service, the margin of error nevertheless remained at least at 50% for the provinces of Annam, 20% to 25% for Tonkin, 15% for Cambodia, and 10% for Cochinchina. "One can therefore state," he wrote in 1937, "that the population of Indochina is calculated to be between 20 and 30 million inhabitants. Within these limits, the (official) number of 23 million hardly represents a more truthful figure than others."[9]

The extent of demographic growth is nevertheless obvious, and it certainly began during the nineteenth century. The statistics are certainly not utterly dependable, considering not only that the sole available numbers are those in the fiscal registries of the Nguyen imperial administration, but also that the authorities of the time did not count women, children, and non-*kinh* (not ethnic Viet) minorities. There were also quite a number of villagers unaccounted for. With these sources, however, we can nevertheless estimate a demographic bracket.

During the reign of Gia Long, the registered population totaled 612,912; 719,510 in 1829; 970,516 in 1840; and it was 1,024,388 in 1848 under Tu Duc. Turc, the French consul at Haiphong, declared that there were roughly 750,000 tax-paying men in Tonkin, while the official registers stated only 532,326. In 1884, there were 400,110 registered in the six provinces of Cochinchina, for a total population of 1,633,824.[10] Therefore, according to Nguyen The Anh, the figures declared by the villages should be multiplied by at least 2.5 to approach the truth. Furthermore, to estimate the total population, the number of registered inhabitants should be multiplied by between 3 and 8, depending on the region and the period. He goes on to state that the Vietnamese population in 1870 can be estimated at around 2 million for Cochinchina, less than 4 million for Annam, and approximately 5 million for Tonkin, which totals to approximately 11 million in all.[11] It is possible therefore to estimate a more or less transient population of 5 to 10 million inhabitants between 1800 and 1858. In any case, it is feasible that the Indochinese population grew at a rate of at least 10‰ a year during the first half of the twentieth century, starting from perhaps 11–12 million around 1880 and reaching 16 million around 1900 (table 6.1).

This global growth probably affected regions and nationalities unequally. Initially, it chiefly affected the Vietnamese peasantry, the largest group in the peninsula, but it experienced serious regional demographic crises until the 1930s. By disrupting the productive system, the long war of "pacification" in Tonkin and northern Annam provoked an upsurge of flooding, scarcities, and epidemics, and the generalization of physical misery created a genuine demographic disaster in these countries, in particular during the terrifying years from 1883 to 1896.[12] Around 1880, the population of Tonkin could reasonably be estimated at about 6 million inhabitants, and that of Annam at 3 million.[13] In the troubled areas, population increase had hardly recovered its regular growth before the 1910–20 decade. This is a far cry

TABLE 6.1 Population of French Indochina: colonial estimates and "censuses,"
1875–1948 (in thousands)

	1875–1880	1913	1921	1926	1931	1936	1943^c	1948^c
Cochinchina	1,502^a	3,165	3,797	4,118	4,484	4,616	5,200	5,628
Annam	3,000	5,000	4,933	5,581	5,122	5,656	7,183	—
Tonkin	6,000	6,000	6,854	7,402	8,096	8,700	9,851	—
TOTAL VIETNAM	10,502	14,165	15,584	17,101	17,702	18,972	22,234	—
Cambodia^b	1,100	1,600	2,403	2,535	2,806	3,046	3,000	3,748
Laos	[400?]	630	819	855	944	1,012	1,100	1,169
TOTAL INDO-CHINA	≈12,000	16,395	18,806	20,491	21,452	23,030	26,334	27,580
By ethnicity								
Vietnamese	—	12,600	13,895	5,581	15,765	16,679	19,479	—
Khmer	—	1,800	2,275	—	2,682	2,925	—	—
Laotian	—	—	428	504	589	—	—	—
Chinese	—	304	293	—	418	326	—	—
Minorities	—	1,810	—	—	2,031	2,462	—	—

SOURCES: H. Brenier, *Essai d'atlas statistique de l'Indochine française* (Hanoi-Haiphong: Gouvernement général de l'Indochine, 1914); *Annuaires statistiques de l'Indochine, 1913–1943*. The 1875–1880 figures for Vietnam are from C. Fourniau, *Les contacts franco vietnamiens en Annam et au Tonkin de 1885 à 1896*, PhD diss., Aix-Marseille, 1983 (Lille: Atelier national de reproduction des thèses, 1984), pp. 2502–3; Cambodia figures are from J. Delvert, *Le Paysan cambodgien* (Paris: Mouton, 1961), p. 427. The estimates for 1943 and 1948 are from *Annuaire statistique de l'Union française d'outre-mer 1939–1949* (Paris, 1951). The figures for 1875–1880 and 1913 are obviously very rough. It should also be noted that health services estimated the population of Indochina at 22,518,020 in 1935 and at 25,086,850 in 1939 (*Rapports annuels de l'Inspection générale de l'Hygiène et de la Santé 1935 et 1939*, Archives du Pharo, Marseille).
^{a}Figure for 1878.
^{b}The regressive series (1900–1962), constructed by R. Prudhomme from the Cambodian census of 1962, gives figures that are relatively close to the results of the colonial population counts, except for the period before 1921 (*L'Economie du Cambodge* [Paris: Presses universitaires de France, 1969], p. 250). The official estimates for 1875 and 1913 (actually 1911) are clearly too low. R. Thomas adopts the following figures: 2,057,000 in 1900, 2,414,000 in 1915, 2,562,000 in 1920, 2,746,000 in 1925, 2,944,000 in 1930, 3,187,000 in 1936, 3,485,000 in 1940 ("L'évolution économique du Cambodge, 1900–1940" [PhD diss., Université de Paris VII, 1978], p. 24).
A retrospective projection of demographic structures (mortality, fertility, population distribution by age and by sex) in contemporary Vietnam formulated by M. Banens in 1999 results in the following figures for colonial Vietnam: 14 million inhabitants in 1884, 16.1 in 1899, 18.7 in 1914, 20.5 in 1924, 23.4 in 1934, 24.4 in 1939, 25.4 in 1944, and 25.9 in 1949. These figures are 14% to 30% higher than those in the colonial censuses. Whether this is an accurate assessment or an inflation of the latter's flaws, the average annual growth rate of the Vietnamese population that these figures imply—13‰—is no different from the rate we propose below. See M. Banens, "Vietnam: A Reconstitution of Its Twentieth-Century Population History," in *Quantitative Economic History of Vietnam, 1900–1990: An International Workshop*, ed. J. C. Bassino, J.-D. Giacometti, and K. Odaka (Tokyo: Institute of Economic Research, Hitotsubashi University, 2000).
^{c}Estimates.

from the extravagant calculations produced by the administration to justify its fiscal needs, which estimated that there were 15 million inhabitants in the two protectorates at the time.[14] We know a few things about other demographic crises, whose complete history remains to be written. The correspondence of the missions indicated recurrent famine and cholera in 1896 in the bishopric of western Tonkin, where, in one year, 1,200 out of 201,000 Christians perished, a mortality rate of 6‰.[15] The serious flooding in Tonkin in the summer of 1926 caused poor harvests at the end of the same year, accompanied by a serious epidemic of smallpox and cholera, which effectively canceled out the natural increase in 1927.[16]

Demographic growth can be chiefly attributed to the fact that, without a corresponding decrease in fertility and the birthrate, death rates rapidly decreased, in part thanks to the slow introduction of a minimum of modern medical care and to vaccination campaigns, however chaotic. The eradication of the "stabilizing epidemics" that periodically reduced the population to sustainable levels started with these campaigns. With colonization, the population of Vietnam, and probably the Khmer and Lao populations, seems to have arrived at the first phase of the demographic transition in which the dependent world, whether colonized or not, was generally engaged during the twentieth century. This was a decisive shift, which early on had the result of regularizing natural growth and giving it a volume it had never reached before. Fertility remained very high, as all the polls undertaken before 1945 suggest: for 100 fertile women questioned when they were over forty-five, there were 520 children (live births) born in southern Annam in 1933, and 565 in Thanh Hoa in 1936,[17] which is more than five per woman. This trend was reinforced by the first efforts to improve sanitation in childbirth, undertaken in the countryside during the 1930s; 113 rural childbirth centers with 195 *ba mu* (rural midwives) opened in Tonkin in 1935. The same tendency characterized the birthrate in Cochinchina, where the rates went from 33.5‰ to 38.1‰ between 1913 and 1936, according to the official figures.

In reality, however, according to Smolski, these rates were actually no lower than 40‰, the number he believed applicable to Annam and Tonkin and one close to the average rate (41.1‰) for the 812,000 Vietnamese Catholics in 1929 and the rate (at least 37.8‰) that Pierre Gourou estimated for Tonkin around 1930.[18] In contrast, the Cochinchinese mortality rate had fallen from a maximum of 28‰ in 1918 (due to the epidemic of so-called Spanish influenza?) to 21.5‰ in 1923, 23.5‰ in 1926, and 22.2‰ in 1936 (25‰ to 30‰, according to Smolski, during the 1930s)— the same as the figure for England in the middle of the nineteenth century—except for brief increases in 1928–29 (26.6‰ in 1928, 25.8‰ in 1929) and in 1935.[19] In Hanoi, the mortality rate, probably underestimated, stood at 25‰ in 1934.[20] Everywhere, infant mortality remained very high—in 1930, close to one out of two children died before they reached the age of five in southern Annam and in Hanoi[21]— but it probably diminished slowly, at least locally.

There is one certainty: natural growth rates increased continuously after 1920 (according to Anthony Reid, they did not exceed 10‰ in nineteenth-century Vietnam), though undoubtedly with substantial regional variations due to the maintenance of higher mortality rates in the protectorates, as is shown, for example, through studies on Phnom Penh.[22] In Cochinchina, these rates probably surpassed the high figure of 12‰ to 13‰ starting in the 1920s (see fig. 6.1) and tended to increase rapidly, perhaps doubling between 1936 and 1945. In Tonkin and Annam, they were roughly 10‰ in the good years, but Gourou estimates the yearly growth in Tonkin around 1931 at about 15‰ (a number higher than that in Japan during its period of maximal demographic growth), with the population increasing each year by some 100,000 in Tonkin and 60,000 in Cochinchina around 1939.[23] The total yearly growth of Indochina's population in the 1930s was 225,000, according to the health services.[24] A survey conducted by the latter in three villages of Annam in 1939 shows a live birthrate of 32‰, a mortality rate of 22.3‰, and the number of persons per household at 5.2.[25] In Laos, an identical study in three villages resulted in still higher rates: respectively, 47‰, 19‰, and an average of 5.5 persons per household.[26] In total, according to the official statistical data, in fifteen years, from 1921 to 1936, the population of colonized Vietnam rose by 21.7% (a rate of average annual growth of 14‰), in Cambodia by 26.7% (17.8‰), and in Laos by 23.5% (15.6‰). These are very unreliable figures, certainly, but they at least serve to roughly situate the starting point of an exceptional demographic explosion. In 1938, it was expected that the population of Indochina would increase by about 300,000 per year in the fifteen years to follow.[27] In 1940, even a rather cautious Vietnamese physician was able to predict in his doctoral thesis that by the 1990s, Indochina would have 65 million inhabitants, a prediction that proved conservative, missing the mark by some 15 million.[28] "The population doubles every thirty-eight years," Jean Bourgoin estimated in 1948. "This is a unique phenomenon in the world, since, even in Bengal, the population does not increase at such a rate."[29]

Vaccinations and Health Care

The motors of this initial explosion merit serious research; the history of agricultural ecology, famine, and scarcity remains to be explored. One of the most important engines of this demographic change was the introduction in Indochina of the Pasteurian revolution. In spite of its limited implementation, through massive vaccination campaigns, it radically circumscribed the catastrophic effects of epidemics. The introduction of vaccines (fig. 6.1) stemmed from a political decision based on the understanding that collective sanitary action was a condition of colonial development. "The propagation of vaccination is not only an essentially philanthropic project," one of its pioneers wrote in 1880, "it is especially and above all a work of high political and social economy. If one considers that more than four-fifths of the rich alluvial plains of the Mekong remain uncultivated and without laborers, if one realizes on the other hand that the European will never be able to take the place of the Annamese in the cultivation of the soil in this kind of climate, it is evident that the future and the prosperity of the colony depends on the growth of the indigenous population. And I do not hesitate to affirm that the diffusion of the virus vaccine is one of the most powerful means at our disposal to ensure this

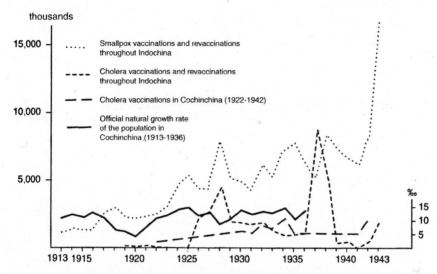

thousands

15,000 — ····· Smallpox vaccinations and revaccinations
                throughout Indochina

        — — — Cholera vaccinations and revaccinations
                throughout Indochina

        — · — Cholera vaccinations in Cochinchina (1922-1942)

10,000 —   Official natural growth rate
        ———   of the population in
                Cochinchina (1913-1936)

5,000 —

                                                          ‰
                                                        ⊢ 15
                                                        ⊢ 10
                                                        ⊢ 5

    1913 1915   1920   1925   1930   1935   1940 1943

FIGURE 6.1. Vaccination and demography, 1913–1943. (Based on data from *Annuaires statistiques de l'Indochine 1913–1943* and, for Cochinchina population, T. Smolski, "Note sur le mouvement de la population en Indochine," *Bulletin économique de l'Indochine*, 1929.)

result."[30] In fact, the essential rupture introduced by colonial medicine in the regime of native mortality was the retreat of smallpox and cholera.

In Cochinchina, from 1871, Jennerian vaccinations against smallpox were theoretically made compulsory for Asians, and in 1878, Navy doctors were given the responsibility of delivering them. This marked the beginning of vaccination en masse: from 1878 to 1881, in seventeen months, Dr. Vantalon vaccinated more than 50,000 children.[31] This theoretically mandatory procedure was generalized to the Indochinese Union in 1908, and Western-style vaccination was slowly substituted for the former methods of *variolisation* and Chinese vaccination sporadically used until then. With colonization, as Laurence Monnais-Rousselot has shown,[32] modern medical practices, a preoccupation with hygiene, and mass prophylaxis slowly started to penetrate rural areas. The production of vaccines and serums started with the foundation, in 1891, of the Pasteur Institute in Saigon by Dr. Albert Calmette, and of another in Nha Trang in 1895 by Dr. Alexandre Yersin (1863–1943). The latter, a brilliant, atypical scientist, had isolated the plague bacillus in Hong Kong the previous year and discovered the vaccine with which to fight it.[33] The spread of vaccination and the establishment of a fundamental medical infrastructure contributed to stopping pandemics and permitted the undertaking of the struggle against malaria.[34] This infrastructure comprised the Hanoi School of Medicine, opened in 1902; about ten thousand free hospital beds and several hundred rural clinics, in place in 1930; 367 physicians working in 1939, with 151 doctors of medicine, and 216 Indochinese physicians, along with 3,623 male nurses and midwives and 760 rural midwives, with 91,000 childbirths to their credit.

If malaria, trachoma (in Phnom Penh, 43% of school-age children suffered from it in 1940–41),[35] and other epidemics remained unbeaten, plague, which had hit Cochinchina, Cambodia, and Annam hard as recently as 1906–8, seems to have become localized in certain regions there by 1930, and it was reported only episodically in Tonkin after 1921. Smallpox lost its virulence after the serious epidemic of 1923–25, which ravaged the entire Far East. Around 1930, there was a forceful, far-reaching smallpox vaccination campaign—for example, in Tonkin 41.6% of the population was vaccinated in 1930[36]—but, nevertheless, a significant part of the rural population did not receive the vaccine (20% according to the Health Services of Thanh Hoa and Nghe An in 1939). "It is always the same ones who are vaccinated," colonial physicians lamented.[37] As a result, smallpox remained endemic, with severe regional outbreaks, as in 1938–39 in Nghe An and Thanh Hoa, as well as in Laos.[38] Around that time, however, intensive provincial vaccination programs were established. There were terrible explosions of cholera in Tonkin and Annam in 1926–27 and from 1926 to 1931 in Cochinchina and Cambodia, causing at least 55,000 deaths.[39] From 1928 to 1930, vaccination was carried out intensively: 1,738,000 vaccinations were delivered in 1931, and 1,733,000 in 1932, and these reinforced the natural mechanisms of the diseases' recession. Cholera then passed, according to regions, into the endemic stage, or else disappeared, and systematic vaccinations were limited to Cochinchina and the zones around towns. The epidemic would later reappear, however, making its way from southern China into Tonkin and Annam between 1937 and 1939.

The Population/Grain Ratio

Added to a mode of development focused on exports, such demographic growth could only accentuate the imbalance in the ratio of cultivated land to grain production and to population (see table 6.2). Two givens are essential. First, climate remained the principal factor determining agricultural production, as it always had been, even though, by its very nature, its effects fluctuated over time and across zones. The indigenous agricultural cycle thus remained an alternation of bad harvests (resulting from droughts or excessive rainfall) with bumper harvests. In consequence, the food balance was often disrupted regionally. Second, in the deltas of northern Annam and Tonkin, in the period between the two world wars, the agrodemographic system began a process of prolonged deterioration, to which colonization could only offer short- or mid-term responses. The only basic solution, the control of population growth and accelerated agricultural modernization of the peasant economy, lay out of its reach.

Aside from the addition of speculative new ventures such as cattle husbandry in Cambodia and corn planting, colonization did not modify the economy of irrigated rice growing of the north and central Vietnamese deltas or the Cambodian plains, which was intensive and skillful and involved a considerable investment of human labor and many risks and hazards during cultivation.[40] For lack of peasant accumulation and agricultural credit accessible to the rural masses, there was hardly any introduction of modern techniques apart from irrigation projects and the rapid expansion of commercial crops like corn. A few new technologies made their appearance: use of R. Jeannin's improved Tonkin plow gradually spread, and small mechanical pumps were to be found here and there in rural areas around 1940. However, chemical fertilizer was not introduced, and there was no scientific selection of paddy lineages; around 1938, more than two thousand varieties were still cultivated—although these were certainly well adapted to the ecological constraints of nonindustrial agriculture—as compared to the few dozen varieties cultivated in Japan. Consequently, agricultural productivity remained very low. "Within the group of rice-growing countries of the Pacific," General Inspector of Agriculture Yves Henry remarked in 1931, "Indochina occupies pretty much the lowest rank in its average output: 12 quintals per hectare, against 18 in Siam, 15 in Java, and 34 in Japan, despite the fact that nothing in the nature of its land and its water resources a priori justifies such a low output."[41] In 1943, outputs were estimated at 13 quintals per hectare in Tonkin, where they had remained unchanged since the beginning of the century, 8 in Cambodia, and 14 in Cochinchina; in Annam they fell from 13 (the average from 1919 to 1922) to 10 quintals (the average in 1942–43). The stagnation of agrarian cultures also played a part in the slow, regional deterioration of the peasant economy's food-producing capacities. As a result of the rise of village production of corn destined for export in certain regions, and of advances in growing rice for export on latifundia in the Mekong Delta, the majority of farmers were left with only a small part of the agricultural product. Even Tonkin and central Annam, which encountered great difficulties in producing enough rice for internal consumption, exported rice during normal years (sometimes up to 200,000 tons in the case of Tonkin), as well as corn (out of 556,000 tons exported in 1938 by Indochina, 100,000 tons were shipped from Haiphong, and 30,000 from Tourane).

Nevertheless, this analysis should be tempered. In Laos and Cambodia, the pressure on the land was infinitely less. As we saw earlier, in Cambodia since the beginning of the twentieth century—thanks notably to the digging of *preks*—the progressive "peasant reconquest"[42] was under way, focusing on uncultivated land, riverbanks, and the peripheral plains of the Tonlé Sap and the Mekong. Likewise, in the province of Battambang, toward 1928–30, a substantial movement of peasant colonization started with the building of the Bovel irrigation networks and with the rise of large rice-growing concessions. Moreover, the vagaries of rice growing

	Area of rice fields (thousands of hectares)	Paddy production (thousands of tons)	Production per inhabitant (quintals)	Yield per hectare (quintals)
Tonkin				
1913 estimate	1,150	1,825	3	15.8
1919–1922 average	1,540	2,100	3	13.6
1926–1930 average	1,200	1,600	2	13
1930–1931 average	1,200	1,600	2	13
1931–1932 average	1,200	1,600	2	13
1942–1943 average	1,487	1,882	1.9	13
Annam				
1913 estimate	467	—	—	—
1919–1922 average	1,100	1,400	3	13
1926–1930 average	800	900	1.9	12
1930–1931 average	800	900	1.9	12
1931–1932 average	800	900	1.9	12
1942–1943 average	946	983	1.6	10
Cochinchina				
1913 estimate	1,800	1,993	11	11
1919–1922 average	2,000	2,700	7	13.5
1926–1930 average	2,300	2,700	6	12
1930–1931 average	2,300	2,700	6	12
1931–1932 average	2,300	2,700	6	12
1942–1943 average	2,303	3,179	5.9	14
Cambodia				
1913 estimate	620	620	3.8	10
1919–1922 average	492	560	2	11
1926–1930 average	800	800	2.9	10
1930–1931 average	800	800	2.9	10
1931–1932 average	800	800	2.9	10
1942–1943 average	987	838	2.7	8
Laos				
1913 estimate	—	—	—	—
1919–1922 average	217	220	3	10
1926–1930 average	400	300	3.3	7
1930–1931 average	400	300	3.3	7
1931–1932 average	400	300	3.3	7
1942–1943 average	446	386	2.9	9
ANNUAL INDOCHINESE AVERAGE				
1913 (excluding Laos)	4,037	—	—	—
1919–1922	5,349	6,980	—	—
1926–1930	5,500	6,300	—	—
1931–1932	5,500	6,300	—	—
1936	5,000	7,000	3	14
1942–1943	6,169	7,270	2.6	11.7

(Source note on facing page)

were more or less cushioned, even in zones of high peasant density, by raising secondary crops; by fishing (for example, on the Khmer Tonlé Sap from December to February); by the omnipresent cottage industries; and by recourse to temporary or permanent wage labor. Finally, there was also the trading of agriculture products between neighboring regions, depending on the agricultural calendar, such as in the zones of contact between the irrigated rice fields of the lower plains and the slash-and-burn agriculture of the highlands. Thus, in the Khmer provinces of Stung Treng and Ratanakiri, Khmer, Jorai, and Tampuon peasants exchanged rice from the plains for crops from the mountains, forest products, pirogues, or elephants.[43] The peasant economy was, in fact, composed of multiple local combinations, with varying degrees of success, of the resources of several interconnected productive sectors.

Land Clearing and Improvement Prior to 1930

If there were admittedly increases in peasant agricultural production, this was growth without modernization. It was due, moreover, to the expansion of agriculture into the reserves of land that still existed in the northern and central Vietnamese deltas, especially those in Cochinchina, where 1,800,000 hectares were opened up to cultivation between 1893 and 1930. In 1943, the acreage devoted to rice growing in the whole of Indochina was evaluated at 6,169,000 hectares, and the production of paddy at 7,270,000 tons. For the three Vietnamese states, the estimate was 4,736,000 hectares and 6 million tons. The *nam tien*, the Vietnamese peasantry's "march toward the south," continued during the colonial era, but at what pace? The dredging and building of canals in western Cochinchina provoked a veritable stampede of poor peasants from central and eastern Cochinchina, but scarcely any came from central and northern Vietnam. In the end, the latter provided more workers for the plantations, and, still, between 1926 and 1930, at the pinnacle of their development, the number of contractual workers recruited every year in Tonkin and in Annam oscillated between only 7,400 and 18,000.

TABLE 6.2 SOURCE: *Annuaires statistiques de l'Indochine, 1913–1943.* The 1891 *Annuaire général de l'Indochine* estimated the surface area of the Cochinchinese rice fields at 880,000 ha, or 78.9% of the total cultivated area (1,100,000 ha). With regard to the data assembled here, see J.-D. Giacometti's interesting commentaries on the colonial agricultural statistics for the three Vietnamese countries: "Sources and Estimations for Economic Rural History of Vietnam in the First Half of the Twentieth Century," and "Bases for Estimation of Agriculture in Central Vietnam before 1954: The Examples of Thanh Hoa and Nghe An Provinces," in Bassino et al., *Quantitative History.* In his critique of the available sources, Giacometti shows that the colonial agricultural statistics were closer to the realities of production and the rural economy than has been assumed, a point confirmed in the same volume by Ta Thi Thuy, "Rice Cultivating and Cattle Raising in Tonkin in the First Half of Twentieth-Century." Giacometti furthermore proposes a reassessment of the cultivated areas and production from 1898 to 1953, which results in a 10%–30% increase (depending on location) in surface area and tonnage vis-à-vis the colonial figures, but with very similar per-hectare yields—within one or two quintals.

Others left for construction sites and commercial or urban activities in Cambodia (191,000 Vietnamese in 1936) and Laos (27,000), while others still sought work on the plateaus of Lang Biang, Djiring, and upper Donnai. As a result, in Cochinchina, in 1926, there were only 35,000 people from Tonkin and 25,000 from Annam.[44] The official attempts at transmigration and implantation of villages populated with immigrants recruited from the two protectorates (Rach Gia in 1907 and, in the 1920s, Ha Tien, etc.) in the Mekong Delta met with little success. As for the reserves of land in Cambodia—around 1940, rice fields occupied barely 5% of its acreage—they remained intact. In fact, one of the great problems that the colonial regime was unable to overcome was its inability to organize the movement of the Vietnamese peasants of the deltas across great distances, rather than a shortage of available land.

In the absence of agricultural change and of massive transmigration of rural populations, over which colonial power had only a weak hold, the ratio between the peasant population and available land in the deltas of Annam and Tonkin became increasingly strained after 1920, as these regions' population density increased. This was only exacerbated by the fact that land improvement policies were implemented belatedly there. Until 1930, the principal goal of colonial water management had been the reinforcement of the dams of the Red River and the establishment of minimal hydrologic security on its delta, as Dominique Vesin has shown.[45] An important study of the river and a reflection on possible models for its control were undertaken. It featured the research of the engineer Normandin, as well as debates by the commissions on dikes regarding the ultimate consequences of embankment, filling-in *(colmatage)*, and deforestation.[46] The three "black" decades from 1900 to 1930, which were marked by at least thirty-five serious breaks in the river's dikes between 1905 and 1926, were decisive in this regard.[47] At the time of the 1913 crisis, for example, nearly thirty local breaches took place.[48] In July 1915, forty-eight breaks took place over more than four kilometers; a quarter of the delta was under water, and the harvest was lost over more than 200,000 hectares.[49] Repeated disasters, notably those of 1893, 1904, 1909, 1911, 1913, 1915, 1924, and 1926 (when the dikes were breached opposite Hanoi) led to general programs of dam reinforcement in 1909, 1918–24, 1926, and 1931. The volume of the dams went from 20 million cubic meters in 1885 to 72 million in 1930 (115 million in 1945), and their width reached fifty meters,[50] as opposed to about twenty in the beginning of the century. After 1927, there were no longer any catastrophic ruptures of dikes in Tonkin, although water levels exceeded twelve meters in 1940, until the dramatic flooding of August 1945 (during which 230,000 hectares were submerged), the most serious of the century.

Overall, however, the conquest of new deltaic land in the northern and central regions had not started before 1905. It would not become a central preoccupation of the Gouvernement général until Albert Sarraut's first mandate (1911–14), and it remained limited until 1930. By then, excluding local work, 60,000 hectares had been prepared in Thanh Hoa, as well as in the two Tonkinese networks of Kep (7,500 hectares from 1906 to 1914) and Vinh Yen (17,000 hectares from 1914 to 1922). Work on the dam was also in progress in the "compartments" *(casiers)* of Song Cau (34,000 hectares from 1922 to 1938) and Son Tay (14,000 hectares from 1924 to 1932), for a total of 132,700 hectares. Larger projects for global management of the Red River and its delta (e.g., the engineer Godard's 1897 project) were left in limbo.[51] In fact, given the rapid population increase, the hydrological development of new agricultural zones could only regionally attenuate or lighten demographic pressures on the food supply.

Disparities in the Peasant Economy

Even before 1930, the northern deltas were approaching saturation. However, because of its desire to preserve the rural community, and because of the fundamental extraversion of its mode of economic development, colonization had not massively destabilized the Vietnamese peasantry, with the important exception, it is true, of temporary worker migrations. "The demographic imbalance in Indochina remains, in sum, as striking as it was on our arrival in the country," Charles Robequain wrote in 1938.[52] At the time, there were fewer than 75 people per square kilometer in the Transbassac, and 160 to 180 in the central Mekong Delta, but more than 300 in Quang Ngai, Quang Nam, Thua Thien, Ha Tinh, and Thanh Hoa, 430 in the Red River Delta (versus 315 in Java), and even more than 1,500 in a zone of 260 square kilometers around Nam Dinh and Ha Dong. Food densities (the ratio between population and cultivated surface) were even higher: 678 in Tonkin, 657 in Annam, 350 in Cambodia, and 188 in Cochinchina.[53] Expressed per capita in cultivated surface, the same ratio continuously deteriorated during the twentieth century. It stood at some 2,000 square meters circa 1885 in Tonkin and Annam.[54] Taking into account the double harvests that were prevalent for at least 54% of the cultivated land, it was on the order of 2,100 square meters in Tonkin around 1936 and 1,000 square meters around 1987. Within a century, two-thirds of it colonial, the population of Vietnam had increased by a factor of six, and the cultivated surface by two.

The balance of population and grain production therefore became extremely uncertain, and the peasants were periodically wracked by agro-ecological crises. In the province of Hung Yen, for instance, out of the twenty-two years between 1905 and 1930 for which data exist, only nine elapsed without calamities.[55] Similarly, from 1916 to 1927, twelve out of twenty-four harvests were lost in Nghe An, and eight out of twenty-four in the region of Ha Nam.[56] Three factors combined to account for this: (a) the persisting high peasant fertility, linked to very high infant mortality, the requirements of irrigated rice growing, which was extremely labor-intensive (as Gourou noted, at harvest time, as when the crop of the tenth month [December] was brought in, there was a shortage of workers in the Red River Delta), and the essentials for taking care of the elderly poor and keeping families together; (b) the lowering of mortality as a result of colonial sanitary action; and (c) the expansion of capitalist exports. As the latter developed, the spiraling growth of the rural population accelerated. These two dynamics did not offset each other, but rather produced cumulative negative social effects. "We are in danger of being overwhelmed by a starving multitude within about fifteen years," the Hue court's finance minister prophesied in 1938. "No political and social force will be able to resist this rising tide."[57]

A certain number of mechanisms, however, cushioned the deterioration of the peasant condition. Some came from outside the rural society, like the offer of wage labor by companies, colonial or not. Others were inherent to this society: access to local land in Annam and Tonkin, familial and village solidarities, and the omnipresence of extra-agricultural activities such as fishing, trade, and especially small rural industries. The latter were industries that needed manpower, which absorbed surpluses of available peasant labor outside of the peak periods of rice cultivation, and as a result "were an essential element in the framework of the farming societies."[58] It is very difficult to trace their evolution during the colonial period, and their decline, often cited, is no more certain, apart from the general regression of domestic cotton spinning.

A 1938 survey provided an inventory of 1,350,000 artisans, of whom 25% labored in food industries, 25% in textiles, 25% in basketwork, and 19% in woodworking and paper preparation.[59] In total, at least 7% of the inhabitants of the Tonkin Delta earned their livelihoods from artisan production. It is certain that craft and domestic production remained very important in the north and in Annam and that high degrees of village specialization occurred. The hulling and bleaching of rice, producing noodles, cakes, and oil, alcohol distilling, small-scale sugar refining, cotton spinning and especially weaving, the winding and weaving of silk, embroidery, lace making, manufacturing fishing nets, building sampans, wood handicrafts, brickyards, lime kilns, stoneworking, pottery, and so forth, provided extra resources to innumerable peasant families. These handicrafts were equally present in Cochinchina (cotton textiles in Go Cong, basketwork in the Plain of Reeds, mat making in the region of Ca Mau, woodworking and ironworking in Thu Dau Mot, pottery in Lai Thieu and Bien Hoa), where a rural micro-capitalism also developed (with minor sugar refineries and small rice mills, tile works, etc.). In Cambodia and Laos, small domestic industries were no less active. As for traditional water transport, it remained astonishingly lively: in 1930, close to 43,000 "indigenous" sailing boats entered Indochinese ports.

On the other hand, contributing to the economic stagnation of the village was the evolutionary tendency of property and farming structures in the Vietnamese countryside.[60] If rural indebtedness progressed considerably in Cambodia, small-scale domestic farming remained largely predominant there. On the other hand, the latifundia system and proletarianization of the peasantry shaped the rural society in the central provinces of Cochinchina, and, still more, in the west. Around 1930, in Cochinchina, 72% of peasants owned less than five hectares—the minimal surface for a family farm in an extensive rice-growing system with only one annual harvest—and one peasant out of four was a landowner. Middle and large holders (those owning more than ten hectares), representing 13.6% of all owners, possessed 87.5% of the cultivated acreage and controlled the mass of farmers (*ta dien*: two-thirds of the rural population) through short-term leases, obligatory advances, and usury. In total, 5,300 big landowners—those who possessed more than fifty hectares—held 44% of cultivated land.

The situation was different in the plains of Annam and Tonkin, where communal lands, which in theory were periodically redistributed among registered persons, still took up, during the same period, more than one-fifth of the cultivated land and where micro-property was the rule: in Tonkin, an area of very intensive agriculture, 91% of the landowners had less than 1.8 hectares, and 586,000 owners (61% of the total) possessed less than a *mau* (0.36 hectare)—less than the minimal surface of one hectare needed to support a family in 1931. Nevertheless, a class of Chinese-type landlords, middle and, more rarely, large landowners (1,070 held more than eighteen hectares and, in total, 17% of the cultivated land), who farmed their land with daily workers or sharecroppers, was clearly on the rise from the beginning of the century.[61] In 1930, 81,000 owners (8.5% of the total) who owned more than five *mau* (1.8 hectares) apiece held 43.2% of the cultivated land, and usury ravaged the rural areas. The result was a shortage of land, escalating prices, high land rents (at least half of the gross product), the extreme uncertainty of agricultural investment, the stagnation of cultivating methods, and peasants' having to sell off their harvests at any price immediately after the crops were in, and to resort to wage labor. In 1937, there were from two to three million agricultural day laborers and more than a million unemployed in the Red River Delta, according to the economist Georges Khérian.[62]

The peasant economy seemed to be stalling as population density increased in the overcrowded deltas of central and northern Indochina at the turn of the 1930s. French colonization launched the industrial era and brought about an enduring demographic transition in Indochina, but it did not transfer the model of industrialization founded mainly on the growth of internal consumption, which would, anyway, have been incompatible with the interests of a certain number of the large metropolitan industries. Technical and economic modernity, accessible to a thin social fringe, coexisted with mass poverty. The consequences of the periodic dysfunctions of the old Vietnamese agro-demographic system were added to those of the new farming imbalances generated by colonial capitalism. A growing peasantry had to search for its subsistence in "restricted" rice growing. Here, we recognize the phenomenon of socioeconomic "involution" described by Clifford Geertz in Java.[63] Starting before 1930, vast areas of rural misery expanded in the regions where the ratio of population to cereal production was the most strained, that is, in the deltas of the Red River, Nghe An, Ha Tinh, and Quang Nai. All colonial surveys noted this phenomenon. In 1928, Yves Henry and Maurice Devisme estimated the average food availability in Indochina at 337 kilograms of paddy per person per year (equal to 219 kilograms of rice, 600 grams per day), but in Tonkin it was only 211 kilograms, whereas the minimal ration was between 220 and 270 kilograms. According to the two agronomists, the Red River Delta was capable of feeding only about 5.2 million inhabitants, and there were already 7 million. Paul Bernard's calculations are even bleaker: for the same region, 128 kilos of rice per person per year, or 350 grams a day; he estimated the number of individuals who could not be fed in Tonkin and northern Annam to stand at 5 million.[64] Malnutrition was chronic:

> Apart from harvest time, the poorest and largest part of the farming population is in general underfed. In the morning around 5 A.M., the peasant eats one or two bowls of rice (100 to 200 g) or some yams or corn cooked in water. Around noon, he takes his only real meal, which consists of rice (with corn or yams sometimes added), seasoned with *tuong* [soy and fermented rice sauce] (50 g), *nuoc cay* (a pickle of small crabs from the rice fields), or *nuoc mam* [fermented fish sauce], a few vegetables, rarely fish, and even more rarely meat. Finally, he eats a little rice in the evening, most often sweet potatoes or cassava with some vegetables.[65]

Elsewhere, in Cochinchina, Cambodia, and Laos, life was less difficult for the peasantry and the townspeople, but even in Cambodia, regional shortages were not rare.[66] In Tonkin and Annam, the downward trend in food production per person had started. Finally, after 1930, colonial development led to the crisis of the peasant economy, without having put in place the necessary means of mastering it.

1930–1940: THE GREAT DEPRESSION AND UNDERDEVELOPMENT

In the decade that preceded World War II, all the elements of a prolonged crisis of the structures of production, exchange, population, and resources became intertwined. The crisis actually preceded and prolonged the effects of the Great Depression, but the latter accentuated it with dramatic violence.

The Collapse of the Colonial Economy

With the global economic depression of the 1930s, the foundations of Indochinese capitalism were undermined.[67] Its dynamism weakened as early as 1928, as the result of a series of events. These included the slump in rubber rates (−57.5% from January to April 1928), which is the true starting point of the Great Depression in Indochina; the fall in the value of gold francs in exports in 1929 (−11.6% in relation to 1928); the sudden increase in bankruptcies in Saigon-Cholon (39 in 1927, 73 in 1928, 95 in 1929) after years of wild speculation financed by advances from banks and exporters; and consequently the first restrictions of credit, starting in September 1929. The price of rice peaked that same month and then started to tumble. After a brief recovery in April 1930, the decrease resumed, henceforth uninterrupted; in July, a collapse began that reached its extreme point in June 1934 (-72% in relation to the gold-franc prices of rice in April 1930) and incited the collapse of the system of provisions, credits, and advances that constituted the financial bedrock of Cochinchinese rice growing. Indochinese rice exports decreased from 1,798,000 tons in 1928 to 960,000 in 1931. In November 1933, the average rate was 3.20 piastres a quintal (100 kilograms), as opposed to 11.56 piastres in 1929. As for rubber rates, they reached their lowest level in 1932, at 3 cents per pound, in comparison to 73 in 1925, representing only 1.70% of their 1910 maximum. The great Indochinese plantation, which had hardly come out of its phase of initial investment, was threatened with extinction. In relation to the preceding year, the decrease of exports in gold francs was 30% in 1930, 39% in 1931, and 9% in 1932. If the reduction of exported tonnage was only relative, except for rice (which fell by 46.6% from 1928 to 1931) the value of Indochinese foreign trade was brought down to the figures of its starting years, 1898–1900. For the first time, in 1930, Indochina's commercial balance began to show a deficit. This remained so in 1931.

Besides the seasonal fluctuations in the harvests of paddy (in large excess in 1928, mediocre in 1929), three factors aggravated the crisis of the colonial economy in Indochina and in all of Southeast Asia: the short-range speculations of Cholon paddy traders and of the banks; the abandonment of the Stevenson plan on November 1, 1928, which was the final failure in the attempt to create a cartel managing global rubber production; and the deterioration of silver rates (they fell 45% in December 1930 in relation to 1929), which dramatically reduced the purchasing power of the Chinese masses. Still, the recovery started in the spring of 1934 and was confirmed in 1935. The conjunction of excellent harvests of paddy in Cochinchina, poor grain harvests in France, and drought in North China increased the prices of number 1 white rice from 3.26 piastres per quintal in 1934 to 7.86 in 1936, and to 13.20 in 1940. The exported tonnage in 1936 (1,763,000 tons) exceeded all figures reached until then. Exports of coal, cement, tin and tungsten, zinc, and rubber (in one year, its price doubled, following the new plan of restrictions signed in London in May 1934) all progressed in like manner. Still, prices did not recover to their previous levels. The page of prosperity had been definitively turned.

These five years of crisis broke the expansion of colonial capitalism, which had been so stunning during the course of the 1920s. Its driving forces had been affected, and would henceforth be consistently indebted. As a consequence, all other economic activities were undermined. Starting in 1928, the number of bankruptcies and liquidations suddenly soared, and would only return to the level of 1927 by 1938: in ten years, from 1928 to 1937, 1,348 bankruptcies and liquidations were declared. According to data compiled by Charles Robequain and "deflated" year by year by coefficients drawn from tables in his work, the overall loss endured by the invested capital stood at 290 million gold francs between 1929 and

1937.[68] The structural effects of the crisis were no less profound. The general budget collapsed from 108 million piastres in 1931 to 60.9 million piastres in 1934, and the five local budgets decreased from 69.6 million piastres in 1930 to 43.6 million in 1934.[69] Compared to its 1930 level, the ordinary revenue of the general budget fell 19% in 1931, 34.7% in 1932, 42% in 1933, 43.6% in 1934, and 41% in 1935. The crisis put the old principle of self-supporting Indochinese finances in check: financially, colonization was caught in a stranglehold. A number of powerful corporations were threatened, such as the Société des Charbonnages de Dong Trieu (Dong Trieu Coal-Mining Company), which, after engaging in an extravagant price war in foreign markets with the rival Charbonnages de Tonkin (Tonkin Coal Mines) for several years, found itself overwhelmed by debt and in a state of virtual bankruptcy by 1936.

There was also a brutal stop in the frantic expansion of the Cochinchinese rice growing economy, notably in the "pioneer" provinces in the West. In 1933, the indebtedness of the rice fields was estimated at 700 million current francs (around 180 million gold francs), an average of 3.50 francs per hectare (1,500 francs in certain provinces of Transbassac), quite a bit more than the average price of land.[70] In 1933, 15% of the rice fields lay abandoned. In these conditions, the development of the national Vietnamese bourgeoisie, who depended on the investment of the product of their land income into commerce, banks, and industries (it was with this aim that the latifundia landowners of the south had founded the Annamese Credit Company in 1927), was broken. Since the Banque de l'Indochine refused to support the Sociétés indigènes de crédit agricole mutuel, the task of assuming and converting rice growers' debts fell once more to the administration. In western Cochinchina, 132,000 hectares of rice fields (13% of the total) changed hands between 1930 and 1934, often to the profit of mortgage creditors, big companies, or *chettiars* from British India.[71] But the disaster also threw into sharp relief the problem of the distribution of colonial profit and brought to life the internal divisions of modern capitalism. The disaster seriously weakened large Chinese traders, injured by the erosion of exchanges with the Far East, as well as French settlers, very important in Cochinchina. Guarantees given to banks for debts lost 70% to 80% of their value, putting the said banks in peril. Rice growers, small and medium planters, tradesmen, and civil servants, who, like the great Vietnamese landowners, had mortgaged their properties to the hilt to finance expansion (it was estimated in 1930 that one-third of the income of the rice fields went to the payment of interests on debts),[72] found themselves ruined and threatened with expropriation.

In 1926–29, the Banque de l'Indochine had multiplied advances and the types of short-term loans that were extended every six months. The bank subsequently entered, starting in October 1930, and in concert with the Gouvernement général, into an inflexible policy of executing mortgage debts that it held on landed prop-

erty, notably that used for rice growing and real estate, a debt that was further burdened by the stabilization of the piastre in May 1931. The violent conflict that erupted
in 1931 between the Banque de l'Indochine and the coalition of French and Vietnamese factions of the Cochinchinese bourgeoisie, culminated with the purchase
at auction by the bank, for 100,000 piastres, on September 28, 1933, of the famous
plantation of La Souchère in Long Thanh, whose value was estimated at two million piastres. "The Banque de l'Indochine has become a new Compagnie des Indes
that is laying its hand on all the good businesses of the country," the Syndicat des
commerçants et industriels de Cochinchine (Union of Merchants and Industrialists of Cochinchina) claimed in August 1933. The relative unity of colonial society
was for a time broken, and from 1933 to 1935, Saigon witnessed pervasive and unusual "anti-capitalist" demonstrations by colonists protesting against deflation, the
Banque de l'Indochine, and the attachment of the piastre to the gold standard.

Coming Out of the Crisis

The general direction of the "anti-crisis" policy adopted by the Gouvernement
général under Governors-General Pierre Pasquier and then René Robin, in direct
accord with the Banque de l'Indochine and metropolitan leaders, is clearly apparent today. It had, it seems, three objectives: protecting the value of invested capital; encouraging the "normal" effects of a cyclical capitalist crisis, that is, the "pu-
rification" of the corporate scene after years of wild speculation, the rationalization
of production, notably rice growing, and, ultimately, linking Indochina more closely
to the French imperial economy. This was about saving "healthy" investment and
modernizing reconstruction, in short, about taking advantage of the crisis to finally
establish, in a rational manner, Albert Sarraut's old project of "developing" the
colonies. But by no means was there an in-depth alteration of the colonial mechanisms of accumulation. The rigorous policy of deflation, of rendering profitable
existing colonial enterprises—or what had to be preserved of them—functioned,
first, through the concession of substantial, though selective and temporary, aid to
rice growers and planters in the form of exceptional advances and loans. The decree of April 26, 1932, created the Service des prêts fonciers (Land Loan Services),
which granted long-term credit and a low interest rate guaranteed by the general
budget. In this way, 99.6 million current francs were lent to rice growers from 1933
to 1942 (only half of these advances had been repaid in 1942). There were 4,000
such requests, of which 1,000 concentrated four-fifths of the agrarian debt, and 351
were granted. Moreover, the creation of the Caisse de compensation du caoutchouc
(Rubber Compensation Fund) in 1931 and the Office de soutien à la production
agricole (Office of Support for Agricultural Production), created by the law of April
1932, placed 96.5 million francs at the disposal of 485 planters between 1930 and
1942, almost totally reimbursing them, albeit in devalued money, by the end of this
period. Peasant taxation had saved the capitalist plantation.

But the principal measure taken to defend capital had been the "stabilization" of the piastre, made official by the decree of May 31, 1931, which linked the Indochinese currency to the gold standard (at 1 piastre to 655 milligrams of gold) at a rate equal to 10 francs (or about 2 francs at the 1914 rate). This measure, in the works since 1928, and accomplished de facto in November 1929, was denounced by the colonists and the latifundists, partisans on the contrary of a strong devaluation of the piastre aimed at alleviating the debt of rice growers and resuming exports to the Far East, and who suddenly saw their debts overvalued. The reappraisal of the piastre, however, aimed to escape the effects of the lasting devaluation of silver and to eliminate the corollary risk of a depreciation of investment in Indochina, which one author estimates in 1934 at about 527 million current francs of capital invested since 1924.[73] In the long term, the point was, while trying to hold firmly onto franc-piastre parity—which was henceforth the dogma of the Gouvernement général—to provide a steady monetary foundation for future investment of capital, for loans, and for metropolitan exports, as well as valuing the profits achieved in Indochina in francs. "The gold standard has restored security to outside capital that wants to involve itself in Indochina," the 1933 Commission monétaire indochinoise (Indochinese Monetary Commission) noted.[74] Monetary reform had a deflationary effect on indigenous consumption and salaries, which seem to have fallen more quickly than the cost of living throughout the colony, and more acutely in the north than in the south. Most important, the reform unhooked the piastre from the Asian currency system. This had less to do with the abandonment of the silver standard—the latter disappeared in the Far East when the Chinese yuan was linked to the pound sterling and to the dollar on November 3, 1935—than with the choice of an elevated gold parity at a time when the pound sterling, the dollar, the Siamese tical, and the Filipino peso were about to be devalued.

Henceforth integrated into the gold block implemented by France between 1931 and 1932, Indochina found itself with a strong currency, in the midst of neighbors and competitors with weakened currencies. For instance, from 1931 to 1932, the exchange rate of the piastre with the Hong Kong dollar grew from 20% to 40%, which obviously led to a temporary reduction in exports to Hong Kong and southern China (they decreased 60% in volume between 1929 and 1936). The revaluing of the piastre temporarily disturbed the flow of Asian foreign trade with Indochina and integrated the colony more tightly into the orbit of French foreign trade. In this regard, 1933 was a significant turning point for Indochina's foreign exchange: the share of France and the empire was henceforth dominant (standing at 50.5% of Indochina's exports) and would remain high until 1938 (when it reached 53.2%). The decrease in Indochina's relative customs autonomy, which it had maintained in spite of the French customs law of 1928 (the so-called Kircher tariff), furthered this trend: in March 1934, the Indochinese special tariff was abolished for half the items it had covered. This was a difficult change, since Indochinese rice exported duty-free to France essentially served as food for livestock, competing with wheat producers and contrary to the policies of the Ministry of Agriculture. Under pressure from these interests, the Gouvernement général was compelled to impose an exit tax on rice destined for the French market.

This drastic deflation, coupled with reinforced protectionism, served to lower prices (there was a decrease of 38.7% in the index of wholesale prices at Saigon between 1930 and 1935), encouraging French exports and compensating for capital depreciation. Furthermore, in the context of its "cleansing" policies, the administration allowed the process of concentration to do its work. Under the energetic direction of Paul Gannay, its true leader in the Far East and one of the most powerful figures in French Indochina from 1927 to 1952, the Banque de l'Indochine tightened its granting of credit and maintained elevated interest rates. Not only did its advances, loans, and discount operations decrease by more than 70% from 1929 to 1933, but its rate of discounts was only lowered to 6.5% in 1932, as shown in official reports of the time. It acquired liquidated estates at low cost and took control of a considerable number of struggling companies, of which the most important was Octave Homberg's Société financière française et coloniale (French and Colonial Financial Company), acquired in 1932.[75] The Banque de l'Indochine's acquisitions of holdings, which stood at around 18–19 annually between 1917 and 1921, increased to 46 in 1928, 39 in 1933, and 53 in 1937.[76] Its business banking operation was considerably strengthened during the crisis. "In sum, the policy of the Banque de l'Indochine since the crisis has been one of taking over all viable enterprises, which, absent due vigilance and proper regulation, will end up forming a vast trust or *konzern* that dominates the colony," Inspector of Colonies G. Lasserre wrote in 1938.[77] A comment added in the margin of the report by someone in the minister's offices reinforced this harsh assessment: "The political influence acquired by the Banque de l'Indochine and the fear that it inspires in civil servants and governors are well known." The crisis made colonial big capital preponderant in the Indochinese economy, to the detriment of the colonists and the Vietnamese bourgeoisie,[78] and blocked the development of the national capitalism that the latter had tried to construct in the 1920s. This rationalization of the colonial economy was furthered by attempts to transform paddy distribution through the creation of bonded warehouses destined to eliminate the Chinese, and the organization of a market on the model of the Bullinger Pool, the powerful private Burmese rice–exporting monopoly, as well as measures of technical modernization of rice growing entrusted to the Office du riz (Rice Office) in April 1930.

The economic policies of the 1930s had uneven results. The measures intended to technically modernize the colonial economy had only minor effects, but deflation, favored by the colonial context, met with relative success. The budgets recovered their balance in 1935. The international accord of May 7, 1934, on rubber, which allotted a quota of 30,000 tons to Indochina, loosened the market and permitted prices to recover. Exports, which did not surpass 10,433 tons in 1930, jumped to 29,574 in 1935. The investments of the large companies resumed, notably those focused on rubber, which established massive grafting programs after 1930. On the other hand, the vast imperial economic project defended by the "autarchist" business milieu, which became one of the defining forces of French capitalism after the Conférence économique impériale (Imperial Economic Conference) of 1934, had difficulty resisting the contradictions of Indochina's multiple interest groups.[79] The economic policy of the Popular Front would to a certain extent result in strained commercial relations between France and its Asian colony. The devaluation of the piastre (by about 50%), following that of the franc, on October 2, 1936, and the abandonment of its convertibility into gold (it was henceforth a currency exchanged according to the franc standard), then the decision taken on June 30, 1937, to let the Indochinese currency float like the franc, clearly provoked inflation and the unbalancing of budgets all over again. But, most important, they gave a boost to trade with the Far East and to the campaign by exporters and colonial businessmen to delink the piastre from the franc, establishing parity with the Hong Kong dollar in order to sustain sales of rice in China, and the customs and commercial autonomy that would mark the economic history of Indochina after 1940. At the same time, the deep dependence of the Indochinese economy on the metropole represented the crossing of a dangerous threshold for the latter, which was henceforth threatened with having to assume the colony's serious deficits.

The Great Depression had dramatically posed the problem of a global change in the colonial economy. Although it was not lacking in clear-sighted minds, colonization had not developed the strengths necessary for such a shift. It had not, for example, modified the fundamental structures of Cochinchinese rice growing, starting with the material, social, and moral subjection of the *ta dien* (farmer) to the great landowner. Any modernization of rice growing, however, presupposed the opening of agricultural credit to the *ta dien,* with the idea that the latter could themselves become small landowners. The course chosen was in fact bound to encourage technical innovation and the concentration of enterprises, to make what existed profitable, instead of truly passing to an "industrializing colonization" on the model of the Japanese colonization of Manchuria, Korea, and Formosa.

The Spiral of Underdevelopment

Overall, the Depression had created the material conditions for a moral secession between the established elite and the popular masses in Vietnamese society, inasmuch as it coincided and joined with the structural crisis of the peasant economy in the overpopulated deltas of Annam and Tonkin. The 1930s actually witnessed the generalization of a situation of acute underdevelopment in the two protectorates. All its symptoms—an acceleration in the pace of population growth, permanent food shortages, massive rural underemployment, the degradation of rural social relations—henceforth took on alarming proportions there. The economic crisis had undoubtedly aggravated overpopulation, while also provoking the return of tens of thousands of workers to rural areas. In 1930–31, close to 11,000 workers were repatriated to Tonkin from the other territories. In Haiphong, the number of inhabitants dropped from 168,000 to 73,000, because half of the Chinese population returned to China between 1931 and 1935 and two-thirds of the Vietnamese population returned to the countryside.[80] The protectorate's sales of rice, certainly much smaller than Cochinchina's, had diminished in value by a factor of 10 from 1929 to 1931.[81] This led to a widespread devaluation of land, to the vertiginous fall of agricultural salaries, and to rising rural underemployment. In Cochinchina, the revenue of the *ta dien* collapsed, as is attested by the administration's reports, as well as by the figures on tax evasion, and many returned to subsistence farming. Even in Cambodia, the peasantry suffered harshly from the effects of the crisis, as is shown by the collapse of the local budget's fiscal revenue: a drop of 44% from 1930 to 1934, the strongest decrease of the five territories. Nevertheless, in the Khmer countries, there were vast reserves of land capable of absorbing periodic crises, and agrarian tensions there remained limited until the 1950s.

In Vietnam, the peasant society undoubtedly possessed efficient defense mechanisms. "The communal and especially the familial structures appear to be both sufficiently solid and elastic to accommodate this influx of mouths to feed, but it has in all likelihood resulted in accentuated poverty."[82] The rise of underdevelopment in the central and northern rural areas was no less evident; even more weakened by this additional weight, and in the absence of modernization of its structures, the old Vietnamese agro-demographic system reached the limits of its elasticity in the overpopulated deltas of Tonkin and Annam, and its mechanisms of internal regulation, the familial and village relationship of dependence and solidarity, were affected. The alarm was sounded by the peasant revolts of 1930 and by the terrible famine that hit the provinces of Nghe An and Ha Tinh in northern Annam in 1931. In the following years, catastrophe threatened several times, notably during the serious drought of 1936.

The great rural surveys of the 1930s, those of Pierre Gourou, Charles Robequain, and René Dumont, and the writings of Paul Bernard and René Bouvier,[83] along with other less well known texts, provide a striking analysis of the peasant condition in Tonkin and Annam, as well as of peasant poverty in Cochinchina. Amid the internal debates about colonial policy, they raised the old theme of the pressure of increasing population on a fundamentally limited foundation. Especially revealing are the gross consumption figures for imported industrial products in Indochina per inhabitant: hardly 1.8 kg of kerosene and 0.4 kg of cotton fabric in 1939. Evoking the unspeakable "misery of the Indochinese rural masses," an official expert would write in 1947: "While families in the Tonkin Delta had no more than 6 piastres per month at their disposal, it was unsettling to see publicists speak before the war of how rich Indochina was. A rich Indochina! Gentlemen, what blasphemy, when millions of people live in fear of a famine that perpetually threatens their families."[84] Certainly, with corn as a supplement and the annual contribution of 30,000 to 50,000 tons of Cochinchinese rice—although counterbalanced by equivalent exports of Tonkin rice to China—grain production in Tonkin roughly corresponded to consumption until 1939. But this came at the cost of chronic undernourishment of a part of the peasantry and an increasing precariousness of the food situation, which was aggravated by the absence of any reserves.

On the eve of World War II, the life of peasants in the ten thousand *xa* (rural communes) of the Red River Delta was terrible. The great anthropologist Nguyen Van Huyen, an excellent observer of the rural condition, estimated in 1939 that production of rice in the delta varied between 18 and 22 million quintals, for an irreducible consumption of 18.5 million. But it is necessary to deduct from this estimate 2 million quintals that were exported and 2 million more for alcohol distilleries, seed, and shipments to the highlands. A million and a half mouths could not be fed. If the deliveries from the south were to cease, there would be shortages. Nguyen Van Huyen's analysis would be confirmed by the terrifying famine of March through May of 1945. The peasant budgets he studied almost always revealed dramatic situations, in which misery and undernourishment were widespread. "In the poor villages," he wrote, "80% of the population has only one meal a day. It is only during times of intense agricultural work, that is, during a third of the year, in particular during the harvest, that they have enough to eat."[85] A family of from five to seven people had to possess 4 to 5 *mau* (1.44 to 1.8 hectares) of rice fields to avoid undernourishment; however, in the province of Nam Dinh, for example, where the population density was between 800 and 1,400 habitants per square kilometer, 79.3% of landowners had less than 1 *mau* (36 acres). Widespread lending at rates that reached as high as from 300% to 400%, the quasi-slavery of indebted peasants, mass rural underemployment, monopolization of communal land by powerful lineages and landowners, who were important especially in the southeastern part of the delta, gambling tragedies, innumerable obligations and festive offerings tied to social pressure in the closed universe of the village community, the recurrent pressure of magical practices and rituals, the martyrdom of peasant women: such were the somber realities, around 1939, of the peasants in the Tonkin area. They found themselves henceforth in the grip of an underdevelopment that the powers in place could no longer master. "In any case," Nguyen Van Huyen wrote,

> the peasant elite, the village notables, are opposed to all true and deep reform. These
> are people who have paid for twenty, thirty, and forty years to attain their social sta-

tus. They are at an age when one can quietly cross one's legs on the *dinh*'s best mats to eat and to drink or knowledgeably to appreciate the way in which young people serve them what they eat and drink. If anyone tries to push through any kind of reform whatsoever, he inevitably attracts merciless spite. Someone puts opium under his roof, or some contraband alcohol in his pigsty or his stable. And nine times out of ten, the framed man is condemned.

The powerful inertia of the village, "this traditional organization that benefits privileged men while increasing the misery of the majority," and the rigid hierarchy upon which it rested, blocked all hope of change. On the eve of the war, many Vietnamese intellectuals felt that to solve the crises of rural society, it was imperative to break the relative autonomy of the *lang* and its institutional tradition, the *xa* (commune), and the power of the great lineages. As Nguyen Van Huyen lamented,

> The introduction of what is called "communal reform" has been in vain. With its council composed of a president, a treasurer, and a secretary, in the image of private associations, [it] has just complicated the situation to the detriment of the central administration against which the village has always risen up.... For the chieftainship is elsewhere. There is a mentality to be changed, an organization rooted in very strong interests, which penetrates the deepest layers of society, that needs to be altered. Otherwise, all effort at reform will be no more than window-dressing."[86]

The colonial regime was precisely not in a position to carry out this transformation. It was, fundamentally, from then on trapped within the sharp contradiction between its two historic functions: ensuring the functioning of the mechanisms that extracted colonial profit and hastening the modernizing transformation of colonized societies. Both presupposed investments and political capacities that the colonial regime could no longer muster. This inadequacy constituted the objective historic foundation for the genesis of future Indochinese nation-states. It was not that the leaders of colonization had not considered the depth of Vietnamese underdevelopment. Their analyses of the rural uprisings of 1930–31 (see chapter 7) attributed them as much "to the imbalance of indigenous social conditions, which is in reality caused by the pauperism peculiar to the Asiatic collectivities," as Governor-General Robin wrote in 1931,[87] as to revolutionary action. "The uprising of the peasantry," added this conservative and austere *haut-fonctionnaire*, "is a veritable struggle between the classes. It was not difficult for the communists to awaken and incite the hatred of these poor peasants.... Can a combined intervention of the colonial power and the Annamese government, through a set of well-conducted reforms, extinguish the virulence of nationalism and balance the social situation while making pauperism disappear, in order to restore the people's confidence in the legal authority?"

The "Peasant" Option and the Colonial Power's Hydraulic Strategy

In the event, the colonial administration would attempt to confront the problem of underdevelopment in a manner consistent with its logic—that is to say, through the only strategy compatible with the administration's policy of "conservative reform" of the existing structures of colonial capitalism. It aimed simultaneously to preserve the extraction of colonial profit and the perpetuation of its social foundation in the Vietnamese rural areas and to prevent or blunt in time the proletarianization of the peasantry. This was the strategy of rural development that would soon be known as the *politique du paysannat* (politics of the peasantry). It involved reorienting part of state investment to the benefit of the peasantry—in short, an attempt to give some reality to the principle advanced by Jules Harmand at the beginning of the century: "The native is the true colonist, the state is the great colonizer."[88] The objective was to rebalance the ratio of grain production to population growth and optimize peasant production without modifying its social structures, with the aid of a minimum of modern inputs, and to loosen the demographic constraint by opening up external outlets. There was an attempt to raise agricultural productivity through a policy of "aid to the rice field" launched in 1932. The Rice Office was created in 1930 and tried to reenergize the rice-growing agronomic stations. In Asia, as in the rest of the Far East, scientific agronomy started, albeit very timidly, to penetrate peasant rice culture, the first germ of the future "green revolutions." Programs of peasant colonization (initiated with the decree of November 11, 1928) were revitalized and amplified; they reutilized the former imperial policy of land clearing, but often went unheeded especially following the economic crisis of the 1930s. The Office of Rural Colonization, created on April 22, 1932, mapped out a policy of peasant transmigration from the northern deltas to the "vacant" lands of the Middle region of Tonkin, of the highlands of the center and south of the Mekong Delta, totaling an estimated 1.2 million hectares in 1938,[89] a policy that was simultaneously to encourage small-scale peasant landowning.

Finally, and particularly in 1930–31, the upper echelons of the colonial state became aware of the vital necessity of moving toward systematic planning of deltas and rationally accepting the hydraulic constraints with the aim of generalizing the double harvest. The hydraulic program of 1931, revised and completed in 1936–37, and financed by loans (1,370 million current francs) authorized by the law of February 22, 1931, aimed most notably, between 1931 to 1940, to equip the *casiers* (drained plots of land with irrigation) of Thai Binh, of the middle delta (Ha Dong–Phu Ly, Nam Dinh, Ke Sat, Hung Yen, Bac Ninh, and the Day barrage, the biggest mobile dam in the world until the mid-1950s), as well as those of Annam (Vinh, Thanh Hoa, Ha Tinh, Thua Thien, Quang Nam, Quang Ngai), Cambodia, and Laos. Between 1931 and 1940, about 42 million piastres were invested in large-scale hydraulic construction projects.[90] By 1945, a total of 377,000 hectares had been

TABLE 6.3   Agricultural hydraulics at the beginning of 1945: an estimate (in hectares)

	Projects completed since the beginning of the century	Projects in progress	Projects under study	Total
Tonkin	377,130	60,500	494,400	932,030
Annam	120,000	37,000	79,000	236,000
Cochinchina	89,000[a]	475,000	—	564,000
Cambodia	19,300	50,000	115,000	184,300
Laos	16,000	—	12,000	28,000
TOTAL	621,430	622,500	700,400	1,944,330

SOURCE: The figures for Tonkin are drawn from D. Vesin, "Histoire du fleuve Rouge: Gestion et aménagement d'un systéme hydraulique au Tonkin des années 1890 jusqu'à la Seconde Guerre mondiale" (MA thesis, Paris, 1992). The remaining figures are from two documents issued by the Indochinese subcommittee of the State Planning Commission's Comité de l'hydraulique agricole: *Rapport d'ensemble,* by Jamme, the chief engineer public works, doubtless from the end of 1946; and *Hydraulique agricole en Cochinchine,* another report from the same date by Jamme, CAOM, Affaires économiques, 577.

[a] This figure refers only to irrigation networks and plots equipped with hydraulic canals.

equipped and improved in the Red River Delta since the beginning of the century (table 6.3 and map 6.1), 60,500 hectares were being outfitted, and the improvement of 494,000 supplementary hectares was being considered.[91] During the previous half century, Tonkin had gained on average 10,000 hectares per year. Production increased substantially, from 300,000 to 633,000 tons of paddy in the protectorate, according to sources.[92] It was an impressive result, and yet disappointing if one considers that in the absence of consistent agrarian and agronomic policies and of a new industrialization of the country, the acceleration of the hydraulic and delta planning only permitted the maintenance of peasant consumption at its existing precarious level, that is at a level that avoided famine but not high enough to lift the rural masses out of their undernourishment and their deepening general underdevelopment.

Those in charge of colonization therefore chose to implement an ambitious "peasant" strategy after 1930. As Governor-General Brevié forcefully stated:

I tried to lay out the main aspects of the land policy that I intended to promote in this country. It was inspired above all by the idea of improving the fate of the peasant masses, which are the most numerous and the most impoverished. For both moral and material reasons, all other preoccupations, all other needs, must give way to this, and I would hope that the imperious demands and the excessive requests of those in Indochina who are better off than our peasants will cease. First, let us turn to life's disinherited; so doing, we shall perform an act of human solidarity that is vital to us all.[93]

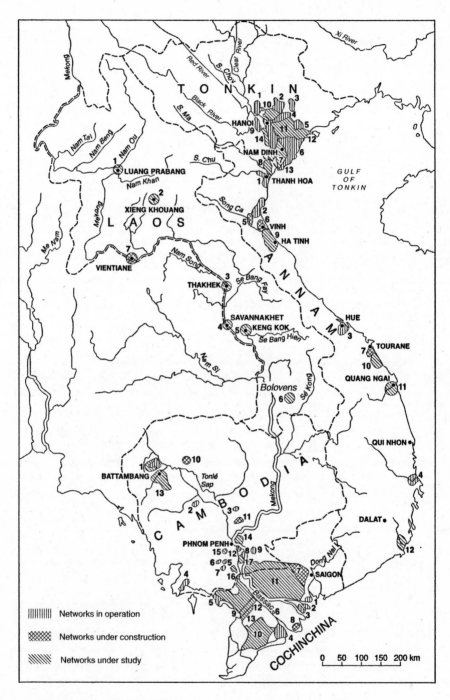

MAP 6.1. Agricultural hydraulics in Indochina, 1945 *(key on facing page).*

This approach, fundamentally similar to that of the ancient Chinese or Vietnamese imperial administration, could at best, however, assure the peasantry the minimum of growth it needed to compensate for its uncontrollable demographic expansion, whose explosive effects were to be curbed by rural development.

In the colonial milieu, this policy became the object of widespread debate at the time, rekindling the controversy over the industrialization of Indochina (see chapter 7) and on the means of confronting the "permanent food crisis in Tonkin and in northern Annam, or the forthcoming one in Cochinchina."[94] In fact, the colonial rulers had clearly conceived a policy of peasant colonization and of support for small familial landowners, which, in many respects, would be continued by the future Vietnamese regimes. What they lacked, however, were the political means necessary to mobilize the peasantry. How could one displace a part of the Vietnamese peasantry of the north toward the mountainous hinterland and toward the vast reserve of available land in Cochinchina and Cambodia, estimated by one author in 1937 at close to 1.2 million hectares, representing a "second delta of the Red River"?[95] Most colonial decision-makers, with the exception of economists like Paul Bernard, a *polytechnicien* engineer and lucid businessman, shared the opinion of the lawyer Georges Khérian: to take action on the birthrate would be impossible for a long time. The only course left was to stimulate peasant migration through the distribution of land that would be set up for the migrants, led by "colonization organizers" recruited from among the notables, the mandarins, and the clergy, while increasing agricultural production. "If one truly wishes to decongest the urban areas of the delta," Khérian wrote, "it is essential to adopt *a fearless policy of managed colonization [colonisation dirigeé]*, which is the only way to realize these massive displacements."[96] He went so far as to evoke the necessity of birth control and to question the quasi-official colonial, and Confucian, dogma of the peasants' unshaken, atavistic attachment to their village.

In reality, the administration encouraged small familial colonization (ordinance of March 6, 1936) and created a Superior Council of Colonization on December 28, 1937—although it does not seem to have been very active. Furthermore, the colonial

---

MAP 6.1. KEY

Tonkin, *networks in operation:* 1. Vinh Yen; 2. Song Cau; 3. Kep; 4. Bac Ninh–East; 5. An Duong; 6. Thai Binh; 7. Nam Dinh–East; 8. Ha Dong–Phu Ly; 9. Son Tay; *under study:* 10. Phuc Yen–Bac Ninh; 11. Ke Sat–Hung Yen; 12. Song Thai Binh; 13. Song Day; 14. Ha Dong–Phu Ly.

Annam, *networks in operation:* 1. Song Chu; 2. Vinh-North; 3. Thua Thien; 4. Tuy Hoa; *under construction:* 5. Do Luong; 6. Vinh-South; 7. Quang Nam–North; *under study:* 8. Song Ma; 9. Cam Xuyen; 10. Quang Nam–South; 11. Quang Ngai; 12. Phan Rang.

Cochinchina, *networks in operation:* 1. Go Cong; 2. Ba Tri; 3. Bang Cung; 4. Thiep Nhut; 5. Ha Tien; 6. An Truong; *under construction:* 7. Cau An Ha; 8. Long Vingh–Long Toan; 9. Chau Doc–Long Xuyen–Rach Gia–Ha Tien; *under study:* 10. Quan Lo; 11. Plain of Reeds; 12. Rach Soi–Bassac–Rach Gia–Long Xuyen; 13. Rach Soi–Bassac–Chung Bau.

Cambodia, *networks in operation:* 1. Bovel; 2. Bamnak; 3. Stung Khya; 4. Prey Nop; 5. Takeo; 6. Bat Rokar; 7. Kompong Sleng; 8. Koki Thom; 9. Kompong Sne; *under construction:* 10. Siem Reap; 11. Cheung Prey; 12. Beng Khnor; *under study:* 13. Banan; 14. Veal Samnap; 15. Kompong Tram; 16. Angkor Borey; 17. Beng Thom.

government planned to open a "Tonkin area" in the Mekong Delta and to establish a certain number of settlement villages in upper Tonkin. None of this met with much success. From very early on, colonization had effectively superimposed a new mobility linked to salaried employment on the earlier networks of peasant mobility based on intervillage and intrafamily relationships, as Andrew Hardy's research demonstrates.[97] After 1930, the Gouvernement général opted for a collective migration, transplanting the village power structures and cults, according to the pattern of nineteenth-century imperial colonization. This choice was in accordance with its ideological presumptions—the atavistic ties of the peasant to his village—as well as with the rigidity of tax levies. However, the administration did not have the means to put into motion a large-scale migration of the delta peasantry, as would be the case in the 1980s in Vietnam, and its options hardly gave rise to consistent results.

For the geographer Pierre Gourou, in contrast, peasant emigration toward the south only offered a temporary outlet, given the population increase in Cochinchina. His vision was pessimistic. "The problem has no solution," he wrote, "if the Tonkin population continues to rise according to its current pace. The overpopulation in Tonkin must be alleviated by other methods, first, through the improvement of agricultural output (selection, fertilizers, hydraulics, new techniques), second, to a lesser extent, through the extension of the craft trades and industries, and finally, through emigration, not only to Cochinchina, but also to other Indochinese territories."[98] In any case, the peasant strategy could not yield immediate results: it presupposed, in addition to enormous investments, that the administration could control the technical system, cultural practices, and the agrarian structures of the village, and that it could rely completely on a modern peasant elite, which still had to be forged. It depended, in short, on the availability of a long stretch of time over which to carry out these policies. It amounted to a desire to fight against time. Because, since the 1930s, the race between rural underdevelopment and the peasant policies of the Gouvernement général was on throughout Indochina, and, in northern and central Vietnam, seemingly unstoppable population growth far outpaced the rural development belatedly envisioned by the colonizers.

. . .

On the eve of World War II, two dominant traits of colonial capitalism were certainly the distortion between, on the one hand, its constituent structures, demography, and the economic evolution of the colonized peasantries, and, on the other, the permanence of these structures, its refusal to change them, and their capacity to survive the Great Depression virtually intact. Inscribed in this logic of permanence and distortion were the magnitude and the violence of the tragedy that was brewing. High Commissioner Émile Bollaert would later tersely summarize the stakes: "We have rights and legitimate interests in Indochina. We have sown a great deal, and we are not ashamed to say that we do not want to be deprived of the harvest."[99]

7

Resistance, Nationalism, and Social Movements, 1900–1939

To wish to colonize Asia is to pursue an illusion and to flirt with danger. You have not fully understood that the Asiatic populations are our equals; that they enjoy a civilization older than ours; that it endures in their memory and their pride. They were free and will want to be free again. It is not difficult to predict that in contact with our civilization, with the wind of ideas of emancipation that are circulating throughout the world, they will quickly feel this need for independence, which is the goal and the honor of all peoples, awaken and ferment. They will revolt one day, and their revolt will necessarily triumph, because it is the immortal privilege of liberty to triumph everywhere.

—JULES DELAFOSSE,
Bonapartist deputy from Calvados, to the Chambre des Députés,
December 22, 1885

Placed in a long-term perspective, the twentieth century was a time of interminable revolutions for the Indochinese peninsula. It was the victory of these revolutions, rather than a relatively peaceful, Anglo-Indian mode of decolonization, which through the extension of World War II, tolled the death knell of French imperialism. There was nothing fortuitous about this: of all of the nationalist and revolutionary movements that appeared in the French empire, those of Indochina were the most precocious, the most diversified, and the most radical.

Already by 1939, many were surprised by their dynamism. It emerged from the fact that Confucian Vietnam, but also Buddhist Cambodia and the Lao, had an ancient national societal structure that rested upon village cohesion, a highly affirmed ethno-cultural identity centered on the figure of the king and on many centuries of continuity in the princely courts and the royal state. But it was as much the result of the depths of the rifts that French colonization incited in these societies. Colonization destabilized the peasantry and generated an urban network and pockets of industrial development, and in so doing, it created situations that favored the implantation of modern political movements. At the same time, however, the colonial regime checked their growth by stubbornly sustaining the premodern powers.

By doing this, it forced the traditionalist components of nationalism into an impasse and condemned its "reformist" currents to failure. This set the stage for the future radical movements. Furthermore, Indochinese societies were less well controlled by colonial power than we think. They evaded its authority in many ways: smuggling, tax and recruitment evasion, passivity. . . . They were, to differing degrees, societies of protest, rebellious societies.[1] A case in point is the conscription of men for World War I: in Cochinchina, in thirteen provinces, crowds marched on the prisons to deliver those unwillingly enlisted.

It is necessary, however, to avoid determinism. Nothing was played out in advance. The radical movements were certainly not the only ones that spread modern national ideas. Recent historiography has shown the importance of peaceful forms of nationalism, of its gradualist and reformist trends, their prolonged engagement in ambivalent collaborations of varying sincerity with the colonial power, an engagement that was not a repudiation of a more or less long-term goal of national emancipation.

The social effects of the colonial situation were contradictory; they were both revolutionary and conservative. In fact, the diverse populations in the peninsula encountered very differentiated political dynamics, marked by major historical shifts, which were nevertheless synchronized. The Vietnamese elite, which suffered the pain of national humiliation, rapidly developed a modern political culture based on the model offered by the new China. Meanwhile, until World War II, the Khmer, the Lao, and the forest people lived in a pre-political sphere separated from the great currents of world culture. These countries were seemingly politically "static," without an active nationalism outside of certain elements of the courts, of modern elites, and of the great families, until late in the century. The historical conditions that led to the possible hegemony of the Vietnamese state over the postcolonial Indochinese space were thus created during the colonial period.

THE RECURRENCE OF TRADITIONAL FORMS OF RESISTANCE TO COLONIZATION

Until the middle of the twentieth century, forms of resistance anchored in the past by their cultural references and by their modes of organization and expression were a major part of Indochinese history.

The Laotian Regions

In the ethnically heterogeneous political construction that was Laos, the only resistance colonization consistently encountered were the revolts of messianic inspiration on the part of the montagnard peoples. Colonization depended upon the collaboration of the Tai ethnic group of Laos—the Lao Lum, or "Lao of the plains"—who were in fact more numerous in Siam than in Laos, where in 1930 they only represented around 45% of the population. In 1907, 525 Vietnamese militiamen and 475 Lao of the Garde indigène led by 26 European commissioned and noncommissioned officers were enough, with five small steamboats, to assure military control of the country.[2] Lao society had poorly recovered from the great nineteenth-century deportations to Siam, and it remained organized through the customary clientele networks of the former *muong*, which provided most of the ministers and dignitaries of the royal court of Luang Prabang and most of the Protectorate's civil servants. The latter were trained at the Pavie secondary school, then at the École de droit et l'administration de Vientiane, which opened in 1928. Nationalism did not exist in Laos because of the long-standing lack of a modern intelligentsia: in 1940, there were only seven thousand primary school students out of a million inhabitants, and the small intellectual elite was descended from the princely families. This historical consolidation of regional "feudalities" is attributable not only to the clientalization practiced by the colonial regime but also to the slowness of transformations in small-scale village production. Trade and credit were in the hands of the Chinese, the staff in mines and offices were Vietnamese, a minority that likewise made up the majority of the population of the small urban centers (53% in Vientiane and 85% in Thakhek in 1943). The towns were largely populated and controlled by Vietnamese and Chinese.

It was almost exclusively among the Vietnamese—minor employees in towns, or miners in Cammon—that the Indochinese Communist Party, totally marginal in relation to the rest of the multi-ethnic society, found support after 1934. Furthermore, Thai expansionism, reactivated around 1937, undermined the strengthening of Lao opposition to the French Protectorate, insofar as the latter long appeared as the necessary counterweight to the aims of Bangkok. Starting during the Pavie period, the colonial regime carefully cultivated its image as protector and renovator of the Lao nation. In fact, in 1941, it created the first newspaper in Lao, the bimonthly *Lao Nhay*. Through this stance it also sought to prevent the progress, on the eve of the war of 1939, of a more radical national consciousness among a younger urban generation, which perhaps developed in relation to the appearance, starting in 1934–35, of communist propaganda in Laotian.

The concept of a Laotian nation had already started to appear as early as the end of World War I among the small Laotian elite with a Western education. It was to coalesce in the 1930s around the Buddhist Institute of Vientiane with the renovation of Theravada Buddhist and Pali studies, the perfecting of the written language, the modernization of the language, and scholarly research on national history and culture. The main figures were Prince Phetsarath Rattanavongsa, the Protectorate's inspector of political affairs, and his learned secretary, Sila Viravong, who undertook the publication of classic Laotian manuscripts and of his own *Phongsawadan Lao* (History of Laos), in which he proves the great age of the Laotian mandala and the continuity of Laotian history. It is evident that Thai nationalist history developed within the circle of Prince Damrong in Bangkok strongly influenced this pair. This phase of cultural nationalism was strongly opposed to the "Vietnamese danger" and Thai irredentism. As early as 1931, in *France-Indochine,* Phetsarath demanded better integration of Laos into the heart of Indochina and the replacement of the Protectorate's Vietnamese personnel by Laotians, who made up only 54% of all civil servants in 1937.[3] Prince Souphanouvong, who in 1937 finished his studies as an engineer at the École nationale des Ponts et Chaussées (National School of Bridges and Roads) in the Paris of the Popular Front, was representative of a group of aristocratic intellectuals who were in sympathy with democratic ideas.

However, non-Lao populations opposed the colonizers in numerous ways, generally in the form of dissident Buddhist movements led by local charismatic figures. Rebellions exploded when colonization threatened the internal equilibrium of the highland societies and their traditional systems of relationships, especially by demands for corvée. The revolt of the Kha (in Thai, "slaves"), in fact, of the Alak, allied to the Lovens, in the southern plateau of the Boloven, was the most tenacious—a real "thirty-year guerrilla war."[4] It was a response to the increase in the recruitment of forced labor, which broke the cycles of *ray* (itinerant slash-and-burn agriculture) and to the resettlement of people in villages near military stations with a view to opening up the rich red soils of the plateau to European plantations, as well as to the relocation of commercial routes previously oriented toward Bangkok and the establishment by the French of unelected tax collectors and chiefs of circumscription *(tasseng),* who were predatory and much loathed. The revolt, which broke out in 1901, spread to the Sedang of Annam, and several thousand montagnards attacked Savannakhet in April 1902. The leader of the rebellion was a former Alak monk named Bak Mi, also known as Ong Kheo (Accumulator of Merit) and Phou mi Boun (Predestined One), who was believed to have magic powers, styled himself Great King *(chau sadet),* and purported to announce the coming of Maitreya, the future incarnation of the Buddha, and the advent of an era of peace. After the administrator Dauplay treacherously killed Bak Mi in November 1910, the guerrilla fighters were led in the Phou Lovan massif by his lieutenant, Komadom, an extraordinary person who dreamed of the unification of the proto-Indochinese tribes into an autonomous Khom *muong,* and to that end invented Khom writing. The rebellion surged up again with renewed force in 1935, and the guerillas were only defeated in September 1936.

Other revolts periodically shook the Laotian mountains: the revolt of the Lu in 1908–10 in the province of Phong Saly; the revolt of the Tai, allied to the Chinese opium merchants, against the exactions of the powerful Deo family, which was a client of the colonial administration, from November 1914 to December 1915; and especially the revolt of the Hmong (Meo), from 1918 to 1922,[5] on both sides of the border between Laos and Tonkin. This border held no meaning for opium farmers settled between 800 and 2,000 meters of it. Their uprising began in January 1918

in Chinese Yunnan, spreading to Indochina in June, directed first against Tai po-
tentates invested with regional power by the French authorities, and against their
exorbitant taxation of the opium produced by the Hmong, then against their colonial protectors. By the end of October 1919, there was a general uprising of the
Hmong over some 40,000 square kilometers, under the direction of the shaman
Batchai. Their aim was the creation of a Hmong kingdom at Dien Bien Phu, which
they set on fire in January 1920. It was only in 1922 that the colonial order was
reestablished by the capture and the execution of Batchai.

The Central Highlanders and Khmer Confront Colonial Power

In Cambodia and especially in the Protectorate of Annam, the resistance of the forest people, whom the precolonial states had barely controlled, was strong. The
Mnong revolted in 1912–14 in the Khmer province of Kratié, and in October 1914,
they killed Henri Maitre, the explorer of the proto-Indochinese tribal regions,
inhabited by the so-called Moï (which in Vietnamese means "slave" or "savage").
They would remain rebellious until the 1930s. In the high plateaus of the Annam-
Cambodia-Cochinchina frontier zone, the struggle of the Moï against the expansion of the great rubber plantations was only with difficulty brought under control
in 1934–36 by the pacification of the Phnong, who lived on the Annamese slope
of the central cordillera, and by the creation of a commissionership of the Moï regions. It had, in any case, delayed the development of a mountainous hinterland
often considered at the time as a second Malaysia for mining and forestry.

If Khmer nationalism, like its Lao counterpart, was slow to form—the two actually only arose in response to the dynamism of Vietnamese nationalism—the image of a passive and docile Cambodia, disseminated by the colonial authorities starting in the years 1904–5, must be seriously nuanced.[6] It is not that Indochinese
communism acquired any influence there before 1945. It is symptomatic of the situation that a movement like the Indochinese Congress, launched in 1936 from
Saigon by the Vietnamese communist and Trotskyist Left, had no echo except in
the Vietnamese diaspora. Still, colonial domination initiated a profound, although
very slow, readjustment of the relations between political powers and social forces.
In acquiring the collaboration of the traditional civil servants and endowing the
rural authorities *(mesrok, mekhum)* with increased powers, the colonial administration damaged the protective relations and reciprocal obligations through which
authority was exercised in Khmer countries. The misappropriation and exactions
of the new elite of bureaucrats, the increase in taxation, the expansion of merchant
agriculture along the river, and the indebtedness in rural areas triggered the first
agrarian tensions.

As Alain Forest has explored,[7] these tensions were expressed in a nonpolitical
form. The first of these was rural robbery in the jungle-covered frontier zones, notably in Battambang and Kratié: "The forest and the *phnom* [mountain] were the

settings in which the idea of rebellion took shape."[8] The chronicle of rural dissidence, which fluctuated according to the harvest cycle, was full of incidents such as the theft of cattle and buffalo destined for either Siam or Cochinchina; bloody attacks on villages or houses—especially Chinese—by bands who then withdrew into Siam. There were also acts of vengeance, various fights, escaping into the forest in order to avoid requisitions, and peasant demonstrations in front of residents' offices to denounce the negligence of their Khmer underlings.[9] But, unlike Laos, colonial Cambodia also experienced local peasant uprisings—notably during the subsistence crisis of 1911–13 (more than 1,500 arrests in 1913), in 1919–20, and during the 1930–34 crisis—which used invulnerability spells and were generally incited by the achars—highly respected lay figures who were in charge of ceremonies at Buddhist monasteries (vat)—or by monks. These upheavals were sporadic and localized, yet violent, and included the movement of the bonze Prak across from Tay Ninh (1896) and repeated uprisings of the former supporters of Prince Si Votha in the provinces of Tonle Repou and Melou Prey (1905, 1906, 1908, 1915) and of Vises Nheou in Battambang (1908–9). Some movements involved a sudden blaze of prophecies of a return of royal legitimacy and the imminent arrival of the Buddha. This was the case in the failed attempt of the Vietnamese traditional healer Ngo Prep in 1898 and most especially in the attack of the former monk Uch—a sort of patriotic bandit—and his band on the residency at Kampot, which was at the time in the midst of the pepper economy crisis of 1909, as well as the attack by the Ta Khwet group on the delegation of Kompong Trach in January 1915.[10] There were also local collective explosions like the murder of Resident Bardez by the population of a village of Kompong Chhnang on April 18, 1924, in response to the increase in tax levies.

The principal response of the Khmer peasant communities to the colonial disruption was to gather around the Buddhist monasteries. The cohesion of rural society, less and less maintained by the old administrative structures, was thus reestablished in a different cultural and spiritual register. In this regard, the attitude of the colonial authorities was in fact ambiguous. They supported Buddhism, but only to better oversee its activities and to put it to use, and also to remove it from the influence of Bangkok, the great regional center of Buddhist spirituality. Between 1914 and 1920, the colonial authorities attempted to centralize the Cambodian monastic Sangha (2,653 vat and 37,353 monks in 1938), until then organized horizontally, and required official authorization for the construction of new pagodas, in order to make the vat coincide with the khum, the basic administrative apparatus of the Protectorate. Specifically, the colonial authorities tried to divert the flow of monks who went to deepen their knowledge of the doctrine in Bangkok by creating a Pali École supérieure (School of higher learning) in Phnom Penh in 1914. They also endeavored to gain control over the nomadism of the monks by requiring, starting from 1916, a certificate of morality and a diploma of ordination for new monks. In 1919, finally, a hierarchical Sangha organization was established, henceforth divided into dioceses, subjected to chiefs of the two main orders of Buddhism, Mohanikay and Thommayut, and placed under the tutelage of the Ministère de l'Intérieur et des Cultes (Ministry of the Interior and Religion). The crowning moment of this policy, aimed at culturally disconnecting Khmer society from Siam, was the foundation of the Institut bouddhique (Buddhist Institute), a center for Buddhist studies, in January 1930; a parallel institution was not really established in Laos until 1947.[11]

The impact of this political double measure should not be underestimated. Until the eve of World War II, there were no multicultural groups of intellectuals in Cambodia. This historical lacuna can be explained by the Protectorate's distrust of modern teaching, but just as much by the resistance of the Sangha to the advancement of the colonial school system, which it feared would undermine Buddhist values and culture. Unlike in Vietnam, there was no initiative on the part of Khmer society to compensate for the lack of Protectorate schools or to promote modern culture and education. In 1920–21, there were only 19 Khmer students at the Indochinese University of Hanoi, as opposed to 268 Vietnamese, 30 Chinese, 5 Laotian, and 3 French;[12] in 1937, there were only 3 Khmer out of 632 students. Only a select few children of important families studied in France. In 1937, the enrollment in the 813 vat schools was 34,853 students, much higher than the figure for the 117 Franco-Khmer schools (11,548). Ten years later, in 1946, the modern Khmer elite included only one science doctorate; one medical doctor; one engineer from the Ecole Centrale; four bachelors of arts, science, and law; one surveyor-engineer; and a small number of agricultural engineers, Indochinese physicians, and veterinarians trained at the University of Hanoi.[13]

Within Cambodia, the attempt to spread scientific culture—to the extent that any such attempt was made—had failed. On the eve of the war, the small group of individuals with degrees were mostly civil servants who had been educated at the École d'administration cambodgienne (Cambodian School of Administration), created in 1917–22 to provide secretarial training and preparation for the examinations for the kromokar and the chaukron (judges). From this pool of civil servants, teachers, and Achar rural elite would come most of the weak political leadership of the future Cambodia under King Sihanouk: of the 320 Khmer ministers and deputies in office from 1945 to 1960, 140 (43.7%) had studied only at the École d'administration in Phnom Penh.[14] There were no Khmer newspapers before 1917; the first novel in Khmer, Tonle Sap, was published in 1938;[15] and Sisowath High School opened in 1936.

Under these circumstances, Khmer nationalism emerged very belatedly. It was expressed for the first time in 1936, through the Nagara Vatta or Nokorwath (literally, "the country of temples") magazine, which had a circulation of 5,000 and quickly gained influence through its famous "Saturday Editorial." This review was launched by Son Ngoc Thanh, a young judge who was a Khmer Krom (a Khmer from Cochinchina) and later a librarian at the Buddhist Institute, and by Pach Chhoeun and Hem Chieu, two professors of Pali at the Buddhist Institute. Encouraged by a small group of French intellectuals (notably Suzanne Karpelès, secretary of the Buddhist Institute), the group issued the call for a "Cambodia for the Cambodians" and acquired a substantial audience in the narrow circles of the new elite of Phnom Penh, made up especially of lower civil servants and students, and among the young monks, anxious about the threat of Westernization.[16]

The initial hotbed was the Buddhist Institute, meeting ground for scholars, writers, intellectuals, and bonzes. The debate that was starting centered on the definition of nationality. Who was Cambodian? The embryonic Khmer nationalism immediately identified itself with a "negative reference" to the Vietnamese control of administrative management and urban economy. "It is the cause of all of our ills," Khemeravanich declared in July 1934 in *La Presse indochinoise.* The debate themes were announced and disseminated within the framework of *krumsamaki*— solidarity groups that arose outside the Buddhist Sangha—constituted after 1930. The most important of these was the Association des anciens élèves du Lycée Sisowath (Sisowath High School Alumni Association), founded by Son Ngoc Thanh, which was deeply rooted in the provinces. These groups exalted Khmer solidarity, the sense of belonging to a nation, the concept of a national monarchy. The alumni association, closely linked to *Nagaravatta,* organized a Sisowath student strike in May 1936 against official attempts to make students over twenty years old pay individual taxes. The outlines of a nationalist project critical of both the Vietnamese and Chinese presence and of the French administration took form in a demonstration in Phnom Penh on July 20, 1942. It looked to a Buddhist revival as the source of a new Khmer national identity and took comfort in the unifying function of Buddhism, which basically held peasant society together and assured its adhesion to the traditional representation of royalty (the king was regarded as a Bodhisattva). Buddhism was a refuge for Khmer national identity, which it imprinted with its own moral code and its tendency to withdrawal and minimal cooperation with the authorities.

These characteristics—connected to the loosening of traditional ties between peasants and the new Khmer civil service, an embryonic privileged class derived from narrow recruitment (there were perhaps 20,000 Khmer civil servants in 1939)— were already directly perceptible in the surprising peasant movement of 1916, which involved a sudden general uprising against the recruitment of increasing numbers of corvée laborers for the completion of a vast program of roadworks launched by the Protectorate in 1912. On November 2, 1915, demonstrations broke out close to Kompong Cham, and two hundred peasants from Ksach Kantal province who had come to Phnom Penh obtained an annulment of their illegal recruitment from the Superior Residency. After January 1916, the movement spread through all of Cambodia, in accordance with the regulations, calling for the possibility of a cash substitution for the ten days of labor that could legally be required. More than a hundred thousand peasants participated, of whom thirty-one thousand walked to Phnom Penh to air their complaints to King Sisowath "in the customary fashion." This was an unprecedented peasant mobilization against the heavy colonial fiscal system and against forced labor, but also against the regulations on the forests and the taxation of fish traps at a time when fishing in the rivers and the Grand Lac was in the process of being monopolized by the Vietnamese, the Chinese, and the Cham. The movement was for the most part peaceful, but some remarkable scenes took place in Phnom Penh: thousands of peasants crossed the Mekong in columns, despite having been prohibited from doing so, entered the royal palace, and, following tradition, joined hands and crouched down before the king, explained their demands, then withdrew. In January 1916, the movement culminated in the provinces, notably in Kompong Cham and Prey Veng. It collapsed after a royal proclamation issued on February 4 confirmed the right to purchase forced labor and promised to punish the exactions of civil servants; it had also been appeased by the king's tour of the provinces. The principal lesson of this "unexpected explosion,"[17] as Forest has shown, was to reveal the division that colonization had created between the peasants and their traditional intermediaries, the notables and royal administrators: in 1916, demonstrators no longer had any recourse but to the address themselves directly to the king.

And so the twofold nature of future Khmer nationalism was established. On the one hand, there was national valorization of royalty, which was, in fact, encouraged by the colonial regime to the extent that it distanced the bureaucratic class from the people, and through its support of the impressive restoration of Angkor by the École française d'Extrême-Orient (French School of the Far East). This royalty was conscious of its political dispossession, practicing a policy of "noninvolvement" and dedicating itself to bolstering its symbolic function. On the other hand, there was the withdrawal of the peasantry into its productive tasks, its celebrations and rituals, its mythical universe.[18] It appeared pacified and had little communication with the modern world in the absence of a social group of intermediaries who could establish this communication and mobilize the peasants for a new historical project. In addition, because of the great amount of available land and the absence of demographic pressure, there were no acute agrarian tensions in Cambodia, except at a few points. Étienne Aymonier's old analysis would remain true until late in the twentieth century: "This race is perennially attached to the idea of not separating its own existence from that of the royal family. The king is the living incarnation, the august and supreme personification of the nation."[19] It was a situation heavy with future dramas.

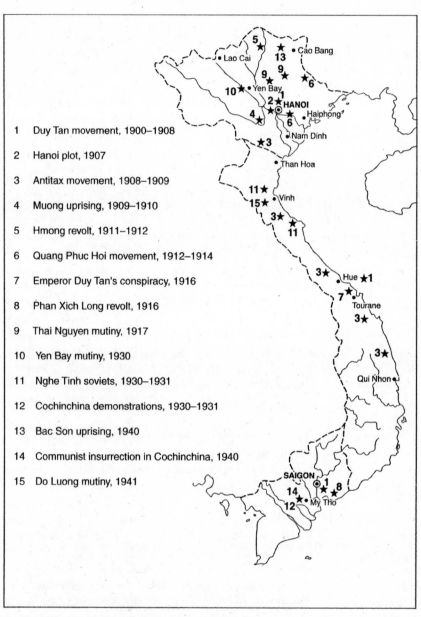

1   Duy Tan movement, 1900–1908

2   Hanoi plot, 1907

3   Antitax movement, 1908–1909

4   Muong uprising, 1909–1910

5   Hmong revolt, 1911–1912

6   Quang Phuc Hoi movement, 1912–1914

7   Emperor Duy Tan's conspiracy, 1916

8   Phan Xich Long revolt, 1916

9   Thai Nguyen mutiny, 1917

10 Yen Bay mutiny, 1930

11 Nghe Tinh soviets, 1930–1931

12 Cochinchina demonstrations, 1930–1931

13 Bac Son uprising, 1940

14 Communist insurrection in Cochinchina, 1940

15 Do Luong mutiny, 1941

MAP 7.1. Twentieth-century revolts against French colonization in Vietnam. (J. M. Pluvier, *Historical Atlas of South-East Asia* [Leiden, 1995], p. 45.)

Secret Societies and Millenarianism in Vietnam

In the Vietnamese lands, the trauma of colonialism reactivated ancient forms of revolt. Heterodox initiatives that aimed to confront the context of moral, national, and social dislocation and to rebuild a utopian, fraternal, "grand unity" retained a powerful mobilizing power until after 1945. During the period of disarray following the end of the Can Vuong movement and the armed resistance in 1897, social dissidence, recurrent in the former Vietnam, seems to have experienced a renewed outbreak, though dispersed. It took the forms of noncollaboration of nonconformist resisting literati, rebelliousness on the part of marginal elements of rural society, and ephemeral revolts by originally Chinese secret societies, or Triads, like the lodges of Nghia Hoa Hoi (Society for Duty and Concord) and Thien Dia Hoi (Society of the Sky and Earth). Firmly implanted where the Chinese were numerous (in the south and in upper Tonkin), these lodges were "Vietnamized" after 1870–75 and would remain very active until around 1920.[20] In 1882–83, the Triads agitated in Cochinchina with the secret support of Hue and the aim of creating a diversion during the French offensive in Tonkin.[21]

There were also periodic upsurges of popular forms of millenarianism, launched by charismatic leaders, Buddhist bonzes, healers, miracle workers, and visionaries claiming to belong to ancient dynasties. These movements brought together the messianic tendencies of Maitreya Buddhism, divination, and utopianism focused on the arrival of the new millennium, exploited peasant mysticism and popular myths, and mobilized crowds of peasants with the help of practices deriving from popular culture. In the north, in 1897, the authorities suppressed the prophetic movement of the Ky Dong (the "Child with the Marvelous Looks"), a young high school graduate who fascinated crowds and distributed mandarin diplomas. This was followed by the plot of Vuong Quoc Chinh, a former member of the Can Vuong who, supported by a network of pagodas, attempted to seize Hanoi on December 5, 1898. In 1912, the authorities were forced to outlaw the cult of the Tam Thanh (Three Spirits) in Tonkin, whose prophecies about the country's liberation had enabled the spread, particularly in the mining population of the Thai Nguyen region, of propaganda by Phan Boi Chau's nationalist group.

The millenarian and apocalyptic culture was especially active in the Mekong Delta, a recently occupied frontier where the imprint of Confucianism was weaker, and above all in western Cochinchina around the region of the Seven Mountains. The Dao Lanh (Religion of Good) sect—which grew out of the Buddhist messianism of the Buu Son Ky Huong (Mysterious Fragrance from the Precious Mountain), preached in the region of Sa Dec in 1849 by Doan Minh Huyen, the "Buddha of Peace in the West"—spurred resistance in Cochinchina until around 1875, then once again during the revolts of 1878 and 1882–83. Mystic sects and Triads were intimately involved in unforeseen explosions, like the uprising of the Triads and Minh sects brought together between 1911 and 1913 by the magician Phan Phat San, an alleged descendant of Ham Nghi and the Ming dynasty, who proclaimed himself emperor under the name Phan Xich Long and unexpectedly attacked Cholon with several hundred of his followers armed with spears on March 28, 1913. This movement resurfaced three years later in a series of local revolts and an attack on the Saigon prison that attempted to free Phan Xich Long.

Far from disappearing in the twentieth century, the millenarian phenomenon persisted, nurtured even during periods of prosperity by the vacuums in rural leadership as it incorporated modern components. In the middle of the decade of the 1920s, a second period of expansion in mystical activity in Cochinchina began with the appearance of Caodaism between 1919 and 1926, and a third followed with the founding of the large Dao Xen (or Hoa Hao) sect in 1939 on the eve of World War II in Europe (see chapter 5). The two served as surrogates for a faltering rural leadership and, at high points of national crisis, turned into anticolonial political-military forces.

Nevertheless, in spite of their vitality, the great popular millenarian movements did not provide an organizing element for Vietnamese opposition to colonization. They could not move beyond the regional context of rural Cochinchina, whose political landscape they nevertheless profoundly marked. Most important, in spite of their underlying anticolonial component, they did not succeed in elaborating a political project. Even as they constituted themselves, nationalism was already at work in the heart and the periphery of the Vietnamese cities.

THE EMERGENCE OF VIETNAMESE NATIONALISM

Vietnamese nationalism found expression starting at the end of the Can Vuong movement, through the convergence of a series of initiatives that would build a new national vision for the future. The colonial challenge would be taken up in political terms with a rare precociousness, one that has no equivalent in the history of the French colonial empire. The defeat of the resistance, the partition of the country, the establishment of the tutelage of the imperial state, dynastic chaos from 1884 to 1886, and the consequent crisis of the idea of the celestial mandate not only made a national revival of crucial importance but also undermined the relevance of Confucian beliefs, especially the ethical view of the world characterized by the subject's will to identify the "correct" position for each situation, that which was appropriate for the context and in line with the norms of the doctrine: filial piety, frugality, straightforwardness, loyalty to one's superiors, and the practice of the "five human relations." These proved themselves impracticable in the midst of the historical debacle of the time: nationalism would be as much cultural as political.

Thinking National Ideology and Action

Starting in the decade of 1900–1910, certain words became charged with new significance. Out of these, a new national mind-set would be collectively constructed. For example, *dan*, which signified "child of the sovereign," acquired the meaning of "citizen." Modern nationalist vocabulary—"patriotism" *(ai quoc)*, "nation" *(quoc dan)*, "compatriot" *(dong bao)*, "national state" *(quoc gia)*, "revolution" *(cach mang)*, "democratic republic" *(dan chu cong hoa)*—penetrated the language. So began the transfer of allegiance on the part of the educated elite from the legitimacy of the king to that of the nation: "The king is still there, but the homeland is no longer there. If there is no longer a homeland, what use is a king?" the reformist scholar Ngo Duc Ke asked in 1924.[22] Starting at the end of the nineteenth century, a shift occurred. The Confucian notion of fidelity, and the former allegiance to an imperial figure, now stripped of meaning through the arrival of colonial tutelage, was transferred to the country and to the idea of the nation. As the latter could no longer refer to the monarchy, which had previously been its organizing principle, it became from then on the object of a slow and difficult redefinition.

The introduction of the nationalist project—which simultaneously comprised a vision of the future organized around the construction of a nation-state and the will to take on the question of "progress" and development, and therefore to accept a reinterpretation of the past—certainly took place under the influence of the model suggested by colonial France, itself produced by a powerful nationalism. More important, however, this took place in the context of an uninterrupted debate profoundly influenced by the "social Darwinist" theories of T. H. Huxley and Herbert Spencer, which were reinterpreted and spread throughout the entire Far East by the great Chinese scholar-modernists of the generation of 1898, including Kang Youwei, Yan Fu, and Liang Qichao. From the perspective of this eastern social Darwinism, the struggle against foreign domination was only a particular case of the general struggle on the part of nations for historical existence. The dilemma was clear: to survive while adapting, through the construction of the national modern state, or to disappear. Its only resolution demanded unprecedented social innovation and a radical redefinition of the content of national identity. This involved both inventing a new culture and spreading modern political forms of national consciousness into a society that was not familiar with them. What was at stake was dramatic and heartrending, since the nationalist project implied a profound rupture with the past, an inescapable "Westernization." How was one to survive and preserve one's identity? How was one to escape from the process of historical annihilation and the exclusion from history evoked in a song of the Chinese revolutionary students of 1911: "Only one thing makes us afraid: being like the Indians who are incapable of defending their land; only one thing makes us afraid: losing all hope of recovery like Annam"? It was a problem that no Vietnamese institution or political movement, communism included, could avoid in the twentieth century.

. Even the high mandarins and the dynasty, despite their participation in the loss of independence, engaged with this problematic.[23] In their view, assuming a partnership with colonization was not only the means to preserve the future of the monarchy but also a way of clearing the path for its modernization, and at the same time, for the development of a neotraditionalist nationalism polarized around the royal figure, perceived as the guardian of national identity. This view was set forth in 1909 by the former regent Hoang Cao Khai:

> The people who find themselves in an inferior situation must accept the support for their development given to them by those who are better off. . . . This is what becomes clear when we consider the past, during which our country was governed by the Chinese for a thousand years. . . . It happened that later, thanks to China, we won our independence. It is a manifestation of a natural law for the strong race to be victorious and the weak one vanquished. It is necessary, if one belongs to the weak race, to have recourse to a stronger one for development.[24]

This vision of the future was also the basis of the gamble of the influential journalist Pham Quynh in the 1920s: a historical pact was possible between the colonial regime and a conservative nationalism that was "wise and reasonable . . . [and] perfectly compatible with a large and liberal French Protectorate."[25] In this view, the revived monarchy had to become, with the support of the Treaty of 1884, the "natural expression of nationalism": "le roi symbole de la nation."[26]

This vision, however, was very quickly surpassed, not only because of the passivity of the dynasty—with the exception of Emperor Duy Tan, who was dethroned in 1915 for conspiracy—but, more important, because of the fact that the nationalist idea initially took root outside of the royal ideology and institutions. Between 1904 and 1908, the debate on the nation began among the members of the generation of literati who had lived through the failure of the resistance to the conquest. This was a heterogeneous and numerically small group—there were perhaps twenty thousand scholars at the end of the nineteenth century—but it was socially hegemonic and in the process of sociological renewal, bringing together the Confucian elite, the first modern intellectuals, who were in conflict with the mandarin establishment, and elements of the wealthy landed and business bourgeoisie that was forming in the south.[27]

Two figures, and two schools of thought, put the nationalist problematic on the agenda. The first of these was Phan Boi Chau (1867–1940). Connected in his youth with the supporters of Phan Dinh Phung, this Nghe An scholar passed the literary examinations but refused the position that was offered to him and devoted his later years to the renewal of the patriotic struggle. He was "the first Vietnamese politician to speak of a Vietnamese nation," Georges Boudarel writes.[28] Phan Boi Chau elaborated the notion of a nation composed of citizens *(quoc dan),* conceived of as a renewed source of legitimacy. He traveled the country from north to south in an attempt in 1902 to bring together patriotic scholars in order to lay out a new project. In February 1905, he chose to exile himself to Japan, from where he led an unremitting struggle against the colonial power. He envisioned the prospect of a pan-Asiatic alliance between the nationalist movements of the Far East and searched for exterior support that he believed was indispensable in the struggle against France. Active exchanges were thus established in Tokyo between his group and pan-Asian Japanese, Sun Yat-sen's Tong Meng Hui (the future Guomindang), Chinese anarchists, and the Chinese constitutionalist movement of Kang Youwei and Liang Qichao.

This activity envisioned the creation of a revolutionary organization abroad, composed of young people who would receive political and military training in Japan. This movement would be capable of spreading among the educated elite of Vietnam, of infiltrating units of fighters, of gathering together the secret societies and what remained of the Can Vuong, and of preparing an uprising aimed at liberation, in sum of forcing the hand of history before it was too late. If the outcome was victorious, a nation-state would be founded that would undertake the development of the country, following the example of Meiji, and the creation of a political system capable of giving the Vietnamese the means of power that was the key condition to their insertion into the world system of states. It was essentially the revolutionary model that Sun Yat-sen conceived and put into practice between 1895 and 1911. In April 1904, with the support of a member of the imperial family, Prince Cuong De, a direct descendent of Gia Long, the founder of the dynasty, Phan Boi Chau created the Viet Nam Duy Tan Hoi (League for the Modernization of Vietnam), often called the Duy Tan League. In November 1906, he drafted a pamphlet that had a great resonance throughout Vietnam, *Lettre d'outre-mer écrite avec du sang* (Letter from Overseas Written in Blood), organized the clandestine distribution of patriotic literature, the creation of trading companies in Hong Kong and in Vietnam to cover clandestine activities, the collection of funds, and the emigration of young people to Tokyo, the so-called exodus toward the East *(dong du).* He also strengthened contacts with the former Yen The guerilla chief Hoang Hoa Tham, with the secret societies of Cochinchina, and with groups of patriotic scholars in central and northern Indochina.

From the 1900s, however, a "reformist" approach developed that was opposed to this historical project of the creation of a state-centered nationalism. The modern Vietnamese press made its appearance with A. Schreiner's *Nam Ky* (The South) and especially with *Nong Co Minh Dam* (Tribune of the Old Peasant Peoples) and *Luc Tinh Tan Van* (News of the Six Provinces), directed by Gilbert Chieu in collaboration with Phan Boi Chau.[29] At the same time, the movement for a new culture affirmed itself, inspired by the son of a scholar from central Vietnam who had fought for Ham Nghi, Phan Chu Trinh (1872–1926). He set out its purpose in his "Mémoire au Gouverneur Paul Beau" (Memoir to Governor Paul Beau) of August 15, 1906, and his "Lettre à mes compatriotes" (Letter to My Compatriots) of March 1907, both of which caused a considerable stir.[30]

Phan Chu Trinh passed the 1901 palace examination, but he resigned from his position in the Ministère des rites (Ministry of Rites) in Hue and met with Phan Boi Chau in 1906 in Tokyo. He returned disappointed and reticent with regard to the new militarist and expansionist Japan, however, and he was no less wary of Confucian traditionalism and premodern forms of popular protest. For him, national construction required a radical rupture with the existing Vietnam. More important, it required that the colonized society borrow the elements necessary for its advancement—science and its technical applications, democracy, and modern economic and trade practices—from its colonial adversary. Priority should be given to apprenticeship in these areas, and it was necessary to put an end to certain institutions (the monarchy, the mandarinate) and forms of domination (such as that exercised by the conservative notables in the rural areas) that blocked this apprenticeship. In contrast to Phan Boi Chau, Phan Chu Trinh and the young graduates who shared his ideas—among them, Tran Quy Cap (1871–1908), Ngo Duc Ke (1878–1929), and Huynh Thuc Khang (1876–1947)—began with a critique of the former Vietnamese regime, which had blocked the path toward a Vietnamese Meiji.

For them, it was necessary to establish a twofold political strategy. The first aspect of it was to encourage progress and democracy within the colonized society, by spreading modern knowledge among the people on a massive scale, which depended on the substitution of roman writing (Quoc ngu) for ideograms and the formation of a network of modern schools, developing a spirit of enterprise through the creation of commercial companies, and, finally, by putting pressure on the colonial power with the help of the modern press in order to elicit the population's participation in political affairs, following the example of the nationalist model offered by the Indian Congress Party. On the whole, the idea was to establish the associative, social, and political structures of a modern civil society and create a public opinion. Phan Chu Trinh was resolutely hostile to any recourse to violence.

It was moreover necessary, in his view, to forge an external alliance, inverse to that advocated by Phan Boi Chau, with the liberal elements among the colonizers, who were active in Indochina notably in the Masonic and radical milieus, and particularly with the democratic forces in France—the Radicals, the Socialists, and the Ligue des droits de l'homme (Human Rights League). In other words, it was necessary to gamble on the logic of modernization at work in the colonial process, and on its potential for decolonization, patiently weighing on history. It was a project that was given some credibility by the policies of Governor-General Paul Beau. After the rigors of Doumer's regime, this Freemason, who was linked to Eugène

Etienne, tried to pacify opinion by modernizing the traditional schools and the literary examinations in Annam through the royal ordinance of 1906. That same year,
he opened the Indochinese University in Hanoi in hope of neutralizing the Dong
Du. He also created the Indigenous Consultative Chamber in Tonkin in 1907.

Phan Boi Chau, like Phan Chu Trinh, fundamentally addressed himself to the
elite, and was convinced that the true interests of the dominant class of the literati
and the rural notables in fact coincided with those of the people. The two conceived
of the social content of the nationalist project in the same way, envisioning the transformation of the literati into a new elite of capitalist entrepreneurs, civil servants,
and modern intellectuals. But Phan Chu Trinh's vision was one of democratic nationalism. He formulated many of the problems that faced the future Vietnamese
society. In his ultimate speech in 1925 in Saigon, Trinh would call for a rejection
of established morals in order to found a social ethics of individual responsibility
(luan ly xa hoi). Phan Boi Chau's vision implicitly rested on the opposite historical gamble—that colonial reform was impossible, and that Vietnamese society, imprisoned in its oppressive conformity and subjected to the overwhelming pressures
of foreign domination, could not organize itself politically. Phan Boi Chau was also
a supporter of a new culture, but the latter seemed to him less an important issue
in itself than a tool for regaining independence and the construction of a state that
would be stronger than society and capable of making it more dynamic. It was a
gamble described well by one of the spiritual fathers of Chinese nationalism, Liang
Qichao: "Imperialism and centralization will be the essential elements of political
life in the twentieth century."

None of the currents of the national movement of the twentieth century would
be in the position to escape this alternative problematic, with which Confucian culture was not capable of dealing. This culture had not disappeared; on the contrary,
it continued to impregnate the collective ethos. The modernizing generations of
1900–20 endeavored to reconcile their innovative views with Confucian moral values in the creation of a "reformed" Confucianism, inspired by readings of Confucius provided by the great Chinese reformers of 1898. A number of the leaders of
the national movement were both nationalistic and Confucian, such as the great
journalist Huynh Thuc Khang, who received his doctorate in 1904 and was a friend
of Phan Chu Trinh, and who, after thirteen years of imprisonment in Poulo Condore, at the age of fifty-one, founded the most enduring of Vietnamese newspapers,
Tieng Dan (The Voice of the People) (1927–43), in Hue. Intellectuals from northern and central Vietnam, such as Tran Trong Kim, author of *Nho Giao* (Confucianism, 1929–30), and especially Pham Quynh, would affirm the relevance of the
"doctrine of the wise men" until the middle of the twentieth century. The Confucian ethic even invested itself in communism, and Ho Chi Minh excelled in its political utilization. Nevertheless, attempts to define the new Vietnamese identity in
Confucian terms did not succeed.

Reformists and supporters of violence maintained a continual dialectical relationship with one another. An ambiguous relationship of "resistance/dialogue" was tightly knotted between them and the colonial power. The conflict between these approaches was not resolved before 1936–39. Yet for a long time, the approach of modernizing democratic nationalism seemed to be the most credible one, as is shown by the events of 1908. Starting in 1906, the modernizers undertook a campaign throughout Indochina, taking advantage of the gathering of scholars for literary competitions. Associated with the members of the Duy Tan league, they created new schools and a network of shops and commercial enterprises (seventy-two in Annam alone in 1908). Their actions culminated in the opening of the Dong Kinh Nghia Thuc (Dong Kinh School for the Just Cause) in Hanoi in March 1907, which had immense repercussions. It marked the beginning of a vast movement for innovation in Tonkin and Annam.

On March 12, 1908, a massive protest began in Quang Nam against the increase in the number of days of corvée owed to the provincial authorities from six to eight, the equivalent of a sudden increase of 18% in the rate of personal tax, but also against the exactions of the mandarinate and the notables, who tended to override the traditional internal arrangements of the village.[31] The reformists attempted to unite the protests behind their project for a new society and seem to have achieved their goal in the Hue region. Authorities were utterly surprised. Thousands of peasants gathered to present their grievances to the *préfectures,* forcing the mandarins to accompany them into the residencies. From Quang Nam, the agitation spread to Quang Ngai, Binh Dinh, and the Hue region, then to northern Annam in May–June. The peasants cut their hair to signal their adherence to new ideas; they demonstrated peacefully, but in April, serious riots broke out in Binh Dinh. The Garde indigène and troops fired into the crowds. In the north, unrest remained hidden and conspiratorial. In Hanoi, on June 27, 1908, there was an attempt to poison the garrison in order to open the way for an attack by Hoang Hoa Tham on the capital, while in Cochinchina, around one hundred suspects were arrested in relation to the "conspiracy" of Gilbert Chieu.

A Colonial Reformism? The "Franco-Annamese Collaboration"

The colonial authorities did not try for compromise. They struck at all their adversaries and chose the tactic of amalgamating the various trends of the nationalist movement. They closed the Dong King Nghia Thuc in January 1908, along with the reformist schools, and ordered forceful repression by the army of peasant protests in central Annam. Hundreds of reformists were condemned in the mandarin courts. Tran Quy Cap faced torture and execution on May 17, and Phan Chu Trinh, condemned to life imprisonment, was exiled to Poulo Condore on April 4, 1908, with sixty or so of his comrades. The new governor-general, Antony Klobukowski (1908–11), temporarily closed the Indochinese University, severely hurt the revolutionary movement, and obtained the expulsion of Phan Boi Chau and Cuong De from Japan, with which France had concluded a political and financial accord in 1907. Under the direction of Resident Jules Bosc, a Bureau des affaires politiques was set up, prefiguring the Sûreté générale.[32] As for the campaign for commercial enterprises, it was a failure.

For a time, the repression seemed to justify the approach of the supporters of armed struggle. Their hopes were shattered, however, by their isolation and the power of the repressive apparatus. It is true that the Phan Boi Chau movement recovered a certain dynamism from 1911 to 1917. The remnants of the Duy Tan League disbanded in January 1912, but, exiled to Canton from 1909 on, Phan Boi Chau reorganized the movement on the basis of a republican approach in May 1912, calling it the Viet Nam Quang Phuc Hoi (Society for the Restoration of Vietnam). It was implanted in South China, Bangkok, and northeastern Siam, as well as in Nghe An, Quang Nam, Quang Ngai, and Tonkin. Its activity consisted of preparing an "Army for the Restoration" in southern China, establishing secret liaisons with the interior of the country, and dispatching armed terrorists there in order to create a climate of unrest. All of this failed, however, as did attacks in December 1912 at Nam Dinh; April 1913 in Hanoi; March 1915 on French posts in the Lang Son region; and September 1915 on the penitentiary (bagne) at Lao Bao. One of the last rebels of the Can Vuong, An Vo, was captured at Nghe Tinh in January 1912, and De Tham was assassinated in an operation organized by the authorities on February 10, 1913.

Even though the colonial authorities had only 2,500 European troops at their disposal at the most difficult point in 1917, they were unshaken not only by local resistance to the recruiting of soldiers and workers for the war in Europe but also by the conspiracy of Tran Cao Van and the young emperor Duy Tan in Hue (May 3, 1916); the uprising of the garrison and inmates of the penitentiary of Thai Nguyen (August 30–31, 1917); the rebellion of Binh Lieu (November 14, 1918, through June 20, 1919) led by the Quang Phuc Hoi; and the plot of Vinh Yen in 1920. In fact, the Quang Phuc Hoi was already essentially dismantled by 1913 for lack of meaningful Chinese support. For the national Vietnamese movement, the attitude of the new Republican China ended up being just as disappointing as that of its imperial predecessor. As Georges Boudarel has shown, the Duy Tan Hoi and the Quang Phuc Hoi were certainly the first modern political parties in Indochina, but they did not succeed in implanting themselves deeply or for the long term.

However, the Thai Nguyen revolt was a turning point.[33] It was headed up by four sergeants of the Garde indigène, by the bandit Ba Chi, and by one of Phan Boi Chau's first partisans, Luong Ngoc Quyen (1890–1917), son of a renowned reformist scholar, Luong Van Can. Quyen, who had received his diploma in 1908 from the Shumbu military academy in Tokyo, had been imprisoned in the Thai Nguyen penitentiary since July 1916. These six men recruited 130 guards, 200 prisoners, and

300 civilians from among the floating population of miners, boatmen, and small-time bandits. Flying the Quang Phuc Hoi's yellow flag with five red stars, they proclaimed independence, slaughtered the French, and took over the small city; it would take six months to reduce the last of the rebels, who had taken refuge in the mountains. The terrible conditions of the prison camp and the sadistic crimes of Resident Darles had unprecedentedly united a brilliant scholar, a sergeant from a peasant family, a gambler and opium smoker, and men from thirty different provinces. For the first time, the regional and social limits of former anticolonial movements were surpassed.

The explosion of this first Vietnamese nationalism had in effect reinvigorated the criticism in France of the Indochinese administration, however, and created a current of thought there favorable to the evolution of the political status of Indochina, leading the Gouvernement général to revise its approach to its indigenous partners. In this respect, it is necessary to detach ourselves from the simple image of a uniquely repressive colonization, entirely deaf to the demands of the colonized. This French colonial "reformism," a colonial extension of the French Republican tradition of social and political reform, seems to have played itself out between 1905, the year the government of Émile Combes in France and its minister of the colonies, Étienne Clementel, officially adopted the policies of "association," and 1929.[34] Starting in 1908, the Ligue des droits de l'homme; its president, Deputy Francis de Pressensé; Jean Jaurès; and the socialist and anarchist press led an active campaign against France's Indochinese policies, for the liberation of those condemned in 1908, and against the colonial scandals. In the beginning of 1911, with the support of Minister of the Colonies Messimy, the Viollette report to the Chamber denounced the methods of the Indochinese administration. On April 9, 1909, following a proposal by de Pressensé, the Chamber voted for an agenda favorable to the "consultative participation of the natives in public affairs" in Indochina, and it adopted an identical resolution on April 6, 1911, after an important debate marked by Jaurès's memorable and prophetic intervention about taxes in Indochina and the regime of concessions in the Congo. In 1911, the new minister of the colonies, Albert Lebrun, relaunched the projects for indigenous representation and entrusted Albert Sarraut with their implementation. Sarraut's two terms in the Gouvernement général (1911–14; 1917–19) probably represented a decisive moment for the future of Indochina, especially since, as minister of the colonies in 1919 and then as a very visible political leader, he was to be one of the principal forgers of French colonial policy in the interwar period. He brought with him a new team of young and often remarkable officers of the Service civil (Civil Service), who already had experience in Indochina: Jules Bosc, Paul Blanchard de La Brosse, and the brilliant Louis Marty, who would be director of political affairs from 1925 to 1934; they were joined in 1917 by Pierre Pasquier and René Robin.

As Agathe Larcher-Goscha has shown, the approach of "Sarrautism" was not simply a tactic, a political gesture, more spoken of than enacted.[35] It was more an audacious gamble on the possibility of progressively "Frenchifying" the upper classes of Vietnamese society and of establishing a durable partnership with them through a progressive transfer of political democracy to the colony. It set in motion a coherent colonial reformism and acted as the expression, within the groups who directed colonization, of a minority current of thought that was an extension of J.-L. de Lanessan's vision. This current of thought was open to the idea of the self-government of the colonized, which did not necessarily exclude the possibility of eventual decolonization, accepted in 1913 by a man like General Théophile Pennequin.[36] Sarraut himself did not entirely dismiss this long-term eventuality. Plans for a "Yellow Army" that would include an officer corps descended from the native elite, presented in 1906 by General Émile Voyron and supported especially by Pennequin, went in this direction. Colonial reformism meant assuming contradictory imperatives: reducing the overly high costs of the Indochinese administration and the too heavy load of taxes, which weighed for the most part on the peasantry, all the while finding large investments to favor colonial development, and, lastly, establishing a coherent partnership with the modern Vietnamese elite. In the face of an emerging nationalism, the idea was to expand the alliances between the colonizers and the budding Vietnamese bourgeoisie. This was likely also the project of the Radical deputy Maurice Long, governor-general from 1920 to 1922, and certainly that of the Socialist Alexandre Varenne, who was put in charge of Indochina from 1925 to 1928 by the Cartel des gauches government.

This gave rise to the policy of "Franco-Annamese collaboration" *(Phat Viet de hue),* a central theme of the colonial discourse after 1911. It consisted of replacing simple, indefinite domination with a very prolonged tutelage of the "backward peoples," while also judiciously extending the representation of the new elite, drawing them into a partnership with the subjugated peoples—albeit a highly unequal one— that the colonizers needed to forge. Phan Chu Trinh was pardoned at the beginning of 1911 by Klobukowski and dispatched, at his request, on a mission to France at the Gouvernement général's expense. In Tonkin, Sarraut reorganized both the Chambre consultative indigène (Indigenous Consultative Chamber) and the conseils provinciaux (provincial councils) of notables, which were extended to Annam in April 1913. He sought to substitute less expensive native personnel for lower-level French functionaries and opened up the colonial civil service to the indigenous elite. The first Vietnamese civil service administrator was appointed in 1913. Sarraut tried to decentralize the administration in favor of the five territories. He also renegotiated the alcohol contract with the Fontaine group. In April 1913, the price of alcohol was lowered, thus both reducing smuggling (and its often-violent repression) and, coincidentally, leading to a rise in the alcohol monopoly's sales and profits. He also gave strong impetus to the Assistance médicale, created in 1905, and made the modern medical system more "indigenous"; commenced reforming judicial procedures and the courts (Penal Code of December 1912); and created the powerful Direction des affaires politiques et indigènes, connected with French diplomatic outposts in East Asia (1912), whose repressive structure was adapted to the new demands by the addition of an efficient system of intelligence. These initiatives were all the more imperative because they served to combat the supporters of an uncompromising nationalism, while compromising with the supporters of a reformist nationalism, and because the collaboration of the mandarinate and the new Vietnamese bourgeoisie would prove indispensable in facilitating the significant fiscal and labor demands placed on the three Vietnamese territories in the context of the war: 91,747 men were recruited, of whom 48,694 were *tirailleurs* (riflemen), 42,744 were workers, and 309 were interpreters.[37]

In 1919, during Sarraut's second term, the audacity of colonial reform reached its pinnacle. The policy of development required a partnership with the Vietnamese elite. Sarraut was advised by Louis Marty, then the presiding official of the Direction des affaires politiques (Political Affairs Directorate), a prototype of the civil servants in Indochina who were sympathetic to Eastern culture, possessed a knowledge of local languages, were open to the dominated societies, and possessed political sense and an inquisitive intelligence. The two encouraged, notably through the expansion of electoral colleges, the affirmation of a current of ideas favorable to the Franco-Annamese collaboration that they thought was capable of capturing national aspirations. This strategy, which the colonists hated and fought against, led to the development of structures of collaboration. It essentially entailed finding a long-lasting historical compromise with a part of the modern nationalists; this compromise was, of course, unbalanced, perpetuating a dynamic and evolving colonization. Thus, on May 1, 1917, on the initiative of Marty and two influential scholars, Nguyen Ba Trac and Pham Quynh, the Gouvernement général sponsored and financed the establishment in Hanoi of *Nam Phong* (Wind of the South), published in three languages (Quoc ngu, Chinese, and French). In February 1919, the Association pour la formation intellectuelle et morale des Annamites (AFIMA, the Association for the Intellectual and Moral Formation of the Annamese) was founded. On February 27, 1919, in a resounding speech at the Van Mieu temple in Hanoi, Sarraut evoked, albeit in ambiguous terms, the need to draw up "a charter, a kind of Indochinese constitution" that would assure the electoral representation of the colonized, who would be given the power to exercise partial control over colonial policies. "It is necessary," he added, "to accord to those whom I call the indigenous citizens an extension of their political rights within the indigenous *cité* [political community]. To put this more clearly: it is necessary to increase indigenous representation where it does not yet exist and to expand the electoral body that can choose representatives."

Certainly, this speech had only a limited concrete application, essentially embodied in the electoral reform of June 9, 1922, in Cochinchina,[38] which increased the indigenous electoral college of the Conseil Colonial (Colonial Council) from 1,800 to 20,000 voters—out of three million inhabitants—and its representation to ten seats out of twenty-six, instead of six. At the beginning of the 1920s, out of all the French colonies, Indochina was the only one in which the colonized elite had electoral representation, though this was admittedly impeded by multiple limitations on its power. Nothing had been played out, but it seemed as if a historical space was opening up for the reformist nationalist project. In fact, this project exerted a genuine attraction for the youth at least until 1923, as is attested, for example, by the first political choice of the young Ho Chi Minh, whose real name was Nguyen Tat Thanh. This son of a revoked mandarin held views close to those of the reformist Phan Chu Trinh when he left for Marseille in June 1911. In September, he presented his candidacy to the École coloniale (Colonial School), which at the time had a section open to Indochinese students, to the president of the Republic.[39] Like the future Ho Chi Minh, from the 1910s on, a number of other young people also undertook the "voyage to the West" *(tay du)* in hope of appropriating the secrets of power and modernity. In Vietnam, after 1911, the reformists and the modern bourgeoisie even founded private schools (there were fifteen in Saigon in 1930) and businesses like the Société annamite de crédit (Annamese Credit Company) (which opened its doors in Saigon in 1927), and a modern press flourished.

Far from having a mass following of the kind enjoyed by the Indian Congress Party, however, reformist nationalism in Indochina was in the end identified with conservative forces. This was due to the historical inadequacy of the Vietnamese bourgeoisie and the failure of the French government to respect the promises it had made in 1919. The policies of Sarraut, who became minister of colonies in 1920, and of his successors in the Gouvernement général, little by little became part of a simple, short-term tactic aimed at turning the new Vietnamese elite into clients of the colonial administration. In fact, the only success of these policies was the creation of the Grand Council of Economic Interests, a simple consultative body, which was dominated by the French business milieu, in 1928. With the Great Depression, all new initiatives disappeared. As for Franco-Annamese collaboration and reformism, they remained the domain of small groups, which were unable to form genuine political parties. Those who remained behind the movement were very divided, for instance, between Nguyen Van Vinh's magazines *Dong Duong Tap Chi* (Indochinese Magazine) (1913–20) and *Trung Bac Tan Van* (News of the Center and the North), which supported a period of direct administration provided that it established democracy, and Pham Quynh's *Nam Phong,* whose considerable influence could not be ignored. Quynh (1895–1945), a remarkable figure, linked to Marty, an excellent scholar, educated at the College of the Protectorate, and an interpreter at the French School of the Far East, pleaded in his magazine for a revival of Confucian culture that would disengage itself from the orthodox neo-Confucianism of Zhu Xi and from the monarchical tradition, accord with modern knowledge and values in the context of a reformed Protectorate, and "help the Annamese monarch create a genuine national government."[40] Although neotraditionalism had a substantial following before 1930, notably as a result of the emergence in Hue of the influential scholar Huynh Thuc Khang's *Tieng Dan*, which in 1927 held partially similar views, it had nevertheless not brought its adherents to the point of collective political action.

In Cochinchina, a constitutionalist movement was organized in 1917–19 around *La Tribune indigène*, launched in 1917 by the agronomist engineer Bui Quang Chieu (1872–1945) with secret subsidies from the administration, and the *Echo annamite*, created in 1919 by Nguyen Phan Long. This first constitutionalism was important, because with it, the colonized began appropriating modern political concepts and practices in order to adapt colonial reformism to their own ends. This political apprenticeship was part of a deep movement through which, during the 1920s, the urban Vietnamese elite began to construct a political society in the colonial context. The constitutionalists, like the neotraditionalists, developed a seemingly modern campaign ("more teachers, more schools"); they organized an anti-Chinese boycott in 1919, denounced the scandals of colonization (like the projected monopoly granted over the port of Saigon in 1923), and easily obtained the support of the landowning big bourgeoisie of the south, whose political representatives they became after their success in the Colonial Council elections of October 1925. By 1923, their chances of succeeding seemed good, and they seemed to be a continuation of the movement of Phan Chu Trinh. But, at the same time, constitutionalism very quickly limited its historical ambitions to the promotion of the interests of the rich propertied classes of the south. In 1917, its spokesman in the Colonial Council, Diep Van Cuong, proposed that the right to vote and naturalization be granted only to the elite, landowners, notables, and those with diplomas, expressly denying political rights to the uneducated masses. The constitutionalist movement also saw itself as part of the Franco-Annamese collaboration, in which it saw the beginnings of a future Vietnamese republican self-government reserved for the elite, with which it would have been satisfied. It never went beyond this. It did not try to mobilize the masses, and all its activities were restricted by its promotion of the enrichment of the powerful families of the south and its attempt to supplant the colonists and the mandarinate as the partners of the colonial authorities. Inasmuch as constitutionalism thought "more in terms of class than in terms of nation,"[41] the possibilities for a democratic nationalism and an evolutionary decolonization seemed singularly reduced from the 1920s on, all the more so because, starting then, two new factors weighed in this direction, as well as in the direction of a rejection of French colonial reformism: the radicalization of the younger generation of intellectuals and the appearance of modern social movements.

FROM NATIONALISM TO NATIONAL COMMUNISM: THE REVOLUTIONARY INTELLIGENTSIA (1923-1929)

Within a few years after 1923, an astonishing mobility of individual and collective identities became evident in the cities, while radical protests emerged and the dynamic of the national movement experienced a rapid acceleration. The outcome was the rise of a new political force, that of the future: communism. The latter drew its founding followers from a new social group: the revolutionary intelligentsia.

New Generations of Intellectuals

Before this period, the active elements of the nationalist movement had primarily been recruited from the old-style literati, who often refused to learn French. In the 1920s, the latter gradually receded into the background of nationalist action, and it was henceforth the social group of intellectuals and semi-intellectuals, with modern educations, who constituted its leading wing. Sociologically, this group was formed following the entrance of a significant number of young Vietnamese into secondary schools. According to David Marr, there were perhaps five thousand intellectuals who had taken a modern, more or less comprehensive, course of studies in 1925, and ten thousand in 1935.[42] The majority were pupils, students, secretaries in the administration or in private companies, teachers, and journalists; they often came from families that belonged to the old educated elite, whose former leadership functions they would in fact take on, first in a radical, then in a revolutionary mode. This intelligentsia—in the sense the Russian Narodniki gave the term— was a lasting phenomenon in Vietnam.[43]

In a historical situation characterized by overwhelming foreign hegemony, the new Vietnamese intellectuals saw themselves prevented from carrying out the essential social functions of the modern intellectual: elaborating and disseminating knowledge and ideologies, directing production and exchange, managing policy by both exercising power and playing oppositional roles at all levels of the state and the civil society. Stuck in a lower social status than colonists and foreign civil servants, and placed in a situation of dramatic cultural alienation, these intellectuals found themselves in an unprecedented impasse as a result of the weak development and political impotence of the national bourgeoisie. Some among them, notably those of the younger generation, confronted this historic alienation through revolution. They embarked on social dissidence, adopting or producing a revolutionary culture, interpreting the realities of the world for the society as a whole, and promoting the historical interests and projects of the modern intellectuals (the transformation of society and culture, industrialization and development, etc.), while politically mobilizing the disinherited classes; in sum, they formed a revolutionary elite—an intelligentsia. The historical function of revolutionary nationalism, in its diverse forms, was precisely to deliver a response to the crisis of the intellectuals.

Two resounding events signaled the arrival of this new historical force.[44] The first of these was a speech delivered in Saigon, on October 15, 1923, by a young man with a law degree, Nguyen An Ninh (1900–1943), on the subject of "Les aspirations de la jeunesse annamite" (The Aspirations of Annamese Youth). It caused a sensation through its audacity, its radical condemnation of Confucianism and of France's "civilizing mission," its appeal to the self-affirmation of youth, and its exaltation of individualism. The second event was the twenty-four-year-old Pham Hong Thai's attempted assassination of Governor-General Pierre Merlin at the Victoria Hotel in Canton on June 19, 1924, organized by a revolutionary group—linked to Phan Boi Chau, who was in China at the time—that was confusedly influenced by the anarchism of *propagande par le fait* (propaganda by the deed) of the Tam Tam Xa (Society of Hearts).[45] Nguyen An Ninh proclaimed the impossibility of separating individual liberation, political emancipation, and social transformation. The intelligentsia henceforth had a historic project.

The revolt of the intellectual youth, the milieu of the Vietnamese society that found itself on the front lines of the confrontation with the West, was at first cultural. It was expressed through an iconoclastic rejection of the Confucian tradition and of its unchangeable values (filial piety, absolute authority of parents and teachers), of the gerontocracy, and of the suffocating family, which they held responsible for Vietnam's backwardness. As Philippe Peycam has shown, a real "journalistic revolution" took place in Saigon between 1917 and 1928.[46] The young intellectuals of the new, often ephemeral, press, for which they wrote both in French and in Quoc ngu, carried out a constant campaign for a radical cultural and social modernization, even as they positioned themselves consistently in opposition to the colonial administration. So began a long process of critiques and cultural reevaluation that would destroy the neotraditionalists' attempts to bring about a Confucian revival. "In the past, Confucianism raised Vietnam up to the rank of a civilized nation," the novelist Ngo Tat To wrote in 1929. "But Confucianism also carried Vietnam to the brink of destruction."[47]

At the same time, a volontarist conception of the celebration of the romantic hero was affirmed, for example, by Nguyen An Ninh, a great admirer of Nietzsche. Many turned with fascination to Western literature, philosophy, and the leftist ideologies of Europe. Pacifism and feminism were a success. As Bui Tran Phuong has shown, vigorous feminism, looking to shake off the masculine and familial yoke, was affirmed among the educated elite, inspiring the most influential of the opposition journals in Saigon at the start of the 1930s, Phu Nu Tan Van (Women's News, 1929–34), founded in May 1929.[48] In October of the same year, the journalist Phan

Khoi published a strident "Indictment of the Annamese family" in it. These dynamic, inventive debates continued in *Dan Ba Moi* (The New Woman, 1934–36) and *Phu Nu Thoi Dam* (Women's Chronicle, 1930–34) in Hanoi, as well as other publications. Radical youth looked to the revolutionary West and to Soviet Russia, but also to India and China. Marxism in its Bolshevik form was attractive, but many were passionate about Gandhi and Tagore, as well as about Sun Yat-sen and Lenin.

Even if it affected only a few thousand individuals, this "revolt of sons against fathers," this anti-Confucian "nihilism" of the educated youth, and the constitution of the youth as a political force—something very unusual for a Confucian country—was one of the major events in the twentieth-century history of Vietnam, because the intelligentsia formed through it would be the leaven for the country's revolution. In 1923, a long journey was only just beginning, which the youth started by going into internal exile in a search for another culture and new ideological responses. There was a multiplication of scholarly circles and associations, a flowering of journalism—from 1917 to 1940, close to 300 periodicals were published in Saigon, where there were 29 printing presses in 1932, of which 23 were Vietnamese—and a flourishing of a series of fleeting but combative radical journals. The most influential of these was *La Cloche fêlée* (December 1923–June 1924), founded in Saigon by Nguyen An Ninh, a journalist and remarkable writer who was the genuine intellectual leader of the generation of 1923. Other publications, like Tran Huy Lieu's *Dong Phap Thoi Bao* (France-Indochina, July 1926–December 1928), were no less influential. A kind of populist practice also took shape. From 1925, even the sons and daughters of the mandarins distanced themselves from their milieu of origin. This was the case with the future communist leaders Nguyen Thi Minh Khai (1910–41), the granddaughter of a provincial governor, who became an employee of the Vinh train station;[49] Nguyen Van Cu (1912–41), said to be descended from the great fifteenth-century scholar Nguyen Trai; Pham Van Dong, born in 1906, whose father headed Emperor Duy Tan's cabinet; and Tran Phu (1904–31), the son of a mandarin in the Quang Ngai district who had committed suicide to protest French demands for corvée. They all became simple teachers.

The Radicals of 1925–1926

The turn of the Indochinese youth to political radicalism in 1925–26 coincided with the definitive failure of the reformists, in particular, the constitutionalists, who had invested all their hopes in the ascent to power in France of the Cartel des gauches. In August 1926, the reformists launched a weekly newspaper, *La Tribune indochinoise*, which carried on *La Tribune indigène* and had a certain success. They attempted to form themselves into a true party in October. The same year, their leader Bui Quang Chieu traveled to France to push for the advancement of their program of gradual political reforms. It was a failure, notwithstanding the nomination of

Alexandre Varenne, leader in Puy-de-Dôme of the French Socialist Party (SFIO), the French branch of the Socialist International, as governor-general in 1925.[50] The main reforms of the Varenne administration (July 1925–January 1928) were the new access of the Vietnamese to certain administrative functions, an amnesty, the adoption of strict contract labor regulations on the rubber plantations (through the three decrees of October 25, 1927), the creation of the Inspection générale du travail,[51] and the renaming of the Protectorate's consultative bodies, which became the Chambres des représentants du peuple (Chambers of the Representatives of the People).

Even though these innovations adjusted the colonial system, they did not modify its political structure. Varenne finally fell, the victim of a campaign by colonists (notably the influential planter Marquis Henri de Montpezat, publisher of *La Volonté indochinoise*), of the veiled opposition of the colonial bureaucracy, and of the failure in France of the Cartel des gauches. Pham Quynh's attempt, in September 1926, to create the Parti progressiste du Vietnam (Progressive Party of Vietnam) with some of those who had been deported to Poulo Condore, like Huynh Thuc Khang, and delegates of the three *ky,* was not authorized. In the end, the reformist nationalists remained timid, conscious of their sociological and political weaknesses, which one of them, Nguyen Phan Long, succinctly outlined in 1924:

> The French revolution of 1789 provides useful lessons. . . . Before the revolution broke out, a new order of things was imperceptibly substituted for the former; the rise of the bourgeoisie had arranged the necessary transition from one to the other. . . . And from among this bourgeoisie, leaders of the crowd emerged, captivating by their audacity and genius. . . . Next to these giants, what are the worth and the weight of our "elite"? Without organizers and known leaders, a revolution is condemned to bloody failure and internal dissidence, even without any foreign intervention. . . . Given the considerations laid out above, emancipation would be harmful for us at present, because it would be premature.[52]

In fact, there was a vacuum in the social leadership of the national movement from then on. A complete rupture between conservative nationalism and intellectual radicalism was unavoidable.

The great turning point came in the spring of 1926. The clashes between the intellectual youth and the colonial authorities intensified after the arrest of Phan Boi Chau in Shanghai in June 1925 and after his condemnation to death in Hanoi on November 25 (he was pardoned by Varenne on December 25). They were aggravated by Nguyen An Ninh's arrest on March 24, 1926, then through the funeral ceremony of Phan Chu Trinh, on April 4, which incited an immense national demonstration. In Saigon, more than 140,000 people participated in the funeral cortege of the great patriot. Several days later, in reaction to the sanctions inflicted upon the students who openly demonstrated their patriotic sentiments, a boycott movement broke out in the schools, which then spread to the center and north of the country. At the end of May 1926, more than a thousand students were expelled in the south, with the approval of traditionalists and the constitutionalists.[53] Strikes and incidents in the schools were unceasing during the three following years.

The Path of Revolution

From then on, activism was the order of the day. The intelligentsia turned with enthusiasm to illegal activity. They attempted to create magazines, which were quickly banned, and printed tracts, appeals, and manifestoes. They emigrated to foreign countries, to China and to France, where hundreds of young people from the south went in 1926. The same movement through which the intelligentsia gained its autonomy created a new generation of revolutionary parties, with ideologies that were still unfocused. Among them were ephemeral groups such as Jeune Annam (Young Annam), which flourished almost everywhere, and the Société secrète Nguyen An Ninh (Nguyen An Ninh Secret Society)—a clandestine movement formed by its namesake in central Cochinchina at the beginning of 1928, modeled to some extent on the old Triads, but with a modern agenda—which brought together youth, peasants, and urban workers. The most important of these parties were the Tan Viet Nam Cach Menh Dang (Revolutionary Party of New Vietnam), which emerged in 1924 from the activities of a group of young people from the regions of Vinh, Tran Mong Bach, Ha Huy Tap, Tran Phu, and Ton Quang Phiet, and would spread to Annam; and the Viet Nam Quoc Dan Dang (VNQDD; National Party of Vietnam), founded in November 1927 in Hanoi by a twenty-seven-year-old former student of the École de commerce (School of Commerce), Nguyen Thai Hoc.[54] The VNQDD was inspired by Sun Yat-sen's Three Principles of the People (san min zhuyi: nationalism, democracy, and people's livelihood, the so-called triple démisme) and the revolutionary model of the Chinese Guomindang. Very dynamic, despite the fact that it was under the surveillance of the Sûreté, the VNQDD rapidly recruited hundreds of militants in Tonkin from among young intellectuals, workers, and women. It was distinguished by the emphasis it placed on armed action. In 1929, the VNQDD launched several terrorist actions against Sûreté agents and campaigned against the recruitment of laborers for the plantations of the south.

This renewal of the revolutionary nationalist parties would, however, represent only a brief period of transition for the intelligentsia toward something beyond nationalism. This transition took place simultaneously with the rise of an especially dynamic communist movement. Until 1925, communism still had limited appeal within the national movement, essentially among the small Vietnamese community in France. It emerged from the Groupe des patriotes annamites (Group of Annamese Patriots), which was established in 1911 by Phan Chu Trinh and a young lawyer, Phan Van Truong, and gained renewed strength in 1918 when it affirmed the idea of a Vietnamese nation in the Wilsonian context of the Versailles Peace

Conference, following the example of the Korean, Tunisian, and Indian national-
ists. This was the crux of the *Revendications du peuple annamite* (Demands of the
Annamese People) drafted in 1919, with the collective signature Nguyen Ai Quoc
(Nguyen the Patriot).

The future Ho Chi Minh (1890?–1969) quickly detached himself from the group
and adopted the pseudonym Nguyen Ai Quoc.[55] Born in Nghe An to a mandarin
father who had been dismissed by the Protectorate, he went to France in 1911 in
the context of the *tay du* (voyage to the West), which Phan Chu Trinh had just inaugurated. Like the latter, Ho Chi Minh was then a modernizer, convinced of the
urgent necessity for the nation to enter the era of progress and technology. An
autodidact, he made a vain attempt to gain admission to the École coloniale. Ho
became interested in technology during the war years, which he spent in London.
After the war, he returned to Paris, probably in June 1919, where like several members of the Groupe des patriotes, he joined SFIO and the Freemasons. In the midst
of this political apprenticeship, close to the French anarchists—he linked himself
to the celebrated anticolonialist Paul Vigné d'Octon, a contributor to the anarchist
Paris newspaper *Le Libertaire*—he submitted short articles to anarchist, socialist,
and union papers that affirmed the existence of an Annamese nation. This activism
found an echo in his much-noticed statement at the SFIO national conference in
Tours in December 1920 in favor of membership in the Comintern. Together with
a handful of French Antilleans, Madagascans, Algerians, and a few young
Vietnamese—in particular, the brilliant chemical engineer Nguyen The Truyen
(1898–1969)—he was one of the first colonial militants of the French Communist
Party (PCF) and participated in the founding of the Union intercoloniale (Intercolonial Union) and its journal *Le Paria* (The Pariah) in April 1922.[56]

The publication by Nguyen Ai Quoc and Nguyen The Truyen of the celebrated
Procès de la colonisation française (Indictment of French Colonization) in 1924,
after the departure of Nguyen Ai Quoc in June 1923 for the conference that founded
the Internationale paysanne (Peasant International) in Moscow, marked the first
affirmation of a different, precociously Third World brand of communism. Starting at this time, Quoc's intellectual path consisted of highlighting the fact within
the communist world that the revolution in Asia—and the colonies—historically
represented the "liberation" of nations, their modernization; that its mainspring
was the mobilization of peasant masses; and that communism should integrate the
rich traditions of non-European cultures. In sum, it was another way of stating that
the future of the world was being decided in Asia and the colonized world.[57] Could
this be considered a premonition?

This tiny communist core reached a certain audience through its activity. This
was the case in Vietnam, first of all, where it was perceived as a patriotic protest
breaking the immense silence in which the colonial regime had enclosed the conquered peoples. In France, it took hold among the several thousand Vietnamese

workers, sailors, students, and soldiers. This led to the constitution, within the sphere of influence of the PCF, of a long-standing focal point for Vietnamese nationalism, which in 1926 took the form of the Viet Nam Doc Lap Dang (Party for the Independence of Vietnam), founded through the initiative of the Colonial Section of the Central Committee of the PCF and led by Nguyen The Truyen.

Thanh Nien

A second pole of Vietnamese communism came into being at the same time in Canton, in the wake of the Chinese revolution of 1924–27 and the beginnings of Chinese communism, and in the context of the interest that the Comintern henceforth had in China, and, consequently, in Indochina. Arriving in Canton in December 1924 as a Comintern representative charged with founding an Indochinese revolutionary organization and as part of the Soviet assistance mission to Guomindang directed by Mikhail Borodin, Nguyen Ai Quoc, alias Ly Thuy, formed the Thanh Nien Cong San Doan (Communist Youth Brigade) with nine members of the Tam Tam Xa, almost all from his native province of Nghe An. This group was the constitutive and leading core of a larger organization, a welcoming structure for the members of the new Nationalist parties called the Viet Nam Cach Menh Thanh Nien Hoi (Association of Revolutionary Vietnamese Youth).[58] Created in June 1925 amid a strategic alliance between the communist movement and the forms of colonial nationalism being established by the Comintern, the organization published and distributed a mimeographed bulletin called *Thanh Nien* (Youth), which had two hundred and eight issues from June 21, 1925 to May 1930. Centralized and disciplined, it took charge, with the support of the Guomindang, of the political formation of the young revolutionaries through courses from three weeks to four months long, given in the Chinese Communist Party building, at 13 Wang Ming Street in Canton. Between 1925 and 1929, some three hundred young Vietnamese took these courses, taught mainly by Ly Thuy, before being admitted to the Thanh Nien and leaving for Indochina to create clandestine groups. Some were sent to the Whampoa Military Academy; several became officers in the Guomindang's Nationalist army, then in the Chinese Red Army;[59] others, like Le Hong Phong (1902–42), left to study at the Université des travailleurs d'Orient (University of the Workers of the East) in Moscow, where fifty Vietnamese students were enrolled in the autumn of 1927.

The Success of Communism among Educated Youth

The endogenous process by which communism won over the young Indochinese revolutionary intelligentsia can basically be explained by the ideological needs of the latter, whose interest in Marxism became apparent in 1926, when radical periodicals began reprinting multiple articles from Europe's communist press. Marx and Engels's *Communist Manifesto* was published in eight installments, from

March 29 to April 26, 1926, by the Saigon magazine *La Cloche fêlée*. Communism offered a coherent and united response to the historical problem faced by intellectual youth, and a global alternative to the hopeless perspective of the nationalists' social Darwinism. It proposed a positive vision of the future for nations and people stripped of history, lost in the colonial century, as well as an alternative, presented as "scientific," to Confucian morals, which seemed bankrupt, and to the complex of popular mystical beliefs. It also offered a model of development and of the reconstruction of society and state—that of the USSR. "After having chased the French from our frontiers," *Thanh Nien* declared in June 1925, "we must destroy counterrevolutionary elements, construct roads for transportation and communication, develop our commerce and industry, educate the people, and bring them peace and happiness." This was an essential factor for a national movement whose foreign alliances (with Japan, China, Germany in 1914, and the French Left) had all been disappointing; adherence to communism held the promise of the concrete and effective solidarity represented by the powerful Comintern world apparatus.

Moreover, communism allowed the intelligentsia to break out of its social isolation and take charge of the new social movements. Since 1925, workers' strikes had sporadically erupted in cities and towns. One of the first was the great strike at the arsenal of Saigon (August 5–14, 1925), which repeated the following year on May 5.[60] Conflicts multiplied on the rubber plantations in the south, while sporadic agrarian disturbances also broke out, like the Ninh Thanh Loi affair in 1928. Communism responded to the misery of the peasants and the workers, to oppression by large landowners and notables, to the difficult experience of colonial exploitation faced by the peasantry and the small yet significant proletariat. For the miserable masses, communism provided a reconstitution of the social net by creating new solidarities in the form of the unions, clubs, and brotherhoods that the intellectuals were organizing, which helped to resolve the daily problems of the popular classes. A model for mass mobilization and the organization of social movements, it put the intellectual youth in contact with the immense ranks of the poor.

"Against a modern political organization of oppression, we must pit a modern organization of resistance," Nguyen An Ninh had written.[61] The Thanh Nien signified the end of a purely conspiratorial era of romanticism and amateurism, and the beginning of an era of revolutionary politics and ideological coherence. It emphasized theory and tried to reconcile nationalism and communism by defining a new program associating national liberation and social liberation. It sought to elaborate concepts for action—for example, in the pamphlet *Duong Cach Menh* (The Path of Revolution), authored by Nguyen Ai Quoc in 1927 in response to a confused Confucian text written by a relative of Phan Boi Chau, Nguyen Thuong Huyen; or through writings in *Thanh Nien* magazine. It created and diffused a political vocabulary. The Thanh Nien not only proposed a political alternative for the intelligentsia in revolt by valorizing the working and peasant masses, but it also provided a genuine ethic of reform, renovating Confucian morals through the transplantation of Soviet communist values. To the image of the emancipated, independent modern woman disseminated by the small urban bourgeoisie, it opposed a revolutionary, militant, egalitarian feminism.

Despite its weakness, the Thanh Nien was the first revolutionary organization to operate continuously throughout all the countries bordering China and Siam (where Nguyen Ai Quoc was at work in the Vietnamese diaspora in 1928–29) and to have a plan of action that was still quite close to that conceived of by the nationalists: a phase of agitation, a phase of mass action, and a phase of insurrection. The organization recruited from schools: for example, from the Albert-Sarraut high school in Hanoi, where Pham Van Dong joined it at the end of 1927; around the same time, Dang Xuan Khu, the future Truong Chinh, also joined the movement at the Franco-Annamese School of Nam Dinh. It also recruited from the nationalist parties, in particular, from the core of the Tan Viet, which, in July 1927, entered into discussions with the goal of fusing with the Thanh Nien. In 1929, the latter had a thousand militants in the three *ky,* 90% of whom were young intellectuals.[62]

The Thanh Nien undertook a particularly intensive action in the peasant and working-class milieu, in the context of a so-called movement of proletarianization launched after the Sixth Comintern Congress in August 1928 adopted the "class against class" approach. Young intellectuals went to work on the rubber plantations, in the urban factories, and in the mines. A Vietnamese version of revolutionary populism, a genuine transfer of the intellectuals' social affiliation, this "proletarianization" aimed simultaneously to educate the members of the Thanh Nien and to organize the people. Through it, the organization was implanted in the towns, in the villages of Nghe An, Ha Tinh, and in central Cochinchina, where it used the networks of the Nguyen An Ninh Secret Society. Proletarianization was a genuine success. On the great Michelin plantation in Phu Rieng, there was a Thanh Nien group in 1928;[63] in numerous locations, in 1929–30, the first worker and peasant unions were formed, while the number of incidents and strikes increased (seven in 1927, twenty-four in 1929).

Starting in 1928, the revolutionary determination of the young intelligentsia, the pressure it exerted with the goal of creating a genuine communist party, overtook and shattered the Thanh Nien, an idiosyncratic, transitory organization in which classical nationalism marked by Confucian culture was still very much evident. In the Thanh Nien's eclectic discourse, communist themes were merged with praise for Confucianism, an appeal for national unity, and even social Darwinist fears of "racial extinction." Priority was given to national liberation over social combat: "The current circumstances," *Thanh Nien* declared on October 24, 1927, "compel the Vietnamese people to nourish a national revolution rather than a class revolution. This is why it is the duty of the rich, the poor, the mandarins, and the population to unite to ensure triumph of the national revolution." However, confronted with the constraints of clandestine action in the popular milieu and, perhaps more important, by the exigencies of its own historical development, the young "proletarianized" intelligentsia, who attentively followed the contemporary debate in the Comintern about China that took place in the wake of the bloody defeat of the Chinese communists in 1927, opted for the new leftist course of the International. In 1928, the surge of the current favorable to the creation of a true communist party became irresistible. It carried the day in France, where, in April, the Vietnam Doc Lap Dang ceded its place to a Vietnamese communist group founded by Nguyen Van Tao and then, at the end of 1929, to a Trotskyist group animated by Ta Thu Thau.[64] On June 17, 1929, led by Ngo Gia Tu (1908–35), the Hanoi group of the Thanh Nien founded an Indochinese Communist Party, Dong Duong Cong San Dang, after having deliberately broken with the leaders of the Thanh Nien at the time of the group's May 1929 congress in Hong Kong. This small organization also took root in Cochinchina.

What was rejected was the compromise between nationalism and communism, the "nationalist communism" that Nguyen Ai Quoc had sought. The preeminence that the Thanh Nien had conferred upon the national struggle seemed to render impossible the mobilization of the poor on the basis of their own interests. Henceforth, they sought to affirm a communism of class struggle, in accordance with the new line of the Comintern that anticipated the creation of communist parties in the colonies. The Thanh Nien dispersed, and its remaining members decided to transform themselves into the Parti communiste de l'Annam (Communist Party of Annam), which was essentially implanted in Cochinchina. As for the Tan Viet, it announced its transformation into the Ligue communiste Indochinoise (Indochinese Communist League) on January 1, 1930. At that time there were three communist groups, none of them recognized by the Comintern. Only the VNQDD escaped the attraction of communism. Nguyen Ai Quoc, then in Siam, where he was the representative of the International for the "South Seas" zone, reunited the representatives of the three groups at a secret conference in Kowloon (Hong Kong) from February 3 to 7, 1930. He managed to unify them into the Dang Cong San Viet Nam (Vietnamese Communist Party) on the basis of the project of national liberation directed toward the working class in the context of a "bourgeois-democratic revolution." But the possibility of accords with the nationalist elites was retained. A young militant who had just returned from the USSR, Tran Phu, was named secretary-general. But by then, with the Communist Party barely born, insurrection had already broken out.

1929–1932: S.O.S. INDOCHINA

The conflicts that, over the course of three years, pitted the Vietnamese nationalists and communists against the colonial power, under conditions aggravated by the Great Depression, brought together all of the tensions at work since the beginning of the century: the agitation of educated youth; the beginnings of workers' activism; the social polarization and underlying discontent against the weight of the colonial fiscal system and the corruption of mandarins and notables in the villages; the monopolization of communal land by the latter (in 1937, in Annam, more than three thousand villages, out of around eight thousand, no longer had any communal land); and the degradation of the relations of patronage and of the mechanisms of traditional solidarity that guaranteed the precarious equilibrium of peasant life.[65] The powder necessary for a collective explosion had accumulated everywhere. But the explosion occurred in four different contexts: the large and mid-sized towns of Tonkin; rural and urban Cochinchina, where capitalist relations were the most developed and where rice prices fell in 1930, then collapsed the following year; the miserable and overpopulated provinces of northern Annam, Nghe An and Ha Tinh (Nghe Tinh), where a series of disastrous harvests had succeeded one another since the middle of 1929; and Quang Ngai, Binh Dinh, and part of Quang Nam, where, as John Kleinen has shown, added to deficits in the paddy harvests, the collapse in October 1929 of sugar-cane exports to China left peasants unable to pay their rents and plunged day laborers into unemployment.[66] The movements in 1930 consequently followed very varied rhythms and used diverse methods. There was no synchronized general uprising as there would be in 1945, and the factors of social and political unity were still operating in favor of the colonial regime.

Yen Bay

A trial of force took place in three acts. The assassination of Bazin, a recruiter of plantation labor, by the VNQDD on February 9, 1929, in Hanoi unleashed a spiral of repression and revolutionary violence. The Sûreté was still poorly informed about the exact nature of its adversaries, and mass trials decimated the Thanh Nien. The assassination by Cochinchinese militants in Saigon of one of their comrades on the rue Barbier in May 1929 provoked the arrest of more than a thousand suspects, among them Pham Van Dong, who had been sent from Hong Kong by *Thanh Nien* to investigate, and after a verdict was delivered on July 3, 1929, tensions suddenly mounted.

So began the revolutionary cycle of the VNQDD. The police arrested nationalist militants by the hundreds in Tonkin, extracted confessions, and infiltrated the organization that the party's terrorist groups championed. In mid-May 1929, the Central Committee of the VNQDD met in Bac Ninh to plan an insurrection for the coming year. In July, there was a large trial of 227 of its militants in Hanoi. In October, an explosion in a secret bomb-manufacturing workshop in Bac Giang alerted the authorities. Henceforth, the VNQDD was hunted down and dismantled bit by bit. On January 26, 1930, those of its leaders who were still at liberty decided to stake their all. At their last meeting, Nguyen Thai Hoc declared:

Life is a game of chance. Chance is against us and the party now risks a complete dissipation of its forces. Once fear enters into the hearts of people, they will lose enthusiasm and faith, and the revolutionary movement will become as cold as the ashes of a long-dead fire. We shall lose all support, and we shall be arrested sooner or later. We shall die slowly, locked in prisons and servitude. Better to die now and leave an example of sacrifice and struggle for future generations. If we fail, at least we shall have become men.[67]

A general uprising was set for February 9. A lightning attack was made at Yen Bay: on the night of February 9–10, forty soldiers of the garrison of the fortress that overlooked the Red River, supported by sixty insurgents from the outside, killed five of their French commissioned and noncommissioned officers and seized their installations. The 550 other soldiers, however, did not join them. Within a few hours, the rebellion had been put down. The insurgents' emissary was arrested in Hanoi, and the insurrection planned for Bac Ninh was aborted. In the delta, five other attempts failed or were quelled, notably the Vinh Bao uprising, led by Nguyen Thai Hoc, on February 15 and 16. Several attempts took place in diverse locations; in Hanoi, militants on bicycles set off bombs on the evening of February 10. The VNQDD uprising was crushed in fifteen days, its leaders and militants arrested en masse. Terror fell upon the north. The Criminal Commission of Tonkin judged 1,086 accused, condemning 80 to death and 594 to forced labor and heavy prison sentences. Nguyen Thai Hoc, captured on February 21, climbed the scaffold on June 17, 1930, with twelve of his comrades, with the cry of "Viet Nam van tue!"—"Long live Vietnam!"

Protests and Popular Uprisings: The "Soviets" of Nghe Tinh

Then, unexpectedly, a second, social, popular phase of insurrection began. It emerged in the regions where the destabilization of the fragile revenues of the peasants and the workers coincided with the implantation of a communist organization—often comprised of members of the literate elite—strong enough to dispute the power of the rural notables.[68] The militants of the young communist party incited strikes on the day of the Tet, February 4, 1930, at the immense plantation of Phu Rieng, "Phu Rieng the Red," which three thousand coolies controlled for three days in March, and at the cotton mill of Nam Dinh, where there were four thousand workers. In April, there were strikes at the sawmills, the matchstick factories, and the rail workshops in the small industrial conglomeration of Vinh / Ben Thuy / Truong Thi, where more than three thousand workers lived. This was the beginning, in Quang Ngai, northern Annam, and Cochinchina, of a vast movement of strikes in almost all the industrial centers, as well as peasant demonstrations. A threshold was crossed on May 1, 1930, especially in Vinh, where the bullets of the Garde indigène inflicted the first deaths. Tracts were distributed, there were nocturnal meetings and gatherings, red streamers and flags were draped in the trees, and marches to the administrative centers took place throughout the summer of 1930. In Cochinchina, where there were some one hundred and twenty-five peasant demonstrations in 1930–31 in thirteen out of the twenty-one provinces, thousands of workers went on strike in the Saigon-Cholon area, and tens of thousands of peasants demonstrated between May and October 1930. After this period, the demonstrations diminished in number and intensity. In Quang Ngai, the demonstrations started in the sugar-cane districts, and on October 8, the *préfecture* of Duc Pho was sacked. Agitation took hold throughout the entire coastal plain, self-defense militias *(tu ve)* were formed, notables were condemned and beaten, and there were bloody battles with the Garde indigène and the Foreign Legion.[69]

Then, in the rural areas of Nghe An and Ha Tinh, a third phase, that of the rural soviets *(xo viet),* began. After the bountiful harvests of 1928 and the fifth month of 1929, the food balance went abruptly askew in the wake of the drought and insufficient harvests of the tenth month of 1929. The shortage would mobilize the peasants and workers in both provinces. Despite the repression of the workers' actions in Vinh, the peasant marches on the administrative centers continued, at the initiative of the communist militants, who redirected their actions toward the villages. Some 1,300 communist militants, generally from the former Tan Viet, were well established in the two provinces, and they organized attacks on administrative centers, the burning of land registries, and the liberation of prisoners, and destroyed the alcohol sales points of the state monopoly company *(régie).* An immense peasant wave surged forward with its own demands against the colonial fiscal system, against corruption and the exactions of the mandarins and notables, against the exploitation of the landowners. In the summer of 1930, the *tu ve* appeared, the administrative fabric disintegrated, the notables fled to the towns, and a political void opened up in the rural areas. On September 12, seemingly without a central decision by the Communist Party, which was still in the midst of organizing itself, the leaders of the Regional Committee of Annam—Le Mao, Nguyen Duc Canh, and Nguyen Phong Sac—established soviets, modeled on those of the Chinese Soviet Republic of Jiangxi, in the districts of Nam Dan and Thanh Chuong, where the mandarinal administration had collapsed. The councils of notables were overturned, taxes and debts were abolished, communal rice fields monopolized by the rich were taken back and redistributed among the poor, rents were reduced, ritual ceremonies were forbidden, and Quoc ngu classes were created. The power of the movement was such that the warnings of the Central Committee, installed in Saigon, had no effect. In an atmosphere of exultation, innumerable village meetings took place in Nghe Tinh. Peasant unions and armed militia were improvised. Between September and December 1930, perhaps seventeen soviets were established in Nghe An, and fourteen others were created in Ha Tinh in January–February 1931.[70]

The leadership of the Communist Party was surprised by the extent of the movement: there were a hundred strikes and more than four hundred peasant demonstrations in 1930. But the Comintern saw the Chinese-modeled "soviet bases" as an effective strategy for the entire continental Far East, and it is probable that the Vietnamese communists thought the same. Meeting in Hong Kong in October 1930 with Nguyen Ai Quoc present, the first plenary of the Central Committee radicalized the movement. It rejected the underlying nationalism of the February proposals made by Nguyen Ai Quoc, and advocated the formation of a labor and peasant government according to the Stalinist scheme of a "bourgeois democratic" revolution with a "proletarian" leadership, which would simultaneously be anti-imperialist and anti-feudal. This would in fact be the strategy of the Party until 1975. The new name, Dong Duong Cong San Dang (Indochinese Communist Party, or ICP), which dropped the Vietnamese reference and adopted the Indochinese horizon for the revolution to come, sanctioned this alignment of Vietnamese communism with the "class against class" approach of the Comintern, which could therefore recognize the ICP as a section with full rights starting on April 11, 1931. Priority had to be given to the reinforcement of the workers' role in the ranks of the Party and its leadership, so the overwhelming predominance of the intellectuals and peasants had to be reduced. In a typically Stalinist vein, the Central Committee maintained, in the beginning of 1931, at the moment when repression hit its peak, that the revolutionary movement was on the rise in Indochina, a judgment it reaffirmed in March 1931 on the eve of its own capture. Clearly, the Party had organized the peasant wave more than it had effectively directed it, and it showed itself incapable of organizing the retreat of the popular movements.

Repression and Punishment

Starting in September 1930, these movements faced a relentless French counteroffensive. After the Yen Bay uprising, the *tirailleur* battalions were purged; 10,000 men changed garrisons.[71] The Foreign Legion and the Tho battalions of Tonkin reinforced the units of the Garde indigène in Nghe Tinh. Airplanes machine-gunned peasant demonstrations; districts where soviets had been established were militarily occupied and partitioned in a network of new posts. "Red" villages were burned, and suspects and prisoners were executed: the cleansing of the rural areas was implacable.

In fact, the peasant movement had already weakened in January–February 1931. It experienced a sudden upsurge in May, but then violence became generalized. After two successive lost harvests (those of the tenth month of 1930 and the fifth month of 1931), famine threatened, then broke out, in northern Annam. The local communist centers launched the "fight for rice," the paddy of well-off peasants was confiscated, the theft of rice between villages and violence increased—130 murders were officially recorded. Then the movement took a turn toward food riots and in so doing isolated itself. In the first two weeks of May, the authorities applied

a so-called plan of resistance and combat, which had a deep impact on rural notables concerned about the generalization of violence. The campaign of support for
Nghe Tinh caused a revival of peasant and worker action in Cochinchina from
February to May 1931, but it did not fully recover its initial dynamism. In July, the
insurrection in northern Annam was defeated. Thousands of suspects filled the prisons. In all, at least 9,000 to 10,000 were imprisoned; there were several thousand
deaths and thousands of convictions. In Nghe Tinh alone, perhaps 3,000 peasants
(1,252 officially) were killed by the Protectorate forces, and there were 3,000 to 4,000
arrests and close to 3,000 convictions. The number of prisoners in Indochina went
from 20,312 in 1930 to 28,097 in 1932.[72] In the meantime, the clandestine apparatus of the ICP had been dismantled by the Sûreté, which managed to capture the
entire Central Committee in Saigon in April 1931, as well as virtually all of the members of the regional committees, shortly before the British police arrested Nguyen
Ai Quoc in Hong Kong on June 6, 1931. The Comintern's underground networks
in Shanghai and Singapore were dismantled after the Chinese police arrested the
representative of its Far Eastern Bureau, Y. Rudnik (alias Noulens), in Shanghai
on June 15.[73] The diverse attempts by militants returning from Moscow to reconstruct the clandestine apparatus of the ICP would fail throughout 1932 due to the
efficiency of repressive operations. All of the members of the Central Committee
and the regional committees were imprisoned or dead.

For Vietnam, 1931 and 1932 were the years of the first great mass repression
of the twentieth century. They also, however, saw the first example of the ICP
taking control of the working classes and the peasantry and, no less important,
saw the irremediable failure of nationalism as an organized political movement.
By denouncing the Yen Bay and the popular uprisings starting in February 1930,
the majority of conservative nationalists, the *Nam Phong* group, and the constitutionalists condemned themselves to being political clients of a colonial power
that mistrusted them. Blood had been spilled between them and the youth. The
possibility of defining nationalism in terms of a reformed Confucianism was
closed off. As for the revolutionary nationalists who succeeded in taking refuge
in China, they were unable to regain a foothold in Indochina after February 1930.
In Vietnam, Yen Bay was the swan song of a historically vanquished classical
nationalism. This failure explains why communism experienced such a powerful advance in 1930–31: many young sympathizers or militants of the VNQDD,
such as Pham Tuan Tai, one of its founders, and Tran Huy Lieu, the leader of the
southern section, had joined or would join the only party that appeared, for a
time, capable of continuing the struggle within Indochina. This did not signify
the end of the nationalist political culture, but rather its immersion in the communist movement. The blossoming of cultural nationalism during this period was
essential, but the communist movement was henceforth colonization's principal

adversary. However, by the end of 1932, the ICP had been put out of action by the Sûreté. For it, too, the future seemed bleak.

THE DEFEAT OF A VICTORY: THE CRISIS OF COLONIZATION (1932–1939)

"The crisis of colonization has opened up everywhere," Albert Sarraut wrote in 1931.[74] This was probably nowhere as evident in the French empire as in Vietnam. It was a prolonged, global crisis, in which it is logical to seek the fundamental reasons of the future war in Indochina. Colonial power, which appeared victorious over its adversaries in 1932, would gradually lose its historical initiative in the following years. By resorting to the police state, it merely deferred another, and henceforth inexorable, test by strength. Governor-General Pasquier summarized the colonial practice of the new decade as: "Watch, punish, and suppress."[75] It was a period during which colonization searched in vain for an alternative to its failures.

A Withdrawal into the Empire

To understand this brutal shrinkage of the colonial state's margin of initiative, we must look to the quasi-impossibility of colonial reform, and, in the final analysis, to the structural evolution of French capitalism during the Great Depression. With foreign markets closing, and the French financial and commercial position in central Europe rapidly deteriorating, the empire—and primarily Indochina, economically the most important colony alongside Algeria—became the principal regulator of the balance of trade and investment, which was in considerable decline. It fell to the colonies to bolster French industries that were losing momentum, such as textiles, metallurgy, and sugar. As is well described, in particular, by Jacques Marseille, a genuine "withdrawal into the empire" started, to which the Conférence économique impériale (Imperial Economic Conference) of 1934–35 and the Conférence des gouverneurs généraux des colonies (Conference of the Governors-General of the Colonies) of November 1936 attempted to give a certain coherence.[76] The "autarchic" conception of an "imperial economy," supported by the powerful cotton, automobile, and metallurgy industries, carried the day. More generally, dominant colonial thought organized itself around the absolute dismissal of any thought of decolonization. Sarraut himself expressed an energetic, determined refusal in 1931: "The European edifice henceforth rests upon colonial stilts.... I denounce with all my strength, for Europe as well as for my own country, all forms through which Western tutelage in the colonies might be evicted.... Nowhere, any more in the Indies than in Java, Indochina, or Africa, is the native capable at this time of assuming the operation of the apparatus of modern civilization and manipulating its mechanism to his own profit."[77] Indochina occupied a central place in this perspective.[78] The Indochinese subcommittee created within the Conseil supérieur des colonies in 1930 affirmed this categorically: "France will not abandon Indochina. Its interest, and the interest of Indochina itself, requires this. Indochina is necessary to France from both a political and an economic point of view, and the sacrifices that our public finances have made there, along with the substantial capital that our businesses, have invested there give it responsibilities."[79] In contrast to the tendencies affirmed by British policies in Burma and in India, the idea of modifying the status of Indochina was less acceptable than ever before, since it meant accepting the possibility of eventual decolonization.

To Renovate Colonization and Industrialize Indochina?

There was no consensus on these choices within the colonial milieu, as is shown by the Indochinese debate of the years 1930–38. Several different economic strategies confronted one another. To counter the policy of political status quo and a simple modernization of the colonial economic structures in the context of an imperial autarky (in essence, neocolonialism, in the historic sense of the word), many high commissioners—including Henri Brenier, former director of the *Bulletin économique de l'Indochine;* Louis Mérat, director of economic affairs in France's Overseas Ministry in 1936; Blanchard de La Brosse, former governor of Cochinchina; Alexandre Varenne; important Indochinese businessmen such as Paul Bernard, an engineering graduate of the École Polytechnique, Ponts et Chaussées engineer, and former artillery officer in Chad, then in Indochina, who became a director of the Société française financière et coloniale (SFFC) after joining it in 1925; and Edmond Giscard d'Estaing, president of the SFFC in 1933—promoted a strategy of rapid industrialization in the colonies, notably Indochina. This was not a new project, but it was forcefully reformulated in the books and remarkable studies of Paul Bernard, which were highly critical of the "pessimistic" analysis of the great geographer Pierre Gourou (which Bernard called "a veritable abdication of intelligence").[80] The plan consisted of modifying the mode of accumulation of colonial profit by exporting French merchandise, instead of capital, to the colony; making Indochina, as a second Japan, the financial and industrial relay point for French capitalism in the Far East, a "platform" for exports to Asia, and the support base for the construction of Nationalist China's infrastructure (this was Alexandre Varenne's wager); expanding the domestic market; using industrialization to combat the rising poverty of the Vietnamese peasantry; and, through gradual political reforms, granting the Vietnamese bourgeoisie and middle classes some political power.

In Tonkin, three out of every four peasants were too many, in Paul Bernard's view, and in Cochinchina, one out of two. By 1948, he predicted, not even the great hydraulic works programs then under way would be able to provide for the eight million inhabitants of the Tonkin Delta, where the population increased by 100,000 each year and a family required a minimum of 3,000 kilos of paddy annually. Consequently, there would be an excess of 2,400,000 peasants. The population transfers (transmigration) envisioned by the Gouvernement général, which required an investment of 10,000 francs per family before the first harvest, would be able to settle at most 40,000 annually, and would thus not be able to absorb this excess. Only massive industrialization could deal with this overpopulation. At the same time, it would provide profits for a new wave of French investment and open new markets in Asia to French industry. This perspective was open to political reforms and, logically, did not exclude an eventual decolonization of Indochina once things had cooled down—something that a handful of other "modernizers" in the business milieu occasionally advocated, although not in any concrete terms. It resulted, under the Vichy regime, in the preparation, within the context of the Groupement des professions industrielles coloniales (1941), of a coherent program of industrialization, which would be the prototype of the "Plan de modernisation et d'équipement de l'Indochine" of 1947. It also led to the creation by French business, in November 1942, of the Société d'études pour le développement industriel de l'Indochine, presided over by Paul Bernard.

With the debate over the industrialization of Indochina, a reevaluation of the hybrid structures of the Indochinese Union also began in the colonial milieu in 1938, in the context of the Japanese advances in Asia. In 1938, Varenne clearly outlined the concept of an Indochinese Federation, perceived as inseparable from the project of industrialization, on which French policy in Indochina would increasingly be based from 1940 to 1947.[81] A way of negating the idea of decolonization, which required the acceptance of the concept of the independence of the colonies, it consisted in bypassing the distinction between the protectorates and the colony of Cochinchina through the creation of five territorial powers that would unite the dominant native elite with the local administration under the control of a highly organized federal government directly linked to the French prime minister's office (présidence du Conseil). Varenne thought it

> necessary to form a policy that gives them a consciousness of the importance of their race and their country, which allows them to perceive certain policies for the future; finally, it is necessary [that they] have the impression that the protection of France will lead them to a new political entity . . . a great Indochinese Federation, in which the Annamese will play an important role, since they are the dominant race, which will create new types of juridical ties between the metropole and the colony but, far from separating Indochina from France, will unite them forever.[82]

However, these two options, which respectively anticipated the strategy of immediate development and the future Union française after 1945, were not pursued. For the majority of the French political milieu, the colonial problem, which the Indochinese uprisings of 1930 had foregrounded, was reduced after 1932 to accelerating the development of the empire and at best modernizing its economic and social structures. Because the industrialization of Indochina would compound the destabilizing effects of the agrarian crisis with mass proletarianization, it went against the interests of France's industries. The empire was considered, implicitly or not, as vital to France's status as a great power. Thus, after 1932, the SFIO, which during the major debate about Indochina in the Chamber in June 6–27, 1930, had defended the concession of self-government to Annam as a prelude to its gradual political emancipation,[83] adopted a policy of silence regarding Indochina, content-ing itself with participation in campaigns against repression. The colonies had an insignificant place in the program of the Popular Front. The only changes projected were an amnesty for the political prisoners of the empire and the creation of an in-vestigative committee on the colonies, on the model of the great British investiga-tive committees in India and Burma.

This strategy of "withdrawing into the empire" had as its first consequence the definitive defeat of the Vietnamese nationalists. Deprived of the means to over-throw the powerful French military and political apparatus in Indochina by force—it would be necessary to wait for Japan to take care of that in 1945—they were also incapable of forcing it to a political compromise on the Indian model.[84] It was nec-essary, in effect, for them to mobilize the masses politically, which the Vietnamese bourgeoisie did not dare do for fear of being overwhelmed by the communist move-ment. To this end, it was also necessary that there be a shift in the structures of French capitalism in the metropole and, by extension, in its different components, that would be compatible with the independence of the colonies.

Toward a Conservative Colonial Reformism

Conservative reform—a historically decisive choice, since it laid the basis for a rev-olutionary situation—was, in fact, what was chosen after 1929 by the high-level civil servants who administered Indochina in Paris and the colony starting in 1928. This group—Pierre Pasquier, governor-general from 1928 to 1934; René Robin, his suc-cessor; Louis Marty; and Georges Grandjean, Marty's replacement as the Gou-vernement général's director of political affairs—had worked for Sarraut from 1911 to 1919. They were determined not to give up anything under pressure and were sure they would succeed.

The 1933 attempt to "renovate" the Vietnamese monarchy is a revealing ex-ample in this regard. In June 1930, Pham Quynh called in France-Indochine for the transformation of the monarchy into a semi-constitutional regime (through the creation of a ministry responsible to the emperor, a single chamber for An-nam and Tonkin, elected through restricted suffrage and granted legislative ini-tiative, and a permanent mission from Annam in Paris) with genuine adminis-trative responsibilities. It seemed possible that this might take place after the trip to Indochina of Paul Reynaud, then minister of the colonies in the Tardieu gov-ernment in 1931, and after the return of the heir, Prince Nguyen Phuc Vinh Thuy (the future Bao Dai), to Hue on September 8, 1932.

The high Indochinese administration and its leader, Pasquier, were conscious of the crisis of political legitimacy and the force of Vietnamese nationalism, and they did not reject the idea of transforming the Nguyen monarchy into a national modernized monarchy—in measured steps—and endowing it with a certain political initiative, the first version of what would become the Associated States of Indochina after 1947. As Pasquier wrote on April 14, 1931:

> To fulfill our engagements will be the most legitimate way to satisfy the aspirations of the Annamese nation, to help it become aware of its personality. The modern adaptation of the domestic sovereignty of Annam . . . this should be the goal of the reorganization . . . its pursuit implies a renovation of the indigenous administrative system. . . . The leader of the state, even in the eyes of the modern Annamese, should remain the privileged being who perpetuates the ancestral culture, personifies the collective soul, and acts as the father and mother of his subjects. . . . The young sovereign . . . will be the first modern monarch of Annam . . . choosing his own ministry, organizing a renovated administration, he will implicitly aid us in applying the Protectorate regime. . . . A new Annam . . . will shine in the midst of the Indochinese group, whose final constitution will be an association of states under French sovereignty.[85]

It was a program of simple conservative restoration of the monarchy and the mandarinate, as well as of the Protectorate, which would unquestionably be overtaken in the race with national communism that was under way.

Enthroned as the ruler with the name of Bao Dai, the new sovereign, talented but irresolute, obtained, on September 10, 1932, the abolition of the convention of 1925, and promised reforms in his first ordinance. In 1932, on the initiative of Huynh Thuc Khang, the Chamber of Representatives of Annam demanded a constitution. A veiled struggle started in the court at Hue between the men whom Governor-General Pasquier had placed close to the emperor—Pham Quynh, promoted to the position of director of the imperial cabinet and minister of education in 1932, and Nguyen De, special secretary to the emperor—on the one side, and the most resolute reformists, on the other. The latter seemed to have scored points in May 1933, when Bao Dai proclaimed that he was taking control of the country's affairs by appointing a series of young ministers, in particular, the Catholic Ngo Dinh Diem, former governor of Binh Dinh, named minister of the interior and secretary of a "commission of reforms." Their initiatives (especially to obtain the rewriting of the 1884 treaty) failed, however, because of pressure from the Protectorate and thanks to the abstention of the neotraditionalists, especially Pham Quynh, and the capitulations of Bao Dai.

On July 17, 1933, Ngo Dinh Diem was dismissed, and Pham Quynh became prime minister. But the fact that the Gouvernement général essentially took only its conservative dimensions into account compromised his project to make the monarchy the beneficiary of self-government and "reconcile indigenous nationalism with French imperialism."[86] The mandarinate was purged and given a new status. The three *ky*, however, remained separate and the superior residences remained omnipotent. The situation had reverted to the governing system prior to the 1925 convention. Reconciling political reform with the perpetuation of a premodern monarchy was impossible. The teaching of Confucian ethics was encouraged, and the teaching of ideograms was reinstated. "Do not destroy anything of the old Asiatic edifice and leave the garden intact as we have found it," Pasquier advised. This was a neo-Confucianism that evoked the Confucian "restoration," which Chiang Kai-shek attempted at the same time in China, and which would take the place of moral rearmament for the French regime, its Vietnamese allies among the mandarins, and the great property owners of the south. As part of this project of a conservative reform of the colonial system, the colonial authorities strove to reconstruct the councils of notables, to fill the gap opened between them and the peasantry in 1930, and to struggle against the seizing of communal lands. It was an immobilizing project, which the governor of Cochinchina defined succinctly in 1935, saying: "There are moments in the life of peoples when progress consists of a return to the past."[87]

This conservative reaction, however, took place in the context of growing economic difficulties, which had disastrous repercussions on the capacity of the Gouvernement général to develop socioeconomic initiatives. The general budgets, deeply diminished by the crisis, went into deficit; while it was imperative to support colonial business, it became impossible to maintain the tax levels. From 1931 to 1935, the general budget was decreased by 52%. The problem of the French officials became where to find the financial means to pursue their long-term objective of modernizing the colonial economy in order to enhance Franco-Indochinese trade. How could they simultaneously finance the enormous water and agricultural projects through which the colonial authorities sought to address a rural underdevelopment that Governor-General Robin called "rural pauperism" in 1931?[88] It was a crucial question. "Can the collaborative intervention of the colonial power and the Annamese government," Robin asked, "through a series of well-conducted reforms, extinguish the virulence of nationalism, bring a balance to the social situation while eliminating poverty, and restore the people's trust in legal authority?" The strategy of rural development chosen by the colonial administration at this time of economic crisis was weighed down by its cost.

The direction taken by the figures responsible for Indochinese colonization in the aftermath of the troubles of 1929–31—refusal to change the status of Indochina, keystone of the empire (how could the French resist the nationalism of the Maghreb if they negotiated with that of Indochina?); stubborn repression of revolutionary opposition; and reconquest of the countryside through a policy of agricultural intensification—was a coherent one. But it presupposed keeping Vietnamese society passive.

The Reconstruction of the Communist Movement

It was precisely this long-term strategy of the colonizers that provided an opportunity for the Vietnamese communist movement, which showed itself capable of filling the political void, and, more important, of surviving the crushing defeat it had suffered almost as soon as it was established.[89] A crucial factor in its survival was the support of the Comintern, which from 1930 to 1935 sent back to Indochina more than twenty Vietnamese political organizers trained in Moscow. Certainly, a number were arrested, but in the spring of 1932, the others established a regional provisional committee for the south, which would be led for a dozen years by Tran Van Giau, returned from the USSR, and in June 1933 they created a Bureau dirigeant à l'extérieur (External Directorate), entrusted to Le Hong Phong and installed on the Chinese border. In France, the French Communist Party had waged a permanent campaign against repression in Indochina starting in 1930, which led to the creation, on March 9, 1933, of the Comité d'amnistie aux Indochinois (Committee for the Amnesty of the Indochinese) organized by Francis Jourdain, Romain Rolland, and Henri Barbusse. Several delegations were also dispatched to Indochina, notably those led by communist members of Parliament, Paul Vaillant-Couturier in April 1933, then Gabriel Peri in February 1934. These initiatives were completed by those of the powerful Ligue des droits de l'homme. This combination would save Indochinese communism.

The initial results of this reconstruction of the ICP were limited. Illegal activity, though it resumed sporadically, essentially in Cochinchina, remained very difficult. There were brief strikes, tracts furtively distributed in the streets, red flags hoisted at night over rural roads. Meanwhile, communism spread in the penal colonies and the prisons, which became genuine "red" universities, where a revolutionary culture was quickly diffused, nourished by the texts of the Comintern and the PCF, where the party recruited new adherents from among the former nationalists, and where it acquired an unfailing ideological homogeneity. "Far from reforming the political prisoners," the Sûreté complained in 1933, "imprisonment seems to strengthen their revolutionary spirit, and each one profits from his time in prison to complete his own education and to teach the other prisoners, including common criminal prisoners. They are all firmly resolved to resume agitation as soon as they are released."[90] From 1930 to 1945, innumerable solidarities, and indeed several of the networks of leaders of the future Vietnam, were formed there. It is possible to speak of a Poulo Condore group (Le Duan, Pham Van Dong, Bui Cong Trung), of a Son La group (Le Duc Tho, Van Tien Dung), a Ba To group (Tran Van Tra, Pham Kiet), and so forth.

La Lutte

The great innovation of the revolutionaries was the opening by the communist movement, in the broadest sense of the term, of a new political front, that of legal action, in Cochinchina. This unforeseen initiative caught the colonial regime by surprise and led to a paradox: illegal, hunted, and in chains, communism was able to take action publicly in Saigon. In truth, the shift to legal action was the result of the initiative of a small group of intellectuals in the south who emerged from the activist nationalism of the years 1923–26. Most of them joined the Trotskyist movement in France around 1928–29 on the basis of a radical critique of nationalism and the ideological ties that, in their eyes, Stalinist communism maintained with it. Sent back to Indochina in May 1930, they worked as teachers in private schools in Saigon and organized several clandestine Trotskyist groups in the spring of 1931, which were decimated by the Sûreté in August 1932.

On the initiative of Nguyen An Ninh, their elder and former mentor, and with the secret agreement and support of the Comintern and the French Communist Party, these brilliant intellectuals formed a front for workers' legal action, including Ta Thu Thau (1906–46), Huynh Van Phuong (1906–70), Ho Huu Tuong (1910–80), Tran Van Thach (1903–45), Phan Van Hum (1902–45), and the remnants of the ICP—two "returnees from France"—Nguyen Van Tao (1908–72), and Duong Bach Mai (1904–65). On April 24, 1933, their French-language workers' weekly, La Lutte (The Struggle), was launched in Saigon (taking advantage of French legislation concerning the press in the colony), along with the group of the same name. They quickly acquired a considerable influence, which was confirmed by the election of two of the members of the group to the municipal council of Saigon on May 7, 1933, and four of them on May 12, 1935. Remarkably knowledgeable, the Lutteurs (Strugglers) undertook an uninterrupted campaign against repression, denouncing the misery of the workers and peasants and the exactions of the administration and the notables, and demanding political democracy and freedom to unionize. They managed not only to turn Vietnamese opinion in the south to their advantage but also to impose a new style of revolutionary action. Until then, the latter had been identified with clandestine combat tied to the activities of secret societies. Henceforth, it also took on the appearance of an open political struggle modeled on those of the great European communist parties.

In 1935, thanks to the group's action, the workers of Saigon-Cholon were capable of resuming their union organizing, and the convicts of Poulo Condore carried out serious hunger strikes. In spite of repeated operations on the part of the Sûreté, which was still on the lookout for opposition forces, the clandestine reorganization of communist groups resumed, especially in Cochinchina, and the ICP was able to hold its first regular convention in Macao on March 27–31, 1935. Although the Comintern had already turned to the strategy of the Popular Front, this convention stuck to the leftist approach, confirming the marginalization of Nguyen Ai Quoc (the future Ho Chi Minh), who had just returned to Moscow, and choosing a new secretary-general, Le Hong Phong, a "returnee from the USSR."

Starting in 1931, dozens of protest movements—strikes against hard labor and hunger strikes—were organized in the prisons by clandestine networks created by the communists. The most notable were those that culminated in 1935, those of March–April (600 strikers) and August–September (over 1,000) at Poulo Condore, and the ten strikes spanning from January to August 1936. As Peter Zinoman has shown, the Indochinese prison system, through its disorganization, its brutality, and confusion of political and common law crimes, was a powerful factor in uniting anticolonial elites. It also drew the criminal subculture into political protest. The prison system benefited the only structure capable of resisting it from the inside: the Communist Party.[91]

Strengthened by the trial by fire of the 1930s and backed by the Comintern, communism appeared in a midst of a phase of repression as a powerful denial of the murky social Darwinist perspective of the nationalists and as an alternative to the "loss of Viet Nam." For the first time in its history, the Sûreté was unable to destroy one of its opponents. During this period of Vietnamese communism, the idea of class became central, and an indestructible, comprehensive project for the future of the society was rooted in the communist conscience. The shift of the intelligentsia was complete: after the radical intellectual came the militant intellectual, a professional organizer of the masses, the future political cadre *(can bo)* of the revolution.

The Popular Front: Indochina in the Hour of Hope

With the rise to power of the Popular Front in France, a point of no return was crossed in Indochina. The entire urban population and an important fraction of the peasantry rose, peacefully, against a colonial power that was isolated and on the defensive. The "June 36" general strike in France and the formation of Léon Blum's government, in which the socialist Marius Moutet was overseas minister, instilled immense hope in Vietnam—and even in Cambodian and Laotian cities—not for a violent and sudden rupture of colonial relations, but for the transfer of French political democracy and social legislation to Indochina. The amnesty of August 27, which liberated around 1,500 political prisoners and reduced many sentences, seemed to validate this hope. It freed for action militants trained in the prisons, among them many of the future Vietnamese communist leaders (Pham Van Dong, Le Duc Tho, Truong Chinh, Nguyen Van Cu, Le Duan, Nguyen Van Linh, etc.). Two great collective movements followed in 1936–37. The first of these was the movement for the creation of an "Indochinese Congress," launched from Saigon by La Lutte on May 27, 1936, with the support of the clandestine ICP, which had aligned itself in July 1936 with the Comintern's "Anti-Imperialist Popular Front" policy and therefore was allied both with right-wing nationalism and with the French Left. The Indochinese Congress also had the support of the Trotskyists and of a portion of the constitutionalists. It involved the preparation of *cahiers de vœux* (wish lists) in preparation for the arrival of the "investigative commission" that was to be sent to the colonies by the Popular Front. To this effect, the La Lutte group established, with the aid of clandestine militants and former political prisoners, close to six hundred "Action Committees" in Cochinchina. If the campaign for the Congress, easily impeded by the administrations of the protectorates, failed in Tonkin and Annam, agitation in Cochinchina in the south was intense in the second half of 1936. Worried by the changing attitudes of the people and the disarray of the rural notables, the Gouvernement général secured the outlawing of the Congress, on September 9, 1936, by Marius Moutet.

By then, the terrain of confrontation between the colonial regime and Vietnamese society had already shifted. On the eve of the Popular Front, the condition of the workers had become economically intolerable. The economic recovery had resulted in a sharp rise in prices during the third quarter of 1936, while workers had endured six years of harsh salary reductions. A wave of strikes, the biggest in the history of Vietnam—a distant echo of the French strikes of June 1936—shook Indochina. Most Vietnamese and Chinese wageworkers were mobilized between the beginning of August 1936 and March 1937. Partial statistics counted some 298 strikes, for perhaps 500,000 to 1,000,000 more or less stable workers, but there were probably nearer to 1,000 between the summer of 1936 and the winter of 1937–38 (fig. 7.1a).[92] The movement was especially intense in the south, where at least 347 strikes took place from June 1936 to August 1937, resulting in the loss of more than 100,000 days of work (fig. 7.1b).

The strikes had three characteristics. They paralyzed traditional small businesses like the sawmills and potteries of Cochinchina, as well as major enterprises like the Naval Arsenal of Saigon, the Compagnie française des tramways (French Tramway Company), the rubber plantations, the coal fields of Hon Gai and Dong Trieu—the strike there lasted for more than a month, from November 3, 1936, to early December—and the great cotton-spinning mill of Nam Dinh. They were peaceful: workers and coolies drafted lists of demands, elected delegates to negotiate with the bosses, and returned to work once their demands were more or less met. Clearly, the model of the European strike had been assimilated. Only the obstinacy of the colonial management and the Chinese and Vietnamese smaller managers prolonged the conflicts, so that they almost attained the dimensions of a general strike. Finally, the strikes of the workers resonated throughout the rural areas, especially in the south. Peasant protests against taxation, against the taxes on tobacco growing, against the monopolization of land by absentee owners of large estates (latifundia), and for the increase of the salaries of daily agricultural workers had resumed in several regions. Rural order was undermined by strikes of harvesters, the pulling up of tobacco plants, land occupations, and the contestation of the authority of the notables.

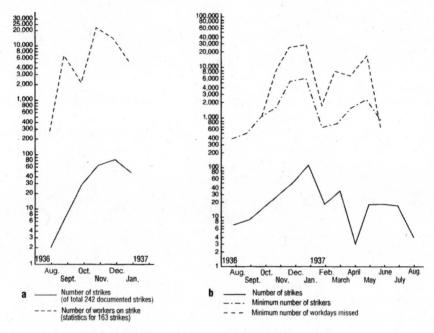

FIGURE 7.1. The strike movement: (a) Indochina, August 15, 1936–January 15, 1937; (b) the South, 1936–1937. (From D. Hémery, *Révolutionnaires vietnamiens et pouvoir colonial en Indochine* [Paris: Maspero, 1975], p. 345.)

At first taken by surprise, the colonial administration quickly evaluated the social movement under pressure from Moutet, who imposed a tactic of arbitration, of nonviolent confrontation with the Vietnamese workers' movement, on the Gouvernement général, which he had just entrusted to Jules Brevié, former governor-general of French West Africa (Afrique occidentale française, or AOF)—and a future Vichy minister—who was reputed to be "liberal" and in any case sensitive to the social dimension of the colonial problem. Moutet and his advisors were conscious of the social crisis smoldering in Vietnamese Indochina, more than in any other territory of the empire. They dreaded the appearance of local or regional famines and a new 1930, and they understood the necessity for an adjustment in peasants' and workers' incomes for a genuine social policy that was the only thing capable, they thought, of stopping the rise of a Chinese type of communism. With regards to the crisis of the strikes, the authorities tended to push for compromise, pressuring the Indochinese bosses to accept the principal demands of the workers, which were more or less satisfied. The strikers thus won a relative victory, securing a 7% to 10% increase in salaries. Moreover, Moutet signed the decree of December 30, 1936, which was essentially a genuine code of free labor and applied a part of the French social reforms of 1936 in Indochina.

The Indochinese Congress, the workers' revolt, and the support for these by the middle classes and the intellectuals had considerable consequences. The historic initiative passed to the side of communism, irrespective of faction. The whole national movement was to remain aligned with the Left for a long time. Legal communism was at its peak. In Saigon, *La Lutte*'s organization, which had supported the strikes, covering them and disseminating firsthand news about them, had by the beginning of 1937 acquired a political authority that made it a model of a political strategy that could be extended to all of Indochina. Two other legal groups appeared, that of the *Nhanh Lua* (Ear of Rice) in Hue in October 1936, led by the communist writer Nguyen Khoa Van, and that of *Travail* in Hanoi in September 1936, organized around a journal of the same name by a group of young communist and Trotskyist intellectuals, including Vo Nguyen Giap and the future Truong Chinh. The clandestine organizations recruited massively in the action committees that had agitated for the Congress and in private and public firms. The ICP was the main beneficiary. The Central Committee of the ICP of the interior, led by Ha Huy Tap, resisted the Comintern-style league of Popular Fronts until the session of August–September 1937, but it gave way in the end. Ha Huy Tap would be pushed aside in March 1938, when the strategy of the "Indochinese Democratic Front" was adopted.[93] The party reconstituted its regional and local clandestine apparatus in many of the provinces, multiplying its groups and peasant unions. In 1937, it was the only party operating on a national scale and unquestionably controlled national opinion in Tonkin and Annam. According to the police, it had perhaps two thousand militants in 1939, divided into a hundred and fifty cells.[94] In the south, the political forces were more diverse. The Trotskyists, who had formed a small clandestine organization in July 1935, were able to provide it with more substance. They formed several dozen unions in the Saigon-Cholon area in the spring of 1937.

At this time, there were probably several hundred semi-legal unions in Indochina; strikes had become commonplace and would continue to be until the war. From then on, the question of the legalization of unions was on the table and, through it, the question of the establishment of democratic rights, which would have forced the colonial administration to recognize a political and social movement largely dominated by diverse communist trends allied to the nationalist Left. There was, furthermore, no extremism among them. Indochina was living through a time of hope and internationalism. Would the Vietnamese push for liberation from the "colonial night" follow the path of a social and political struggle? At the beginning of 1937, this question was unavoidable; as the campaign for the creation of an Indochinese Congress resumed, the great worker demonstrations of May 1 were being prepared, and the former minister Justin Godart, who had been appointed colonial labor delegate (*délégué au Travail*) by the French government, and the new governor-general, Jules Brevié, were welcomed in Saigon and Hanoi in January 1937 by impressive crowds of people with raised fists.

The hopes of the summer of 1936 were dashed during the summer of 1937. Popular Front governments tenaciously opposed the historic dynamism of Vietnamese society. For Moutet and the leaders of the SFIO, subjected to pressure from the Radicals, given that the world war was looming on the horizon, it was no time for political change in the colonies, and even less for the industrialization of Indochina. They focused instead on the French cotton industry. For them, it was simply a matter of reinforcing colonial relations through renovation of the socioeconomic structures of the empire and, in Indochina, of accelerating the restoration of agrarian relations through the immediate implementation of an irrigation program. Any reform of political status was out of the question. What was affirmed by the Popular Front was the continuity of the neocolonial policy put in place after 1930. Renouncing de facto its former claims from the 1930s of self-government for Indochina, the SFIO, except for its left-wing Pivertists, was regressing toward a neocolonialism tinged with social reformism, "democratic colonization."

The French communists, although anticolonial on principle, downplayed the issue from 1936 to 1937. The ministry tolerated political activity in the colony, but it did not legalize it. A decisive test came when a project to legalize the unions, examined in March 1937, was shelved, and unions remained clandestine. At the same time, repression resumed at a slower pace and led in June 1937 to a trial of force with legal communism, notably with *La Lutte,* which had been the most active wing of the political and social movement for the past four years. Ta Thu Thau, Nguyen An Ninh, and Nguyen Van Tao were condemned and imprisoned on July 20, 1937. The administration thus helped rupture the unity of the revolutionaries that had endured since the great repression of 1931. The general strike of the railroad workers of the Transindochinois, from July 3 to August 9, 1937, was broken; hundreds of arrests were made. The Popular Front was in the end merely the final lost chance of peaceful decolonization.

1936–1939: The Forgotten Turning Point in Vietnamese History

In the colonial history of France and the colonized societies of Indochina, the historical split of 1936–37 would be of prime importance, even in Cambodia and Laos, where modern nationalisms emerged. It was, however, in Vietnam that the future of the peninsula would be reoriented by the closing down of the historic possibility that had seemingly opened up in 1936—that of a gradual decolonization carried out through an accord between the French Left and a Vietnamese national movement reoriented toward the Left. One symptom of this closure was the polemic that developed between the communists and Trotskyists starting in the spring of 1937 on the conduct to observe regarding the Popular Front and, more generally, about the orientation of the historic project of "national liberation." It led in the beginning of June 1937 to the rupture of the unified front that had associated them, since 1937, under the umbrella of *La Lutte.* Henceforth, an ideological war raged between the Trotskyists and the Stalinists. The Trotskyists supported a primarily political combat in the form of social and political struggles that were to lead to political democracy and urban revolution. Skeptical of the possibility of gradual decolonization and constrained by its allegiance to the Comintern to apply (despite its discomfort with this) the strategy of support for the French Popular Front, the ICP opposed to the Trotskyist approach a path that was increasingly close to that taken by Maoist communism in China: the construction of a National Front under communist hegemony, the implantation of the Party among the peasantry as well as among the urban masses, a patient conservation of its forces, and the gathering of diverse currents of the national movement together into a network of mass organizations formed and controlled by the communists.

In this way, a vigorous "national communism" affirmed itself, adopting the approach of what was called the "Indochinese Democratic Front," which was implemented by the ICP starting in March 1938 and led to the Viet Minh strategy in 1941. The creation of a single national party was under way. Undoubtedly, this change involved difficult debates. In 1938–39, it led the ICP to be content with limited objectives (social reforms, democratic freedom), to propose a political accord of all the classes and all the French in Indochina against the Japanese threat, and to substitute a multitude of workers' associations, study groups, clubs, and cooperatives that could operate semi-legally for the red unions. They also developed, in the three *ky,* a Vietnamese press *(Tuong Lai, Ban Dan, Doi Moi)* and a French press *(Demain, Le Peuple)* and sought to be represented in the official institutions; in the elections for the Chamber of Representatives in Tonkin in 1938, the lists supported by the ICP obtained fifteen seats. But the new strategy also led to a great deal of confusion: was it necessary to choose between French imperialism and the Japanese peril? Should the national future be conceived of in terms of Indochina or Vietnam? The ICP was unable to deliver a clear answer to this dilemma, and in 1938–39, it defended an ambiguous "anti-fascist front" policy that confused more than a few of its militants.

This encouraged the fragmentation of the national political field on the eve of war. The Trotskyist opposition, itself split between those who rejected any compromise with the Stalinists and those who, like Ta Thu Thau, did not exclude some dialogue with them, did well in the south, where its press acquired great influence, and on April 30, 1939, Trotskyist candidates won four seats on the Colonial Council of Cochinchina, defeating their Stalinist and constitutionalist adversaries. The VNQDD sought to organize itself in Nationalist China. In Hanoi, a new nationalist revolutionary generation—the belated heirs of Phan Boi Chau, equally influenced by the political models of Japan and European fascisms, and also anticommunist—tried to renew the theme of the "survival of the people" inspired by social Darwinism. This evolved in intellectual and student circles in Hanoi around the figure of Nhat Linh (Nguyen Tuong Tam) and organized itself into small, secret groups. The most notable was the Dai Viet Quoc Dan Dang (Nationalist Party of Greater Vietnam), founded in 1939 by the law student Truong Tu Anh.[95] In Cochinchina, Caodaism consolidated its position, while in Chau Doc region there appeared the blazing frontier "millenarianism" (J. Chesneaux) of Hoa Hao, steeped in the millenarian tradition of western Cochinchina and based on the mystical experience of a young man of nineteen, Huynh Phu So, who on July 4, 1939, started preaching a reformed Buddhism, a new path to community salvation that quickly mobilized hundreds of thousands of peasants.[96]

At this time, World War II had been going on in China for close to two years, and Indochina was suddenly in the immediate rear of the front lines. This rear seemed much weakened to the colonial high administration, given the magnitude of Japanese threat, certainly, but equally because the Vietnamese link in the colonial chain was now more brittle. In combination with the political hegemony of an especially dynamic communism, nationalist culture exerted a profound influence on Indochina's evolving modern civil society. Since 1923, the advance of political consciousness in Vietnamese society had been considerable. In this regard there is no better, more lucid testimony than that offered by the future director-general of the Sûreté, Georges Grandjean, in January 1931:

> We no longer have anyone with us. The mandarins, to whom we have only ever given an insufficient moral and material position, serve us only out of prudence, and anyway cannot do very much. The bourgeoisie probably does not want communism, but it still considers that it could be—as in China—put to excellent use externally, even if it is worthless internally. The educated youth is entirely against us, as is the immense and miserable population of workers and peasants. Truly, something more than simple repression is needed here. It is undoubtedly necessary to reform the material order. But it is no less necessary and urgent to restore calm to people's souls. For that, it is necessary to govern and not be content with shortsighted administration. The reforms needed must be carried out immediately.[97]

This analysis was more pertinent than ever in 1937.

The ten years that followed this prophetic warning were lost. From then on, the Indochinese colonial regime, even though it held on solidly to Indochina, was on the defensive. Caught between the neocolonialism of a French capitalism in crisis, the vitality of the Vietnamese political and social movements, and the Japanese threat, it was pushed into a situation in which it could only use the repressive arm, the ultimate recourse in a situation of political paralysis. The requests presented by Emperor Bao Dai to Minister of the Colonies Georges Mandel in the course of the former's visit to France in June 1939—the return of Tonkin to the effective authority of Hue and self-government for the Protectorate—were stymied by the imperative of a more rational development of the empire: "to reduce our budget deficit and thus stop the hemorrhaging of gold," in Mandel's words.[98] The limited promotion policy of the Hue monarchy was maintained in Paris. There was an obvious attempt to invent the future. Already in April 1931, Pasquier envisaged an "association of states under French rule,"[99] and in 1938, Varenne put forward his proposal for an "Indochinese Federation."[100] The outlines of France's two Indochinese policies of 1945 were already visible. However, in 1939, Mandel only contemplated the participation of the "protected" government of Annam in the management of Tonkin through the creation of a High Chamber common to both protectorates. This was still nothing more than using the Vietnamese monarchy as a rampart against the risk of a revolution. A decree of September 26, 1939, outlawed all the communist organizations: hundreds of arrests destroyed the Trotskyist groups and the remnants of the nationalist parties and drove the ICP completely underground. The penal colonies filled up again. But all the evidence suggested that the final test of strength had only been deferred between underground Indochina and a colonial project with no future.

8

The Decline and Fall of the French Empire in the Far East

World War II sounded the death knell of the old European colonial empires. In the Far East, Japanese military expansion began with the annexation of Manchuria (1931) and continued with the invasion of China (1937). Successive French governments witnessed the crystallization of the menace weighing upon Indochina. Remote geographically, France would be hard pressed to confront a potential Japanese invasion; especially inasmuch as a strong Vietnamese national movement had rapidly developed during the 1930s. The war in Europe, France's surrender to Germany in June 1940, and the refusal of the British and Americans to commit to eventual cooperation with the French colonial enterprise made Indochina an easy target for the Japanese. Meanwhile, given the circumstances and coinciding political interests, including their common hostility to communism, liberalism, and democracy, the Vichy regime signed an agreement with Tokyo. This collaboration between governments, paralleling that between Vichy and Berlin, not only gave French domination of Indochina a reprieve but also left the French with the illusion of a durable sovereignty.

In the Far East, however, French positions progressively disappeared. In China, Vichy maintained parallel relations with the governments of both Chiang Kai-shek, which had withdrawn to Chongqing, and Wang Jingwei, established by the Japanese in Nanking, The French concessions in Hankou, Tientsin, and Canton, and then Shanghai, were retroceded to Wang Jingwei's regime in 1943.[1] During the same period, the Japanese took control of the French concession of Guangzhouwan. With the return of the leased concessions to the Chinese, political and legal privileges, and the attached economic interests, were also affected. In reprisal, the Chongqing government seized the Yunnan railroad. The Free French government, basing its political reforms for the empire upon the 1944 Brazzaville Declaration (meant essentially for Africa), pretended that French possessions in Asia were not beginning to disintegrate. French policy reflected the will to restore France's status as a world power. Deputy Gaston Monnerville issued a reminder that without an empire, France was only a liberated country, but with its empire, it would once again be a great power, and General Philippe Leclerc, commander of the Corps expéditionnaire français en Extrême-Orient, conceived of his arrival in Hanoi as the final act of France's liberation. In Indochina, however, the reality of independence prevailed over the fiction of a restored empire. France, which no longer had the means to implement the policies of a great world power, would go against world trend and exhaust itself in a war that was the first step toward the extinction of its colonial empire.

THE CRUCIAL YEARS

After France's defeat in World War II, Indochina was plunged into a play of antagonistic forces from which the French were practically absent. The links between the metropole and its Asian colonies were disrupted by Japanese occupation of the Indochinese peninsula and further strained by the Allied division of the theater of operations in the Far East between the Americans (the Pacific and China) and the British (Southeast Asia). This situation had a considerable impact on the internal evolution of the peninsula. When war was declared in Europe, Indochina's defensive forces numbered thirty-two thousand men, to which should be added seventeen thousand auxiliary troops, guards, and partisans. Motorized and armored equipment, artillery, and means of communication were, overall, decrepit or insufficient. Modern aviation was limited to seventeen underequipped Morane aircraft. The Navy demonstrated its capabilities against the Thai fleet at Koh Chang in 1941, but strategically and materially, the colonial army in Indochina lacked the capacity to face a foreign enemy alone.

Indochina as a Stake in the Conflict in the Far East

In Japan's expansion at the expense of China, its forces reached the northern frontiers of Indochina in 1939. Thanks to the Yunnan railroad, this region—like parts of Burma that were accessible by road—was one of the arteries that supplied the Chinese Nationalist government in Chongqing. For the Japanese, bringing a decisive end to the Chinese conflict meant preventing military materials from transiting through Haiphong and along the Yunnan railroad. This was Japan's primary "interest" in Indochina. In 1940, a second motive was added: Indochina, in the broadest sense, as well as Insulindia (the Dutch East Indies), was included in the Japanese government's planned new map of Asia. Japanese control of the natural resources of Southeast Asia was prettied up as emancipation of those still under

the yoke of Western colonialism. It is important to recall that Japan was shelter-
ing Prince Cuong De, the nationalist pretender to the Vietnamese imperial throne.
Japanese agents such as Matsushita Mitsuhiro, operating under the cover of the
commercial firm Dai Nan Koosi, had already established contact with individuals
and nationalist groups, such as the Cao Dai sect of Tay Ninh. France's defeat by
Germany in 1940 dealt a hard blow to French authority and prestige. This first shock
was soon aggravated by two other related events. Japan took advantage of France's
surrender to penetrate Indochina: in September 1940, the Japanese army stormed
across the border of Tonkin to Lang Son and disembarked close to Haiphong. In
1941, the imperial army occupied the remainder of Indochina.

Franco-Japanese State Collaboration

The compromise between the Vichy government and Tokyo formed the base for
the new political context of Indochina. Acting Governor-General Georges Catroux
had already closed the frontier with China by June 20, 1940, to stop the flow of
matériel and fuel destined for the Chinese Nationalist government in Chongqing.
The agreement of August 30, 1940, granted the use of military facilities to the Japanese troops so that they could liquidate Chinese resistance. A military agreement,
signed in Hanoi on September 22, placed three airfields at the disposal of Japanese
aviation and authorized the stationing of 5,000 to 6,000 soldiers north of the Red
River. A protocol signed in Vichy by Admiral Jean-Francois Darlan and Ambassador Kato Sotomatsu on July 29, 1941, multiplied the initial concessions: Japanese military units could freely be stationed in and move about all of Indochina.
Moreover, the French government accepted the principle of "mutual defense"
against outside aggression. These arrangements acquired their coercive force after
the attack on Pearl Harbor in December of the same year. Finally, the conventions
of January and May 1941 tied the Indochinese economy to Japan's. In exchange,
the latter "recognized French sovereignty over Indochina" and committed to respecting its territorial integrity. The new political configuration obliged the French
government to accept Japanese mediation to put an end to the brief Franco-Thai
war, started by Bangkok with the goal of annexing a part of the Mekong's right bank.
The peace treaty of May 9, 1941, severed from Indochina two Laotian territories
of this bank, and the Cambodian province of Battambang—a total of seventy thousand square kilometers. Once again, the tutelary nation found itself diminished in
the eyes of its protégés.[2]

THE IMMEDIATE INTERNAL REPERCUSSIONS,
1940-1941

Certain opponents of colonization perceived these three successive French defeats
as an opportunity to put a definitive end to colonial domination. A contingent of

Vietnamese Phuc Quoc Hoi (National Restoration) nationalists entered Lang Son with the Japanese army, believing they were initiating the liberation of the country; but they were simply the dupes of the Franco-Japanese accords of September 23, 1940. Those who refused to withdraw to Guangxi with the Japanese were killed or captured by French troops. It was a cruel surprise for the militants and combatants, who had counted on Japan; however, it did not destroy the illusions of Japanophiles such as Prince Cuong De or the writer Nhat Linh. Until March 9, 1945, "pro-Japanese" Vietnamese nationalists of all allegiances (Dai Viet [Great Viet], Phuc Quoc Hoi) conducted their activities under Japanese cover and protection, while under the constant surveillance of the French police.[3]

The Indochinese Communist Party (ICP) also believed that the moment had come to launch an insurrection. Strongly repressed since September 1939, it had substituted the politics of the Anti-Imperialist Front for those of the Indochinese Democratic Front of 1938. In 1940, the ICP's Central Committee and "Committee of Countries" *(xu uy)* (i.e., Cochinchina, Annam, Tonkin) started planning for armed struggle, a policy change influenced by international and local factors. The Comintern and the government of the Soviet Union, in a period of "non-aggression" with Hitler's Germany, reverted to their denunciation of British, American, and French imperialism, as well as to the idea that the war declared in 1939 was a war between imperialisms, which the communists should take advantage of. In Indochina, the arrival of the Japanese in Tonkin and the first armed operation of communists in Bac Son (near Lang Son); the military hostilities with Thailand and French difficulties on the Cambodian front; and finally the apparent receptiveness of *tirailleurs* (colonial army riflemen) to communist propaganda indicated that the Russian scenario of 1917—war defeatism leading to revolutionary insurrection—was applicable in Indochina.

On November 22, 1940, the ICP's Committee of Cochinchina *(xu uy Nam bo)* gave the signal for the uprising, while the Central Committee, meeting in Tonkin, 1,800 kilometers away, agreed to defer all insurrections. The messenger from the Central Committee arrived in Saigon too late for the first order to be countermanded, however. Eleven out of the twenty-one provinces were in turmoil over several weeks. The infantry, the Navy, and the Air Force crushed the communists. Many were condemned to death and publicly executed in 1941. By the beginning of that year, the colonial order had been reestablished and the ICP was decimated; its secretary-general, Nguyen Van Cu, and three members of the Central Committee, Nguyen Thi Minh Khai, Ha Huy Tap, and Vo Van Tan, were shot. Henceforth, the ICP took advantage of its "withdrawal" to regroup and reorganize its militants and to come up with a political line more clearly suited to the Asian conjuncture in the new international situation created by the Nazi invasion of the USSR and the entry of the United States into the Pacific War.[4]

The Government of Admiral Decoux

Governor-General Catroux rallied to the Free French forces after having been relieved of his functions by the Vichy Government, and the direction of France's Indochinese possessions was therefore entrusted to Admiral Jean Decoux.[5] The fundamental task, and the most important in the eyes of Decoux, was to maintain French
sovereignty and to respect the commitments to which he was bound by the Franco-
Japanese agreement. The admiral and his closest collaborators, like Georges Gautier
and Claude de Boisanger, played a subtle game, trying to preserve what they considered as France's interests while respecting the accords with the Japanese government, in other words, ceding as little as possible to Japanese demands. Nevertheless,
Decoux's team did not realize that, for the Japanese, the colonial authorities were primarily interlocutors who disposed of the administrative and military personnel necessary to the maintenance and successful economic exploitation of Indochina for the
Japanese war effort. The French may have understood the situation, but they had no
choice other than to comply. Before pursuing their "push toward the south" *(nanjin)*,
the Japanese had managed to secure a protected rear guard without bearing the burden of complete responsibility in Indochina.

On the other hand, the presence of the Japanese, the appeal they had for a part
of Indochinese opinion, their propaganda activities, and their collusion with the Indochinese nationalists constituted a danger the French had to counter. In a report
dated April 1943, the administrator Renou noted that the principal issue occupying the administration was the Japanese impact upon the population and notably
the elite, which forced it to grant a great deal of importance to Franco-Annamese
relations.[6] This concern dictated a series of initiatives regarding the colonized to officials in the Gouvernement général.

The Imported "National Revolution"

Although he wrote in his memoirs that he was not linked to Marshal Pétain, but
rather to the only legal and legitimate government of France,[7] Admiral Decoux affirmed his allegiance to the Vichy "National Revolution" in other ways. His politics were not only the product of circumstances, but were equally inspired by a
nationalist and authoritarian ideology. He took an extreme stand in relation to those
he considered "anti-French," repressing the Indochinese communists and nationalists; to this he added sanctions against Gaullists, Freemasons, and Jews. One would
think his discriminatory zeal might have been curbed by the smallness of the French
community and the remoteness of the metropole. The historian Eric Jennings has
pertinently analyzed the results of Vichy policies in Indochina as the tacit convergence of the conservative, if not reactionary, ideologies of Vichy, imperial Japan,
and the Indochinese establishment.

The pro-Vichy French and the Japanese had a mutual interest in preserving the political and administrative status quo in the peninsula during the war. However, this collaboration, the result of certain affinities, but even more imposed by the circumstances, repressed a temporarily stifled rivalry between empires.[8] The Decoux administration combined antidotes to the Japanese presence with colonial and Vichy principles. It manifested respect for the elite—the sovereigns and mandarins—and reinforced the status and the standard of living of civil servants, while recruiting Indochinese in greater numbers. In addition, it demonstrated a vigilant solicitude toward the young, supervising them with care. The first part of this program was essentially concerned with appearance and nomenclature. Since the name "Indochinese Union" hinted of centralism, it was replaced by "Indochinese Federation." The admiral especially wanted to heighten the prestige of the monarchies, and he urged the sovereigns Bao Dai, Norodom Sihanouk, and Sisavang Vong to appear in public as often as possible, although his encouragement did not aim to make them take actual political initiative. Decoux had carefully distributed the roles. To the natives, he assigned management, execution, and even authority; for the French, he retained control, command, and security.[9] The monarchs' activities were chiefly ceremonial, such as the Nam Giao celebration, the "inauguration of the chrysanthemums," in Vietnam. In Cambodia, the Festival of the Waters, Bon Om Tuk, was particularly appreciated. Rites and trips aside, Sihanouk resigned himself to the "role of playboy": "I dedicated myself to horses, movies, the theater, water-skiing, basketball, not to mention my love affairs . . . in short, I lived without purpose."[10]

As for Bao Dai, he acknowledged that Decoux was concerned by the "problem of accelerating the training of a native elite" but also noted that "the resident superior always presides over the Council of Ministers and remains the actual head of the imperial government. . . . In Indochina, the sovereigns reign and the admiral governs."[11] The latter had only contempt for democracy and what he called "its decay." Assemblies like the Colonial Council of Cochinchina and the Chamber of Representatives of the people of Annam, forums in which a wide array of opinions were expressed, became nothing more than legislative rubber stamps and were finally dissolved on grounds that they were foci of demagogy, "especially since the Popular Front."[12] The Federal Council, created in 1941, then the Grand Federal Council established in 1943—comprising representatives of the Indochinese majority, but nominated by the governor—played only an advisory role. An exceptional situation called for exceptional power: an authoritarian figure, Decoux reserved to himself the power to decide quickly, and alone. Since the Council no longer gave its opinion on important questions,[13] the admiral defined himself as "France's last proconsul in the Far East."

Nevertheless, imperative necessities drove Decoux to recruit more Indochinese civil servants, some of them to positions of responsibility, and to reduce the disparity of pay between the Indochinese and the French. In fact, decrees by Minister of the Colonies Mandel in 1938 and 1939 had already opened schools and army officer careers to young Indochinese, and ordered the recruitment of Indochinese civil servants with pay equal to that of French civil administrators. An evolution had therefore been initiated on the eve of the war. In 1940, the chief of the local service of the Cochinchinese police signaled the discontent of graduates and cited six people, "returned from France," whose professional incomes were derisory: two former students of the Polytechnic School earned 100 piastres per month, as did the architect Nguyen Van Duc, whereas his French colleague, who had started on the same level, had a much higher income of 400 piastres.[14] Decoux recognized the anomaly represented by such situations: "Even in my Gouvernement général, the salary of a grade one *tong doc* [provincial governor] was inferior to that of a deputy sergeant of the French Customs."[15] The salary increases were also considered a means of eliminating the corruption of the civil servants and heightening the image the population held of the administrative authorities. A 1941 decree increased the resources of the mandarins: a prefect *(tri-huyen)* of the third mandarinal class received 300 instead of 142 piastres, a grade one governor, 700 instead of 488 piastres.[16]

The Vichy government accorded particular attention to schooling for the young. In an article in the *Revue des Deux Mondes* of August 2, 1940, Marshal Pétain reproached the schools of the Third Republic for having only known how to instruct, instill ideas, and generate skepticism, but not to educate. This judgment was seconded by certain thinkers in Indochina, who lamented the passing of the traditional, predominantly moral, form of education, and blamed the ideals of liberalism, of democracy, and of Bolshevism for having engendered negativity, nationalistic agitation, and the communist gangrene. The ideology of the Vichy National Revolution was disseminated not only through the schools but also to the general population. Pétain's speeches were broadcast on the radio and published in the press, and his portrait was displayed at public crossroads and projected in cinemas. Special emphasis was given to Pétain's role of father figure, because the authorities believed it would be well received by people who accepted a hierarchy of preeminence founded upon age and wisdom. The cult of Pétain was associated with exaltation of the mother country, France. The daily saluting of the tricolor flag and chorusing of the anthem "Maréchal, nous voilà!" in schools were part of a program in which the marshal's aphorisms furnished the subject matter for moral lessons and French essays. Schools and youth organizations participated in great gatherings where young Indochinese and French found themselves side by side and in athletic games, marching parades, and songs commemorated heroes (who were also portrayed on postage stamps): Joan of Arc was associated with the Trung sisters, who had led a revolt against China in the first century C.E., and the sacrifice of Captain Do Huu Vi for France during the Great War was celebrated.[17]

In the official mindset, the strength of nation and empire depended on training both body and mind. The Commission of Youth and Sports, under Navy Commandant Jean Ducoroy, had as its motto *Mens sana in corpore sano* (a sound mind in a sound body). A physical education training college was opened at Phan Thiet in Annam. Along with Scouting organizations, the Commission created an official youth organization similar to the Compagnons de France and, in 1944, six hundred thousand youths participated in the activities of these organizations.[18] Jamborees, Saigon-Hanoi cycling races, and torch races all aimed at instilling a sense of Indochinese solidarity into the young. They did confirm to the Vietnamese that their country was indeed unified from north to south. In Cambodia, the Gouvernement général created Yuvan, a youth movement that encouraged irredentism with regard to the territories annexed by Siam. It founded a "Foyer de Battambang" (Battambang Home) in Phnom Penh in the hopes of attracting and retaining the better subjects of the Battambang province and to "facilitate their training according to French discipline."[19] In Laos, propaganda, clearly aimed at the Laotians of Thailand, exalted the theme of the "Grand Foyer lao" (Great Laotian Home).

Admiral Decoux's policies were two-edged. The initiatives of the French government undeniably contributed to cultivating and reinforcing a patriotic and even nationalistic sentiment among Indochinese. The enlisting and indoctrination of the youth with the goal of channeling their energy toward objectives favorable to metropolitan France had as its primary consequence the reinforcement of a preexisting inclination, dating back to before the war, toward organization and collective action, preparing for its diversion toward other goals. The same held true in the cultural domain, where Decoux perpetuated the administrative tradition weighing upon cultural evolution. The war, and the necessity of "counteracting treacherous Japanese propaganda," could only reinforce this will to intervene.[20] Decoux created the Service de l'information, de la propagande, et de la presse (IPP) and entrusted its direction to Navy Commandant Marcel Robbe. The IPP was also responsible for the official Alexandre de Rhodes publishing house. A literary prize of the same name was awarded to authors. Intellectual activity manifested itself less through the daily newspapers than through the distribution of periodicals of general interest and literary magazines. The magazine *Indochine*, published in French, was not without interest, but it never transgressed the conformity imposed by its official origins. The key publications for the future emanated from Vietnamese intellectual circles in Hanoi.

The Intellectual Elite's Return to Its Roots

A group of scientists led by the engineer, École polytechnique graduate, and *agrégé* in mathematics Hoang Xuan Han (author of the first scientific dictionary in Quoc ngu), created the *Bao Khoa Hoc* (Journal of Sciences) to disseminate scientific knowledge to an educated readership in Quoc ngu. The magazine *Tri Tan* (New Knowledge), whose driving force was the scholar Nguyen Van To, a researcher at the École française d'Extrême-Orient, presented studies of philology, ancient history, and classical literature. Although it was considered too academic by some, this did not prevent *Tri Tan* from contributing to a deepening of the knowledge of civilization and national history. *Thanh Nghi* (Enlightened Opinion) complemented *Tri Tan*. Its contributors, generally younger, were mostly lawyers (Vu Van Hien, Vu Dinh Hoe), but the magazine also published scientific and historical contributions by Hoang Xuan Han, the poets of the Xuan Thu Nha Tap (Spring-Autumn) and Tu Luc Van Doan (Autonomous Literary Group) schools, and the novelist Nguyen Tuan. The *Thanh Nghi* group had as its common denominator the quest for and the creation of a Vietnamese modernity, drawing essentially on French and European cultural sources.[21] Politically, these modernizers were liberals who accepted ideological debate with Marxists. Their spokesman, Dang Thai Mai, was a teacher and a literary critic. Thanks to him the Chinese novelist Lu Xun's *True Story of Ah Q* was translated and published in the magazine. He also publicized the controversy between the communist ideologist Zhou Yang and the writer Hu Feng, and debated with Vu Van Hien on the role of the individual in history and that of the writer in society. The *Thanh Nghi* group, meanwhile, pursued a deepening of national culture while searching for areas of convergence or synthesis with European culture. The magazine's editors were concerned with Vietnamese realities, which they approached through investigations and reports, notably about rural life, questions of industrialization, crafts, and the education of the young.

In another register, the Marxist Truong Tuu (alias Nguyen Bach Khoa), considered a Trotskyist, founded the Han Thuyen publishing house and published numerous poetic works, novels, and essays, including a Marxist-Freudian interpretation of Vietnam's national epic, Nguyen Du's *Kim Van Kieu* (*The Tale of Kieu*) and, in 1944, a Marxist analysis of Vietnamese society by Luong Duc Thiep. Dang Thai Mai, meanwhile, provoked a major scandal, similar to the uproar that greeted Victor Hugo's romantic drama *Hernani*, by translating and producing the Chinese playwright Cao Yu's play *The Storm*, a work about the decadence and disintegration of a family of notables. In 1943, *The Night of Lam Son* and *The Debt of Me Linh*, the first operas with patriotic themes, written by Huynh Van Tieng, with music by Luu Hu Phuoc, were staged in the municipal theater of Saigon. This rich literary output and the diverse interpretations of the cultural stakes can only be explained by the progressive lightening of censorship, motivated by the desire to prevent Vietnamese intellectuals from succumbing to the lure of Japanese propaganda. A communist writer would recognize, twenty years later, that in 1942, a faction of Vietnamese intellectuals had been entirely seduced by the Japanese.[22]

Quoc ngu was the vehicle for these creations and exchanges, which in return reinforced its intellectual and national status. The urban and rural literacy movement disseminated the national written language even further among the population. The Association for the Expansion of Quoc Ngu (Hoi Truyen Ba Quoc Ngu), founded in

1938, was by then flourishing. Even though the scholar Nguyen Van To was the president, the key member, in the beginning at least, was the future general-secretary of the ICP, Truong Chinh. The association was well established in Tonkin and Annam, and an analogous organization existed in Cochinchina. It estimated the number of people who learned Quoc ngu as the result of its work at fifty-one thousand in Tonkin alone, of whom thirty-one thousand were from Hanoi and its vicinity.[23] Nguyen Van To estimated that young Vietnamese, especially the intellectuals, knew their maternal language better than before; he was proud that one no longer encountered intellectuals who prided themselves on knowing how to write French better than their mother tongue.[24] In his attempt to detect the influence of French literature upon modern Vietnamese literature, the linguist and essayist Phan Ngoc has identified the period 1930–40 as the most fertile in the literary history of Vietnam. Writers had "Europeanized" the Vietnamese language in order to remedy its inadequacies when expressing discursive and scientific thought, he contends. As a consequence, literary production was not simply a matter of copying or adopting literary genres, but rather required the creation of an adequate tool of expression for the transition from a "fixed language to a inflectional one." This change necessitated the use of "locutions employed as articulations of discursive thought, all modeled on French." This process, he argues, was achieved in the 1960s and permitted the translation of Vietnamese into Western languages as easily as European languages were translated into other Western languages.[25]

In 1943, the ICP drafted and distributed a cultural manifesto, *De Cuong Van Hoa*, urging writers and artists to participate in the elaboration of a "national, scientific and proletarian culture" and outlining its objectives and criteria. During the same period, young intellectuals such as the writer Nguyen Dinh Thi and the geographer Nguyen Thieu Lau considered the peasantry the incarnation of the nation and its culture as the foundation of the national culture. There was, then, a general movement toward a return to origins and a reevaluation of tradition. The cultural evolution of the Vietnamese during the four years of war accomplished an important step toward political maturity. A maturity analogous to that of political ideas manifested itself in a renewal in the visual arts that paralleled that in literary ones. Vietnamese genius was affirmed in the works of painters trained at the École supérieure des beaux-arts in Hanoi. The talents of Le Pho, Mai Trung Thu, Vu Cao Dam, Bui Xuan Phai, and Nguyen Phan Chanh, to name only a few, were already recognized. They were able to reconcile European and Asian artistic influences, and undoubtedly this synthesis explains why their art did not attract the French public of artists, critics, connoisseurs, and collectors fond of "primitive"—that is, African and Oceanic—art.[26] In 1943, in the twilight of French rule, the Gouvernement général organized an art exhibit in Hanoi where the works of To Ngoc Van, Tran Van De, and Bui Xuan Phai, among others, were displayed next to those of French painters of the seventeenth, eighteenth, and nineteenth centuries. Covering this exposition in the official magazine *Indochine* on December 9, 1943, the critic Claude M. wrote: "The Annamese have no need to blush at the French origin of their artistic movement."[27] These kinds of transformations prepared the ground for the national revolution of 1945.

INDOCHINA'S ACHILLES' HEEL: THE ECONOMY

Indochina was not a battlefield; only certain cities and the north-south railway fell victim to Allied bombardment. The war exerted its trauma principally through the collapse of the economy. More than the economic crisis of 1931, the war revealed the vulnerability of a colonial economy that was not only piloted by a foreign power but also depended on world prices and outlets for exports. The different regions of Indochina had undergone uneven development: Cochinchina exported rice and rubber, and Tonkin coal, while Indochina imported all of its fuel, machinery, and also textile raw materials and cloth and chemical products. By 1939, exports had risen to 4,700,000 tons, which broke down to 2,100,000 tons of rice and corn, 1,790,000 tons of coal, 215,000 tons of various ores, and 158,000 tons of cement. Imports totaled about 587,000 tons: 100,000 tons of fuel, 100,000 tons of chemical and metal products necessary to local industries and crafts, 30,000 tons of industrial equipment (railroad cars, automobiles, machine tools), and 30,000 tons of European foodstuffs (powdered or condensed milk, flour, wine).[28]

The war affected the economy in three main phases. It started to wean Indochina away from its privileged ties with France. During the period 1940–41, Indochina was able to trade with its usual Far Eastern partners: Singapore, Hong Kong, and the Dutch East Indies, but the war in the Pacific put an end to these relationships. In a second phase, the Indochinese economy was subsumed into the Japanese war economy and a part of its resources were drained to sustain the Japanese war effort. Then, starting in 1943, Allied control of the seas and skies interrupted shipment between Indochina and the countries within the Japanese sphere, as well as communications between Cochinchina and Tonkin, whose economies were interdependent. When the 1945 agreement on rice delivery to Japan was signed in March, the Japanese had more than 100,000 tons in stock that they had been unable to transport. The Gouvernement général had to tackle the formidable task of making the economy function in such a way as to satisfy Indochinese needs while respecting the economic accords signed between Vichy and Tokyo. Making matters even more difficult, on August 31, 1941, and then again on December 30, 1942, the Japanese troops stationed in Indochina demanded large supplies of foodstuffs and raw materials and requisitioned transportation equipment.

It was necessary to make the population work to ensure its own means of subsistence. The program to set up infrastructures established before the war, was actively encouraged, notably in the development of "rice-growing areas" in order to settle peasants and expand cultivation. The research and production of substitute products, especially those developed to make up for the absence of fuel, was a success: the administration encouraged the development or expansion of land reserved for castor-oil plants and peanuts. Their acreage increased from 17,500 hectares in 1939 to 59,000 in 1942 and 68,000 in 1944.[29] To meet the demand for textiles, the acreage reserved for cotton increased from 7,000 hectares before the war to 19,000 in 1942 and 52,000 in 1944.[30] The ingenuity of chemists was extended to pharmaceutical products, infant food products, and even to winemaking. The increase in cultivated acreage, the imposed delivery to Japan of certain products (castor oil, cotton, and rice), price controls, and rationing required the implementation of a command economy. With this goal, the government created, on a Vichy model, a series of organizations, the principal ones being the Comité des céréales (for grains) and the Comptoir du charbon (for coal). This type of heavy-handed and often inefficient organization, aimed to preserve the control of domestic and foreign trade with the Japanese, and to regulate an economy sensitive to the effects of speculation and the black market. Expenditure on infrastructure (*grands travaux*) and, in particular, piastres allocated to the Japanese troops (58 million piastres in 1941, 117 million in 1943, 363 million in 1944) aggravated inflation. Fiduciary circulation—364 million piastres in banknotes and coins in 1942—had risen to 1.5 billion piastres by March 1945.

In spite of increases in incomes and salaries, the population felt the effects of shortages and the price increases more and more strongly. A high-level government official noted:

> In spite of regulation and repression, shortages can only translate into a constant increase in prices, which has increased the discontent among the masses. Starting from a basis of 100 in 1925, the index of wholesale prices in Saigon increased to 182 in 1943, and to 329 in December 1944; the general European cost-of-living index rose from 100 in 1925 to 199 in 1943 and to 338 at the end of 1944. The same index in Hanoi was 356 in 1943 and 740 in December 1944. The increase in the cost of living was worse for the [indigenous] working class. The index in Saigon was 236 in 1943, but 437 at the end of 1944; in Hanoi, it went from 541 to 1,040 during the same period. This growth, which was becoming dizzying at the end of 1944, finally became administratively unmanageable.[31]

The Indochinese economy was "on the verge of industrial collapse" in 1944. "What can we say about the year 1945?" asked the Inspection générale des mines et de l'industrie (General Inspectorate of Mines and Industry). "The only recommendation to make would be to give up all new projects, even if these projects only used manpower, because rice must be found to feed workers, and paying them increases inflation."[32]

The situation was dire. Communications and transport, vital for the survival of overpopulated Tonkin, were cut off by Allied air raids and the operations of

American submarines. In the course of the first seven months of 1944, only 8,600 tons of rice destined for Tonkin was loaded in Saigon (compared to 80,000 tons in 1940). A poor rice harvest during the winter of 1944–45 plunged Tonkin and northern Annam into a terrible famine (the number of victims was estimated at 2 million by Ho Chi Minh, and at 1 million by Decoux). In September 1945, when the English inventoried the rice supply in Cholon, they estimated 69,000 tons in the Japanese warehouses of the Mitsui Company, and 66,000 in stores of the Comité des céréales. Japanese stocks in Cochinchina, Cambodia, and northern Annam amounted to 25,000 tons; private stocks in Cochinchina were assessed at 100,000 tons, and those of Cambodia at 50,000 tons.[33] The famine in the north provided an ideal basis for denouncing the deficiencies of the colonial regime, and even a supposed Franco-Japanese collusion aimed at physically liquidating the Vietnamese population. The Viet Minh used this not only as a weapon of propaganda, but also to mobilize and to organize the population in order to seize stocks stored by the French, which were in Japanese hands after March 9, 1945.

MARCH 9, 1945

On the night of March 9, 1945, Japanese troops moved throughout Indochina to disarm the French and take over the administration of the whole country. After localized, though sometimes very fierce, conflicts (notably in Lang Son), the Japanese thus put an end to more than three-quarters of a century of European domination. Some French military units were able to slip into Chinese territory, though because of the incomprehension or the prejudices of the Chinese authorities and the Americans, this did not end their problems.[34] Was this takeover the result of circumstances or part of a premeditated, long-term plan? Since 1943, the war in the Pacific and Southeast Asia had taken a favorable turn for the British and the Americans. In 1944, in a free France, General de Gaulle's government was preparing for the liberation of Indochina from Japanese occupation. The new French government named General Eugène Mordant, who had been the commander of the French Indochina Army, as its representative. Mordant's powers surpassed those of Decoux, who remained the titular governor-general during this time. The Japanese knew that French Resistance networks in Indochina were in contact with the Allies and that, in the event of an American landing, they would open an interior front. The Japanese offensive aimed to prevent this possible, if not probable, stab in the back. It reconciled its initially divided perpetrators with the idealistic objective of the liberation of Asia, while putting an end to the ambiguous situation that had reigned until then.[35] The immediate consequence was the collapse of French tutelage. It was, in the eyes of the Indochinese, a belated but definitive indication of France's decline as an imperialist power. March 9, 1945, also had another immediate consequence: the Americans in China could no longer count on French net-

works for information and possible operations against the Japanese, and the Indochinese section of the American OSS (Office of Strategic Services) entered into
contact with the Viet Minh.[36] The latter, which is to say, the ICP, deemed that the
moment had come to take the initiative on the political and military fronts.[37]

The Japanese government granted independence to the kingdoms of Annam-
Tonkin, Cambodia, and Laos in April 1945. The fate of Cochinchina remained in
abeyance, because the Japanese assessed that it was under claim by both the Cambodians and the Vietnamese. The entirety of the various populations remained
skeptical of this independence accorded by an occupying power they all knew to
be in a very delicate situation. Indeed, the certainty of a Japanese defeat became
more apparent each day. The Japanese authorities themselves allowed a parallel
structure to flourish alongside the official one. The Indochinese government was
without financial and military power. Between the concession of independence
by the Japanese and their surrender, the Indochinese governments, especially that
of Vietnam, only had five months to establish their authority, to elaborate and
implement political and economic initiatives.[38] After the surrender of Japan in
August 1945, disarray and then anarchy took hold. The political movements and
parties that had waited for the most "opportune moment" took advantage of this
situation.

THE REVOLUTION OF AUGUST 1945 IN VIETNAM

Political disintegration was much greater in Vietnam, since it was the only country in Indochina that had been developed according to the Western criteria of
modernity. Vietnam had a genuine and dynamic political life; it was where the national struggle was strongest, but also where internal rivalries were sharpest. Above
all, the ICP was in fact a Vietnamese party, and the international communist network obedient to the Soviet Union gave the Indochinese political situation a global
dimension. Who, in Indochina, would take advantage of the situation created by
the Japanese surrender to the Allies? The power of the pro-Japanese nationalist
groups was uneven. Two among them imposed themselves because they were more
than political "parties" and were supported by new religions: Caodaism and Hoa
Hao, whose leaders each claimed a million followers. The importance of these so-
called political-religious sects was due not only to their appeal for the rural masses
but also to the fact that their prophets and priests had used the period that followed
March 9, 1945, to organize their supporters on a territorial, paramilitary, and political basis. These political-religious forces were the only ones capable of counterbalancing the dynamism of the ICP and eventually of opposing it. The nationalists of the Viet Nam Quoc Dan Dang, who had taken refuge in China rather than
collaborate with the Japanese, remained under the influence of the Guomindang.
They were relying on the long-anticipated entrance of Chinese troops into the

north of the country, which finally took place in October 1945. As a result, they were unable to take autonomous initiatives.

The ICP was the only political organization that had a clearly defined strategy. This had been halted since 1940, when its recruitment was limited; it numbered only around five thousand members, of whom more than a thousand were in prison, and it was absent in certain districts and even some provinces. At the end of 1940 and the beginning of 1941, the ICP, busy tending its wounds, was at its lowest ebb. In the south, the failure of the uprising had destroyed it; in the center and the north, militants were either underground or guerrillas. Time and their geographic situation undoubtedly gave the communist militants the opportunity to interpret, to inflect, and even to modify the general principles and directives of their superiors.[39]

In the context of the Japanese occupation of Indochina and the invasion of the USSR by the Wehrmacht, Ho Chi Minh, having returned from the Soviet Union and stayed at Chinese Red bases during China's United Front against Japan, initiated a new direction in the strategy of the ICP. The Eighth Plenum of the Central Committee of the ICP, meeting in Pac Bo (upper Tonkin) on May 10–14, 1941, was an event of great importance. It defined a new political line, in which the social revolution (class struggle and agrarian revolution) was adjourned in order to prioritize the "revolution of national liberation." The logic of the latter accorded a central role to the Viet Minh. This front of national unity was different from the previous anti-imperialist front in that it rallied to the Allies' struggle against "fascist" states.[40]

After having adopted this strategy of national liberation, associating the French and the Japanese as a common target, it founded its instrument: the Viet Nam Doc Lap Dong Minh (Alliance for the Independence of Vietnam), known by the abbreviation "Viet Minh." It aimed at uniting all political and patriotic forces around— in fact, under the control of—the ICP. Liberation was conceived of as a process of armed struggle, and survivors of the surrender of Bac Son (September 1940) would constitute one of the two military cores of the Army of National Salvation.[41] This army, and the Party, had developed a base in upper Tonkin, in a liberated zone known as Viet Bac. The French Army failed to eradicate these guerrilla bases, despite "pacification" operations from 1943 to 1944. The region was sparsely populated and then only by ethnic groups such as the Tai and the Dao, but it was favorable to ambushes and escape. Viet Bac also provided a route to China and therefore links with the Chinese Communist Party and probably with the Comintern (until 1943, when it was dissolved).

In 1945, the communists were implanted throughout the entire peninsula and led hundreds of committees of national salvation (hoi cuu quoc), which could probably count on tens of thousands of followers. These committees were both vehicles for spreading ICP influence and tools of political and eventually military ac-

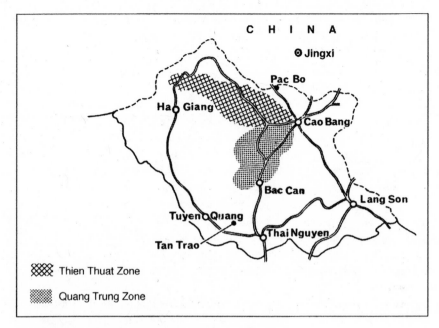

MAP 8.1. Zones of the revolutionary movements in Viet Bac.

tion. Communist leaders put these assets to use, realizing that they had to seize the opportunity. From March 9, 1945, the Viet Minh had elbow room, so to speak, and its armed groups had already advanced to Thai Nguyen, at the entrance of the Red River Delta.[42]

Nguyen Ai Quoc, who took the name of Ho Chi Minh in 1941, had established his headquarters in Tan Trao, a village seventy kilometers from Hanoi. There, the Viet Minh reaped the fruits of its cooperation with the OSS. Not only did the Deer Team of Major Allison K. Thomas, who arrived at Tan Trao on July 16, 1945, establish ties with the Viet Minh, but they also equipped them with new arms, which increased the prestige of the Vietnamese communists. When Ho Chi Minh and his comrades learned from their radio of the surrender of Japan, they were therefore able to act accordingly. At the announcement of Japan's surrender, a national convention, meeting in Tan Trao on August 16 and 17, placed Ho Chi Minh at the head of a temporary government of national salvation. The Army of National Salvation (Cuu Quoc Quan) set out for Hanoi. There, the Viet Minh Committee had decided to seize vital locations and buildings. It did this without firing a shot on August 19, 1945, after having secured the complicit neutrality of the mandarin Pham Ke Toai, the representative of Emperor Bao Dai in Tonkin.[43]

The only uncertainty was what the reaction of the Japanese military command would be. The occupying army was not a true obstacle, however, according to the account of the president of Hanoi's Revolutionary Military Committee. The fall of the Tonkin superior residence and the barracks and weapons of the Civil Guard (the former Garde indigène in the protectorates and Garde civile in Cochinchina) took place without difficulties, although "the Japanese army had mobilized substantial forces, set up four tanks to block the crossroads, and advanced infantrymen up to the palisade of the barracks of the Civil Guard." At that point a face-to-face confrontation began between the crowd, militiamen of the ICP, and the Japanese. The Vietnamese revolutionaries exhorted the Japanese soldiers to wait for their repatriation without becoming involved in Vietnamese domestic affairs. "In the evening," wrote Nguyen Khang, "before our resolute strength, the Japanese were forced to retreat."[44]

The Japanese watched the Liberation Army units enter Hanoi after reaching Gia Lam (the city's airfield) on the morning of August 26.[45] Ho Chi Minh had discreetly entered the city on August 21. On September 2, he proclaimed the independence of Vietnam, henceforth to be called the Democratic Republic of Vietnam. Vo Nguyen Giap describes the city in jubilation and the rally at the Ba Dinh square: "Red brightens Hanoi. Flags, lights, flowers fill the sky as far as one can see. Red banners float above houses; the stores and small shops are closed. Markets are not held. All the activities of commerce and production of the town have ceased. The population of the capital—the old, the young, men and women—is in the streets. All have understood that they must participate in this first great gathering of their homeland."[46] After the reading of the declaration of Vietnamese independence, the crowd was called to take an oath: "If the French conquer Vietnam, we vow: not to come to their service; not to work for them; not to supply them; to block their path. There were a million people, a million voices that rose up as one."[47]

In Hue, the Thanh Nien Tien Tuyen (First Line Youth) of the scoutmaster Ta Quang Buu controlled the imperial capital, where, on August 22, a Viet Minh committee was put in place. On August 25, Emperor Bao Dai abdicated. In Saigon, a similar scenario was played out the same day. An administrative committee of Nam Bo, with the communist Tran Van Giau presiding, organized the seizure of power with the help of a mass organization, the Thanh Nien Tien Phong (Avant-garde Youth), founded and controlled by another communist, Dr. Pham Ngoc Thach. There, as elsewhere, the Japanese authorities did not intervene.[48] In the provinces, the predominantly communist Viet Minh or the nationalists (Viet Nam Quoc Dan Dang, Phuc Quoc Hoi / National Restoration) were either in sole control or else in competition with each other. Since it was better organized, and because it had not compromised itself with the Japanese and could claim to represent domestic resistance, the ICP became an invaluable interlocutor for the Allies and benefited from a certain prestige among the population.

In the summer of 1945, the French expeditionary corps that was being organized to reoccupy Indochina was still not ready. The procrastination caused by the hostility of President Franklin D. Roosevelt to France's colonial policies, especially its Indochinese policies, ceased after his demise. At the Potsdam conference, on July 12, 1945, the Allies accepted the participation of French troops in the theater of Asian operations and yet, at the same time, decided to entrust the British with the disarmament of the Japanese troops south of the 16th parallel. The newly founded Vietnamese state was already prey to intrigues and rivalries. The British considered France the legitimate administrator of Indochina, and their representative in Saigon, General Douglas D. Gracey, judging the Vietnamese to be incapable of maintaining order, rearmed French troops at the end of September 1945. On September 23, the Nam Bo Executive Committee called upon the population to leave Saigon and embark on resistance. The first war of Indochina was beginning in Cochinchina.

North of the 16th parallel, the Chinese Army of Yunnan, under the command of General Lu Han, marched into Tonkin and Laos. Would the course of the Vietnamese revolution change? Would the nationalists seize power thanks to the support of the Chinese? In the end nothing came of it, because the government of Chiang Kai-shek had to renounce its designs on Indochina. Major Archimedes Patti and some of his OSS comrades in Indochina were attentive and strongly sympathetic to Ho Chi Minh. However, aside from the fact that not all the executors of American politics in Asia shared this sentiment, Roosevelt's successor, Harry Truman, progressively modified the course of U.S. policies toward Indochina. It was no longer a question of the international trusteeship of Indochina, a formula to which Roosevelt had remained faithful until the end, according to the historian Stein Tønnesson. The Soviet danger and the growing importance of Gaullist France in the international context pushed the American government to recognize French sovereignty over Indochina in 1945 (in a declaration of policy of the State Department dated June 22). On October 5, a telegram from Secretary of State Dean Acheson clearly affirmed that the United States did not oppose the return of France to Indochina, and the chief of the OSS, William Donovan, stated that it was necessary to maintain the European colonial empires in the face of communism.[49]

There remained the French, whose government was represented in Hanoi by a group led by Jean Sainteny, who had arrived on August 22, 1945, with the Patti mission. Sainteny was in a very delicate situation: how to avoid meeting and holding discussions with (and in so doing recognizing) an independent Vietnamese power, all the while pursuing his mission of restoring French authority? On the one hand, he was urged on in the latter respect by the French community in Hanoi, who were anxious and frustrated over their lost colonial power and who were humiliated daily in individual incidents. On the other hand, he was blocked by Major Patti and the Chinese command, which restricted him to a minor, auxiliary role, denying him all negotiating and decision-making capacities.[50] The administrators

Jean Cédile and Pierre Messmer were parachuted into Cochinchina and Tonkin, respectively, as commissioners of the French Republic. The expansion of "police operations" that the French attempted in Saigon with the help of the British enlightened the Vietnamese about the overt intention of the government of the Fourth Republic to take back control of Indochina.

In Cambodia and Laos, both of which were declared independent states after March 9, 1945, the events following the Japanese surrender took a different turn. In the two kingdoms, the monarchy was maintained and the sovereigns, Norodom Sihanouk and Sisavang Vong, were still respected. Earlier, the Japanese had restored the nationalist leader Son Ngoc Thanh to Phnom Penh, though he had been compromised by the so-called demonstration of the umbrellas (July 20, 1942), when some two thousand people, mostly Buddhist monks, high-school students, and teachers, demanded the liberation of Hem Chieu, a venerable Buddhist suspected of collusion with the Japanese, who was imprisoned in Poulo Condore (where he died). On August 9, 1945, in a coup d'état, Son Ngoc Thanh separated the king from the Council of Ministers and took over the actual control of Cambodia until October 1945.[51]

In Laos, starting in September 1945, the king decided to reestablish ties with France, while Prince Phetsarath, his stepbrothers Souvanaphouma and Souphanouvong, and other leaders reaffirmed the independence of a unified Laos and created the Lao Issara movement. The large Vietnamese community, notably in Thakhek, but also in Savannakhet and in Vientiane, had already been won over to the idea of independence, the Viet Minh having mobilized and organized it into self-defense militias. The Vietnamese of northeastern Thailand organized themselves in the same way until Phibun Songkhram took power in 1948.[52] Prince Souphanouvong, who was an engineer of public works in Vietnam, returned to Laos with a Viet Minh escort, who provided him with his first advisors and cadres of the armed forces of Pathet Lao. One of them related:

> On October 1, 1945, six officers and myself were summoned by the directors of Special Operations. We had been chosen to escort his Royal Highness Prince Souphanouvong to Vientiane according to the instructions of President Ho Chi Minh. We took with us five soldiers, fifteen old rifles, and an old Bren light machine gun . . . generous aid considering the resources of the Liberation Army at the time. . . . The following day, we made our first stop at Khe Sanh. There, the prince solemnly ordered us to remove our (Viet) Liberation Army badges and to replace them with the Laotian badges that had been manufactured in Hanoi.[53]

The author of these lines, a Vietnamese who thereafter organized the Intelligence Services in Pathet Lao, notes further:

> My first impression of Savannakhet was one of a Vietnamese town: we heard Vietnamese voices and the thousands of people who welcomed us were for the most part Vietnamese. . . . The Vietnamese community was proud of us and the majority thought

we were the vanguard of a conquering army. The Laotian leaders . . . manifested great distrust of us. We had not foreseen this and came up against numerous difficulties in pursuing our work. First of all, neither the Laotians nor the Vietnamese understood the peculiarity of our situation [of being Vietnamese in Laotian uniforms].[54]

As soon as Japan had surrendered, the countries that had been under French domination were in a state of moral and political secession from metropolitan France. The nationalist leaders and the majority of the people were convinced that this path was irreversible. But the will to resist was uneven: of the three countries, Vietnam had the best resources, and its revolutionary leaders early on envisioned their use throughout the entirety of Indochina.[55]

RESTORING FRENCH SOVEREIGNTY

Domestic French politics weighed heavily on the policies France pursued in Indochina at the end of World War II. The Fourth Republic's instability prevented its increasingly divided governments from devising a coherent and firm policy in Indochina. The principles of reform and liberal orientation laid out at Brazzaville were rapidly obliterated by the desire to reconstruct French imperial grandeur, and subsequently by anti-communism. In reexamining the period from 1946 to 1948, Governor Henri Laurentie recognized that France and its decision-makers were too weak to conduct a "massive operation to win hearts and minds" in Indochina.[56] Above all, contrary to the illusions of French liberals, or of their Dutch counterparts who signed the Linggadjati Agreement with the unilaterally declared Republic of Indonesia in March 1947, the nationalism of the dominating nation could not be reconciled with that of the colonized.

General de Gaulle dispatched men to Indochina bearing directives directly based on the Brazzaville Declaration of 1944 and, more particularly, on the French government's declaration on Indochina of March 24, 1945, which stated France's intention to establish a new regime in Indochina: it would henceforth be reorganized as the Indochinese Federation, itself integrated into a new federal unit, the French Union. The particular degree of autonomy to be granted to the French possessions was chosen in such a way as to preserve the authority of France and its decision-making power in vital areas, such as the economy, foreign relations, and defense. This redesigning of ties between the colonies and France could more or less satisfy those colonies remaining in France's immediate orbit. Indochina, however, so geographically distant from France, was in a situation that excluded a return to political dependence: Vietnam (i.e., the Democratic Republic), Laos, and Cambodia were already independent. To enter into the French Union was to accept an illogical regression. The incompatibility of the opposing points of view was exemplified in the case of Vietnam, where, early on, messages were exchanged and meetings were organized between the emissaries of the French government, on the one hand, and the Viet Minh and various Vietnamese personalities, on the other.[57]

The French, who ignored and misjudged the evolution of mind-sets and of the relations of power, never pronounced the word "independence," not even as a long-term goal. As for the Vietnamese, particularly among the Viet Minh, who were the inevitable interlocutors of the French, the future envisioned for Indochina by de Gaulle's government was unacceptable. The governmental declaration of March 24, 1945, affirmed that France would not abdicate its sovereignty in Indochina, intending to transform it into an autonomous federation of states. The ex-emperor of Annam, Duy Tan, saw in this declaration the work of the civil servants of the Ministry of the Colonies "attached to the status quo." In what most call his "testament," the exiled ex-monarch, whom de Gaulle had planned to return to Indochina, emphasized that it was "impossible, after the war, to come empty-handed to Indochina and especially Annam, offering nothing but promises. It is absolutely necessary to offer these men a true sacrifice that testifies both to the generosity of France and to the boldness of the accomplishments of the Fourth Republic."[58]

The ICP's organ, Co Giai Phong (The Flag of Liberation), stated its position in February 1944, denouncing the Gaullist refusal to recognize the independence of Vietnam.[59] When Captain Paul Mus returned from an information mission at the start of 1945, he noted that there was no flow of communication between the Vietnamese and de Gaulle.[60] However, the relations of power would drive all participants to moderate their principles and postpone the complete and immediate execution of their respective projects. When, at the end of 1945, the French wanted to resume activity in Indochina, they did not have enough room to maneuver, and only the British supported them. In the north, the Chinese had their own objectives. Among the Americans, the anticolonialism of Roosevelt and his entourage was still potent, though they did not go so far as to offer support to Ho Chi Minh's government, as French accusations have stated. As for Ho Chi Minh and his government, they were in a critical situation. The Soviet Union was too far away to be of much help to them; the Chinese communists were on the brink of engaging in a war, whose outcome was uncertain, with the Guomindang. The latter occupied Vietnam to the 16th parallel and favored their friends of the VNQDD. Ho Chi Minh undoubtedly had amicable ties with OSS Major Patti, who advised him and transmitted to Washington (via Chongqing) messages in which Ho invoked the liberal and democratic ideas of the United States. Patti's sympathy carried little weight with the U.S. government, however, and his superiors in the OSS and Ambassador Patrick Hurley rebuked him for compromising himself with the communists.[61]

In contrast, the evolution of France's domestic policies caught the attention of the communist-controlled Vietnamese government. The participation of communist ministers in the French government, and the prestige and influence of the French Communist Party in the wake of the Resistance, certainly influenced the shift in Ho Chi Minh's policies, inclining him to negotiate with the French rather than opting for immediate frontal conflict. Meanwhile, the troops of the Corps expéditionnaire français en Extrême-Orient (CEFEO) had landed in Cochinchina, not only in Saigon but also in the Mekong Delta, where the 2nd Armored Division, led by General Leclerc, had begun to penetrate. The resistance had to face considerable firepower with very limited means. In Cambodia, Leclerc's troops captured Son Ngoc Thanh on October 15, 1945, without a military operation or any real difficulty. In the lower part of Laos, the French benefited from the support of the princely family of Champassak and the weakness of Lao Issara; the only resistance came from the Vietnamese organized by the Viet Minh. Thus, the autumn of 1945 was the beginning of what could be called the reconquest.

HO CHI MINH OPTS FOR TEMPORIZATION

Through the mediation of Sainteny—named French commissioner in Tonkin— triangular negotiations were begun between the governments of France, the Democratic Republic of Vietnam, and China. Under pressure from Vietnamese nationalists to get rid of the Chinese troops, Ho Chi Minh agreed to sign the accords of March 6, 1946, with France. The Guomindang agreed to withdraw its troops from upper Vietnam once France had given up all its concessions and privileges in China. French troops were allowed to replace them. Through the preliminary convention of the March 6 agreement, France recognized Vietnam as a "Free State," with its own government, parliament, army, and economy, yet still belonging to the Indochinese Federation and the French Union. One important feature of the agreement was France's acceptance of the principle of the reunification of Tonkin, Annam, and Cochinchina, subject to a consultation of the population by referendum. The annex agreement stated that French and Vietnamese troops would replace Chinese troops, and that the French would withdraw within five years.

The precise details of the appendix to the agreement compensated for the absence of the word "independence" in the March 6 accords, but it was the work of the French negotiators in Hanoi. The government in Paris would learn of this only later. This double process, which some called deceitful, would reappear subsequently. The protagonists maintained opposing positions, and their acts and decisions were sometimes contradictory. General Leclerc, commander in chief of France's army in Indochina, was from the beginning in favor of the application of the accords, while High Commissioner Admiral Georges Thierry d'Argenlieu was first reticent about, then openly hostile to, the Vietnamese government. As for the French administrators in Indochina and those in Paris responsible for France's Indochina policy, they favored great firmness toward the colonized and deemed that internal autonomy was the maximum that could be conceded them. None of France's representatives in Indochina were in favor of "letting go" of the colony.

Their differences were essentially tactical, even when they went with a general philosophy. Thus, General Leclerc was in favor of negotiation because he did not dispose of sufficient military means for reconquest and was persuaded that a military solution could not be substituted for a political solution. He was suspected and even accused of utterly accommodating Vietnamese demands, whereas he had simply taken stock of the aspirations to independence of the Vietnamese and their resolution to defend themselves. Hoping to preserve a French presence in Indochina, Leclerc was favorable to a compromise with Ho Chi Minh.

The conduct of the majority of the French in Indochina, which had evolved between their leaving France and their confrontation with the reality of Indochina, was underpinned by the vision of what we would call today a "new world order," but seen in the context of the disputes between the United States and the old European empires, between the latter and the Soviet Union, and also between various groups of French (parliamentary staff, civil and military high commissioners, and economic and financial circles). In other words, the state and the groups controlling French capitalism had a neocolonial perspective on how to modernize the structures and forms of their activities, notably by industrializing Indochina in order to ensure its reform and perpetuation, but the different sides could not agree on the ways and means to achieve this.

As for the Vietnamese, Ho Chi Minh favored negotiations, but he did not lose sight of his goal, still fragile but partially realized, of creating an independent Vietnamese state. This did not prevent the nationalists from trying to outbid the Vietnamese leader and accusing him of treason.[62] Cochinchina was a stumbling block, for Ho Chi Minh had affirmed in an intangible and irreversible way that it was an integral part of Vietnam. As a result, the military resistance led by Nguyen Binh and French "pacification" continued in the south, whereas coexistence—albeit difficult—was instituted in Vietnam above the 16th parallel in the spring of 1946.

The French Maneuver

In Indochina, it was High Commissioner Thierry d'Argenlieu who torpedoed the accords of March 6 by opposing the measures intended to bring France closer to the Democratic Republic of Vietnam. He envisioned the use of military force to achieve what he considered were objectives in line with France's interests: "To forbid, in principle, a recourse to force would be to risk the loss of Indochina and gravely compromise the primary aim of our mission, which is to reestablish France's authority there not only in law but in reality."[63] In concert with Commissaire de la République Jean Cédile, he organized an autonomous Cochinchinese government. According to Cédile, the accords of March 6, 1945, were only a "local agreement" and did not imply any recognition on behalf of the French government of a single government grouping together the three countries of Annam, Tonkin, and Cochinchina. Twenty days after the signature of the accords of March 6, a Cochinchinese Consultative

Council elected Dr. Nguyen Van Thinh as head of the provisional government of the Republic of Cochinchina. The social foundation for this Cochinchinese autonomy was limited to a fraction of the southern middle class, and the French abandoned this initiative during the summer of 1946, leading Dr. Thinh to commit suicide in November of the same year. The events in Cochinchina reflected the implementation of two irreconcilable and diametrically opposed projects. Other events would confirm for some the ulterior motives that they attributed to others, and vice versa. The first Dalat conference between the French and the Vietnamese, in April 1946, revealed the absence of common ground, as much on principles as on the question of Cochinchina. The Fontainebleau conference, in July 1946, resulted simply in a modus vivendi that Ho Chi Minh signed on the eve of his return to Vietnam. On October 23, 1946, in a public meeting in Hanoi, Ho took stock of the situation:

> I went to Paris in order to resolve the question of our independence and the reunification of Vietnam. The present situation in France does not yet allow for the resolution of these two questions. It will be necessary to wait. But I am able to affirm definitively that sooner or later, Vietnam will be independent, and the north, center, and south reunified. The Franco-Vietnamese conference has not finished its work. It will resume next January. But the modus vivendi of September 14 has made things easier for both parties and cleared the road for the continuation of the negotiations in a more friendly atmosphere.

Was it therefore possible to avoid war as the fatal solution to this tense face-off? General Raoul Salan, who accompanied Ho Chi Minh to France, was persuaded that war would break out: "I had a last conversation [with Ho] there, and I repeated what I said at the first dinner: we are going to fight and it will be very hard."[64] Furthermore, the French military command had prepared its plans since March–April, and Vo Nguyen Giap had undoubtedly done the same. While the Vietnamese president was in France, Thierry d'Argenlieu convened a second conference in Dalat, in August 1946, to define the constitution of the Indochinese Federation. The admiral took advantage of the agreement concluded between the French government, on the one hand, and the Laotian and Cambodian governments, on the other, in the first eight months of 1946. These pacts recognized the autonomy of the two monarchies; in return, they accepted a special relationship with France and their entrance into the Indochinese Federation. Furthermore, the French negotiated with Thailand the retrocession of territories yielded to it in 1941. France, therefore, appeared as the protector of the two kingdoms against its ambitious neighbors, starting with Vietnam.

Toward War

The Hanoi government's mistrust was based on events in Cochinchina, as well as what it considered to be limits placed upon its sovereignty. This was the result of the expansion of the French Army in Tonkinese territory, its occupation of the coal mines of Campha in April 1946, its installation in the highlands among certain ethnic minorities, its occupation of the coastal zone of the Sino-Vietnamese border region, and daily incidents, of which some were deadly, such as the ambush of the French in Bac Ninh on August 3, 1946. The French did not limit themselves to military operations and the protection of possessions and members of the French community. To take one example, uncontrolled exports and purchases of weapons in China by the Hanoi government caused the depreciation of the Indochinese piastre, the colonial currency shared by all of Indochina. The accords of March 6 had not foreseen this type of problem, and French intervention with regard to customs seemed an intolerable intrusion into Vietnamese domestic affairs. Concretely, it was the cause of many incidents between French soldiers and Vietnamese customs officers.

The withdrawal of the Chinese was an opportunity for the Vietnamese communists to reinforce their political hegemony. From June to July 1946, they eliminated the anticommunist nationalists of Dong Minh Hoi and Viet Nam Quoc Dan Dang both politically and physically: some of them were murdered, others were ousted and had to follow the withdrawing Guomindang troops. Thus strengthened, the government prepared for a confrontation with the French, which they deemed inevitable. In the middle of 1946, the French military authorities estimated that Vo Nguyen Giap, head of the army, had organized sixty thousand men, of whom twelve thousand were in Cochinchina, into thirty-five "regiments" of infantry and three of artillery (not including the self-defense militia), with a significant supply of weapons turned over by the Japanese at their disposal. In July 1946, General Leclerc returned to France convinced that the Viet Minh were preparing for war against the French. The French military and political leaders who remained in Indochina (High Commissioner Thierry d'Argenlieu and General Jean-Étienne Valluy) were all the readier to fight the Viet Minh. Valluy's directive no. 2 (April 10, 1946) accorded with Thierry d'Argenlieu's logic, setting up "a plan of action to maneuver against the city . . . to be completed as early as possible with a study of a series of measures, which should have as their goal progressively to modify and transform the scenario of a purely military operation into one of a coup d'état." This directive led the historian Philippe Devillers to place the blame for Franco-Vietnamese hostilities (December 1946) on the French command.[65] The modus vivendi was either not applied (in Cochinchina) or seriously strained (in Tonkin). An important step toward the war was taken in November 1946. A customs incident in the harbor of Haiphong triggered a shooting by the self-defense militia; the French responded with a deadly bombardment (six thousand victims according to Vietnamese, three hundred according to the French), and another bloody battle broke out in Lang Son. These two outbursts confirmed the mutual suspicions of the French and the Vietnamese.[66]

Convinced that the use of force was unavoidable, the French command occupied all of Haiphong after five days of combat. It was too late for either side to turn back. Haiphong seemed to be a prelude to the French reoccupation of Tonkin. Meanwhile, the Vietnamese leaders prepared aggressions against the French. On December 19, 1946, the People's Army and Self-Defense Militias attacked the French in Hanoi; other assaults occurred simultaneously against French garrisons elsewhere.[67] Ho Chi Minh launched a call for national resistance: "Whoever has a rifle must use his rifle! Whoever has a sword must use his sword! And if you don't have a sword, take up picks and sticks! Each person must fight with all his might against colonialism and save our Homeland." The following day, he concluded another call "to the Vietnamese people, to the French people, and to the people of the Allies" in this way: "The French colonialists intend to reoccupy our country. This is obvious, unquestionable." In Paris, the dramatic decision to declare war fell to the socialist Léon Blum, who had just formed the new government: "I did not deserve this," he said, bursting into tears. The war was now openly fought, extending to the entire Vietnamese territory, and soon throughout all of Indochina.

THE FIRST PHASE OF THE WAR: A COLONIAL RECONQUEST?

The period from 1947 to 1950 was characterized by uncertainty. On the military front, the French obtained only partial advances rather than decisive results. On the political front, there was a search for an alternative that was both nationalist and anticommunist, the so-called Bao Dai solution, which was hard to formulate. For his part, however, High Commissioner Léon Pignon interpreted it to mean: "Our objective is clearly defined: to pursue our quarrel with the Viet Minh party on the internal Annamese level."[68] The war had begun locally, but progressively, and inexorably, it invaded all the Indochinese countries. The Vietnamese fought for independence. Did France have an equally clear strategy? Was it about colonial reconquest in the most literal sense? All the while acknowledging the necessity of declaring war, Léon Blum, the head of the French government, sent Minister of the Colonies Moutet and General Leclerc to Indochina to take stock of the situation. Using different terms, the two arrived at the same conclusion: military action was necessary to reach a political solution. This solution, however, implied expanding military strength and armaments. From the outset, therefore, questions arose that would continue to confront the French government: first, which political solution should be adopted, and how to apply it firmly? In the meantime, how to finance the war effort? Whatever the option, the answer to these questions depended more on a continuity of political views than on military ones, and on the material situation as well as on the mind-set of the French nation. Other factors, however, such as the situation in Europe and the remainder of the world, would soon influence the evolution of this war.

In 1947, the French political parties in power were divided: the communists and a minority of the socialists favored negotiations with Ho Chi Minh, which the majority of the socialists and the Mouvement républicain populaire (MRP) opposed. Thus, the socialist prime minister Paul Ramadier failed to adopt a well-defined policy. Throughout the conflict, French domestic policies continuously influenced decisions concerning Indochina. Strategies changed, and the "États associés d'Indochine" (Associated States of Indochina) replaced the Indochinese Federation. The new high commissioner, Émile Bollaert, a civilian, was directed to deal with these Associated States, Cambodia, Laos, and even Cochinchina, within the framework of the French Union. The French expeditionary corps took charge of the military side of an operation of exploration and political expansion within the anti-communist Vietnamese nationalist milieu. In April 1947, Ho Chi Minh's proposal to negotiate was rejected, and a visit to the Vietnamese leader by Paul Mus, Leclerc's advisor, on May 12, 1947, failed. Bollaert then turned resolutely toward finding a *contre-feu nationaliste* (nationalist riposte) in Vietnam. His successor, Léon Pignon, would be left to finish the task. The exclusion of the French communists from the governmental coalition accentuated the anti–Viet Minh policies of the Ramadier cabinet. The French Communist Party was free to oppose the government's Indochinese policies openly and to proclaim its "solidarity with the Vietnamese people." The political divides in France and the course of the conflict in Indochina coincided and hardened, paralleling the evolution of the international context.

On the military front, General Valluy continued to work on a plan that prioritized the defeat of the Viet Minh. This military objective was founded on a classic sociopolitical vision: the "passive" and "versatile" "Annamese masses" would quickly abandon a militarily vanquished Viet Minh. On this point, Valluy was in conflict with High Commissioner Bollaert, who had at one time considered proposing to negotiate with the Viet Minh again. But when French military command tried to determine where to focus the military effort, it too was divided. Should the French dedicate all of their energy to the complete pacification of Cochinchina, the richest of the Indochinese states, where they could depend on more political support than elsewhere, and where they had installed a government? Or would it be better to attempt to destroy the political and military apparatus of the Viet Minh where it was based, that is, in Tonkin? In Tonkin itself, was it more profitable to deliver decisive blows in the heart of the upper region, to the national stronghold of the Democratic Republic of Vietnam, or to cut it off from the Red River, the Viet Minh's source of food and manpower?

At the end of 1947, the troops of the French Union had regained a foothold in Tonkin and Annam, in the zones considered most vital—highly populated areas of major economic activity (the Tonkin coal basin, the industrial cotton zone of Nam Dinh, the coastline from Faifo to Dong Hoi). At the end of 1950, the Red River Delta was occupied, but its "pacification" remained superficial. In 1947, the French offensive aimed at eliminating the national stronghold in the north broke up the Viet Minh forces by destroying their logistical bases, but it failed to annihilate them.

Taking into account the size of its forces (100,000 men) and the available matériel, the French command did not have the capacity to repeat this kind of attack against the central political-military bases of the Vietnamese resistance. These operations, however, reinforced France's conviction that their adversaries were strategically weak and possessed negligible military strength, underestimating the Viet Minh. They should have remembered what the General Weygand had said in 1920 about Indochinese soldiers: "The warlike atavism of the Annamese and their respect for the hierarchy make them good fighters if they are well commanded." To the regular and regional fighters of the Democratic Republic of Vietnam, whose number was estimated at 80,000, should be added the local forces of an armed population, the presence of political leadership at all levels, intensive propaganda, and possible recourse to terrorism. But the resistance had to consider the long-term course of the war and could not move beyond the stage of guerrilla conflict as long as outside factors did not intervene to the tip the balance in its favor.

The French succeeded precisely where they depended on networks of organization and action analogous to those of their adversaries. In Cochinchina, this meant developing alliances with the Caodaists and the Hoa Hao (which were, however, subject to deadly reversals), and the pacification of Bentre by Colonel Leroy and his mobile units of the Défense des chrétientés (Christian militia). In Tonkin, the French managed to shield the Catholic bishoprics of Bui Chu and Phat Diem from the influence of the Viet Minh by organizing them into autonomous administrative and defense units. From 1947 to 1949, the balance of power between the antagonists tended to even out, in the sense that neither side managed to win a decisive victory. But in 1950, the victory of the Chinese Communist Party over the Guomindang and the arrival of the People's Liberation Army on Indochina's northern frontier, starting in December 1949, dramatically modified the course of the war.

A Nationalist Riposte

In this last period, the quest for a military solution permitting a political end to the conflict had failed. Simultaneously, the nationalist alternative to the Viet Minh was developing very slowly and with significant difficulty. Ex-Emperor Bao Dai, who had become the citizen Vinh Thuy and been named special counselor in Ho Chi Minh's government, and who arrived in Hong Kong in 1946, hinted on July 5, 1947, at his potential role as mediator in the conflict. This attracted the attention of the French government, but negotiations between the two parties stagnated: Bao Dai demanded recognition of independence and the union of Cochinchina with Tonkin and Annam:

> Truly, the French do not understand what has happened in the Far East in the course
> of these past two years. Without a doubt, war is ruinous for a convalescent country

like France, which also fears the consequences of a possible communist victory in China, a victory that seems increasingly certain; I therefore understand its urge for a swift resolution and its desire for peace. But it is France's responsibility to eliminate the Viet Minh hypothesis, and there is only one way to do so: grant to me what they do not want to grant to them.[69]

The French government balked at this solution because the recognition of independence would have unavoidable repercussions in Cambodia, Laos, and the remainder of the colonial empire. In 1947, it still clung to the principle of internal autonomy for Vietnam with the status simply of an "Associated State."

It was only on June 5, 1948, after numerous negotiations, that an agreement was initialed on the cruiser *Duguay-Trouin*, anchored in Ha Long Bay. With the signature of High Commissioner Bollaert, France "solemnly recognized the independence of Vietnam, which was free to realize its complete unity." Bao Dai, however, refused to return to Vietnam as long as the French authorities delayed the transfer of administrative powers to the government of General Xuan, heir to the Republic of Cochinchina. It was therefore only the following year, on March 8, 1949, that Bao Dai met the president of the Republic, Vincent Auriol, at the Elysée. Both were unaware of various accords that clarified the terms of those signed at Ha Long. The signed conventions had limited objectives: the internal independence of Vietnam was proclaimed, but the monetary, economic, and customs union with Laos and Cambodia was reaffirmed. French military bases were maintained in the territory, and Vietnamese diplomacy had to conform itself to the directives of the High Council of the French Union. In his journal, dated March 14, 1949, Auriol confirmed the intention that had driven the French to choose the "Bao Dai solution": "Whatever the decision of the Indochinese, there is no doubt that had we dealt with Ho Chi Minh, he would have joined with the Chinese; but it is preferable that the French Union be installed with Bao Dai, so that our sovereignty is affirmed and the Chinese, and notably Mao Tse-tung, will hesitate before doing anything in Indochina."[70]

Nevertheless, in April 1949, the union of Cochinchina, Tonkin, and Annam was sealed. On April 28, Bao Dai returned to Vietnam, but the nationalist alternative did not function any better than before. Undoubtedly, this resulted from the rifts between the nationalist parties, but also because Bao Dai did not sufficiently affirm his governmental authority. The new chief of state considered that the agreements with France had an "evolutionary character." He devoted his efforts to their completion, rather than to the war against the Viet Minh, believing that it was through negotiation that genuine independence would be achieved, and that war was therefore pointless. The French, lacking confidence in them, were slow to hand over power to the nationalists; Auriol blamed "civil servants who do not want to let go of their position."[71] All was therefore far from being won for the new partners: the real independence of Vietnam as much as the unequivocal engagement of the nationalists against the communists. The Indochinese conflict was increasingly divided into two camps, in parallel with the evolution of the world situation.

THE SECOND PHASE OF THE WAR: INDOCHINA AS A HOT SPOT IN THE COLD WAR

The victory of Mao Zedong in China in 1949 modified the political and strategic balance in Far East Asia and the conditions of the Indochinese war. The "socialist camp" henceforth extended from the Elbe to the Sino-Indochinese border. The Vietnamese communists were "on the frontline of the anti-imperialist front," but they benefited from a "strong rearguard," the People's Republic of China, without which the armed struggle could not evolve from guerrilla warfare to a people's war, according to the ideas of Vo Nguyen Giap. Along the 1,400 kilometers of the common border, weapons and supplies could move unhindered. Starting on February 10, 1950, a liaison organization installed at Nanning (Guangxi province) directed the transportation of military matériel to Vietnam. In October 1951, the railroad from Nanning to Nam Quam (close to Lang Son) was completed: Chinese, Czech, and East German matériel transited through there. The French command evaluated the matériel from China at seven hundred tons per month. Training and rest camps, hospitals of Guangxi, Yunnan, Guandong, and the island of Hainan became Chinese "sanctuaries." Moral and diplomatic support was added to this material aid, despite the fact that the People's Republic of China was perfectly aware that France would delay recognizing its legitimacy due to this aid. In January 1950, the Chinese government accepted the establishment of diplomatic relations with the Democratic Republic of Vietnam. The recognition of the Democratic Republic of Vietnam by the Soviet Union soon followed.

Also in 1950, the French Communist Party (which convened its Twelfth Congress in April), the Confédération générale du travail (General Confederation of Labour; CGT), the Union of Young Republicans of France, and the Union of Young Women of France launched an active campaign against the "dirty war" and for "peace in Vietnam." Militants protested against the dispatch of troops, and dockworkers at the ports of Marseille and La Rochelle went on strike, refusing to load war matériel destined for the Far East. The campaign for the liberation of the sailor Henri Martin, a communist who had distributed antiwar tracts, received a great deal of attention.[72] The far Left intensified its opposition to France's Indochinese policies by mobilizing a portion of the ever-increasing anticolonial and/or pacifist French, without ever, however, succeeding in creating a "mass struggle" against the war.

The War Becomes International

In 1950, the new arrangement of forces in Asia led the government of the United States to adopt the principle of granting military aid to oppose communism in Vietnam. At the same time, however, the American leaders pressured the French government to accelerate its "nationalist solution." In June 1950, the first American fighter planes were delivered to the French in Saigon. On June 25, the North Korean army, invading South Korea, triggered the armed intervention of the United States. At opposite ends of the Far East, the existence of two similar fronts gave the war of Indochina a new dimension, without, however, totally eclipsing the former one, at least in French opinion: in official statements, the repression of international communism was substituted for the restoration of French supremacy. In reality, successive French governments stubbornly adhered to the "Associated States" formula of recognizing only internal autonomy. The Vietnamese prime minister, Tran Van Huu, pressured by the nationalists, accused France of failing to apply the accords of March 8, 1949, in a just and expedient fashion. In April 1953, Cambodia's king, Norodom Sihanouk, launched a "crusade for independence" to obtain the transfer of political and military power from the French to the Cambodians. The Laotian government had a more moderate attitude, but it moved toward the same goal.

The general evolution of the colonized countries of Asia (India, Indonesia, the Philippines, Burma) stimulated the rise of nationalism in Cambodia and Laos, where the sovereigns saw their legitimacy questioned by political parties or by personalities such as Son Ngoc Thanh and Prince Souphanouvong. In 1951, a united Indochinese Front regrouped the Viet Minh (now called the Lien-Viet), the Issarak Khmer, and the Issara Lao. The existence of guerrilla troops in Cambodia and Laos, supported by Vietnamese units, became ever more problematic for the French as the Viet Minh expanded operations to create a diversion and to allow its ally, the Pathet Lao, to establish a territorial base in northern Laos. The conference of the Associated States held in Pau, on June 29, 1950, rendered public the disagreement between the government of Prime Minister René Pleven and the Indochinese delegations. The latter denounced the excessively centralizing role of France in the French Union. During the conference, there were also confrontations between various national visions of questions common to the Federation, such as the navigation on the Mekong, interstate migration, finances, and so on. Two years later, the radical Prime Minister René Mayer would provide proof that the French government still controlled Indochinese affairs: on May 9, 1953, he decided, unilaterally and without even consulting the "Associated States," to devalue the piastre.[73]

Over the years, it became clear that the French expeditionary corps would not win. From 1950 to 1954, successive French governments, in a climate of repeated parliamentary crises, all chose not to resolve the Indochinese problem, allowing the country to get increasingly bogged down in a conflict led by a French command, which never obtained supplementary forces or matériel. Reacting to the disaster of Cao Bang, on October 3, 1950, President Vincent Auriol wrote in his journal: "For the past year and a half, we have been following piecemeal policies."[74] The former prime minister Paul Reynaud, returning from Asia in April 1953, told Auriol: "I believe that it is a crime against France to continue to maintain this hemorrhage that is the war in Indochina." Auriol replied: "I fully agree, and if I have made the irrevocable decision not to run for office again, it is because I too do not agree with the government. I am not able to say it, but I will say it later."[75]

In its beginnings, the war had primarily been an anti-guerrilla action, with torture and summary executions of prisoners and hostages. It had consisted of brutal clean-up operations (burning of villages, pillaging, and massacres), partly because it was impossible for French troops to distinguish between one Vietnamese and another, between a fighter and a non-fighter. To gain credibility for their policy of "nationalist riposte," the governing French demanded, like High Commissioner Bollaert in 1949, that French military command energetically repress the various attacks on the local population. The "dirty war" probably never disappeared completely but, after 1950, this conflict more and more resembled a conventional war.

The Balance of Military Forces Reverses Itself

The opponents of the expeditionary corps had increased their military and political forces and acquired a strategic capacity that enabled them to go beyond guerrilla warfare. Toward the middle of 1950, the French expeditionary corps was therefore confronted with a transformed People's Army of Vietnam (PAVN). Without a doubt, this was still an army of infantrymen—"the best infantrymen of the world," according to General Raoul Salan—but it was completely reorganized all the way to the "brigade" level, and all the echelons were equipped with heavy weapons: cannon, mortars, machine guns, and anti-aircraft guns. This reorganization took place from top to bottom, from regular units to regional units, down to local guerrillas. As a result, the PAVN's firepower nearly matched that of the French army. At the same time, the military command, after five years of harsh "natural selection," had improved. Furthermore, following the example of the Chinese, sessions of "ideological rectification," called *chinh huan,* were organized to reinforce the moral cohesion of the fighters and the commanders. The vigor and the keenness of the PAVN appeared starting in 1950 and made the French command aware that the conflict had moved into a new phase. The "Cao Bang disaster" followed by the abandonment of Lang Son in October 1950, provoked disbelief and disarray among the French.[76]

China's material assistance was certainly considerable from 1950 to 1954; both the Vietnamese and the Chinese recognize this. Furthermore, it was not limited to military aid. Numerous Chinese economic and financial experts followed closely on the heels of the military advisors to strengthen the currency, among other things. What is less certain are the respective roles of Vietnamese and Chinese strategists, notably in conceiving battle plans. If one believes Chinese sources, notably the *Journal* of General Chen Geng, who headed the Chinese military mission, the Chinese developed the battle plans for the "campaign of the borders." However, General Vo Nguyen Giap claims that he was the one who did so.[77]

Without a doubt, the arrival of the Chinese communists on the northern border of Vietnam not only provided relief to the PAVN but also gave it a second wind, reinforcing it considerably and providing it with a sanctuary. This gave the PAVN an immeasurable boost; but it was the PAVN itself that won the victories (along Route 4 and at Dien Bien Phu) and suffered the defeats (at Na San).

Since China had become communist and started regularly supplying the government and the troops of Ho Chi Minh, occupation of the strongholds from the coastline to Cao Bang and along the length of the Chinese frontier proved to be expensive, perilous, and inefficient; the French high command thus ordered their evacuation. A rushed operation, panic, and very bad coordination transformed the withdrawal into a disaster. There were 4,800 killed and missing, and 10,000 weapons fell into the hands of the PAVN. A historian of the war wrote: "The disaster is a moral one. . . . The repercussions of such an event surpass the material result. Cao Bang was for the war of Indochina what [the battle of] Bailén [in 1808] was for Spain's war against Napoleon I, [and the battle of] Valmy [in 1792] for the French Revolution."[78]

From then on, the only possible strategy for the French was to cling to the Red River Delta. The PAVN took initiative on a number of fronts: in Laos, in the Tai territories (in upper Tonkin), in the southern part of the Red River Delta, in Cochinchina, and on the high plateaus of central Annam. However, it did not immediately repeat the exploit of Cao Bang. The appointment of General Jean de Lattre de Tassigny as commander in chief of the French troops in Indochina dealt a blow to the PAVN's progress. First, de Lattre put an end to the discouragement that had settled in among the French. All the while clearly putting the military back on track in Tonkin (at the battles of Vinh Yen and Dong Trieu) in 1951, de Lattre actively pushed the Indochinese toward military and political engagement. His speech during the distribution of prizes to pupils of the Chasseloup-Laubat School issued a veiled injunction: "Be men, by which I mean if you are communist, join the Viet Minh. With them, individuals fight well for bad reasons. But if you are patriots, fight for your homeland, because this war is yours."[79] De Lattre's trip to the United States was distinguished by his remarks to the Americans concerning France's sacrifice for the "free world," which ensured that U.S. financial and military aid would finally be delivered regularly.

Would the war take on a new turn? General de Lattre's abrupt retirement owing to illness (he died in January 1952) left his efforts uncompleted. The United

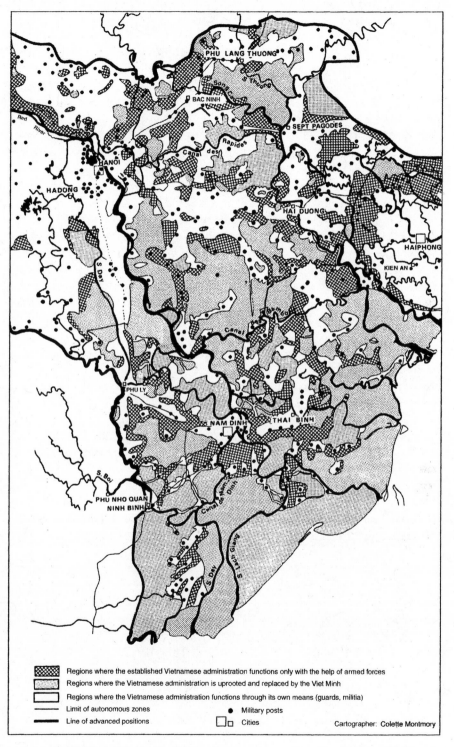

Regions where the established Vietnamese administration functions only with the help of armed forces

Regions where the Vietnamese administration is uprooted and replaced by the Viet Minh

Regions where the Vietnamese administration functions through its own means (guards, militia)

Limit of autonomous zones

Line of advanced positions

● Military posts

▢▫ Cities

Cartographer: Colette Montmory

MAP 8.2. Pacification of the Tonkin Delta on January 14, 1953. (Based on the wall map at French headquarters, now in the map library, CAOM.)

States delivered 85 billion francs worth of supplies in 1952; by 1953, the figure had reached 119 billion. Even though America was then assuming 40% of all military expenses in Indochina, the military situation worsened for the French. Vo Nguyen Giap undertook the conquest of the highlands of Tonkin. At the same time, Viet Minh units infiltrated the Red River Delta, demonstrating that pacification had been only very partial or superficial (map 8.2). In 1953, the plan of the new commander in chief, General Henri Navarre, was to start by "prohibiting" the PAVN from operating in the northern delta and completely "pacifying" the south (map 8.3) and the center. Carrying out the "Navarre plan" required reinforcements that the government refused to provide. Persuaded that it would be possible for them to beat the PAVN on a conventional battlefield, the French generals came up with the idea of constructing entrenched camps in order to attract the PAVN troops and thus "break" them. Dien Bien Phu fell into this category, but Navarre considered it more as a blockade preventing the PAVN from entering Laos. Therefore, when Vo Nguyen Giap rose to the challenge, and when it became clear that the siege was serious and the defensive situation worsening, Navarre refused to grant absolute priority to Dien Bien Phu. After a heroic resistance that lasted for two months, the entrenched camp surrendered on May 7, 1954.

It became clear that the defeat of Dien Bien Phu, although in itself less serious than that of Cao Bang, was the greatest and most decisive battle of the war in Indochina. Influenced by this defeat, the French command quickly ordered the evacuation of An Khe (in the high central plateaus), which ended in a "second Cao Bang." The evacuation of the southern region of the northern delta, on the other hand, was a success, allowing the Corps expéditionnaire to entrench itself in the enclave of Haiphong. But the series of military defeats weighed heavily on French policy and on the negotiations begun in Geneva to conclude a peace treaty in Korea and discuss the Indochinese situation. A new French prime minister, Pierre Mendès France, took advantage of this dramatic state of affairs by presenting the National Assembly with his famous gamble to achieve peace in Indochina within a month.

THE GENEVA PEACE: ONLY A TRUCE?

The Geneva agreement of July 21, 1954, temporarily divided Vietnam into two zones, on either side of the 17th parallel, until general elections could be organized that would decide the fate of the country. Laos was essentially divided between the royal government and Prince Souphanouvong's Pathet Lao, allied with the Democratic Republic of Vietnam. Only Cambodia regained its territorial and political integrity. What was signed on July 21 was not an actual treaty but a "mutual declaration." It presented the principles upon which a political end to the Indochinese conflict was to be based. This procedure was the result of the refusal of the United

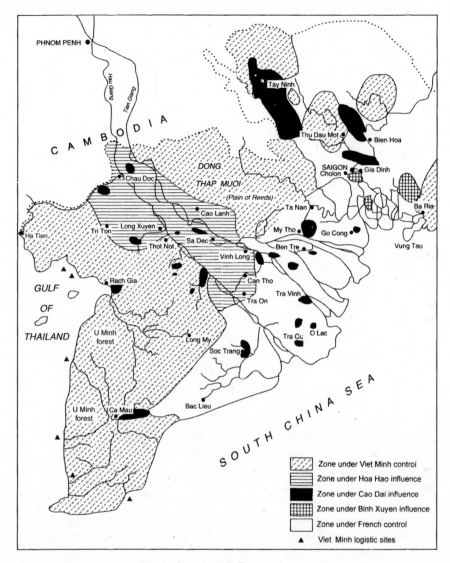

Zone under Viet Minh control
Zone under Hoa Hao influence
Zone under Cao Dai influence
Zone under Binh Xuyen influence
Zone under French control
▲ Viet Minh logistic sites

MAP 8.3. Nam Bo in 1953. (Service historique de l'Armée de terre, Vincennes.)

States and the Vietnamese nationalist government to ratify the final document of the conference. On July 22, Ngo Dinh Diem, chief of the nationalist government of the state of Vietnam, solemnly protested against the agreement, which "left half of Vietnam to the communists." He expressed the hope that one day the country would be "reunited and free." On October 23, 1954, General Dwight Eisenhower, president of the United States, assured Ngo Dinh Diem of his unconditional support against communist subversion. As a result, new protagonists came into play and put a new deal into place. At the end of the conference, however, the problems of Indochina were anything but resolved. The meeting at Geneva had validated the place of each group on the political scene, recognizing their victories and confirming their losses. A decade later, the question of Indochina would arise all over again.

The Results of the War

The total number of victims of the war is estimated at 500,000. On the French Army, the conflict exacted a toll of 59,745 killed and missing, of whom 2,005 were officers. The financial cost had risen to 2,385 billion francs.[80] Although no conscripts were sent to fight, the majority of the French no longer agreed with the aims of the war. The outcome of the conflict alleviated their weariness, but the incapacity of the Fourth Republic governments (which succeeded one another through numerous crises) to end the war contributed to the discrediting of its leaders and institutions. "The Republic died at Dien Bien Phu" is doubtless an oversimplification, but that disaster was an instant blow to the French colonial empire and shook the parliamentary Republic. Moreover, this first defeat in a colonial war traumatized the French military—above all, the officer corps, some of whom sought to learn from it. Rallying civilian populations to the cause became the major preoccupation of the supporters of the "psychological warfare" that was systematized in Algeria. From the art of the "people's war," some officers retained only recipes: physical partitioning and psychological rape through intensive propaganda. The Vietnamese had used such methods on the general population and French prisoners of war, but they had been combined with other actions aimed at making them acceptable to Vietnamese, if not to foreigners.

Furthermore, the other entities in the French Union absorbed the shock waves of the war and the French defeat. Important contingents of the expeditionary force consisted of Moroccans, Algerians, and Senegalese riflemen. The portion of overseas recruitment increased from 38% in 1947 to 60% in 1952, but it fell to 55% in 1954. In addition to the 55,000 West Africans and 110,000 North Africans, the Foreign Legion contributed 65,000 men.[81] Those who were captured underwent anticolonial indoctrination. The prestige of the Vietnamese revolution had grown in the world. The Geneva conference had hardly ended when the insurrection began in French North Africa.

A New Geopolitical Situation

The war, essentially Franco-Vietnamese, had taken place in a geopolitical, economic, and social space that had been organized by the French colonizers. The belligerents used its resources in the pursuit of unity and solidarity or division and antagonism. The French accentuated the differences and the distances that existed within the social body of the three countries of Indochina. They first captured and held the urban centers. "The countryside surrounded the town," said Le Duan, one of the members of the ICP's political bureau. Did it really? In fact, ethnic and religious divisions raged as much in the countryside as in the towns and allowed the French to find allies or partners there: Tai, Nung, Hmong, Rhade, Jarai, Khmer and Lao, Catholics, Caodaists, and Hoa Hao. There were 59,000 killed and missing in the Indochinese armed forces that fought alongside the French expeditionary corps, almost as many as the losses of the latter. However, it was also thanks to the classic cleavages and ideological options that the PAVN acquired supporters among the Tho, the Kha, the Khmer, and the Lao. The Indochina war had at least two sociopolitical consequences, the first being migration from rural areas to the city. The population of Saigon-Cholon increased from 500,000 in 1945 to 1,200,000 in 1949 and 2,000,000 in 1954. During the same year, at least 1,000,000 Tonkinese, Catholics for the most part, escaped, often dramatically, to the south, where they settled in homogeneous pockets, transforming the ethnic and sociopolitical landscape. In another development, Vietnamese bridgeheads in Cambodia and Laos engendered native communist cells there.

At the same time, the peninsula was divided between four states whose common official doctrine was one of greatness and national security. The Pax Gallica disappeared, and there was no longer an authority to regulate relations between the national communities. Would the Vietnamese, the most aggressive, and those who had defeated the French, claim for themselves the role of hegemony and tutelage previously occupied by the French? They were in any case constrained to reject any exterior interference, whether traditional (by a reunited China) or new and perceived as bringing with it neocolonial dependency (by the United States).

The war generated social transformations, especially when it succeeded in creating new states, and therefore a new political class, a body of civil servants and soldiers, a middle class, and a technostructure. The PAVN and the armies created to fight communism in Vietnam, Cambodia, and Laos provided paths of social promotion for peasants and the lower middle class, and at the same time were instruments of nation-building and consolidation. The administration and the specific structure of the Communist Party provided other means to achieve ascension and social involvement. This structure was not only replete with ideology but also facilitated particular methods of disseminating and inculcating ideology. For example, "rectification" *(chinh huan)*, indoctrination, and forcing people to conform became commonplace both within the PAVN and among civilians. This technique incorporated some Sino-Vietnamese cultural values, such as the art of popular war, and was itself a modernized reactivation of older Sino-Vietnamese cultural practices. Through the war, the PAVN turned to national, that is to say, Sino-Vietnamese, sources of culture. In the same period, the "Chinese angle" tended to become dominant once again in the Far East. National liberation was in fact a social revolution. Even if this was not the stated intention and even if it was not accompanied by agrarian reforms in favor of the landless peasantry, the reversal of the "authority of the white man" in Indochina empowered the native social classes with whom the French had previously refused to share any power. The greatest revolution of all, however, was psychological. The war broke the stereotypes of the colonized as eternal minors, incapable of military heroism, inept in organization and creation, and so on. The war acted as a gigantic psychodrama, creating among the colonized what they had lacked at the very beginning of the colonial century: confidence in themselves.

Land of Lost Opportunities

Indochina Ablaze

If we are to believe one of the last governors-general of Indochina, Jules Brevie, "Progress depends on the endurance of suffering, and the greater the suffering, the greater the progress."[1] It is not easy to make due allowances for suffering and progress in the historical balance of Indochinese colonization, for, as this book shows, it is difficult even to evaluate this balance satisfactorily, given that reliable information is missing on essential data such as colonial profit and its distribution, the evolution of standards of living and the consumption of colonized populations, the change of ecosystems, the evolution of the village, the diffusion of modern knowledge, and the crisis of ancient cultures and values. The history of Indochina during recent decades leads one to believe, however, that any "progress" there was not worth the price paid by the colonized. It was an almost exemplary price: to emerge from "the colonial night," the peoples of Indochina would have to assume and undergo one of the longest and cruelest wars of the twentieth century. That the genesis of this suffering was colonization is the crux of the colonial reality.

COLONIZATION: DREAMS AND REALITIES

In Indochina, as elsewhere, the road to colonization was paved with good intentions. At the time of triumphant imperialism, there were many, both among its active agents and among its sternest critics, who conceived of it as the "human form of progress," as a way for France to come into nonantagonistic, mutually beneficial contact with Asian and African societies. During the 1911 debate on Indochina and the Congo in the Chamber of Deputies, the great French socialist leader Jean Jaurès dreamed of "instituting a colonial policy not in contradiction with the spirit of humanity and democracy that is not just France, but the best part of France's genius." Of this best part, the colonized only savored a fleeting taste. As Jaurès perceptively added:

> The natives whose taxes you doubled, tripled, and quintupled, whose resources and hope you devoured on a daily basis, natives who had perhaps hesitated when you arrived, who perhaps said of France's renown: "These are armed men, but perhaps also friends who have arrived." Well! You took their resources from them, you built, not useful, modest works for them, such as irrigation schemes for their rice fields, or roads for their personal traffic or for that of their poor vehicles, you built superb railroads that were the pretext for fruitful loans, for shameless enterprises. Why? Because you were party to this false principle: that it was necessary, from the beginning, that colonies be a source of profit for France.[2]

For the most part, this process had to remain valid until the end of the colonial period. Certainly, the dream of a humanist colonization motivated more than one colonial. French Indochina had its philanthropists, its disinterested figures, its courageous personalities, devoted to the colonized, alongside a European majority that was much less so. However, the mirage of a liberating colonization would until the bitter end remain a utopian, albeit important, act of faith.

French Indochina was first and foremost an enterprise of political domination. Its establishment was incredibly violent, a state of affairs that continued periodically in order to maintain the colonial regime. However, at the same time, the colonial enterprise presented itself as the historical vector of modernization and everything this word signified at that time: industry, science, wage labor, machines, and a market economy. This enterprise sought to be the messianic incarnation of "progress." Domination, oppression, humiliation, racism, violence, modern schooling, modern medicine (for a limited population), industrialization, an export economy, and even the first democratic experiences ... all of this was inextricably and contradictorily melded and intertwined with the dynamics of colonial globalization.

French Indochina was one of the important pillars of France's power in the world. It was certainly a source of profit, one of the cogs in the colonial regulation of dysfunctions of French society and capitalism. On the basis of public investments financed by taxing peasant production, abundant capital, both French and local, was invested there. The great success of Indochinese colonization was fundamentally the success of ends determined by its promoters: plantations and mines, banks and trading firms. Success resulted from the precocious implantation of a "state machine" more demanding than any precolonial political system, the referee of conflicts between the principal Indochinese interests and an organizer of the colonial enterprise, thanks to the transplantation of the modern state's rationale into the dominated societies. It was the origin of a continuous flux of profits, benefits, pensions, and balances, swelling individual fortunes, inheritances, and the portfolios, great and small, of colonial businesses, the ruling class, and the French middle class.

From this point of view, the colonization of Indochina was only a particular case of the grand failure, in the nineteenth and twentieth centuries, of the quest for an equal exchange between the civilizations and peoples of Europe, Asia, and Africa, the need for which was glimpsed by only a few isolated individuals and minorities, far off the colonial track. Ships in the night . . . Could it have been any different? Today, this question is more topical than ever.

THE COLONIAL CONTRACT

If colonization was singularly costly to the Indochinese societies who nourished it with their natural resources and their labor, it was no less of a determining factor in their future. First, it united them in a new historic space, whose heart was Vietnamese. Auguste Pavie's project of reconstructing a great Lao state on the middle Mekong, which would encompass the Lao of northeastern Siam, was abandoned before 1900. Until the end of the twentieth century, Laos and, to a lesser degree, Cambodia would be considered territorial reserves of an Indochina thought of as fundamentally, first, "Annamese," then Vietnamese. Second, Indochina was a historic, transient, yet coherent, structure that inserted native peasantries forcefully into a foreign French universe: the economic market, limited industrialization, machines, wage labor, science, and so on. In sum, their often marginal entry was forced into the only "modernity" that history knew until then: that of a capitalist world economy.

For these societies, Indochinese colonization was therefore a fundamental historic rupture, which left them forever in upheaval, although very unequally, as shown by the survival, in numerous regions of Vietnam and throughout Cambodia and Laos, of precapitalist social forms: the extended family, lineage, and village communities. During this transition, notably in Vietnam, a new social stratification, elements of new social classes, although often embedded in older, yet still vital domestic structures—an embryonic proletariat, modern intellectual elites—were constituted in the cities, while the peasantry to varying degrees underwent training in the monetarization of their material cultures and their proletarianization.

These elements of general modernization, limited but very real, created the ambiguity of colonial Indochina. The latter, besides, always claimed, if only in the discourse that it delivered to the colonized elites, who were not necessarily unresponsive, that its aim was only to modernize. The other side of the colonial process was that it evoked participatory responses, not only among the elite but also, to a certain extent, among the people. The establishment of colonial power was thus not merely the result of conquest from the outside; it was also an internal process of the colonized societies, arising from multiple gulfs that divided them and tore them apart. The Indochinese colonial regime, besides, could not function without securing a partnership, however fragile, with the dominant classes and the old and new colonized elites, who hoped to use its modernizing capacities for their own ends, which were in the long run anticolonial. Colonization did not cause only attitudes of resistance among the colonized; the latter invested their own projects, and their own strategies in it, depending on the circumstances. This fragile partnership was founded on a feeling of unavoidable necessity among the elites and on the clear understanding they had of their own interests, which the colonial regime knew how to maintain, at least until the end of the 1920s. As a result, in spite of a permanent and tenacious anticolonialism among the Vietnamese, French Indochina was constructed on the evolutionary meeting of solidarities and antagonisms, hopes and deceptions, between the dominant and the dominated. It was, up until the 1930s, a provisional historic compromise, strongly unequal, of course, but not fictional, to such an extent that a number of Vietnamese ended up, at least for several decades, also thinking of themselves as "Indochinese."

FROM INDOCHINA TO MODERN NATIONS

In the space delimited by the Indochinese construct, however, the colonial regime, despite itself, could not help but contribute to another mutation: the maturation of the modern Indochinese nations. In Cambodia and Laos, whose ancient affiliation to the Thai world had been severed by the colonial regime, leaving them quasi-isolated in relation to the rest of the world, this maturation was delayed, as it clearly was too among the montagnards. It had to take place in response to both the expansion of Thailand and the rise of Vietnamese nationalism. On the other hand, in Vietnam, maturation was rooted in conquest itself, and in the moral and physical trauma that accompanied it. "We have conquered Indochina," Pennequin lucidly observed in 1913, "and we have pacified it, but we have not won the souls. . . . We are still encamped in this country: there are always winners and losers."[3] To win the hearts and minds would be the futile quest of colonialism, the inaccessible grail that would torment even the Pentagon in the 1960s. In Vietnam, between the winners and losers—at least most of them—the compromise was always fragile and was only transiently instituted, in the three crucial decades from 1900 to 1930, whereas Vietnamese intellectuals had since the first years of the twentieth century elaborated the concept of a modern nation, made sublime by resistance to colonization, nourished by the threefold will to escape the community of fate with the domineering foreigner, to promote political democracy, and, consequently, to reinvent the national community. The modern national idea became dominant very early on in the new Vietnamese society, and it took shape outside of the royal function, notwithstanding the attempts of the emperors Duy Tan (in 1916) and Bao Dai (first in 1932 and then in 1945) to control it. Repeatedly, in 1911, 1919, 1925, and 1936, one might have thought that a dialogue of decolonization was finally going to open up between France and the nations of Indochina. So many lost opportunities!

From then on, the colonial compromise broke down under the weight of the great crisis of the 1930s. With Indochina in mind, Sarraut wrote in 1931: "Our overseas Empire only dates back half a century, and already Friday now takes Robinson's measure there."[4] At the same time, French imperialism's neocolonial coming to grips with the crisis—the intransigent rejection of any notion of decolonization or political democratization—checked Vietnamese nationalism. Yet from the unforeseen there also emerged youthful nationalists who adhered to the revolutionary model of the Third International, and the nationalist problematic came to embody the most vigorous, although uncertain and divided, colonial communism, to which the inability of colonial power to remedy rural underdevelopment and to envisage its own overtaking, joined with the "overdue" defeat of France in the Far East in the 1940s, would provide opportunities. The national idea and the democratic idea gradually parted ways. From before 1939, an irremediable conflict arose between colonial France and the national Vietnamese movement thus renewed by the communist project, establishing the dynamic of a trial by force. World War II and the Japanese occupation created the conditions for this.

In the fateful year 1945, a liberated but still would-be imperial France confronted the prospect of the liberation of the Indochinese nations. French colonial imperialism, in the midst of acquiring a new historical shape and a neocolonial project, finally found the political will to take on the issues concerning the development of colonized peoples. It was just then that imperial France was overtaken in Indochina by the unforeseeable: a national, communist revolution that was radically decolonizing and pregnant with another historical project.

By 1945, French colonization had become intolerable to all Indochinese. In the entirety of its colonial space, French imperialism was in search of a new breath of air, a renovation whose chances were played out precisely in the confrontation with the Indochinese nations. As a result, the liberation of the national state throughout Indochina would come at the heavy price of a revolutionary war lasting thirty years and pitting the nation's development against that of democracy.

As early as 1911, Jaurès had raised a prophetic cry of alarm: "If we carry on, we will reap nothing from these lands but hatred and disappointment."[5] Three decades later, this warning had become a reality. In Indochina, there was not decolonization but a revolution that quickly turned into a new form of domination. Imperial France never recovered. And in Indochina, the "human form of progress" had still not been found, any more than it had been anywhere else.

Vietnamese Resistance to French Conquest

From Colonel Henri Frey, Pirates et rebelles au Tonkin, nos soldats au Yenthé *(Paris: Hachette, 1892), pp. 39–40, 83–86.*

In Indochina, the European indifferently confuses under the name of "pirate," not only marauders, highway robbers, and smugglers, as well as all sorts of adventurers who, giving into the temptation of a roaming life and defying the powerlessness of the law, prey in bands on land, on the coast, and on the rivers of Tonkin, but also the natives who, rebelling against French domination, fight to regain their national independence. . . . There are among the latter those who are uniquely motivated in their struggle against our authority by the hatred of foreigners and by a pure feeling of patriotism, contrary to those authors who pretend that the word "homeland" does not have an equivalent in the Annamese language and that the races of the Far East are not capable of letting themselves be carried along by this noble sentiment, which renders the masses and individuals capable of the grandest things. The strength, the courage with which a number of these pirates confront the executioner's blade, after having sometimes been the object, at the hand of their judges, of the most atrocious forms of torture; the harangues that some of them address to the public in the moments before their execution, declaring with the fervor of martyrs dying for their faith that they are guilty of no act of plundering or banditry, that they have fought and have sacrificed their lives to deliver their country from foreign oppression; the respectful reverence with which the crowds attend the executions . . . all of this attests to the fact that we are in the presence of true rebels. What is more, history is there to testify that in another era, during the Chinese occupation, this sentiment manifested itself among the populations of Tonkin in explosions of hatred and anger, which, more than once, were fatal to the conquerors. . . .

One must therefore recognize that a national party struggling against French influence indeed exists in Tonkin and Annam. This party is encouraged and favored by important figures in Annam and China; its importance grows each day, and it will soon constitute a most serious threat to our protectorate if pacification is slow to come. This party has, in all of the provinces, representatives chosen from among former mandarins or renowned literati, who obey the watchword of one of their higher-ups, whose authority is uncontested and who heads the anti-European movement. The chiefs of the large pirate bands also obey him.

APPENDIX 2

The Colonizers and
the Annamese Nation

From Dr. Jules Harmand, "Note sur la répartition de nos forces militaires en Indochine,"
Mémoires et documents Asie 57 *(July 15, 1885): 12–15, quoted in Philippe Devillers,*
Français et Annamites: Partenaires ou ennemis? 1856–1902 *(Paris: Denoël, 1998), pp.*
484–85.

We must never forget that the Annamese nation, whose homogeneity is without equal in all of Asia, constitutes a truly fearsome entity for a conqueror very far from its base of operations, a people whose history, from the remotest of times to today, shows the observer that they possess to the highest degree the sentiment of patriotism or, more exactly, the concept of race, and it would be very dangerous for us to see them all reunite in a common hatred of which we would be the object.

I would never let a chance go by of fighting a prejudice whose only foundations are utterly superficial observations, the interested statements of a handful of unscrupulous adventurers, or the illusions of ignorant or credulous missionaries, and which has unfortunately taken root with us. I am talking of the opinion that presents the Annamese people as divided into two enemy nations, the Annamese and the Tonkinese. This is an absolute error and has been altogether pernicious for us. Let us be clear about one thing, and that is that there is, for all intents and purposes, only one Annamese, from Kouang-Si [i.e., Guangxi province in South China] to the frontiers of Cambodia and Siam, that all the Annamese have the same ideas, the same customs, the same aspirations, the same rancor, and the same [social] organization, just as they have the same language and the same laws. There is less real antagonism between the Annamese of Tonkin and their southern brothers than there is, here in France, between a Breton and Provençal; and there is not a single "Tonkinese" who wishes to see his "Annamese" mandarins replaced by French chiefs. Let it be known once and for all that Tonkin is governed exactly like the rest of Annam, and that if the Tonkinese are not governed by mandarins of Tonkinese origins, it is only in obedience to an administrative law derived from China. It is to conform to this rule—which, moreover, allows for many exceptions—that the "Tonkinese" literati fulfill their functions in the southern provinces, while their colleagues of southern origins come, in a normal to-and-fro, to administer the provinces of Tonkin. . . .

There is not, in Annam, a single scholar or a single schoolchild, a single common man who does not know the names and deeds, which have become legendary, of the kings and the chiefs of bands that for centuries have raised high the flag of revolt against the Chinese invaders and who finally drove them out. The same is true of the least incident of our conquest of Cochinchina or of the present campaign. These are signs that no politician can look on with indifference.

It is for these reasons that we should do everything possible to avoid a general rebellion. From the beginning, to obviate these dangers or try to lessen their gravity, I have advised, then demanded insistently, the occupation of favorable points to divide Annam into several sections, to separate it especially from southern Tonkin. It is also because of this that I asked for the occupation, at the time easily accomplished, of southern Tonkin, and that I annexed Binh Thuan to Lower Cochinchina. My goal was to disrupt the cohesion of Annam, to cut it up, so to speak, into a series of segments or sections, in such a way that it could never reunite all of its forces against us. How recent events prove that I was right and make me deplore the fact that I was not understood!

Colonial Assemblies in Indochina, 1868–1940

Assembly	Date created	Composition	Attributions and modes of designation
Colonial Council of Cochinchina	February 8, 1880	Initially 12 Europeans and 6 "natives." Since the January 6, 1922 decree: • 10 French members elected by direct vote; 10 native members elected by restricted vote (electoral college [minimum age: 25]: landowners paying at least 10 piastres in land taxes; individuals subject to high trading dues; graduates of *primaire supérieur*, secondary, or university level; secondary- and superior-level civil servants with 5 years of seniority; industrial or commercial employees with a primary school or professional certificate with 10 years of seniority; notables, canton chiefs, and their assistants with at least 3 years of seniority); • 2 representatives of the Chamber of Commerce of Saigon and 2 delegates of the Chamber of Agriculture, equally divided between "natives" and Europeans; • Out of the 7 members of the Permanent Commission, only 2 can be "native."	Deliberating powers for • the management of the colony's private domain (except for free concessions or through mutual agreement) and public works, • the vote on local budgets subject to the approval of the General Government (but the Council cannot initiate expenditures other than optional expenses).

(continued)

Assembly	Date created	Composition	Attributions and modes of designation
Indigenous Consultative Assembly of Cambodia (became the Chamber of the People's Representatives on April 10, 1940)	March 8, 1913 (statutes revised in 1928)	41 elected members (as of 1924) • 2 elected by the neighborhood leaders of Phnom Penh; • 39 representatives of the provinces: 1/8 appointed, the rest elected by counselors and former counselors of the Residencies, civil workers in service or retired, those with diplomas starting at the second degree.	Consulting power only: Examine the protectorate's budget and questions submitted to the Assembly by the administration.
Indigenous Consultative Assembly of Tonkin (became the Chamber of the People's Representatives in 1926)	Instituted May 4, 1907; eliminated December 1908; reorganized March 19, 1913	The number of members and its composition varied. Beginning in 1928: • 1/4 of the Chamber made up of appointed civil servants and notables; • an electoral college (minimum age: 21) elects the other members: civil servants of the native administration, chiefs and deputy chiefs of cantons, graduates of French or Franco-indigenous schools; individuals of literary or mandarin rank; retired army officers; delegates of the Council of notables; secretaries and interpreters of the French administration; individuals subject to high trading dues.	Idem
Indigenous Consultative Assembly of Annam (became the Chamber of the People's Representatives in 1927)	April 19, 1920	33 members. Electoral college: Native civil servants of French and Annamese administration, university graduates, chiefs and deputy chiefs of cantons, delegates of the Council of Notables chosen by the Co Mat within the councils, individuals of mandarin rank, individuals subject to high trading dues.	Same attributions as in Tonkin. The Chamber gives its opinion on all questions of interest to the native population; it must be consulted on the budget, construction projects, and new taxes.

Indigenous Consultative Assembly of Laos	April 27, 1923	Same as in Cambodia, but assembly also includes members appointed by the resident superior (1 for each of the 10 provinces) and 2 representatives of the king of Luang Prabang.	Same attributions as in Tonkin
Indigenous Consultative Assembly of Quang Tcheou Wan (Guangzhouwan)	September 14, 1922	Elected by a restricted electoral college with varying requirements for rural and urban representatives.	Idem
PROVINCIAL COUNCILS			
District councils of Cochinchina	March 5, 1889	Elected in each canton by the councils of notables and French representatives of the economic chambers appointed by the governor (since 1930).	Consultative powers for examination of budgets and for economic and administrative affairs
Residence's council of Cambodia	August 27, 1903	Idem	Idem
Provincial Councils of notables of Tonkin	Created May 1, 1907; reorganized March 9, 1913	2 French councillors appointed; district representatives (*phu* and *huyen*) elected by chiefs and deputy chiefs of cantons, by presidents and vice-presidents of the Councils of notables, and by the *ly truong*.	Idem
Provincial Councils of notables of Annam	April 29, 1913	¼ of the members appointed. Representatives of the *phu* and *huyen* elected by chiefs and deputy chiefs of cantons (in office or retired) and by delegates of the Councils of notables (1 for every 30 registered).	Idem
Indigenous Consultative Council of Laos	October 13, 1920	No elections. Made up of native civil servants; 2 members appointed by the *muong*.	Idem

(continued)

Assembly	Date created	Composition	Attributions and modes of designation
MUNICIPALITIES			
Municipality of Saigon	April 1867: municipal commission appointed, then elected December 1870; municipal council electd; created May 16, 1877	• French representation (8 incumbent and 4 replacements) and native representation (instituted in 1881: 6 incumbents); all elected by direct vote. • Mayor elected by the municipal council.	
Municipality of Hanoi	July 19, 1888	• French representation (1891, 10 councillors) elected by direct vote; • Native representation (1891, 6 councillors) elected by an electoral college whose members filled a tax quota (at least 15 piastres of direct taxes) or demonstrated the requisite capacities (secretaries, graduates, literati of the third class, etc.).	
Municipality of Haiphong	July 19, 1888	Idem	
ECONOMIC ASSEMBLIES			
Chambers of commerce: Saigon Haiphong Hanoi	September 30, 1868 June 3, 1886 June 3, 1886	16 French and 4 natives elected by shopkeepers subject to trading dues.	
Chambers of agriculture: Cochinchina Tonkin	April 30, 1897 February 10, 1894	4 natives out of the 16 incumbents, 4 French replacements. 4 natives out of the 16 incumbents.	

Mixed chambers of commerce and agriculture:		
Tourane (Da Nang)	May 4, 1897	
Vinh	October 30, 1925	
Phnom Penh	April 30, 1897	
Vientiane	April 28, 1928	
In the Protectorates, French economic and financial interests	November 4, 1928	Composed of French representatives of the assemblies and economic chambers.
Grand council of economic and financial interests of Indochina	November 4, 1928	Mixed assemblies: 28 French members, of whom 22 elected by the assemblies and economic chambers and 6 appointed; 23 native members designated by elected assemblies and economic chambers, except for 5 nominated by colonial authorities.

Public Investments in Indochina, 1920–1938

Year	Participation funds	Supporting funds	Military spending contribution	Roads, trails, bridges	Railroads	Ports and sea access	Inland navigation	Hydraulics, agriculture, animal husbandry	Town planning, public health	Mining prospects	Communications, meteorology, aviation	Total (in thousands) piastres	Total (in thousands) current francs	Total (in thousands) 1914 francs
1920	25	—	10,016	4,114	123	335	128	3,025	3,122	—	271	21,159	244,809	48,960
1921	18	—	8,575	4,236	317	298	68	4,953	3,417	—	312	22,194	152,486	45,745
1922	—	—	6,875	5,237	1,405	163	108	3,373	4,927	—	1,008	23,096	156,753	50,631
1923	20	—	8,180	5,215	1,463	386	148	3,312	4,867	—	1,142	24,733	209,241	52,310
1924	17	—	9,173	5,860	2,793	482	370	3,577	5,270	—	1,308	28,850	290,808	61,942
1925	343	—	8,688	5,020	3,477	293	246	3,886	4,870	—	521	27,344	326,856	59,814
1926	—	—	10,071	5,089	2,618	561	488	3,516	5,222	—	418	27,983	475,711	69,453
1927	—	—	10,522	6,667	5,436	329	313	5,618	5,731	—	735	35,351	465,292	74,446
1928	—	—	11,351	7,726	2,370	264	3,715	3,068	7,297	—	561	36,352	464,215	74,274
1929	—	—	8,690	6,731	2,860	311	274	6,321	5,458	—	780	31,425	360,130	58,341
1930	—	—	10,958	6,550	7,706	1,313	1,855	4,422	5,196	—	2,077	40,077	400,870	73,359
1931	—	—	10,150	7,063	8,568	693	1,684	4,078	4,433	—	1,717	38,386	383,950	76,790
1932	—	—	10,810	2,890	10,570	357	670	4,545	2,511	—	928	33,281	333,810	77,777
1933	—	—	6,942	683	17,348	52	35	4,016	1,595	—	3,144	33,815	338,150	86,566
1934	4	—	7,066	1,299	14,273	780	721	4,088	1,525	—	362	30,118	301,180	80,113
1935	84	—	4,004	1,820	7,020	710	740	3,888	1,972	—	223	20,461	204,610	61,383
1936	—	30	4,011	2,737	5,107	630	965	3,346	2,090	—	381	19,297	192,970	48,242
1937	60	99	3,923	3,599	1,763	609	724	2,898	3,240	—	170	17,085	170,850	30,069
1938	329	—	15,660	4,404	2,818	181	95	9,390	4,330	—	703	37,910	379,150	59,147
TOTAL	900	129	165,665	186,945	98,035	9,047	13,377	81,320	77,074	—	16,766	548,917	5,851,841	1,189,362

SOURCE: Ministère des Colonies, *Investissement des fonds publics aux colonies: Indochine,* CAOM, Affaires politiques, 2640 (2).

NOTE: All figures are in thousands of piastres, which, in the last two columns, have been converted to current francs and 1914 francs.

APPENDIX 3

Annual Mobilization of Capital Stocks by Indochinese Companies in Various Economic Sectors, 1880–1940

Year	Industry		Transport		Plantations		Mines		Commerce		Property and real estate		Banks		Misc.		Total	
	1	2	1	2	1	2	1	2	1	2	1	2	1	2	1	2	1	2
1880–1890	—	—		268		120		—		200		—		1,200		—		1,788
1891–1900	[3,100]	310		55		110		50		—		200		2,400		—		3,125
1901–1914	[26,227]	2,622		2,870		5,538		1,082		1,762		—		2,400		—		16,726
1915–1923	[183,075]	7,363	2,594	939	16,308	5,903	8,735	3,162	11,400	412	6,500	261	6,000	2,172			66,103	23,929
1924	49,374	10,516	31,800	6,773	118,350	25,208	30,280	6,449	37,820	8,055	21,000	4,473	10,000	2,130	396	84	299,020	63,691
1925	37,945	11,716	2,625	496	67,500	12,757	17,400	3,288	29,998	5,669	—	—	10,000	1,890	—	—	165,864	31,348
1926	49,770	7,266	4,000	584	164,549	24,024	68,300	9,971	39,481	5,764	27,575	4,025	40,000	5,840	—	—	393,675	54,476
1927	47,009	7,521	27,100	4,336	363,749	58,199	85,508	13,681	18,000	2,880	38,150	6,104	20,000	3,260	1,709	273	601,225	96,196
1928	62,158	9,945	45,850	7,336	138,083	22,093	115,610	18,497	28,050	4,488	120,500	19,280	20,000	3,200	640	102	530,891	84,942
1929	34,517	5,591	28,175	4,565	143,689	23,277	128,750	20,857	20,700	3,353	172,200	27,896	36,000	5,832	960	155	564,991	91,528
1930	29,080	5,321	14,350	2,662	80,160	14,669	47,110	8,621	78,007	14,275	12,024	2,200	1,200	219	800	146	262,731	48,079
1931	21,600	4,320	—	—	7,111	1,422	9,035	1,807	1,000	200	500	100	48,000	9,600	250	50	87,796	17,559
1932	23,380	5,447	370	86	29,900	6,966	39,980	9,315	11,656	2,715	603	140	—	—	470	109	106,359	24,781
1933	60,110	15,388	—	—	13,250	3,392	13,275	3,398	10,018	2,564	23,040	5,898	5,000	1,280	10	2	124,703	31,923
1934	618	164	—	—	19,200	5,107	8,437	2,244	24,650	6,556	600	180	11,000	2,926	140	37	63,905	16,998
1935	1,800	540	—	—	34,785	10,435	3,000	—	1,450	362	7,219	1,804	6,500	1,625	—	—	37,375	11,212
1936	43,980	10,995	—	—	49,598	12,399	500	750	3,825	578	5,475	9,636	—	—	—	—	121,747	30,436
1937	67,640	11,922	19,250	4,812	70,575	12,421	—	88		4,863	—	93	7,020	—	20	3	166,845	29,364
1938	26,476	4,130	2,500	390	16,000	2,496	13,208	2,060	31,175	2,314	600	1,185	45,000	—	5,080	792	140,039	21,846
1939	19,625	2,943	1,610	241	3,500	525	40,994	6,149	15,430	708	7,900	—	—	—	20	3	89,079	13,361
1940	35,549	4,265	19,250	2,310	3,000	360	2,670	320	3,900	—	—	—	—	—	—	—	64,369	7,724

KEY TO COLUMN SUBHEADS: 1 = In thousands of current francs. For 1880–1890, 1891–1900, 1901–1914, and 1915–1923, the survey furnishes only global figures for each decade, which we have converted into annual averages. 2 = In thousands of 1914 (gold) francs. The conversion indexes used are the reevaluation coefficients of fixed assets defined by the March 19, 1960, decree (see J. Aubert-Krier, *Comptabilité privée* (Paris: Presses universitaires de France, 1962), pp. 27–38.

SOURCE: 1943 survey, CAOM, Affaires économiques, 52.

The Banque de l'Indochine's Shareholdings, June 1937

1. Indochinese Banks and Financial Companies:
   Crédit foncier d'Indochine (4.66%)
   Crédit mobilier indochinois (9,417)
   Union immobilière indochinoise (85,745)
2. Railroads and Public Services:
   Compagnie française des chemins de fer de l'Indochine et du Yunnan (13.1%)
   Chemins de fer du sud de l'Indochine (3,976)
   Messageries fluviales de Cochinchine (2.2%)
   Société indochinoise d'électricité (24%)
   Compagnie franco-indochinoise de radiophonie (1,000)
   Fourniture des eaux dans le Nord-Annam (20%)
3. Public Works:
   Société française d'entreprises de dragages et de travaux publics (10%)
   Syndicat d'études pour l'irrigation du Centre-Annam (1)
4. Industrial Companies:
   Distilleries de l'Indochine (30.3%)
   Manufacture indochinoise de cigarettes (5,100)
   Engrais azotés et chutes de Da Ninh (11)
   Établissements Delignon (1.72%)
   Société franco-annamite pour l'industrie de la soie (375)
   Compagnie générale des soies de France et d'Indochine (0.33%)
   Société industrielle de chimie d'Extrême-Orient (0.12%)
   Salines de l'Indochine (1,243)
   Outillage du port de Saigon-Cholon (850)
   Ciments Portland artificiels de l'Indochine (0.12%)

5. Mines:

Société française des charbonnages du Tonkin (0.83% of ordinary stock; 1.1% of stocks at plural votes)

Indochinoise de charbonnages et mines métalliques (12.3%)

Compagnie minière et métallurgique de l'Indochine (0.15%)

Étains du Cammon (25.5%)

Étains de l'Indochine (100)

Étains et wolframs du Tonkin (11.73%)

Mines de fer du Cambodge (2,333 + 867 + 645)

Société générale de prospection (100)

Société d'études pour l'industrie métallurgique en Indochine (20)

Exploitations minières et agricoles (673)

6. Real Estate Companies, Plantations:

Société foncière saigonnaise (100%)

Société foncière du Cambodge (0.5%)

Société du Phnom Deck (2)

Syndicat des planteurs de caoutchouc (1)

Bienhoa industrielle et forestière (9.52%)

Société industrielle et agricole de Cam Tien (6.57%)

Caoutchoucs de Binh Loc (17.1%)

Caoutchoucs de l'Indochine (2.41%)

Société indochinoise des cultures tropicales (852)

Plantations de Long Thanh (plantation de la Souchère 45,185 + 3,726)

Plantations d'hévéas de Prek Chlong (25.4%)

Caoutchoucs de Phuoc Hoa (10,000)

7. Commercial Companies:

Union commerciale indochinoise et africaine (0.04%)

SICAF, Société indochinoise de commerce, d'agriculture et de finance (63.6% of class A stocks; 11.5% of class B stocks)

8. China:

Compagnie Olivier Chine (7.40%)

Crédit foncier d'Extrême-Orient (2.5%)

Chinese Central Railways (4.60%)

Anglo-French China Corporation (1,000; in liquidation)

Oriental Industrial Monopolies (10,000; in liquidation)

Compagnie française des tramways et d'énergie électrique de Shanghai (17,000)

Établissements Belin

Société d'études minières d'Extrême-Orient

Société d'entreprises et d'exportations en Chine (100)

9. Other Colonies:

Banque d'État du Maroc (1.1%)

Compagnie générale du Maroc (1.24%)

Société internationale de régie co-intéressée des Tabacs au Maroc (0.57%)

Compagnie franco-espagnole du chemin de fer de Fez à Tanger (1.58%)

Crédit foncier à l'Ouest africain (32%)
Crédit industriel africain (100)
Compagnie du chemin de fer franco-éthiopien de Djibouti à Addis-Abeba (18.1%)
Compagnie impériale des chemins de fer éthiopiens (10,097)
Salines de Djibouti, Sfax et Madagascar (10.8%)
Caledo-Nickel (10)
Le Nickel (4,128 + 2,512)
Domaine de Tabeluyl (68,443)
Compagnie du Pacifique (31)
Cotonnière des Nouvelles-Hébrides (225)
Société de l'Afrique-Orientale maritime et commerciale (1,000)
Compagnie navale et commerciale Océanie (10)
10. France:
Crédit national (649)
Crédit colonial (13.1%)
Banque française d'acceptation (2,500)
Air France (6.92%)
Équipements des voies ferrées et grands réseaux électriques (1,000)
Électrocâble (1,000)
Compagnie commerciale des sels marins (200)
Compagnie minière coloniale (4.73%)
Mines d'or de Litcho (14%)
Mines d'or d'outre-mer (17,032)
Agence coloniale française (2)
Union coloniale française (20)

NOTE: The companies in italic are ones that had a representative of the Banque de l'Indochine on their board of directors. Not all the board members could be identified, however. When it was impossible to calculate the percentage of the Bank's participation in the capital, we have simply indicated in parentheses the number of stocks it held.

SOURCE: This list was compiled by comparing the January 19, 1938 report ("Étude sommaire sur les participations financières de la Banque de l'Indochine," CAOM, Affaires économiques, 598) with data in the *Annuaire financier France-Extrême-Orient, 1928–1929.*

The Société française financière et coloniale's Shareholdings, 1937

Crédit foncier de l'Indochine, Compagnie immobilière et foncière France-Indochine

Industrielle de chimie d'Extrême-Orient, Sucreries et Raffineries de l'Indochine, Entreprise de dragages et de travaux publics, Eaux et Électricité d'Indochine, Énergie électrique indochinoise, Indochinoise d'électricité, Coloniale d'éclairage et d'énergie, Cotonnière de Saigon, Verreries d'Extrême-Orient, Indochinoise de charbonnages et de mines métalliques, Mines d'or de Bao Lac, Chalandages et Remorquages de l'Indochine, Papeteries de l'Indochine, Imprimerie d'Extrême-Orient, Établissements Delignon, Salines de l'Indochine, Voies ferrées de Loc Ninh et du Centre indochinois, Société nouvelle des phosphates du Tonkin, Tramways du Tonkin

Société des caoutchoucs de l'Indochine, Indochinoise des cultures tropicales, Plantations indochinoises de thé, Société agricole franco-annamite

Plantes à parfum de Madagascar, Société malgache de cultures, Générale des graphites, Minerais de la Grande-Ile, Gemmes de Madagascar

Le Caoutchouc industriel, Société d'impression nouveauté sur étoffes, Établissements Pierre Bloche, Vautheret, Gros et Laforge, Soieries Ducharne

SOURCE: *Annuaire de la Cote Desfossés*, 1937.

The Société financière des caoutchoucs' Shareholdings (Rivaud Group), 1937

Compagnie financière des colonies, Union tropicale de plantation

Indochina: Plantation des Terres-Rouges, Plantation d'An Vieng, Caoutchoucs de Padang, Compagnie du Mékong, Compagnie du Cambodge

Malaya and the Dutch East Indies: Cultuur M. "Waringin," Sennah Rubber Co., Plantations du Nord-Sumatra, Asahan Cultuur Mij, Huileries de Deli, Soenghei Lipcet, Compagnie du Selangor, Palmboomen Cultuur Mopoli, Scefin Co., Beyabang, Huileries de Sumatra

Central Africa: Compagnie générale de l'Équateur, Equatorial Produce, Compagnie agricole de l'Angola, Compagnie agricole de Cazengo, Plantations de l'Abyssinie, Plantations de Nyombe-Penja, Plantations de la Sangra, Companhia Cervejas de Angola

South Africa: Brakpan, Crown Mines, Langlaate, Robinson Deep, Springs Mine, West Springs, M'Zaita, Kunstyde Unic

SOURCE: *Annuaire de la Cote Desfossés,* 1937.

The Banque de l'Indochine's Profits, 1875–1939

Year	A Capital paid (in thousands of current francs)	B Profits (in thousands of current francs)	C Profits (in thousands of 1914 francs)	D Original rate of profit (col. C/col. A)[b]
1875	2,000	18	18	0.9
1876	—	197	197	9.85
1877	—	270	270	13.5
1878	—	228	228	11.4
1879	—	291	291	14.55
1880	—	402	402	20.10
1881	—	308	308	15.40
1882	—	367	367	18.35
1883	—	345	345	17.25
1884	—	645	645	32.25
1885	—	711	711	35.55
1886	—	599	599	29.95
1887	—	655	655	32.75
1888	3,000	1,006	1,006	33.50
1889	—	734	734	24.46
1890	—	775	775	25.83
1891	—	691	691	23.03
1892	—	838	838	27.93
1893	—	1,099	1,099	36.63
1894	—	1,030	1,030	34.33
1895	—	935	935	31.16
1896	—	1,148	1,148	38.26
1897	—	771	771	25.70
1898	—	1,430	1,430	47.66
1899	—	1,504	1,504	50.13
1900	6,000	2,459	2,459	40.98
1901	—	3,154	3,154	52.56
1902	—	3,544	3,544	59.06
1903	—	4,276	4,276	71.26
1904	—	4,972	4,972	82.86
1905	—	4,321	4,321	72.01
1906	9,000	5,011	5,011	55.67
1907	—	6,722	6,722	74.68

(continued)

Year	A Capital paid (in thousands of current francs)	B Profits (in thousands of current francs)	C Profits (in thousands of 1914 francs)	D Original rate of profit (col. C/col. A)[b]
1908	—	5,327	5,327	59.18
1909	—	6,136	6,136	68.17
1910	12,000	7,542	7,542	62.85
1911	—	8,140	8,140	67.83
1912	—	10,504	10,504	87.53
1913	—	10,362	10,362	86.35
1914	—	7,844	7,844	65.36
1915	—	8,263	5,784	48.20
1916	—	9,566	5,984	2.48
1917	—	11,549	4,226	35.21
1918	—	19,140	5,742	47.85
1919	45,600 (13,224)[a]	21,323	6,162	46.59
1920	68,400 (19,836)[a]	25,872	7,502	37.82
1921	—	46,460	13,938	70.26
1922	—	44,242	14,290	72.04
1923	—	53,598	13,399	67.54
1924	—	62,889	13,395	67.52
1925	—	76,795	14,591	73.55
1926	—	113,335	16,546	83.41
1927	—	91,488	14,638	73.795
1928	—	76,017	12,162	61.31
1929	—	90,481	14,657	73.89
1930	—	87,748	16,057	80.94
1931	120,000 (24,000)[a]	61,581	12,316	51.31
1932	—	39,810	9,275	38.64
1933	—	37,387	9,571	39.87
1934	—	38,851	10,334	43.05
1935	—	45,507	13,652	56.88
1936	—	56,681	14,170	59.04
1937	—	61,524	10,828	45.11
1938	—	73,029	11,392	47.46
1939	—	111,870	16,780	69.91

SOURCE: The figures in column B are from Yasuo Gonjo, *Franku-Teiko Kushugi To Asia; Indoshina-Ginkoshi-Kenkyû* (Tokyo, 1985; typescript French translation: "La Banque de l'Indochine [1875–1939]: histoire d'une banque d'outre-mer française," pp. 132, 172, 327, 349, 478). Gonjo established four statistical series for profits: Profits I (profits minus operating costs); Profits II, or gross profits (Profits I minus the redemption of initial investments and the director's fees); Profits III, or net profits (Profits II minus the redemptions and provisions); Profits I' (Profits I minus losses and various administrative expenses, generally minimal), which best reflect the financial situation of the bank and come closest to the concept of base profit. We have used the figures of Profits I' to create this table, deflating them from 1914 on according to the method indicated in note 71 to chapter 3.

[a] Figures in parentheses are 1914 francs.

[b] For this calculation the figures in column A (capital paid) are first converted to 1914 francs.

Franco-indigenous School System in Indochina, 1930 and 1942

Levels of schooling (in 1930)	Teaching staff (in 1930)	Number of students		Language of instruction (in 1930)	Diplomas (in 1930)
		1930	*1942*		
Franco-indigenous elementary schooling: • elementary cycle at 397 full-course schools • classes at 2,835 elementary schools • classes at 4,531 establishments of academic initiation: renovated pagoda schools, etc.	Official schools: • 4,727 assistant schoolteachers and instructors (often educated at Franco-indigenous *primaire supérieur* schools) Establishments of academic initiation: • 5,452 teachers (former ideogram teachers, graduates of elementary and sometimes primary cycles, pagoda school teachers)	338,379	546,504	Native language, with an initiation to French in most elementary schools (85,000 students in all)	Certificate of indigenous elementary primary studies. Created in 1924, it included optional exams in French or Chinese.
Franco-indigenous primary schooling: 397 full-course schools	1,572 schoolteachers: graduates from teacher training colleges, holding either a diploma of *primaire supérieur* school studies or a *primaire supérieur* school teaching certificate and a certificate of pedagogical aptitude	40,367	63,611	French, with study of the native language and Chinese (Pali in Cambodia and Laos)	Certificate of Franco-indigenous primary studies, including native language, Chinese, or Pali exams.

(continued)

Levels of schooling (in 1930)	Teaching staff (in 1930)	Number of students		Language of instruction (in 1930)	Diplomas (in 1930)
		1930	1942		
Franco-indigenous *primaire supérieur* schooling: 21 establishments (*primaire supérieur* school classes, schoolteacher training colleges, first cycles of Franco-indigenous middle and high schools)	126 French and native *primaire supérieur* teachers	4,615	6,163	French, with study of the native language and Chinese or Pali	Diploma of Franco-indigenous *primaire supérieur* studies (approximately equivalent to the French elementary school certificate)
Franco-indigenous secondary schooling (3 years): Franco-indigenous high school of the Protectorate (Hanoi), Petrus-Ky Franco-indigenous high school (Saigon), Quoc Hoc middle school (Hue)	314 French and native graduate teachers	157	697	French, with study of the native language and Chinese or Pali	Certificate of qualification in Franco-indigenous secondary instruction, or the local baccalaureate in two parts, made equivalent to the French baccalaureate (except in medicine) in January 1930
Professional schooling	137 instructors and foremen	1,680	3,461		Professional diplomas
TOTAL	12,328, of which 12,014 are native (8,891 in the three Ky)	385,198	620,436		

Currency Conversion

1914 Francs (Gold Francs) and Current Francs

In this work, the term "current francs" indicates francs of variable value in the years following 1919. Up to 1914, the currency is called "1914 francs" (also known as "gold francs").

The term "1914 francs" refers to the franc created in 1803, which remained in circulation until 1914. Throughout this period, the franc's value in gold remained the same as in 1803 (namely, 1.00 F = 290 mg pure gold), as did its parity in international currency exchange with the British pound sterling (£1.00 = 25 F) and the U.S. dollar ($1.00 = 5 F). Thus, for one century, the franc was a strong and stable currency.

During the First World War, the unprecedented growth of the supply of banknotes in circulation (an eightfold increase from 1914 to 1918), together with state loans, France's debts to the United States and the United Kingdom, and price inflation, resulted in the decline of the real gold-value of the franc, which lost 30 to 40% of its value in relation to the dollar and the pound sterling. The crisis of the franc, concealed during the war by the financial and monetary solidarity of the Allies, broke out in March 1919, when that solidarity had ended. The franc suddenly collapsed on the currency market: in December 1919 the dollar was worth 11 F and the pound worth 42 F.

Throughout the twentieth century, the franc repeatedly depreciated. During the Third, Fourth, and Fifth Republic to 1999 (when the euro was introduced), the government had to devalue the franc periodically in order to reestablish a minimum of currency stability, albeit temporarily, at a lower exchange rate. The first devaluation occurred in 1928, reducing the legal gold value of the 290-mg pure gold franc to 65.5 mg. From 1919 on, the "current franc" thus became unstable and continued to lose its real value.

Historians cannot assess the real changes in prices, profits, salaries, production costs, and so on without using a stable standard currency. For the nineteenth century, this is not a problem because the franc was stable. For the twentieth, we convert "current francs" (whose value continually falls) to "gold francs" through coefficients that combine various series of statistical data. This operation is called "deflating" (prices, salaries, profits, etc.). There are several methods of deflating, each using different coefficients. In this book, we have used the coefficients fixed by the decree of March 19, 1960, published by the statistician J. Aubert-Krier in 1962 (see the table source note below). Thus, the statistics drawn from historical documents, in current francs, have been deflated year by year according to these coefficients.

The table below presents an example of possible equivalences that take into account inflation, the evolution of prices, and the buying power of French currency during the twentieth century. Conversion of current francs into euros is the subject of much debate, and the figures given in the table are only hypothetical.

Value of Current Francs in 1914 Francs
(with Equivalence in 1999 Francs and in Euros)

Current Francs	1914 Francs	1999 Francs	Euros
1F 1914	1.0	17.281	2.63
1F 1920	0.289	4.891	0.75
1F 1923	0.250	—	—
1F 1928	0.160	3.161	0.48
1F 1933	0.256	—	—
1F 1936	0.176	3.703	0.56
1F 1940	0.150	2.057	0.31
1F 1945	0.020	0.646	0.10
1F 1950	0.0065	—	—

SOURCES: Figures for current francs to 1914 francs are from J. Aubert-Krier, *Comptabilité privée* (Paris, 1962), pp. 37–38; for current francs to 1999 francs and euros, Institut national de la statistique et des études économiques (INSEE), Département des statistiques financières, taken from *CFDT [Confédération Française Démocratique du Travail] Magazine*, June 2001.

NOTES

FOREWORD

1. The original French version, *Indochine: La colonisation ambiguë, 1858–1954,* appeared in 1995.

2. Georges Boudarel arrived in Indochina in 1948 to teach high school philosophy. A member of the French Communist Party, he was opposed to the Indochina War and crossed over to the Viet Minh in 1950. During this time, he was involved in Vietnamese propaganda and the "reeducation" of captured French troops. Thanks to a general amnesty, he returned to France in 1968 and taught history at the Université de Paris VII. In 1991, the French Far Right, led by former prisoners of war of the Viet Minh, attacked Boudarel publicly, accusing him of torture and crimes against humanity during the Indochina War. Highly mediatized, the "Boudarel Affair" set off a wide range of debates in France, including one over the historical meaning of French colonization and decolonization.

3. Georges Balandier, *L'Afrique ambiguë* (1967; Paris: Pocket, 2008); C. Goscha, telephone conversation with Daniel Hémery, 16 July 2008. Hémery and Brocheux were equally influenced by Paul Mus's work on Vietnamese nationalism and French colonialism. Pierre Brocheux told us that Mus's *Viet Nam: Sociologie d'une guerre* was the most influential book he read early on in his career. See Daniel Hémery's essay on Paul Mus in *L'espace d'un regard: L'Asie de Paul Mus (1902–1969),* ed. C. E. Goscha and D. Chandler (Paris: Les Indes savantes, 2006).

4. See Daniel Rivet, "Le fait colonial et nous: Histoire d'un éloignement," *Vingtième siècle* 33 (1992): 127–38. Significantly, the publication of Brocheux and Hémery's study of "ambiguous Indochina" was followed by Daniel Rivet's *Le Maghreb à l'épreuve de la colonisation* (Paris: Hachette, 2002). And if Balandier and Mus inspired Hémery and Brocheux, it's clear that Jacques Berque, a specialist on North Africa, did similar things for Daniel Rivet.

INTRODUCTION

1. Georges Taboulet's two-volume *La geste française en Indochine: Histoire par les textes de la France en Indochine, des origines à 1914* (Paris, 1955–56) is the most erudite example of this historiography and still unsurpassed.

2. Malte-Brun titled the first part of vol. 12 of his *Géographie mathématique, physique et politique de toutes les parties du monde,* published in Paris in 1804 with Edme Mentelle, "Pays indo-chinois ou royaumes de Tonquin, de Cochinchine, de Laos, etc." Subsequently, in his *Précis de la géographie universelle ou description de toutes les parties du mondes sur un plan nouveau d'après les grandes divisions naturelles du globe* (Paris, 1813), 4, bk. 72, pp. 168–69, he gave a definition of "Indo-Chine." As Malte-Brun himself notes in the preceding work, John Leyden published a long article titled "On the Languages and Literature of the Indo-Chinese Nations" in vol. 10 of *Asiatic Researches,* the journal of the Asiatic Society of Bengal (Calcutta, 1808), and uses the notions of "Indo-Chinese languages" and the "Indo-Chinese Continent" with regard to Arakan, Siam, and Laos in his *Comparative Vocabulary of the Burma, Malayu, and Thai Languages* (Serampore, 1810). The *Larousse du XXe siècle* (Paris, 1953), still used the name "Indochine" in the sense that Malte-Brun and Leyden had given it. See D. Hémery, "Inconstante Indochine . . . L'invention et les dérives d'une catégorie géographique," *Revue française d'histoire d'outre-mer* 87, 326–27 (2000): 137–58.

3. K. Malte-Brun, *Précis de géographie universelle* (1813), 4: 168–69.

4. "Dai Nam" (Great State of the South) was the name adopted by the Hue court in 1838, but Chinese merchants and voyagers, and Europeans in the nineteenth century, used the old Chinese name "An Nam" (Pacified South), which the French adopted. The seal sent in 1803 by the Chinese emperor to the Vietnamese sovereign Gia Long bore the inscription *Yue-nan wang tche nin,* "Seal of the King of Yue of the South" (i.e., "of Vietnam").

5. P.-Y. Manguin, *Les Nguyen, Macau et le Portugal: Aspects politiques et commerciaux d'une relation privilégiée en mer de Chine, 1773–1802* (Paris, 1984); Nguyen The Anh, "L'Angleterre et le Vietnam en 1803: La mission de J. W. Roberts," *Bulletin de la Société des études indochinoises* 11, 4 (1965); A. Lamb, *The Mandarin Road to Old Hue: Narratives of Anglo-Vietnamese Diplomacy from the 17th Century to the Eve of the French Conquest* (Hamden, Conn., 1970).

6. C. Fourniau, *Vietnam: Domination coloniale et résistance nationale, 1858–1914* (Paris: Les Indes savantes, 2002).

7. J. Kleinen, *Facing the Future, Reviving the Past: A Study of Social Change in a Northern Vietnamese Village* (Singapore, 1999), p. 190; id., "The Village as Pretext: Ethnographic Praxis and the Colonial State in Vietnam," in J. C. Breman, P. Kloos, and A. Saith, eds., *The Village in Asia Revisited* (New Delhi, 1997). See likewise Nguyen The Anh, "Village versus State: The Evolution of State-Local Relations in Vietnam until 1945," in *Tonan Ajia Kenkyu* (Southeast Asian Studies) 41, 1 (June 2003); Diep Dinh Hoa, "A New Approach to Village Philosophies in the Red River Delta" (typescript, Australian National University, 1998); Hy Van Luong, *Revolution in the Village: Tradition and Transformation in North Vietnam 1925–1988* (Honolulu, 1992); M. Grossheim, *Nordvietnamesische Dorfgemeinschaften: Kontinuität und Wandel* (Hamburg, 1997); G. Boudarel, L. Prin, and Vu Canh, eds., *Propriété privée et propriété collective dans l'ancien Vietnam* (Paris, 1987).

8. In Vietnam, the drafting of cadastres in 1836 led to the establishment of 20,000 village registers. See Nguyen Dinh Dau, "Remarques préliminaires sur les registres cadastraux

(*dia ba*) des six provinces de Cochinchine," *Bulletin de l'École française d'Extrême-Orient* 78 (1991): 278n5. In 1924, a cadastre civil servant registered 21,991 "villages" (probably *xa*, or communes): 10,488 in Tonkin, 9,685 in Annam, and 1,818 in Cochinchina. See likewise P. Alinot, *Géographie générale de l'Indochine française* (Saigon, 1924), pp. 14–16.

9. Nguyen The Anh, *Monarchie et fait colonial (1875–1925)* (Paris, 1992); E. Poisson, *Mandarins et subalternes au nord du Vietnam: Une bureaucratie à l'épreuve (1820–1918)* (Paris: Maisonneuve & Larose, 2004).

10. D. P. Chandler, *History of Cambodia* (Oxford, 1992); Khin Sok, *Le Cambodge entre le Siam et le Vietnam de 1775 à 1860* (Paris, 1991).

11. Po Dharma, *Le Panduranga (Campa), 1802–1835: Ses rapports avec le Vietnam* (Paris, 1987).

12. Nguyen The Anh, *Kinh te va xa hoi Viet Nam duoi cac vua trieu Nguyen* (Saigon, 1970); id., "La réforme de l'impôt foncier de 1875 au Vietnam," *Bulletin de l'École française d'Extrême-Orient* 78 (1991): 287–96.

13. P. Langlet, *L'ancienne historiographie d'état au Vietnam* (Paris, 1992), xiv.

14. Nguyen The Anh, *Monarchie et fait colonial*, p. 311.

15. Langlet, *Ancienne historiographie*.

16. P. Langlet, "Point de vue sur Nguyen Truong To et le réformisme vietnamien au milieu du XIX siècle," *Études interdisiciplinaires sur le Vietnam* 1 (Saigon, 1974); Nguyen The Anh, "Tradition et réformisme à la cour de Hue dans la seconde moitié du siècle," in P. Brocheux, ed., *Histoire de l'Asie du Sud-Est: Reforme, révolte, révolution* (Lille, 1981), pp. 110–23; G. Boudarel, "Un lettré catholique vietnamien du XIX siècle qui fait problème: Nguyen Truong To," in A. Forest and Y. Tsuboi, eds., *Catholicisme et sociétés asiatiques* (Paris, 1988), pp. 159–203.

17. Nguyen The Anh, *Monarchie et fait colonial*, pp. 17–25.

18. A. B. Woodside, *Vietnam and the Chinese Model: A Comparative Study of Nguyen and Ch'ing Civil Government in the First Half of the Nineteenth Century* (Cambridge, Mass., 1971), p. 290; Langlet, *Ancienne historiographie*.

19. Quoted in Nguyen The Anh, "Tradition et réformisme."

20. Le Thanh Tuong, *Un patriote annamite admirateur de la France: Essai sur la vie de Phan Thanh Giang, vice-roi de Cochinchine* (Hanoi, 1938), p. 92.

21. P. Bairoch, "La place de la France sur les marchés internationaux au XIX siècle," in *La position internationale de la France: Aspects économiques et financiers, XIX–XX siècles* (Paris, 1977).

22. Ibid.

23. Quoted by Taboulet, *Geste française en Indochine*, 1: 242.

24. Marseille Chamber of Commerce, letter to the ministre de la marine et des colonies, May 9, 1865, Centre des archives d'outre-mer, Aix-en-Provence [CAOM], AFJ, d. 11.

CHAPTER 1

1. See part 1 of Charles Fourniau's major study *Vietnam: Domination coloniale et résistance nationale, 1858–1914* (Paris, 2002).

2. Vo Duc Hanh, *La place du catholicisme dans les relations entre la France et le Vietnam de 1851 à 1870* (Leyden, 1969); id., *La place du catholicisme dans les relations entre la*

France et le Vietnam de 1870 à 1886 (Berne, 1993); N.-D. Le, *Les missions étrangères et la pénétration française au Vietnam* (Paris, 1975); Cao Huy Thuan, *Les missionnaires et la politique coloniale française au Vietnam (1857-1914)* (New Haven, Conn., 1990); C. Prudhomme, *Missions chrétiennes et colonisation XVI*e*-XX*e *siècles* (Paris, 2004), and id., ed., *Une appropriation du monde: Mission et missions, XIX-XX*e *siècle* (Paris, 2004).

3. A. Forest, *Les missionnaires français au Tonkin et au Siam (XVII*e*-XVIII*e *siècles): Analyse comparée d'un relatif succès et d'un échec certain* (Paris, 1997); L. Burel, "Le contact colonial franco-vietnamien dans le Centre et le Nord du Vietnam, 1856-1883" (PhD diss., Paris, 1997).

4. Burel, *Contact protocolonial franco-vietnamien.*

5. J. F. Cady, *The Roots of French Imperialism in East Asia* (New York, 1967).

6. See, e.g., the work of Abbé P. Raboisson, *Études sur les colonies et la colonisation au regard de la France* (Paris, 1877).

7. Quoted by Forest, *Missionnaires français au Tonkin et au Siam,* p. 725n13.

8. On this commission, see Vo Duc Hanh, *Place du catholicisme,* and P. Devillers, *Français et Annamites: Partenaires ou ennemis? 1856-1902* (Paris, 1998).

9. Commander Gatier's report, October 20, 1880, AN CC3, 1183.

10. C. de Montigny, *Manuel du commerce français en Chine* (Paris, 1846).

11. I. Hedde (delegate of Lyon silk industry), *Étude pratique du commerce d'exportation de la Chine* (Paris, 1848).

12. E. Denis, *Bordeaux et la Cochinchine sous la Restauration et le second Empire* (Bordeaux, 1965). On Lyon, see J.-F. Klein's noteworthy study, "Soyeux en mer de Chine: Stratégies des réseaux lyonnais en Extrême-Orient (1843-1906)" (PhD diss., Lyon, 2002).

13. G. Durand and J.-F. Klein, "Marseille et la Chine: Une liaison impossible? (1832-1853)," in *Les échanges Franco-Chinois au XIX*e *siècle: La mission de Lagrené en Chine (1843-1846),* symposium at the Collège de France, June 4, 2004; English version being translated for *The China Journal,* published by the Australian National University, Canberra.

14. P. Cayez, *Crises et croissance de l'industrie lyonnaise, 1850-1900* (Paris, 1980); J.-F. Laffey, "Les racines de l'impérialisme français en Extrême-Orient," *Revue d'histoire moderne et contemporaine* 16 (April-June 1969); id., "Roots of French Imperialism in the XIXth Century: The Case of Lyon," *French Historical Studies* 6, 1 (Spring 1969); id., "Municipal Imperialism in Nineteenth Century France," *Historical Reflections* 1 (1974); "Municipal Imperialism in France: The Lyon Chamber of Commerce, 1900-1914," *Proceedings of the American Philosophical Society* 119, 1 (February 21, 1975); and, above all, Klein, "Soyeux en mer de Chine."

15. Conseil supérieur de l'agriculture, du commerce et de l'industrie, *Enquête sur la marine marchande* (Paris, 1863), 1: 362.

16. Taboulet, *Geste française en Indochine,* 1: 416.

17. P. Devillers, "Au Sud-Vietnam, il y a cent ans," *France-Asie,* Winter 1965-66; M. W. McLeod, "Truong Dinh and Vietnamese Anticolonialism 1859-1864: A Reappraisal," *Journal of Southeast Asian Studies* 24, 1 (March 1993).

18. It was marked by the brochures of *[Lieutenant de vaisseau]* Rieunier, published under the pseudonym Abel, *Solution pratique de la question de Cochinchine ou fondation de la politique française en Extrême-Orient* and *La question de Cochinchine au point de vue des intérêts français* (Paris, 1864), and by those written by Francis Garnier under the pseudonym

G. Francis, *La Cochinchine française en 1864* (Paris, 1864) and *De la colonisation de la Cochinchine* (Paris, 1865).

19. P. Lamant, "Les prémices des relations politiques entre le Cambodge et la France vers le milieu du XIX siècle," *Revue française d'histoire d'outre-mer* 72, 267 (1985): 167–98.

20. *Exploration de l'Indochine de 1866 à 1868 par une commission française présidée par le capitaine de frégate Doudart de Lagrée et publiée sur l'ordre du Ministère de la Marine . . .* (Paris, 1873); M. E. Osborne, *River Road to China: The Mekong River Expedition, 1866–1873* (London, 1975); J. Valette, "L'expédition du Mékong (1866–1868) à travers les témoignages de quelques-uns de ses membres," *Revue historique,* no. 502 (April–June 1972); and esp. J.-P. Gomane, *La Mission Doudart de Lagrée–Francis Garnier (1866–1868)* (Paris, 1995), and Francis Garnier, *Voyage d'exploration en Indochine,* ed. J.-P. Gomane (Paris, 1985). On Garnier, see P. Petit-Brûlefert, "Francis Garnier: Une vie (1839–1873)" (PhD diss., Perpignan, 1997).

21. J. Valette, "Les relations politiques entre la France et le Vietnam de 1867 à 1875" (PhD diss., Poitiers, 1971).

22. Y. Tsuboi, *L'empire vietnamien face à la France et à la Chine* (Paris, 1987); M. W. McLeod, *The Vietnamese Response to French Interventions, 1862–1874* (New York, 1991); Bui Tran Phuong, "La politique de paix préconisée par Nguyen Truong To face au défi occidental au XIXe siècle" (MA thesis, Université de Paris VII–Denis Diderot, 1995).

23. Devillers, *Français et Annamites.*

24. Admiral Léonard Charner, letter of March 24 to the king of Cambodia, quoted by Devillers, *Français et Annamites,* p. 85.

25. E. Renan, *La réforme intellectuelle et morale de la France* (Paris, 1871).

26. Jules Ferry to the Chamber of Deputies, July 28, 1885.

27. J. Valette, "L'expédition de Francis Garnier au Tonkin," *Revue d'histoire moderne et contemporaine,* April–June 1969, p. 189–200. On the geographic movement, see D. Lejeune, *Les sociétés de géographie en France et l'expansion coloniale au XIXème siècle* (Paris, 1993).

28. A. Murphy, *The Ideology of French Imperialism, 1871–1880* (Washington, D.C., 1948), pp. 40–70.

29. J. Harmand, *L'Indochine française: Politique et administration* (Paris, 1887); id., *Domination et colonisation* (Paris, 1910); J. Chailley-Bert, *La colonisation de l'Indochine: L'expérience anglaise* (Paris, 1892); J. Ferry, *Le Tonkin et la mère patrie* (Paris, 1890); J.-L. de Lanessan, *L'expansion coloniale de la France* (Paris, 1886); id., *L'empire d'Annam* (Paris, 1889); id., *L'Indochine française: Étude politique, économique et administrative* (Paris, 1889); id., *La colonisation française en Indochine* (Paris, 1895); P. Doumer, *Situation de l'Indochine, 1897–1901* (Paris, 1902), and *L'Indochine francaise (Souvenirs)* (Paris, 1905).

30. Alfred Rambaud, *La France coloniale: Histoire, géographie, commerce* (Paris: A. Colin, 1886).

31. C. Fourniau, *Vietnam: Domination coloniale et résistance nationale, 1858–1914* (Paris, 2002).

32. François Fournier was the author of an anonymous brochure, *Les Colonies nécessaires: Tunisie, Tonkin, Madagascar. Par un marin* (Paris, 1885), and an article published in May 1885 in the *Nouvelle Revue,* "La question du Tonkin: Les objectifs de la France en Indochine." See P. Masson, "La stratégie navale française de 1850 à 1914," *Revue maritime* (1968).

33. Figures cited by J. Thobie, *La France impériale, 1860-1914* (Paris, 1983). See also Y. Breton, A. Broder, and M. Lut Falla, *La longue stagnation en France: L'autre Grande Depression, 1873-1897* (Paris, 1997).

34. See Y. Gonjo, *Banque coloniale ou banque d'affaires: La Banque de l'Indochine sous la IIIe République* (Paris, 1993), and Marc Meuleau, *Des pionniers en Extrême-Orient: Histoire de la Banque d'Indochine, 1875-1975* (Paris, 1990).

35. Lanessan, preface to id., *Expansion coloniale de la France.*

36. D. Brötel, *Französischer Imperialismus in Vietnam: Die koloniale Expansion und Errichtung des Protektorates Annam-Tongking, 1880-1885,* and the articles by Laffey cited in n. 14 above.

37. F. Garnier, "Des nouvelles routes de commerce avec la Chine," *Bulletin de la Société de géographie,* February 1882.

38. Klein, "Soyeux en mer de Chine."

39. Laffey articles cited in n. 14 above.

40. Quoted by E. Delbard, "Les chemins de fer du Tonkin," *Annales de l'Extrême-Orient et de l'Afrique,* January 1889. On this penetration, see C. Fourniau, "Politique coloniale ou 'politique mondiale': Doumer et le Yunnan," in *Histoire d'outre-mer: Mélanges en l'honneur de J.-L. Miège* (Aix-en-Provence, 1992), 49-72, and M. Bruguière, "Le chemin de fer du Yunnan, Paul Doumer et la politique d'intervention française en Chine, 1889-1902," *Revue d'histoire diplomatique* 77 (1963).

41. Georges Clemenceau, speech of December 24, 1885, quoted by C. Fourniau, *Les contacts franco vietnamiens en Annam et au Tonkin de 1885 à 1896,* PhD diss., Aix–Marseille, 1983 (Lille, 1984), p. 463.

42. Pierre Rheinart, note of August 25, 1885, quoted by Fourniau, *Contacts franco vietnamiens,* p. 635.

43. On Liu Yong Fu and the Black Flags, see H. Macaleavy, *Black Flags in Vietnam: The Story of a Chinese Intervention* (London, 1968), and "La formation d'un rebelle: Liu Yong Fu et la création de l'armée des Pavillons Noirs," in J. Chesneaux, F. Davis and Nguyen Nguyet Ho, eds., *Mouvements populaires et sociétés secrètes en Chine aux XIXe et XXe siècles* (Paris, 1970); E. Laffey, "French Adventures and Chinese Bandits in Tonkin," *Journal of Southeast Asian Studies* 6, 1 (March 1975).

44. Jules Ferry, letter to his wife, quoted by G. Guillen, *Politique étrangère de la France,* vol. 1: *L'expansion 1881-1898* (Paris, 1985), p. 189. On the war with China, see also C. Fourniau, "L'amiral Courbet," *Revue d'histoire des armées,* no. 3 (1985).

45. Fourniau, *Contacts franco vietnamiens,* p. 482.

46. Ibid., pp. 455-58.

47. *Le Télégraphe,* December 25, 1885, quoted by Fourniau, *Contacts franco vietnamiens,* p. 486.

48. B. Lavergne, *Les deux présidences de Jules Grévy, 1879-1887* (Paris, 1966). See the stimulating analyses of Devillers, *Français et Annamites,* pp. 280-318, and Fourniau, *Contacts franco vietnamiens,* pp. 674-785.

49. Nguyen The Anh, "The Withering Days of the Nguyen Dynasty," in Institute of Southeast Asian Studies, Singapore, *Research, Notes, and Discussions,* no. 7 (May 1978); and esp. id., *Monarchie et fait colonial au Vietnam (1875-1925): Le crépuscule d'un ordre traditionnel* (Paris, 1992), chaps. 1, 3, and 4.

50. M. Osborne, *The French Presence in Cochinchina and Cambodia: Rule and Response, 1859–1905* (Ithaca, N.Y.: Cornell University Press, 1969), pp. 206–28; A. Forest, *Le Cambodge et la colonisation française: Histoire d'une colonisation sans heurts (1897–1920)* (Paris, 1980), chap. 1; Ke Khi You, "L'insurrection générale de 1885–1886 au Cambodge" (MA thesis, Université de Paris-VII, 1971); D. P. Chandler, *A History of Cambodia* (Oxford, 1992), chap. 8.

51. Ferry, *Tonkin et la mère patrie*, p. 275, quoted by D. Hémery, "L'Indochine de la conquête à la colonisation (1885–1914)," in J. Ganiage, *L'expansion coloniale de la France sous la IIIeme République (1871–1914)* (Paris, 1968), pp. 354–96.

52. J. Blancsubé, *À propos du Tonkin et de l'Indochine* (Paris, 1886).

53. Lanessan, *Indochine française*, p. 682.

54. Quoted by Fourniau, *Contacts franco vietnamiens*, p. 561.

55. Colonel F. Bernard, *L'Indochine, erreurs et dangers* (Paris, 1901), p. 32.

56. General H. Frey, *Pirates et rebelles au Tonkin* (Paris, 1891), p. 43.

57. Ibid., p. 15.

58. Ibid., p. 56.

59. Fourniau, *Contacts franco vietnamiens*, p. 925.

60. J. Dupuis, *Le Tonkin de 1872 à 1886* (Paris, 1910), p. 564.

61. Fourniau, *Contacts franco vietnamiens*, p. 925.

62. On Ba Dinh, see Fourniau, *Contacts franco vietnamiens*, pp. 907–23, and Captain J. Masson, *Souvenirs de l'Annam et du Tonkin* (Paris, 1903).

63. Quoted by Fourniau, *Contacts franco vietnamiens*, p. 2551.

64. Garnier, *De la colonisation de la Cochinchine*, p. 13.

65. In the words of J. Chesneaux, "Stages in the Development of the Vietnam National Movement, 1862–1940," *Past and Present*, no. 7 (1955): 63–75.

66. Lanessan, *Indochine française*.

67. F. Baille, *Souvenirs d'Annam (1886–1890)* (Paris, 1890), p. 72.

68. According to Clemenceau, quoted by Fourniau, *Annam-Tonkin, 1885–1896*, p. 20.

69. Data calculated by Fourniau, *Contacts franco vietnamiens*, p. 1723.

70. Quoted in M. Blanchard, "L'Indochine française de 1886 à 1889," *Études d'histoire moderne et contemporaine* 5 (1953): 187.

71. Fourniau, *Contacts franco vietnamiens*, p. 1809.

72. Harmand, *L'Indochine française*, p. 35.

73. Fourniau, *Contacts franco vietnamiens*, p. 1809.

74. L. Bonhoure, *L'Indochine* (Paris, 1900), p. 181.

75. D. G. Marr, *Vietnamese Anticolonialism, 1885–1925* (Berkeley, 1971).

76. Proclamation found on 30 November 1890 by Captain Pélissier in a refuge of the Yen The, quoted by Matgioi [A. de Pouvourville], *La Politique indochinoise* (1894), p. 207. See also the texts quoted by J. Chesneaux, *Contribution à l'histoire de la nation vietnamienne* (Paris, 1955), chap. 8.

77. Fourniau, *Contacts franco vietnamiens*, p. 931.

78. Paul Bert, letter quoted by R. Marle, "La pacification du Tonkin," *Bulletin de la Société des études indochinoises* 1 (1972): 54.

79. Quoted by Fourniau, *Annam-Tonkin, 1885–1896*, p. 72. On Paul Bert's government, see P. Isoart, "Paul Bert, resident général de France en Annam-Tonkin (Janvier–Novembre 1886)," *Approches-Asie* 10 (1989–90).

80. J. Kim Munholland, "The French Army and the Imperial Frontier in Tonkin, 1885–1897," *Proceedings of the 3rd Annual Meeting of the French Colonial Historical Society* (Montreal, 1977).

81. Commandant P. Famin, *Au Tonkin et sur la frontière du Kwang-Si* (Paris, 1895).

82. See Fourniau, *Contacts franco vietnamiens*, p. 1848ff.

83. J.-L. de Lanessan, *La lutte pour l'existence et l'évolution des sociétés* (Paris, 1903).

84. D. Deschamps, "Les sources scientifiques de la politique indochinoise de J.-L. de Lanessan (1891–1894)," in *Vietnam. Sources et Approches: Colloque Euroviet* (Aix-en-Provence, 1996), p. 279ff.

85. J.-L. de Lanessan, *Indochine française*, p. 719.

86. J.-S. Galliéni, *Gallieni au Tonkin* (Paris, 1899), p. 91.

87. E. Poisson, *Mandarins et subalternes au nord du Viêt Nam: Une bureaucratie à l'épreuve (1820–1918)* (Paris, 2004).

88. Centre national de la recherche scientifique, *Histoire des frontières de la péninsule indochinoise*, ed. P.-B. Lafont, vol. 1, *Les frontières du Vietnam* (Paris, 1989).

89. C. L. Keeton, *King Thebaw and the Ecological Rape of Burma: The Political and Commercial Struggle between British India and French Indo-China in Burma, 1878–1886* (Delhi, 1974); P. J. Tuck, *The French Wolf and the Siamese Lamb: The French Threat to Siamese Independence 1858–1907* (Bangkok, 1995); D. Brötel, *Frankreich in Fernen Osten: Imperialistiche Expansion und Aspiration in Siam und Malaya, Laos, und China, 1880–1904* (Stuttgart, 1996); V. Grabowsky, "Chiang Khaeng 1893–1896: A Lue Principality in the Upper Mekong Valley at the Centre of Franco-British Rivalry," in C. E. Goscha and S. Ivarssøn, eds., *Contesting Visions of the Lao Past: Lao Historiography at the Crossroads* (Copenhagen, 2003).

90. C. Hirschfeld, "The Struggle for the Mekong Banks, 1892–1896," *Journal of Southeast Asian History* (Singapore), March 1968.

91. P. J. N. Tuck, "Auguste Pavie and the Exploration of the Mekong Valley 1886–1895," *Terrae Incognitae* 14 (1982); A. Pavie, *Mission Pavie: Géographie et voyages* (Paris, 1901–11); id., *Au pays des millions d'éléphants et du parasol blanc* (1921; reprint, Paris, 1995); H. Simon, *Auguste Pavie, explorateur en Indochine* (Rennes, 1997); A. Goscha-Larcher, "On the Trail of an Itinerant Explorer: French Colonial Historiography on Auguste Pavie's Work in Laos," in Goscha and Ivarssøn, *Contesting Visions*, pp. 209–38.

92. Gabriel Hanotaux, letter to Pavie, quoted by Guillen, *Expansion*, p. 367. See also Fourniau, "Politique coloniale ou 'politique mondiale.' "

93. Guillen, *Expansion*, pp. 376–77.

94. C. Charle, *La crise des sociétés impériales: Allemagne, France, Grande-Bretagne, 1900–1940: Essai d'histoire sociale comparée* (Paris, 2001).

95. Forest, *Cambodge et la colonisation française; Osborne, French Presence in Cochinchina and Cambodia*.

96. Bernard, *Indochine*, p. 39.

CHAPTER 2

Epigraph: Joseph d'Ariès quoted in Fourniau, *Vietnam: Domination et résistance nationale*, p. 111.

1. Albert Sarraut, *Grandeur et servitude coloniales* (Paris, 1931).

2. Osborne, *French Presence in Cochinchina and Cambodia.*

3. Fourniau, *Contacts franco vietnamiens,* p. 1186.

4. Joseph Chailley-Bert quoted by P. Isoart, "Paul Bert, résident general de France en Annam-Tonkin (January–November 1886)," *Approches-Asie,* no. 10 (1989–90).

5. J. Chailley-Bert, *Paul Bert au Tonkin* (Paris, 1897), p. 336.

6. L. Rouyer, *Histoire militaire de l'Annam et du Tonkin depuis 1799* (Paris, 1897), p. 185.

7. Lanessan, *Colonisation française en Indochine,* p. 13.

8. Ibid.

9. Fourniau, *Contacts franco vietnamiens,* p. 2249.

10. Ibid., p. 782.

11. Louis de Grandmaison, *L'expansion française au Tonkin: En territoire militaire* (Paris, 1898), p. 179.

12. P. Isoart, "La création de l'Union indochinoise," *Approches-Asie,* no. 11 (1992): 45–71.

13. Ibid.

14. Lanessan, *L'Indochine française,* p. 678.

15. Fourniau, *Vietnam: Domination coloniale et résistance nationale,* p. 193.

16. E. Millot, *Le Tonkin* (Paris, 1888), p. 189.

17. Fourniau, *Contacts franco vietnamiens,* pp. 1586–87.

18. Camille Pelletan quoted by Harmand, *Indochine française,* p. 35.

19. Vu Van Hien, "Les institutions annamites depuis l'arrivée des Français: L'impôt personnel et les corvées de 1862 à 1936," *Revue indochinoise juridique et économique,* no. 1 (1940).

20. Acting Governor-General Bideau quoted by Lanessan, *Colonisation francaise en Indochine,* p. 1.

21. Fourniau, *Vietnam: Domination coloniale et résistance nationale,* p. 453.

22. See ibid., pp. 539–657, and A. Lorin, *Paul Doumer, gouverneur-général de l'Indochine (1897–1902): Le tremplin colonial* (Paris, 2004), 248.

23. J. Harmand, preface to a translation of *India* by Sir John Strachey (London, 1888), *L'Inde* (Paris, 1892), p. xxx; see also Harmand, "L'Indo-Chine française" (1887 lecture in Paris to the Association républicaine pour la célébration du centenaire de 1789), and H. L. Wesseling, "The Dutch Colonial Model in French Colonial Theory, 1890–1914," in *Proceedings of the IInd Annual Meeting of the French Colonial Historical Society* (Milwaukee, 1976).

24. L. Mossy, *Principes d'administration générale de l'Indochine* (Saigon, 1924); J. de Galembert, *Les administrations et services publics indochinois* (Hanoi, 1931); J.-B. Alberti, *L'Indochine d'autrefois et d'aujourd'hui* (Paris, 1934); R. Pinto, "Aspects de l'évolution gouvernementale de l'Indochine française," in *Études indochinoises et extrême-orientales* (Paris, 1946).

25. Harmand, preface cited in n. 23 above, p. xlvi.

26. Bernard, *Indochine,* p. 43.

27. A. Messimy, *Notre œuvre coloniale* (Paris, 1910), p. 149.

28. A. Métin, *L'Indochine et l'opinion* (Paris, 1916), p. 97.

29. B. Eli, *Paul Doumer in Indochina (1897–1902)* (Heidelberg, 1967).

30. P. Doumer, *Situation de l'Indochine de 1897 à 1902* (Paris, 1902), p. 89.

31. L. Cury, *La société annamite* (Paris, 1910), p. 70.

32. Letter of August 31, 1897, quoted by Forest, *Cambodge et la colonisation francaise,* p. 63.

33. See P. Lamant, *L'affaire Yukanthor: Autopsie d'un scandale colonial* (Paris, 1989).

34. Harmand, *Indochine francaise*, p. 36.

35. Ibid.

36. Ngo Duc Ke in *Hoi Gia Long (Demandez à Gia Long)*, quoted by Nguyen The Anh, *Monarchie et fait colonial au Vietnam*, p. 245; see also in ibid., analysis on pp. 279-84.

37. See the arguments of Forest, *Cambodge et la colonisation francaise*, and M. E. Osborne, "History and Kingship in Contemporary Cambodia," *Journal of Southeast Asian History*, March 1966.

38. B. Gay, "Approche du système colonial: Histoire des contestations 'ouvertes' du haut Laos et du bassin de la rivière Noire (novembre 1914-mars 1916)" (PhD diss., Paris, 1982); M. Stuart-Fox, *A History of Laos* (New York, 1997).

39. Ibid.

40. G. Condominas, "Essai sur l'évolution des structures politiques thai," in *L'Espace social à propos de l'Asie du Sud-Est* (Paris, 1980); C. Taillard, *Le Laos: Géographie d'un état-tampon* (Montpellier, 1989); M. Stuart-Fox, *Laos, Politics, Economics and Society* (London, 1986), and id., *History of Laos*.

41. K. G. Izikowitz, *Lamet: Hill Peasants in French Indochina* (Göteborg, 1951).

42. See Léopold Sabatier, *Palabre du Serment au Darlac. Assemblée des chefs de tribus, 1e janvier 1926* (Hanoi, 1930).

43. E. Poisson, *Mandarins et subalterns au Nord du Vietnam: Une bureaucratie à l'épreuve, 1820-1918* (Paris, 2004).

44. P. Pasquier, *L'Annam d'autrefois: Essai sur la constitution de l'Annam avant l'intervention française* (Paris, 1907, reprint 1930), p. 117.

45. Doumer, *Situation de l'Indochine*, p. 90.

46. Cury, *Société annamite*, p. 80.

47. Prime minister of Annam quoted by L. Salaun, *Essai sur l'organisation de l'Indochine* (Paris, 1901), p. 99.

48. Messimy, *Notre œuvre coloniale*, p. 108. See also J. Morel, "Contribution à l'histoire financière du Tonkin (1884-1909)," *Revue indochinoise*, no. 1 (1909), and H. Guermeur, *Le régime fiscal de l'Indochine* (Hanoi, 1909).

49. Salaun, *Essai sur l'organisation de l'Indochine*, p. 134.

50. H. Brenier, *Essai d'atlas statistique de l'Indochine française: Indochine physique, population, administration, finances, agriculture, commerce, industrie* (Hanoi-Haiphong, 1914), p. 8.

51. C. Descours-Gatin, *Quand l'opium finançait la colonisation en Indochine: L'élaboration de la régie générale de l'opium (1860 à 1914)* (Paris, 1992), p. 210; P. Le Failler, "Le mouvement international anti-opium et l'Indochine (1905-1940)" (PhD diss., Aix-en Provence, 1993); *Opiums: Les plantes du plaisir et de la convivialité en Asie*, ed. A. Hubert and P. Le Failler (Paris, 2000); Y. Bision, "Le monopole des stupéfiants" (thesis, Université de Paris X, 1993); J. Dumarest, "Les monopoles de l'opium et du sel en Indochine" (thesis, Lyon, 1939).

52. Descours-Gatin, *Quand l'opium finançait la colonisation*; Le Failler, "Mouvement international anti-opium."

53. Francis, *De la colonisation de la Cochinchine*, p. 27; Descours-Gatin, *Quand l'opium finançait la colonisation*, p. 101.

54. B. Peyrouton, *Les monopoles en Indochine* (Paris, 1913), p. 78; on the monopoly on alcohol, see also R. Monier, *La question du monopole de l'alcool au Tonkin et dans le Nord-Annam* (Paris, 1913).

55. Fourniau, *Vietnam: Domination coloniale et résistance nationale*, p. 618.

56. J. Mordaing, "Le monopole des alcools indigènes au Tonkin et dans le Nord-Annam," *Revue indochinoise*, June 1913.

57. Forest, *Cambodge et la colonisation française*, p. 222n2.

58. Salaun, *Essai sur l'organisation de l'Indochine*, p. 71.

59. Brenier, *Essai d'atlas statistique de l'Indochine*, graph no. 34

60. See *Annuaires économiques de l'Indochine*, 1930–31 and 1940–42, as well as P. Bernard, *Le problème économique indochinois* (Paris, 1934), p. 14.

61. Bernard, *Problème économique*, p. 50.

62. This is based on the estimate of 60 million quintals for 5 million hectares of rice fields presented in Y. Henry in his *Économie agricole de l'Indochine* (Hanoi, 1932), p. 338.

63. Forest, *Cambodge et la colonisation francaise*, pp. 223–25; M. Comte, "Économie, idéologie et pouvoir: La Société cambodgienne (1863–1866)" (PhD diss., Lyon, 1980), pp. 303–19. R. Thomas, "L'Évolution économique du Cambodge, 1900–1940" (PhD diss., Paris, 1978), pp. 236–38, reaches similar conclusions.

64. Harmand, *Indochine française*, p. 35.

65. On the *xa*, see Philippe Papin, "Des villages dans la ville aux villages urbains: L'espace et les formes du pouvoir à Hanoi de 1805 à 1940" (PhD diss., Paris, 1997); on the French vision of the Vietnamese village, see L. Dartigues, "Les représentations françaises du monde social vietnamien à travers les textes savants, 1860–1940: Essai d'anthropologie historique de la connaissance coloniale du Vietnam" (PhD diss., Marseille, 2001).

66. P. Kresser, *La commune annamite en Cochinchine* (Paris, 1935).

67. Nguyen Huu Khang, *La commune annamite: Étude historique, juridique et economique* (Paris, 1946), p. 55. On the Vietnamese village before the colonial period, see "Le village traditionnel," *Études vietnamiennes* (Hanoi), no. 61 (1980) and no. 65 (1981).

68. H.G., "L'évolution des institutions communales au Tonkin (1921–1941)," *Revue indochinoise juridique et économique* (Hanoi, 1942).

69. Anon., "Note sur les institutions communales en Annam," Centre des archives d'outre-mer, Aix-en-Provence [CAOM], Fonds Guermut, B1.

70. P. Papin, "Who Has Power in the Village? Political Process and Social Reality in Vietnam," in G. Bousquet and P. Brocheux, *Viêt Nam Exposé: French Scholarship on Twentieth-Century Vietnamese Society* (Ann Arbor, Mich., 2002), pp. 21–60.

71. See Ang Choulean, "La communauté Khmère du point de vue du sacré," *Journal asiatique*, nos. 1–2 (1990).

72. G. Condominas, *Nous avons mangé la forêt de la Pierre-Génie Gôo: Chronique de Sar Luk, village mnong gar, tribu proto-indochinoise des hauts-plateaux du Viêt-Nam central . . .* (Paris, 1957).

73. M. Guerin, A. Hardy, Nguyen Van Chinh, and Stan Tan Boon Hwee, *Des montagnards aux minorités ethniques: Quelle intégration nationale pour les habitants des hautes terres du Viêt Nam et du Cambodge?* (Paris and Bangkok, 2003).

74. Nguyen The Anh, *Monarchie et fait colonial au Viêt-Nam (1875–1925)*, p. 280.

75. Forest, *Cambodge et la colonisation française*, p. 110.

76. Ibid., pp. 82–84.

77. A. Larcher-Goscha, "La légitimation française en Indochine: Mythes et réalités de la 'collaboration franco-vietnamienne' et du réformisme colonial (1905–1945)" (PhD diss., Paris, 2000).

78. Harmand, preface cited in n. 23 above, pp. xxviii and lx.

79. Ibid.

80. G. de Gantès, "Coloniaux et gouverneurs en Indochine française, 1902–1914" (PhD diss., Paris, 1994), p. 501.

81. J. Betz, *Bartholdi* (Paris, 1954), p. 217.

82. Speech by Pham Quynh at the proclamation of results of the *tri huyen* examinations, Hanoi, December 1941, quoted in P. Bezançon, *Un colonisation éducatrice? L'expérience indochinoise (1860–1945)* (Paris: L'Harmattan, 2002).

83. Anon., "Note sur les institutions communales en Annam," p. 337.

84. Pasquier, *Annam d'autrefois*, p. 337.

85. Anon., "Note sur les institutions communales en Annam."

86. P. Zinoman, *The Colonial Bastille: A History of Emprisonment in Vietnam, 1862–1940* (Berkeley, 2001), p. 63; D. Hémery, "'Terre de bagne en mer de Chine: Poulo Condore (1862–1953)," in Proceedings of Colloquium, "Colonisation et répression," Université de Paris VII, 2008 (forthcoming).

87. P. Morlat, *La répression coloniale au Vietnam, 1908–1940* (Paris, 1990).

88. J. Obrecht, "Le problème de l'identification et l'organisation des services d'identité en Indochine," *Revue indochinoise juridique et économique* 17 (1942): 1–51. On the repressive aspects of the colonial system, see Morlat, *Répression coloniale*, and D. Hémery, *Révolutionnaires vietnamiens et pouvoir colonial en Indochine: Communistes, trotskystes, nationalistes à Saigon de 1932 à 1937* (Paris, 1975), chap. 4.

89. Quoted by Obrecht, "Problème de l'identification."

90. J.-D. Giacometti, "La question de l'autonomie de l'Indochine et les milieux coloniaux français, 1915–1928" (PhD diss., Aix-Marseille, 1997).

91. See A. Sarraut, *La mise en valeur des colonies françaises* (Paris, 1923).

92. Huynh Van Tong, "Histoire de la presse vietnamienne jusqu'en 1930" (PhD diss., Paris, 1971), and D. Hémery, "Journalisme révolutionnaire et système de la presse au Vietnam dans les années 1930," *Cahiers du Centre universitaire de recherches sociologiques d'Amiens*, no. 8 (1978): 55–85.

93. J. Robinard, "La Franc-maçonnerie et la colonisation sous la III République de 1904 à 1936" (PhD diss., Aix-en-Provence, 1971); J. Dalloz, "Les Vietnamiens dans la Franc-maçonnerie coloniale," *Revue française d'histoire d'outre-mer*, 85, 320 (1998): 103–18.

94. D. Hémery, "L'Indochine, les droits humains, 1898–1954: Entre colonisateurs et colonisés, la Ligue des droits de l'homme," *Outre-mers: Revue d'histoire* 88, 1st semester (January) 2001.

95. *Bulletin socialiste de la Cochinchine* (Saigon), 1905.

96. See Hémery, *Révolutionnaires vietnamiens et pouvoir colonial,* and the socialist press of French Indochina, notably the weekly *Agir* (Saigon), 1936–39.

CHAPTER 3

1. The central works remain C. Robequain, *L'evolution économique de l'indochine française* (Paris, 1939); P. Gourou, *L'utilisation du sol en Indochine française* (Paris, 1940); Y. Henry, *Économie agricole de l'Indochine* (Hanoi, 1932); P. Bernard, *Le problème économique indochinois* (Paris, 1934). A. Agard, *L'Union indochinoise française ou Indochine orientale: Régions naturelles et géographie économique* (Hanoi, 1935), provides useful information. M. J. Murray, *The Development of Capitalism in Indochina (1870–1940)* (Berkeley, 1940), p. 685, advances a certain number of interesting hypotheses, but gives more weight to ideological preoccupations than to systematic historical research. The economic history of French Indochina is currently enjoying a boom: see, e.g., *L'esprit économique impérial, 1830–1970: Groupes de pression et réseaux du patronat colonial en France et dans l'empire,* ed. H. Bonin, C. Hodeir, and J.-F. Klein (Paris, 2008), which contains many contributions about French entrepreneurs in Indochina, and P. Brocheux, *La palanche et le camion: Une histoire économique du Vietnam de 1850 à nos jours* (in press).

2. F. Leurence, *Étude statistique sur le développement économique de l'Indochine de 1899 à 1923* (Hanoi, 1925).

3. Robequain, *Évolution économique,* p. 189.

4. Ho Hai Quang, "La formation du secteur de production capitaliste au Vietnam méridional (1859–1918): La théorie des capitaux importés à l'épreuve des faits," *Revue d'histoire d'outre-mer,* 2nd trimester 1985.

5. Forest, *Cambodge et la colonisation française,* chaps. 12–13.

6. Ibid.

7. Ibid.

8. Paul Doumer quoted in ibid., p. 240.

9. Acting Governor-General Joost van Vollenhouven, letter to the minister, May 31, 1914, quoted in Gay, "Approche du système colonial," p. 136n2.

10. In addition to the writings of Robequain, Gourou, and Murray, see Nguyen Tan Loi, "L'économie commerciale du riz en Indochine" (PhD diss., Paris, 1934); Y. Pégourier, *Le marché du riz d'Indochine* (Paris, 1936); J. Decaudin, "Un essai d'économie dirigée: Le marché du paddy et le marché du riz en Cochinchine, 1941–1944," *Bulletin économique de l'Indochine,* 1944; I. Nørlund, "Rice Production in Colonial Vietnam, 1900–1930" in *Rice Societies: Asian Problems and Prospects,* ed. id., S. Cederroth, and I. Gerdin (London, 1986); and esp. P. Brocheux, "L'économie et la société dans l'ouest de la Cochinchine pendant la période coloniale (1890–1940)" (PhD diss., Paris, 1969); id., "Grands propriétaires et fermiers dans l'ouest de la Cochinchine pendant la période coloniale," *Revue historique,* July–September 1971; and id., *The Mekong Delta: Ecology, Economy and Revolution, 1860–1960* (Madison, Wis., 1995).

11. Robequain, *Évolution économique,* p. 124. See also J. Brassford, "Land Development Policy in Cochinchina under the French" (PhD diss., University of Hawaii, 1984); Brocheux, *Mekong Delta;* Vo Tong Xuan and Shigeo Matsui, eds., *Development of Farming Systems in the Mekong Delta of Vietnam* (Ho Chi Minh City, 1998); D. Briggs, "Problematic Progress: Reading Environmental and Social Change in the Mekong Delta," *Journal of Southeast Asia Studies* 34, 1 (February 2003).

12. Nguyen Dinh Dau, "Remarques preliminaires sur les registres cadastraux (*dia ba*) des six provinces de Cochinchine," *Bulletin de l'École française d'Extrême-Orient* 78 (1991).

13. Ta Thi Thuy, *Viec nhuong dat khan hoang o Bac Ky tu 1919 den 1945* (Hanoi, 2001); see also Pham Cao Duong, "L'accaparement des terres pendant la période coloniale," *Revue française d'histoire d'outre-mer*, 1985.

14. Estèbe, *Problème du riz en Indochine*, pp. 68ff.

15. *Bulletin économique de l'Indochine*, 1907, p. 243.

16. Robequain, *Évolution économique*, p. 300.

17. I. Nørlund, *Interplay between Craft and Industry in a Vietnamese Province: Nam Dinh, 1900-1945* (Copenhagen, 1991), pp. 184-201.

18. T. R. Dawson and P. Schidrowitz, *History of the Rubber Industry* (Cambridge, 1952); M. Boucheret, "Les plantations d'hévéas en Indochine (1897-1954)" (PhD diss., 2008), the first sound—and very well documented—history of rubber plantations in Indochina, as well as of French colonial capitalism; A. McFadyean, *The History of Rubber Regulation, 1934-1943* (London, 1944); C. Whittlesey, *Governmental Control of Crude Rubber* (Princeton, N.J., 1928); P. Carton, *Le caoutchouc en Indochine* (Hanoi, 1924); H. Tardy, *Économie et politique du caoutchouc* (PhD diss., Paris, 1928); J. Vaxelaire, *Le caoutchouc en Indochine* (Hanoi, 1939); and C. Bonneuil, "Mettre en ordre et discipliner les tropiques: Les sciences du végétal dans l'Empire français, 1870-1940" (PhD diss., Paris, 1997), chap. 5, pp. 277-372.

19. Resident E. Desenlis, report, August 1927, quoted by J. Tully, *France on the Mekong: A History of the Protectorate in Cambodia, 1863-1953* (Lanham, Md., 2002), p. 316. See also the often-quoted 1929 report of Work Inspector Delamarre, which appears in an appendix to J. Goudal, *Labour Conditions in Indo-China*, ILO Studies and Reports, Series B, no. 26 (Geneva, 1938).

20. Secrétariat d'État aux Colonies, "Le problème du caoutchouc" (note dated April 23, 1941), Centre des archives d'outre-mer, Aix-en-Provence [henceforth cited as CAOM], Affaires économiques, 59 (7).

21. D. W. Del Testa, "'Imperial Corridor': Association, Transportation, and Power in French Colonial Indochina," in special issue of *Science, Technology, Society* (Delhi), December 1999; and "Paint the Trains Red: Labor, Nationalism, and Railroads in French Colonial Indochina, 1898-1945" (PhD diss., University of California, 1999).

22. G. Raffi, "Haiphong: Origines, conditions et modalités du développement jusqu'en 1921" (PhD diss., Aix-Marseille, 1993).

23. E. Denis, *Bordeaux et la Cochinchine sous la Restauration et le Second Empire* (Bordeaux, s.d.), p. 80.

24. A. Chevalier, "Les améliorations scientifiques et techniques réalisées par la France en Indochine," *Revue de botanique appliquée et d'agriculture tropicale*, November-December 1945; Bonneuil, "Mettre en ordre," chap. 5, pp. 277-372. On colonial forest management, see M. Buchy, "Histoire forestière de l'Indochine (1850-1954): Perspectives de recherches," *Revue française d'histoire d'outre-mer*, no. 299 (1993): 219-49; F. Thomas, "Écologie et gestion forestière dans l'Indochine française," *Revue française d'histoire d'outre-mer*, no. 319 (1998): 59-86; id., *Histoire du régime et des services forestiers français en Indochine de 1862 à 1945* (Hanoi, 1999); M. Cleary, "Managing the Forest in Colonial Indochina, c. 1900-1940," *Modern Asian Studies* 39, 2 (2005): 257-83. For a more general comparison, see D. R. Headrick, *The Tentacles of Progress: Technology Transfer in the Age of Imperialism, 1850-1940* (New York, 1988).

25. "Rapport sur les services de l'agriculture en Indochine," June 1924, CAOM, Affaires économiques, 880.

26. J. Prades, *Déboisements, incendies, rays: Préservation et reconstitution de la forêt* (Hanoi, 1921); M. Cleary, "Managing the Forest in Colonial Indochina, c. 1900–1940," *Modern Asian Studies* 39, 2, (2005).

27. A. George, "Autonomie économique, coopération internationale, et changements de structure en Indochine" (PhD diss., Paris, 1953), p. 256.

28. Ibid.

29. *La Quinzaine coloniale,* May 25, 1937.

30. See J. Marseille, *Empire colonial et capitalisme français: Histoire d'un divorce* (Paris, 1984).

31. Quoted by J.-D. Giacometti, "La question de l'autonomie de l'Indochine et les milieux coloniaux français, 1915–1928" (PhD diss., Aix-en-Provence, 1997); see also S. Pesenti, "De l'administration à la mise en valeur: Les tentatives de modernisation d'une agriculture coloniale. Annam-Tonkin (1886–1919)" (MA thesis, Aix-en-Provence, 1994).

32. See the analysis of C. Coquery-Vidrovitch, "Vichy et l'industrialisation des colonies," *Revue d'histoire de la Seconde Guerre mondiale,* no. 114 (1979).

33. On the history of the *sapèque,* see A. Schroeder, *Annam: Études numismatiques* (Paris, 1905); F. Thierry, *Monnaies d'Extrême-Orient,* vol. 2, *Vietnam-Japon* (Paris, 1986); J. Delambre, "Un technicien méconnu: René Mercier et la sapèque Bao Dai, 1933," *Bulletin de la Société française de numismatique* no. 4 (1980); A. Buu Sao, *La sapèque vietnamienne face aux monnaies étrangères* (PhD diss., Paris, 1992). On the money in circulation at the beginning of the twentieth century, see J. Silvestre, "Notice sur les monnaies circulantes dans les pays d'Extrême-Orient (1908)," *Bulletin de la Société de géographie de Rochefort,* 1909.

34. The classic work on the subject remains W. F. Spalding, *Eastern Exchange Currency and Finance* (London, 1917).

35. *Rapport de la Commission monétaire indochinoise* (Paris, 1920), p. 22.

36. Letter of July 22, 1938, CAOM, Affaires économiques, 518.

37. A. Sabes, *Le renouvellement du privilège de la Banque de l'Indochine* (PhD diss., Paris, 1931), p. 44.

38. *Dépêche coloniale,* July 27, 1928.

39. *Rapport de la Commission monétaire indochinoise* de 1933 (Paris, 1934), p. 3.

40. G. Lasserre, "Les banques en Indochine, vers 1945," CAOM, Affaires économiques, 598.

41. "Rapport sur les monts-de-piété" (1945), CAOM, Affaires économiques, 598.

42. M. Meuleau, *Des pionniers en Extrême-Orient: Histoire de la Banque de l'Indochine, 1875–1975* (Paris, 1990); Y. Gonjo, *Banque coloniale ou banque d'affaires: La Banque de l'Indochine sous la IIIe République* (Paris, 1993). See also J. Bouvier, F. Furet, and M. Gillet, *Le mouvement du profit en France au XIX siècle: Matériaux et études* (Paris, 1965), pp. 219–49, 448.

43. After the crash in copper, the CEP was transformed in 1889 into the Comptoir national d'escompte de Paris (CNEP).

44. H. Bonin, "Le CNEP, banque impériale (1848–1940)," *Revue française d'histoire d'outre-mer* 78, 293 (1991).

45. Gonjo, *Banque coloniale ou banque d'affaires,* chap. 8.

46. On this project, see G. Lasserre, "Les banques coloniales," CAOM, Affaires économiques, 190 (B).

47. Meuleau, *Des pionniers en Extrême-Orient,* p. 358.

48. W. Oualid, *Le privilège de la Banque de l'Indo-Chine et la question des banques coloniales* (Paris, 1923).

49. Ibid., p. 61.

50. R. Vally, "Les banques coloniales françaises d'émission, un point de vue historique et critique" (PhD diss., Paris, 1924), p. 135; Lasserre, "Banques en Indochine."

51. Meuleau, *Des pionniers en Extrême-Orient,* p. 338.

52. Lasserre, "Banques en Indochine."

53. Oualid, *Privilège de la Banque de l'Indo-Chine,* p. 122.

54. Lasserre, "Banques en Indochine."

55. Oualid, *Privilège de la Banque de l'Indo-Chine,* p. 122.

56. Lasserre, "Banques en Indochine."

57. Gonjo, *Banque coloniale ou banque d'affaires,* pp. 412–13.

58. Lasserre, "Banques en Indochine."

59. H. Baudoin, *La Banque de l'Indo-Chine* (Thèse de droit, Paris, 1903), p. 161.

60. Meuleau, *Des pionniers en Extrême-Orient,* chaps. 5–8.

61. N. Shinonaga, "La formation de la Banque industrielle de Chine," *Le Mouvement social,* April–June 1991; J.-N. Jeanneney, "La Banque industrielle de Chine et la chute des frères Berthelot, 1921–1923," in *L'Argent caché: Milieux d'affaires et pouvoirs politiques dans la France du XXᵉ siècle,* 2nd ed. (Paris, 1984), pp. 128–68; Meuleau, *Des pionniers en Extrême-Orient,* chap. 8.

62. Gonjo, *Banque coloniale ou banque d'affaires,* p. 276.

63. W. Oualid, *Le privilège de la Banque de l'Indo-Chine,* p. 276.

64. Gonjo, *Banque coloniale ou banque d'affaires,* p. 330.

65. Oualid, *Privilège de la Banque de l'Indo-Chine,* p. 106.

66. Gonjo, *Banque coloniale ou banque d'affaires,* p. 342.

67. Ibid., pp. 506–7.

68. Oualid, *Privilège de la Banque de l'Indo-Chine,* pp. 110–11.

69. P. de Feyssal, *L'endettement agraire en Cochinchine: Rapport au gouverneur général de l'Indochine* (Hanoi, 1943).

70. A. Lotzer, "Note pour servir à l'histoire du paysan indochinois," *Bulletin économique de l'Indochine,* 1943.

71. In this book, notably in chapter 3, in order to deflate the amounts given in francs at the current rate, I used the coefficients for the reevaluation of conversions fixed by the decree of March 19, 1960, as restated in J. Aubert-Krier, *Comptabilité privée* (Paris, 1962), pp. 37–38. The statistics presented in current francs and used to establish the tables and graphs were deflated year by year using these coefficients. See app. 11 for a table of conversion between current francs, 1914 francs, 1999 francs, and (for reference) euros.

72. "Enquête de 1943 sur les investissements dans les colonies," CAOM, Affaires économiques, 52.

73. Commissariat général au Plan, Commission de modernisation et d'équipement des Territoires d'outre-mer, sous-commission Indochine, *Note sur les données économiques et financières d'un plan d'équipement de l'Indochine,* April 25, 1947, report of P. Bernard and J. Bourgoin, CAOM, Affaires économiques, p. 578.

74. Marseille, *Empire colonial et capitalisme français*, p. 103.

75. Ibid., p. 96.

76. "Enquête de 1943 sur les investissements dans les colonies," CAOM, Affaires économiques.

77. Leurence, *Étude statistique*.

78. Ministère des Colonies, *Investissement des fonds publics aux colonies: Indochine de 1919 à 1934*, CAOM, Affaires politiques, 2640 (2). The amounts presented in current piastres were converted into current francs year by year at the official exchange rate and the results obtained deflated according to the method described in n. 71 above.

79. Ministère des Colonies, *Sommes dépensées pour la mise en valeur de l'Indochine de 1919 à 1934*, CAOM, Affaires politiques, 2640 (2).

80. A. Schreiner, "Étude sur la constitution de la propriété foncière en Cochinchine," *Bulletin de la Société des études indochinoises*, 1902, pp. 3–303.

81. Marseille, *Empire colonial et capitalisme français*, p. 115. On the various orientations of state developmentalism, see J.-D. Giacometti, "La compétitivité des productions indochinoises et les plans de mise en valeur," *Outre-mers: Revue d'histoire*, no. 330–31 (2001): 71–90.

82. CAOM, Indochine, Nouveau Fonds, 262.

83. P. Bernard, *Nouveaux aspects du problème économique indochinois* (Paris, 1937), p. 21; for the financing of the equipment for the railroads, see the synthesis of F. Bobrie, "Le financement des chemins de fer coloniaux: Un exemple de l'investissement public outre-mer entre 1860 et 1940," *Cahiers d'histoire* (Lyon, 1977), n. 2.

84. Leurence, *Étude statistique*.

85. M. Fall, "Investissements publics et politique économique en Indochine, 1898–1930" (PhD diss., Paris, 1985).

86. See Denis, *Bordeaux et la Cochinchine*; G. de Gantès, "Le particularisme des milieux d'affaires cochinchinois (1860–1910): Comment intégrer un comptoir asiatique à un empire colonial protégé," in *Esprit économique impérial*, ed. Bonin et al., 737–47.

87. See Ho Hai Quang, "Le rôle des investissements français dans la création du secteur de production capitaliste au Vietnam méridional" (PhD diss., Reims, 1982); and id., "Formation du secteur de production capitaliste" (cited n. 4 above). Although convincing for the nineteenth century, this author's thesis loses its believability for the period after 1900 because of the lack of a precise study of the importation of capital after that date.

88. J.-P. Aumiphin, "La presence financière et économique française en Indochine, 1859–1939" (PhD diss., Nice, 1981).

89. See J.-F. Klein, "Lyon et la colonisation: Du discours fédérateur à l'oubli collectif," in *Identité et régionalité: Être lyonnais hier et aujourd'hui*, ed. A. Vingtrinier et al. (Lyon, 2005), and id., "Soyeux en mer de Chine."

90. See J.-F. Klein, "De la Compagnie lyonnaise à l'Union Commerciale Indochinoise: Histoire d'une stratégie d'entreprises," in *Lyon et l'Extrême-Orient*, special issue, *Cahiers d'histoire* 40, no. 3–4 (1995): 349–67.

91. Klein, "Soyeux en mer de Chine."

92. Robequain, *Évolution économique*, p. 180.

93. Marseille, *Empire colonial et capitalisme français*, p. 100. Robequain, *Évolution économique*, p. 181, cites 492 million gold francs in private investment for the period

1888–1918. In 1913, the reporter of the colonial budget to the Chamber of Deputies, Messimy, estimated capital investments in Indochina in 1905 at 544 million gold francs, which is to say 29.5% of private investment in the colonial empire (1.8 billion francs).

94. *Bulletin économique de l'Indochine* (1934): 389. On the dynamics of creation and the disappearance of Indochinese limited liability companies *(sociétés anonymes)*, see J. Serre, "Vie et mort(s) des entreprises en Indochine française (1875–1944)," *Revue française d'histoire d'Outre-mer*, 1st semester 2001, pp. 159–76.

95. T. Smolski, "Les investissements de capitaux privés et les émissions de valeurs mobilières en Indochine au cours de la période quinquennale 1924–1928," *Bulletin économique de l'Indochine* 32 (1929): 804–20.

96. Robequain, *Évolution économique,* table 12, p. 183.

97. Marseille, *Empire colonial et capitalisme français,* p. 102.

98. A. Sarraut, *La mise en valeur des colonies* (Paris, 1923), pp. 349–50.

99. *Tribune indochinoise,* July 8 and 13, 1932. See also Estèbe, *Problème du riz en Indochine,* pp. 60–61.

100. See Ho Hai Quang, *Rôle des investissements français.*

101. T. Smolski, "Les investissements de capitaux en Indochine," *Bulletin de l'Agence économique de l'Indochine* (1929): 314.

102. Ho Hai Quang, *Rôle des investissements français,* p. 382.

103. Commissariat général au Plan, *Note sur les données économiques et financiers.*

104. D. Barjot and M. Merger, *Les entreprises et leurs réseaux: Hommes, capitaux, techniques et pouvoirs, XIXᵉ–XXᵉ siècles* (Paris, 1998); P. Morlat, "Les réseaux patronaux français en Indochine (1918–1928)," in *Esprit économique impérial,* ed. Bonin et al.

105. Meuleau, *Des pionniers en Extrême-Orient; Annuaire financier France–Extrême-Orient, 1928–1929,* pp. 63–67.

106. J. Boudet, *Le monde des affaires* (Paris, 1952), p. 49.

107. Report of January 7, 1930, CAOM, Affaires économiques, Concessions, 190.

108. J. Bourgoin, "Exposé sur les conditions générales d'un plan d'équipement de l'Indochine devant le Comité économique de l'Indochine, Dalat, novembre 1947," *Notes documentaires et études,* January 21, 1948.

109. H. Simoni, "Le rôle du capital dans la mise en valeur de l'Indochine" (PhD diss., Paris, 1929), p. 90.

110. Fourniau, *Vietnam: Domination et résistance,* p. 758.

111. Marseille, *Empire colonial et capitalisme français,* p. 131.

112. Commissariat général au Plan, *Notes sur les données économiques et financières.*

113. Meuleau, *Des pionniers en Extrême-Orient,* p. 307.

114. Ibid., p. 395.

115. H. Lanoue, "Structure de l'Indochine," *Cahiers internationaux,* October 1950.

116. Commissariat général au Plan, *Notes sur les données économiques et financières.*

117. E. Picanon, "Rapport sur la navigation en Indochine en 1910," *Bulletin économique de l'Indochine,* no. 89 (1911).

118. Nguyen Huu Khang, "La commune annamite" (PhD diss., Paris, 1946), p. 183.

119. *Vues d'ensemble sur les liens économiques entre la France et ses colonies,* app. 14, CAOM, Affaires économiques, 59 (4).

120. Statistique générale de la France, *Annuaire statistique de la France, 1941,* pp. 159, 277.

121. Gouvernement général, Service de la statistique générale, *Annuaire statistique de l'Indochine,* 1932-33.

122. *Balance commerciale des colonies,* CAOM, Affaires économiques, 51.

123. Gouvernement général, Service de la statistique générale, *Annuaire statistique de l'Indochine,* 1941-42.

124. Giacometti, "La question de l'autonomie de l'Indochine et les milieux coloniaux français."

125. Robequain, *Évolution économique,* p. 371.

126. Great Britain, Department of Overseas Trade, *Economic Conditions in China to 1st September 1929* (London, 1930).

127. Conférence économique de la France métropolitaine et d'outre-mer, *Rapports généraux et conclusions d'ensemble* (Paris, 1935).

128. P. Bernard, *Le problème économique indochinois* (Paris, 1934), pp. 38-39.

129. V. Talon, *Le régime douanier de l'Indochine* (Paris, 1932), p. 156.

130. "Note du 12 avril 1924 de l'Union coloniale au president du Conseil à propos des demandes japonaises en vue d'obtenir le tariff minimum," CAOM, Fonds du Comité de la France d'outre-mer, 305. See also I. Nørlund, "Franco-Indochinese Trade Relations, 1885-1930, with a Special Reference to the Textile Trade" (unpublished paper, 1986).

131. Association de l'Industrie et de l'Agriculture françaises, "Note sur la question de l'octroi aux produits japonais du tarif minimum en Indochine," October 21, 1916, CAOM, Comité de la France d'outre-mer, 305.

132. Administration des Douanes et Régies, *Tableau du commerce extérieur de l'Indochine, années 1935 à 1938* (Hanoi, 1939).

133. Statistique générale de la France, *Annuaire statistique de la France, 1941,* p. 173.

134. G. Khérian, "La balance des comptes de l'Indochine," *Revue indochinoise juridique et économique,* 1939.

135. "Note sur la situation monétaire de l'Indochine," October 1931, CAOM, Affaires politiques, 2467 (5).

136. Ibid.

137. *Bulletin économique de l'Indochine,* 41, 1 (1939): 17.

138. *Dépêche coloniale,* 12 June 1934.

CHAPTER 4

1. Centre des archives d'outre-mer, Aix-en-Provence (hereafter cited as CAOM), NF 2639, "Note du 28.4.1931 concernant le personnel européen et indigène en Indochine."

2. E. du Vivier du Streel, former director of the Congrès de l'Exposition coloniale, in *L'urbanisme aux colonies et dans les pays tropicaux,* ed. Jean Royer (Paris, 1932-35), 2: 12.

3. L. Imbert, *La Cochinchine au seuil du XXᵉ siècle* (Bordeaux, 1900), pp. 28-29.

4. P. Billotey, *L'Indochine en zigzags* (Paris, 1929), p. 21.

5. R. Serène, "Des préjugés aux amitiés," in *L'homme de couleur* (Paris, 1939), p. 8.

6. P. Loti, *Journal intime* (Paris, 1930), p. 106.

7. H.-P. d'Orléans, "Hanoï la jolie," in *Journal des Voyages* (1893), p. 210.

8. Dr. Hocquard, "Trente mois au Tonkin," *Le Tour du Monde* 61 (1885): 327.

9. "L'Indochine française," in *Géographie universelle Quillet* (Paris, 1929), 2: 467.

10. E. Hébrard, "L'Urbanisme en Indochine," *L'Architecture,* February 1928; reprinted in *Urbanisme,* March 1932. See also G. Wright, *The Politics of Design in French Colonial Urbanism* (Chicago, 1991), esp. chap 4.

11. R. Parenteau and L. Champagne, eds., *La conservation des quartiers historiques en Indochine* (Paris, 1997), pp. 66–77; P. Papin, *Histoire de Hanoi* (Paris, 2001).

12. *Compartiments* were buildings of one or more storeys whose rooms and courtyards extended back deeply behind their narrow façades.

13. CAOM, Agence FOM, carton 236, and also *Articles et documents,* no. 292 (July 13, 1939).

14. R. Dorgelès, *Sur la route mandarine* (Paris, 1925), pp. 191–92.

15. J. Ajalbert, *Les destinées de l'Indochine* (Paris, 1911), pp. 40, 43.

16. F. Vertran, *Portrait d'un colon* (pamphlet, n.p., n.d.).

17. Governor-General Admiral Pierre de la Grandière, personal letter, August 28, 1864, CAOM, Fonds Indochine A30 (6).

18. CAOM, Fonds Affaires politiques, carton 1482, "Note sur les soldes des Européens en Indochine" (1931).

19. NF Indochine 2639. The writer, Do Huu Thinh, *commis principal hors classe* at the Trésorerie d'Indochine and *chevalier* of the Legion of Honor, belonged to a family of Cochinchinese notables with French nationality; his brothers included the World War I hero *Capitaine-aviator* Do Huu Vi (for more on whom, see chapter 8) and Colonel Do Huu Chanh.

20. P. Franchini has remarkably described the sentiment of psychological unease of Eurasians in *Continental Saigon* (Paris, 1976). From 1937 to 1939, the newspaper of the Eurasian G. Bazé, *Blanc et Jaune,* denounced discrimination against Eurasians and "naturalized" Vietnamese and demanded equal treatment for these two categories. He sought to develop a common cause with the *Pondichériens* of French India. And see also D. Rolland, *De sang mêlé: Chronique de métissage en Indochine* (Bordeaux, 2006); E. Saada, *Les enfants de la colonie: Les métis de l'Empire français, entre sujétion et citoyenneté* (Paris, 2007).

21. A. Viollis, *Indochine S.O.S.* (Paris, 1935; reprint, 1949).

22. Serène, "Des préjugés aux amitiés," p. 8.

23. These pamphlets were edited with the help of the Ministère des Colonies around 1900.

24. *Le Moniteur des Provinces,* January 26, 1905.

25. Quoted in P. Brocheux, "Le prolétariat des plantations d'hévéas 1927–1937," *Le Mouvement social,* no. 90 (January–March 1975).

26. Governor-General Alexandre Varenne, interview in *La Dépêche coloniale,* CAOM, Agence FOM, 918.

27. Minister of the Colonies Albert Sarraut, confidential circular, March 14, 1933, CAOM, Affaires publiques, 1734.

28. Nguyen Vy, *Tuan, chang trai nuoc Viet* [Tuan, a Guy from Vietnam] (Glendale, Calif., n.d.), 1: 298ff.

29. Trung tam Luu tru Quoc gia 2 [National Archives Center 2, Ho Chi Minh City; hereafter Luu tru 2], Fonds TDBCPNV, EO3 312.

30. Nguyen Vy, *Tuan,* vol. 1, chap. 15; vol. 2, chap. 22.

31. Ibid., 1: 298–99.

32. Ruche d'Orient lodge, Saigon, meeting of May 21, 1927; on the agenda: "Étude de la situation nouvelle créée par les rapports tendus entre les Annamites et les Français," CAOM, Agence Fom 919/2795.

33. Comité maçonnique d'études franco-annamites, *Histoire des troubles sociaux qui ont affecté l'Indochine de 1886 à 1926,* vol. 4 (Saigon, 1927).

34. J. Dalloz, "Les Vietnamiens dans la Franc-maçonnerie coloniale," *Revue française d'histoire d'outre-mer* 85, 320 (1998): 103–18.

35. D. Langlois, *L'Aventure indochinoise d'André Malraux* (Paris, 1967).

36. For Babut, see D. Danzon, "Di tim dau vet Babut" (On the Trail of Babut), *Xua Nay,* no. 79B (September 2000): 22–23, 42; for Nguyen Cong Hoan, see his *Nho va ghi* (Notes and Reminiscences) (Hanoi, 1978); and for E. Ganofsky, see Ngo Van, *Au pays de la cloche fêlée,* chap. 4, n. 44.

37. *Annuaire Didot-Bottin,* 1939.

38. G. C. Hickey, *Sons of the Mountains: Ethnohistory of the Vietnamese Highlands to 1954* (New Haven, Conn., 1982).

39. R. Trinquier, *Le Temps perdu* (Paris, 1978), and J. Leroy, *Fils de la rizière* (Paris, 1977).

40. Ajalbert, *Destinées de l'Indochine,* p. 175.

41. CAOM, NF Indochine 1567.

42. G. Groslier, "Rapport sur les arts indigènes au Cambodge" (a historical study of the Service des arts cambodgiens from 1918 to 1924), CAOM, Agence FOM 911.

43. See P. Brocheux, "Vietnamiens et minorités en Cochinchine pendant la période coloniale," *Modern Asian Studies* 6, 4 (1972), and J. Delvert, *Le Paysan cambodgien* (Paris, 1961).

44. Subprefect of Binh Luc (Tonkin), letter to *tuan phu* (provincial chief), October 4, 1934, Trung tam Luu tru Quoc gia 1 [National Archives Center 1, Hanoi; hereafter Luu tru 1], Fonds Resuper, L4, 74973.

45. Cited by A. Woodside, "The Development of Social Organisations in Vietnamese Cities in the Late Colonial Period," *Pacific Affairs* 44, 1 (1971).

46. Luu tru 2, Fonds Goucoch, no. 3528, "Notes du commandant d'Ariès sur les réformes des villages annamites de Saigon." D'Ariès was in charge of *Affaires indigènes.*

47. Forest, *Cambodge et la colonisation française.*

48. A number of copies of letters and petitions addressed to the French resident superior in Annam and even to the governor-general are in files 26667, 19142, 21787, and 26773 of the Fonds Indochine of the CAOM at Aix-en-Provence.

49. Luu tru 2, Fonds Goucoch, file E. 20.

50. Luu tru 1, archives from the provinces of Sadec, Thudaumot, and Bentre (1924 and 1925).

51. J. Godart, "Rapport de mission," CAOM, Fonds Guernut, A XVIII.

52. *Doc hoc* [mandarin in charge of education] Ngo Giap Dau, "Monographie de Nam-Dinh" (typescript, 1916), Luu tru 1.

53. CAOM, NF Indochine, Commission Morché.

54. P. Brocheux, "Grands propriétaires et fermiers dans l'Ouest de la Cochinchine," *Revue historique,* no. 499 (July–September 1991).

55. Godart, "Rapport de mission."

56. CAOM, P. A. 28, file 52.

57. *Médecin-colonel* Peltier, "La Protection de la maternité et de l'enfance dans les colonies françaises," part 4: "L'Indochine." CAOM, Agence FOM 238.

58. Subprefect of Binh Luc, letter cited n. 44 above.

59. Hy Van Luong, *Revolution in the Village: Revolution and Transformation in North Vietnam, 1925–1988* (Honolulu, 1992).

60. J. Goudal, *Problémes du travail en Indochine* (Geneva, 1937).

61. Inspection générale des mines et de l'industrie, 1941 annual report.

62. Letter to the resident superior, April 28, 1933, Luu tru 1, Fonds Résidence supérieure du Tonkin, M. 11 71972. The reference is to the Société des charbonnages of Dong Trieu, which employed 3,200 laborers.

63. Dinh Van Duc, "Con duong Song," in *Chi mot con duong: Hoi ky cach mang* (There Is Only One Path: Memories of Revolution) (Hanoi, 1974).

64. Indochinese Communist Party document quoted by Thi Sanh, *Lich su phong trao cong nhan mo Quang Ninh* (History of the Quang Ninh Mine Workers' Movement) (Quang Ninh, 1974), pp. 297, 298, 299, and the documents in SLOTFOM III 49, register 6 (for Hanoi), CAOM.

65. Luu tru 1, Fonds Province de Nam Dinh, M. 11 3181. By August 1930, the number of employees and workers hired in the factories of Nam Dinh under French management had risen to 5,238 (2,146 men and 3,092 women).

66. *Articles et documents,* no. 292 (July 13, 1939).

67. Documents captured by the Sureté in Hanoi, December 6, 1930, (poorly) translated in SLOTFOM III 49, register 6.

68. Luu tru 1, Fonds Resuper, M. 17.77177.

69. CAOM, NF Indochine 2634.

70. Governor of Cochinchina, letter to the governor-general, March 16, 1937, CAOM, P.A. 28; carton 2, file 15.

71. Resident Superior Thibeaudeau, report, CAOM, NF Indochine 2664.

72. Decoux, "Note sur la situation en Annam," NF Indochine 1198.

73. Viollis, *Indochine S.O.S.* (1949 ed.), p. 80.

74. A profile of this class can be found in P. Brocheux, "Les grands *dien chu* de la Cochinchine occidentale," in *Traditions et révolution au Vietnam,* ed. J. Chesneaux et al. (Paris, 1971).

75. Brocheux, "Grands propriétaires et fermiers."

76. R. Smith, "Bui Quang Chieu and the Constitutionalist Party in French Cochinchina, 1917–1930," *Modern Asian Studies* 3, 2 (1969).

77. Brocheux, "Vietnamiens et minorités."

78. Pham Le Bong, note to Governor-General Decoux, August 9, 1940, p. 8, CAOM, P.A. 14, carton 2. Pham Le Bong was a member of the Tonkin middle class and his businesses (a shop and a firecracker factory) were managed by his wife. He owned two newspapers, one in French *(La Patrie annamite),* the other in Quoc ngu *(Viet Bao),* but his main activity consisted of his seat in the Chambre des représentants du peuple du Tonkin, where he appeared as a supporter of the monarchy. See Vu Bang, *40 nam noi lao* (Forty Years of Lies) (Paris, 1984), pp. 154–56.

79. P. Brocheux, "Note sur Gilbert Chieu, patriote vietnamien et citoyen français," *Approches Asie,* no. 11 (1992).

80. P. Brocheux, "Élite, bourgeoisie, ou la difficulté d'être," in *Saigon, 1925–1945* (Paris, 1992).

81. *Xa Hoi Viet Nam trong thoi Phap-Nhat* (Vietnamese Society under French-Japanese Domination), vol. 2 (Hanoi, 1957).

82. *Bulletin économique de l'Indochine, 1944,* parts 3–4.

83. Pham Quynh, *Mot thang o Nam Ky* (A Month in Cochinchina) (Hanoi, 1916).

84. P. Brocheux, "Crise économique et société en Indochine française," *Revue française d'histoire d'outre-mer* 63, 232–33 (1976).

85. Prefect of Duy Tien (Tonkin), report, October 5, 1934, Luu tru 1, Fonds Resuper, L4, 74973.

86. Luu tru 2, Fonds Goucoch 1573.

87. CAOM, NF Indochine 632.

88. Forest, *Cambodge et la colonisation française,* app. 6, p. 506.

89. Luu tru 2, Fonds Goucoch (divers) 3421.

90. CAOM, Agence FOM 858.

91. Programme d'organisation des services d'assistance et d'hygiène en Indochine, CAOM, commission Guernut, carton 22 Bb.

92. In their columns, and even in feature articles, *L'Argus indochinois, La Tribune indochinoise,* and *Blanc et Jaune* denounced the racist, insulting, and brutal behavior of which the Vietnamese were often the victims.

93. CAOM, Agence FOM 923.

94. CAOM, Agence FOM 918. The Third Estate was at the bottom rung of the three-part social hierarchy in Ancien régime France, beneath the Church and the aristocracy. Lacking the privileges of those two groups, it demanded equality in 1789, which led to the French Revolution.

CHAPTER 5

1. R. Vanlande, *L'Indochine sous la menace communiste* (Paris, 1930).

2. Wright, *Politics of Design,* pp. 199–200.

3. Pierre Pasquier, memorandum to Governor-General Merlin, "L'enseignement primaire en Annam," December 31, 1922.

4. Bezançon, *Colonisation éducatrice?*

5. See G. P. Kelly, *Franco-Vietnamese Schools, 1918–1938: Regional Development and Implications for National Integration* (Madison, Wis., 1982), and "Colonial Schools in Vietnam, 1918 to 1938," in *Proceedings of the 2nd Annual Meeting of the French Colonial Historical Society* (Milwaukee, 1976); Gouvernement général de l'Indochine, *Le Service de l'Instruction publique en Indochine en 1930* (Hanoi, 1930).

6. "Situation de l'enseignement indigène," report of P. Beau to the minister of the colonies, 2 July 1907, Centre des archives d'outre-mer, Aix-en-Provence [henceforth cited as CAOM], Fonds du Gouvernement général, 2579.

7. P. Beau, *Situation de l'Indochine de 1902 à 1907* (Paris, 1908), p. 315.

8. *Annuaire statistique de l'Indochine, 1939–1946.* According to the "Tableau statistique de l'enseignement en Indochine," CAOM, NF Indo. 1323, there were a total of 1,528 students in 1944 (1,210 of them in the sciences, medicine, pharmacy, and law.)

9. Quoted in V. Floquet, "Étude de la vie rurale au Tonkin d'après les rapports des résidents supérieurs (1908–1930)" (MA thesis, Aix-en-Provence, 1992), p. 70.

10. Note from the Ministry of the Colonies, Service de l'Indochine, to the Inspection générale de l'instruction publique, November 11, 1919, quoted by P. Bezançon, "La rénovation des écoles de pagodes au Cambodge" (MA thesis, Paris, 1992).

11. R. Jacques, "Le Portugal et la romanisation de la langue vietnamienne: Faut-il réécrire l'histoire?" *Revue française d'histoire d'outre-mer* 85, 318 (1998): 21-54.

12. M. Pietri of the École française d'Extrême-Orient to the governor-general regarding the doctoral examination of 1910, Hanoi, February 3, 1911.

13. *Code annamite: Lois et règlements du royaume d'Annam* (Paris, 1865), 1: vi.

14. Parliamentary debate on the budget for the colonies, January 1930.

15. Quoted by Marr, *Vietnamese Anticolonialism*, p. 149.

16. Governor-general, letter to the minister of the colonies, September 15, 1917, CAOM, NF Indochine 56.

17. L. Marty, "Au sujet de la revue *Nam Phong*," CAOM, NF Indochine 56.

18. Pham Quynh, *Nam Phong*, no. 20 (February 1919).

19. Bezançon, "Rénovation des écoles de pagodes."

20. G. Groslier, "Rapport sur les arts indigènes du Cambodge," CAOM, Agence FOM 911, 1925.

21. Ibid.

22. Resident superior of Annam to governor-general, "Rapport sur les industries d'art indigènes," CAOM, Agence FOM 911, April 1925.

23. *Les écoles d'art de l'Indochine* (report produced for the Exposition internationale des arts et technique de Paris, Section coloniale), CAOM, Agence FOM 911, 1937, p. 8.

24. *Truong dai hoc my thuat Hanoi, 1925-1990* (The École supérieure des beaux-arts of Hanoi, 1925-1990) (Hanoi, 1990).

25. Governor-general, report to the minister of the colonies, CAOM, Affaires politiques 1733, 27.9.1932.

26. CAOM, Affaires politiques 1734.

27. CAOM, Affaires politiques 1733.

28. "Note sur le cinéma scolaire en Annam," CAOM, Affaires politiques 1733, 2.6.1932.

29. *Van Tho Dong kinh Nghia thuc: Prose et poésies du DKNT* (Hanoi, 1997), pp. 180-81.

30. Tran Huy Lieu et al., *Lich Su thu do Ha-noi* (History of the Capital of Hanoi) (Hanoi, 1960).

31. Dao Duy Anh, *Nho nghi chieu hom* (Memoirs and Reflections of the Evening) (Ho Chi Minh City, 1989). A lively press was the main means by which Cochinchinese urbanites participated in public life, as P. Peycam highlights in "Intellectuals and Political Commitments in Vietnam: The Emergence of a Public Sphere in Colonial Saigon, 1916-1928" (PhD diss., London, 1999).

32. See C. Rageau's catalogue of the collection of documents in Quoc ngu in the Bibliothèque nationale, or D. G. Marr, *Vietnamese Tradition on Trial, 1920-1945* (Berkeley, 1981).

33. Nguyen Van Ky, *La société vietnamienne face à la modernité: Le Tonkin de la fin du XIXᵉ siècle à la Seconde Guerre mondiale* (Paris, 1995).

34. Viollis, *Indochine S.O.S.*, p. 78.

35. Dang Phuc Thong, *La femme dans la société annamite* (Hanoi, 1931), p. 3. The responses of Vietnamese women to the challenges they had to face are soundly analyzed by

Bui Tran Phuong, "Viêt Nam, 1918–1945: Genre et modernité. Émergences de nouvelles perceptions et expérimentations" (PhD diss., Lyon, 2008).

36. CAOM, Agence Fom 238.

37. Ibid.

38. H. Célarié, *Promenades en Indochine* (Paris, 1937), pp. 176–77.

39. Truong Tuu, in *Tao Dan*, no. 1 (March 1939): 25.

40. Trinh Van Thao, *L'école française en Indochine* (Paris, 1995), pp. 179–80.

41. *Su Phat trien cua tu tuong o Vietnam tu the ky XIX den cach mang Thang Tam,* vol. 2: *He Y thuc Tu san va su bat luc cua no truoc cac nhiem vu lich su* (The Ideological Evolution of Vietnam from the Nineteenth Century to the August Revolution, vol. 2: Bourgeois Thought and Its Powerlessness in the Face of the Historical Tasks) (Ho Chi Minh City, 1993). See also *History of Buddhism in Vietnam*, ed. Nguyen Thai Thu (Hanoi, 1992), part 5.

42. C. Lange, "L'Église au Vietnam," in *Les prodromes de la décolonisation de l'Empire français 1936–1956* (Paris, 1986).

43. Nguyen Tran Huan, "Histoire d'une secte religieuse au Vietnam: Le caodaisme," in *Tradition et révolution au Vietnam* (Paris, 1971); J. S. Werner, *Peasant Politics and Religious Sectarianism: Peasant and Priest in the Cao Dai in Vietnam* (New Haven, Conn., 1981).

44. Hue Tam Ho Tai, *Millenarianism and Peasant Politics in Vietnam* (Cambridge, Mass., 1983).

45. This section is based on M. M. Durand and Nguyen Tran Huan, *Introduction à la littérature vietnamienne* (Paris, 1969); *Littératures contemporaines de l'Asie du Sud-Est*, ed. P.-B. Lafont and D. Lombard (Paris, 1974), particularly the contribution of Nguyen Tien Lan; Bui Xuan Bao, *Le roman vietnamien contemporain: Tendences et évolution du roman vietnamien contemporain, 1925–1945* (Saigon, 1968); and Vu Ngoc Phan, *Nha van hien dai* (1942; reprint, Glendale, Calif., 1980).

46. Phan Khoi, "Le poète Tan Da et moi," *Tao Dan Tap Chi*, nos. 9–10 (July 16, 1939).

47. Ten thousand copies of the magazine *Phong Hoa* (Mores and Customs) were printed in 1933.

48. Rim Kin quoted by Khin Hoc Dy, "Le développement économique et la transformation littéraire dans le Cambodge moderne," *Mondes en développement*, no. 28 (1979): 798. Rim Kin's novel *Suphat*, translated by Gérard Groussin, has been published in French under the title *Sophat: Ou les surprises du destin* (Paris, 1994).

49. E. Pujarniscle, "Philoxène ou de la littérature coloniale," in *Le Roman colonial* (Paris, 1987).

50. On November 15, 1929, an exhibition of painting and sculpture was inaugurated in Hanoi. New aesthetic tendencies inspired by the West were remarked upon. One French journalist wrote of the "birth of the Annamese school of beaux arts"; see *Nam Phong*, December 1929.

51. René Crayssac, *Extrême-Asie: Revue indochinoise*, July 1930; for the period after 1930, see R. Cornevin, "La vie culturelle: la littérature d'expression française," in Académie des sciences d'outremer, Commission Indochine, *Indochine, alerte à l'histoire: Ni opprobre, ni oubli* (Paris, 1985), pp. 197–208.

52. See H. Copin, *L'Indochine dans la littérature française, des années vingt à 1954: Exotisme et altérité* (Paris, 1996), and B. Hue et al., *Littératures de la péninsule indochinoise* (Paris,

1999), a book published within the framework of the history of francophone literature that testifies to the richness of colonial literature, yet at the same time restricts its social and cultural impact. Indeed, is this literature a minor key of twentieth-century French literature? Can its authors aspire to a universal dimension or are their works of only documentary value?

53. N. André-Pallois, *L'Indochine: Un lieu d'échange culturel? Les peintres français et indochinois (fin XIXè–XXè siècle)* (Paris, 1997), p. 193.

CHAPTER 6

1. Following J. S. Furnivall, *Netherlands India: A Study of Plural Economy* (Cambridge, 1939).

2. J. C. Scott, *The Moral Economy of the Peasant: Rebellion and Subsistence in Southeast Asia* (New Haven, Conn., 1976); S. L. Popkin, *The Rational Peasant: The Political Economy of Rural Society in Vietnam* (Berkeley, 1979).

3. This follows many previous studies, such as those of Vu Quoc Thuc, *L'économie communaliste au Vietnam* (Hanoi, 1951), and, in another register, the fundamental work of P. Mus, *Vietnam: Sociologie d'une guerre* (Paris, 1952).

4. Governor-General Jules Brevié, report, June 17, 1937, Centre des archives d'outre-mer, Aix-en-Provence [henceforth cited as CAOM], Indochine Nouveau Fonds, 2280.

5. According to M. Banens, "Vietnam: A Reconstitution of Its Twentieth-Century Population History," in *Quantitative Economic History of Vietnam, 1900–1990: An International Workshop,* ed. J. C. Bassino et al. (Tokyo, 1999), p. 10; the quotation is from T. Smolski, "Note sur le mouvement de la population en Indochine," *Bulletin économique de l'Indochine* (1929).

6. P. Gourou, *Les paysans du delta tonkinois: Étude de géographie humaine* (Paris, 1936), p. 185.

7. Inspection générale de l'hygiène et de la santé, annual report, 1939, Archives du Pharo Marseille; *Les maladies pestilentielles observées dans les colonies françaises en 1939,* special issue of *Médecine tropicale,* no. 6 (1941).

8. P. Gourou, "La densité de population dans le delta du Tonkin," in *Congrès international de la population, Paris, 1937,* vol. 6 (Paris, 1938).

9. T. Smolski, "Les statistiques de la population indochinoise," in *Congrès international de la population,* vol. 6. The most recent work is Nguyen Shui Meng, *The Population of Indochina* (Singapore, 1974).

10. Nguyen The Anh, *Kinh te va xa hoi Viet-Nam duoi cac vua trieu Nguyen* (Economy and Vietnamese society under the Nguyen Dynasty) (Saigon, 1970), pp. 25–27.

11. Nguyen The Anh, *Viet-Nam thoi Phap do ho* (Vietnam under French domination) (Saigon, 1970), p. 230. See also id., "Quelques aspects économiques et sociaux du problème du riz au Vietnam dans la première moitié du XIXe siècle," *Bulletin de la société des Études indochinoises* (Saigon), 1967, nos. 1–2; id., "Monarchie et fait colonial au Viêt-Nam (1875–1925)," pp. 17–20.

12. Fourniau, *Contacts franco vietnamiens,* pp. 2141–50.

13. Ibid., pp. 2502–3. One of the earliest demographic surveys is L. Cadière, "Documents relatifs à l'accroissement et à la composition de la population en Annam," *Revue indochinoise,* 1908: 303–21, 517–30, 650–53. Henri Brenier evaluates the birthrates in the villages

of the Catholic missions in *Le problème de la population dans les colonies françaises: Cours professé à la Semaine sociale de Marseille (session de 1930)* (Lyon, 1930).

14. Fourniau, *Contacts franco vietnamiens*, p. 2503n1.

15. Ibid.

16. Smolski, "Note sur le mouvement de la population en Indochine."

17. Investigation of Dr. Pierre Chesneau, cited by H. Ulmer, "Quelques données démographiques sur les colonies françaises," in *Congrès international de la population indochinoise.*

18. Smolski, "Statistiques de la population indochinoise." See also M. Chevry, "Naissances et décès dans la ville de Hanoi," *Bulletin économique de l'Indochine,* 1936; Brenier, *Problème de la population;* P. Gourou, "La densité de population dans le delta du Tonkin," in *Congrès international de la population;* id., *Paysans du delta,* part 2, chap. 3.

19. *Annuaires statistiques de l'Indochine;* Chevry, "Naissances et décès dans la ville de Hanoi." For Annam, see Nguyen Thieu Lau, "Introduction à l'étude démographique des plaines maritimes de l'Annam," *Bulletin de l'Institut indochinois pour l'étude de l'homme,* 1941: 183–213.

20. Chevry, "Naissances et décès dans la ville de Hanoi."

21. Ibid.; Dr. Chesneau, "Natalité et mortalité infantile au Cammon (Laos), au Sud-Annam et au Nord-Annam," in *Congrès international de la population.*

22. A. Reid, "The Population Growth and Its Causes in Pre-Colonial Southeast Asia," in *Death and Diseases in Southeast Asia: Explorations in Social, Medical and Demographic History,* ed. G. Owen (Singapore, 1987); Dr. Darbes, "Accroissement apparent et réel de la population de Phnom Penh de 1931 à 1936," in *Congrès international de la population.*

23. Smolski and Gourou cited in nn. 16 and 18 above; P. Gourou, "La population rurale de la Cochinchine," *Annales de géographie,* January–March 1942.

24. Inspection générale de l'hygiène et de la santé, annual report, 1935, Archives du Pharo, Marseille.

25. Ibid., annual report, 1939.

26. Ibid.

27. P. Blanchard de La Brosse, "Rapport à la commission économique du Conseil supérieur de la France d'outre-mer" (ca. 1938), CAOM, Fonds du Comité central de la France d'outre-mer, 125.

28. Dr. Bui Kien Tin, *Le médecin en face du problème démographique de l'Indochine* (Paris, 1940).

29. J. Bourgoin, *Notes documentaires et études* (French government publication) (Paris: Présidence du Conseil, 1948).

30. Dr. Vantalon, "Rapport sur la vaccination en Cochichine pendant l'année 1880," *Excursions et reconnaissances* (Saigon, 1880), p. 230.

31. Ibid.

32. L. Monnais-Rousselot, *Médecine et colonisation. L'aventure indochinoise, 1860–1939* (Paris, 1999).

33. Dr. Gaide, *L'Assistance médicale et la Protection de la santé publique* (Hanoi, 1931); P. Bernard, *Les Instituts Pasteur d'Indochine* (Saigon, 1922); H.-H. Mollaret and J. Brosselet, *Alexandre Yersin ou le vainqueur de la peste* (Paris: Fayard, 1985); P. Pluchon, *Histoire*

des médecins et des pharmaciens de la Marine et des Colonies (Toulouse, 1985), Monnais-Rousselot, *Médecine et colonisation.*

34. Inspection générale de l'hygiène et de la santé, annual report, 1939. See chiefly Monnais-Rousselot, *Médecine et colonisation,* as well as *Médecin-Colonel* Le Gall, *La situation sanitaire de l'Empire français pendant l'année 1940* (Paris, 1943); B. Metral, "La politique de santé en Cochinchine de 1858 à 1930" (MA thesis, Paris, 1990); L. Monnais-Rousselot, "La variole et la vaccine en Indochine française (1860–1939)," *Revue française d'histoire d'outre-mer,* 4th trimester 1995; and A. Guenel, "Lutte contre la variole en Indochine: Variolisation contre vaccination," *History and Philosophy of the Life Sciences,* no. 17 (1995).

35. J. Tully, *France on the Mekong: A History of the Protectorate in Cambodia* (Lanham, Md., 2002), p. 225.

36. *Maladies pestilentielles . . . 1939;* and see also Monnais-Rousselot, *Médecine et colonisation.*

37. *Maladies pestilentielles . . . 1939.*

38. Inspection générale de l'hygiène et de la santé, annual report, 1939.

39. Ibid., annual report, 1932.

40. Y. Henry, *Économie agricole de l'Indochine* (Hanoi, 1932); R. Dumont, *La culture du riz dans les deltas du Tonkin* (Paris, 1935); Gourou, *Paysans du delta;* id., *L'utilisation du sol en Indochine française* (Paris, 1940).

41. Y. Henry, inaugural address, Office indochinois du riz, Hanoi, 1931.

42. The term "peasant reconquest" is from J. Delvert, in *Le paysan cambodgien* (Paris, 1961).

43. See M. Guérin's excellent study, "Essartage et riziculture humide: Complémentarité des écosystèmes agraires à Stung Treng au début du XXème siècle," *Aseanie,* December 2001.

44. Smolski, "Statistiques de la population indochinoise."

45. See D. Vesin's fascinating "Histoire du fleuve Rouge: Gestion et aménagement d'un systéme hydraulique au Tonkin des années 1890 jusqu'à la Seconde Guerre mondiale" (MA thesis, Paris, 1992).

46. Ibid., pp. 27ff., 68 ff.

47. Governor-General Brévié, report to the minister of the colonies, November 19, 1937, CAOM, Fonds des travaux publics, 907; Vesin, "Histoire du fleuve Rouge."

48. J. Gauthier, *Les digues du Tonkin* (Hanoi, 1916).

49. N. Peytavin, *Rapport sur la crue du fleuve Rouge* (Hanoi, 1916).

50. A.-A. Pouyanne, *L'hydraulique agricole au Tonkin* (Hanoi, 1931), p. 26; Commissariat général au Plan, sous-commission de l'Indochine, *L'hydraulique agricole en Indochine,* CAOM, Affaires économiques, p. 577.

51. Vesin, "Histoire du fleuve Rouge," pp. 125–30.

52. C. Robequain, *L'évolution économique de l'Indochine française* (Paris, 1939), p. 70.

53. G. Khérian, "Le problème démographique indochinois," *Revue indochinoise juridique et économique* (Hanoi), 1937; id., "Les méfaits de la surpopulation deltaïque," ibid., 1938.

54. Fourniau, *Contacts franco-vietnamiens,* p. 341.

55. Pouyanne, *Hydraulique agricole au Tonkin,* p. 121.

56. Y. Henry and M. Devisme, *Documents de démographie et de riziculture* (Hanoi, 1928), p. 49.

57. Ho Dac Khai, "Contribution à l'étude de la colonisation annamite," *Revue indochinoise juridique et économique*, 1938.

58. Robequain, *Évolution économique*, p. 271.

59. *Bulletin économique de l'Indochine*, no. 1 (1939).

60. Henry, *Économie agricole de l'Indochine*, pp. 66–113, 152–95, and Gourou, *Utilisation du sol*, pp. 227–39, 272–83, 305–7.

61. Gourou, *Utilisation du sol*, p. 230ff.

62. Khérian, "Méfaits de la surpopulation deltaïque."

63. C. Geertz, *Agricultural Involution: The Process of Ecological Change in Indonesia* (Berkeley, 1963).

64. Henry and Devisme, *Documents de démographie et de riziculture*, p. 32. See likewise P. Bernard, *L'Indochine et la crise: Le problème du riz* (Paris, 1936).

65. Report of the delegation of French Indochina to the Conférence d'hygiène rurale des pays d'Orient (August 1927), quoted by Botreau-Roussel, "Note sur l'alimentation du paysan du delta tonkinois et les améliorations qu'il est possible de lui apporter," *Bulletin de l'Institut indochinois pour l'étude de l'homme* 5, 1 (1942): 59–66.

66. R. Thomas, "L'évolution économique du Cambodge, 1900–1940" (PhD diss., Université de Paris VII, 1978), p. 45.

67. See P. Brocheux, "The State and the 1930s Depression in French Indochina," and I. Nørlund, "Rice and the Colonial Lobby: The Economic Crisis in French Indo-China in the 1920s and the 1930s," in *Weathering the Storm: The Economies of Southeast Asia in the 1930's Depression*, ed. P. Boomgaard and I. Brown (Singapore, 2000), pp. 252–70.

68. Robequain, *Évolution économique*, p. 186.

69. *Le financement public de l'équipement des colonies*, CAOM, Affaires politiques, 2640.

70. P. Blanchard de La Brosse, *L'Indochine et la crise*, Institut colonial international, XXII session (Lisbon, 1937), p. 257.

71. P. Brocheux, "Crise économique et société en Indochine française," *Revue française d'histoire d'outre-mer* 68, 232–33 (1976).

72. Y. Pégourier, *Le marché du riz d'Indochine* (Paris, 1936), p. 17.

73. P. Estèbe, *Le problème du riz en Indochine* (Paris, 1934), p. 165.

74. Commission monétaire indochinoise, April 1934 report, p. 3.

75. According to Meuleau, *Des pionniers en Extrême-Orient*, twenty-seven Indochinese companies were added to the bank's portfolio between 1930 and 1937. See the reports of G. Lasserre on *Les banques coloniales*, CAOM, Affaires économiques, 190 (B), written in 1938, and on *Les banques en Indochine*, CAOM, Affaires économiques, 598, written in 1945.

76. Meuleau, *Des pionniers en Extrême-Orient*.

77. Lasserre, *Banques coloniales*.

78. Brocheux, "The State and the 1930s Depression in French Indochina."

79. J. Marseille, *Empire colonial et capitalisme français: Histoire d'un divorce* (Paris, 1984), chaps. 8 and 12.

80. Brocheux, "Crise économique et société"; id., "The State and the 1930s Depression in French Indochina."

81. Pégourier, *Marché du riz d'Indochine.*

82. Brocheux, "Crise economique et société."

83. Robequain, *Évolution économique de l'Indochine française;* Gourou, *Paysans du delta;* id., *Utilisation du sol;* Dumont, *Culture du riz;* P. Bernard, *Le problème économique in-dochinois* (Paris, 1934); id., *Nouveaux aspects du problème économique indochinois* (Paris, 1937); R. Bouvier, *La misère du paysan tonkinois* (Paris, 1937).

84. J. Bourgoin, presentation to the Comité économique de l'Indochine, Dalat, November 1947, in id., *Notes documentaires et études.*

85. Nguyen Van Huyen, "Le problème de la paysannerie annamite au Tonkin," *Est* (Hanoi), February 1939.

86. Nguyen Van Huyen, *Recherches sur la commune annamite,* presented at the Institut indochinois pour l'étude de l'homme (Hanoi, 1939).

87. D. Hémery, "Aux origines des guerres d'indépendance vietnamiennes: Pouvoir colonial et phénomène communiste en Indochine avant la Seconde Guerre mondiale," *Mouvement social,* October–December 1977.

88. J. Harmand, *Domination et colonisation* (Paris, 1910), p. 150.

89. Blanchard de La Brosse, "Rapport à la commission économique du Conseil supérieur de la France d'outre-mer."

90. Secrétaire d'État aux Colonies, report, 1941, CAOM, Affaires politiques, 2681.

91. Vesin, *Histoire du fleuve Rouge,* pp. 243–44.

92. Ibid.

93. Cited in Khérian, "Méfaits de la surpopulation deltaïque." See also J. Brévié, *Le déblo-quement des régions surpeuplées d'Indochine* (Société belge d'études et d'expansion, December 1938), and A. Lotzer, *La surpopulation du Tonkin et du Nord-Annam: Ses rapports avec la colonisation de la péninsule indochinoise* (Hanoi, 1941).

94. Governor-General Brévié, speech to the Conseil supérieur de colonisation, June 30, 1938, *Bulletin de l'ARIP,* July 1, 1938.

95. Khérian, "Méfaits de la surpopulation deltaïque au Tonkin."

96. Ibid.

97. A. Hardy, *Red Hills: Migrants and the State in the Highlands of Vietnam* (Copenhagen, 2003), chap. 2.

98. Gourou, *Utilisation du sol,* p. 148.

99. High Commissioner Émile Bollaert, speech on taking office in 1947, quoted by A. Laurent, *La Banque de l'Indochine et la piastre* (Paris, 1954), p. 25.

CHAPTER 7

1. P. Le Failler, "Village Rebellions in the Tonkin Delta, 1900–1905," in G. Bousquet and P. Brocheux, eds., *Viêt Nam Exposé: French Scholarship on Twentieth-Century Vietnam* (Ann Arbor, Mich., 2002), pp. 61–86.

2. *Situation politique, economique et financière du Laos en 1907,* Centre des archives d'outre-mer, Aix-en-Provence [henceforth cited as CAOM], Fonds de la résidence supérieure du Laos, D3.

3. M. Stuart-Fox, *A History of Laos* (New York, 1997); S. Ivarsson, "Bringing Laos into Existence: Laos between Siam and Indochina, 1860–1945" (PhD diss., Copenhagen, 1999).

4. François Moppert, "La révolte des Bolovens, 1901–1936," in *Histoire de l'Asie du Sud-Est: Révoltes, réformes, révolutions,* ed. P. Brocheux (Lille, 1981). See also J. B. Murdoch, "The 1901–1902 Holy Man's Rebellion," *Journal of the Siam Society,* January 1974.

5. Isabelle Alleton, "Les Hmong aux confins de la Chine et du Vietnam: la révolte du Fou (1918–1922)," in *Histoire de l'Asie du Sud-Est,* ed. Brocheux.

6. Forest, *Cambodge et la colonisation francaise.*

7. Ibid., p. 410.

8. Ibid. See also A. Souyris-Rolland, "La piraterie du Cambodge," *Bulletin de la Société des études indochinoises,* 4th trimester 1950.

9. Forest, *Cambodge et la colonisation francaise.*

10. Ibid., p. 398.

11. See ibid.

12. Ibid., p. 162n3.

13. *Le Démocrate* (Phnom Penh), August 12, 1946, quoted by P. Preschez, *Essai sur la démocratie au Cambodge* (Paris, 1961), p. 7.

14. Phouk Chhay, "Les élites politiques du Cambodge contemporain" (thesis, Phnom Penh, ca. 1965), p. 87.

15. D. Chandler, *A History of Cambodia* (Oxford, 1992), p. 159. See also J. Nepote and Khing Hoc Dy, "Samapheavi de Rim Kin," *Péninsule* 43, 2 (2001).

16. On the beginnings of Khmer nationalism, see Chandler, *History of Cambodia,* and P. Edwards, "Cambodia: The Cultivation of a Nation, 1860–1945" (PhD thesis, Monash University, 1999). F. Joly, "Les débuts du nationalisme au Cambodge" (typescript, École nationale de la France d'outre-mer, 1954); V. M. Reddi, *A History of the Cambodian Independence Movement, 1863–1955* (Tirupati, Andhra Pradesh, India, 1970).

17. A. Forest, "Les manifestations de 1916 au Cambodge," in *Histoire de l'Asie du Sud-Est,* ed. Brocheux.

18. This mythical universe is described in E. Porée-Maspero's remarkable *Étude sur les rites agraires des Cambodgiens* (1941; Paris: Mouton, 1962, 1964, 1969).

19. É. Aymonier, *Le Cambodge* (Paris, 1900–1904), 1: 56.

20. G. Coulet, *Les sociétés secrètes en terre d'Annam* (Paris, 1926).

21. Nguyen The Anh, "Sociétés secrètes, Cour de Hue et gouvernement de Cochinchine à la veille de la mort de Tu Duc (1882–1883)," *Approches-Asie,* December 1978–January 1979.

22. "Demandez à Gia Long," poem translated and published by Nguyen The Anh in id., *Monarchie et fait colonial au Vietnam,* p. 245. Concerning these questions, see Marr, *Vietnamese Tradition on Trial,* p. 304.

23. See Nguyen The Anh, *Monarchie et fait colonial au Vietnam.*

24. Hoang Cao Khai, *Nam su Kinh ou Guong su Nam: Miroir de l'histoire du Vietnam* (Hanoi, 1910).

25. Pham Quynh, "Vers une doctrine nationale," in *Nouveaux essais franco-annamites* (Hanoi, 1938).

26. Ibid.

27. Gilbert Chieu is very representative of this phenomenon. See P. Brocheux, "Note sur Gilbert Chieu (1867–1919), citoyen francais et patriote vietnamien," *Approches-Asie* (Paris), no. 11 (1992).

28. See G. Boudarel, "Phan Boi Chau et la société vietnamienne de son temps" and "Mémoires de Phan Boi Chau," *France-Asie* (Paris), nos. 194–95 (1968) and 199 (1969); and D. G. Marr, *Vietnamese Anticolonialism, 1885–1925* (Berkeley, 1971). See also Masaya Shiraishi, *Phan Boi Chau in Japan, 1905–1909: The Solidarity among the Asian People of the Same Sickness* (The Hague, 1980).

29. Brocheux, "Note sur Gilbert Chieu."

30. Phan Chu Trinh's "Mémoire au Gouverneur Paul Beau" (August 15, 1906) and "Lettre à mes compatriotes" (March 1907) were published in the *Bulletin de l'École française d'Extrême-Orient,* March–June 1907. On Phan Chau Trinh (a.k.a. Phan Chu Trinh), see the excellent documentary work of Le Thi Kinh (Phan Thi Minh), *Phan Chau Trinh qua nhung tai lieu moi* (Phan Chau Trinh through New Sources) (2 vols.; Da Nang, 2001).

31. See J. Kleinen, "Do Not Pay Taxes: The Anti-Tax Revolt in Central Vietnam, 1908," in *A Comparative Study of Peasant Unrest in Southeast Asia,* ed. L. E. Bauzon (Singapore, 1991); R. Lorrin, *Le mouvement social contre l'impot en Annam en 1908* (Paris, n.d.).

32. See P. Morlat, *Les affaires politiques de l'Indochine (1895–1923): Les grands commis du savoir au pouvoir* (Paris, 1995).

33. See P. Zinoman, *The Colonial Bastille: A History of Imprisonment in Vietnam, 1862–1940* (Berkeley, 2001).

34. See D. Hémery, "En Indochine française, réformisme colonial et nationalisme vietnamien au XXᵉ siècle: Le Sarrautisme et ses avatars," *Cahiers d'études indochinoises,* 1992; id., "Indochine, les droits humains"; A. Larcher-Goscha, "La légitimation française en Indochine: Mythes et réalités de la collaboration franco-vietnamienne" (PhD diss., Paris 2000). On Sarraut's team, see Morlat, *Affaires politiques de l'Indochine.*

35. See A. Larcher, "Réalisme et idealisme en politique coloniale: Albert Sarraut et l'Indochine, 1911–1914" (MA thesis, Paris, 1992).

36. Général Pennequin, "Pour garder l'Indochine," *Revue de Paris,* December 1, 1913. On Pennequin, see Mireille Favre–Le Van Ho, "Un milieu porteur de modernisation: Travailleurs et tirailleurs vietnamiens en France pendant la Première Guerre mondiale" (Ph.D. thesis, Paris, 1986).

37. See Favre–Le Van Ho, "Milieu porteur de modernisation"; Duong Van Giao, *L'Indochine française pendant la guerre de 1914–1918: Contribution a l'étude de la colonisation indochinoise* (Paris, 1925).

38. Hue Tam Ho Tai, "The Politics of Compromise: The Constitutionalist Party and the Electoral Reforms of 1922 in French Cochinchina," *Modern Asian Studies,* July 1984.

39. D. Hémery, "À propos de la demande d'admission du jeune Ho Chi Minh à l'École coloniale en 1911," in *La bureaucratie au Vietnam,* ed. G. Boudarel (Paris, 1983), pp. 26–30.

40. Pham Quynh, *Essais franco-annamites* (Paris, 1930). On Nguyen Van Vinh, see C. Goscha, "Le barbare moderne: Nguyen Van Vinh et la complexité de la modernité occidentale au Vietnam colonial," *Outre-mers: Revue d'histoire,* 2nd semester 2001.

41. Hue Tam Ho Tai, "Politics of Compromise." On Constitutionalism, see R. B. Smith, "Bui Quang Chieu and the Constitutionalist Party in French Cochinchina, 1917–1930," *Modern Asian Studies,* April 1969; M. Cook, *The Constitutionalist Party in Cochinchina: The Years of Decline, 1930–1942* (Victoria, Australia, 1977); Brocheux, "Élite, bourgeoisie, ou la difficulte d'être."

42. Marr, *Vietnamese Tradition on Trial, 1900–1945*, p. 32.

43. D. Hémery, "Ta Thu Thau: L'itinéraire politique d'un révolutionnaire vietnamien pendant les années 1930," in *Histoire de l'Asie du Sud-Est*, ed. Brocheux, pp. 192–222; id., "Le communisme national: Au Vietnam, l'investissement du marxisme par la pensée nationaliste," in *Les aventures du marxisme: Actes du colloque international pour le centenaire de Marx* (Paris, 1984); Trinh Van Thao, *Le Vietnam du confucianisme au marxisme* (Paris, 1992).

44. See Hue Tam Ho Tai, *Radicalism and the Origins of the Vietnamese Revolution* (Cambridge, Mass., 1992); Hémery, "Ta Thu Thau"; and id., "Saigon la Rouge," in *Saigon, 1925–1945* (Paris, 1992).

45. G. Boudarel, "L'extrême-gauche asiatique et le mouvement national vietnamien (1905–1925)," in *Histoire de l'Asie du Sud-Est*, ed. id.

46. P. Peycam, "Intellectuals and Political Commitment in Vietnam: The Emergence of a Public Sphere in Colonial Saigon" (PhD diss., London, 1999).

47. Ngo Tat To, *Thoi Vu*, no. 9.

48. S. Quinn-Judge, "Women in the Early Vietnamese Communist Movement: Sex, Lies and Liberation," *Southeast Asia Research* 10, 1 (March 2002).

49. Ibid.

50. W. F. Frederick, "Alexandre Varenne and Politics in Indochina, 1925–1926," in *Aspects of Vietnamese History*, ed. W. F. Vella (Honolulu, 1973), pp. 96–159; F. Koerner, "Un socialiste auvergnat gouverneur général de l'Indochine: Le cas d'A. Varenne, 1925–1928," *Revue historique*, January–March 1981.

51. M. Boucheret, "Le pouvoir colonial et la question de la main d'oeuvre en Indochine dans les années 1920," *Cahiers d'Histoire*, no. 85 (2001).

52. Nguyen Phan Long, *L'Echo annamite*, June 6, 1924.

53. Daniel Hémery, "Ta Thu Thau."

54. Gouvernement général de l'Indochine, *Le Viet Nam Quoc Dan Dang, ou Parti national annamite au Tonkin (1927–1932)*, vol. 2 of *Contribution à l'étude des mouvements politiques de l'Indochine française* (6 vols.; Hanoi, 1933–34).

55. P. Brocheux, *Ho Chi Minh* (Paris, 2000); id., *Ho Chi Minh: Du révolutionnaire à l'icône* (Paris, 2003), trans. as *Ho Chi Minh: A Biography* (New York, 2007); W. Duiker, *Ho Chi Minh* (New York, 2000); D. Hémery, *Ho Chi Minh de l'Indochine au Vietnam* (Paris, 1990); id., "Jeunesse d'un colonisé, genèse d'un exil: Ho Chi Minh jusqu'en 1911," *Approches-Asie*, no. 11 (1992); Thu Trang-Gaspard, *Ho Chi Minh a Paris (1917–1923)* (Paris, 1992); A. Ruscio, *Ho Chi Minh: Textes 1914–1969* (Paris, 1990).

56. C. Liauzu, *Aux origines du tiers-mondisme: Colonisés et anticolonialistes (1919–1939)* (Paris, 1982).

57. D. Hémery, "Du patriotisme au marxisme: L'immigration vietnamienne en France de 1926 à 1930," *Mouvement social*, January–March 1975; Brocheux, *Ho Chi Minh*.

58. Huynh Kim Khanh, *Vietnamese Communism, 1925–1945* (Ithaca, N.Y., 1981); N. Azéma, "Le mouvement et le journal, 'Thanh Nien,' 1925–1930" (MA thesis, Paris, 1982); Hue Tam Ho Tai, *Radicalism*.

59. C. Goscha, "Building Force: Asian Origins of Twentieth-Century Military Science in Vietnam (1905–1954)," *Journal of Southeast Asian Studies* 34, 3 (October 2003).

60. J. F. Giebel, "Ba Son 1925: The Strike at the Arsenal of Saigon. A Closer Look at Events and Their Interpretations" (MA thesis, Ithaca, N.Y., 1989).

61. Nguyen An Ninh, *La Cloche fêlée,* November 26, 1926.

62. Huynh Kim Khanh, *Vietnamese Communism,* p. 111.

63. Cf. P. Brocheux, "Le prolétariat des plantations d'hévéas au Vietnam méridional: Aspects sociaux et politiques (1927-1937)," *Mouvement social,* January-March 1975.

64. Hémery, "Du patriotisme au marxisme"; id., "Ta Thu Thau."

65. Notable among contemporary studies are L. Roubaud, *Viet-Nam: La tragédie indochinoise* (Paris, 1931), and Viollis, *Indochine S.O.S.*

66. J. Kleinen, "Sugar and Blood: Was the Quang Ngai Revolt of 1930-1931 an Exception to the General Rules of Agrarian Revolt?" (paper read at the 12th Conference of the International Association of Historians of Asia, University of Hong Kong, Hong Kong, June 24-28, 1991).

67. Viet Dan, Hoang Van Dao, *Viet Nam Quoc Dan Dang* (The Vietnamese National Party) (Saigon, 1965), pp. 90-91.

68. The two essential studies are P. Brocheux, "L'implantation du mouvement communiste en Indochine française: Le cas du Nghê Tinh (1930-1931)," *Revue d'histoire moderne et contemporaine,* January-March 1977, and Ngo Vinh Long, *Peasant Revolutionary Struggles in Vietnam in the 1930's* (Cambridge, Mass., 1978), p. 747. See also Tran Huy Lieu, *Les soviets du Nghê Tinh de 1930-1931 au Vietnam* (Hanoi, 1960); Gouvernement général de l'Indochine, *La terreur rouge en Annam,* vol. 5 of *Contribution à l'étude des mouvements politiques de l'Indochine française* (Hanoi, 1933-34); and D. Hémery, *Révolutionnaires vietnamiens et pouvoir colonial en Indochine: Communistes, trotskystes, nationalistes à Saigon de 1932 à 1937* (Paris, 1975).

69. Kleinen, "Sugar and Blood."

70. Tran Huy Lieu, *Soviets du Nghê Tinh;* Tran Van Giau, *Giai Cap Cong Nhan Viet Nam: Tu Dang Cong San Thanh Cap den Cach Mang Thanh Cong* (The Vietnamese Working Class: From the Formation of the Communist Party to the Success of the Revolution) (Hanoi, 1962-63), 1: 124-25.

71. T. Rettig, "French Military Policies in the Aftermath of the Yen Bay Mutiny (1930)," *Southeast Asia Research* 10, 3 (November 2002).

72. *Annuaire statistique de l'Indochine,* 1930 and 1932. However, the prison sentences resulting from the increase in crime during the Great Depression need to be kept in mind.

73. F. S. Litten, "The Noulens Affair," *China Quarterly,* June 1994.

74. A. Sarraut, *Grandeur et servitude coloniales* (Paris, 1931), p. 219.

75. Governor-General Pierre Pasquier, telegram, May 16, 1930, CAOM, Indochine Nouveau Fonds, 2636.

76. See J. Marseille, *Empire colonial et capitalisme français: Histoire d'un divorce* (Paris, 1984), esp. chaps. 7, 8, 9, 10, 14.

77. Sarraut, *Grandeur et servitude,* pp. 260-76.

78. On French policy in Indochina from 1930 to 1939, see D. Hémery, "Aux origines des guerres d'indépendance vietnamiennes: Pouvoir colonial et phénomène communiste en Indochine avant la Seconde Guerre mondiale," *Mouvement social,* October-December 1977.

79. Ibid.

80. Bernard, *Problème économique indochinois*; id., *Nouveaux aspects du problème économique indochinois*, p. 159; Gourou, *Paysans du delta tonkinois.*

81. A. Varenne, *Politique étrangère*, February 1938.

82. Ibid.

83. Hémery, *Aux origines des guerres d'indépendance.*

84. Cook, *Constitutionalist Party in Cochinchina.*

85. Letter to Minister of Colonies Paul Reynaud, CAOM, Indochine NF 2939.

86. *France-Indochine*, 30 October 1931.

87. Governor Pierre Pagès, letter, August 19, 1935, CAOM, Indochine Nouveau Fonds, 1836.

88. "Rapport sur la situation politique de l'Annam au mois de mai 1931," CAOM, Indochine Nouveau Fonds, 1597.

89. See Hémery, *Révolutionnaires vietnamiens et pouvoir colonial.*

90. Sûreté quoted ibid., p. 188.

91. Zinoman, *Colonial Bastille*, chap. 7. See also Hémery, "Terre de bagne en mer de Chine: Poulo Condore (1862–1953)," in Proceedings of Colloquium, "Colonisation et répression," Université de Paris VII, 2008 (forthcoming).

92. Hémery, *Révolutionnaires vietnamiens et pouvoir colonial*, part 3.

93. As demonstrated by S. Quinn-Judge, *Ho Chi Minh: The Missing Years* (London, 2003), pp. 222–28.

94. Hémery, *Révolutionnaires vietnamiens et pouvoir colonial*, p. 396.

95. See F. Guillemot, "Révolution nationale et lutte pour l'indépendance au Vietnam: L'échec de la troisième voie 'Dai Viet' (1938–1955)" (PhD diss., Paris, 2003).

96. See P. Bourdeaux, "Emergence et constitution de la communauté du Bouddhisme Hoa Hao: Contribution à l'histoire sociale du delta du Mékong (1935–1955)" (PhD diss., Paris, 2003).

97. Georges Grandjean, letter, January 22, 1931, CAOM, Marius Moutet papers, PA28, C3.

98. Minister of the Colonies Georges Mandel, speech at Longpont, 1939.

99. Governor-General Pierre Pasquier, report to the minister of the colonies, April 14, 1931.

100. *Revue politique et parlementaire*, October 1938.

CHAPTER 8

1. F. Mercier, *Vichy face à Tchang Kai-shek: Histoire diplomatique* (Paris, 1995).

2. On the military events, see C. Hesse d'Alzon, "L'armée française d'Indochine pendant la Seconde Guerre mondiale: 1939–1945," in *L'Indochine française, 1940–1945*, ed. P. Isoart (Paris, 1982).

3. M. Shiraishi, "La présence japonaise en Indochine 1940–1945," in *Indochine française, 1940–1945*, ed. Isoart.

4. On these events, see P. Brocheux, "L'occasion favorable 1940–1945," in *Indochine française, 1940–1945*, ed. Isoart. The outcome of the insurrection and repression in Cochinchina was more than 100 dead, according to the French, or 5,248, according to Vietnamese historians. Different sources assert that between 6,000 and 8,000 were imprisoned.

5. On the Decoux government, see P. Isoart, "Aux origines d'une guerre: L'Indochine française 1940–1945," in *Indochine française, 1940–1945*, ed. id.

6. Trung tam Luu tru Quoc gia 2 [National Archives Center 2, Ho Chi Minh City], Fonds TDBCPNV, EO3 312.

7. J. Decoux, *À la barre de l'Indochine, 1940–1945* (Paris, 1949). He is contradicted by C. de Boisanger, *On pouvait éviter la guerre d'Indochine: Souvenirs 1941–1945* (Paris, 1977).

8. See the examples in *Indochine française, 1940–1945*, ed. Isoart, p. 2. The number of civil servants punished is given in P. Lamant, "La révolution nationale dans l'Indochine de l'amiral Decoux," *Revue d'histoire de la Seconde Guerre mondiale* 138 (April 1985): 21–41. See also E. Jennings, *Vichy in the Tropics: Pétain's National Revolution in Madagascar, Guadeloupe and Indochina, 1940–1944* (Stanford, Calif., 2001); and *L'empire colonial sous Vichy*, ed. J. Cantier and E. Jennings (Paris, 2004).

9. Decoux, *À la barre*, p. 390.

10. N. Sihanouk, *L'Indochine vue de Pékin: Entretiens avec Jean Lacouture* (Paris, 1972), pp. 33–34.

11. Bao Dai, *Le Dragon d'Annam* (Paris, 1980), p. 97.

12. Decoux, *À la barre*, p. 392.

13. Ibid., p. 391.

14. Note no. 45453 of June 27, 1941, CAOM, PA 14, carton 1.

15. Decoux, *À la barre*, p. 399.

16. Trung tam Luu tru Quoc gia 1 [National Archives Center 1, Hanoi; hereafter Luu tru 1], Fonds Resuper, E7, 81417.

17. After having been invalided out of the Air Force as the result of a crash, *Capitaine-aviator* Do Huu Vi was killed leading a company of the Foreign Legion on the Somme in July 1916.

18. Admiral Decoux, telegram to Vichy, February 10, 1944, CAOM, NF Indochine 2435. Cambodia had its own organization, the "Jeunesses Yuvan."

19. Decoux, *À la barre*, p. 408.

20. Ibid., p. 381.

21. On Hanoi's intelligentsia and the crucial 1941–44 period, see *Thanh Nghi Hoi Ky* (Hanoi, 1999), the memoirs of Vu Dinh Hoe, who was the driving force behind *Thanh Nghi*. For a study of the magazine, see P. Brocheux: "La revue *Thanh Nghi*: Un groupe d'intellectuels vietnamiens confrontés aux problèmes de leur nation 1941–1945," *Revue d'Histoire moderne et contemporaine* (1987), no. 21, and id., "La revue *Thanh Nghi* et les questions littéraires, 1941–1945," *Revue française d'Histoire d'Outre-mer*, no. 280 (1988).

22. Hoc Phi, "Dom lua ban dau" (The Start of Decomposition), *Tap chi Van hoa* (Literary Magazine), September 3, 1963, p. 57. On this period, see also Mai Van Bo, *Luu Huu Phuoc Con Nguoi va Su Nghiep* (Luu Huu Phuoc: The Man and His Work) (Ho Chi Minh City, 1989), and Tran Do, *Ben song don sung* (Waiting for Weapons along the River) (Hanoi, 1980).

23. Tran Huy Lieu, Nguyen Luong Bich, and Nguyen Khac Dam, *Xa hoi Viet Nam trong thoi Phap Nhat, 1939–1945* (Vietnamese Society during the Franco-Japanese Period, 1939–1945) (Hanoi, 1957).

24. Interview with Le Thanh in *Cuoc phong van cac van* (Interviews with Writers) (Hanoi, 1942).

25. Phan Ngoc, "À la rencontre de deux cultures: L'influence de la littérature française au Vietnam," *Aséanie* 1 (1998) (Bangkok): 123-43.

26. André-Pallois, *L'Indochine: Un lieu d'échange culturel?* pp. 223-36.

27. Quoted by N. Taylor, "Orientalism/Occidentalism: The Founding of the Ecole des Beaux Arts d'Indochine and the Politics of Painting in Colonial Viet Nam, 1925-1945," *Crossroads* 11, 2 (1997): 1-33.

28. J. Martin, director of the Services économiques de l'Indochine, account in *Revue d'histoire de la Seconde Guerre mondiale*, no. 138 (April 1985).

29. J. Martin, report to the Conseil du gouvernement, dated February 3, 1945, CAOM, Nouveau Fonds Indochine 1267.

30. Ibid.

31. Martin, in *Revue d'histoire de la Seconde Guerre mondiale*, p. 91.

32. Inspection générale des Mines et de l'Industrie, note of April 18, 1944, Luu tru 1, Fonds du gouvernement général, L. 41, 7067.

33. High Commissioner G. Thierry d'Argenlieu to the minister of the colonies, December 7, 1945, CAOM, Affaires économiques, carton 14. In addition, the annexation of the province of Battambang by the Thai in 1941 had deprived Indochina of around 500,000 tons of paddy between 1941 and 1946. See Bui Minh Dung: "Japan's Role in the Vietnamese Starvation of 1944-45," *Modern Asian Studies* 29, 3 (1995), as well as the collection of personal accounts *Nan doi nam 1945 o Viet Nam: Nhung chung tich lich su,* ed. Van Tao and Furuta Mota (Hanoi, 1995).

34. J. Maigre and R. Charbonneau, *Les parias de la victoire: Indochine-Chine, 1945* (Paris, 1980). On the situation of the French Indochinese army, see d'Alzon, "L'armée française d'Indochine."

35. In addition to Shiraishi, "Présence japonaise," see also Kiyoko Kurusu Nitz, "Independence without Nationalists: The Japanese and Vietnamese Nationalism during the Japanese Period, 1940-1945," *Journal of South East Asian Studies* 15, 1 (March 1984), and id., "Japanese Military Policy towards French Indochina during the Second World War: The Road to Meigo Sakusen (9 March 1945)," ibid. 14, 2 (September 1983).

36. A. Patti, *Why Vietnam? America's Albatross* (Berkeley, 1980).

37. "The Japanese and the French fighting each other, that's what we want to bring about." Directive of the Permanent Bureau of the Central Committee of the ICP, March 12, 1945.

38. D. G. Marr notes this in *Vietnam 1945: The Quest for Power* (Berkeley, 1995), pp. 150-51, contrasting Vietnam with Indonesia, where Sukarno had "several years to begin to devise alternatives to the colonial system." The time factor is often underestimated or overlooked by historians.

39. Marr, ibid., pp. 238ff., emphasizes this.

40. Ibid., pp. 164ff.

41. *Lich su Quan Doi Nhan Dan V.N.* (History of the Vietnamese People's Army) (Hanoi, 1977); P. Brocheux, "Le mouvement indépendantiste vietnamien pendant la seconde guerre mondiale, 1939-1945," in *L'Empire colonial sous Vichy,* ed. J. Cantier and E. Jennings (Paris, 2004), pp. 266-85; Bui Diem, *In the Jaws of History* (Bloomington, Ind., 1999), pp. 16-89.

42. *Le Khu Quang Trung dans les activités révolutionnaires du mois d'août 1945 au Viet*

Bac (Hanoi, 1972); *Le Khu Tien Thuat dans les activités révolutionnaires du mois d'août 1945 au Viet Bac* (Hanoi, 1972).

43. Nguyen Khang, "Hanoi rises up," in *Mo Ky Nguyen Tu Do* (Opening the Era of Freedom) (Hanoi, 1980), p. 298.

44. Ibid., p. 307.

45. Vo Nguyen Giap, "Mot sang Ba Dinh" (Dawn on Ba Dinh Square), in *Mo Ky Nguyen Tu Do* (Opening the Era of Freedom), p. 397.

46. Ibid., p. 397.

47. Ibid., pp. 400–401.

48. On the revolutionary events in Hue, see *Mot con gio bui* (The Torment) by Tran Trong Kim, the prime minister of the period (Saigon, 1969), p. 107. On Saigon, see the point of view of Tran Van Giau quoted by P. Brocheux, "Les sentiers de la révolution," in *Saigon, 1925–1945,* pp. 197–209.

49. A. Patti, *Why Vietnam?*; W. Duiker, "Les États-Unis et l'Indochine française, 1940–1945," in *Indochine française, 1940–1945,* ed. Isoart, pp. 177–213. See also S. Tønnesson, *The Vietnamese Revolution of 1945: Roosevelt, Ho Chi Minh and de Gaulle in a World at War* (London, 1991), esp. chaps. 4, 5, and 7.

50. J. Sainteny, *Histoire d'une paix manquée: Indochine, 1945–1947* (Paris, 1967).

51. N. Sihanouk, *Souvenirs doux et amers* (Paris, 1981).

52. See *Lao Issara: The Memoirs of Oun Sananikone* (Ithaca, N.Y., 1975), and *Iron Man of Laos: Prince Phetsarath Ratanavongsa* (Ithaca, N.Y., 1978), both trans. J. B. Murdoch, ed. D. K. Wyatt. And see also J. Deuve, *Le Laos, 1945–1949: Contribution à l'histoire du mouvement Lao Issara* (Montpellier, 1994). On activities in Thailand, see Hoang Van Hoan, *Giot nuoc trong bien ca* (A Drop of Water in the Ocean) (Beijing, 1986), pp. 281–315.

53. Tran Van Dinh, "La naissance de l'armée du Pathet Lao," in *Laos: War and Revolution,* ed. N. S. Adams and A. W. McCoy (New York, 1970), p. 425.

54. Ibid., pp. 427–29.

55. "On these two occasions, I asked Truong Chinh and Hoang Minh Giam to clarify the obvious contradiction present in their vocabulary between Vietnam as a nation and the use of Indochina as a term—Indochinese Communist Party. Both argued that the terms were compatible because the three Nation-States had developed, under French domination, common geographical, political and economic interests. Therefore the name Vietnam was applicable as well to the Indochinese Federation." Patti, *Why Vietnam?* p. 568 n2.

56. Henri Laurentie quoted by M. Shipway, *The Road to War: France and Vietnam, 1944–47* (Providence, R.I., 1996), p. 274.

57. *Indochine française, 1940–1945,* ed. Isoart; Sainteny, *Histoire d'une paix manquée;* P. Mus, *Hô Chi Minh, le Vietnam, l'Asie* (Paris, 1971).

58. Published in the newspaper *Combat* on July 16, 1947. See also P. Brocheux, "De l'empereur Duy Tan au prince Vinh San: L'histoire peut-elle se répéter?" *Approches-Asie,* no. 10.

59. Editorial by Truong Chinh, general-secretary of the Party, in *Ngon co Giai Phong* (The Flag of Liberation) (Hanoi, 1976).

60. CAOM, Nouveau Fonds Indochine 1219, "Note sur la crise morale franco-indochinoise," August 1, 1945.

61. Patti, *Why Vietnam?*

62. On this entire period and its events, see Sainteny, *Histoire d'une paix manquée*; J.-J. Fonde, *Traitez à tout prix: Leclerc et le Vietnam* (Paris, 1971); *Le Général de Gaulle et l'Indochine, 1940–1946*, conference of the Institut Charles-de-Gaulle (Paris, 1982); *Leclerc et l'Indochine, 1945–1947*, conference of the Fondation Leclerc-de-Hauteclocque (Paris, 1992); and G. Thierry d'Argenlieu, *Chronique d'Indochine, 1945–1947* (Paris, 1985). However, the latest and most complete analytic survey of the subject is F. Turpin, *De Gaulle, les gaullistes et l'Indochine, 1940–1956* (Paris, 2005).

63. D'Argenlieu, *Chronique*, p. 283.

64. R. Salan, *Mémoires: Fin d'un empire* (Paris, 1970), 1: 404.

65. Valluy's directive no. 2 is quoted in P. Devillers, *Paris, Saigon, Hanoi: Les archives de la guerre, 1944–1947* (Paris, 1988), p. 179.

66. For a view of the "dirty war," see P. A. Thomas's testimony, *Combat intérieur*, vol. 1. (Paris, 1998). G. Einaudi associates it with testimony of other soldiers of the CEFEO in *Vietnam! La guerre d'Indochine, 1945–1954* (Paris, 2001). An opposing perspective can be found in A. Thévenet, *La guerre d'Indochine* (Paris, 2001).

67. See the excerpts of General Vuong Thua Vu's memoirs and those of Ho Chi Minh's secretary Vu Ky (trans. P. Brocheux) in *Leclerc et l'Indochine*, pp. 190–294. S. Tønnesson, *1946: Déclenchement de la guerre d'Indochine. Les vêpres tonkinoises du 19 décembre* (Paris, 1987), and Devillers, *Paris, Saigon, Hanoi*, both support the thesis that French officials had premeditated doing away with the government of Ho Chi Minh. They conclude that the Vietnamese could not have triggered the offensive of December 19, 1946. Since 1988, the Vietnamese have officially claimed responsibility for the decision to attack.

68. High Commissioner Léon Pignon, *Note d'orientation* no. 9, January 4, 1947, quoted in Devillers, *Paris, Saigon, Hanoi*, p. 334.

69. Bao Dai, *Dragon d'Annam*, p. 213.

70. V. Auriol, *Mon septennat, 1947–1954* (Paris, 1970).

71. Ibid., October 10, 1950, p. 295. Auriol's explanation is oversimple.

72. A. Ruscio, *Les communistes francais et la guerre d'Indochine, 1944–1954* (Paris, 1985). Georges Boudarel provides important testimony about the path of a French anticolonialist and his life in the bush with Vietnamese resistance in his *Autobiographie* (Paris, 1991).

73. Meuleau, *Des pionniers en Extrême-Orient*, pp. 500–507.

74. Auriol, *Mon septennat*, p. 293.

75. Ibid., p. 518.

76. L. Bodart, *La guerre d'Indochine: L'humiliation* (Paris, 1965).

77. Qiang Zhai, *China and Vietnam Wars, 1950–1975* (Chapel Hill, N.C., 2000). On the diplomatic level, the PRC became the obligatory intermediary between the DRVN and the USSR after the latter had recognized the DRVN in 1950, according to B. de Treglode, "Les relations entre le Viet-Minh, Moscou et Pékin à travers les documents soviétiques (1950–1954)," *Revue historique des Armées*, no. 4 (2000). This chaperoning resulted at the Geneva conference in the DRVN delegation having to submit to the initiatives of Zhou Enlai and Molotov, see F. Joyaux, *La Chine et le réglement du premier conflit d'Indochine, Genève 1954* (Paris, 1979).

78. Y. Gras, *Histoire de la guerre d'Indochine* (1979; repr. Paris, 1992), p. 354.

79. General Jean de Lattre de Tassigny, Chasseloup-Laubat School, Saigon, July 11, 1951, remarks reprinted in a brochure entitled *Appel à la jeunesse vietnamienne*.

80. Gras, *Histoire de la guerre d'Indochine*. On the war in Indochina, see also A. Ruscio, *La guerre française d'Indochine* (Paris, 1992); P. Franchini, *Les guerres d'Indochine*, vol. 1 (Paris, 1988); J. Dalloz, *La guerre d'Indochine, 1945–1954* (Paris, 1987). On the involvement of the United States in the war, see D. Artaud and L. Kaplan, *Dien Bien Phu* (Lyon, 1989); D. Anderson, *Trapped by Success: The Eisenhower Administration and Vietnam, 1953–1961* (New York, 1991); and K. C. Statler, *Replacing France: The Origins of American Intervention in Vietnam* (Lexington, Ky., 2007). On the negotiations in Geneva, see J. Lacouture and P. Devillers, *La fin d'une guerre* (Paris, 1960). On the passage from the French war to the American war, the same authors also published *Viet Nam: De la guerre française à la guerre américaine* (Paris, 1969). The Vietnamese revolution and the Indochina war within their Southeast Asian geopolitical framework are analyzed by C. Goscha, *Thailand and the Southeast Asian Networks of the Vietnamese Revolution, 1885–1954* (Richmond, Surrey, UK, 1999). For an overview of the economic war and the economic and financial legacy of the conflict for the states of the Indochinese peninsula, see H. Tertrais, "L'économie indochinoise dans la guerre (1945–1954)," *Outre-mers: Revue d'histoire* 88, 330–31 (2001), and id., *La piastre et le fusil: Le coût de la guerre d'Indochine* (Paris, 2002). See also C. Hodeir-Garcin, *Stratégies d'empire: Le grand patronat colonial face à la décolonisation* (Paris, 2003).

81. See M. Bodin, *Les Africains dans la guerre d'Indochine* (Paris, 2000). On the French *Corps expéditionnaire* in Indochina, see id., *La France et ses soldats: Indochine, 1945–1954* (Paris, 1996), and *Soldats d'Indochine, 1945–1954* (Paris, 1997).

CONCLUSION

1. Governor-General Jules Brevie quoted by J.-P. Aumiphin, "La présence financière et économique française en Indochine, 1859–1939" (PhD diss., Nice, n.d.), p. 104.

2. Jean Jaurès in "Débats parlementaires," *Journal officiel,* April 6, 1911, p. 1773.

3. General Théophile Pennequin, presentation to the officers of the Groupe d'Indochine, CAOM, A 30 (22), quoted by Fourniau, *Contacts franco vietnamiens,* p. 2584.

4. Sarraut, *Grandeur et servitude coloniale,* p. 283.

5. Jaurès cited in n. 2 above.

Vietnamese diacritics are not used in the text but are given in the alphabetical list below. Note that the Vietnamese letter Đ follows D.

áo xanh
Ba Đình
Ba Rìa
Bắc Ninh
Bắc Sơn
Bạch Thái Buổi
Bảo Đại / Vĩnh Thủy
Báo Khoa Học
Biên Hoà
Bui Bằng Đoàn
Bui Chu
Bui Công Trung
Bui Henriette Dr
Bui Quang Chiêu
Bửu Sơn Kỳ Hương
Cần Thơ
Cần Vương
Cao Bằng
Cao Đài
Cao Triều Phát
cây mít
Châu Đốc
Chế Lan Viên

Chí Hoà
chính huận
Chợ Lớn
chữ nôm
Cờ Giải Phong
Cờ mật viện
Côn Đảo
cổng điền
cổng thổ
cũ nâu
Cường Để
cứu dân độ thê
Cứu Quốc Quân
Diêp Văn Cương
Dục Đức
Dương Bạch Mai
Duy Tân emperor
Duy Tân Hội
Đà Nẵng
Đại Nam
Đại Nam Quốc Âm tự vị
Đại Việt
Đạm Phương

Đặng Thai Mai
Đăng Xuân Khu
Đào Duy Anh
Đạo Lành
Đào Minh Huyên
Đề cương Văn hóa Việt Nam
Đề Thám
địa bạ / địa bộ
Điện Biên Phủ
điền chủ
Đinh Bộ Lĩnh
Đình Công Tranh
Đốc Ngữ
Đời Nay
đồn điền
đồng
Đông Du
Đông Dương Cộng Sản Đảng
Đông Dương Tạp Chí
Đổng Khánh
Đông Kinh Nghĩa Thục
Đông Pháp Thời báo
Đuốc Nhà Nam
Gia Định Báo
giáp
Hà Nội
Hải Phòng
Hải Triều
Hàm Nghi
Hàn Mặc Tử
Hàn Thuyên
hát cải lương
hát chèo
Hiệp Hòa
Hồ Biểu Chánh
Hồ Chí Minh / Nguyễn Ái Quốc (Nguyễn
  Tất Thành)
Hồ Hữu Tường
Hồ Ngọc Can
Hòa Hảo
Hoàng Cao Khải
Hoàng Đạo
Hoàng Hoa Thám / Đề Thám
Hoàng Kế Viêm

Hoàng Tích Chu
Hoàng Trọng Phu
Hoàng Xuân Hãn
hội cứu quốc
hồi ký
hội truyền bá quốc ngữ
Hòn Gai
Huế
hương ước
Huỳnh Phú Sổ
Huỳnh Thúc Kháng
Huỳnh Tịnh Của / Paulus Của
Huỳnh Văn Phương
Huỳnh Văn Tiếng
Khải Định
Khai Hóa Nhật Báo
Khái Hưng
Khâm Thiên
Khoa Học Phổ Thông
Khoa Học Tạp Chí
Kim Văn Kiều
kinh lược
Kỳ Đồng
kỳ mục
Lạng Sơn
Lao Bảo
Lào Cay
Lê Duẩn
Lê Đức Thọ
Lê Lợi
Lê Phát An
Lê Phát Vinh
Lê Pho
Lê Văn Khôi
Lê Văn Trung
lính cơ
luận lý xã hội
Lục Tỉnh Tân Văn
Lương Đức Thiệp
Lương Tam Ky
Lưu Hữu Phước
Lưu Trong Luu
Lưu trữ
Lưu Vĩnh Phức

lý trưởng
Minh Mạng
Nam Phong Tạp Chí
Nam Xương
Ngày Nay
Nghệ Tỉnh / Nghê An ~ Hà Tỉnh
Ngô Đình Diệm
Ngô Đình Thục
Ngô Đức Kế
Ngô Gia Tự
Ngô Tất Tố
Ngô Văn Chiêu
Nguyễn (dynasty)
Nguyễn Ái Quốc (Nguyễn Tất
    Thành) / Hồ Chí Minh
Nguyễn An Ninh
Nguyễn Ánh
Nguyễn Bá Tong
Nguyễn Bá Trac
Nguyễn Bỉnh Khiêm
Nguyễn Cat Tương
Nguyễn Công Hoan
Nguyễn Công Tiểu
Nguyễn Đình Chiểu
Nguyễn Đình Thi
Nguyễn Đức Canh
Nguyễn Hiêp
Nguyễn Hiêp Hồng
Nguyễn Hữu Độ
Nguyễn Huu Khang
Nguyễn Phan Chánh
Nguyễn Phan Long
Nguyễn Phong Sắc
Nguyễn Phú Khai
Nguyễn Thái Học
Nguyễn Thế Truyển
Nguyễn Thị Minh Khai
Nguyễn Thiệu Lâu
Nguyễn Trãi
Nguyễn Tri Phương
Nguyễn Trong Hiêp
Nguyễn Trường Tộ
Nguyễn Tuân
Nguyễn Văn Cư

Nguyễn Văn Đức
Nguyễn Văn Tạo
Nguyễn Văn Thính
Nguyễn Văn Tố
Nguyễn Văn Vĩnh
nhà ngói
nhà quê
Nhanh Lúa
Nhất Linh
Nho giáo
Pác Bó
Phạm Công Tắc
Phạm Duy Tốn
Phạm Hồng Thái
Phạm Ngọc Thạch
Phạm Quỳnh
Phạm Văn Đồng
Phan Bội Châu
Phan Chu Trinh
Phan Đình Phùng
Phan Kế Bính
Phan Kế Toại
Phan Khôi
Phan Ngọc
Phan Phat San
Phan Thanh Giản
Phan Văn Hùm
Phan Văn Trường
Phan Xích Long
"Pháp Việt đề huề"
Phật giáo Thanh Niên
Phật Thầy Tây An
Phong Hóa
Phủ Nư Tân Văn
"quan phan tối rượu sam banh sáng
    sửa bò"
Quảng Ngãi
Quốc Học
quốc hồn
Quốc ngữ
quốc tuý
Quốc Văn Giáo Tư
Sơn La
tá điền

Tạ Quang Bửu
Tạ Thu Thâu
Tạ Tỵ
Tâm Tâm Xã
Tâm Thành
Tản Đà / Nguyễn Khắc Hiếu
Tân Trào
Tân Việt Nam Cách Mạng Đảng
Tây Du
Tây Nguyên
Thanh Nghị
Thanh Niên Cách Mạng Đông
   Minh Hội
Thanh Niên Cộng Sản Đoàn
Thanh Niên tiền phong
Thanh Niên tiền tuyến
Thành Thái
Thế Lữ
Thiên Địa Hội
Thiên Tử
Thiếu Sơn
Thiệu Trị
thôn
Thực Nghiệp Dân Báo
Tiếng Dân
tỉnh
Tố Hữu
Tô Ngọc Vân
Tô Tâm
tộc biểu
Tôn Đức Thắng
Tôn Thất Tuyết
tổng đốc
Trần Bá Lộc
Trần Cao Vân
Trần Chánh Chiếu / Gilbert Chiếu
Trần Hữu Độ
Trần Huy Liệu
Trần Phú
Trần Quí Cáp

Trần Quốc Tuấn
Trần Trọng Kim
Trần Văn Đê
Trần Văn Giàu
Trần Văn Thạch
Trần Văn Trà
Tri Tân
Trịnh Đình Thảo
Trinh Văn Thảo
Trung Bắc Tân Văn
Trung Lập Báo
Trương Công Định
Trương Tửu / Nguyễn Bách Khoa
Trương Vĩnh Ký / Petrus Ký
Tự Đức
Tự Lực Văn Đòan
Tú Mỡ / Hồ Trọng Hiếu
tự vệ
tuần phủ
Văn Miếu
Văn Thân
Việt Nam Cách mạng Thanh Niên Hội
VN Duy Tân Hội
VN Độc Lập Đảng
VN Độc Lập Đồng Minh Hội
VN Đồng Minh Hội
VN Quang Phục Hội
VN Quốc Dân Đảng
Vũ Bằng
Vũ Đinh Chi
Vũ Đinh Hoè
Vũ Được Khuê
Vũ Trọng Phụng
Vũ Văn Hiển
xã
Xô Viêt
xứ uy
Xuân Diệu
Xuân Thu Nhã Tập
Yên Báy

This bibliography essentially comprises recently published works, as well as a certain number of older works that are still useful and often essential. This book is the result of the study not only of the available historical writings but also of the files of the Centre des archives d'outre-mer (CAOM) in Aix-en-Provence and the Service historique de la Défense (SHD) in Vincennes, of private and national archives in Vietnam, and of works in Vietnamese, most of which are listed in the notes, rather than here.

Adams, N. S., and A. W. McCoy. *Laos: War and Revolution.* New York: Harper & Row, 1970.

Agard, A. *L'Union indochinoise française ou Indochine orientale: Régions naturelles et géographie économique.* Hanoi: Imprimerie d'Extrême-Orient, 1935.

Ageron, Ch.-R., and P. Devillers, eds. *Les guerres d'Indochine de 1945 à 1975.* Les Cahiers de l'IHTP, no. 34. Paris: Institut d'histoire du temps présent, 1996.

Ajalbert, J. *Les destinées de l'Indochine: Voyages, histoire, colonisation.* Paris: Louis-Michaud, 1911.

Alberti, J. B. *L'Indochine d'autrefois et d'aujourd'hui.* Paris: Société d'éditions géographiques, maritimes et coloniales, 1934.

Anderson, D. L. *Trapped by Success: The Eisenhower Administration and Vietnam, 1953–1961.* New York: Columbia University Press, 1991.

André-Pallois, N. *L'Indochine: Un lieu d'échange culturel? Les peintres français et indochinois (fin XIXe–XXe siècles).* PEFEO monograph no. 184. Paris: École française d'Extrême-Orient, 1997.

Ang Choulean. "La communauté khmère du point de vue du sacré." *Journal asiatique* 1, 2 (1990).

Artaud, D., and K. Kaplan, eds. *Diên Biên Phu: L'Alliance atlantique et la défense du Sud-Est asiatique.* Lyon: La Manufacture, 1989.

Aumiphin, J.-P. *La présence financière et économique française en Indochine, 1859–1939.* Hanoi: Éditions des statistiques du Vietnam, 1997.

Auriol, V. *Journal du septennat, 1947–1954.* 7 vols. Paris: A. Colin, 1970–80.

Aymonier, É. *Le Cambodge.* 3 vols. Paris: E. Leroux, 1900–1904.

Baille, F. *Souvenirs d'Annam (1886–1890).* Paris: E. Plon, Nourrit & Cie, 1890.

Bao Dai. *Le Dragon d'Annam.* Paris: Plon, 1980.

Bassino, J.-P., J.-D. Giacometti, and K. Odaka, eds. *Quantitative Economic History of Vietnam, 1900–1990: An International Workshop.* Tokyo: Hitotsubashi University, Institute of Economic Research, 2000.

Bayly, S. "French Anthropology and the Durkheimians in Colonial Indochina." *Modern Asian Studies* 34, 3 (2000): 581–622.

Bernard, P. *Nouveaux aspects du problème économique indochinois.* Paris: Fernand Sorlot, 1937.

———. *Le problème économique indochinois.* Paris: Nouvelles éditions latines, 1934.

Betz, J. *Bartholdi.* Paris: Éditions de Minuit, 1954.

Bezacier, L. *Manuel d'archéologie d'Extrême-Orient, Asie du sud-est.* Vol. 1: *Le Cambodge;* vol. 2: *Le Viêt-Nam.* Paris: A. & J. Picard, 1966, 1972.

Bezançon, P. *Une colonisation éducatrice? L'expérience indochinoise, 1860–1945.* Paris: L'Harmattan, 2002.

———. "La rénovation des écoles de pagodes au Cambodge." MA thesis, Université de Paris VII, 1992.

Bibliography of Asian Studies. Annual supplement of the *Journal of Asian Studies* (Ann Arbor, Mich.).

Billotey, P. *L'Indochine en zigzags.* Paris: Albin Michel, 1929.

Bodinier, G., ed. *1945–1946: Le retour de la France en Indochine. Textes et documents.* Vincennes: Service historique de l'Armée de Terre, 1987.

———. *Indochine 1947: Règlement politique ou solution militaire. Textes et documents.* Vincennes: Service historique de l'Armée de Terre, 1989.

Bonin, H., C. Hodeir, and J.-F. Klein, eds. *L'esprit économique impérial (1830–1870): Groupes de pression et réseaux du patronat colonial en France et dans l'Empire.* Paris: Publications de la SFHOM, 2008.

Bonneuil, C. "Mettre en ordre et discipliner les Tropiques: Les sciences du végétal dans l'Empire français, 1870–1940." 2 vols. PhD diss., Université de Paris VII, 1997.

Booth, A. "Economic Development of Southeast Asia: 1870–1985." In *Exploring Southeast Asia's Economic Past,* special issue, *Australian Economic History Review* 31, 1 (March 1991).

Boucheret, M. "Les plantations d'hévéas en Indochine (1897–1954)." 2 vols. PhD diss., Université de Paris I–Panthéon–Sorbonne, 2008.

Boudarel, G. *Autobiographie.* Paris: Jacques Bertoin, 1991.

———. *Giap.* Paris: Atlas, 1977.

———. "Influences and Idiosyncrasies in the Line and Practice of the Vietnam Communist Party." In *Vietnamese Communism in Comparative Perspective,* ed. W. S. Turley. Boulder, Colo.: Westview Press, 1980.

———. "L'insertion du pouvoir central dans les cultes villageois au Vietnam: Esquisse des problèmes à partir des écrits de Ngô Tât Tô." In *Cultes populaires et sociétés asiatiques:*

Appareils culturels et appareils de pouvoir, ed. A. Forest, Y. Ishizawa, and L. Vandermeersch. Paris: L'Harmattan, 1991.

———. *Phan Boi Chau et la société vietnamienne de son temps.* Special issue of *France-Asie* 199 (1965).

———, ed. *La bureaucratie au Vietnam.* Paris: L'Harmattan, 1983.

Boudet, P., and R. Bourgeois. *Bibliographie de l'Indochine française.* 4 vols. Hanoi: Imprimerie d'Extrême-Orient, 1913–35.

Boulbet, J. *Paysans de la forêt.* Paris: École française d'Extrême-Orient, 1975.

Bourdeaux, P. "Émergence et constitution de la communauté du Bouddhisme Hoa Hao: Contribution à l'histoire sociale du delta du Mékong (1935–1955)." PhD diss., École pratique des hautes études, Paris, 2003.

Bousquet, G., and P. Brocheux, eds. *Viêt Nam Exposé: French Scholarship on Twentieth-Century Vietnamese Society.* Ann Arbor: University of Michigan Press, 2002.

Bradley, M. P. *Imagining Vietnam and America: The Making of Postcolonial Vietnam (1919–1950).* Chapel Hill, N.C.: University of North Carolina Press, 2000.

Brassford, J. *Land Development Policy in Cochinchina under the French.* PhD diss., University of Hawaii, 1984.

Brébion, A. *Dictionnaire de bio-bibliographie générale, ancienne et moderne de l'Indochine française.* Paris: Société d'Éditions géographiques, maritimes et coloniales, 1935.

Brenier, H. [chef du Service des affaires économiques au Gouvernement général]. *Essai d'atlas statistique de l'Indochine française: Indochine physique, population, administration, finances, agriculture, commerce, industrie.* Hanoi-Haiphong: Gouvernement général de l'Indochine, 1914.

Briggs, D. "Problematic Progress: Reading Environmental and Social Change in the Mekong Delta." *Journal of Southeast Asia Studies* 34, 1 (February 2003).

Brocheux, P. "Une adolescence indochinoise." In *De l'Indochine à l'Algérie: La jeunesse en mouvement des deux côtés du miroir colonial, 1940–1962,* ed. Nicolas Bancel, Daniel Denis, and Youssef Fatès, 32–53. Paris: La Découverte, 2003.

———. "Courants nationalistes au Vietnam" (73–80); "Déception et méfiance vietnamiennes" (228–42); "Témoignages vietnamiens sur le déclenchement du drame du 19 décembre 1946" (291–94). In *Leclerc et l'Indochine, 1945–1947: Quand se noua le destin d'un empire,* ed. Guy Pedroncini and Philippe Duplay. Paris: Albin Michel, 1992.

———. "Crise économique et société en Indochine française." *Revue d'histoire d'outre-mer* 63, 232–33 (1976).

———. "L'Économie et la société dans l'Ouest de la Cochinchine pendant la période coloniale (1890–1940)." PhD diss., École pratique des hautes études, Paris, 1969.

———. "Élite, bourgeoisie, ou la difficulté d'être." In *Saigon, 1925–1945.* Mémoires, 17. Paris: Autrement, 1992.

———. "L'empreinte de la domination coloniale française sur l'Indochine (1860–1954)." In NORAO, *Identités territoriales en Asie orientale,* 1: 175–83. Paris: Les Indes savantes, 2004.

———. "L'expédition de reconquête de l'Indochine en 1945–1946 et celle de Saint Domingue en 1802–1803: Essai de mise en parallèle." In *1802 en Guadeloupe et à Saint Domingue: Réalités et mémoire. Actes du colloque de Saint-Claude, 2–3 mai 2002.* Gourbeyre: Archives départementales [de la Guadeloupe], 2003.

———. "Les grands *dien chu* de la Cochinchine occidentale." In *Tradition et révolution au Vietnam*, ed. Jean Chesneaux, Georges Boudarel, and Daniel Hémery. Paris: Anthropos, 1971.

———. "Grands propriétaires et fermiers dans l'Ouest de la Cochinchine pendant la période coloniale." *Revue historique*, July–September 1971.

———. "Une histoire croisée: L'immigration politique indochinoise en France, 1911–1945." *Hommes & migrations*, no. 1253 (January–February 2005): 26–39.

———. "L'histoire de la péninsule indochinoise: Un état des lieux." *Cahiers d'histoire immédiate*, no. 8 (Autumn 1995): 129–42.

———. *Une histoire économique du Viet Nam, 1850–2007: La palanche et le camion*. Paris: Les Indes savantes, 2009.

———. *Ho Chi Minh*. Paris: Presses de Sciences po, 2000.

———. *Ho Chi Minh: Du révolutionnaire à l'icône*. Paris: Payot & Rivages, 2003. Published in English as *Ho Chi Minh: A Biography*, trans. Claire Duiker. New York: Cambridge University Press, 2007.

———. "L'implantation du mouvement communiste en Indochine française: le cas du Nghê-Tinh (1930–1931)." *Revue d'histoire moderne et contemporaine*, January–March 1977.

———. *The Mekong Delta: Ecology, Economy, and Revolution, 1860–1960*. Monograph 12. Madison, Wis.: Center for Southeast Asian Studies, University of Wisconsin–Madison, 1995.

———. "Moral Economy or Political Economy? The Peasants Are Always Rational." *Journal of Asian Studies* 42, 4 (August 1983): 791–803.

———. "Note sur Gilbert Chieu (1867–1919), citoyen français et patriote vietnamien." *Approches-Asie*, no. 11 (1992).

———. "L'occasion favorable, 1940–1945: Les forces politiques vietnamiennes pendant la guerre mondiale." In *L'Indochine française, 1940–1945*, ed. P. Isoart, 131–78. Paris: Presses universitaires de France, 1982.

———. "Le prolétariat des plantations d'hévéas au Vietnam méridional: Aspects sociaux et politiques (1927–1937)." *Mouvement social*, no. 90 (January–March 1975).

———. "La question de l'indépendance dans l'opinion vietnamienne de 1939 à 1945." In *Les chemins de la decolonisation de l'empire français, 1936–1956*, ed. Ch.-R. Ageron, 201–7. Paris: Éditions du Centre national de la recherche scientifique, 1986.

———. "The State and the 1930s Depression in French Indochina." In *Weathering the Storm: The Economies of Southeast Asia in the 1930s Depression*, ed. P. Boomgaard and I. Brown. Singapore: Institute of Southeast Asian Studies, 2000.

———. *Vietnamese Communism and the Peasants: Analogy and Originality in Vietnamese Experience. Vietnamese Communism in Comparative Perspective*, ed. W. Turley. Boulder, Colo.: Westview Press, 1980.

———. "Vietnamiens et minorités en Cochinchine pendant la période coloniale." *Modern Asian Studies* 6, 4 (1972).

———, ed. *Histoire de l'Asie du Sud-Est: Révoltes, réformes, révolutions*. Lille: Presses universitaires de Lille, 1981. Study of the Hmong revolts between 1918–1922 (I. Alleton); those of the Bolovens between 1901 and 1936 (F. Moppert); peasant demonstrations in 1916 in Cambodia (A. Forest); Vietnamese peasant movements (Nguyen Xuan Linh); traditionalism and reform under the Nguyen (Nguyen The Anh); Vietnamese nationalism's Asian ties between 1905 and 1925 (G. Boudarel); the Vietnamese intelligentsia in the 1920s and the Trotskyist leader Ta Thu Thau (D. Hémery); and the relations between the communists and Vietnamese peasants (P. Brocheux).

Brötel, D. *Französischer Imperialismus in Vietnam: Die koloniale Expansion und die Errichtung des Protektorates Annam-Tongking, 1880–1885*. Zurich: Atlantis, 1971.

Brown, I. *Economic Change in South-East Asia, c. 1830–1980*. New York: Oxford University Press, 1997; reprint, 1999.

Bruno, G. [pseud. of Augustine Fouillée]. *Le tour de la France par deux enfants: Devoir et patrie: Livre de lecture courante*. Cours complet de lecture et d'instruction morale et civique. Paris: Belin, 1877.

Bui Tin. *1945–1999: Vietnam, la face cachée du régime*. Paris: Kergourd, 1999.

Bui Tran Phuong. "La politique de paix préconisée par Nguyen Truong To face au défi occidental au XIXᵉ siècle." MA thesis, Université de Paris VII–Denis Diderot, 1995.

———. "Viêt Nam, 1918–1945: Genre et modernité. Émergences de nouvelles perceptions et expérimentations." PhD diss., Université de Lyon II–Louis Lumière, 2008.

Bui Xuan Bao. *Le roman vietnamien contemporain: Tendences et évolution du roman vietnamien contemporain, 1925–1945*. Saigon: Tu sach Nhan-van Xa hoi, 1968.

Burel, L. "Le contact colonial franco-vietnamien dans le Centre et le Nord du Vietnam, 1856–1883." 3 vols. PhD diss., Université de Paris VII, 1997.

Burguière, M. "Le chemin de fer du Yunnan: Paul Doumer et la politique d'intervention française en Chine, 1889–1902." *Revue d'histoire diplomatique,* January–March, April–June, July–September 1963.

Buttinger, J. *Vietnam: A Dragon Embattled*. 2 vols. London: Pall Mall, 1967.

Cady, F. *The Roots of French Imperialism in Eastern Asia*. Ithaca, N.Y.: Cornell University Press, 1954.

Cantier, J., and E. Jennings, eds. *L'empire colonial sous Vichy*. Paris: Odile Jacob, 2004.

Cao, Huy Thuan. *Les missionnaires et la politique coloniale française au Vietnam, 1857–1914*. Yale Southeast Asia Studies 13. New Haven, Conn.: Yale Center for International and Area Studies, 1990.

Careghi, J.-C. *Le statut personnel des Vietnamiens en Indochine de 1887 à 1954*. Aix en Provence: Presses universitaires d'Aix-Marseille, 2002.

Catalogue des périodiques vietnamiens de la BN. Edited by J.-C. Poitelon and Nguyen Tat Dac. Paris: Bibliothèque nationale, 1993.

Catalogue du fonds indochinois (Livres vietnamiens imprimés en quôc ngu, 1922–1954). Edited by Ch. Pasquel-Rageau. Microfilm. Paris: Bibliothèque nationale, 1991.

Catalogue du fonds vietnamien, 1890–1921. Edited by Le Thi Ngoc Anh. Paris: Bibliothèque nationale, 1987.

Cayez, P. *Crises et croissance de l'industrie lyonnaise, 1850–1900*. Paris: Éditions du CNRS, 1980.

Cesari, L. "La menace d'intervention militaire américaine pendant la conférence de Genève et la stratégie des États-Unis en 1954." *Vingtième siècle,* July–September 1989.

Chandler, D. P. *A History of Cambodia*. Oxford: Allen & Unwin, 1992.

Charle, C. *La crise des sociétés impériales: Allemagne, France, Grande-Bretagne, 1900–1940: Essai d'histoire sociale comparée*. Paris: Seuil, 2001.

Chen, K. C. *Vietnam and China, 1938–1954*. Princeton, N.J.: Princeton University Press, 1969.

Chesneaux, J. *Contribution à l'histoire de la nation vietnamienne.* Paris: Éditions sociales, 1955.

Chesneaux, J., G. Boudarel, and D. Hémery, eds. *Tradition et révolution au Vietnam.* Paris: Éditions Anthropos, 1971.

Clauzel, J. *La France d'outre-mer (1930–1960): Témoignages d'administrateurs et de magistrats.* Paris: Karthala, 2003. French Indochina, pp. 445–90, 700–713.

Cleary, M. "Managing the Forest in Colonial Indochina, c. 1900–1940." *Modern Asian Studies* 39, 2 (2005): 257–83.

Clementin-Ojha, C., and P. Y. Manguin. *Un siècle pour l'Asie: L'École française d'Extrême-Orient (1898–2000).* Paris: École française d'Extrême-Orient, 2001.

Condominas, G. *L'espace social à propos de l'Asie du Sud-Est.* Paris: Flammarion, 1980.

———. *Nous avons mangé la forêt de la Pierre-Génie Gôo: Chronique de Sar Luk, village mnong gar, tribu proto-indochinoise des hauts-plateaux du Viêt-Nam central.* Paris: Mercure de France, 1957.

Congrès international de la population, Paris, 1937. Paris: Hermann, 1938–39.

Conseil supérieur de l'agriculture, du commerce et de l'industrie. *Enquête sur la marine marchande.* 3 vols. Paris: Impr. impériale, 1863.

Cook, M. *The Constitutionalist Party of Indochina, 1930–1942: The Years of Decline.* Monash Papers on Southeast Asia, no. 6. Victoria, Australia: Centre of Southeast Asian Studies, Monash University, 1977.

Cooper, N. *France in Indochina: Colonial Encounters.* Oxford: Berg, 2001.

Copin, Henri. *L'Indochine dans la littérature française des années vingt à 1954: Exotisme et altérité.* Paris: L'Harmattan, 1996.

Cordier, H. *Bibliotheca Indosinica: Dictionnaire bibliographique des ouvrages relatifs à la péninsule indochinoise.* 5 vols. Paris: Imprimerie nationale, 1912–15.

Corre, A. *L'ethnographie criminelle d'après les statistiques judiciaires recueillies dans les colonies françaises.* Paris: C. Reinwald, 1894.

Dalloz, J. *Dictionnaire de la guerre d'Indochine, 1945–1954.* Paris: A. Colin, 2006.

———. *La guerre d'Indochine, 1945–1954.* Paris: Seuil, 1987.

———. "Les Vietnamiens dans la franc-maçonnerie coloniale." *Revue française d'histoire d'outre-mer* 85, 320 (1998): 103–18.

Dartigues, L. *L'orientalisme français en pays d'Annam, 1862–1939.* Paris: Les Indes savantes, 2005.

Del Testa, D. W. "'Imperial Corridor': Association, Transportation, and Power in French Colonial Indochina." In special issue of *Science, Technology, Society* (Delhi), December 1999.

———. "Paint the Trains Red: Labor, Nationalism and Railroads in French Indochina, 1898–1945." PhD diss., University of California, 1999.

———. "Railroad Development and Market Contraction in French Colonial Indochina, 1898–1954." In *Working Papers* of the Asian Historical Statistics Project, Hitotsubashi University, Tokyo, Japan, 2000.

Delvert, J. *Le paysan cambodgien.* Paris, The Hague: Mouton, 1961.

Denis, E. *Bordeaux et la Cochinchine sous la Restauration et le second Empire.* Bordeaux: Delmas, 1965.

Descours-Gatin, C. *Quand l'opium finançait la colonisation en Indochine: L'élaboration de la régie générale de l'opium, 1860 à 1914.* Paris: L'Harmattan, 1992.

Descours-Gatin, C., and H. Villiers. *Guide de recherches sur le Vietnam: Bibliographie, archives et bibliothèques de France.* Supervised by G. Boudarel, P. Brocheux, and D. Hémery. Paris: L'Harmattan, 1983.

Deuve, J. *Le royaume du Laos (1949–1965).* Paris: École française d'Extrême-Orient, 1984.

Devillers, P. *Français et Annamites: Partenaires ou ennemis? 1856–1902.* Paris: Denoël, 1998.

———. *Histoire du Viêt-nam de 1940 à 1952.* Paris: Seuil, 1952.

———. *Paris, Saigon, Hanoi: Les archives de la guerre, 1944–1947.* Paris: Gallimard–Julliard, 1988.

Diep Dinh Hoa. "A New Approach to Village Philosophies in the Red River Delta." Typescript. Australian National University, 1998.

Dorgelès, R. *Sur la route mandarine.* Paris: Albin Michel, 1925.

Doumer, P. *Situation de l'Indochine de 1897 à 1902.* Hanoi: F. N. Schneider, 1902.

Dreyfus, G., *Lettres du Tonkin, 1884–1886.* Paris: L'Harmattan, 2001.

Duiker, W. J. *Historical Dictionary of Vietnam.* Lanham, Md.: Scarecrow Press, 1998.

———. *Ho Chi Minh.* New York: Hyperion Press, 2000.

———. *The Rise of Nationalism in Vietnam, 1900–1941.* Ithaca, N.Y.: Cornell University Press, 1976.

Dumont, R. *La culture du riz dans le delta du Tonkin.* 1935. Rev. ed. Pattani, Thailand: Prince of Songkla University, 1995.

Duong Trung Quoc, et al., eds. *Viet-Nam: Nhung sukien Lich Su* [Vietnam Historical Chronology, vol. 4: From the Origins to 1858, 1858–1918, 1919–1945, 1945–1975]. Hanoi: NXBGD / Publishing House of Education, 2002–3.

Durand, B., P. Langlet, and Nguyen Chanh Tam. *Histoire de la codification juridique au Vietnam.* Montpellier: Université de Montpellier, Faculté de droit, 2001.

Durand, G. "Le commerce extérieur de l'Indochine française." In *Études indochinoises* 3. Études et documents, no. 25. Aix-en-Provence: Institut d'histoire des pays d'outre-mer, 1993.

Durand, M. M., and Nguyên Tran Huan. *Introduction à la littérature vietnamienne.* Paris: Maisonneuve & Larose, 1969.

Duteil, J.-P. *L'ombre des nuages: Histoire et civilisation du Vietnam au temps des Lê et au début de la dynastie Nguyên, 1427–1819.* Paris: Éditions Arguments, 1997.

Edwards, P. "Cambodia: The Cultivation of a Nation, 1860–1945." PhD thesis, Monash University, Clayton, Australia, 1999.

Einaudi, G. *Vietnam! La guerre d'Indochine, 1945–1954.* Paris: Le Cherche-Midi, 2001.

Elliott, Duong Van Mai. *The Sacred Willow: Four Generations in the Life of a Vietnamese Family.* New York: Oxford University Press, 1999.

Fall, B. *Le Viet-Minh: La République démocratique du Viêt-Nam, 1945–1960.* Paris: A. Colin, 1960.

Fall, D. *Bernard Fall: Memories of a Soldier Scholar.* Washington, D.C.: Potomac Books, 2006.

Fall, M. "Le chemin de fer de l'Indochine: 'L'acier du rail, l'argent du budget commun.'" *Revue d'histoire des chemins de fer* 7 (Autumn 1992).

Feray, P. R. *Le Viêt Nam au XXe siècle.* Paris: Presses universitaires de France, 1979.

Ferro, M., ed. *Le Livre Noir du colonialisme, XVIe–XXIe siècle: De l'extermination à la repentance*. Paris: Robert Laffont, 2003. Indochina and Vietnam, pp. 351–91.

Folin, J. de. *Indochine, 1940–1945: La fin d'un rêve*. Paris: Perrin, 1993.

Forest, A. *Le Cambodge et la colonisation française: Histoire d'une colonisation sans heurts, 1859–1905*. Paris: L'Harmattan, 1980.

———. *Les missionnaires français au Tonkin et au Siam (XVIIe–XVIIIe siècles): Analyse comparée d'un relatif succès et d'un échec certain*. 3 vols. Paris: L'Harmattan, 2000.

Fourniau, C. *Les contacts franco vietnamiens en Annam et au Tonkin de 1885 à 1896*. PhD diss., Aix–Marseille, 1983. Lille: Atelier national de reproduction des thèses, 1984.

———. *Vietnam: Domination coloniale et résistance nationale, 1858–1914*. Paris: Les Indes savantes, 2002.

Fourniau, C., and Trinh Van Thao, eds. *Le contact colonial franco-vietnamien: Le premier demi-siècle, 1858–1911*. Aix-en-Provence: Université de Provence, 1999.

Franchini, P. *Les guerres d'Indochine*. 2 vols. Paris: Pygmalion, 1988.

———. *Les mensonges de la guerre d'Indochine*. Paris: Perrin, 2005.

Galliéni, J.-S. *Gallieni au Tonkin (1892–1896)*. Paris: Berger-Levrault, 1941.

———. *Trois colonnes au Tonkin (1894–1895)*. Paris: R. Chapelot, 1899.

Gantès, G. de. "Coloniaux et gouverneurs en Indochine française, 1902–1914." PhD diss., Université de Paris VII, 1994.

Garnier, Francis [pseud. G. Francis]. *La Cochinchine française en 1864*. Paris: E. Dentu, 1864.

———. *De la colonisation de la Cochinchine*. Paris: E. Dentu, 1865.

———. *Voyage d'exploration en Indochine*. Edited by J.-P. Gomane. Paris: La Découverte, 1985.

Gazquez, D., and A. Larcher-Goscha. *Publications officielles de l'Indochine française*. Paris: Bibliothèque nationale, 2005.

Géographie universelle Quillet illustrée: Physique–économique–humaine. Edited by Maurice Allain. 4 vols. Paris: Librairie Aristide Quillet, 1923–26.

Giacometti, J.-D. "La question de l'autonomie de l'Indochine et les milieux coloniaux français, 1915–1928." PhD diss., Université de Aix–Marseille, 1997.

Girardet, R. *L'idée coloniale en France de 1871 à 1962*. Paris: La Table ronde, 1972.

Girault, A. *Principes de colonisation et de législation coloniale*. Paris: L. Larose, 1895.

Gomane, J. P. *La Mission Doudart de Lagrée–Francis Garnier (1866–1868)*. Paris: L'Harmattan, 1995.

Gonjo, Y. *Banque coloniale ou banque d'affaires: La Banque de l'Indochine sous la IIIe République*. Paris: Comité pour l'histoire économique et financière de la France, 1993. Originally published as *Fransu-teikoshugi to Asia: Indoshina Ginkoshi-Kenkyu* (Tokyo, 1985).

Goscha, C. E. "Le contexte asiatique de la guerre franco-vietnamienne: Réseaux, relations et économie (août 1945–mai 1954)." 2 vols. PhD diss., École pratique des hautes études, Paris, 2000.

———. *Thailand and the Southeast Asian Networks of the Vietnamese Revolution, 1885–1954*. Richmond, Surrey, UK: Curzon Press, 1999.

———. *Vietnam or Indochina? Contesting Concepts of Space in Vietnamese Nationalism, 1887–1954*. Copenhagen: Nordic Institute of Asian Studies, 1995.

Goscha, C. E., and S. Ivarssøn, eds. *Contesting Visions of the Lao Past: Lao Historiography at the Crossroads*. Copenhagen: Nordic Institute of Asian Studies, 2003.

Gourou, P. *Les paysans du delta tonkinois: Étude de géographie humaine.* Paris: Éditions d'Art et d'Histoire, 1936.

————. *L'Utilisation du sol en Indochine française.* Centre d'études de politique étrangère, Travaux des groupes d'études, no. 14. Paris: Paul Hartmann, 1940.

Gouvernement général de l'Indochine. Direction des services économiques. Service de la statistique générale. *Annuaires statistiques de l'Indochine.* 10 vols. 1914–45.

Grandmaison, L. de, General. *L'expansion française au Tonkin. En territoire militaire. . . . Avec une lettre du général Galliéni.* Paris: E. Plon, Nourrit & Cie, 1898.

Gras, Y., General. *Histoire de la guerre d'Indochine.* Paris: Plon, 1979. Rev. ed. Paris: Denoël, 1992.

Grossheim, M. *Nordvietnamesische Dorfgemeinschaften: Kontinuität und Wandel.* Hamburg: Mitteilungen des Instituts für Asienkunde Hamburg, 1997.

Guérin, M. "Des casques blancs sur le Plateau des Herbes: La pacification des aborigènes des hautes terres du Sud-Indochinois, 1859–1940." PhD diss., Université de Paris VII, 2003.

————. "Essartage et riziculture humide: Complémentarité des écosystèmes agraires à Stung Treng au début du XXᵉ siècle." *Aséanie: Sciences humaines en Asie du Sud-Est* (Bangkok), no. 8 (December 2001).

Guérin, M., A. Hardy, Nguyen Van Chinh, and S. Tan Boon Hwee. *Des montagnards aux minorités ethniques: Quelle intégration nationale pour les habitants des hautes terres du Vietnam et du Cambodge.* Paris: L'Harmattan; Bangkok: Institut de recherche sur l'Asie du Sud-Est contemporaine, 2003.

Guermeur, H. *Le régime fiscal de l'Indochine.* 1909. Rev. ed., ed. C. Descours-Gatin. Paris: L'Harmattan, 1999.

Guide des fonds d'archives d'époque coloniale conservées au centre no. 1 des Archives nationales. Bilingual ed. Hanoi: Nha Xuat Ban Khoa Hoc Xa Hoi [Social Sciences Publishing House], 1995.

Guillemot, F. "Révolution nationale et lutte pour l'indépendance au Vietnam: L'échec de la 3e voie 'Dai Viet' (Dai Viet Quoc Dan Dang 1938–1955)." PhD diss., École pratique des hautes études, Paris, 2003.

Guillen, P. *L'expansion, 1881–1898.* Vol. 1 of *Politique étrangère de la France.* Paris: Imprimerie nationale, 1985.

Gunn, G. *Political Struggles in Laos, 1930–1954: Vietnamese Communist Power and the Lao Struggle for Independence.* Bangkok: Duang Kamol, 1998.

————. *Rebellion in Laos: Peasants and Politics in a Colonial Backwater.* Bangkok: White Lotus Press and École française d'Extrême-Orient, 2003.

Hardy, A. *Red Hills and the State in the Highlands of Vietnam.* Honolulu: University of Hawai'i Press; Copenhagen: Nordic Institute of Asian Studies, 2003.

Hartingh, B. de. *Entre le peuple et la nation: La République démocratique du Viet Nam de 1953 à 1957.* PEFEO monograph no. 189. Paris: École française d'Extrême-Orient, 2003.

Hémery, D. "Asie du Sud-Est, 1945: Vers un nouvel impérialisme colonial? Le projet indochinois de la France au lendemain de la Seconde Guerre mondiale." In *L'ère des décolonisations: Sélection de textes du Colloque "Décolonisations comparées," Aix-en-Provence, 30 septembre–3 octobre 1993,* ed. Ch.-R. Ageron and M. Michel. Paris: Karthala, 1995.

———. "Aux origines des guerres d'indépendance vietnamiennes: Pouvoir colonial et phénomène communiste en Indochine avant la Seconde Guerre mondiale." *Mouvement social,* October–December 1977.

———. "Le communisme national: Au Vietnam, l'investissement du marxisme par la pensée nationaliste." In *Les aventures du marxisme,* ed. R. Galissot. Paris: Syros, 1984.

———. "Décoloniser la France le syndrome indochinois en métropole, 1944–1954." In *Culture impériale: Les colonies au cœur de la République, 1931–1961,* ed. P. Blanchard and S. Lemaire. Paris: Autrement, 2004.

———. "Du patriotisme au marxisme: L'immigration vietnamienne en France de 1926 à 1930." *Mouvement social,* January–March 1975.

———. "En Indochine française, réformisme colonial et nationalisme vietnamien au XXe siècle: Le sarrautisme et ses avatars." In *Études indochinoises* 3. Études et documents, no. 25. Aix-en-Provence: Institut d'histoire des pays d'outre-mer, 1993.

———. "Générations . . . Au Vietnam, des intellectuels en situation coloniale." *Approches-Asie,* no. 11 (1992).

———. *Hô Chi Minh: De l'Indochine au Vietnam.* Paris: Gallimard, 1990.

———. "Inconstante Indochine . . . L'invention et les dérives d'une catégorie géographique." *Revue française d'histoire d'outre-mer* 87, 326–27 (2000): 137–58.

———. "L'Indochine, les droits humains, 1899–1954: Entre colonisateurs et colonisés, la Ligue des droits de l'homme." *Outre-mers: Revue d'histoire* 88, 1st semester (January 2001).

———. "Jeunesse d'un colonisé, genèse d'un exil. Hô Chi Minh jusqu'en 1911." *Approches-Asie,* no. 11 (1992).

———. *Révolutionnaires vietnamiens et pouvoir colonial en Indochine: Communistes, trotskystes, nationalistes à Saigon de 1932 à 1937.* Paris: F. Maspero, 1975.

———. "Saigon la Rouge." In *Saigon, 1925–1945.* Mémoires, 17. Paris: Autrement, 1992.

———. "Terre de bagne en mer de Chine: Poulo Condore (1862–1953)." In Proceedings of Colloquium, "Colonisation et répression," Université de Paris VII, 2008. Forthcoming.

Henley, D. E. F. "Ethnographic Integration and Exclusion: Indonesia and Indochina." *Comparative Studies in Society and History* 37, 2 (1995): 286–324.

Henry, Y. *Économie agricole de l'Indochine.* Hanoi: Gouvernement général de l'Indochine, 1932.

Henry, Y., and M. Devisme. *Documents de démographie et de riziculture.* Hanoi: Publications du Bulletin économique de l'Indochine, 1928.

Hickey, G. C. *Sons of the Mountain: Ethnohistory of the Vietnamese Central Highlands to 1954.* New Haven, Conn.: Yale University Press, 1982.

Histoire des frontières de la péninsule indochinoise. Edited by P.-B. Lafont. Vol. 1, *Les frontières du Vietnam.* Paris: L'Harmattan, 1989.

History of the August Revolution. Hanoi: Éditions en langues étrangères, 1972.

Hoang, Van Dao. *Viet Nam Quoc Dan Dang: Lich su tranh dan can dai (1927–1954)* [The VNQDD: The History of a Contemporary Struggle]. Saigon: n.p., 1970.

Ho Chi Minh. *Écrits.* Hanoi: Éditions en langues étrangères, 1971.

Hodeir-Garcin, C. *Stratégies d'empire: Le grand patronat colonial face à la décolonisation.* Paris: Belin, 2003.

Hue, B., et al., eds. *Littératures de la Péninsule indochinoise*. Paris: Karthala-AUF, 1999.

Hue Tam Ho Tai. *Millenarianism and Peasant Politics in Vietnam*. Cambridge, Mass.: Harvard University Press, 1983.

Huynh, Kim Khanh. *Vietnamese Communism, 1925–1945*. Ithaca, N.Y.: Cornell University Press, 1982.

Huynh, Ly. *Phan Chau Trinh: Than The va su nghiep* [Phan Châu Trinh: The Man and the Work]. Da Nang: Nha xuat ban Da Nang, 1992.

Huynh Van Tong. *Lich su bao chi Viet Nam tu khoi den nam 1930* [History of the Vietnamese Press to 1930]. Saigon: Tri Dang, 1973.

Hy Van Luong. *Revolution in the Village: Tradition and Transformation in North Vietnam, 1925–1988*. Honolulu: University of Hawai'i Press, 1992.

Hyvanluong, Diepdinhhoa. "Culture and Capitalism in the Pottery Enterprises of Bien Hoa, South Vietnam (1878–1975)." *Journal of Southeast Asian Studies* 22, 1 (March 1991).

Imbert, L. *La Cochinchine au seuil du XXᵉ siècle*. Bordeaux: J. Durand, 1900.

Indochine, alerte à l'histoire: Ni opprobre, ni oubli. Paris: Académie des sciences d'outre-mer, 1985.

L'Indochine de 1940 à 1945. Special issue of the *Revue d'histoire de la Seconde Guerre mondiale et des conflits contemporains*, no. 138 (April 1985), with a bibliography by J. Valette.

Institut Charles de Gaulle. *De Gaulle et l'Indochine, 1940–1946*. Paris: Plon, 1982.

Isoart, P. "La création de l'Union indochinoise." *Approches-Asie*, no. 11 (1992).

———. *Le phénomène national vietnamien: De l'indépendance unitaire à l'indépendance fractionnée*. Paris: Librairie générale de droit et de jurisprudence, 1961.

———, ed. *L'Indochine française, 1940–1945*. Paris: Presses universitaires de France, 1982. Essays on the origins of the Indochina war (P. Isoart), the attitude and strategies of Vietnamese movements during World War II (P. Brocheux), etc.

Ivarsson, S. "Bringing Laos into Existence: Laos between Siam and Indochina, 1860–1945." PhD diss., University of Copenhagen, 1999.

Jennings, E. *Vichy in the Tropics: Pétain's National Revolution in Madagascar, Guadeloupe and Indochina, 1940–1944*. Stanford: Stanford University Press, 2001.

Journoud, P., and Tertrais, H., eds. *1954–2004: La bataille de Dien Bien Phu entre histoire et mémoire*. Paris: Société française d'histoire d'outre-mer, 2003.

Joyaux, F. *La Chine et le règlement du premier conflit d'Indochine (Genève, 1954)*. Série internationale 9. Paris: Publications de la Sorbonne, 1979.

Kelly, G. P. *Franco-Vietnamese Schools, 1918–1938: Regional Development and Implications for National Integration*. Madison, Wis.: Southeast Asia Publications, 1982.

Khin Sok. *Le Cambodge entre Siam et Vietnam de 1775 à 1860*. Paris: École française d'Extrême-Orient, 1991.

Kim Huyng-Jun, ed. *Religion, Ethnicity and Modernity in Southeast Asia*. Seoul: National University Press, 1998.

Klein, J.-F., "Lyon et la colonisation: Du discours fédérateur à l'oubli collectif." In *Identité et régionalité: Être lyonnais hier et aujourd'hui*, ed. A. Vingtrinier, B. Benoît, and G. Gardes. Lyon: Jacques André Éditions, 2005.

———. *Un Lyonnais en Extrême-Orient, Ulysse Pila: vice-roi de l'Indochine, 1837–1909*. Lyon: Lugd, 1994.

———. "Soyeux en mer de Chine: Stratégie des réseaux lyonnais en Extrême-Orient, 1843–1906." PhD diss., Université de Lyon II, 2002. Paris: Les Indes savantes, forthcoming.

Kleinen, J. "'Do Not Pay Taxes': The Anti-Tax Revolt in Central Vietnam, 1908." In *A Comparative Sudy of Peasant Unrest in Southeast Asia*, ed. L. E. Bauzon. Singapore: Institute of Southeast Asian Studies, 1991.

———. *Facing the Future, Reviving the Past: A Study of Social Change in a Northern Vietnamese Village*. Singapore: Institute of Southeast Asian Studies, 1999.

———. "Sugar and Blood: Was the Quang Ngai Revolt of 1930–1931 an Exception to the General Rule of Agrarian Revolt?" Paper read at the 12th Conference of the International Association of Historians of Asia, University of Hong Kong, June 24–28, 1991.

———. "The Village as Pretext: Ethnographic Praxis and the Colonial State in Vietnam." In *The Village in Asia Revisited*, ed. J. C. Breman, P. Kloos, and A. Saith. New Delhi: Oxford University Press, 1997.

Kleinen, J., et al., eds. *Lion and Dragon: Four Centuries of Dutch-Vietnamese Relations*. Amsterdam: Broom, 2008.

Kratoska, P. H. "The British Empire and the Southeast Asian Rice Crisis of 1919–1921." *Modern Asian Studies* 24, 1, 1990.

Lacouture, J., and P. Devillers. *La fin d'une guerre*. Paris: Seuil, 1960.

Laffey, J. F. "Municipal Imperialism in Nineteenth-Century France." *Historical Reflections* 1, 1 (1974).

Lafont, P. B. *Bibliographie du Laos*. 2 vols. Paris: École française d'Extrême-Orient, 1964–78.

Lamant, P. *L'affaire Yukanthor: Autopsie d'un scandale colonial*. Paris: Société française d'histoire d'outre-mer, 1989.

———. *Bilan et perspectives des études khmères (langue et culture)*. Paris: L'Harmattan, 1997.

Lanessan, J.-L. de. *La colonisation française en Indo Chine*. Paris: Alcan, 1895.

———. *L'empire d'Annam, son organisation sociale et politique*. Paris: Impr. de Chaix, 1889.

———. *L'expansion coloniale de la France: Étude économique, politique et géographique sur les établissements français d'outre-mer*. Paris: Alcan, 1886.

———. *L'Indochine française: Étude politique, économique et administrative*. Paris: Alcan, 1889.

———. *La lutte pour l'existence et l'évolution des sociétés*. Paris: Alcan, 1903.

Lange, C. "L'Église au Vietnam." In *Les prodromes de la décolonisation de l'Empire français 1936–1956* (Paris: Éditions du CNRS, 1986).

———. *L'Église catholique et la société des Missions étrangères au Vietnam: Le vicariat apostolique de Cochinchine aux XVIIe et XVIIIe siècles*. Paris: L'Harmattan, 2005.

Langlet, P. *L'ancienne historiographie d'État au Vietnam*. 2 vols. Textes et documents sur l'Indochine 14. Paris: Publications de l'École française d'Extrême-Orient, 1992.

———. *La tradition vietnamienne: Un état national au sein de la civilisation chinoise*. Special issue of the *Bulletin de la Société des études indochinoises* 44, 2–3. Saigon: Société des études indochinoises, 1970.

Langlet, P., and Quach Thanh Tam. *Atlas historique des six provinces du Sud (Nam Ky) du Viet Nam*. Paris: Les Indes savantes, 2001.

Larcher-Goscha, A. "La légitimation française en Indochine: Mythes et réalités de la 'collaboration franco-vietnamienne' et du réformisme colonial (1905–1945)." 2 vols. PhD diss., Université de Paris VII, 2000.

Lavergne, B. *Les deux présidences de Jules Grévy.* Paris: Fischbacher, 1966.

Lawrence, Mark Atwood, and Fredrik Logevall, eds. *The First Vietnam War: Colonial Conflict and Cold War Crisis.* Cambridge, Mass.: Harvard University Press, 2007.

Le, N. D. *Les missions étrangères et la pénétration française au Viet Nam.* The Hague: Mouton, 1975.

Le Failler, P. *Monopole et prohibition de l'opium en Indochine: Le pilori des chimères.* Paris: L'Harmattan, 2001.

Le Failler, P., and J.-M. Mancini, eds. *Viet Nam: Sources et approches.* Proceedings of the Euroviet II conference, Aix-en-Provence, May 3–5, 1995. Aix-en-Provence: Publications de l'Université de Provence, 1996.

Le Thanh Khoi. *Histoire du Vietnam des origines à 1858.* Paris: Sudestasie, 1981.

———. *Le Viet Nam: Histoire et civilisation.* Paris: Éditions de Minuit, 1955.

Leroi-Gourhan, A., and J. Poirier, with A.-G. Haudricourt and G. Condominas. *Ethnologie de l'Union française: Territoires extérieurs.* Vol. 2: *Asie, Océanie, Amérique.* Paris: Presses universitaires de France, 1953.

Leurence, F. *Étude statistique sur le développement économique de l'Indochine de 1899 à 1923.* Hanoi: Impr. d'Extrême-Orient, 1925. Reprinted from the *Bulletin économique de l'Indochine* 171, n.s., 2 (1925).

Li, Tana. *Nguyen Cochinchina: Southern Vietnam in the Seventeenth and Eighteenth Centuries.* Ithaca, N.Y.: Cornell Southeast Asia Program, 1998.

Lin Hua. *Chiang Kai-shek, De Gaulle contre Hô Chi Minh: Viêt-Nam 1945–1946.* Paris: L'Harmattan, 1994.

Littératures contemporaines de l'Asie du Sud-Est. Colloque Littératures de l'Asie du Sud-Est du XXIXe Congrès international des orientalistes. Dir. P.-B. Lafont and D. Lombard. Paris: À l'Asiathèque, 1974.

Lockhart, B. M. *The End of the Vietnamese Monarchy.* New Haven, Conn.: Yale Center for International Studies, 1993.

Lockhart, G. *Nations in Arms: The Origins of the People's Army of Vietnam.* Sydney: Allan & Unwin, 1989.

Lorrin, A. *Paul Doumer, gouverneur général de l'Indochine (1897–1902): Le Templin colonial.* Paris: L'Harmattan, 2004.

Loti, P. *Journal intime.* Paris: Calmann-Lévy, 1930.

Lyautey, H. *Du rôle colonial de l'armée.* Paris: A. Colin, 1900.

Manguin, P.-Y. *Les Nguyen, Macau et le Portugal: Aspects politiques et commerciaux d'une relation privilégiée en mer de Chine, 1773–1802.* Publications de l'École française d'Extrême-Orient, 84. Paris: PEFEO, 1984.

———. *Les Portugais sur les côtes du Viet Nam et le Champa: Étude sur les routes maritimes et les relations commerciales, d'après les sources portugaises (XVIe, XVIIe, XVIIIe siècles).* Publications de l'École française d'Extrême-Orient, 81. Paris: PEFEO, 1972.

Mantienne, F. *Monseigneur Pigneau de Béhaine, évêque d'Adran, dignitaire de Cochinchine.* Études et documents 8. Paris: Églises d'Asie, 1999.

Marin, C. *Le rôle des missionnaires français en Cochinchine aux XVIIe et XVIIIe siècles.* Études et documents 9. Paris: Églises d'Asie, 1999.

Marquet, J. *Les cinq fleurs: L'Indochine expliquée*. Collection des livres classiques à l'usage des écoles élémentaires indigènes. Hanoi: Direction de l'instruction publique en Indo-Chine, 1928.

Marr, D. *Vietnam*. World Bibliographical Series 147. Oxford: Clio Press, 1992.

———. *Vietnam 1945: The Quest for Power*. Berkeley: University of California Press, 1995.

———. *Vietnamese Anticolonialism, 1885–1925*. Berkeley: University of California Press, 1971.

———. *Vietnamese Tradition on Trial, 1920–1945*. Berkeley: University of California Press, 1981.

Marseille, J. *Empire colonial et capitalisme français (années 1880–années 1950): Histoire d'un divorce*. Paris: Albin Michel, 1984.

McConnell, S. *Leftward Journey: The Education of Vietnamese Students in France, 1919–1939*. New Brunswick, N.J.: Transaction Publishers, 1989.

McHale, S. F. *Print and Power: Confucianism, Communism, and Buddhism in the Making of Modern Vietnam*. Honolulu: University of Hawai'i Press, 2004.

McLeod, M. W. "Truong Dinh and Vietnamese Anti-Colonialism (1859–1864): A Reappraisal." *Journal of Southeast Asian Studies* (Singapore) 24, 1 (March 1993).

———. *The Vietnamese Response to French Intervention, 1862–1874*. New York: Praeger, 1991.

Mercier, F. *Vichy face à Tchang Kai Shek: Histoire diplomatique*. Paris: L'Harmattan, 1995.

Meuleau, M. *Des pionniers en Extrême-Orient: Histoire de la Banque de l'Indochine, 1875–1975*. Paris: Fayard, 1990.

Meyer, C. *La vie quotidienne des Français en Indochine, 1860–1910*. Paris: Hachette, 1985.

Michaud, J. "The Montagnards and the State in Northern Vietnam from 1802 to 1975: A Historical Overview." *Ethnohistory* 47, 2 (Spring 2000).

Monnais-Rousselot, L. *Médecine et colonisation: L'aventure indochinoise, 1860–1939*. Paris: CNRS Éditions, 1999.

Morlat, P. *Les affaires politiques de l'Indochine, 1895–1923: Les grands commis, du savoir au pouvoir*. Paris: L'Harmattan, 1995.

———. *Indochine années vingt*, vol. 1: *Le balcon de la France sur le Pacifique*. Paris: Les Indes savantes, 2001.

———. *Indochine années vingt*, vol. 2: *Le rendez-vous manqué: La politique indigène des grands commis au service de la mise en valeur*. Paris: Les Indes savantes, 2006.

———. *La répression coloniale au Vietnam, 1908–1940*. Paris: L'Harmattan, 1990.

Murray, J. *The Development of Capitalism in Colonial Indochina, 1870–1940*. Berkeley: University of California Press, 1980.

Mus, P. *Hô Chi Minh, le Vietnam, l'Asie*. Edited by Annie Nguyen Nguyet Ho. Paris: Seuil, 1971.

———. "The Role of the Village in Vietnamese Politics." *Pacific Affairs*, September 1949.

———. *Vietnam, sociologie d'une guerre*. Paris: Seuil, 1952.

Ngo Kim Chung and Nguyen Duc Nghinh. *Propriété privée et propriété collective dans l'ancien Vietnam*. Edited by Georges Boudarel, Lydie Prin, Vu Can, et al. Recherches asiatiques. Paris: L'Harmattan, 1987.

Ngo Tat To. *Quand la lampe s'éteint*. Hanoi: Éditions en langues étrangères, 1959.

Ngo Van. *Au pays de la cloche fêlée: Tribulations d'un Cochinchinois à l'époque coloniale*. Paris: l'Insomniaque, 2000.

———. *Viêt-nam, 1920-1945: Révolution et contre-révolution sous la domination coloniale.* Paris: l'Insomniaque, 1996.

Ngo, Vinh Long. *Before the Revolution: The Vietnamese Peasants under the French.* Cambridge, Mass.: MIT Press, 1973.

Ngo Vinh Long and Nguyen Hoi Chan. *Vietnamese Women in Society and Revolution.* Vol. 1, *The French Colonial Period.* Cambridge, Mass.: Vietnam Resource Center, 1974.

Nguyen An Tinh, ed. *Nguyen An Ninh.* Ho Chi Minh City: Tre, 1996.

Nguyen Dinh Thi and Tran Ngoc Bich. *Bibliographie vietnamienne.* 2 vols. Paris: Sudestasie, 1975-82.

Nguyen Hien Le. *Dong kinh nghia thuc.* Saigon: La Bôi, 1968.

Nguyen Khac Vien and Huu Ngoc. *Anthologie de la littérature vietnamienne.* 4 vols. Hanoi: Éditions en langues étrangères, 1972-1977.

Nguyen Shui Meng. *The Population of Indochina.* Singapore: Institute of Southeast Asian Studies, 1974.

Nguyen Thanh. *Lich su Bao Tieng Dan,* Da Nang: Nha xuat ban Da Nang, 1992.

Nguyen Thanh Nha. *Tableau économique du Vietnam aux XVIIe et XVIIIe siècles.* Paris: Cujas, 1970.

Nguyen The Anh. *Bibliographie critique sur les relations entre le Vietnam et l'Occident des origines à 1954.* Paris: Maisonneuve & Larose, 1967. New ed., Paris: Les Indes savantes, forthcoming.

———. "L'élite vietnamienne et le fait colonial dans les premières années du XXᵉ siècle." *Revue française d'histoire d'outre-mer* 268 (1985).

———. "Into the Maelstrom: Vietnam during the Fateful 1940s." In *Vietnam Culture Series,* no. 3: 201-13. Westminster, Calif.: Institute of Vietnamese Studies, 2005.

———. *Kinh te va xa hoi Viet-Nam duoi cac vua trieu Nguyen* [Economy and Vietnamese Society under the Nguyen Dynasty]. Saigon: Lua Thiêng, 1970.

———. *Monarchie et fait colonial au Viet Nam (1875-1925): Le crépuscule d'un ordre traditionnel.* Paris: L'Harmattan, 1992.

———. "Quelques remarques sur l'état des études historiques sur le Vietnam." *Approches-Asie,* no. 15 (1997).

———. "Sociétés secrètes, cour de Huê et gouvernement de Cochinchine à la veille de la mort de Tu Duc (1882-1883)." *Approches-Asie,* no. 13 (December 1978-January 1979).

———. "Village versus State: The Evolution of State-Local Relations in Vietnam until 1945." *Tonan Ajia Kenkyu (Southeast Asian Studies)* 41, 1 (June 2003).

Nguyen The Anh and A. Forest, eds. *Guerre et paix en Asie du Sud-Est.* Paris: L'Harmattan, 1998.

Nguyen The Anh and Y. Ishizawa. *Commerce et navigation en Asie du Sud-est (XVIIIe-XIXe siècles).* Paris: L'Harmattan, 1999.

Nguyen Van Huyen. *La civilisation annamite.* Hanoi: Imprimerie d'Extrême-Orient, 1943.

Nguyen Van Khanh. *Viet Nam Quoc Dan Dang trong lich su cach mang Viet Nam* [The National Democratic Party of Vietnam in Vietnamese history]. Hanoi: Nha xuat ban Khoa hoc xa hoi, 2005.

Nguyen Van Ky. *La société vietnamienne face à la modernité: Le Tonkin de la fin du XIXᵉ siècle à la Seconde Guerre mondiale.* Paris: L'Harmattan, 1995.

Nguyenvan Phong. *La société vietnamienne de 1882 à 1902.* Paris: Presses universitaires de France, 1971.

Nguyen Vy. *Tuan, chang trai nuoc Viet* [Tuan, a Guy from Vietnam]. 1969. 2 vols. Glendale, Calif.: Dai Nam, n.d.

Nhung Tuyet Tran and A. Reid, eds. *Vietnam: Borderless Histories.* Madison: University of Wisconsin Press, 2006.

Niollet, D. *L'épopée des douaniers en Indochine, 1874–1954.* Paris: Kailash, 1998.

Norindr, P. *Phantasmatic Indochina: French Colonial Ideology in Architecture, Film, and Literature.* Durham, N.C.: Duke University Press, 1996.

Nørlund, I. "The French Empire, the Colonial State in Vietnam, and Economic Policy: 1885–1940." In *Exploring Southeast Asia's Economic Past,* special issue, *Australian Economic History Review* 31, 1 (March 1991).

———. *Interplay between Craft and Industry in a Vietnamese Province: Nam Dinh, 1900–1945.* Copenhagen: Nordic Institute of Asian Studies, 1991.

———. "Rice and the Colonial Lobby: The Economic Crisis in French Indochina in the 1920s and 1930s." In *Weathering the Storm: The Economies of Southeast Asia in the 1930s Depression,* ed. P. Boomgaard and I. Brown. Singapore: Institute of Southeast Asian Studies, 2000.

———. "Rice Production in Colonial Vietnam, 1900–1930." In *Rice Societies: Asian Problems and Prospects,* ed. id., S. Cederroth, and I. Gerdin. London: Curzon Press, 1986.

———. "Textiles Productions in Vietnam, 1880–1940: Handicraft and Industry in a Colonial Economy." PhD diss., University of Copenhagen, 1994.

Osborne, M. E. *The French Presence in Cochinchina and Cambodia: Rule and Response (1859–1905).* Ithaca, N.Y.: Cornell University Press, 1969.

Oualid, W. *Le privilège de la Banque de l'Indo-Chine et la question des banques coloniales.* Paris: Marcel Giard, 1923.

Papiers Georges Thierry d'Argenlieu: 517 AP. Inventory by M.-F. Limon. Paris: Centre historique des Archives nationales, Paris, 2001.

Papin, P. " 'Des villages dans la ville' aux 'villages urbains': L'espace et les formes du pouvoir à Hanoi de 1805 à 1940." 2 vols. PhD diss., Université de Paris VII, 1997.

———. *Histoire de Hanoi.* Paris: Fayard, 2001.

———. "Who Has Power in the Village? Political Processes and Social Reality in Vietnam." In *Viêt Nam Exposé: French Scholarship on Twentieth-Century Vietnamese Society,* ed. G. Bousquet and P. Brocheux. Ann Arbor: University of Michigan Press, 2002.

Papin, P., and P. Le Failler, eds. *Dong Khanh dia du chi: Géographie de l'empereur Dong Khanh.* Hanoi: Thong Nhat, 2001.

Patti, A. L. A. *Why Viet Nam? Prelude to America's Albatross.* Berkeley: University of California Press, 1980.

Pégourier, Y. *Le marché du riz d'Indochine.* Paris: Librairie technique et économique, 1937.

Peycam, P. "Intellectuals and Political Commitment in Vietnam: The Emergence of a Public Sphere in Colonial Saigon." PhD diss., SOAS, University of London.

Pham Thi Ngoan. "Introduction au *Nam Phong,* 1917–1934." Special issue of the *Bulletin de la Société des études indochinoises* 48, 2–3. Saigon: Société des études indochinoises, 1973.

Phan Boi Chau. *Mémoires.* Edited and translated by G. Boudarel. *France-Asie,* 1968.

Phan Ke Binh. *Viêt-Nam Phong-Tuc (Mœurs et coutumes du Vietnam)*. Edited by N. Louis-Hénard. 2 vols. Collection de textes et documents sur l'Indochine, 11. Paris: Publications de l'École française d'Extrême-Orient, 1975–80.

Pluvier, J. M. *Historical Atlas of South-East Asia*. Leiden: E. J. Brill, 1995.

Poisson, E. *Mandarins et subalternes au nord du Vietnam: Une bureaucratie à l'épreuve (1820–1918)*. Paris: Maisonneuve & Larose, 2004.

Popkin, S. L. *The Rational Peasant: The Political Economy of Rural Society in Vietnam*. Berkeley: University of California Press, 1979.

Qiang Zhai. *China and the Vietnam Wars, 1950–1975*. Chapel Hill: University of North Carolina Press, 2000.

Quinn-Judge, S. *Ho Chi Minh: The Missing Years*. London: Hurst, 2003.

Rambaud, A. *La France coloniale: Histoire, géographie, commerce*. Paris: A. Colin, 1886.

Rettig, T. "Indochinese Soldiers in the Service of France, 1927–1939." PhD diss., SOAS, London University, 2005.

Robequain, C. *L'évolution économique de l'Indochine française*. Centre d'études de politique étrangère, 13. Paris: Paul Hartmann, 1939.

———. *Le Thanh Hoa: Étude géographique d'une province annamite*. 2 vols. Paris: G. Van Oest, 1929.

Rocolle, P. *Pourquoi Dien Bien Phu?* Paris: Flammarion, 1968.

Romo-Navarrete, M. "Pierre Mendès-France: De l'héritage colonial à la marche vers le progrès." PhD diss., Université de Paris IV–Sorbonne, 2007.

Rotter, A. *The Path to Vietnam: Origins of the American Commitment to Southeast Asia*. Ithaca, N.Y.: Cornell University Press, 1987.

Roubaud, L. *Viet-Nam: La tragédie indochinoise*. Paris: L. Valois, 1931.

Rouyer, L.-F.-E. *Histoire militaire et politique de l'Annam et du Tonkin depuis 1799 jusqu'en 1897*. Paris: H. Charles Lavauzelle, [1906?].

Ruscio, A. *Les communistes français et la guerre d'Indochine, 1944–1954*. Paris: L'Harmattan, 1985.

———. *Dien Bien Phu: La fin d'une illusion*. Paris: L'Harmattan, 1986.

———. *Histoire de la guerre française d'Indochine*. Brussels: Éditions Complexe, 1992.

———. "Orientation bibliographique. La guerre française d'Indochine (1945–1954)." Institut d'Histoire du temps présent, *Bulletin trimestriel*, no. 28 (June 1987): 22–58.

———, ed. *La guerre "française" d'Indochine, 1945–1954: Les sources de la connaissance. Bibliographie et filmographie*. Paris: Les Indes savantes, 2001.

———, ed. *Ho Chi Minh: Textes, 1914–1969*. Paris: L'Harmattan, 1990.

———, ed. *Viet Nam: L'histoire, la terre, les hommes*. Paris: L'Harmattan, 1989.

Ruscio, A., and S. Tignères. *Dien Bien Phu, mythes et réalités: Cinquante ans de passions françaises, 1954–2004*. Paris: Les Indes savantes, 2005.

Russier, H. *L'Indochine française: Atlas indochinois*. Hanoi: Imprimerie d'Extrême-Orient, 1931.

Saada, E. *Les enfants de la colonie: Les métis de l'empire français entre sujétion et citoyenneté*. Paris: La Découverte, 2007.

Sage, W. W., and J. A. N. Henchy. "Laos Bibliography." Institute of South East Asian Studies, Singapore, *Library Bulletin*, no. 16 (1986).

Sainteny, J. *Histoire d'une paix manquée: Indochine, 1945–1947*. Paris: Amiot-Dumont, 1954.

Salemink, O. "Beyond Complicity and Naivete: Contextualizing the Ethnography of Vietnam's Central Highlands, 1880–1990." PhD diss., Amsterdam, 1999.

Sarraut, A. *Grandeur et servitude coloniales*. Paris: Éditions du Sagittaire, 1931.

———. *La mise en valeur des colonies françaises*. Paris: Payot, 1923.

Scott, J. C. *The Moral Economy of the Peasant: Rebellion and Subsistance in Southeast Asia*. New Haven, Conn.: Yale University Press, 1976.

2nd International Conference on Khmer Studies, 26–28 January 2000: Proceedings. Phnom Penh: Royal University of Phnom Penh, 2000.

Serène, R. "Des préjugés aux amitiés." In id., et al., *L'Homme de couleur*. Paris: Plon, 1939.

Shipway, M. *The Road to War: France and Vietnam, 1944–1947*. Providence, R.I.: Berghahn Books, 1996.

Shiraishi, M. *Phan Boi Chau in Japan, 1905–1909: The Solidarity among the Asian Peoples of the Same Sickness*. The Hague: Institute of Social Studies, 1980.

Singaravelou, P. *L'École française d'Extrême-Orient, ou l'institution des marges, 1898–1956: Essai d'histoire sociale et politique de la science coloniale*. Paris: L'Harmattan, 1999.

Smith, R. B. "Bui Quang Chieu and the Constitutionalist Party in French Cochinchina, 1917–1930." *Modern Asian Studies* 3, 2 (1969).

———. "The Vietnamese Elite of French Cochinchina, 1943." *Modern Asian Studies* 6, 4 (1972).

Statler, K. C. *Replacing France: The Origins of American Intervention in Vietnam*. Lexington: University Press of Kentucky, 2007.

Stuart-Fox, M. *A History of Laos*. New York: Cambridge University Press, 1997.

———. *The Lao Kingdom of Lan Zang: Rise and Decline*. Bangkok: White Lotus, 1998.

———. *Laos: Politics, Economics and Society*. London: France Pinter, 1986.

Taboulet, G. *La geste française en Indochine*. 2 vols. Paris: A. Maisonneuve, 1955–56.

Taillard, C. *Le Laos: Stratégies d'un état-tampon*. Montpellier: GIP Reclus, 1989.

Talon, V. *Le régime douanier de l'Indochine*. Paris: Domat-Montchrestien, 1932.

Tarling, G. *The Cambridge History of Southeast Asia*. Vol. 2. New York: Cambridge University Press, 1992.

Ta Thi Thuy. *Les concessions agricoles françaises au Tonkin de 1884 à 1918*. Hanoi: The Gioi, 2001.

Tertrais, H. *La piastre et le fusil: Le coût de la guerre d'Indochine, 1945–1954*. Paris: Comité pour l'histoire économique et financière de la France, 2002.

Teston, E., and M. Percheron. *L'Indochine moderne: Encyclopédie administrative, touristique, artistique et économique*. Paris: Librairie de France, 1931.

Thévenet, A. *La guerre d'Indochine*. Paris: France-Empire, 2001.

Thierry D'Argenlieu, G., Admiral. *Chroniques d'Indochine*. Paris: Albin Michel, 1985.

Thiollier, L. *La grande aventure de la piastre indochinoise*. Saint-Étienne: J. Bruyère, 1930.

Thobie, J. *L'impérialisme à la française*. Paris: La Découverte, 1986.

Thomas, F. *Histoire du régime et des services forestiers français en Indochine de 1862 à 1945*. Hanoi: Éditions The Gioi, 1999.

Thu muc Dong bang song Cu Long [Bibliography of Cuu Long]. Mekong Deltam Thu Vien Khoa hoc Xa Hoi. Ho Chi Minh City, 1981.

Tønnesson, S. *1946: Déclenchement de la guerre d'Indochine. Les vêpres tonkinoises du 19 décembre.* Translated by Bruno Metz. Paris: L'Harmattan, 1987.

——. *The Vietnamese Revolution of 1945: Roosevelt, Ho Chi Minh and de Gaulle in a World at War.* London: Sage Publications, 1991.

Tønnesson, S., and H. Antlöv. *Imperial Policy and Southeast Asian Nationalism, 1930–1950.* Copenhagen: Nordic Institute of Asian Studies, 1995.

Touzet, A. *L'économie indochinoise et la grande crise universelle.* Paris: Marcel Giard, 1934.

Tran Huy Lieu. *Les soviets du Nghe Tinh de 1930–1931 au Vietnam.* Hanoi: Éditions en langues étrangères, 1960.

Tran, My-Van. *A Vietnamese Royal Exile in Japan: Prince Cuong De (1882–1951).* New York: Routledge, 2005.

Tran Thi Lien, C. "Les Catholiques vietnamiens pendant la guerre d'indépendance (1945–1954): Entre la reconquête coloniale et la résistance communiste." PhD. diss., Sciences po, Paris, 1990.

Tran Van Giau. *Su phat trien cua tu Tuong o Viet-Nam tu The ky XIX den Cach Mang Thang Tam* [The Development of Thought in Vietnam from the Nineteenth Century to the August Revolution]. Hanoi: Khoa Hoc Xa Hoi, 1973–1975.

Tréglodé, B. de. *Héros et révolutionnaires au Vietnam.* Paris: L'Harmattan, 2001.

Trinh Van Thao. *Les compagnons de route de Ho Chi Minh: Histoire d'un engagement intellectuel au Vietnam.* Paris: Karthala, 2004.

——. *L'École française en Indochine.* Paris: Karthala, 1995.

——. *Vietnam, du confucianisme au communisme: Un essai d'itinéraire intellectuel.* 1990. Rev. ed. Paris: L'Harmattan, 2007.

Tsai, Maw-Kuey. *Les Chinois au Sud-Vietnam.* Ministère de l'Éducation nationale, Comité des travaux historiques et scientifiques, Mémoires de la section de géographie, 3. Paris: Bibliothèque nationale, 1968.

Tsuboi, Y. *L'empire vietnamien face à la France et à la Chine.* Paris: L'Harmattan, 1987.

Tuck, P. J. N. *French Catholic Missionaries and the Politics of Imperialism in Vietnam, 1857–1914: A Documentary Survey.* Liverpool: Liverpool University Press, 1987.

——. *The French Wolf and the Siamese Lamb: The French Threat to Siamese Independence, 1858–1907.* Bangkok: White Lotus, 1995.

Tully, J. *France on the Mekong: A History of the Protectorate of Cambodia.* Lanham, Md.: University Press of America, 2002.

Turpin, F. *De Gaulle, les gaullistes et l'Indochine, 1940–1956.* Paris: Les Indes savantes, 2005.

UNESCO. *Sources de l'histoire de l'Asie et de l'Océanie dans les archives et les bibliothèques françaises.* Paris: UNESCO, 1981.

Valette, J., *La guerre d'Indochine, 1945–1954.* Paris: A. Colin, 1994.

——. *Indochine, 1940–1945: Français contre Japonais.* Paris: SEDES, 1993.

"Le Village Traditionnel." In *Études vietnamiennes* (Hanoi), nos. 61 and 65 (1981).

Viollis, A. *Indochine S.O.S.* Paris: Gallimard, 1935. Reprint. Paris: Éditeurs français réunis, 1949.

Vo Duc Hanh. *La place du catholicisme dans les relations entre la France et le Viet-Nam de 1851 à 1870.* 3 vols. Leiden: Brill, 1969.

——. *La place du catholicisme dans les relations entre la France et le Viet-Nam de 1870 à 1886.* 3 vols. Bern: Peter Lang, 1993.

Vo Nguyen Giap, General. *Chien Dau trong vong vay* [Fighting against Encirclement]. Hanoi: NXBQDBD [Publishing House of the People's Army], 2001.

———. *Dien Bien Phu diem hen lich su* [Dien Bien Phu, an Appointment with History]. Hanoi: NXBQDBD [Publishing House of the People's Army], 2000.

———. *Duong toi Dien Bien Phu* [On the Way to Dien Bien Phu]. Hanoi: NXBQDBD [Publishing House of the People's Army], 1999.

———. *Nhung nam thang khong the nao quen* [Unforgettable Years and Months]. Hanoi: NXBQDBD [Publishing House of the People's Army], 2001.

Voraphet Kham. *Commerce et colonisation en Indochine, 1860–1945.* Paris: Les Indes savantes, 2005.

Vu Ngoc Phan, *Nha van hien dai: Phe binh van hoc.* 5 vols. 1942. Reprint, Glendale, Calif.: Dai Nam, 1980. On cover: "Biography of Contemporary Vietnamese Authors: Literary Criticism."

Vu Ngu Chieu. "Political and Social Change in Vietnam between 1940 and 1946." PhD diss., University of Wisconsin–Madison, 1985.

Werner, J. S. *Peasant Politics and Religious Sectarianism: Peasant and Priest in the Cao Dai in Vietnam.* New Haven, Conn.: Yale University Press, 1981.

White, C. "The Peasants and the Party in the Vietnamese Revolution." In *Peasants and Politics: Grass Roots Reaction to Change in Asia,* ed. D. B. Miller. London: Edward Arnold, 1979.

Woodside, A. B. *Community and Revolution in Modern Vietnam.* Boston: Houghton Mifflin, 1976.

———. "The Development of Social Organizations in Vietnamese Cities in the Late Colonial Period." *Pacific Affairs* 44, 1 (1971).

———. *Lost Modernities: China, Vietnam, Korea, and the Hazards of World History.* Cambridge, Mass.: Harvard University Press, 2006.

Wright, G. *The Politics of Design in French Colonial Urbanism.* Chicago: University of Chicago Press, 1991.

Zelinsky, W. "The Indochinese Peninsula: A Demographic Anomaly." *Far Eastern Quarterly,* February 1950.

Zinoman, P. *The Colonial Bastille: A History of Imprisonment in Vietnam, 1862–1940.* Berkeley: University of California Press, 2001.

INDEX

Italic page references indicate illustrations.

Africa, 147, 150, 320; French colonies in, 68, 337; influence on French arts, 249, 345; rubber plantations, 169, 396. *See also* AOF (Afrique occidentale française)

agriculture, 8, 212; agro-industrial plantations, 125–28; bank financing of, 147; colonist farmers, 189; colonization of, 118; deficiencies of credit for, 150–51; demographic change and, 256, 258–61, 263; French, 36; Great Depression and, 315; hydraulics and, 276–77, *278,* 279–80; land clearing and improvement, 261–63; "plant-based civilizations" and, 4, 132; precolonial decline of, 12; red-soil zones, 118, 126, 164; rice cultivation, 122–23; scientific modernization and, 132–34; as "traditional" economic sector, 250–51. *See also* plantations

agronomists, 126, 127–28, 132, 133, 266, 276

Ajalbert, Jean, 198

Alak highlanders, 284

alcohol monopoly, 92, 93–94, 104, 165, 301–2

Algeria, 21, 97; Algerians in French Communist Party, 310; "Arab kingdom" under French rule, 73; colonial status of, 71; exports, 176; French investment in, 152, 179; importance to French empire, 320; Indochina as new version of, 26; Mitidja, 188; Vietnamese exiled to, 53; war of insurrection in, 372

anarchism, 295, 300, 306, 310

Ang Duong, king, 10, 27

An Giang/Chau Doc (province), 26, 27

Angkor (province/temple complex), 66, 67, 107, 233, 289

Anglo-French rivalry, 9, 14, 17, 28, 41, 64; in Africa, 42, 66, 67; along Mekong River, 65, 66; Siam and, 66

Annam, 3, 34, 42, 251, 404n4; administrative costs, 83; anticolonial resistance in, 52, 381; census data, 252, 253, 254, 256; cinema in, 232; civil administration of, 81; colonial administration of, 77, 78; colonial reformism and, 323–24; communal lands in, 202, 203, 265, 315; disease epidemics, 258; education, 220, 225; in Franco-Vietnamese War, 362; French annexation of Tonkin and, 44; French colonists, 183; hydraulics in, 277, *278;* Indigenous Consultative Assembly, 386; investments in, 159; Japanese wartime policy and, 349; mines and factories, 208; peasant economy, 264, 266, 272; police, 111; provinces of, 88; resident superior of protectorate, 84; rice cultivation, 259, 260; taxation in, 91, 92, 97, 100; trade commodities, 38; village community in, 102

Annam-Tonkin protectorate, 47, 49, 85; administration of, 76; association, as colonial policy, 62; division of, 77; end of military regime, 73; financial cost of colonization, 78, 80

467

Comintern (Communist [Third] International), 310, 311, 312, 314, 379; "class against class" approach, 313, 318; dissolution of, 350; Popular Front strategy, 327, 328, 333; rural "soviet base" strategy in Far East, 318; survival of Vietnamese communist movement and, 326

Comité des forges (Ironworks Committee), 39, 67, 80

commerce, chambers of, 388–89

Commission spéciale de la Cochinchine (Special Commission for Cochinchina), 14, 20

communism, 297, 305; "bourgeois-democratic revolution" and, 314, 318; in Cambodia, 373; educated youth attracted to, 311–14; events of 1920s in China, 311, 314; in Laos, 373; legal action and, 326–27, 332; national communism, 324, 333; peasant masses of colonized nations and, 310; prison networks, 326, 328; Quoc ngu and, 225; reconstruction of movement, 326; soviet bases in China and Vietnam, 317–18; Stalinist–Trotskyist split, 332–33; unions and, 127, 210, 327; U.S. support for European colonial empires and, 353

Communist Manifesto (Marx and Engels), 311–12

Communist Party, Chinese, 311, 350, 356, 363

Communist Party, French (PCF), 310, 311, 326, 403n2; Franco-Vietnamese War and, 361, 362, 365; *Lutteurs* (Strugglers) and, 327; prestige from Resistance in World War II, 356

Communist Party, Indochinese (ICP), 314, 373, 440n55; and *ao xanh/cu nau* labor distinction, 208; August 1945 revolution and, 349–50; cultural initiatives, 345; decolonization strategy, 333; formation of, 318; French repression of, 319–20, 335; ideology and structure of, 373–74; Popular Front and, 331; reconstruction of, 326; restoration of French sovereignty and, 356; sailors and, 207; Vietnamese of Laos and, 283; women's emancipation and, 239; World War II insurrection and, 339

Communist Party, Vietnamese (Dang Cong San Viet Nam), 314, 317–18

Compagnie de Fives-Lilles, 39

Compagnie des charbonnages de Trang Bach (Trang Bach Coal-Mining Company), 210

Compagnie générale d'électricité, 39

Compagnie générale des soies (General Silk Company), 118, 165

Compagnie générale du Tonkin et du Nord-Annam, 94

Compagnie lyonnaise indochinoise, 38, 162

Compagnie universelle du canal de Suez (Universal Suez Canal Company), 24

compradore system, 166–67, 199, 213

concessions, agricultural, 125–26

concubines *(con gai)*, 195

Condominas, Georges, 104

Conférence économique impériale (Imperial Economic Conference), 272, 320

Confucianism, 5, 6, 11, 69; Can Vuong movement and, 59–60; Caodaism and, 243; Catholic Church in conflict with, 18–19; collapse of, 241; communist response to, 312–13; condemned by revolutionary intellectuals, 306, 312; filial piety as virtue, 292, 306; literati and, 12; mandarins' defense of, 59; mobilized in support of colonial regime, 76; orthodox neo-Confucianism, 304; patriarchal authority as value, 241; peasant village and, 279; "reformed," 297, 319; renovation of Nguyen dynasty and, 325; science and, 236, 238; in southern Vietnam, 73; traditional examination system and, 211, 222; Vietnamese literature and, 246; Vietnamese nationalism and, 292, 293, 296, 297. *See also* literati, Vietnamese; mandarin class; mandate, celestial

Congrès international de géographie, 1878, 42

Constans, Jean, 57

constitutionalists, 196, 304, 307, 309, 319, 328

coolies, 53, 57, 59, 127, 184, 193

Corneille, Pierre, 246

corvée labor, 91, 100, 201, 298, 307

cotton industry, 38, 113, 162, 347; as colonial lobby, 107; factories, 125; foreign trade and, 178, 179

Coulet, Georges, 196

Courbet, Adm. Amédée, 21, 44, 46

court system, 110, 302

Crayssac, René, 248

culture, transformation of: arts and crafts revival, 229–31; assimilation and cultural relativism, 218–19; customs and ideas, 237–41; education system, 219–23, 224, 225; French initiatives, 217–18; ICP manifesto (*De Cuong Van Hoa*), 345; language as issue in, 225–29; modern literature in Vietnam, 245–47; radio and cinema, 232–33; religion and, 241–45; "return" to traditional values, 241–43